AppleScript
The Definitive Guide

Other Macintosh resources from O'Reilly

Related titles

AppleScript: The Missing
   Manual

Learning Unix for Mac OS X
   Tiger

Mac OS X Tiger for Unix
   Geeks

Mac OS X Tiger in a Nutshell

Mac OS X Tiger Pccket Guide

Running Mac OS X Tiger

Essential Mac OS X Panther
   Server Administration

PowerBook Fan Book

iBook Fan Book

iPod Fan Book

Mac OS X: The Missing
   Manual

Office 2004 for Macintosh:
   The Missing Manual

Switching to the Mac:
   The Missing Manual

**Macintosh Books
Resource Center**

mac.oreilly.com is a complete catalog of O'Reilly's books on the Apple Macintosh and related technologies, including sample chapters and code examples.

A popular watering hole for Macintosh developers and power users, the Mac DevCenter focuses on pure Mac OS X and its related technologies, including Cocoa, Java, AppleScript, and Apache, to name just a few. It's also keenly interested in all the spokes of the digital hub, with special attention paid to digital photography, digital video, MP3 music, and QuickTime.

Conferences

O'Reilly Media brings diverse innovators together to nurture the ideas that spark revolutionary industries. We specialize in documenting the latest tools and systems, translating the innovator's knowledge into useful skills for those in the trenches. Visit *conferences.oreilly.com* for our upcoming events.

Safari Bookshelf (*safari.oreilly.com*) is the premier online reference library for programmers and IT professionals. Conduct searches across more than 1,000 books. Subscribers can zero in on answers to time-critical questions in a matter of seconds. Read the books on your Bookshelf from cover to cover or simply flip to the page you need. Try it today for free.

SECOND EDITION

AppleScript
The Definitive Guide

ELMHURST COLLEGE LIBRARY

Matt Neuburg

O'REILLY®

Beijing · Cambridge · Farnham · Köln · Paris · Sebastopol · Taipei · Tokyo

AppleScript: The Definitive Guide, Second Edition
by Matt Neuburg

Copyright © 2006 Matt Neuburg. All rights reserved.
Printed in the United States of America.

Published by O'Reilly Media, Inc., 1005 Gravenstein Highway North, Sebastopol, CA 95472.

O'Reilly books may be purchased for educational, business, or sales promotional use. Online editions are also available for most titles (*safari.oreilly.com*). For more information, contact our corporate/institutional sales department: (800) 998-9938 or *corporate@oreilly.com*.

Editor: Chuck Toporek	**Compositor:** Matt Neuburg
Production Editor: Claire Cloutier	**Cover Designer:** Ellie Volckhausen
Copyeditor: Nancy Kotary	**Interior Designer:** David Futato
Proofreader: Lindsay Frost	**Cover Illustrator:** Susan Hart
Indexer: Matt Neuburg	**Illustrators:** Robert Romano, Jessamyn Read, and Lesley Borash

Printing History:

November 2003:	First Edition.
January 2006:	Second Edition.

ISBN: 0-596-10211-9
[M]

Table of Contents

Part II. The AppleScript Language

Preface

If you use a Macintosh, there's something amazing lurking under the hood of your computer, and something even more amazing on the surface. Under the hood, there's a system-level mechanism for applications to communicate with one another, order each other about, get information from each other, and generally collaborate to avail themselves of each other's strengths and abilities. On the surface, there's Apple-Script, which puts the power of this mechanism into the hands of ordinary users, letting them program the computer for themselves by writing and executing code in the AppleScript language, as a way of automating the behavior of applications, reducing many steps to one, throwing the burden of repetition and calculation onto the computer, and combining the powers of multiple applications into a seamless united workflow. AppleScript can be used to construct a simple brief automation or a massive complex chain of events. It's a brilliant labor-saving device—and saving labor is what computers are all about.

AppleScript is one of the greatest innovations of Mac OS, one of its most notable distinguishing features—and one of its most practical. Users from lone amateurs to mighty corporations have come to depend on it. Yet AppleScript was long treated by Apple itself as something of an unwanted, troublesome stepchild, and has even (according to apocryphal legend) at times come perilously near to being tossed onto the scrapheap. With the rise of Mac OS X, however, AppleScript has prospered, enjoying a kind of Golden Age, being embraced and acknowledged as one of Apple's star technologies. It is noted on Apple's own web pages as a major element of Mac OS X (for example, see *http://www.apple.com/macosx/overview/*). The Script Editor has been rewritten as a Cocoa application. Scripts may be run from a systemwide menu. More and more of Apple's own new applications are scriptable. Integration with Unix scripting has been provided. Automator (new in Tiger) lets users effectively assemble, customize, and run scripts without having to deal with any code. Even applications that are not technically scriptable can be targeted with Apple-Script. Users can actually write a genuine application with a full-fledged Aqua user interface, using AppleScript as their programming language, thanks to the astounding AppleScript Studio. And it all comes for free as part of Mac OS X.

In this context, with interest in AppleScript waxing anew, the need for a complete explanatory manual and reference is greater than ever. In that spirit, this book has been offered. It is hoped that it will prove helpful to AppleScript's beginning and veteran users alike. Neither prior knowledge of AppleScript nor any previous programming experience is assumed, so that the complete beginner can use this book to learn AppleScript from the ground up; at the same time, the book aims at a degree of technical depth and completeness that will satisfy the needs of those who wish to consult it to check some point of syntax, or to gain a firmer understanding of such advanced arcana as how the scoping rules operate, how terminology is resolved, or what an Apple event really is.

The Scope of This Book

What should be the scope of a book about AppleScript? This is a tricky problem, and one that earlier books, in my view, have not always dealt with satisfactorily. The trouble is that AppleScript is really two subjects. First, there is what one may call AppleScript itself, a system-level technology and a "little language," not particularly useful or powerful on its own, but ready to talk to scriptable applications and to take advantage of *their* utility and power. Second, there is AppleScript as extended and implemented by particular scriptable applications: how to use AppleScript to talk to the Finder, how to use AppleScript to talk to Adobe Photoshop, how to use AppleScript to talk to QuarkXPress, and so forth.

On the whole, this book makes no attempt to treat this second aspect of AppleScript. This may be surprising to readers accustomed to some earlier books, but I believe it to be the right decision nonetheless. AppleScript as implemented by particular applications is a massive, encyclopedic subject. It would be easy to write an entire book of techniques, tricks, and tips for scripting just *one* major application. And the scope of any attempt to do this for *every* scriptable application would be open-ended, because it is impossible to know what scriptable applications the reader has or might acquire, and because new applications, any of which might be scriptable, are being developed all the time. Also, such treatment is largely unnecessary. Every scriptable application includes a dictionary telling the user about how it extends the language; the user can employ this, together with trial and error, and possibly examples from documentation and the Internet, to obtain pretty fair mastery over the art of scripting that application. There might even be books on the exact subject the reader is interested in. It is far better that the reader should consult a book entirely devoted to scripting, say, Adobe Illustrator than that the present book should attempt to compress a treatment of the same material into some reduced and undoubtedly inadequate form (Appendix C lists a few such books).

My choice, therefore, is between concisely teaching the reader to fish and giving the reader a large pile of possibly quite unnecessary fish. Readers who know anything of my work (or anything about fish) will know instantly which choice I would make.

Rather than trying to encompass the details of scripting every application, my approach in this book has been *to explain AppleScript itself*, explicating the technology, documenting the language, describing how a dictionary works and what a user can and can't learn from it, and providing supplementary examples from across the range of applications that I actually use, so that the reader will be mentally equipped and educated and able to study and experiment independently with scripting any application.

Besides, books about the first aspect of AppleScript—about AppleScript itself—have been surprisingly few and far between. It is here that the need exists. The fact is that I have never seen the AppleScript language taught, explained, and documented in what I would regard as a clear, rigorous, and helpful way. Considering how long AppleScript has been around, it is hard to explain this lack. It may have partly to do with the absence of any clear and full explanation from Apple itself. After all, Apple wrote AppleScript, and only the folks at Apple have access to AppleScript's inner workings. Yet the only Apple manual of AppleScript, the *AppleScript Language Guide*, generally lacks explanatory depth.

There is a kind of unspoken myth—we may call it the "ease of use" myth—that tries to give the impression that AppleScript is so easy and intuitive that it doesn't really need explanation. Apple possibly didn't want users to see AppleScript as a full-fledged programming language, with all the precision, complexity, and sophistication that this entails, because that would be something that users would have to *learn*, exercising those parts of their brain to which a Macintosh, with its windows and icons and colorful buttons, isn't supposed to appeal. Instead, AppleScript is supposed to be so simple, so thin, so easy, so English-like, so intuitive, that there is hardly anything to learn in the first place; just pick up an application and its dictionary and presto, you're ready to script it.

Nothing could be further from the truth. First you must learn the language; only then will a dictionary make sense and be useful. AppleScript is not a mere veneer, an intuitive and obvious "glue" for hooking together the terms from an application's dictionary into sentences that will script that application as the user desires. On the contrary, it's a real programming language—a really interesting, fairly complicated, sometimes sophisticated, often opaque and quirky programming language. To conceal this fact from the potential user of AppleScript does that user no favor whatsoever. Every day I see on the Internet users who are starting AppleScript, who seem to imagine that with a few tiny "hints" they're just going to "pick it up"—that their AppleScript code will somehow just write itself. Well, it won't. A beginning user who expects to cut to the chase, to pick up an application's dictionary and just start scripting, is likely to give up in frustration. As Socrates said of virtue, AppleScript isn't something we all somehow are born knowing; it must be learned, and therefore it must be taught. There is nothing about AppleScript that makes it any less susceptible to scrutiny, careful description, and ordered, Euclidean exposition and definition than any other computer language.

In this light, I have written the AppleScript book that I have for so long myself wished to read. Before writing this book, I always found myself rather confused about AppleScript; I could use it with reasonable effectiveness, but I was always somewhat hazy on the details. So writing this book was first and foremost an opportunity for me to dispel my own confusion. My technique, aside from asking a few experts a lot of questions, has been one of sheer open-ended experimentation; essentially ignoring the Apple manual and the existing books and other expositions that have reproduced its myths and mistakes, I have subjected AppleScript to every test I could think of, trying to work out by empiricism and rational deduction the logic of the "little black box" concealed inside it. The result is a reasoned, rigorous, step-by-step presentation of the AppleScript language, intended for instruction and for reference—a studious, patient, detailed, ordered exposition and compendium of the facts as they really are. This book presents AppleScript as a programmer, a student, and a thinker would learn it. In short, it's just what I've always wanted! This book has helped me tremendously. Before I wrote it, I didn't really quite understand AppleScript; now I believe I do. I hope it will do the same for you.

Versions

Things change. All things change. And software often changes faster than the ability of printed books to keep up with it. It will therefore be useful for the reader to know what versions of software I was looking at when I wrote this edition of the book. The first draft was written using Mac OS X 10.4.2 ("Tiger") and AppleScript 1.10; the book was finished under Mac OS X 10.4.3 and AppleScript 1.10.3. Apple's Script Editor was at version 2.1 (later 2.1.1). Late Night Software's Script Debugger 4 was still in beta. (This means that screen shots of Script Debugger 4 don't quite match the finished product.) There may be further changes in Tiger, and possibly even in AppleScript, by the time the book goes to print, but if so, it seems unlikely that these will affect the book's content; still, the reader should be alert to the possibility of slight discrepancies between what I describe and the now-current state of things.

The book is written entirely from the perspective of Mac OS X. This is a deliberate design decision. There is an important sense in which Mac OS 9 really is frozen, if not downright moribund; very few new applications of any importance are being written for it, it is not likely to evolve further to any significant extent, and Apple has begun to produce computers that won't even boot in it (and will soon move to a system where Classic will not run at all). If you are not using Mac OS X, this book might still be useful to you, but please keep in mind that it isn't geared primarily to your situation.

This second edition is written entirely from the perspective of Tiger. Not much attention has been paid to differences between the Tiger version of AppleScript and earlier versions. Where a feature is new in Tiger, I say so. But if you are still using Panther (or Jaguar), you should stick with the first edition of this book.

How This Book Is Organized

This book is divided into four sections, as follows.

Part I, AppleScript Overview

Part I consists of general introductory material, explaining what AppleScript is, motivating the reader with examples of various ways and means for putting AppleScript to use, and defining fundamental terms that the reader will need to understand.

Chapter 1, *Why to Use AppleScript*
> Provides some motivational guidelines and real-life examples intended to answer such big existential questions as what AppleScript is good for and why you would want to use it anyway.

Chapter 2, *Where to Use AppleScript*
> Surveys the various areas of the computer where AppleScript can be employed—for example, by running a script in the Script Editor, by calling into AppleScript from some application's internal scripting language, or by way of a Unix scripting language like Perl.

Chapter 3, *Basic Concepts*
> An explanation of the technologies underlying AppleScript and a glossary of fundamental terms. This is where the technical discussion starts. The rest of the book depends upon the facts and definitions laid down in this chapter.

Part II, The AppleScript Language

Part II develops AppleScript as a programming language. Learners should read the chapters in order; experienced users may employ this section as a linguistic reference.

Chapter 4, *Introducing the Language*
> A subjective description of what AppleScript is like as a language, just to give you a sense of what you're getting into.

Chapter 5, *Syntactic Ground of Being*
> Describes some fundamental externals of the language, such as lines and comments.

Chapter 6, *A Map of the World*
> Surveys the consituent parts of an AppleScript program (as discussed in detail in the ensuing four chapters).

Chapter 7, *Variables*
> Discusses how to assign and define variables and how their names should look.

Chapter 8, *Script Objects*
> Discusses script objects (scripts within scripts), including how to refer to them, how to load and save them dynamically, and how inheritance works.

Chapter 9, *Handlers*
> Shows how to declare and call handlers (subroutines), along with some powerful and interesting advanced devices for passing parameters and returning values.

Chapter 10, *Scope*
> Discusses the visibility and storage of declared and undeclared variables, along with some advanced techniques involving free variables and closures.

Chapter 11, *Objects*
> Describes how objects are targeted and how their attributes (properties and elements) are referred to.

Chapter 12, *References*
> Describes a device for encapsulation and delayed evaluation of expressions targeting objects and referring to their values.

Chapter 13, *Datatypes*
> A guide to the built-in value classes (such as numbers, strings, lists, and records).

Chapter 14, *Coercions*
> Explains how one datatype can be turned into another explicitly or implicitly.

Chapter 15, *Operators*
> Catalogues the various ways to test and combine values, such as addition, comparison, and concatenation.

Chapter 16, *Global Properties*
> Catalogues some predefined variables, such as (believe it or not) pi.

Chapter 17, *Constants*
> Catalogues enumerations and classes that behave as reserved words.

Chapter 18, *Commands*
> Catalogues the few built-in verbs not previously covered.

Chapter 19, *Control*
> Surveys the linguistic structures for determining the flow of an AppleScript program, such as branching, looping, and error handling.

Part III, AppleScript in Action

Part III describes aspects of AppleScript in practice and in relation to the wider world.

Chapter 20, *Dictionaries*
> Talks about the mechanism whereby applications make themselves scriptable through AppleScript by extending the AppleScript language, and explains how terminology is resolved and how to read and understand a dictionary.

Chapter 21, *Scripting Additions*
> Explains the scripting addition mechanism; surveys the built-in scripting additions and provides some additional technical details.

Chapter 22, *Speed*

Collects some tips for optimizing the speed of AppleScript code.

Chapter 23, *Scriptable Applications*

Explains how to drive applications with AppleScript, on the same or a different computer, including certain kinds of web services. Also mentions some useful scriptable applications that come with Mac OS X.

Chapter 24, *Unscriptable Applications*

Talks about how AppleScript can be used together with the system's Accessibility API to automate the interface of applications that are not directly scriptable.

Chapter 25, *Unix*

Talks about how AppleScript can call the Unix shell command line and how Unix scripting languages can call AppleScript.

Chapter 26, *Triggering Scripts Automatically*

Describes ways that an application or process can find and call your script automatically, including folder actions, CGI, and attachability.

Chapter 27, *Writing Applications*

Discusses ways to turn an AppleScript program into a standalone application, ranging from a simple applet (written with AppleScript alone) to a full-fledged application with a true user interface or an Automator action (written with AppleScript Studio). Also introduces the techniques whereby a developer can add scriptability to an Objective-C Cocoa application.

Part IV, Appendixes

Appendix A, *The AppleScript Experience*

A brief hands-on tutorial or walkthrough, illustrating what it's like to plan and implement a task using AppleScript in real life.

Appendix B, *Apple Events Without AppleScript*

Lists some alternatives to AppleScript for creating and sending Apple events.

Appendix C, *Tools and Resources*

A list of references and further readings.

Conventions Used in This Book

The following conventions are used in this book:

Italic

Used for file and folder names, URLs, and new terms when they are defined.

`Constant width`

Used for code examples and the names of variables, handlers, and commands.

Constant-width italic
> Used for placeholders in code, where the programmer would supply the actual name of something.

Constant-width bold
> Used in code examples, for user input from the command line; often seen in conjunction with %, which symbolizes the shell prompt.

-- *code comment in italic*
> Used in code examples, for my comments to the reader about the code or its effect.

-- **code comment in bold**
> Used in code examples, to represent the result (output) of executing the line.

vertical bar |
> Used in syntax templates to indicate alternatives.

[square brackets]
> Used in syntax templates to indicate that something is optional.

¬
> Used to indicate a line of code that continues; these lines will be unbroken in your code but were too long to fit on the printed pages of this book.

 This icon represents a tip relating to the nearby text.

 This icon represents a warning relating to the nearby text.

How to Contact Us

The book-writing process is long and arduous, and the examples have been tested and retested. However, mistakes do creep in from time to time. If you find any errors in the text or code examples, please write to:

> O'Reilly Media, Inc.
> 1005 Gravenstein Highway North
> Sebastopol, CA 95472
> 800-998-9938 (in the United States or Canada)
> 707-829-0515 (international/local)
> 707-829-0104 (fax)

We have a web page for the book, where we list any additional information. You can access this page at:

> *http://www.oreilly.com/catalog/applescpttdg/*

To comment or ask technical questions about this book, send email to:

bookquestions@oreilly.com

For more information about our books, conferences, software, Resource Centers, and the O'Reilly Network, see our web site at:

http://www.oreilly.com

The author maintains a web page with the source code for this book in downloadable form, along with a list of errata and supplementary comments:

http://www.tidbits.com/matt/

Safari® Enabled

 When you see a Safari® Enabled icon on the cover of your favorite technology book, that means the book is available online through the O'Reilly Network Safari Bookshelf.

Safari offers a solution that's better than e-books. It's a virtual library that lets you easily search thousands of top tech books, cut and paste code samples, download chapters, and find quick answers when you need the most accurate, current information. Try it for free at *http://safari.oreilly.com*.

Acknowledgments (First Edition)

In a completely just world, Mark Alldritt of Late Night Software would probably have his name on the cover of this book. In fact, he really ought to have written the book himself, since in all probability no one outside of Apple knows more about AppleScript than he does. I have benefited from his knowledge in three ways: he wrote Script Debugger, without which much of AppleScript's behavior would have remained opaque to me; he provided untiring assistance and advice while I was writing; and he performed a thorough and valuable technical review of the first draft.

Paul Berkowitz also acted as technical reviewer, a task which he performed with brilliance and insight, combining a long and thoughtful experience of AppleScript with diligence and critical perspicacity. He corrected many errors of fact, and gave excellent advice from the perspective of a model reader. Those who find this book useful should know that much of the credit is his. Chuck Sholdt also made several helpful suggestions and provided much-needed encouragement.

All the members of the AppleScript team at Apple who were present at Apple's 2003 WWDC were extremely generous with their time despite the many other demands upon it. Some of them provided important technical advice that has greatly increased the book's accuracy.

It remains only to add that the responsibility where I have not taken or understood the advice of my technical reviewers must rest with me.

My editor, Chuck Toporek, did all the right things. He assigned me the book, he monitored the signals emerging from Apple, he enabled me to attend Apple's 2003 WWDC and put me in touch with the AppleScript team, and he displayed forbearance, confidence, and patience while I was writing, leaving me to wrestle with problems of form and content on my own, never criticizing an early draft that he knew I would eventually rip to shreds myself, while at the same time providing encouragement when needed and advice when requested. Having as copyeditor my old friend Nancy Kotary made this stage of the process a pleasure instead of a trial; she brought to the task her characteristic combination of sound judgement, sharp eyes, and a kind heart, and a number of passages read more clearly thanks to her intervention. Genevieve d'Entremont oversaw the production in a thoroughly professional manner. My thanks to them and to all at O'Reilly Media who participated in the making of this book.

Acknowledgments (Second Edition)

With this second edition I have produced the version of this book I would have preferred all along but failed to produce the first time around, owing to limitations of time and to my own sheer ignorance. (Sorry about that; the same thing happened with my REALbasic book, which required a second edition in order to achieve its proper form.) The presentation has been heavily reorganized, nearly every paragraph has been thoroughly rewritten, many facts about AppleScript that were misapprehended or left in doubt in the first edition have been at last sussed out and presented definitively and correctly, and of course everything has been thoroughly updated to reflect Tiger and other innovations two years on. I have also (as I did for the second edition of my REALbasic book) written the index myself.

My thanks go most particularly to readers of the first edition who provided corrections, criticism, feedback, and suggestions; I have taken their input very much to heart. Also I wish to thank the denizens of Apple's AppleScript-Users mailing list for letting me play in their sandbox; they have often opened my eyes to facts and possibilities that would not otherwise have occurred to me. I am grateful once again to Apple's own AppleScript team, who provided many a helpful and entertaining hour at the AppleScript Pro Sessions in Monterey, California, in May 2005 and at WWDC in San Francisco a month later. As always, I have benefitted from personal correspondence from many people, especially Mark Alldritt, Paul Berkowitz, Hamish Sanderson, and the daring duo of William Cook and Warren Harris. Michael Terry performed a truly incisive technical review, and I have been inspired by many of his suggestions. Nancy Kotary once again helped immensely with her clear-eyed copyediting. Finally I wish to thank my editor, Chuck Toporek, and the entire team at O'Reilly Media, for their patience, encouragement, expertise, assistance, adaptability, and industry.

AppleScript Overview

Part I introduces AppleScript. What is it? How does it work? Where can I use it? What can I do with it? These are the sorts of questions this part answers.

If you already have a notion of what AppleScript is and just want to get on with studying the language, you can skip the first two chapters; but you should read Chapter 3, because it contains fundamental information and definitions that are not repeated later, and on which the rest of the book depends.

The chapters are:

Chapter 1, *Why to Use AppleScript*
Chapter 2, *Where to Use AppleScript*
Chapter 3, *Basic Concepts*

Why to Use AppleScript

If you've never used AppleScript before, you're probably in need of motivation as much as information. You'd like to know: "What is AppleScript?" You'd also like to know: "And why should I care, anyway?"

Those are good questions, and they are best answered by a brief explanation of what AppleScript is for. Therefore, this first chapter classifies the main uses of Apple-Script, along with some examples.

By presenting AppleScript in action, in some typical real-life contexts, I hope to inspire you to imagine how you might use AppleScript in your own life. AppleScript is a big subject, and your best incentive to press ahead is a vision of some task you actually want to accomplish with it. At the same time, you'll have a far easier, more enjoyable experience of AppleScript if your aims are consonant with its nature and abilities.

 In this chapter, the examples are not intended for you to run on your own computer. This is real-life code that works on my machine, but is not expected to run elsewhere. Nor are you expected to understand the code at this point. I'm just showing it to you for purposes of illustration, so glance over it and move on! When you've read more of the book and have learned some AppleScript, you'll understand how to adapt these examples to your own purposes.

The Nature and Purpose of AppleScript

Consider the many and various applications on your computer, and how you typically make them do things. With your hands, you choose menu items, click buttons, and generally wield the mouse and keyboard in the usual way. You also use applications as a source of information; you typically get this information by reading it off the screen, and you can communicate information from one application to another by copying and pasting. Mediating between your hands, your eyes, and the application is your brain: as your eyes get information from the application, your brain decides what to do next, and instructs your hands accordingly.

With AppleScript, you make applications do things *programmatically*. An AppleScript program has the power to give commands to the application, taking the place of your hands on the mouse and keyboard, and it has the power to ask the application questions, taking the place of your eyes reading the screen; the program itself makes the decisions about what to do next, thus taking the place of your brain. Thus, AppleScript lets you *automate* the sorts of things you're accustomed to making applications do manually.

Why is that a good thing? For the same reason that any automation is good. AppleScript performs the same tasks you could perform manually, but it performs them faster, more accurately, and without your direct involvement—you needn't even be sitting at the computer. Some tasks, when performed manually, are tedious or repetitive or error-prone; it's downright annoying for you to have to perform them, whereas the computer never gets bored and never makes a mistake in calculation, and (let's face it) can perform them better than you.

For example, suppose you've got a folder full of image files and you want to change their names in a systematic way to *image01.jpg*, *image02.jpg*, and so forth. It isn't as if you don't *know* how to do this: you select the first image file with the mouse, press Return to start editing its name, type image01.jpg, and press Return again; then you select the next image file with mouse, and do it again, and so forth. The trouble is that you don't *want* to do it. The trouble is with that "Do it again," which rapidly becomes tiresome and error-prone; before long, your eyes are starting to go out of focus, or you are just plain bored out of your skull, and you start to make mistakes. The whole thing is simultaneously too easy (it's an annoying waste of time and brain-power) and too hard (it's easy to make a mistake). It's just not a fit task for a human being. But it's a perfect task for a computer, which won't get bored or make a mistake no matter how many files are in that folder. AppleScript lets you assign to the computer tasks that are better suited to it than to a human being. And that example was a tiny one; AppleScript is just as useful for assembling massive workflows, driving big applications through massive tasks, feeding information from one to the other, processing and reformatting it in complex ways.

To find reasons to use AppleScript, just leave your mental annoyance meter turned on. Does something feel slow, repetitious, clumsy, boring, error-prone? Do you feel that a program isn't quite doing what you want? Does a series of steps need to be reduced to one? Has the computer got you trained, like some sort of laboratory animal, to perform a sequence of set tasks in a certain way? That's just not right. The computer should work for you—not the other way around! Maybe AppleScript can turn the tables.

I've been talking about "AppleScript," and in particular about an "AppleScript program" that's going to replace your hands and brain and make the computer do the work for you. But where does this program come from? Someone has to write it. That "someone" could be someone else: you can find lots of AppleScript programs that might be useful to you, already written and floating around on the Internet, where there's an entire community and culture of AppleScript users, sharing their work and benefiting from one another's experience. On the other hand, that "someone" could be you. That's why this book is here; it teaches you to write programs using AppleScript. That way, you'll be in charge of the automating power of your computer—a power which even now is lurking there, just waiting for you to take advantage of its vast potential. (And, as you'll see in Chapter 2, it's lurking in a lot of places.)

The rest of this chapter will illustrate the following general principles about what AppleScript is good for:

- AppleScript is appropriate primarily when you want to *automate an application*.
- AppleScript is good for expressing *calculated* and *repetitive* activity.
- AppleScript is a means of *reducing the number of steps* needed to perform an action.
- AppleScript is a way of *customizing an application*.
- AppleScript lets you *combine specialties*: by automating more than one application, you make them work together, letting each application do what it's good at and uniting their several powers.

Is This Application Scriptable?

AppleScript isn't just a language; it's an underlying technology supporting that language. Because this technology is present as part of the system, you get it for free—so you may as well take advantage of it. And because you know this technology will be present on any Mac OS computer, you can share with others any useful AppleScript program you happen to write.

So AppleScript is omnipresent. But it's not omnipotent. AppleScript, remember, is all about telling an application to do automatically things of the sort you might make it do manually. But AppleScript does not let you tell every application to do everything it is capable of. AppleScript works by sending messages to the applications you are automating; these messages are called *Apple events*. You cannot send just any old Apple event to any old application. (Well, you can, but it might not have any effect.) The application to which you're sending an Apple event must recognize and respond to that Apple event. The ability to recognize and respond to a set of Apple events is a feature of the application. Giving the application this ability is up to the developers of the application—it isn't something that's within your power (unless you are also the developer of the application). An application that has this ability is said to be *scriptable*. If an application isn't scriptable, you're probably not going to be able to use AppleScript to automate it. (As you'll see in Chapter 24, there is sometimes a way around this limitation, but it should probably be used only as a last resort.) So, before you consider using AppleScript at all, you should have in mind some scriptable application that you want to automate with it.

Not only is AppleScript not omnipotent; it isn't even all that potent. AppleScript is a genuine programming language with some interesting and valuable features, but it's not very powerful or useful on its own. It takes some scriptable application to give AppleScript any real muscle. So, for instance, AppleScript's numeric abilities are limited (it has no built-in trigonometric or logarithmic functions) and its facilites for text processing are fairly rudimentary (it doesn't support regular expressions, and it isn't even very good at extracting substrings). Granted, these shortcomings aren't as significant as they used to be. Mac OS X is loaded with other scripting languages, such as Perl, which are expert at regular expressions—and AppleScript can drive Perl (and vice versa), so success might simply be a matter of combining specialties appropriately. Nevertheless, the general spirit and intention of AppleScript is that the power should be invested mostly in various scriptable applications, not in AppleScript itself.

Thus it becomes crucial to be able to ascertain whether an application *is* scriptable. You'd think this would be an easily answered, black-and-white, yes-or-no question. But in fact it turns out to be frustratingly difficult to know whether an application is scriptable. (This book points out many instances of AppleScript's making something simple into something frustratingly difficult.)

You can obtain an initial overall survey of the situation by means of Apple's Script Editor program (it's in */Applications/AppleScript*): choose File → Open Dictionary, which displays a list of applications present on your computer that the Script Editor thinks are scriptable. You should, however, regard this list with a bit of suspicion, and confirm that a particular application really is or is not scriptable. To do so, choose Window → Library, and in the Library window, press the "+" button (or Control-click to get the contextual menu, and choose Add). You'll see a standard Open dialog. Navigate to an application, select it, and press Open. One of two things will happen:

The application is reported as not scriptable
> An error dialog may appear, stating: "Unable to add the application or extension because it is not scriptable." In this case, the application is definitely not scriptable and that's the end of that.

The application is added to the Library window
> This means that the application *might* be scriptable. But you might have a false positive. To find out, double-click the application's listing in the Library window. This should open the application's dictionary display (see Figure 2-2).

Even if it does, you *still* might have a false positive. Explore the dictionary, clicking the various Suites (in the first column of the browser) and looking through the classes and commands (in the second column) to make sure that these actually *do* something appropriate to the function of that particular application.

A good example is the application called, appropriately enough, Dictionary (located in */Applications*). In Script Editor, you can open the Dictionary application's dictionary display; this dictionary has about two dozen entries. But it's a false positive; the Dictionary application is not really scriptable. What you're seeing are merely some classes and commands inherent in any Cocoa application, merely by virtue of being a Cocoa application. The way you know this is that none of these classes and commands has anything to with the primary function of the Dictionary application—namely, looking up the definition of a word.

What you're looking for, in other words, are applications whose scriptability exposes their true power so that AppleScript can automate them usefully. The scriptable applications I use with some regularity include many of those supplied by Apple as part of Mac OS X, such as Address Book, iCal, iTunes, Mail, Safari, Apple System Profiler, and the Finder. Then there are important third-party programs like Microsoft Word, Excel, and Entourage, FileMaker Pro, Interarchy, BBEdit, StuffIt Expander, and GraphicConverter. You might also have QuarkXPress, or any of the heavily scriptable Adobe applications such as Photoshop, Illustrator, InDesign, or Acrobat. A delightful recent trend is that Apple has made it increasingly easier to add scriptability to Cocoa applications, so new applications are tending to be scriptable. Examples are OmniOutliner and OmniGraffle, Hog Bay Notebook, Intaglio, and many others.

(As you read this book—for example, in Chapter 2, Chapter 3, and especially Chapter 20—you'll learn much more about an application's dictionary, how to navigate it, what it does, and what it tells you. See Chapter 23 for more about the scriptable applications included with a default Tiger installation.)

Calculation and Repetition

Computers are good at calculation and repetition. Humans, on the other hand, are liable to calculate inaccurately, and all the more so in the face of repetitive activity, which can make them careless, bored, and angry. Calculation and repetition on a computer should be performed by the computer—not by a human.

Here's an example straight off the Internet, where someone writes: "I want to rename a whole lot of image files based on the names of the folders they're in." One's eyes glaze over at the prospect of doing this by hand. Yet with AppleScript, it's a snap. The task would make a good droplet—a little application, written with Apple-Script, with a Finder icon onto which you can drop files and folders you want processed. (More details appear in "Applet and Droplet" in Chapter 3 and "Applets" in Chapter 27.) Here's the AppleScript code for such a droplet; you drop a folder or folders onto its icon in the Finder, and it renames all items in each folder using that folder's name followed by a number:

```
on open folderList
    repeat with aFolder in folderList
        if kind of (info for aFolder) is "Folder" then
            renameStuffIn(aFolder)
        end if
    end repeat
end open
on renameStuffIn(theFolder)
    set ix to 0
    tell application "Finder"
        set folderName to name of theFolder
        set allItems to (get every item of theFolder)
        repeat with thisItem in allItems
            set ix to ix + 1
            set newName to folderName & ix
            set name of thisItem to newName
        end repeat
    end tell
end renameStuffIn
```

The parameter `folderList` tells us what was dropped onto the droplet. We process each dropped item, starting with a sanity check to make sure it's really a folder. If it is, we give each item in the folder a new name based on the folder's name along with a number that increases each time.

Reduction

Even when a task doesn't involve repetition and calculation, it may involve many steps. If you can get AppleScript to perform many or all of those steps, you reduce the number of steps *you* have to perform. This can make for a noticeable improvement in your relationship with your computer, even if you perform this task fairly infrequently. Another advantage of reduction is that you no longer have to remember a sequence of steps; your AppleScript program remembers it for you.

Here's an example involving URLs. Often, working in some application, I see a URL that I'd like to "go to" in the appropriate manner. If it's an http URL, my default browser should open and fetch that page. If it's an email address, my email program should create a new message to that addressee. In some applications you can just click a URL and the right thing happens, but many applications provide no such facility, so I have to resolve the URL manually. This means I must look at the URL and decide on the appropriate helper program; then I select and copy the URL; then

I somehow start up the helper program; finally, I paste the URL into the appropriate location. In a browser, I must hit Return afterwards, in order to go to that URL; in an email program, I must create a new message first, in order to have something to paste into. This doesn't sound like very many steps, but it's all very annoying, especially in comparison to those applications where the right thing just happens with a single click.

The solution is an AppleScript program. I've assigned it a keyboard shortcut (ways of doing this are discussed in Chapter 2), so the procedure is this: select and copy the URL, then press the keyboard shortcut. That's a significant savings in time and trouble. Here's the script:

```
set theProc to (get path to frontmost application as Unicode text)
tell application "Finder"
    activate
    delay 1 -- give time for clip to convert from Classic
    set theURL to (get the clipboard as string)
end tell
ignoring application responses
    try
            open location theURL
    end try
end ignoring
activate application theProc
```

The switch to the Finder is to force the clipboard contents to convert themselves to a usable form (and the delay is to give this time to happen); this seems to be needed particularly when working in a Classic application. At the end of the script I switch back to the application I was using at the outset. The heart of the script is the open location command, which does the "right thing" with the URL.

Customization

No application in the world can meet everyone's desires and expectations, because whatever the application's features, it is impossible for the developers of that application to anticipate everything that every user will wish to do with it. AppleScript can be a solution to this problem. Scriptability can provide, in essence, an entire alternative user interface: instead of the graphical user interface of buttons and menus, it's a programming interface. An application's scriptability says to you: "Here are all the types of thing this application operates on, and here are the operations you can perform on them; if none of this application's menu items and buttons and other graphical interface items performs just the sequence of operations you desire, feel free to use AppleScript to create a sequence that does."

Here's a real-life example. On the Internet, someone asked about assigning track numbers in iTunes. A track number is an attribute of a song, which can be set in that song's Get Info dialog; it can be made to appear in the playlist display, and you can sort on it. Thus, track numbers can be used to control the order of playback in a playlist. This user wanted to assign track numbers immediately after "ripping" a CD to iTunes, so that the order in which the tracks appeared on the original CD, and in which they appeared in the initial playlist derived from that CD, could easily be restored within iTunes later on. In essence, the user was saying: "The tracks are already in their correct order within this playlist; how can I use that order to assign all the tracks a track number, in a single move?"

My response was: "Use AppleScript." Here's a script that does it:

```
set i to 1
tell application "iTunes"
    tell (get view of browser window 1)
        repeat with aTrack in (get every track)
            set track number of aTrack to i
            set i to i + 1
        end repeat
    end tell
end tell
```

An interesting philosophical debate then ensued. The user thanked me, but expressed regret that this was the "only way" to accomplish this task; iTunes, he said, should include this feature natively. My attitude was just the opposite: thanks to scriptability, iTunes *does* effectively include this feature natively. "Instead of berating the developers of iTunes for not including that one magic menu item that would do just what you want," I said, "you should be applauding them for making the application scriptable and letting you implement the functionality yourself." Through its scriptability, iTunes is customizable; you can give it features that are within its powers but are missing from its graphical user interface. And this, surely, is the way it should be. If iTunes included a menu item for every task every user on earth would like it to perform, it would have thousands of menu items. Instead, it has a graphical user interface for the tasks that most users want to perform, and leaves the rest up to the individual and AppleScript. iTunes even gives you a way to add your scripts to its graphical interface; put them in *~/Library/iTunes/Scripts/* and they show up automatically in iTunes' Script menu.

Similarly, Microsoft Entourage, an email application, lacks any menu item or keyboard shortcut that truly deletes an email message. Deleting a message that's already in the trash folder (called "Deleted Items") does truly delete it, but deleting any other message merely moves it into the trash folder. This is spectacularly annoying when, for example, you are ready to delete spam messages that have been categorized into the Junk E-Mail folder. But Entourage is scriptable, and it has a Script menu to which you can add your own scripts. So I've written a script to delete all currently selected messages:

```
tell application "Microsoft Entourage"
    display dialog "Really delete selected messages completely?"
    set theMessages to current messages
    try
        delete theMessages
```

```
        delete theMessages
    end try
end tell
```

Some scriptable applications provide a means for customization at an even deeper level, by letting you modify what happens when you choose one of the application's own menu items or perform some other action in that application. For example, the Finder can be set up with Folder Actions that take over automatically when you do things such as move a file into a certain folder. (See "Automatic Location" in Chapter 2 and "Folder Actions" in Chapter 26.)

Combining Specialties

Different applications are good at different things. Most users don't perform all tasks in a single application. For example, in a word processor, you wouldn't expect to perform extensive editing of pictures: a document might include pictures, but you'd create and edit them in some other program, and then incorporate them into the word processing document. That's how it should be, and that's how users typically like it, especially on Mac OS X where (in contrast to previous systems) there is no significant penalty to running several applications at the same time. "Swiss Army knife" programs that try to be all things to all users generally seem bloated with unnecessary features (such as Microsoft Word, with its Photoshop-like "graphics enhancement" features).

When it comes to assisting applications to combine their separate specialties, Apple-Script really shines. Thanks to AppleScript, data can be moved back and forth between applications so that each can operate upon it in the appropriate manner. The result is a workflow in which multiple applications are coordinated, often without the intervention or even the awareness of the user.

Take, for example, SpamSieve. This superb application uses Bayesian algorithms to distinguish between spam and nonspam email messages with astonishing accuracy— far better than those email client programs, such as Entourage and Apple Mail, that include spam filtering of their own. But SpamSieve is not itself an email client. So in order to filter out spam as your email client application receives it, that email client application and SpamSieve must cooperate. The email client receives the mail messages, and hands them over to SpamSieve for evaluation; if SpamSieve marks a message as spam, it tells the email client application, which can then take appropriate action (such as moving the message into a Spam folder). Whenever you check for new mail messages, the two-way communication between your email client and SpamSieve takes place automatically, seamlessly, swiftly, invisibly—and entirely through AppleScript. Thus AppleScript effectively incorporates SpamSieve's brain and its special kind of intelligence into your email application; the two specialties (receiving email messages and storing them in folders, on the one hand, and knowing what is spam and what isn't, on the other) are combined.

An interesting variation on the theme of combining specialities arises when one of the specialized applications isn't on your computer. This is feasible because Apple-Script can send messages to remote applications (for details, see Chapter 23). For this example, we'll have the remote application be a web service. AppleScript supplies a built-in way to talk to a web service implementing an XML-RPC or SOAP interface.

 A good clearinghouse for finding and exploring SOAP-enabled web services is *http://www.xmethods.net*.

Suppose that in creating an email message, we'd like to append a random quotation in place of our normal signature. There are random quotation generators on the Internet, so we can incorporate one of these into a script that creates an email message. The example uses Entourage to create the email message. (I wanted to use Apple's Mail application, but at the time of this writing, scripting of signature creation and modification was hopelessly broken.)

```
try
    tell application "http://www.boyzoid.com/comp/randomQuote.cfc"
        set returnValue to call soap ¬
            {method name:"GetQuote", parameters:{HTMLformat:false}}
    end tell
    set L to |item| of returnValue
    repeat with anItem in L
        if |key| of anItem is "AUTHOR" then
            set auth to value of anItem
        end if
        if |key| of anItem is "QUOTE" then
            set quot to value of anItem
        end if
    end repeat
    set s to "-- " & return & quot & return & " -- " & auth
on error what
    set s to "No signature today, sorry."
end try
tell application "Microsoft Entourage"
    set sig to signature id 1
    set oldSig to (content of sig)
    set content of sig to s
    tell (make new draft window)
        set signature type to other
        set other signature choice to sig
    end tell
    set content of sig to oldSig
end tell
```

The script starts by calling a web service to generate a random quote. The result comes back as a record containing a list of two records (see Chapter 13); we then parse that structure to generate a signature. If anything goes wrong, there's no harm done; a dummy signature is used instead. A new Entourage outgoing message must use an existing signature, so we modify an existing signature, create the new message and apply the modified signature, and finally restore the signature's original text. Figure 1-1 shows the result of running the script.

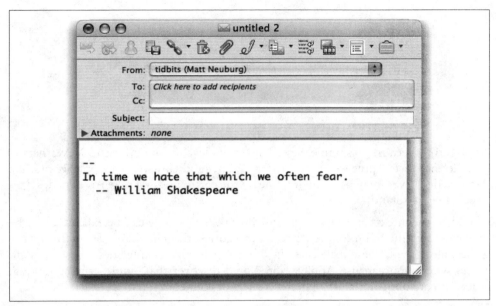

Figure 1-1. Mail message with a quotation supplied by a web service

For yet another example of combining specialties, see "Internally Scriptable Application" in Chapter 2, where a database supplies the email address for a new message in an email client program.

CHAPTER 2

Where to Use AppleScript

AppleScript, because it is implemented at system level, is omnipresent. Nevertheless, you do not use AppleScript at just any time and any place. AppleScript, like Archimedes' lever, may permit you to move the earth; but first, like Archimedes, you need a place to stand.

The various contexts and milieus in which AppleScript code can be executed may be conveniently grouped into a few general categories; this chapter presents these categories, along with some examples. In other words, this chapter describes the main *places* where you can use AppleScript. You'll discover that AppleScript is lurking, ready and at your command, in many corners of your computer.

The taxonomy presented here is somewhat artificial, and my names for the various kinds of context in which AppleScript can be used are mostly made up, but I don't think this makes the discussion any less useful. Bear in mind that the example scripts in this chapter are for the most part deliberately simple and contrived; the emphasis here is not on actual uses for AppleScript (as described in Chapter 1), but on places from which you can put it to use.

Script Editor

A *script editor* is an application such as Apple's own Script Editor (located in */Applications/AppleScript*)—a general development environment where the user can create, edit, test, and run AppleScript code. A script editor application will almost certainly be central to your experience of AppleScript. Although you may use AppleScript code in other contexts, those contexts will generally provide no facilities for working on that code. Thus, no matter where you intend to use your code, you will first develop it in a script editor; if you wish to use it in some other context, you'll transfer it to that context from the script editor when you are satisfied that it is ready. If, using it in that other context, you discover there's a problem with it, you'll probably bring the code back into your script editor to test and improve it.

A script editor application will usually allow you to do things such as the following:

- Edit a script in a convenient interface
- Display a scriptable application's dictionary, which describes how to talk to it with AppleScript
- Record user actions in AppleScript form, if a scriptable application is recordable
- Compile a script, and display the compiled script in pretty-printed format (compilation is a necessary intermediate step between editing and running AppleScript code, and functions as an initial check on that code's validity)
- Run the script's code
- View the result, if any, of running the script's code
- Save the script in any of the standard AppleScript formats

(Technical terms in this list are formally introduced in Chapter 3.)

There are three main candidates for use as a script editor: Apple's Script Editor, the freeware Smile, and the commercial Script Debugger. Each has its own advantages and peculiarities. You needn't feel confined to any single script editor; compiled scripts are a standard format, so any script editor can read the files of any other. (As of this writing, however, Smile still can't deal with bundle-formatted scripts.)

Using the AppleScript Utility application, located in */Applications/ AppleScript*, you can specify a default script editor application—the application that will open compiled script files when they are double-clicked from the Finder.

There are two hazards. First, the presence of Classic interferes somewhat; if anything but Script Editor is made the default editor, Script Editor files may try to open with the Classic Script Editor. Second, and more important, the distinction between files created by the different script editor applications is effectively destroyed; for example, if you use AppleScript Utility to set Script Editor as the default script editor, then a compiled script file subsequently created with Script Debugger may open in Script Editor when double-clicked.

Apple's Script Editor

Figure 2-1 shows a very short script being edited in Apple's Script Editor. The script has been compiled using the Compile button, which appears at the center of the toolbar at the top of the window; thus the script is pretty-printed with nice formatting and syntax coloring. The script has also been run, using the Run button in the toolbar; the result is shown in the lower half of the window. The script asks the Finder for the names of all mounted volumes; the response is a list of strings (see Chapter 13). Also shown is the Result History window, which logs the result of every execution of every script.

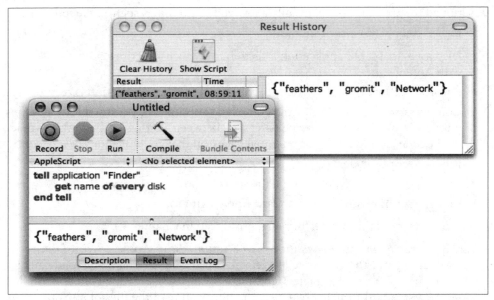

Figure 2-1. Apple's Script Editor

The lower pane of the script window consists of three tabs. The first tab, Description, lets the user enter a comment to be stored with the script. The second tab, the Result tab, is showing in Figure 2-1. The third tab, Event Log, records all outgoing commands and incoming replies—that is, of all lines of AppleScript that equate to Apple events sent to other applications, and the responses returned by those applications. The Event Log is operative only if the Event Log tab is selected when a script is run; but another window (not shown), the Event Log History window, can be set to operate even when it is not open. Both the Event Log History window and the Result History window are particularly useful while developing and testing a script.

The Script Editor includes some facilities for helping you navigate and edit your scripts. At the top of the window, at the right side below the toolbar, is a popup menu for navigating among handlers (subroutines) within the script. The contextual menu that appears when you Control-click in the window gives access to various utility scripts that drive Script Editor itself (which is scriptable) to modify the text in useful ways. (You can edit these scripts, or add utility scripts of your own; they live in */Library/Scripts/Script Editor Scripts*.) When the Script Assistant feature is turned on (in Script Editor's preferences), text is autocompleted as you type; press the Esc key to view or accept an offered completion.

Figure 2-2 shows an application's dictionary as displayed by the Script Editor. A dictionary contains (among other things) classes clumped into groups called "suites"; the dictionary window lets you navigate the resulting hierarchy. The figure illustrates two available navigation modes: you can use an outline at the left (front window) or a browser at the top (rear window). Here, the information for the disk class is being retrieved. Hyperlinks, a Back/Foward button in the toolbar similar to that of a web browser (rear window), and a Search field assist with navigation. The segmented button in the toolbar (rear window, left of the Print button) lets you display two further hierarchies in the browser: the containment chain (object model) and the inheritance chain.

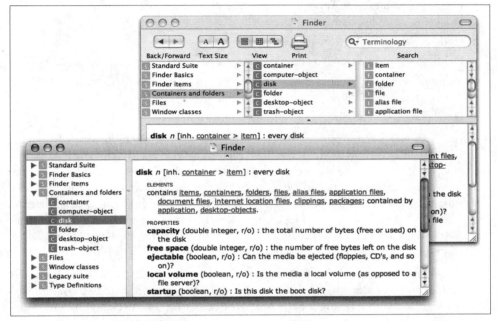

Figure 2-2. A dictionary in Script Editor

Smile

Another free script editor application is Satimage's Smile. It provides an excellent working environment, including fine text-editing and navigation facilities, full script-ability, and some remarkable features to help you in developing scripts, including:

- Execution of selected text
- Automatic persistence of variables and readily accessible global context
- Translation to raw four-letter codes (see Chapter 20)
- Display of AppleScript's own dictionary (see Chapter 20)
- Global terminology searching
- Integrated facilities for constructing custom dialogs and displaying graphics

Script Debugger

A third alternative is Late Night Software's Script Debugger. This is a commercial program, but its features can easily justify the price if you're planning on doing any serious AppleScript development; this book could not have been written without it. Among other things, Script Debugger provides:

- Display of script-level entity values
- Display of values and Apple events in several formats, with browser windows for analyzing complex datatypes
- Code coverage indication and timings
- Debugging facilities such as breakpoints, stepping, tracing, and expressions
- Superior dictionary display, with incorporation of inherited attributes, graphical class charts, and extensive cross-referencing
- Display of actual attributes of running applications

Figure 2-3 shows a script paused at a breakpoint in debug mode in Script Debugger (Version 4). The column at the left shows the line where we are currently paused—actually two lines, because we are paused while a handler is being called—with lines that have been executed shaded blue (code coverage). The drawer at the right displays the datatype and value of the most recently executed statement, the handler call stack, and the values of all variables and top-level entities currently in scope (including AppleScript's own properties—see Chapter 16). A complex datatype (a list) is shown in hierarchical format, with icons indicating the owner of object references.

Figure 2-4 shows Script Debugger's unique Explorer view, displaying the hierarchy of actual current Finder objects. The Finder's disk objects are listed among its top-level elements, and the listing for the first disk object has been opened further, drilling down the hierarchy two additional levels. The code needed to refer to the currenly selected object is displayed at the bottom of the window. At the right, a drawer charts the containment hierarchy in graphical form. This concrete display of a scriptable application's actual objects at a given moment is a very instructive and helpful means to understanding the repertory of things one can say to it.

Internally Scriptable Application

Some applications implement automation not through AppleScript but by means of some other language (possibly one unique to that application) that effectively operates entirely within that application. Such an application is *internally scriptable*. But even though such an application does not use AppleScript for its internal scripting, the developers might still wish it to be able to communicate with other applications. That means Apple events, and AppleScript is a convenient way (convenient both for the developers and for the end user) to construct and send Apple events. The internal scripting language can most likely operate on text, so a typical approach is to give

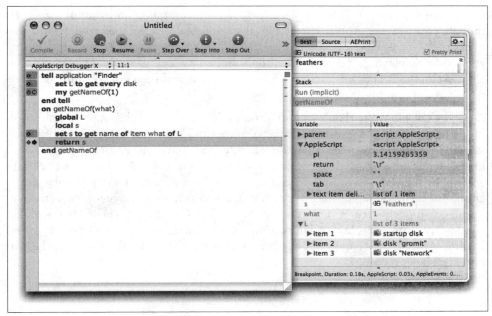

Figure 2-3. Script Debugger in action

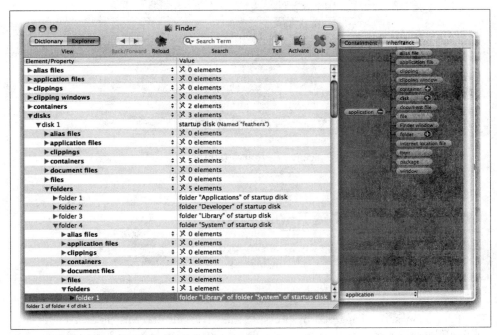

Figure 2-4. Explorer view in Script Debugger

it the ability to treat text as AppleScript code (by compiling and running it). Even though you can use AppleScript code in an internally scriptable application, you wouldn't want to develop it there, as there is no provision for editing and testing your code, displaying a target application's dictionary, and so forth. Thus you'll usually develop your code in a script editor application and then copy it into the internally scriptable application.

A good example is the database application FileMaker Pro. It has an internal scripting language that can execute text as AppleScript. This text can be static or constructed dynamically ("calculated"). Figure 2-5 shows a case in point, with FileMaker Pro being used to communicate via AppleScript with Apple's Mail program. The idea is that you might like to store your contacts in a true database program, but then you might like to create and send an email message to one of them in a true email client (see "Combining Specialties" in Chapter 1). Thus, the FileMaker window (in front) displays a database of contacts; pressing the "To" button causes Mail to create a new email message (in back) using the email address from the current FileMaker record.

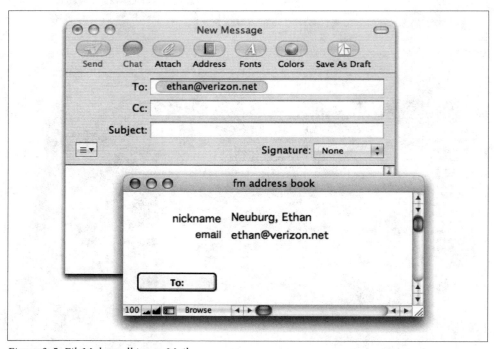

Figure 2-5. FileMaker talking to Mail

The FileMaker script triggered by pressing the "To" button consists of a single step, telling FileMaker to treat a piece of calculated text as AppleScript (entered by way of FileMaker's usual annoying cascade of modal dialogs, as shown in Figure 2-6):

```
    "set theAddress to \"" & fm address book::email & "\"
tell application \"Mail\"
    tell (make new outgoing message)
        set visible to true
        make new to recipient at end of to recipients ¬¶
            with properties {address:theAddress}
    end tell
end tell"
```

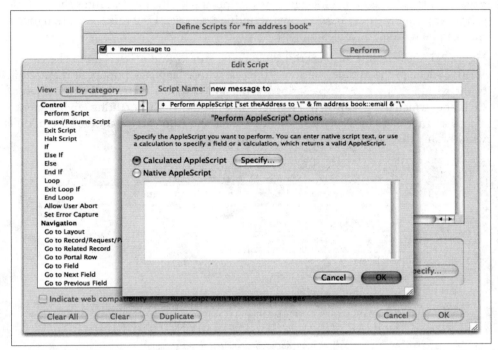

Figure 2-6. Specifying a calculated AppleScript step in a FileMaker script

The code is particularly ugly (and difficult to write), because it isn't AppleScript: it's the instructions, in FileMaker's internal calculation language, for constructing a string that will be treated as AppleScript. This string consists of three pieces—two literal strings, surrounded by quotation marks, and a reference to the current record's email field. The three strings are joined by FileMaker's concatenation operator (&, just as in AppleScript). But the constructed string must itself include quotation marks around the contents of the email field and around the name of the Mail application; to indicate these within a string literal, they have to be "escaped" by preceding them with a backward slash (\). This accounts for the rather bizarre appearance of the first and second lines of the code. But cheer up: things could be worse. At least FileMaker permits return characters within a string literal, so the code can be laid out in lines that reflect how the real AppleScript code would look. (The trick in the fifth line, allowing a line of AppleScript code to wrap in the middle by following AppleScript's line-continuation character with FileMaker's carriage-return character, is so bizarre that I won't even try to explain it.)

Another internally scriptable application is Radio UserLand, the inexpensive "little brother" of UserLand Frontier (for our purposes the two programs are essentially identical). It's a multipurpose scripting program, typically used for creating web pages and for maintaining blogs. It stores scripts internally, and executes them; these scripts are usually in UserLand's own scripting language, UserTalk, but alternatively they can be written in AppleScript.

Figure 2-7 shows some AppleScript code being run in Radio UserLand. The Apple-Script code is in the middle window—the one whose language popup, at the bottom of the window, is set to "AppleScript." (You should ignore the triangles at the left of each line, which are a feature of Frontier's outline-based script editing environment.) The UserTalk code in the bottom window calls the AppleScript code in the middle window and displays the result in the top window.

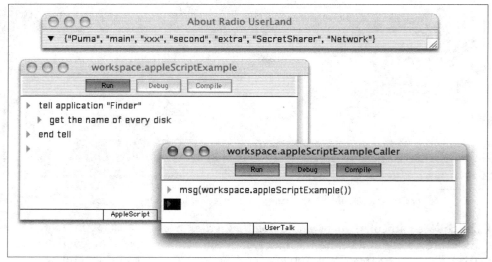

Figure 2-7. Radio UserLand

Script Runner

An application without facilities for editing or compiling scripts may nevertheless offer to execute compiled scripts for you on demand by way of some convenient interface, such as a menu. Such an application might be called a *script runner*. There is usually a requirement that a compiled script file be placed beforehand in some particular location where the script runner can find it. Because the script is compiled beforehand, a time-consuming step (compilation) is skipped, and execution typically proceeds considerably faster in a script runner than it does in an internally scriptable application where the code must be compiled from text on the fly.

Many scriptable applications act as script runners, typically by means of a special Script menu. This behavior is helpful because, having developed a script that drives such an application in a useful way, you might like some convenient interface for executing that script on future occasions; the application's Script menu provides such an interface. Scripts in an application's Script menu do not have to target that application, but the feature makes sense, and is provided, in the expectation that they will do so. (And when a script in an application's Script menu does target that application, there is sometimes a tremendous speed advantage over running that same script from elsewhere; see Chapter 22.)

For instance, as mentioned under "Customization" in Chapter 1, if you put scripts into *~/Library/iTunes/Scripts/*, iTunes will generate a Script menu listing them and permitting you to run them; so that's a good place to store and access your scripts that customize iTunes.

BBEdit is a particularly fine example of a script runner. Whatever compiled scripts you place in *~/Library/Application Support/BBEdit/Scripts/* will appear as menu items in BBEdit's Script menu, where a script can be run by choosing its menu item. For even more convenient access, BBEdit lets you assign keyboard shortcuts to these menu items. BBEdit also implements some further conventions that have become a sort of *de facto* standard: you can edit a script by holding Option as you choose it from the Script menu, and you can reveal a script file in the Finder by holding Shift as you choose it from the Script menu. BBEdit also provides some useful naming conventions for setting the order of the items in the Script menu (otherwise the scripts would always appear in alphabetical order, because that's how the Finder supplies them); read the BBEdit manual to learn more. As an alternative interface, BBEdit also lists and lets you access scripts in a floating window.

Some other programs that act as script runners through a Script menu are Script Debugger, Smile, Microsoft Entourage, Tex-Edit Plus, and various Adobe applications. Apple's Script Editor takes a different approach: instead of a Script menu in the menu bar, it lets you access the compiled script files in a specific location by way of the contextual menu (see "Apple's Script Editor," earlier in this chapter).

An application can act as a script runner in a noncustomizable way as well. For example, an application might incorporate scripts as ordinary menu items. This makes sense when an application is scriptable and can best implement a command's functionality by taking advantage of its own scriptability. Mail's File → Import Mailboxes menu item works this way.

There is also a Script Menu provided by Apple that gives systemwide access to scripts; this is particularly helpful when a script needs to be available from every application, or when its target application has no Script menu of its own. It appears as a status menu item (on the right side of the menu bar) in the form of a black scrolled s-shaped icon. If you don't see it, you can turn it on with the AppleScript Utility. The menu items in the Script Menu represent the folders and script files inside */Library/Scripts* and *~/Library/Scripts*; AppleScript Utility provides an option for toggling the visibility of the */Library/Scripts* items. The menu is global, but there is a special convention for specifying that a script should appear only when a particular application is frontmost: create a folder called *~/Library/Scripts/Applications/ <AppName>* (where for "AppName" you supply the name of some application), and put the script inside that. The Script Menu can also run Unix shell scripts, including Perl scripts. The Script Menu follows the BBEdit conventions for the Option and Shift keys.

 Apple's global Script Menu is a nice idea, but it should not, in my view, be seen as preferable to Script menus in individual applications (especially in view of the latter's speed advantage). Unfortunately, it is beginning to look as if that's just how Apple does see it. Apple's Mail program had a Script menu in Panther, but in the Tiger version this has been removed. I'm guessing that this is because Apple would prefer that you use the global Script Menu. If this is a trend, it's an ominous one.

A utility similar to the Script Menu, with some advantages such as keyboard menu shortcuts and easier creation of application-specific folders, is Red Sweater's Fast-Scripts. An alternative of a completely different kind, using contextual menus instead of a drop-down menu in the menu bar, is Ranchero's Big Cat. And Xendai's Bellhop lets you run a script from the Services menu that appears in most applications.

Still another script runner interface is provided by a *launcher* application. A launcher is a utility used to open things (folders, applications, files); many launchers will "open" a compiled script file by running it. My favorite is DragThing. DragThing's primary interface is a "dock" with clickable icons, where each icon is a file or folder; launching a compiled script with DragThing either runs it or opens it for editing, depending on whether you're holding down the Option key. An icon can also be assigned a keyboard shortcut that launches it, and docks can be set to be active only in a particular application or set of applications. Other examples of launchers are iKey and Keyboard Maestro.

Automatic Location

An *automatic location* is much like a script runner. But there's a significant difference. A script runner finds compiled script files in a prearranged location and offers you an interface so that you can run them when *you* want to. An automatic location is a place where an application finds compiled script files and runs them *automatically*, with no intervention on your part. The application runs the script when *it* wants to—typically in reponse to the occurrence of certain events or stimuli. This doesn't mean you've no involvement, though; you were involved when you arranged for the application to find this script in this location, or to look for it in response to this particular event or stimulus.

BBEdit is an example. I've mentioned (in the previous section, "Script Runner") that BBEdit will use a menu to let you run scripts it finds in a *Scripts* folder within *~/Library/Application Support/BBEdit/*. BBEdit looks for two additional folders in that location—*Startup Items* and *Shutdown Items*. These are repositories for scripts that BBEdit will run automatically in response to being launched and being quit, respectively. Similarly, when you choose from any of BBEdit's built-in menus, BBEdit will run an appropriately named script located in the *Menu Scripts* folder. Now, all these scripts and folders did not come into existence by themselves; you put them there. But once you've done that, since these are automatic locations, BBEdit runs the scripts automatically when the appropriate events occur.

Email clients, such as Apple's Mail and Microsoft Entourage, have "rules," which are essentially filter actions to be applied to mail messages. The usual configuration is to have these rules applied automatically when new mail arrives. One of the things such a rule can do is to run an AppleScript file. Again, these applications do not spontaneously invent the rules or include AppleScript files in them; you do that. But once you've done it, the application turns to the AppleScript file automatically in response to the arrival of new mail. iCal, too, can run an AppleScript file when the alarm for an upcoming event is triggered.

There are also "folder actions," a mechanism whereby a folder in the Finder can be set up to watch for when certain events occur within that folder—that folder's window is opened, closed, or moved, or something is put into or removed from that folder—and can respond to those events by running an associated script.

Some applications use automatic locations as their life's blood. For example, Salling Clicker is all about running AppleScript files in response to your pressing the buttons on a mobile phone or PDA. And Ovolab Phlink is all about running AppleScript files in response to phone calls arriving on your phone line, identification of the caller ID, the caller pressing buttons on a touchtone phone, the caller hanging up, and so forth.

For fuller treatment of the various ways in which a script can be triggered automatically (including an example of a folder action), see Chapter 26.

Application

The reasons why an application might want to employ AppleScript are the same as the reasons why anyone else would—the application wishes to communicate with some other application by way of Apple events (see "Is This Application Scriptable?" in Chapter 1). It is possible to write an application that forms and sends raw Apple events directly, without using AppleScript; but AppleScript makes the task much easier for the developer of an application, just as it does for anyone else.

To write an application that uses AppleScript, you don't have to be a professional developer who spends 15 hours a day at the computer and wears a beanie with a propeller. (Of course, the beanie can't hurt, either.) In fact, writing an AppleScript application could be as simple as saving a script from a script editor application. It may be useful to distinguish three different "levels" of application into which AppleScript can be incorporated: an applet, an AppleScript Studio application, and a standard compiled application that happens to call AppleScript. I'll just briefly survey all three levels here; the first two are revisited in more detail in Chapter 27.

Applet

An *applet* is just a compiled script saved with a tiny application framework wrapped around it. This application framework is just sufficient to turn the script into a stand-alone application. You can make an applet very easily: save your script from within a script editor application, and as you do so, choose to save it as an Application. (You make this choice in the Save dialog; if the script has already been saved, you may need to choose File → Save As to bring up the Save dialog.) The result is an application that, when it runs, behaves almost exactly like your script when *it* runs.

If an applet behaves like the script it contains, why would you bother to make one? Why not simply leave the script as a compiled script file? One reason would be that you want the script to run in some context where merely opening a compiled script file would not run it. One obvious example is the Finder. Let's say there's some operation you frequently need to perform, and the way you want to perform it is by double-clicking something in the Finder. Perhaps you find the Script Menu too much trouble; perhaps you like having an icon right on your desktop, where you can see and access it easily by double-clicking it. Or perhaps you don't want it on your desktop; perhaps you'd like to put it in the toolbar area of your Finder windows. (The toolbar is the area of a Finder window above the files but below the titlebar.) Single-clicking a toolbar item is exactly like double-clicking the same item on the desktop or in a Finder window. But double-clicking a compiled script file in the Finder doesn't run it; it opens the script for editing in a script editor application. On the other hand, double-clicking an applet (or single-clicking it in the toolbar) does run the script. (Indeed, Apple provides, at *http://www.apple.com/applescript/toolbar*, some example scripts for you to put into your Finder window toolbar, and guess what? They're all applets.)

Similarly, suppose you have a script that you'd like to run automatically when you log in to your computer. To run things automatically when you log in, as you doubtless already know, you put them into the list of Login Items in the Accounts preference pane. But it's no use putting a compiled script into that list; this is not an automatic location, where a compiled script, if found, will be run. The Login Items list is not, for example, like BBEdit's Startup Items folder discussed earlier in this chapter. What the Login Items list expects is an application. Well, you can turn a script into an application by making it an applet; so that's what you do.

Another advantage of applets over compiled scripts is that an applet can be a *droplet*—an application onto which you can drag and drop Finder items (files and folders) in order to process them with your script. An example appeared in "Calculation and Repetition" in Chapter 1.

AppleScript Studio

A compiled script or an applet has essentially no user interface. Your script can present a few basic dialogs for the user to interact with (as explained in Chapter 21), but that's all. This is usually not a problem, but sometimes it would really help to have some slightly more sophisticated user interface.

In this situation, AppleScript Studio can be helpful. AppleScript Studio is a way of writing a standard Cocoa application, with Mac OS X–native windows and interface widgets, when the only programming language you know is AppleScript—there is no need to know Objective-C, the default Cocoa programming language, and you don't need a very extensive understanding of the Cocoa application framework. AppleScript Studio doesn't give you direct AppleScript access to everything that Cocoa can do, not by a long chalk; but it can be an easy and rapid way to wrap an interface around some AppleScript code.

For example, Figure 2-8 shows an AppleScript Studio application containing a window that lists the user's hard disks. Here's the code:

```
on awake from nib theObject
    tell application "Finder"
        set L to (get name of every disk)
    end tell
    set content of table view 1 of scroll view 1 of window 1 to L
end awake from nib
```

Figure 2-8. A Cocoa application written with AppleScript Studio

That's all there is to it. The code is recognizable AppleScript; indeed, within the awake from nib handler, the first three lines are essentially the same as the script in Figure 2-1, asking the Finder for the names of the disks. The only addition is the fourth line, starting with set content, which populates the interface with the Finder's reply.

Cocoa

As an example of incorporating AppleScript into a standard application, I'll recreate the previous example as a Cocoa application written in Objective-C. The task is more involved than in AppleScript Studio, because we must twice "cross the bridge" between Objective-C and AppleScript: from Objective-C we must summon Apple-Script, and we must translate the response from AppleScript to Objective-C (whereas with AppleScript Studio there's no need for any of that, because the program is already written in AppleScript).

Cocoa has an NSAppleScript class that accepts and executes AppleScript code. There are two approaches: you can start with a string and compile and execute it, or you can start with a compiled script and execute that. Here's code demonstrating the first approach:

```
- (void) awakeFromNib {
    [self willChangeValueForKey:@"diskList"];
    diskList = [[NSMutableArray alloc] init];
    NSAppleScript* scpt = [[[NSAppleScript alloc] initWithSource:
        @"tell application \"Finder\"\r"
        "get name of disk 1\r"
        "end tell"]
        autorelease];
    NSAppleEventDescriptor* result = [scpt executeAndReturnError: nil];
    if ([result descriptorType] == 'utxt')
```

```
        [diskList addObject: [result stringValue]];
    else if ([result descriptorType] == 'list') {
        int i, u = [result numberOfItems];
        for (i=1; i<=u; i++)
            [diskList addObject: [[result descriptorAtIndex: i] stringValue]];
    }
    [self didChangeValueForKey:@"diskList"];
}
```

Even if you don't know any Objective-C, you can get a sense of what's going on here. Within the awakeFromNib method, the first two lines and the last line have essentially to do with the interface, and needn't concern us except to say that there is an instance variable diskList (an NSMutableArray) and whatever we put into it is going to show up in the interface as a line of the list displayed in our window. There are three lines where we form a literal string constituting our AppleScript code (the same code used in Figure 2-1); this string is slightly complicated because we must "escape" its quote characters, just as in the FileMaker code earlier in this chapter ("Internally Scriptable Application"), and we must explicitly insert "escaped" return characters. The next line (starting with the word NSAppleEventDescriptor) is where we ask for this AppleScript code to be compiled and executed.

After that, we have to do a surprising amount of work (and in fact we should be doing even more—I've deliberately omitted error checking, to condense the presentation). The problem is that when the reply comes back, we have to parse it differently depending on its type. This is all stuff that's taken care of for us when we get a result in a script editor application, but here we have to do it ourselves. If there's only one disk, the result will be a string; we insert that into diskList and that's that. If there's more than one disk, the result will be a list of strings, so we have to cycle through that list and insert each string into diskList. (The main surprise here for an experienced Cocoa programmer is that list indexes in an Apple event, unlike Objective-C collections, are 1-based!)

The other approach, probably faster, would be to compile the AppleScript code beforehand and incorporate the compiled script file into the project. When the application is built, the compiled script file is copied into its bundle as a resource. Instead of constructing the AppleScript code as a string, we retrieve the compiled script file from the bundle. So, for example, if the compiled script file is called *askFinder.scpt*, the relevant line of code (where we create our NSAppleScript object) would be changed to this:

```
NSAppleScript* scpt = [[[NSAppleScript alloc] initWithContentsOfURL:
    [NSURL fileURLWithPath:
        [[NSBundle mainBundle] pathForResource: @"askFinder" ofType: @"scpt"]]
    error: nil] autorelease];
```

The result when the application runs is a window that appears identical—and I do mean identical—to Figure 2-8; so I won't bother to repeat the screenshot.

Unix

Mac OS X, under the hood, is Unix. It is possible to use AppleScript from the Unix command line in the Terminal and from shell-related environments such as Perl and Ruby scripts, by means of the osascript command. osascript can execute a compiled script file or can compile and execute a string (indicated by the -e switch).

You can enter script text directly at the command line by typing osascript and a return character, then typing the text, and finally signalling the end of the text with Control-D. There isn't much likelihood you'd want to do this, but at least it proves that osascript is working, and the code looks exactly like normal AppleScript:

```
% osascript -ss
tell app "Finder"
get name of every disk
end tell
^D
{"feathers", "gromit", "Network"}
```

(The -ss flag causes the result to appear in the familiar way that AppleScript usually formats a list of strings.)

Use of a literal string on the command line raises some difficulties of escaping characters parallel to those we've seen earlier in this chapter; there are various solutions, depending on what shell you're using. In a language such as Perl, you can take advantage of the language's "here document" facility, which makes it easy to enter a multiple-line script without having to escape any quotes. Once again, the code looks exactly like normal AppleScript:

```
#!/usr/bin/perl
$s = <<DONE;
    tell app "Finder"
        get name of every disk
    end
DONE
print `osascript -e '$s'`;
```

Chapter 25 contains full details about calling AppleScript from Unix, as well as communication in the reverse direction (through AppleScript's do shell script command).

Hyperlinks

You can embed AppleScript code in an HTML hyperlink. The user can't actually execute AppleScript code by clicking such a link (the ability to do so would constitute a serious security hole). Rather, when the user clicks that link, the code is displayed in a script editor, ready to execute if the user desires.

The mechanism involved is the applescript URL protocol. The href attribute of the link's <a> tag must begin like this:

```
applescript://com.apple.scripteditor?
```

The specification of Script Editor's bundle identifier is apparently a security measure; it is required, but it is also superfluous, because applescript URLs cannot be made to target any other script editor application by changing this value.

 applescript URLs can be made to target a desired application (or applet) by means of a preference set by the user at system level. Apple provides no interface for setting this preference; but the freeware RCDefaultApp preference pane is an excellent way to do it (*http://www.rubicode.com/Software/RCDefaultApp/*).

The next component of the URL is one of the following three expressions:

```
action=new&
action=insert&
action=append&
```

They signify, respectively, that AppleScript code should be inserted in a new Script Editor window, placed at the insertion point in the currently frontmost Script Editor window, or appended to the end of the currently frontmost Script Editor window. (If no Script Editor window is currently open, all three have the same effect.)

Finally, the AppleScript code itself appears, in this format:

```
script=theCode
```

As this is a URL, illegal characters in *theCode* must be URL-encoded using a percent sign and the character's ASCII value in hexadecimal; for example, a space must be encoded as %20, a quote must be encoded as %22, and a return character must be encoded as %0D. At *http://www.apple.com/applescript/scripteditor/12.html*, Apple provides a utility script that URL-encodes text that has been copied to the clipboard, and embeds it in an applescript protocol <a> tag. Naturally, the script is provided as a link that uses, itself, the applescript protocol!

Thus, for example, this script:

```
tell application "Finder"
    get name of every disk
end tell
```

could be included in a web page as a link from the words "click me" using the following HTML (ignore the line breaks and other formatting, which are used here for clarity but would not be present in real life):

```
<a href="applescript://com.apple.scripteditor?action=new&script=
tell%20application%20%22Finder%22%0D
    %09get%20name%20of%20every%20disk%0D
end%20tell">click me</a>
```

A web page is not the only place you can put an applescript link; certain other contexts will permit links that specify non-HTTP protocols. For instance, you can include such a link in a PDF document; this would allow the reader to click in the PDF in order to capture in the Script Editor some code that you have embedded into the link; this device is extensively used in the Take Control electronic book series as a way of letting the reader obtain and run a utility script with no need to copy and paste from the PDF book (see *http://www.takecontrolbooks.com*). Similarly, you can include such a link in a QuickTime movie (for an example, see *http://brennan.young. net/Comp/LiveStage/GenerateASpath.html*) and in various other contexts.

Automator

Automator is a utility application, new in Tiger, that allows the user to construct a script (called a *workflow*) from a series of steps (called *actions*) in a graphical interface without knowing a programming language. The default actions are in */System/ Library/Automator/*; additional actions may be installed into */Library/Automator/* or *~/Library/Automator*, or they may be included in an application's bundle, where Automator can see them directly. Workflows can be saved as files to be run by Automator, as applications to be run independently (rather like an AppleScript applet), or as plug-ins for use by various applications: for example, a workflow saved as a Finder plug-in becomes a Finder contextual menu item, and a workflow saved as a Script Menu plug-in becomes a menu item in the Script Menu.

The default actions include a Run AppleScript action, which lets the user incorporate AppleScript code directly into a workflow. Even more interesting, an Automator action can easily be written using AppleScript, and instructions for doing this appear in Chapter 27. An action is a useful way to distribute a piece of AppleScript code to users. You can't know, after all, exactly what a user would like to do with your code, and some users don't understand programming well enough to customize Apple-Script code in a script editor themselves. An Automator action can help to solve these problems. An action can easily be positioned among other actions in a workflow that the user constructs in order to achieve a desired result. Furthermore, an action has a graphical interface, which lets the user set various parameters to the AppleScript code without coming into direct contact with that code.

Figure 2-9 shows a simple Automator workflow; it puts up a dialog asking the user to chooose a folder, and lists the pathnames of the items within that folder into a new TextEdit document. Notice the graphical interface that allows the first action to be customized so that the dialog asks for a folder, not a file. Notice also the dataflow paradigm that links the actions: each action produces an output, which functions as the input to the next action in the sequence. The second action produces a list of files and folders (as aliases), but the third action expects text; nevertheless the workflow succeeds because Automator coerces from one type to another as necessary (here, turning a list of aliases into POSIX pathnames separated by return characters).

Automator is in its infancy as of this writing, and it shows. The interface is extraordinarily clumsy: among other things, it's difficult to find the action you want, because the interface, in a misguided attempt to make this easier, causes the order in which

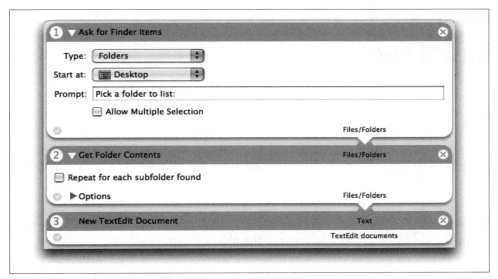

Figure 2-9. An Automator workflow

actions are listed to change constantly (and there's no way to see them simply listed in alphabetical order). There is no provision for branching or looping, so workflows are necessarily very simple. Worst of all, Automator suffers from a serious dearth of useful actions. This, however, is a shortcoming that you, the AppleScript programmer, are in a position to correct. For example, Figure 2-10 shows a workflow that gets the song currently playing in iTunes, retrieves its name, and shows that name as the iChat status message seen by online buddies. (This particular workflow isn't really needed, as iChat now has an option to show the currently playing song as its status message automatically.) Automator doesn't include an action to get an iTunes song's name, nor does it include any actions having to do with iChat. These omissions, however, are easily remedied: I wrote those actions myself, in about five minutes. After you've read Chapter 27, you'll be able to do the same.

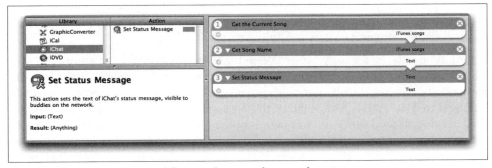

Figure 2-10. An Automator workflow involving two homemade actions

CHAPTER 3
Basic Concepts

Previous chapters have been pure introduction. Chapter 1 has shown what Apple-Script is good for; Chapter 2 has toured the places on your computer where you can use AppleScript. If you're new to AppleScript, you should now be feeling informed and motivated and ready to begin sinking your teeth into some solid facts. If you already have some familiarity with AppleScript, you may be leafing forward through this book, looking for the serious part to begin. Either way, look no further. This is it. The solid, serious stuff starts here.

This chapter formally defines and describes AppleScript—what it is, why it exists, where it lives, and how it works—along with all the basic terms and concepts connected with it. Subsequent chapters will provide further details about some of what's here, but they all presuppose the basis laid out in this chapter. Whether you think of it as an introduction, a survey, or a glossary, to understand this chapter is to know AppleScript's world.

Apple Events

AppleScript would be pointless without Apple events. Apple events lie at the heart of what AppleScript is, what it does, how it works, and why you're going to use it. From writing more efficient AppleScript code to understanding an application's dictionary, a basic acquaintance with Apple events will help you.

A long time ago, in a galaxy far away—actually it was probably in about 1989, in Cupertino, California—some very smart people were completely redesigning and modernizing the Macintosh operating system, creating what was to become System 7 (released in May 1991). And some of these people had a brilliant idea. The system, they decided, should support a messaging system, a way of letting one running application communicate with another. Such communication is called *interapplication communication*, and the messages sent between applications are called *Apple events*.

There are two parties to an interapplication communication: the application that initiates the message, and the application that receives it. I like to refer to these as the *sender* and the *target*, respectively; I find this clearer and more instructive than the more technical terms "client" and "server."

An Apple event is an astonishingly powerful thing. Hermes-like, it crosses borders: two completely independent applications, with no prior arrangement or synchronization, are suddenly talking to each other. What's more, Apple events work across a network, including the Internet, so these two applications can be on different computers. Or, just the opposite, an application can send an Apple event to itself. (Why would it want to do that? You'll find out, in the section "Recordability," later in this chapter.)

The breadth of what may be expressed in an Apple event is also quite amazing. Their structure amounts to a remarkably sophisticated grammar: Apple events are like little sentences, possessing (so to speak) verbs and nouns and modifiers, and this grammar is so cleverly and flexibly devised that individual Apple events can be constructed to say surprisingly complicated things, such as (speaking to a word processing program), "Look at the text of your first window and give me a reference to every line of it whose second word begins with the letter t," or (speaking to an email program), "Look in the mailbox where the incoming mail is, find the first mail message with a subject that starts with the word 'applescript,' and move it into the 'AppleScript' mailbox." Much of the grammar of the AppleScript language is as it is because of the grammar of Apple events.

Reply

Every interapplication communication (under normal circumstances) results in a *reply* from the target application. The reply is itself an Apple event.

This comes as something of a surprise to the naïve user. As human beings, we naturally tend to feel that there are, broadly speaking, two reasons for sending an interapplication communication: either we tell the target to do something or we ask the target a question. Therefore an interapplication communication can be thought of as either a *command* or a *query*. We expect a reply from a query—that's the purpose of the query—but not from a command. Under the hood, however, there is no real technical distinction here; either way, it's the same kind of message, and either way, there will be a reply.

What's the use of a reply from a command? Well, for one thing, even a command might result in some information useful to the sender. For example, the AppleScript make command creates a new entity—a document or a word, for example—but it also generates a reply, which is a reference to the newly created entity. That's useful because the usual reason for creating something is to do something with it, and it might be tricky to get a reference to the newly created entity otherwise.

There is also a solid technical reason why every interapplication communication generates a reply. Remember, these two applications are running independently, so they have to be coordinated somehow if they are to interact coherently. The sender, having sent a command to the target, typically doesn't want to proceed to its own next step until the target has finished obeying that command. The reply informs the sender that the command has been carried out (or, alternatively, that an error has occurred).

When two independently running applications communicate with each other, things can go wrong. The sender sends a message to the target, and then what? The target application might try to obey the message, and crash—leaving the sender in a state of limbo, waiting for a reply that will never come. The target might obey the message, but require a great deal of time to do so. The target might be busy or otherwise not in a position to receive the message in the first place. The sender needs a way to hedge his bets in order to cope with such possibilities. Apple events provide some bet-hedging mechanisms.

Timeout value

> The sender may attach to the message a *timeout* value, a statement of how long he is willing to wait for an answer. If a reply doesn't come back within the specified time, the sender receives a reply anyway—a reply saying that, for one reason or another, no reply came back in time. Thus the sender has an opportunity to respond coherently to the situation. (Meanwhile the target is probably still performing his time-consuming task, blissfully unaware that the sender has lost interest.)

Ignore reply

> The sender may signal up front that he won't be interested in the reply (presumably this is a command, not a query); he doesn't care to know what the reply is or whether there is one, or even whether the command was carried out. In this case the sender does not wait; the message is sent, and the sender immediately proceeds to the next step of his own process. The sender will never find out in any direct way what became of the Apple event. This devil-may-care approach is rather rarely used, but there are times when it comes in very handy.

Scriptability

Not just any old Apple event can be sent to any old application. Well, it can, but the result could easily be an error message instead of the desired result. The target application needs to have been constructed in the first place in such a way that the particular Apple event you send is one to which it is prepared to respond. Such an application defines internally a *repertory* of Apple events that it understands. The application is then said to be *scriptable*.

The thing to understand clearly here is that a scriptable application is scriptable just with respect to the particular repertory of Apple events that the application itself defines. To a remarkable degree, every scriptable application gets to make up its own repertory; one scriptable application's repertory of acceptable Apple events doesn't necessarily resemble that of any other scriptable application. This presents something of a problem for the sender, as every possible target application is picky in a different way about what can be said to it.

This problem washes over into AppleScript, and is in fact one of the single greatest challenges facing the AppleScript programmer. It would be an exaggeration to claim that the AppleScript language is different with respect to every scriptable application—it's the vocabulary that changes, while the underlying language remains the same—but certainly a programmer trying to drive a particular target application for the first time often feels that all previous experience has suddenly been made irrelevant. (For a vivid account of a real-life user struggling with this challenge, see Appendix A.)

The knowledge of what Apple events a scriptable application can respond to, and what it will do in response to them, is an implicit fact built into its workings, not an explicit fact written somehow on its face. How, then, is it possible to know what a scriptable application's repertory is? Some secondary document is clearly needed to expose this information. In the AppleScript world, this document is the application's *dictionary*, a resource built in to the application for the specific purpose of describing its repertory. There is a section about dictionaries later in this chapter, and an entire chapter devoted to them later in the book (Chapter 20).

The Life of an Apple Event

There's obviously more to the story of interapplication communication than just the sender application and the target application. For example, earlier it was said that the sender normally receives a reply even if the target isn't even listening. How is this possible? It's possible because the system itself functions as the intermediary through which all interapplication communications happen. The sender doesn't speak directly to the target, but to the system. It is the system that is responsible for passing the message on to the target, and for letting the sender know how things went.

Figure 3-1 shows in more detail the process whereby an Apple event is sent and a reply is returned.

1. The sender application (at the left of the figure) constructs the Apple event. The Apple event is rather like a letter inside an envelope that you post in the mail. It has information about how it is to be directed—who the target application is, and whether the sender intends to wait around for the reply, and if so, what the timeout value is. This information is intended for the system, and is rather like the stuff that goes on the outside of the envelope. Then there is the content—the details as to what kind of Apple event this is and the particular data that it involves. This information is intended for the target application, and is rather like the letter inside the envelope.

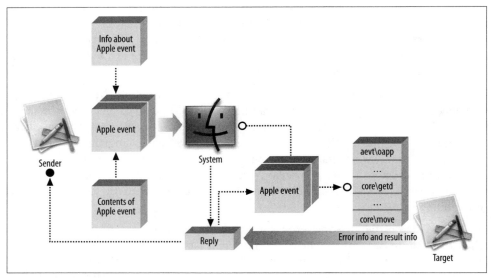

Figure 3-1. Life of an Apple event

2. The sender application calls the system (in the middle of the figure) and hands it the Apple event. The system, rather like the postal service, examines the Apple event and looks at the information about how it is to be directed. Using this information, the system tries to locate the target application. Let's presume that it succeeds in doing this.

3. The target application (at the right of the figure) is portrayed as having a repertory of Apple events to which it is prepared to respond. These Apple events are listed using pairs of four-letter codes. (Apple events really are identified by pairs of four-letter codes, and the Apple events shown in the diagram are genuine, common Apple events.)

4. The system contacts the target application, handing it the Apple event supplied by the sender. The system also attaches to this Apple event a reply Apple event. It is rather as if, when the post office delivers a letter to you, it were to provide a stamped addressed envelope for you to put your reply into. The system holds out this reply event to the target application, but doesn't let go of it.

5. The target application (presuming it is well behaved) responds to whatever the Apple event asks it to do, either doing it successfully or generating an error message; then it puts the result into the reply event. There are two parts to this result. First, the target application must supply a value signifying whether things succeeded. Second, the target application may insert into the reply any other information to be returned. If there was an error, it can insert a message describing the problem; if things succeeded and a result is expected, it can insert that result.

6. The target application now signs off, and the system is left holding the reply Apple event (of which, as we said, it never let go). The system now delivers the reply Apple event to the sender application, and the story ends.

What an Apple Event Looks Like

An Apple event was never meant for human eyes. It is meant to be machine-constructible and machine-parsable. Nevertheless, it is possible to encode all the facts about an Apple event in a textual format. One commonly used format is called *AEPrint*. Let's examine an AEPrint representation of a real live Apple event, to get an idea of what a typical Apple event looks like. The Apple event we'll use is a rather elaborate one I mentioned earlier, an Apple event that means: "Look in the mailbox where the incoming mail is, find the first mail message with a subject that starts with the word 'applescript', and move it into the 'AppleScript' mailbox." Example 3-1 displays that Apple event in AEPrint format.

Example 3-1. A raw Apple event

```
core\move{
    insh:insl{
        kobj:obj {
            form:'name',
            want:'Mbox',
            seld:"appleScript",
            from:'null'()
        },
        kpos:'end '
    },
    ----:obj {
        form:'indx',
        want:'cobj',
        seld:1,
        from:obj {
            form:'test',
            want:'msg ',
            from:obj {
                form:'prop',
                want:'prop',
                seld:'unBX',
                from:'null'()
            },
            seld:cmpd{
                relo:'bgwt',
                obj1:obj {
                    form:'prop',
                    want:'prop',
                    seld:'subj',
                    from:exmn($$)
                },
                obj2:"applescript"
            }
        }
    }
}
```

I don't want to burden you with a full explanation of Example 3-1 (especially since the whole point of AppleScript is that you shouldn't have to worry about what a raw Apple event looks like), but a few characteristic points are of interest.

First, notice the predominance of four-letter codes. Nearly everything seems to consist of exactly four letters: core, move, insh, insl, kobj, form, want, seld, from, prop, kpos, indx, cobj, test, and so forth. Even some things that appear to be only three letters are actually four letters: obj and end and msg, for example, actually have a fourth character (a space).

> These four-letter codes are actually integers. An integer is four bytes, while a character from the ASCII range is one byte, so an integer can express four "packed" characters. The expression of this integer as a four-letter string is simply a convenience for the human reader. The use of single quotes to delimit a four-letter code is a standard convention, and I'll use it in later parts of this book.

Second, observe the overall structure of the Apple event, which is actually quite simple. The command itself is specified in the first line: core\move, exactly as shown in Figure 3-1. Just about every Apple event has at least one parameter, known as the direct object; this is symbolized by ---- (can you find it?), and this particular Apple event also has a second parameter, symbolized by insh.

Finally, you've probably already spotted the repeating pattern form, want, seld, from, which appears throughout the Apple event. This is how an Apple event specifies an object (such as "the 'AppleScript' mailbox"), something that it very commonly needs to do; we'll talk more about the AppleScript avatar of this pattern later on ("Element Specifiers" in Chapter 11).

Go and Catch an Apple Event

What I did to capture the Apple event displayed in Example 3-1 was to turn on the Apple Event Log in Script Debugger, which has an option to display Apple events sent from Script Debugger in AEPrint format. Even if you don't have Script Debugger, you can do something similar. In fact, you can do something even better: you can capture and view *any* Apple event as it flies through the system on its way from sender to target. The system, as we have seen, plays the central role of postman whenever an Apple event is sent. Now imagine that Apple events are secret messages, and that you are an international spy who would like to get a look at them when they are sent. In effect, you would like to waylay the postman, bonk him over the head, snatch the letter out of his hand, and glance at its contents. Well, you can.

First, open the Console; that's where certain Apple events are going to be reported to us. Next, go into the Terminal and enter the following (I'm assuming your shell is bash, the default in both Panther and Tiger):

```
% export AEDebugSends=1; export AEDebugReceives=1
```

These commands turn on the environment settings that cause Apple events to be intercepted and reported. These settings will apply only within this shell session, and only with respect to applications that are launched from within this process. So, let's launch one:

```
% open /Applications/Safari.app
```

Now any Apple events sent to Safari will be logged. Let's send one. Possibly you were unaware that the Unix open command is implemented in Mac OS X with Apple events; you're about to discover that it is. Say this:

```
% open http://www.apple.com
```

(I'm assuming here that Safari is your default browser.)

Within the Terminal, the process started by the open command sends an Apple event, and this fact is reported within the Terminal. Immediately afterwards, Safari receives this Apple event, and this fact is reported within the Console. The two Apple events are exactly the same event. As reported in the Console, when Safari receives it, it will look something like this:

```
AE2000 (556): Received an event:
------oo start of event oo------
{ 1 } 'aevt':  GURL/GURL {
            return id: 38666240 (0x24e0000)
       transaction id: 0 (0x0)
   interaction level: 112 (0x70)
       reply required: 0 (0x0)
   target:
     { 1 } 'psn ':  8 bytes {
       { 0x0, 0x3e0001 } (open)
     }
   optional attributes:
     < empty record >
   event data:
     { 1 } 'aevt':  - 1 items {
       key '----' -
         { 1 } 'TEXT':  20 bytes {
           "http://www.apple.com"
         }
     }
}

------oo  end of event  oo------
```

The Apple event is displayed in a slightly different text format from Example 3-1. I don't know the official name for this text format, so let's call it AEDebug format. AEDebug format is more verbose (and more informative) than AEPrint format, but the same basic elements are clearly present: this is a GURL\GURL event with just one parameter, namely the direct object designated by ---- (which turns out to be the actual URL that Safari was asked to open).

Another way to send an Apple event from the Terminal is to use AppleScript directly, by way of the osascript command (already mentioned under "Unix" in Chapter 2, and formally discussed in Chapter 25). In the Terminal, enter this:

```
% osascript -e 'tell app "Finder" to get disks'
```

This command causes the Terminal to spew out large amounts of information, most of it having to do with the mechanics of compiling and running AppleScript code, and culminating in the Apple event sent to the Finder, along with the Finder's reply. It should look something like this:

```
AE2000 (811): Sending an event:
------oo start of event oo------
{ 1 } 'aevt':  core/getd {
           return id: 53149700 (0x32b0004)
       transaction id: 0 (0x0)
   interaction level: 64 (0x40)
       reply required: 1 (0x1)
   target:
     { 2 } 'psn ':  8 bytes {
       { 0x0, 0xc0001 } (Finder)
     }
   optional attributes:
     { 1 } 'reco':  - 1 items {
       key 'csig' -
         { 1 } 'magn':  4 bytes {
           655361 (0x10000)
         }
     }

   event data:
     { 1 } 'aevt':  - 1 items {
       key '----' -
         { 1 } 'obj ':  - 4 items {
           key 'form' -
             { 1 } 'enum':  4 bytes {
               'indx'
             }
           key 'want' -
             { 1 } 'type':  4 bytes {
               'cdis'
             }
           key 'seld' -
             { 1 } 'abso':  4 bytes {
               'all '
             }
           key 'from' -
             { 4 } 'null':  null descriptor
         }
     }
   }

------oo  end of event  oo------
```

Once more you can see the characteristic parts of an Apple event. This event is called core\getd; it has one parameter, the direct object designated by ----; and that direct object is an object specifier comprising the standard form, want, seld, and from.

What All This Has to Do with AppleScript

A raw Apple event in AEPrint or AEDebug format isn't impossible to read, but it isn't exactly easy either. Constructing one is even harder. Raw Apple events are meant primarily for computers, not for humans, to construct and to read. But now look at this:

```
move item 1 of (every message of incoming mail ¬
    whose subject begins with "applescript") ¬
    to end of mailbox "appleScript"
```

That is the very same Apple event from Example 3-1, but this time it's expressed in an English-like form. It's quite legible, and you can probably imagine constructing something like this for yourself. I certainly hope you can imagine it, because that's what this book is all about. That code is AppleScript.

Now you understand why AppleScript exists. AppleScript is a programming language whose chief purpose is to allow Apple events to be constructed and presented in an English-like form that is fairly intuitive and accessible to a human being. Thanks to AppleScript, you can take advantage of the power of Apple events, constructing and sending them for yourself.

The Open Scripting Architecture

When System 7 was being created, along with Apple events and many other new technologies, it was already Apple's plan to create a language, AppleScript, that would give end users access to the power of Apple events. But, much to the disappointment of users and developers, there wasn't time to create AppleScript before the release of System 7 in mid-1991, and the bulk of the work was postponed until 1992–1993.

One of the conundrums facing the founders of AppleScript at this time was the architectural question of where the language should live. They could have made AppleScript the internal scripting language of a single application, like HyperCard's HyperTalk, but this would mean that the user would run AppleScript code entirely from within this one application, which was unacceptable. AppleScript needed to be available everywhere, and thus would somehow have to be part of the system. But what part? There was no good place, so a new one was created: the resulting structure is the *Open Scripting Architecture* (OSA).

Components

Under the OSA, a scripting language is implemented by a something called a *component*. (Components were not invented specially for the OSA; they existed already in connection with QuickTime.) Think of a component as a piece of self-contained functionality made available at system level so that any program can hook up to it and use it. One thing that's special about components is that they can be installed and uninstalled dynamically. So an OSA-savvy program doesn't necessarily think in terms of any particular scripting language; it asks the system—in particular, the Component Manager—what scripting languages are presently installed, and if it wants to use one, the Component Manager provides access to it.

Because components are installed dynamically, this installation must actually take place while the computer is running. AppleScript is installed as the computer starts up and simply left in place, so that it's always available. You may recall that under Mac OS 9 there was an extension called AppleScript (in the Extensions folder of the system Folder). Its job was to install AppleScript as a component under the OSA as the computer started up. On Mac OS X, the same function is performed by a file called *AppleScript.component*, which is in */System/Library/Components*; this type of file is called a *component file*.

One nice consequence of this architecture is that Apple can easily release upgrades to AppleScript, and the user can easily install them, with no effect on any other part of the system. AppleScript itself has a version number, which refers to the version number of the installed component that implements it; you can find out what this is by running the following one-word script in the Script Editor:

```
version
```

At the time of this writing, the result is "1.10.3".

Other Scripting Languages

One of Apple's purposes in designing the Open Scripting Architecture was to provide a place for other scripting languages that already existed, and for yet others that might exist in the future—hence the "Open" in its name. AppleScript is the only OSA language supplied by Apple, and in fact is designated the *default scripting component*, the one that is used when no particular scripting component is specified. Still, in theory there can be others.

In actual fact there have never been many other OSA languages. This may be because developers have not felt much need to supply them. (It also may be because the OSA itself hasn't quite lived up to its original promise.) Here are a few that I know of:

- UserTalk, the internal scripting language of UserLand Frontier
- QuicKeys Script, the scripting language of CE Software's QuicKeys
- JavaScript, by way of Late Night Software's JavaScript OSA

- AppleScript Debugger, the debuggable version of AppleScript used by Late Night Software's Script Debugger

- The OSABridge components, created by Philip Aker

JavaScript OSA and AppleScript Debugger come in both a Mac OS 9 form (extensions called *JavaScript* and *Script Debugger Nub*) and a Mac OS X form (component files called *JavaScript* and *ScriptDebugger*). UserTalk and QuicKeys Script were available only on earlier systems. (UserTalk was truly dynamic, being loaded and available to other applications only when Frontier itself was running. On Mac OS X, UserTalk is still Frontier's internal scripting language, but it is not available as an OSA language. Similarly, QuicKeys Script is not present as an OSA language in the Mac OS X version of QuicKeys.)

Let's take JavaScript OSA as an example. (It's free, so you can easily try it out.) You put the *JavaScript* component file into */Library/Components*; you then log out and log in. The effect is that JavaScript is now available as an OSA scripting language on your machine. This means that any OSA-savvy environment can see it. For example, in Apple's Script Editor, there's an OSA language popup menu at the left side of the top of the window, below the toolbar (in Figure 2-1 this says "AppleScript"); this popup menu now displays "JavaScript" as an alternative language, meaning that you can switch to JavaScript and compile and run a JavaScript program, right within Script Editor. This behavior illustrates the dynamic and generalized nature of the Open Scripting Architecture.

(A cool feature of JavaScript OSA is that it adds to the JavaScript language some classes allowing Apple events to be expressed. Thus it enables JavaScript to be used as an alternative to AppleScript for driving scriptable applications. See Appendix B.)

A slightly different approach is taken by the OSABridge components. They do not, of themselves, implement a language; rather, they act as a bridge (hence the name) from the OSA to the text-based shell scripting languages already present in Mac OS X (Perl, Ruby, Python, PHP, sh, and Tcl). Among other things, this bridge makes it easy to package a script in one of these languages as an applet or droplet (see "Applet and Droplet," later in this chapter), and the Tcl component lets your script implement a graphical user interface.

Talking to a Scripting Component

Knowledge of an OSA scripting language resides in the component, not in the OSA-savvy application that uses it. For example, earlier we said, in the Terminal:

```
% osascript -e 'tell app "Finder" to get disks'
```

The phrase 'tell app "Finder" to get disks' is an AppleScript expression; when we gave this command in the Terminal, it was obeyed—references to all mounted volumes were displayed in the Terminal. But the Terminal doesn't know AppleScript.

The shell, to which we're talking in the Terminal, doesn't know AppleScript. And the osascript program, which we call from the shell, doesn't know AppleScript either. So who does know it? The AppleScript scripting component, of course.

Similarly, the Script Editor, even though it is the place where users mostly work with the AppleScript language, does not in fact know any AppleScript. The Script Editor is merely a conduit, a front end to the AppleScript scripting component, where all the work of compiling and running scripts actually takes place. That is why, in the previous section, the Script Editor was willing to stop compiling and running AppleScript and start compiling and running JavaScript instead.

There are two approaches that an application can take when it wants to gain access to a scripting component. An OSA-savvy application like the Script Editor wants to be able to access any scripting component at all, indiscriminately. For this purpose, the OSA supplies a special component called the *Generic Scripting Component* (GSC). The program asks the Component Manager to let it talk to the GSC, and after that the GSC routes communications between the program and the appropriate scripting component such as AppleScript. Alternatively, an application might ask the Component Manager for direct access to one particular scripting component. Either way, once it's in communication with the appropriate scripting component, the application can do scripting in that scripting language.

Figure 3-2 diagrams a typical chain of events by which a program turns text into a runnable script, runs it, and is able to display the result, under the OSA:

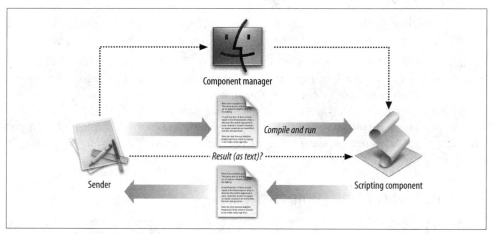

Figure 3-2. The OSA in action

1. The program asks the Component Manager to put it in touch with the scripting component.

2. The program obtains some text and hands it to the scripting component with instructions to compile and run it. If any of the expressions in this script are

equivalents of Apple events, those Apple events will be generated and sent, and we will then be in the world of Figure 3-1.

3. The program asks the scripting component for the result as text; the scripting component complies.

The process diagrammed in Figure 3-2 is how a script editor application such as the Script Editor works. In fact, you can even build a simple working version of the Script Editor yourself, using the developer tool Interface Builder. With the example application shown in Figure 3-3, I can enter text, compile it, display it pretty-printed, and run it; yet, in creating this application, I didn't write a single line of code. This isn't because Interface Builder knows any AppleScript, but because the project uses an OSAScriptController to mediate between the Open Scripting Architecture and the text field in the window.

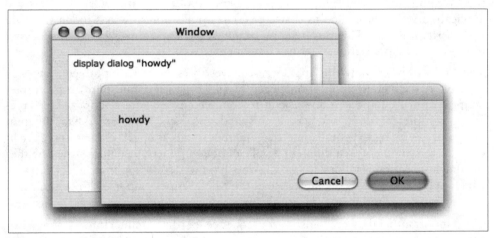

Figure 3-3. Rolling your own Script Editor

Maintenance of State

One of the structural problems that the Open Scripting Architecture was intended to solve was that of simultaneity. In those early days, remember, System 7 had only just introduced a way of letting more than one application run at the same time (cooperative multitasking), without which Apple events and AppleScript would clearly be impossible. Now imagine the following scenario. Application A starts to run an AppleScript program, and will yield time to the AppleScript engine until the program is finished. The AppleScript engine encounters a line involving an Apple event, and will itself yield time, while the system delivers the Apple event to application B. But now suppose that, in the course of responding to this Apple event, application B were to start running some AppleScript code. The system can't say: "No, don't do that; my AppleScript engine is busy!" Rather, the system will have somehow to accommodate the possibility that two or more AppleScript programs may run simultaneously; every running AppleScript program thus needs somehow to be accorded the same status as a real application, with its own context and state that can be preserved while it is paused to give time to other processes.

Components are implemented in a special way that helps to solve this problem, which is one reason why components lie at the core of the Open Scripting Architecture. I'll describe metaphorically how it works. Imagine the AppleScript scripting component as a kind of little universe, a universe where the knowledge of AppleScript resides. And imagine that this universe can make copies of itself. When an application asks the Component Manager for access to the AppleScript scripting component, as at the top of Figure 3-2, it isn't simply given a telephone line to the one master copy of the AppleScript universe sitting in the system; instead, it's as if the Component Manager makes a copy of the AppleScript universe and gives the application a telephone line to that copy. The application now has its *own private AppleScript universe*. This private copy of the AppleScript universe is technically an *instance* of the AppleScript scripting component.

You can readily see how this architecture solves the simultaneity problem. Suppose we have two different applications, each of which gets a connection to the AppleScript scripting component and asks it to compile and execute a script. The AppleScript component does not get all flustered and say, "Oh, gosh, two different programs are trying to get me to do two different things at once!" Rather, there are in effect at that moment two different AppleScript component instances—the one that the first application is talking to and the one that the second application is talking to. Each application asks its own instance of the AppleScript component to compile and execute its script, and there is no conflict or confusion at all.

One important and characteristic consequence of this architecture is that each instance of a component has a memory of its own. When paused, it remembers what it was doing. We say that a component can *maintain state*. When it is handed a script to compile, it remembers the script. After compilation, it remembers the compiled version of the script. After the script is executed, it remembers the result. And this is true of each individual instance of the component, separately; state is maintained *individually for each instance*. The component to which a program gets a connection is like an instance in the world of object-oriented programming (that's why it's called an instance). In terms of our analogy, each little AppleScript universe remembers what goes on in it. Thus an application is able to return again and again to its same AppleScript universe and refer back to things that happened earlier. Multiple applications can do this at the same time, and yet the AppleScript scripting component maintains state for each of them without getting confused at some global level, because it isn't operating at a global level. It's operating at a local level—local to the application that summoned it.

You can see this happening in Figure 3-2. Recall that from the calling application's point of view, there are two separate steps: first the application hands the AppleScript scripting component some text to be compiled and executed; then, after execution is completed, the application asks for the result. The fact that the application can come back a second time and ask for the result of an execution that took place earlier is an example of the AppleScript scripting component's ability to maintain state. Similarly, although this does not appear in Figure 3-2, it would be possible to introduce a third step: we could have our application initially hand the text to the AppleScript component and ask it to compile it, but not (at that time) to execute it. Our application could then later return to the AppleScript component and say: "Hey, remember that script I had you compile a little while ago? Now I'd like you to execute it." And this will work, because the AppleScript component remembers the compiled version of the script.

Back in the world of System 7, on a computer where memory was tight and under a system architecture where context switching was slow, this approach was downright elegant. Virtually no information passes between the calling application and the AppleScript component instance unless the calling application explicitly demands it. Thus, for example, when the application asks for some text to be compiled, it does not receive a copy of the compiled code unless it asks for it. Then later, when the application comes back and asks that the compiled script be run, there is no overhead of handing across a lot of compiled code; the AppleScript component already has the compiled code, and is ready to rock and roll (as a computer scientist would say) with no further ado.

An application *can* ask the AppleScript component for a copy of the compiled code in various forms, though; and there are certain occasions when it will wish to do so. A script editor application, for example, immediately after compilation, will ask for a pretty-printed version of the code, for display in the script window. And then there's the problem of extended persistence. The internal memory of an AppleScript scripting component instance, after all, will not persist forever. The lifetime of one of these instances can be no longer than that of the application that summoned it. When that application quits, any of these little component universes that it may have created must also fade away, and all the stuff that a component instance has been remembering escapes like the air from a popped balloon. So if an application asks the AppleScript scripting component to compile a script and then wants the compiled version to persist somehow after the application itself quits, it must take special steps to obtain the compiled version from the AppleScript component and save it to disk. This in fact is just what a script editor application does when you save a compiled script file.

Script

The word "script," like a number of terms associated with AppleScript, is liable to be tossed rather loosely about in a bewildering variety of senses. Some of its meanings are technically important and therefore indispensable, so it will help if we pause to clarify its chief uses explicitly.

Script as Drive

To "script" an application is to automate it, to drive it, to target it. People say, "I'd like to script the Finder to rename some files automatically." There is an implication that the Finder already has the power to do things to files, and that we are merely taking advantage of this power by dictating programmatically a sequence of actions that the Finder should take. This, after all, is why the Finder is said to be "scriptable" in the first place.

This sense of "script" is formalized in the way some sources define a "scripting language." This quotation comes from the ECMAScript Language Specification (*http://www.ecma-international.org/publications/standards/ECMA-262.htm*):

> A scripting language is a programming language that is used to manipulate, customise, and automate the facilities of an existing system. In such systems, useful functionality is already available through a user interface, and the scripting language is a mechanism for exposing that functionality to program control. In this way, the existing system is said to provide a host environment of objects and facilities, which completes the capabilities of the scripting language.

That is a perfect description of AppleScript. It has few powers of its own; it is meant primarily for controlling the powers of existing applications.

Script as Program

The preceding quotation from ECMA continues:

> A scripting language is intended for use by both professional and nonprofessional programmers. To accommodate nonprofessional programmers, some aspects of the language may be somewhat less strict.

This leap is common enough, but in my view it is unwarranted. Most languages commonly referred to as scripting languages are full-fledged programming languages, and make no particular concession to informality or inexperience. There is arguably nothing easy, and certainly nothing simplistic, about Tcl, Perl, or Scheme. As far as ease of use is concerned, any distinction between a scripting language and a programming language is a distinction without a difference.

Unfortunately this false distinction has played a major role in the history of Apple-Script, especially in Apple's own official propaganda. Even today, Apple's main web page on AppleScript (*http://www.apple.com/applescript/*) talks about how you "write script files" that "make decisions"—along with many other such extraordinary verbal contortions clearly intended to avoid using the word "program" (which never appears).

The term "script" has thus ended up as an acceptable synonym for the politically incorrect "program." Ostensibly, you do not program with AppleScript; you script with it. What you write are not programs; they're scripts. You're not a programmer; you're a scripter. This, I feel, is just silly. AppleScript is a programming language (and, I happen to think, not a particularly easy one). You are a programmer, and you will write programs with AppleScript.

Script as Script Object

Many AppleScript programs that you write or read will contain the term `script` used to demarcate part of their code. Here's an example:

```
script myScript
    display dialog "Hello from " & (get my name) & "!"
end script
run myScript -- dialog says: Hello from myScript!
```

The first three lines are a block of code starting with the word `script`. Such a section of code is often called a *script object*.

In fact, it turns out that an AppleScript program as a whole is itself a script object. This may sound confusing, but in fact it's quite a cool and sophisticated aspect of AppleScript. Thus it is reasonable and rigorously correct to speak of an AppleScript program as a whole as a script, not as a way of avoiding the fact that it is a program, but as a way of expressing its ontological status within the world of AppleScript. As you'll learn later, a script as a whole and a script object within a script have exactly the same ontological status. The script-as-a-whole does have some special features of its own, because it is the ultimate container of any other script objects; it is the top-level script object. But it is not different in kind from script objects that it may contain. (We'll fully explore the details of script objects later in the book, especially in Chapter 8.)

Script as Scripting Component Operand

The term "script" also refers in a completely technical and rigorous sense to a unit of operation between an application that asks for some AppleScript code to be compiled or executed and the scripting component that does the actual work. When such a program sends the scripting component a bunch of text for compilation, as in Figure 3-2, that bunch of text is assigned an identifying number. This number points to the code that is being remembered by the scripting component, and is called its *script ID*. It is by this arrangement that the application and the scripting component can continue to talk about the code while it persists over time, as described earlier in this chapter ("Maintenance of State"). The code itself, the thing being remembered by the scripting component, is thus technically a script, because that's what the scripting component itself calls it. A script is a kind of entity that the scripting component holds on to and can perform various operations on, such as compiling it or executing it.

Script as File

The individual code file is an important and meaningful unit in AppleScript. Unlike some programming environments, where multiple files are assembled through a "make" or some other build process into a separate object file embodying the complete program, with AppleScript the individual file *is* the complete program. An Apple-Script program and the file containing it are thus coterminous. But, as we have just seen, an AppleScript program is a script, because it is a script object. In fact, it will turn out that any script object can be saved as a file (see "Compiled Script Files as Script Objects" in Chapter 8). Just the other way around, any saved compiled script file can be handed to an AppleScript scripting component (as a script) and executed. There is thus a natural and meaningful correspondence between scripts and files, and it makes sense to speak of the file in which your code is saved as itself a script. We see this use of "script" in many places. The script file icon in the Finder seems to represent the script. One says, "Double-click the script to open it in the Script Editor." The Script Editor itself speaks of saving your code as a script.

Compiling and Decompiling

To compile your AppleScript code is a necessary intermediate step between editing it and running it. This section explains what this means, and then discusses some of the implications for you, the AppleScript programmer.

Compiling

To *compile* code means to transform it from editable text to a form that is understood by some engine that will run the code. The particular form depends upon the nature of the particular engine. At one end of the spectrum, the engine might be the computer's central processing unit (CPU), in which case the code is turned from text to machine-language instructions; that, for example, is how Fortran and C work. At the other end of the spectrum, one can postpone compilation until the program is actually running and a line of code is encountered; for example, in some implementations of BASIC, such as the one that came with the original Apple II, the runtime engine accepts pure text, compiling and executing that text one line at a time. A language that works this way is said to be *interpreted*.

In the early days of computers, most language implementations fell into one camp or the other, being either compiled or interpreted. These days, however, many popular scripting languages (such as Perl, Python, and Java) are implemented through a compromise technique where the entire program is initially compiled into an intermediate representation, which is then fed to a runtime engine that accepts and executes it a chunk at a time. In effect, such languages are compiled, then interpreted. Apple-Script works this way.

Like those other scripting languages, AppleScript code is compiled into *bytecode*, meaning that, roughly speaking, the nouns and verbs of the original text are translated into a sort of compressed, coded equivalent, called *tokens*. These tokens are meaningful to the AppleScript scripting component's runtime engine (and illegible to everyone else). The runtime engine interprets the bytecode, parsing whatever tokens it meets along its path of execution, accumulating them into chunks, and translating these chunks further, as necessary, in order to execute them.

There is sometimes a prejudice against interpreted languages as being slow. It is true that the compiled code must be processed further while being run before it can *really* be run, but this need not make the language particularly slow—no one complains, for example, that Perl is slow. The AppleScript runtime engine, however, probably does run a good deal slower than it should. Whether you'll perceive this slowness in practice depends on the nature of the script and on the speed of your computer; with today's fast computers, the observable bottleneck will typically be the time required to send Apple events to the target application and for that application to respond, more than the overall speed of the AppleScript runtime engine. (Tips for improving script speed appear in Chapter 22.)

The AppleScript compiler is what's called a *single-pass compiler*; this is a fairly simple-minded approach to compilation, but it helps to ensure that your script has a certain level of legality and overall consistency *before* runtime. (Of course, even a legal, successfully compiled script could still choke at runtime, but this would be for a different kind of reason; you'll see many examples over the course of this book.) Consequently, the runtime engine has less work to do, and is therefore smaller and faster, than if AppleScript were not compiled at all.

Also, the use of compilation makes AppleScript a better language. For instance, the following AppleScript code is legal:

```
sayHowdy( )
on sayHowdy( )
    display dialog "Howdy"
end sayHowdy
```

In this code, we call a handler, sayHowdy( ), before we've defined it. If AppleScript code were not compiled intially, this would not be possible, because upon encountering this reference to a handler it has not yet met, the runtime engine simply wouldn't know what to do.

Just a reminder: all AppleScript code must be compiled before it can be executed. In a script editor application, if you edit code in a script window and then ask to run the script, the script editor application will attempt to compile it first. AppleScript will refuse to run even a single line of a script if it cannot first compile the whole thing (though the script editor application Smile gives you a way around this, because it permits compilation and execution of individual lines of code in a text window). Code that has already been compiled doesn't have to be compiled again in order to be executed *as long as it is not edited*. If you edit *any* of the code in a script, the *entire* script must be compiled anew before it can be executed.

Decompiling

A curious feature of AppleScript is that it not only compiles scripts, it decompiles them, turning compiled bytecode back into human-readable text. Decompilation is not an unknown procedure in the computer world, but it's usually a kind of hacker tool (used, for example, to steal someone else's code); I don't know any other computer language where decompilation is a routine behavior of the language implementation itself.

AppleScript decompiles on two main occasions: right after you compile a script, and when you open a compiled script file for display in a script editor application. The procedure in both cases is essentially the same. When a compiled script is displayed to a human user, it is pretty-printed, with indentation to reflect the script's structure, and different kinds of word shown in different fonts, sizes, styles, and colors. This pretty-printing, as we have seen, is performed by the AppleScript scripting component, not by the script editor application (the script editor application merely asks the AppleScript component for the pretty-printed script and displays it). The AppleScript scripting component generates the pretty-printed version of the script, not from the original text, but from the compiled bytecode. In other words, in order to generate the pretty-printed text, it decompiles the bytecode.

 The way different kinds of word are formatted for pretty-printing depends upon your formatting preferences. You set these in a script editor application; for example, in Script Editor, you use the Formatting pane of the Preferences window. Your choices here are remembered by the AppleScript scripting component itself, and thus are truly global, affecting all scripts displayed in all script editor applications.

This behavior has some curious consequences. The pretty-printed code that you see when you compile your text in a script editor application is not, you understand, a colorful version of *your* text; it's a completely *different* text, supplied by decompiling the compiled script's bytecode. Therefore, some of the words constituting your script may actually differ before and after compilation. For example, suppose you type this code into a script editor application:

```
tell app "Finder" to get ref disk 1
```

Compile that code. Now your code is displayed like this:

```
tell application "Finder" to get a reference to disk 1
```

The reason is that some AppleScript terms have abbreviations that are acceptable for purposes of compilation, but the scripting component substitutes, at compile time, a token signifying the canonical form of the term; thus, when it decompiles the bytecode, what you see is the canonical form.

AppleScript may even, in the course of decompilation, rebreak your code's lineation. AppleScript allows you to break long lines into shorter lines through the use of a

---

continuation character (¬); at compile time AppleScript will sometimes undo your attempts to use this feature, removing your continuation characters or putting them somewhere else. If I compile this code:

```
do shell script "echo 'hi'" ¬
    password "myPassword"
```

AppleScript rebreaks it like this:

```
do shell script ¬
    "echo 'hi'" password "myPassword"
```

The reason is that the bytecode contains no information about whitespace, so the new formatting imposed by the decompilation process may not correspond to your original whitespace. This looks like a trivial annoyance, but if the line were longer it wouldn't be so trivial. Fortunately, the current version of the Script Editor wraps long lines, so the problem is far less disruptive than it was in the past because there isn't much need to use the continuation character any more.

(Some more examples of this odd behavior of AppleScript's will appear in "Abbreviations and Synonyms" in Chapter 5 and elsewhere, including "Variable Names" in Chapter 7.)

Compiled Script Files

A compiled script file is just what you think it is: it's a file containing the bytecode of a compiled script. Unlike text, a compiled script file can be executed without being compiled (because it's already compiled); the runtime engine is fed the bytecode and can leap into action immediately. A lengthy script can take several seconds to compile, so a compiled script file clearly saves some time and overhead when the script is executed. Obviously this architecture is advantageous when the script is not going to change and therefore will not need compiling ever again—when you distribute the script to others, for example. Applications that act as script runners typically operate on compiled script files (see "Script Runner" in Chapter 2). Script editor applications save a script as a compiled script file by default. When an application has asked the AppleScript scripting component to compile some text, a compiled script file is the only way for the compiled script to outlive that instance of the AppleScript scripting component, which will go out of existence when the host application quits.

(There is actually more to a script, and therefore there can be more to a compiled script file, than the compiled bytecode. I'll discuss these further contents of a compiled script file in "Persistence of Top-Level Entities" in Chapter 8 and "Closures and Stored Script Objects" in Chapter 10.)

You cannot save as a compiled script file code that, for whatever reason, will not compile. This seems tautological, but it can be surprising nevertheless, so it is worth mentioning.

Compiled Script File Formats

To make things more complicated, a compiled script file can come in not one, not two, but three different formats:

Resource-fork file
> The bytecode is kept in the file's resource fork; there is no data fork. The type is 'osas'; the extension is *.scpt*. Historically, this is the oldest form. Script Editor will not create a file in this form (though Script Debugger can), but if Script Editor encounters such a file it can open, edit, and save it in the same form.

Data-fork file
> The bytecode is kept in the file's data fork. (There may be a resource fork, but it's for other things, such as the script's description and window state.) The type is 'osas'; the extension is *.scpt*. This is the default form created by Script Editor, where it is called simply "script"; Script Debugger calls it "Compiled Script (Data Fork)."

Script Bundle
> The bytecode is kept in the data fork of a file called *main.scpt*, which has no resource fork and lives inside the *Contents/Resources/Scripts* folder of a bundle. (A *bundle* is a folder that is presented through the graphical user interface as a file.) Other information is stored in the data fork of other files in the bundle; the description, if any, lives in a file called *description.rtfd*, and window state is stored in the bundle's *Info.plist*. The bundle can be used to hold further ancillary resources (an example appears in Chapter 25). Script Editor calls this format "script bundle"; Script Debugger calls it "Compiled Script (Bundle)."

Originally there was just one compiled script format—the resource-fork file. Life was simple: any context that might open a compiled script file in order to run it (technically known as *loading* the script) could be relied upon to deal with any compiled script file whatsoever. Then when Mac OS X came along, there was a general move to eliminate use of the resource fork everywhere; this resulted in the data-fork file format. Finally, Panther introduced the script bundle format, along with some system functionality that in theory would allow an application to load a compiled script file without worrying about its format.

> A resource-fork script file and a data-fork script file look exactly the same from the outside, so to distinguish them you have to be sneaky. You can do it using the command line in the Terminal; an easy GUI-based alternative is HexEdit (*http://www.ifd.com/hexedit*).

> The wholesale deprecation of resource forks early in the history of Mac OS X has now, ironically enough, been countered by a move in the opposite direction, generalizing the resource-fork mechanism to allow multiple, arbitrarily named forks. See John Siracusa's article on file metadata in Tiger: *http://arstechnica.com/reviews/os/macosx-10.4. ars/6.*

Two kinds of problem have resulted from this proliferation of compiled script file formats. The first has to do with backwards compatibility. A script bundle can't be opened on any system before Panther (Mac OS X 10.3). A data-fork file can't be opened on most pre–Mac OS X systems. But those are the only two formats that Apple's Script Editor can create, so any compiled script file created by Script Editor will lack some backwards compatibility.

(To be precise about data-fork file compatibility, a data-fork file created by the current Script Editor can usually be opened by Script Editor 1.8.3 on a pre–Mac OS X system. But if you go back any further, to Script Editor 1.4.3—which was the standard as recently as the early days of Mac OS 9—it won't be able to open it.)

The second problem is that some applications in common use predate the development of one or both of the more recent formats, or for some other reason fail to take proper account of the multiplicity of possible formats. So, for example, Entourage X can't deal with data-fork scripts, and Entourage 2004 can't deal with script bundles. (In fact, iTunes doesn't deal very well with script bundles either.) NSAppleScript (used by Cocoa applications to load compiled scripts) can deal with resource-fork files in Tiger, but couldn't do so in Jaguar (Mac OS X 10.2). This puts the onus on the programmer to make sure the intended script file format will work properly in the particular context where it is to be run, while longing for the good old days when a script was a script was a script.

Run-only Scripts

Normally, a compiled script actually contains two kinds of information:

- The tokens (bytecode) needed to run the script
- Further information needed to decompile the script and display it to the user

For example, let's say you put a comment into your script. This comment is nothing that the runtime can execute; that's what it means to be a comment. But clearly you don't want this comment thrown away merely because you compile the script; the compiled script therefore retains it, so that when the script is decompiled, you can still read the comment. Similarly, the names of variables are intended entirely for humans; as far as bytecode is concerned, it would be sufficient to assign them numbers, and that's probably what AppleScript bytecode does. But you want to be able to read your variable names the next time you edit the script, so they are saved as part of the compiled script, even though they aren't needed for execution.

A compiled script can optionally be saved as *run-only*. (In Script Editor, this option appears as a checkbox in the Save dialog; in Script Debugger, choose File → Export → Run-Only Script.) In this case, the tokens needed merely to decompile the script and display it to the user are not written into the resulting compiled script file. This makes the compiled script file much smaller and probably causes it to run a bit faster, but it cannot be opened for display or editing.

Be careful when saving a script as run-only. If you have not retained a separate copy that *isn't* run-only, *you will never again be able to read or edit that script.*

The usual reason for saving a script as run-only is to keep it from prying eyes—you want to be able to send the script to other people so they can use it, without their being able to read it. There are, however, alternative ways to accomplish the same goal, which may be easier or friendlier. The scripts in an Automator action or an AppleScript Studio application are run-only; but these built products are separate from the original scripts, which remain editable on your machine.

Script Text File

A script text file is exactly that: it's an ordinary text file, such as can be opened by any word processor, consisting of the uncompiled text of your script. Any script editor application will typically offer an option for saving a script as text. No bytecode is saved into the file, and the script need not be capable of compilation in order to be saved as text—as opposed to a compiled script file, which by definition can't be saved unless the script can be compiled. (Apple's Script Editor does also attempt to compile the script when you save it as text, and will report any compilation errors even though saving succeeded; this seems like a bug.) The conventional extension for a script text file on Mac OS X is *.applescript*, but it is still of type 'TEXT'.

Most script runners will refuse to execute a script text file; they generally expect a compiled script file, whereas a script text file is not compiled (and the script runner is not willing to do the compilation).

A script text file is described by Apple's documentation as a kind of low-grade, last-resort alternative to a compiled script file. But it does have certain advantages. For one thing, obviously, you can save it even though you can't compile the script, so if you're developing a script that won't compile or that you'd rather not compile just now, you have a way to save it. Also there are matters of compatibility and portability. Recall that Apple's Script Editor can't create a compiled script file that will work on early versions of Mac OS 9 or before. And (as I'll discuss later in this chapter) a compiled script file can face difficulties if AppleScript can't locate a needed external referent, which can happen particularly when the script is moved to another computer. A script text file overcomes all these difficulties; it's just text, and therefore is absolutely portable to any machine running any system. Some version of Apple-Script and the Script Editor will be present on just about any machine running Mac OS, so the file can be opened and, if the code is valid, the script can be compiled there.

A valuable feature of Script Debugger is that it saves the original text (as a resource) even into a compiled script file. It's like having two files in one, a compiled script file and a script text file, with all the advantages of both. If there's a problem with the compiled script file (for example, if external referents can't be located or are incorrectly identified by AppleScript), the script text can still be recovered.

Applet and Droplet

An *applet* is an application with very little graphical user interface, consisting essentially of a compiled script along with a minimal amount of standalone executable code, called the *bootstrap code*, along with some other resources necessary to make the application scriptable. The bootstrap code, which runs when the applet is launched, simply summons a scripting component called the Script Application Component; this component does the rest, handing the compiled script over to the AppleScript scripting component for execution, and taking care of such application-like functionality as putting up the applet's menu and its description window if there is one. Thus an applet is a tiny application which, when launched, runs a compiled script embedded within it. A script editor application will allow you to make an applet as simply as saving a compiled script file, just by choosing applet format (called "application") when you save (or choose File → Save As).

When you save your script as an application, the script editor application looks to see whether it has an open handler. If it does, the application becomes a *droplet*. A droplet is just like an applet, except that it has a different creator type (the creator type for an applet is 'aplt', while for a droplet it's 'dplt') and a slightly different icon; functionally, the difference is that a droplet does something when file or folder icons are dropped onto its icon in the Finder. Typically, a droplet responds to the dropped items by processing them in some way (for an example, see "Calculation and Repetition" in Chapter 1). A droplet can also function like an applet: as a droplet, it does something when items are dropped onto its icon, while as an applet, it does something when it is launched from the Finder.

An applet's script remains editable unless you save it as run-only. Unlike a compiled script file, you can't edit an applet's script by opening the applet from the Finder, because that launches the applet. Instead, you open it from within a script editor application, using File → Open, or by dropping the applet's icon on the script editor application's icon in the Finder. A running applet may also display some graphical interface offering a chance to edit its script.

An applet (or droplet) may alternatively be saved in bundle format; it is then an *applet bundle*. (Apple's Script Editor calls this format "application bundle.") This format is parallel to a bundle script; it has the same advantages (the bundle can contain other resources) and the same compatibility limitations (it cannot be used on a system earlier than Panther, Mac OS X 10.3). It also has an additional advantage of great importance: an applet bundle can contain and use a scripting addition, thus solving a longstanding limitation of scripting additions; this advantage is shared with AppleScript Studio applications, which are, after all, also a kind of bundle. (See "Scripting Addition" in this chapter, and "Loading Scripting Additions" in Chapter 21. An example of an applet bundle in action appears in "Persistence" in Chapter 27.)

An applet (not an applet bundle) created by Apple's Script Editor can be both executed and edited on any earlier system. Amusingly, this makes an applet a much more portable format than a compiled script file. (An option that was present in earlier versions of the Mac OS X Script Editor, such as version 1.9, to make an applet "require Classic," was confusing and unnecessary and is now mercifully gone. For the same effect, simply use the "Open in the Classic environment" checkbox in an applet's Finder Info window.)

But what about compatibility in the other direction? An applet created in an sufficiently early system obviously can run only in Classic. In (Classic) Script Editor 1.4.3, by which time Mac OS X was already on the rise, there is an option to save as a Mac OS X applet, but in fact the resulting applet won't open in Mac OS X. Finally, in (Classic) Script Editor 1.8.3, this distinction was abolished; an applet saved with this version of Script Editor runs in Classic or in Mac OS X.

For further details about how to make and write applets and droplets, as well as to learn how to use AppleScript Studio to write more sophisticated AppleScript-based applications with a user interface, see Chapter 27.

Scripting Addition

AppleScript is a little language, and at a very early stage it was felt to be a bit *too* little. An architecture was therefore devised whereby Apple, as well as third-party developers, could extend the language by means of *scripting additions*. A scripting addition is a code library, typically written in a compiled lower-level language such as C, whose purpose is usually to endow AppleScript with some functionality that can be implemented in this lower-level language (possibly by calling into the Macintosh Toolbox) but is otherwise missing from AppleScript itself. On Mac OS 9 and before, a scripting addition is a resource file of type 'osax'; on Mac OS X it can also be a bundle with extension *.osax*. Therefore it is common parlance to refer to a scripting addition as an *osax* (official plural, *osaxen*).

When an instance of the AppleScript scripting component comes into existence, it loads any scripting additions found in any of several locations, namely */System/ Library/ScriptingAdditions* and the corresponding folders in */Library* and *~/Library*.

(On Mac OS 9 and before, there is just one location, the Scripting Additions folder of the System Folder. Observe the lack of a space in the Mac OS X folder name *ScriptingAdditions*; the tale of how that happened is gory and not to be recounted here, and in any case it's too late now to change it.) If a script depends upon a scripting addition, it is up to the end user to install that scripting addition first on any machine where that script is to run. Unfortunately, end users can't be relied upon to do this, which makes it hard to share your scripts with other users if your scripts depend upon any third-party scripting additions. Fortunately, an applet bundle or an AppleScript Studio application will also load scripting additions contained within its own bundle, an innovation that nicely solves the problem.

Tiger comes with just two scripting additions installed by default: StandardAdditions and Digital Hub Scripting. Some earlier systems came with half a dozen scripting additions from Apple, which was confusing; the StandardAdditions osax incorporates most of the functionality of these earlier files.

Communication between a running script and a scripting addition takes place by way of Apple events, just as for a scriptable application. But a scripting addition is not an application, so it doesn't have to be running in order for a script to talk to it. There is also an important linguistic difference to the AppleScript programmer between a scripting addition and a scriptable application, having to do with how the terminology is resolved. To talk to a scriptable application using terminology defined in that application's dictionary, a script must explicitly target that application. But the terminology defined in a scripting addition's dictionary is simply present as part of the language, without the programmer's targeting anything at all. (In fact, you *can't* target a scripting addition.) This sounds cool, but in practice over the years it has become something of a nightmare, because the more scripting additions you've got installed, the more likely it is that vocabulary terms implemented in a scripting addition will clash with terms you'd like to use, with terms of another scripting addition, with terms of some scriptable application, or even with the core AppleScript language. (This point is taken up again in detail in Chapter 20.)

Dictionary

AppleScript is a little language. It is also an extensible language. The purpose of AppleScript is to communicate with scriptable applications by means of Apple events; each such application can extend the terminology of the language in its own way, defining a repertory of Apple events to which it is prepared to respond, along with the English-like AppleScript terms to which these Apple events and their various parts correspond. To be scriptable with AppleScript, the application must publish information about this repertory. The mechanism by which this publication takes place is a resource called a *dictionary*.

The AppleScript scripting component uses the dictionary when compiling and decompiling a script, for two purposes:

- To confirm, at compile time, that the English-like terms used by the AppleScript programmer are legal
- To translate, at compile time and at decompile time, between English-like terms and Apple event structures

Not only does a scriptable application have a dictionary; a scripting addition does too, and for the very same reasons. (In fact, AppleScript itself has a dictionary.)

Dictionary Formats

A dictionary may be expressed in any of three formats:

The 'aete' resource
> The `'aete'` resource is present in scriptable applications in Mac OS 9 and before, and in Carbon applications in Mac OS X (and optionally in Cocoa applications as well). For information about its format, see:
>
> *http://developer.apple.com/documentation/mac/IAC/IAC-308.html*
>
> In Xcode, to see a header file defining some relevant constants, choose File → Open Quickly and enter **AEUserTermTypes.h**.
>
> An `'aete'` resource may be static or dynamic. AppleScript can read a static `'aete'` resource directly off the disk; but it has to ask the application for a dynamic `'aete'` resource (which it does by sending the application an Apple event, of course), which means that the application must be running in order for its `'aete'` resource to be read. The advantage of the dynamic approach is that the dictionary can be constructed in real time, in response to current circumstances.

The scriptSuite and scriptTerminology files
> This pair of files are an innovation of Cocoa Scripting, a technology intended to allow a developer to write a scriptable application in Cocoa fairly easily. They are XML (property list) files with extensions *.scriptSuite* and *.scriptTerminology*. For information about their format, see:
>
> *http://developer.apple.com/documentation/Cocoa/Conceptual/Scriptability/Tasks/SuiteDefs.html*
>
> These files are not directly usable by AppleScript. Rather, the Cocoa engine translates them into a dynamic `'aete'` resource when the application launches. Because of this, a Cocoa application that uses these files to implement its scriptability must be running in order for AppleScript to consult its dictionary; this is why certain applications are launched when you compile a script that targets them. For this reason, and because Cocoa's rendering of these files can result in a "substandard" `'aete'` resource (Apple's word, not mine), some Cocoa applications include a static `'aete'` resource as well.

The sdef file

An sdef (pronounced "ess-deaf") is an XML file expressing dictionary information. It was invented as part of Panther (Mac OS X 10.3); there, however, it could not be used directly as a dictionary. Instead, it was merely a convenient way to construct a dictionary; the sdef file had then to be translated into either or both of the other two formats by way of a provided tool called sdp.

On Tiger, things are greatly improved. First, the sdef specification has been changed in such a way as to allow it to express aspects of a dictionary that were impossible with the earlier sdef type, or even with an 'aete' resource. Second, a Cocoa application's sdef can be read directly by AppleScript. Thus, on Tiger, an sdef is a better dictionary—better than a dictionary has ever been before. The downside is that a Cocoa application that expresses its dictionary solely through a new-format sdef is scriptable only on Tiger. For more information, type **man sdef** in the Terminal. Chapter 27 contains an example of how to make a Cocoa application scriptable using an sdef.

Dictionary Troubles

A scriptable application's dictionary is exposed in human-readable form in a script editor application (see Figure 2-2). It may be said that nine-tenths of the art of programming with AppleScript is figuring out what a targeted application expects and permits you to say to it. You might think that this would be no art at all, since there's the dictionary giving you this information straight out. But it turns out that a dictionary is a remarkably poor device for communicating to a human user the information that is really needed. There are three main problems:

• Because each scriptable application defines its own terminology, learning to script a new application sometimes feels like having to learn an entirely new version of the AppleScript language.

• The dictionary is inadequate to express what the programmer needs to know in order to script the application successfully. Some of this inadequacy is due to poorly written dictionaries. Some of it is due to the inherent structure of all dictionaries, just as a mere list of vocabulary is insufficient for learning a human language. Some of it is due to the way dictionaries are displayed in a script editor application. (This is one reason to use Script Debugger, which supplies a superior dictionary view.)

• At any given point in a script, up to four sets of vocabulary are in force: the target application's dictionary, the dictionaries of all loaded scripting additions, AppleScript's own dictionary, and any other terms created and used by the programmer in the course of the script. These namespaces are not readily distinguished, and collide in confusing and frustrating ways.

For a vivid demonstration of how an AppleScript programmer's time is spent wrestling with the target application's dictionary, please pause and read Appendix A. Dictionaries and the problems associated with them are studied in depth in Chapter 20. Some alternative tools for displaying the contents of an 'aete' resource are listed in Appendix C.

Missing External Referents

AppleScript is a little language, leaving it up to externals such as scriptable applications and scripting additions to extend the vocabulary of the language as needed. A consequence of this architecture is that at various crucial moments during the life of a script, such as when it is compiled, decompiled, or executed, AppleScript will look for externals, and may complain if it can't find them. This section talks what happens on these occasions.

Application Missing at Compile Time

When a script is compiled, AppleScript needs each application targeted by that script, so that it can obtain its dictionary to verify the legality of the terms the script is using and to translate those terms into Apple events in bytecode. If it can't find a targeted application, it will present a dialog asking you, the human user, to locate it. At this point, one of three things can happen:

You cancel out of the dialog.
     The script won't compile.
You locate the correct application.
     The script compiles, and is modified to point to the application you nominated.
You locate some other application.
     The script won't compile.

What consitutes "the correct application" is any application whose dictionary defines the terminology AppleScript is trying to verify. To see what I mean, let's start with code like this:

```
get disk 1
```

If that's all your script says, it won't compile at all, because the term disk isn't part of the AppleScript language. You can use it this way only while targeting a scriptable application that extends the AppleScript language to include a class called disk. Now, suppose we pretend there is such an application, making up a name for this application when in fact we have no application by that name. Let's call it NoSuchApp.

```
tell application "NoSuchApp" to get disk 1
```

When you try to compile this, you're presented with a dialog listing every application, and posing the question: "Where is NoSuchApp?" AppleScript has realized that although the term disk is meaningless in the AppleScript language proper, it might be meaningful in the context of the application NoSuchApp. AppleScript therefore attempts to find the application. (I do not know the exact steps used in the search.) But NoSuchApp can't be found, because there's no such app. So AppleScript turns to you for help. If you cannot at this moment locate NoSuchApp—if, for example, you cancel out of the dialog—the script will simply not compile.

Instead of cancelling, you can nominate an application as NoSuchApp—*any* application, even if it isn't called NoSuchApp. This makes sense because the problem might merely be that the name has changed or you've typed it wrong. For example, you could claim that NoSuchApp is Address Book (just select Address Book in the dialog, and click Choose). However, this does not fool AppleScript for long, because it immediately turns to Address Book's dictionary and investigates its vocabulary. AppleScript quickly concludes you were lying, because Address Book doesn't know what a disk is after all—and the script still won't compile.

Now suppose we try again to compile, and this time, when AppleScript asks us about NoSuchApp, we tell it that NoSuchApp is the Finder. The script now compiles successfully, because the Finder *does* know what a disk is. Also, when the script is decompiled for display, you'll find that the name "NoSuchApp" has changed to "Finder"; I explained earlier, under "Decompiling," how that sort of thing happens.

I'll talk about how you specify a target application in your script, and how to do so in such a way that AppleScript stands the best chance of just compiling the script without asking for human assistance, in "Tell" and "Using Terms From" in Chapter 19, and in "Application" in Chapter 13.

Application Missing at Decompile Time

Decompilation takes place when you open a compiled script file for editing; the byte-code of the compiled script file is illegible, so it must be decompiled in order to be displayed (and pretty-printed). When a compiled script file is decompiled, Apple-Script needs each application targeted by that script, but for the opposite of the reason why this happens at compile time. When a script is compiled, AppleScript needs a dictionary so that it can translate the English-like AppleScript code into Apple events in the bytecode. When a script is decompiled, AppleScript needs a dictionary so that it can translate the Apple events of the bytecode into English-like Apple-Script code.

Once again, AppleScript starts by trying to find the application on its own. And again, I do not know the exact steps involved here, but experimentation shows that if the application is actually running at decompile time or is present on disk and its name has not changed, AppleScript usually finds it easily. The compiled script also contains an alias to the application, which means that even if you change the application's name, or move it to a different folder on the same volume, the compiled script should continue to keep track of it.

Nevertheless, there can be circumstances under which AppleScript cannot find the application on its own—perhaps you moved the application to a different volume, or the script is being opened on a different machine where the application is missing or has another name—so when you try to open the script in your script editor application, you'll get the dialog asking you to locate it. At this point, one of three things can happen:

You cancel out of the dialog.
> The script editor application fails to open the compiled script file.

You locate the correct application.
> The compiled script opens; the script is modified so that the reference to the application points at it in its current location.

You locate some other application.
> The compiled script opens; the script is modified so that the reference points to the application you located, and any terms not resolved by the nominated application's dictionary are shown in raw form.

 In the second and third cases, even though the script is modified, this does not "dirty" the script file itself. So you can then close the script window, and the script editor application will not ask whether you want to save; therefore the knowledge of the application's new location won't be written into the compiled script file, and you'll have to go through the whole rigmarole again the next time you open the file. I regard this as the fault of AppleScript, which apparently has no way to alert the script editor application that the compiled script has changed. The workaround is to modify the script manually—just insert a space somewhere—and compile and save it.

The third possibility is surprising. Recall that when you try to compile a script, if AppleScript asks you to locate an application and you locate some other application, one that doesn't resolve the terms used, AppleScript knows you're lying, and compilation fails. But when you decompile a script, if AppleScript asks you to locate an application and you locate some other application, decompilation succeeds. This can be quite useful, because it means you can open a script for editing, and even read most of it, even if you're missing one of the applications needed to run it.

For example, consider this script targeting Eudora:

```
tell application "Eudora"
    get subject of message 1 of mailbox "Trash"
end tell
```

Let's say we compile this script and send it to a friend who doesn't have Eudora. Our friend tries to open the script in a script editor application. AppleScript can't find Eudora, so it asks our friend where it is. At this point, let's say our friend nominates another application—let's say it's the Finder. The script opens, but the terms subject, message, and mailbox aren't defined in the Finder's dictionary, so some raw four-letter Apple event codes are displayed (and the Finder is substituted for Eudora as the targeted application):

```
tell application "Finder"
    get «class euSu» of «class euMS» 1 of «class euMB» "Trash"
end tell
```

Our friend can now read and edit the script. Those things in funny double angle-brackets are actually raw four-letter codes from the Apple event stored in the byte-code. (See "What an Apple Event Looks Like," earlier in this chapter; raw four-letter codes are further discussed in Chapter 20.) The script is already compiled, so now it is possible to run it—though it probably won't run properly, because the Finder will complain when it is sent an Apple event it doesn't understand.

 Once in a while, AppleScript will misidentify a target application when a compiled script file is moved to a different machine. I don't know the exact causes, but I've seen it happen, and when it does, it's very bad, because not only does the script not work properly, but also, when you open the script to investigate, AppleScript has changed the name of the target application during decompilation—so you have no way to learn what the correct target application is.

Application Missing When a Compiled Script Runs

When a compiled script file is executed directly *without* opening it for editing—as, for instance, in a script runner—it is *not* decompiled, and so it does not face quite the same issues as it does during decompilation. AppleScript in this case doesn't look for an application until the script is already running and it encounters code referring to that application. Thus, a targeted application may be missing, but if the code referring to it is never actually executed, there is no problem.

So, for example, this compiled script file runs perfectly well in a script runner on a machine without Eudora:

```
if 1 = 2 then
    tell application "Eudora"
        get subject of message 1 of mailbox "Trash"
    end tell
else
    display dialog "No problem!"
end if
```

The reason is that because of the branching code (and because 1 is not 2) the material about Eudora is never encountered, so the issue of where Eudora is and what all those terms mean never even arises.

If, on the other hand, such material *is* encountered, and the AppleScript scripting component can't find the target application on its own, what happens depends upon the context. Sometimes the dialog appears asking you to locate the application (as, for example, in BBEdit); but sometimes it doesn't (under Apple's Script Menu, for example, the script will simply fail silently). Furthermore, having helped the AppleScript scripting component find the application, you'd like that information to be saved back into the script so that next time the script will run without assistance. Again, sometimes this happens and sometimes it doesn't, depending upon the context. (If all this inconsistency seems confusing and annoying, that's because it is.)

A run-only script obviously presents a special case, because it can't be modified. Thus, if a run-only script, while executing, encounters a reference to a targeted application that AppleScript can't locate on its own, then even if the dialog asking for the application appears, and even if the user can locate the application (in which case the script will then continue executing), this information cannot be saved back into the script; the next time the script runs, the dialog will appear again.

Application Missing When an Applet Launches

An applet contains a compiled script, and when the applet is launched, the compiled script runs without being decompiled, so you might think it would behave just like a compiled script that is executed directly. You'd be wrong. Instead, when an applet is launched, all its external referents are sought then and there, just as if you were compiling the script.

If an applet, as it launches, asks you to locate a missing application and you do locate it, the applet may proceed to run correctly. But knowledge of the missing applications location is not written into the applet, so the same thing will happen next time the applet is launched. The only solution is to open the applet for editing (if it hasn't been saved as run-only) and fix it in a script editor application.

A puzzle therefore arises of how to permit an applet, if it contains code that might never be executed and that targets an application that might be missing, to run at all—in other words, how to make an applet behave like a compiled script file in this regard, postponing the question of where an application is until the script runs and code referring to that application is actually encountered. This puzzle used to be rather difficult to solve, but with the invention of the terms block (one of the few major linguistic changes in the history of AppleScript), there is in fact a rather slick workaround. I'll explain what it is in "Using Terms From" in Chapter 19.

Scripting Addition Missing

Up to now we've been talking just about missing applications. But what if what's missing is a scripting addition? AppleScript can't present any kind of dialog pointing out that such-and-such a scripting addition is missing, because it has no idea where the troublesome terminology was supposed to come from. This is because you don't target a scripting addition; you just use its terminology directly as if it were part of the language. So if the scripting addition isn't there, then this terminology *isn't* part of the language, and that's all AppleScript knows about what the problem is. You're talking illegally, but AppleScript doesn't know why. So what happens? It depends on what you're trying to do:

You're trying to compile the script.
> The script simply won't compile. In the absence of the scripting addition that defines a certain term, that term is illegal, and a script that uses illegal terminology can't be compiled.

You're trying to decompile the script.
> All other things being equal, you'll succeed. The terminology from the missing scripting addition is shown in raw four-letter form; AppleScript can't find the scripting addition's dictionary to resolve it back into English-like AppleScript code, so it just shows you the Apple event that's stored in the compiled script's bytecode. This makes sense, because if AppleScript refused to decompile the script merely because it contains an unknown Apple event, you'd probably never be able to read the script again, since AppleScript has no way of knowing or informing you of what the problem is—namely, that a certain scripting addition is missing. Of course, now that you've seen the raw four-letter code of the Apple event, *you* probably have no way of knowing what the problem is either. Even if you can guess that a scripting addition is missing, how can you know what scripting addition it is, unless you've got a list of all the raw four-letter codes of all possible scripting additions? (This is just one of many ways in which scripting additions are troublesome.)

You're trying to execute the script.
> The script will run until it comes to the offending Apple event, and then things will probably choke. That's because this Apple event is going to be sent either to some target application or to AppleScript itself, and either way it isn't going to be defined in the repertory, so an error message will come back. Unless the script handles this error, execution will come to a stop and the error message will be displayed; it may well include the four-letter code of the Apple event (for all the good that's going to do you).

Modes of Scriptability

An application is *scriptable* if it defines a repertory of Apple events to which it is prepared to respond and publishes that repertory as a dictionary. The dictionary should contain terms that expose the application's core functionality (that caveat is intended to handle the case of applications that publish a dictionary but are not in fact scriptable in any meaningful way; see "Is This Application Scriptable?" in Chapter 1).

There are two additional modes (or levels, or aspects) whereby an application can be scriptable:

Recordable

> An application is *recordable* if it can generate AppleScript code when the user performs ordinary actions in its graphical user interface. This ability can be useful for helping the programmer learn to script the application. There is no way to find out whether and to what extent an application is recordable, other than by trying to record it.

Attachable

> The term *attachable* is somewhat ambiguously defined. Strictly, an attachable application is one that allows the user to customize, by means of a script, what happens when the application receives an Apple event. But it may also be said that an application that allows the user to customize any of its event responses through a script is attachable.

Recordability

As an example of a recordable application, let's take BBEdit. In a script editor application such as Script Editor or Script Debugger, make a new script window, and choose Script → Record (or press the Record button). In BBEdit, press ⌘-N to make a new window. Back in the script editor application, choose Script → Stop (or press the Stop button). In the the script window, the following compiled script has appeared:

```
tell application "BBEdit"
    activate
    make new text document
end tell
```

BBEdit has recorded the actions you performed; you switched to it and made a new window, and BBEdit has provided the AppleScript code you would have to execute in order to cause the same actions to occur through a script. Obviously, this can be a good way to learn how to script an application. A scriptable application, in effect, has two interfaces: a graphical user interface and the scripting interface. But it isn't always obvious how they intersect. What would I have to say to BBEdit using AppleScript to get the same effect that I see when I press ⌘-N? Recording that action answers that question. Unfortunately, very few applications are recordable (far fewer on Mac OS X than in previous systems).

Recording is implemented partly by AppleScript and partly by the scriptable application. Pressing the Record button in a script editor application signals to AppleScript that it should start watching for recordable events. When it sees a recordable event,

AppleScript decompiles it and sends the decompiled text to the script editor application, which displays the text.

But precisely what constitutes a recordable event? The answer turns out to be surprisingly simple: it's any Apple event that *an application sends to itself*. In fact, an application is allowed to send itself a "fake" Apple event just so that if recording happens to be turned on, this Apple event will be detected and treated as the AppleScript equivalent for whatever else is occurring in the application.

The developers of an application can elegantly implement both scriptability and recordability by factoring the application as they develop it. A *factored* application is one that responds to events in the graphical user interface by sending itself Apple events. So, in BBEdit when you press ⌘-N (or choose File → New), BBEdit does not simply obey by creating a new text window; rather, it sends itself the Apple event that commands a new text window to be created. BBEdit then receives this Apple event—and *that* is what causes it to create a new window. Under this factored architecture, it makes no difference whether a user presses ⌘-N or a script says "make new text document"; BBEdit ultimately receives the same Apple event in either case, without knowing or caring whether it came from its own graphical user interface or from a script. Picture a factored application as being scriptable at a deep level, with the user interface wrapped around that.

Attachability

The most deeply attachable applications I know are the script editor applications Smile and the earlier version of Script Debugger (version 3). For example, Script Debugger implements attachability through a special compiled script file called *Attachments*. Let's say you edit this file to give it an execute handler. This means that every time Script Debugger is about to perform its own execute functionality, it performs the code in this handler instead. Script Debugger's execute functionality is what it does when it runs a script in one of its script windows. It doesn't matter whether you trigger this functionality by choosing Script → Run, by pressing the Run button in a script window, or by scripting Script Debugger with AppleScript (telling it to "execute" a certain window)—in all of these cases, Script Debugger does what your customizing code tells it to do, rather than what it would normally do. In other words, Script Debugger is factored, and it permits you to customize all the actions that you could normally perform either through the graphical user interface or through the scripting interface.

Now consider an application like BBEdit. Recall (from "Automatic Location" in Chapter 2) that BBEdit has a factored menu implementation: when you choose a menu item in BBEdit, if there is an appropriately named script in BBEdit's *Menu Scripts* folder, that script is called, so you can customize what happens in response to that menu item. Is BBEdit attachable? Well, it's certainly not as deeply attachable as Script Debugger, because you can't modify what happens when BBEdit receives the "make new text document" Apple event; if BBEdit receives an Apple event, it's going to do what it normally does, and you have no way to customize that. On the other hand, you can modify what happens when a menu item is chosen, so you are certainly customizing how BBEdit responds to an event in its own graphical user interface. So it seems silly to deny BBEdit attachability on the grounds that it is not *fully* attachable; it merely implements a milder form of attachability than Script Debugger.

Another application that's attachable in a manner similar to BBEdit is Creator, a layout program from MultiAd. It will call a handler in your script when a document is created, opened, closed, saved, or printed, and your script can override the application's default behavior. (Creator is scriptable in other powerful ways as well. You can dynamically add and remove menu items in the menu bar and in the contextual menu, each menu item having its own scripted functionality; and your scripts can even create dialog boxes and other utility windows, with interface widgets that respond interactively through scripts.)

The sign of an application's being truly attachable, I think, is that a user's script can effectively break the application. A simple script given the special name *File•Save* and placed in BBEdit's *Menu Scripts* folder can prevent BBEdit from saving files at all. Thus true attachability is dangerous, which is perhaps one reason why it is so rare. The other applications mentioned in "Automatic Location" in Chapter 2 are willing to run your script at a set moment as a way of customizing their overt behavior, but this is not attachability in the classic sense. Apple Mail, for example, will run a script as part of obeying a rule—that is, as a way of answering the question, "How should I respond when a mail message of a certain type arrives?" But mail will still arrive and rules will still be obeyed. What your script is doing here, therefore, amounts to no more than an elaborate way of setting a preference, and doesn't come under the rubric of true attachability. (See also Chapter 26.)

The AppleScript Language

Part II is the heart of the book; it describes the AppleScript programming language.

This part is intended for use both as a reference and as a source of instruction. The order of exposition is pedagogical, and the chapters are meant to be read in order.

The chapters are:

CHAPTER 4

Introducing the Language

Part I of this book describes AppleScript as a *technology*—why and where and how you use it (Chapter 1 and Chapter 2), the Apple events that lie behind it, the AppleScript scripting component that implements it, the kinds of file it creates and some of the details of working with those files, and the means and modes whereby applications make themselves scriptable with it (Chapter 3). But AppleScript is also a *language*, a programming language that you'll want to learn and understand in order to create and edit AppleScript code on your own. Part II of this book teaches it to you.

This chapter serves as a starting point for your journey through the AppleScript language. The longest journey, it is said, begins with a single step. But even before that, sometimes it's a good idea to contemplate the road. That's what this chapter does. It describes the nature of the AppleScript language in very general terms. What sort of language is it? What is it like to learn and to use?

The AppleScript language deserves contemplation, and often gets it. AppleScript's users seem to spend as much time and energy venting their feelings about AppleScript as they do writing and editing AppleScript code. It's that kind of language. It frequently evokes an emotional reaction, and that emotion can range from frustration through exasperation to fury. Yet at the same time AppleScript has some surprisingly clever behaviors and abilities, and some remarkably sophisticated features.

I've never created a computer language, but I suspect it must be a special sort of labor, both satisfying and frustrating, a blend of artistry and engineering, calling for vision, philosophy, planning, determination, sweat, time, and sheer technological expertise. A computer is just a machine, but a computer language is a human creation. You might expect it to be dry, cold, and logical, but it isn't. Every computer language bears the stamp of its makers, and to learn a computer language is to experience, in some measure, the forces and ideas and goals that went into its creation. In short, AppleScript has a flavor. This chapter tries to describe that flavor.

(If you haven't read Appendix A, I would urge you to take a moment to do so right now. It displays, by actual example, what it's like to work with AppleScript, and shows why it's important to have a solid grounding in the language before trying to get any serious work done toward scripting a target application.)

A Little Language

The "little language" philosophy, as represented by such computer languages as LOGO, Smalltalk, and Scheme, comes in various forms but the very words "little language" tell you most of what you need to know. Littleness can be a virtue in a number of ways. A little computer language can fit in a small space and be run by a small interpreter. A little computer language can be easy to learn, just because there's less of it to learn. A computer language is a tool to make tools, so the initial tool itself can be quite minimal, provided it has the power to make any other tools that may prove necessary.

All of these notions apply to AppleScript. AppleScript was to be easy for users to learn, so the less there was of it, the better. AppleScript appeared at a time when the idea of a computer with as much as four megabytes of random-access memory still felt rather strange and extravagant. To minimize expenditure of time and space resources, it had to compile with just a single pass. In these days of hundreds of megabytes of RAM and dozens of processes running simultaneously, it's easy to forget that AppleScript comes from a day when running more than one application at once on your Macintosh was a relatively new experience, and liable to tax the computer's resources to the utmost. At the time, AppleScript itself needed to be small simply to stay out of the way of other applications. The first version of AppleScript could load a scripting component instance and run a heavily recursive script in less than 300K of RAM.

And the purpose of AppleScript, after all, was to tell *other* programs to do things. Thus AppleScript itself could afford to be so minimal as to have little or no power of its own. AppleScript has minimal string-munging and number-crunching facilities, but then AppleScript is not intended for munging strings or crunching numbers—it's made for driving applications, and *they* can munge the strings and crunch the numbers if need be.

So *is* AppleScript's littleness a virtue? Probably not—at least, not any more. Thanks to Moore's Law and the passage of time, we no longer need AppleScript to be so tiny. Its small size certainly makes it easier to learn than, say, Perl (a language so big and so full of options and functions it can make your head swim), but it is not an easy language at all; on the contrary, it's tricky and quirky and needs a big book like this one to explain it. And if you're used to a full-fledged scripting language, AppleScript comes as something of a disappointment. Perl, for example, has some hundreds of built-in functions; AppleScript has about a dozen, and seems to be missing some extremely basic functionality. Perl has built-in support for powerful string manipulation, regular expressions, and trigonometry; AppleScript doesn't. Just as you don't miss the water until the well runs dry, the "little language" philosophy seems very cute just until you actually need to get something done. On the other hand, if you don't try to misuse it, AppleScript seems quite adequate, especially since it can now (under Mac OS X) avail itself directly of the power of Perl and other built-in Unix tools. As I said in Chapter 1, success may be simply a question of combining specialities appropriately.

Extensibility and Its Perils

As part and parcel of its power to communicate with other applications, AppleScript concedes to those applications an ability to extend the language. Such linguistic extensions appear temporarily to be part of AppleScript, only while your program is talking to the application that provides them. We thus have a language that grows and shrinks and mutates depending on what application it is talking to. For example, AppleScript itself knows nothing of a disk or a folder, but the Finder does. So as long as your AppleScript code is talking to the Finder, it can speak of a disk or a folder. The moment it is no longer talking to the Finder, it can't.

This architecture, as we saw in Chapter 3, has its practical consequences. An Apple-Script program that talks to a particular application can be severely hampered by the absence of that application. Even if you know all about BBEdit and how it extends the AppleScript language, you can't compile a script that talks to BBEdit unless you have BBEdit present on your machine at the time. If you send your friend a compiled script file that talks to BBEdit and your friend doesn't have BBEdit, your friend can't even *read* the script, let alone run it.

For the programmer, the main consequence of AppleScript's extensibility is that it is not one language but many—as many as there are applications to which you might wish to speak. (You can see this consequence in action in Appendix A, where all my knowledge of AppleScript is as nothing compared to my ignorance of how to talk to one particular application.) Thus the AppleScript programmer, no matter how expert, remains something of a perpetual neophyte. Even the most AppleScript-savvy programmer I know has said to me, "I hate trying to figure out the scripting quirks of every app." AppleScript thus displays some tendency to discourage its most devoted users from doing the very thing it was intended to do.

Perhaps even worse than all of this is the everlasting conflict between the various namespaces: terms in a target application, terms in scripting additions, terms in AppleScript itself, and terms you make up for your own use. You just never know when you'll try to say something in AppleScript and it will fail at compile time or at runtime with a mysterious error message, all because an already defined term of whose existence you had no inkling or warning has stepped on your toes. I've mentioned this before ("Dictionary" in Chapter 3) and I'll talk at length about it again ("Terminology Clash" in Chapter 20).

The "English-likeness" Monster

As we have already seen, AppleScript is English-like. Its vocabulary appears to be made up of English imperative verbs, nouns, prepositional phrases, and even an occasional relative clause.

Whether this English-likeness is a good thing is debatable. It is probably responsible for attracting users who would otherwise be frightened by the rigid-looking pseudo-mathematical terseness of a language like Perl, with its funny variable names, its braces and brackets and semicolons and other impenetrable punctuation. Personally, though, I'm not fond of AppleScript's English-likeness. For one thing, I feel it is misleading. It gives one the sense that one just knows AppleScript because one knows English, but that is not so. It also gives one the sense that AppleScript is highly flexible and accepting of commands expressed just however one cares to phrase them, and that is *really* not so. This sense is reinforced by AppleScript's abundance of synonyms. For example, instead of saying:

```
if x <= y
```

you can say:

```
if x is less than or equal to y
```

You are also allowed to use the word "the" wherever it feels natural. And nouns even come with plurals:

```
get the first word of "hello there"
get the words of "hello there"
```

Nevertheless, none of this is due to AppleScript's knowing any English. AppleScript actually has no natural language intelligence at all. AppleScript is every bit as mathematically structured, rigid, and unforgiving as Perl or any other computer language. If you step outside its rules by a tiny fraction of an inch, AppleScript slaps your hand just as any computer language would. The trouble here, I suggest, is that it was AppleScript's similarity to English that tempted you (subconsciously perhaps) to break the rules in the first place.

For example, later in the book I will have to leap up and down and wave my arms wildly to warn the reader not to confuse these two constructs:

```
get words 1 thru 4 of "now is the winter of our discontent"
get text from word 1 to word 4 of "now is the winter of our discontent"
```

The natural tendency to meld these two constructs (which do very different things) into an illegal blend such as "get words 1 to 4" or "get text from words 1 thru 4" is almost overwhelming. That's because in English these notions are too similar to one another. If they were represented by harsh mathematical symbols, there would be no danger of confusing them, but because they look like English, the part of one's brain that speaks English takes over and tries to soften the boundaries between these expressions in the same way that the boundary between them is soft in the world of natural language.

Often, too, AppleScript vocabulary looks like a certain English part of speech when it can't in fact be used as that part of speech would be in English. For example, in the Finder there is an application file property called has scripting terminology. This phrase looks like a predicate and so naturally one tries to say something like this:

```
if theApplication has scripting terminology
```

That won't compile; rather, you have to say this very un-English-like phrase:

```
if has scripting terminology of theApplication
```

Another problem with AppleScript's English-likeness is that with so many English words floating around the language, it can be hard to think up a meaningful variable name that isn't already in use for something else. (This is the same point I made at the end of the previous section.) The following lines of code are all illegal:

```
set name to "Matt"
set feet to 7
set count to 9
set center to 1.5
```

The trouble here is that so much of the English language has been reserved by Apple-Script for its own private use.

Then there is the verbosity of English. In most computer languages, you would make a variable x take on the value 4 by saying something like this:

```
x = 4
```

In AppleScript, you must say something wordy like one of these:

```
copy 4 to x
set x to 4
```

Doubtless not everyone would agree, but I find such expressions tedious to write and hard to read. In my experience, the human mind and eye are very good at parsing simple symbol-based equations and quasimathematical expressions, and I can't help feeling that AppleScript would be much faster to write and easier to read at a glance if it expressed itself in even a slightly more abstract notational style.

Nonetheless, I must reiterate that whenever I put forward these heretical views in a conclave of hard-working AppleScript users, suggesting that we'd all be better off making and sending Apple events in some other less subliminally misleading fashion, I'm invariably greeted with jeers and groans. Users are emotionally (I would say, irrationally) attached to AppleScript's English-likeness; it attracted them to the language in the first place, and they are invested in it now. Those who agree with me, on the other hand, may want to explore the alternatives listed in Appendix B.

Object-likeness

In many computer languages, values are things that you talk about. In AppleScript, values are things that you talk *to*. The following is a legal way (though no one in his right mind would actually talk like this) to add 4 and 5 in AppleScript:

```
tell 4
    get it + 5
end tell
```

The use of `tell` (we are addressing the number 4), `get` (we are ordering the number 4 about), and `it` (which means "whoever I am now addressing") shows the nature of the idiom. To be sure, one can (and will) add 4 and 5 by saying something much simpler:

```
4 + 5
```

Yet this second way of talking works only because, behind the scenes, AppleScript is supplying the `tell` and the `get` for you, to make your life simpler. In AppleScript, whether you know it or not, you are *always* talking to some value and telling it to do something.

One might therefore suppose that AppleScript is an object-oriented language and that all values in AppleScript are objects. Perhaps, one thinks, AppleScript will turn out to be like Smalltalk, where "everything is an object." AppleScript also has certain values that are explicitly called "objects," and refers to the datatypes of all values as "classes." Plus, in a couple of areas AppleScript implements a kind of "inheritance" between one object (or class) and another. All of these things add to the impression that AppleScript might be object-oriented. Plus, Apple's own documentation states flatly that it is.

Nonetheless, I remain skeptical. I don't think AppleScript is really object-oriented or even object-based. I've come to think of AppleScript as merely having values with certain *object-like* aspects. Perhaps the reason for the object-likeness of AppleScript's values has something to do with the fact that AppleScript is all about sending messages (Apple events) to scriptable applications (see "Apple Events" in Chapter 3). Having devised a syntax for representing this message-sending architecture in an English-like way, AppleScript's inventors seem to have generalized this syntax to pervade the language.

LISP-likeness

A number of features of AppleScript seem to suggest that someone on the original AppleScript team was devoted to LISP, or to some LISP dialect such as Scheme. As I myself am fond of Scheme, I rather like these features.

For example, AppleScript has lists, which are ordered collections of any values whatsoever. It provides certain primitive operations for dealing with these lists, such as taking the first element, taking everything but the first element, and joining two lists into one (like Scheme's car, cdr, and cons). And AppleScript permits recursion (a subroutine calling itself).

Thus, it is possible to write AppleScript code that bears an extraordinary resemblance to Scheme code. To give an example, here's a little Scheme program that defines a routine for removing the *n*th element from a list, and then tests the routine:

```
(define remvix
    (lambda (ix ls)
        (cond
            ((null? ls)
                '())
            ((= ix 1)
                (cdr ls))
            (else
                (cons (car ls) (remvix (- ix 1) (cdr ls)))))))
(remvix 2 '(mannie moe jack))
```

And here's the same thing done in just the same style in AppleScript:

```
on remvix(ix, ls)
    if ls is {} then
        return {}
    else if ix is 1 then
        return rest of ls
    else
        return {item 1 of ls} & remvix(ix - 1, rest of ls)
    end if
end remvix
remvix(2, {"Mannie", "Moe", "Jack"})
```

Even if you don't know any Scheme or any AppleScript, the structural and stylistic similarity of these approaches is unmistakeable; they are in fact move-for-move identical, the only differences between them being matters of syntactic detail. To be sure, I've stacked the deck by deliberately writing the AppleScript routine in a Scheme-like style; but the point is that AppleScript is capable of that style, and invites it.

AppleScript also can generate closures (subroutines that remember their global environment). And there is a sense in which all the components of a script—variables, handlers, and script objects—possess the same first-class status; for example, any of them can be passed as a parameter to, or returned as a result from, a subroutine. All of this has a markedly LISP-like flavor.

The Learning Curve

In this chapter I've argued that AppleScript isn't easy just because it's small or just because it's English-like, and I've mentioned that AppleScript borrows some features from object-oriented languages and LISP that you may never have heard of and whose mere mention may have made your eyes glaze over. So perhaps at this point you're starting to worry that AppleScript is difficult to learn. But that isn't what I mean either! What I'm telling you is that AppleScript is a computer language, like any other computer language. You weren't born knowing it, and you aren't going to be able to use it without learning it. And, thanks to this book, you *will* learn it. AppleScript is a straightforward computer language, and can be taught and learned in a straightforward manner; if I didn't believe that, this book wouldn't exist.

AppleScript is extensible, so this book will tell you how to read a scriptable application's dictionary, warn of possible pitfalls, and give plenty of examples. AppleScript is English-like, so the book will teach a clean, concise style, and will wave a red flag when an analogy with natural language threatens to mislead. AppleScript values are object-like; this book tells you how to talk to them. AppleScript has some LISP-like features; this book elicits these features where they are relevant, but where they seem too advanced, you can always skip a section and return to it later on. If this book occasionally comments on the odd way AppleScript does certain things, it is not to frighten or frustrate the reader, but rather to gain the reader's trust. It's just my way of saying, "Don't worry if this seems weird; it *is* weird."

So approach AppleScript without fear. It deserves respect, appreciation, and perhaps a little wonder. After all, it's amazingly old. Thanks to the Mac OS X revolution, Apple has thoroughly modernized a system that was breaking under its own accumulated weight of years; yet AppleScript remains, to all intents and purposes, its same old self. The fact that AppleScript works at all in this brave new world of Unicode text and POSIX paths is simply amazing. But it does, and until a new broom comes along to sweep it clean, having to negotiate some accumulated quirks and cobwebs dating from the creation seems a small price to pay.

CHAPTER 5

Syntactic Ground of Being

This chapter is about the basic facts of AppleScript language syntax. These are the facts you must be aware of before you can read or write any AppleScript code at all.

Lines

AppleScript is a line-based language. There is no visible command terminator, such as a semicolon; a command ends with and is separated from the next command by a line break. For example:

```
set x to 1
copy x + 1 to y
display dialog y
```

You can't have one complete command and then another complete command in the same line, but you can have one command nested inside another command, because most commands in AppleScript have a result (see "Result," later in this chapter), and most commands have at least one parameter, so the result from one command can often be used as the parameter to another command, in the same line. So, for example, in the second line of this code:

```
set x to 1
copy (display dialog x) to y
```

The only commands that can't be nested inside other commands in this way are a few special verbs implemented deep inside AppleScript, such as set and copy.

It is legal for a line to be completely blank. Extra whitespace (spaces, tab characters) is legal and will be ignored.

Line-Break Characters

In a decompiled script, the breaks between lines are all Macintosh return characters (\r, ASCII character 13). This is somewhat ironic, because in a present-day script editor application such as Script Editor or Script Debugger, when you press the Return key what you're entering is a Unix newline (\n, ASCII character 10). Thus the line-termination character goes into the compiler as a Unix line break and comes back out on decompilation as a Macintosh line break.

Indeed, in a script text file (or other text to be treated as AppleScript code) it doesn't matter whether the line-break character is the Macintosh line break, the Unix line break, or even the Windows line break (\r\n). If the code is valid, AppleScript will be able to compile it regardless (and all the breaks between lines of code will end up as Macintosh line breaks internally).

Line-Break Characters in Strings

It is legal to type a line break in a literal string (that is, between matched pairs of double quotes). This represents a line-break character within the string. For example:

```
set pep to "Manny
Moe
Jack"
```

The line-break character being inserted here is the line-break character you get when you press the Return key. What character that is depends upon the editing environment and the era. In the old days it was the Macintosh line break (\r); nowadays, as I mentioned already, it is the Unix line break (\n).

AppleScript also permits the representation of line-break characters through the return global property (see Chapter 16) and the "escaped" characters \r and \n (see "String" in Chapter 13). Thus your code can construct a string value containing a line-break character by using these representations. When you display such a string value, it will be shown (in most contexts) with a visible line break. For example:

```
set pep to "Manny" & return & "Moe"
return pep
```

The result (the value of pep) is displayed like this:

```
"Manny
Moe"
```

So too for a decompiled string literal containing an "escaped" line-break character. The change happens right within your script. If you type this:

```
set pep to "Manny\rMoe\nJack"
```

then when you compile (and decompile) you'll see this:

```
set pep to "Manny
Moe
Jack"
```

This behavior, by general agreement, is annoying, not least because (as the example illustrates) you have no way of knowing whether the line break in the decompiled representation is a Macintosh or a Unix line break. (Script Debugger solves this problem; it lets you view invisible characters in your script, and permits a literal string value to be displayed with "escaped" characters.)

Continuation Character

Long lines of code are inconvenient if your script editor application does not wrap them. In such an environment, if your code contains long lines and you want to be able to read them without scrolling horizontally, you need a way to break long lines. Because a line is a meaningful syntactic unit, you cannot do this merely by inserting a return character. Rather, you must also enter a *continuation character*.

> The problem the continuation character solves is no longer much of a problem, though, because current script editor applications *do* wrap long lines.

The continuation character appears as the "logical not" sign; it is MacRoman codepoint 194, Unicode (and WinLatin1 and ISOLatin1) codepoint 172. This character is usually typed on Macintosh as Option-L; but as a convenience, in a script editor application, typing Option-Return enters both the logical-not character and a return character, and is the usual way of continuing a line. For example:

```
set a to ¬
    1
```

It is a compile-time error for anything to follow the continuation character on the same line other than whitespace.

It is a compile-time error for the line following the continuation character to be blank, unless what precedes the continuation character is a complete command, as in this very silly example:

```
set a to 1 ¬

set b to 2
```

A continuation character inside a literal string is interpreted as a literal logical-not character. To break a long literal string into multiple code lines for legibility without introducing unwanted return characters into the string, you must concatenate multiple literal strings:

```
set s to "one very long line " & ¬
    "deserves another"
```

Under some circumstances, AppleScript will move or remove your continuation characters at compile time. There's nothing you can do about this; it's an effect of the decompilation process. See "Decompiling" in Chapter 3.

> In this book, long lines are manually broken for legibility. Continuation characters are inserted to indicate such breaks, without regard for whether AppleScript would move or remove these continuation characters in a compiled version of the script.

Result

At runtime, a line of AppleScript code that actually executes an expression—that is, it isn't blank, a comment, or mere flow control (looping and branching)—will usually generate a *result*. This result is some sort of value; the particular value depends upon what the line does.

The line need not be a command; any valid AppleScript expression constitutes a valid line, even if it does nothing. For example, this is a valid line of AppleScript code, and it has a value (can you guess what it is?):

```
5
```

A line's result may be captured in two ways: explicitly or implicitly. The next two sections describe them both. As you'll see, my view is that in general you should not make any use of the fact that a line of code has a result. However, the exception proves the rule, so I will also suggest that in just one situation (while developing your code) capturing a line's value implicitly is useful.

Explicit Result

The result of a line after it is executed may be captured explicitly by using the keyword result in the next line that is executed. For example:

```
5
display dialog result -- 5
```

One sees this technique used typically after fetching a value in a context of interapplication communication. For example, this is a fairly common style of coding:

```
tell application "Finder"
    get the name of every folder
end tell
set L to the result
```

Here's another example:

```
tell application "Finder"
    count folders
end tell
set c to the result
```

Why is this technique so common? It may be a habit derived from HyperTalk, where this was a standard idiom. Or people may feel that a line is more legible and understandable if it consists of a single command. Nonetheless, this technique is unnecessary. You can execute a command and capture its result in the same line by nesting commands, as I mentioned in the previous section:

```
tell application "Finder"
    set L to (get the name of every folder)
    set c to count folders
end tell
```

What's more, using result is, I would argue, a downright bad idea. To use result is to be dependent upon AppleScript's rules about what a statement's result is. But you may not know these rules as clearly as you suppose. Your intuitions can lead you astray. For example:

```
set L to {"Mannie", "Moe"}
set end of L to "Jack"
```

After these two lines, L is {"Mannie", "Moe", "Jack"}, but result is "Jack". If you were expecting result to be the same as L, you'll be wrong, and code that depends upon this assumption won't work. That's a simple example; for more complicated code, the chances increase that you may be mistaken about what result represents. Why risk this sort of mistake when in fact it is never necessary to use result in the first place?

Also, result is volatile. It changes after the execution of every expression. If you get into the bad habit of not capturing values when they are generated, because you intend to pick them up later using result, you are just asking for trouble. You might, in the course of further developing your code, insert a line between the line where the value is generated and the line where you pick it up as result; the value of result will then be different from what you expect. This kind of mistake is very difficult to debug. So I recommend that you not get into the habit of using result at all.

Implicit Result

The result of a line's execution is captured implicitly if it is the last line executed in a handler or script. This means that in theory there is no need to return a value explicitly (using the keyword return) from a handler or script. For example, instead of this:

```
on add(x, y)
    return x + y
end add
display dialog add(1, 2)
```

it is possible to say this:

```
on add(x, y)
    x + y
end add
display dialog add(1, 2)
```

This technique suffers from the same drawbacks as using result. The keyword return has two great advantages: you know exactly *what* you're returning (because that's the value of whatever follows the word return) and *when* you're returning it (because the handler exits the moment return is encountered). To rely on an implicit result is to know neither of these things. A line's result, as we've seen, may not be what you think it is. And the value returned by a handler or script is not the value of its physical last line, but rather the value of whatever line happens to be executed last; where there is flow control (loops and branches), you might not know what line this will be.

However, I do make use of the implicit result in one particular context—when developing and testing a script. If a script does not explicitly return a result (using return), a script editor application always displays the implicit result after execution. To check whether the script is working as expected, I specify the value whose implicit result I want to see:

```
on add(x, y)
    x + y
end add
set z to add(1, 2)
z
```

The last line here causes the value of z to be displayed after the script executes; thus, I can check that z is taking on the expected value. The last line is a way of saying return z, only better. To see why, let's suppose you return the value of z explicitly, like this:

```
on add(x, y)
    x + y
end add
set z to add(1, 2)
return z
```

You now proceed with developing the script, appending additional code after this snippet, and are very surprised when it doesn't work as expected. The reason is that you've accidentally left this line in the script:

```
return z
```

When that line is encountered, execution terminates (because that's part of what return means); the code that follows it is never executed. You will probably be confused as to what's gone wrong; in fact, you might continue developing your script, not realizing that anything has gone wrong, and imagining that the result shown by your script editor is the implicit result from a later line! By contrast, the nice thing about this expression:

```
z
```

is that it has no effect at all on the behavior of your script, even if further code is subsequently appended.

Comments

AppleScript permits two kinds of comment: single-line comments and delimited comments. Everything including and after two successive hyphens on a line is a *single-line comment*. For example:

```
set a to 1 -- this a comment on the same line as a command
-- this a comment on a line by itself
```

The *comment delimiters* are (* and *). Everything between comment delimiters is a comment. Such a comment may span multiple lines. This code contains three stretches of text that are legally commented out with comment delimiters:

```
set a to 1 (* because we feel like it;
tomorrow we may not feel like setting a to 1 *)
(* in fact things could be very different tomorrow,
but I really can't speak to that issue just now *)
set b to 2 (* this seems a good idea too *)
```

A comment delimited with comment delimiters may not interrupt a command, nor precede a command on the same line. Neither of these lines will compile:

```
set a to (* because we feel like it *) 1
(* here's a good idea *) set a to 1
```

Comment delimiters attempt to be "intelligent." Comments may be nested, in which case the delimiters must match in pairs. Thanks to this rule, you can easily comment out a stretch of script that already contains some comments:

```
(* outer comment
(* inner comment *)
rest of outer comment *)
```

A rather weird side effect of this "intelligence" is that quotation marks and vertical bars inside comment delimiters must also match in pairs:

```
(* "this works fine" and so does |this| *)
```

If you remove one quotation mark or one vertical bar from inside that comment, the code won't compile.

Single-line comments take precedence over everything (they cause the rest of the line to be ignored, with no attempt at "intelligence"). Thanks to this rule, you can easily comment out comment delimiters. You might wish to do this while testing, as a quick way of effectively removing and restoring some code. Here, the line of code is commented out and is not executed:

```
(*
set a to 7
*)
```

Here, the comment delimiters are commented out, so the line of code *is* executed:

```
--(*
set a to 7
--*)
```

But be careful. This code won't even compile:

```
(* set a to 1 -- and why not? *)
```

That's because the closing comment delimiter is itself commented out as part of the single-line comment, so the opening comment delimiter is unbalanced.

Abbreviations and Synonyms

Many AppleScript terms permit other terms to be substituted for them. For example, the following expressions are equivalent in pairs, assuming that a and b are defined:

```
a is less than b
a < b

a is b
a = b
```

Some terms have a very large number of equivalents. For example, these expressions *all* amount to the same thing:

```
a ≤ b
a <= b
a less than or equal b
a is less than or equal to b
a is not greater than b
a isn't greater than b
a does not come after b
a doesn't come after b
```

To add to the confusion, upon decompilation, AppleScript might substitute one equivalent for another (see "Decompiling" in Chapter 3). So the code in the previous example compiles, but afterwards it looks like this:

```
a ≤ b
a ≤ b
a is less than or equal to b
a is less than or equal to b
a is not greater than b
a is not greater than b
a does not come after b
a does not come after b
```

I call terms that are functionally equivalent to one another *synonyms*. I call terms that are replaced by other terms on decompilation *abbreviations*.

Code in this book is compiled before being pasted into the page, so you won't see any abbreviations in the book's code examples (except, as here, with the explicit purpose of displaying an abbreviation). In fact, this book does not even list abbreviations, except where I find them particularly handy when typing code. For example, in real life I never type the word application because I know the abbreviation app will do; so I tell you about this abbreviation ("Application" in Chapter 13).

I don't tell you about all synonyms either, and on the whole I try not to use them. I feel that it's good style, and makes your AppleScript code more legible, to adopt just one synonym for each term and stick with it. In general my personal preference is the shortest synonym, but not always; for example, of the following two expressions, I prefer the second:

```
a ≠ b
a is not b
```

And in a very small number of cases I do use two synonyms indiscriminately. For example, I'm equally likely to use either of these expressions:

```
a = b
a is b
```

To sum up: wherever there are synonyms, I have a favorite (or, in a very small number of cases, a couple of favorites). My favorites are the versions of each term that I tell you about, and they are the ones I use in code.

Blocks

A *block* is one or more lines of code demarcated from its surroundings as having a separate nature or purpose. A block is announced by a line stating what type of block it is; then comes the code of the block; and finally the block is terminated by a line starting with the keyword end. Blocks can occur within blocks.

It's very easy to spot a block in AppleScript code, because in decompiled code its lines are indented from the announcement line and the termination line. For example:

```
myHandler()
on myHandler()
    repeat 3 times
        display dialog "Howdy"
    end repeat
end myHandler
```

That code contains two blocks. One is announced with the on myHandler line, and is terminated by the end myHandler line; everything in between them is the code of that block. That code consists of another block, announced with the repeat line and terminated by the end repeat line; the line of code in between them is the code of that block.

In this book I frequently refer to such blocks by their announcement keyword; for example, I might say "a repeat block."

Some blocks (just two, actually—tell blocks and if blocks) have single-line variants. This permits some rather twisted condensed syntax. For example:

```
tell application "Finder"
    if exists folder "Mannie" then
        reveal folder "Mannie"
    end if
end tell
```

You can reduce one or both of those blocks to a single line. So, this is legal (but I never talk this way, and I don't recommend you do either):

```
tell application "Finder" to if exists folder "Mannie" then
    reveal folder "Mannie"
end if
```

 When typing a block, don't bother to type the name of the block a second time in the end line. Just type end for that line; the compiler will fill in the name of the block. (For example, don't type end repeat; just type end, on a line by itself, and the compiler will see that this corresponds to a preceding repeat line and will fill in the full end repeat for you.) This is not just a time-saving device; it's also a way to ensure that your blocks are structured correctly.

The only blocks you can make in AppleScript are those for which keywords are supplied; you cannot indent arbitrarily for clarity, as you can in UserTalk or C. So, for example, in UserTalk you can say this:

```
local (x)
bundle
    x = 4
msg (x)
```

The keyword bundle here does nothing except to allow some code to be indented for clarity. It also provides a further level of local scope. In AppleScript the scoping issue doesn't arise, but a way of indenting for clarity might still be nice. To achieve it you would need to misuse an existing block type. For example:

```
local x
repeat 1 times
    set x to 4
end repeat
display dialog x
```

The

AppleScript allows you to use the word the before almost anything. This is pure syntactic sugar, and I never use it. For example, this is perfectly legal:

```
set the x to the 9
display dialog the (get the the the the x + the 1)
```

Now, really.

CHAPTER 6

A Map of the World

Every AppleScript program is a script. This chapter describes the structure of a script. A script is composed of certain definite building blocks, and they go together in a certain way. The next several chapters will return to each of these building blocks individually and explain them in full detail, but first we need an introduction to the entire cast of characters that constitute a script. That's what this chapter is for. It provides the crucial overall map of a script's world, so that in our explorations during subsequent chapters you'll know where we're going and how the geography fits together.

Scope Blocks

Recall (from "Blocks" in Chapter 5) that a pretty-printed script displays its structure by means of indentation. Every set of indented lines is introduced by an on line and terminated by a corresponding end line. The whole thing is a *block*. For example, this is a repeat block:

```
repeat 3 times
    display dialog "Howdy"
end repeat
```

It turns out that two types of block are very special in AppleScript: a *script object definition* and a *handler definition*. They are special in many ways. These are the only blocks that function as what I'll call *top-level entities* in a script. They are not merely blocks; they are also variable definitions. There are special rules for where they occur in a script. Most obviously, they are the regions of scope in a script; for this reason, I call them the *scope blocks*.

Scope will be fully discussed in Chapter 10, but the idea is very simple. Some parts of a script are divided off from other parts by a kind of magic wall of impenetrability. Even if the parts can see each other, they cannot necessarily see inside one another. The word *scope* is the technical term for the visibility of part of a script: the scope of a thing is precisely equivalent to the rules for what parts of a script can see that thing. A script object definition and a handler definition are the only two kinds of block with the ability to put up these walls. They delimit—and in essence, are—the regions of scope within a script, the regions that are divided from one another by special rules as to who can see what. No other blocks have this magic power.

So what do they look like, these two special types of block? That's very simple. A script object definition is a block announced by the keyword script:

```
script scriptName
    -- commands within the script object
end script
```

A handler definition is a block announed by the keyboard on:

```
on handlerName()
    -- commands within the handler
end handlerName
```

And what do they actually do? They define, respectively, a script object and a handler. But what's a script object and a handler? That's a bit harder to explain: it's pretty easy to understand what a script object is or what a handler is through examples showing them in action and illustrating the full set of rules for how they work, but it's not so easy to see, out of context, what they're for and how they differ. But here are some quick descriptions, just to satisfy your natural curiosity:

handler
> A handler is a subroutine, or what some languages call a function. It's a block of code that has a name, and the code can be executed (called) by saying the name. A handler can also receive parameters, which are values that it should operate on when it is executed. A handler is a convenient and powerful way to distinguish and give a name to some code, often to avoid needless repetition when you're going to execute the same code on different occasions (instead of repeating the whole code, you just repeat the handler call—basically a single word), or just as a way of improving the organization and development of a script.

For example, suppose a handler definition defines a handler called capword which takes any string and capitalizes each word of the string. Then any time you want to capitalize the words of any string in your script, you just call capword. Whatever string you hand to capword is its parameter. If you call capword with "hello there" as the parameter, it returns "Hello There".

script object
> A script object is also a named block of code, like a handler, but it's more all-inclusive, more independent, and more persistent. As its name implies, a script object is essentially an entire script within a script.

That definition of a script object wasn't very helpful, but it will have to do for now. Later we'll talk about all that a script object is and all that it can do. It might be useful at present, though, for you to keep in mind the following. In some ways a handler and a script object are rather similar. They are both units or packages of code.

And they are both units of code that you can talk to; you can say to a handler, "Execute the code that's within you," and it will turn out that you can say much the same thing to a script object. But there are some important differences in *how* you talk to them. Asking a handler to execute its code is *all* you can say to handler; you call the handler and that's it. But you don't call a script object; you send a message to it, and that message can be anything. It's almost as if a script object is itself a little scriptable application and you're talking to it with Apple events. That's not exactly the case, but it's got the right flavor, and will give you something to chew on until we reach the formal presentation in Chapter 8.

 What is the cumbersome word "definition" doing in my explanation of an on block and a `script` block? Strictly speaking, there is a real distinction to be drawn here. A handler or a script object is some code; a handler definition or a script object definition is a block stating what that code is. This distinction will become important later in the book, when it turns out that a script object or a handler is really just a value like any other value (like the number 5 or the string "howdy"), whereas the block is really just a way (and not the only way) of *creating and giving a name* to that value. Nevertheless, the bare terms "handler" and "script object" (without "definition") are very often used loosely and conveniently to mean the blocks, and I will use them this way too where there is no danger of confusion.

Levels and Nesting

Looking at how blocks are indented, we can think of them as arranged in levels. For example, in this code the `if` block is one level down from the on block (the handler definition), and the `repeat` block is two levels down from the on block:

```
on myHandler()
    if weekday of (get current date) is Monday then
        repeat 3 times
            display dialog "Howdy"
        end repeat
    end if
end myHandler
```

Code that occurs directly inside a block may be said to be at the *top level* of that block. In the preceding code, the `if` block is at the top level of the handler.

Of course, what's at the top level of a block needn't be another block. So in the preceding code, the `display dialog` command is at the top level of the `repeat` block. But when a block *is* at the top level of another block, we can describe the two blocks in relation to one another as *nested*. So in the preceding code, the `repeat` block is nested in the `if` block, and the `if` block is nested in the handler.

Most blocks can just be nested in one another indiscriminately. But the rules for nesting handler and script object definitions are special (and this is part of what makes them special types of block, and why they are the subject of this chapter). In particular, there's a special rule for where a handler definition can appear:

A handler may be defined only *at the top level of a script object* (or of a script as a whole).

This rule is enforced by the AppleScript compiler. So, this code won't compile:

```
repeat 3 times
    on sayHowdy()
        display dialog "howdy"
    end sayHowdy
end repeat -- compile-time error: Expected "end" but found "on"
```

The rule also means, obviously, that you can't nest a handler directly within a handler. This code won't compile:

```
on outer()
    on sayHowdy()
        display dialog "howdy"
    end sayHowdy
end outer -- compile-time error: Expected "end" but found "on"
```

But there's a way out of these limitations. A script object definition can appear anywhere. So to define a handler in a handler, define it in a script object in a handler:

```
on outer()
    script s
        on sayHowdy()
            display dialog "howdy"
        end sayHowdy
    end script
end outer
```

We'll use this trick in some powerful ways later in the book.

The Top Level

The top level of all is the script as a whole. (Okay, I lied. There are actually some secret levels even higher than that. But just pretend, for now, that there aren't.) What's more, the script as a whole *is itself a script object*, even though it has no name and is not defined by a block.

This strange-sounding fact is actually extremely cool. It gives your script a sort of overall uniformity. For example, a handler definition can't occur anywhere except at the top level of a script object. So why is it possible for this to be a script?

```
on sayHowdy()
    display dialog "howdy"
end sayHowdy
sayHowdy()
```

There's a handler definition sitting there, not nested in a script block. But that doesn't break the rule; it accords with it, because the script as a whole is itself a script object, so this handler definition is in fact at the top level of a script object, precisely where it should be.

Code and the Run Handler

So far, we've talked about blocks, and in particular about script object and handler definitions, as the constituents of a script. But of course there's more to a script than that: there's the actual code, the commands, the stuff that does something. From a visual point of view, code can appear anywhere. But wherever code appears, if you work your way up the levels of nesting, sooner or later you'll always come to either a handler or a script object. That's what the code is really inside of.

For example:

```
set x to 1
on outer()
    set xx to 1
    script s
        set xxx to 1
        on sayHowdy()
            display dialog "howdy"
        end sayHowdy
        set xxxx to 1
    end script
    set xxxxx to 1
end outer
set xxxxxx to 1
```

That script is exactly the same as an earlier example, except that I've added code lines, so that given the structure of the script (a handler in a script object in a handler), at least one line of code appears in every place where code can possibly appear. All the lines of code are set commands, except for the display dialog command in the middle. So now consider the line "set xx to 1." Where is it, structurally? It's inside the handler outer. You can do this for every line of code.

This little game is significant because the regions demarcated by the handler and script object definitions are also regions of scope. The line "set xx to 1" talks about a variable called xx. Because of how and where this line occurs, there are strict rules about what parts of the script can and can't see this variable xx. (Those are the rules I'll talk about in Chapter 10.)

Now, here's a curious fact. Strictly speaking, code doesn't occur just anywhere. *Code can occur only in a handler.* Once again, this may sound weird, but it is actually very elegant, because it makes the structure of a script nice and uniform. There's just one problem: it looks like I must be lying. Surely the first line of the script, "set x to 1," is not in a handler, right? It's in a script object, because it's at the top level of the script and the script as a whole is itself a script object. Similarly, the line "set xxx to 1" is at the top level of a script object, and not in a handler. Right?

Wrong. It turns out that there's a secret kind of handler you can't see. The rule is that *every* script object has a handler called run. This special handler is called the script object's *run handler*. If you like, you can actually express this run handler explicitly. The script object is then said to have an *explicit run handler*.

Here is a script with an explicit run handler:

```
on run
    display dialog "howdy"
end run
```

You will observe that the on run statement lacks any parentheses, unlike other handler definitions we've seen. The run handler is special and doesn't use parentheses.

If a script object has no explicit run handler, then it has an *implicit run handler*. Here is a script with an implicit run handler:

```
display dialog "howdy"
```

Those two scripts are almost exactly the same. They are both scripts with a run handler containing exactly one line of code (the display dialog command). They both do exactly the same thing. The difference is that in one case the run handler is explicit, and in the other the run handler is implicit.

When a script (or script object) runs, *what runs is its run handler*. This will be much more significant to you when I talk more about script objects, but for now just concentrate on your script as a whole. When you execute a script, whether by pressing the Run button in a script window in a script editor application, or by giving a compiled script file to a script runner and calling the script through the interface, or whatever, what runs is that script's top-level run handler, whether implicit or explicit. The two previous scripts with display dialog do exactly the same thing, whether the run handler is implicit or explicit.

A script object (including a script as a whole) has exactly one run handler. Therefore it *cannot have both an explicit and an implicit run handler*. That would be ridiculous. It would also be illegal. This code will not compile:

```
on run
    display dialog "howdy"
end run
display dialog "howdy"
```

If you try to compile that, you will get one of the very few truly informative error messages in the whole of AppleScript: "The run handler is specified more than once, or there were top-level commands in addition to the run handler."

So, if there is an explicit run handler in a script object, that script object cannot have any top-level code. If there is no explicit run handler in a script object, that script *can* have top-level code and the lines of that code *are* its run handler (implicit).

A script object definition or a handler definition are not code. (This is another way in which these blocks are special.) The code inside them is code, of course; but they themselves are not. Thus the following script is legal and does not constitute an attempt to have two run handlers:

```
on run
    display dialog "howdy"
end run
on sayHowdy()
    display dialog "hello"
end sayHowdy
script s
    display dialog "bonjour"
end script
```

When a run handler is implicit, a script object definition or a handler definition at the top level is in some sense not really inside it. They really are at the top level. One way you know this is that otherwise you could never define a handler at the top level of a script. Remember, a handler nested directly in a handler is illegal. But this code is legal even though there's an implicit run handler, because the sayHowdy handler definition isn't really inside it.

```
on sayHowdy()
    display dialog "howdy"
end sayHowdy
```

But this won't compile:

```
on run
    on sayHowdy()
        display dialog "howdy"
    end sayHowdy
end run -- compile-time error: Expected "end" but found "on"
```

The run handler is explicit, and the sayHowdy definition *is* nested inside it—and a handler in a handler is illegal.

We thus have something of a paradox, because an implicit run handler can surround a handler definition without containing it in a way that makes it illegal:

```
set x to 1
on sayHowdy()
    display dialog "howdy"
end sayHowdy
set x to 2
```

In that script, the first line and the last line are in the implicit run handler, but the sayHowdy handler definition is at the top level.

For most purposes, it's not important to be constantly aware of the implicit run handler. It's easier to pretend that code can occur at the top level of a script object. So, for example, when we talk about scope, it will make most sense to speak of "set x to 1" in the preceding example as being at the top level of the script. For purposes of scope (and in other ways) an implicit run handler and an explicit run handler don't behave exactly alike. But you can't have both, so you do need to know they exist.

Variables

To complete our map of the world of a script, we must include variables. A *variable* is an association (formally, a *binding*) between a name and a value. You can think of it as a shoebox with a label on it, into which something is placed for storage. The shoebox's label is the variable's name; what's inside the shoebox is the variable's value. For example, when we say:

```
set x to 5
```

it is as if we had a shoebox labeled "x" into which we place the number 5.

Naturally, variables are very useful things, which is why just about all computer languages have them. To be able to assign your own names to things makes your program clearer and easier to maintain. And in a way any computer program is all about manipulating values, so it's nice to have a place to put each value when you're not using it, so that you can retrieve it again later. A variable's value is like the coffee in your cup when you set the cup on the table, do something else, and then pick up the cup and take a sip. The cup is like the variable; without it, the coffee would just flow onto the floor when you're not using it.

Variables and code are intimately related. Code is where variables are defined; code is where variables are given their values and where those values are retrieved.

Variables and scope blocks (handler definitions and script object definitions) are intimately related. Variables are what scope is all about: they are the "things" that other regions of the code either can or can't see, depending on the rules of scope, the location of the code, and the nature of the walls constructed by the scope blocks. In fact, we can go even further and say that every variable "lives" at the top level of a handler or a script object (and those are the only places where a variable can "live"). In fact, we can go even further than that: handlers and script objects live at the top level of a script object too, and this is because handlers and script objects are themselves variable values. This may sound confusing right now, but after you've read a few more chapters, it will all seem perfectly natural.

Script objects, handlers, variables, and code constitute the entire structure of a script. There is nothing else. Together they are AppleScript's "gang of four," the sole and supreme rulers of the AppleScript world. We have now mapped that world completely. Let's review. At the top is the script object; the script itself is a script object. At the top level of a script object there can be variables, handlers, and script objects. At the top level of a handler there can be variables and script objects, but a handler cannot be nested directly in a handler. Handlers and script objects are the scope blocks, determining where their variables can be seen. Code can go only in a handler, but that handler might be a script object's implicit run handler, so in that sense code can go in a script object too.

CHAPTER 7

Variables

This chapter describes the rules for assignment, declaration, typing, initialization, and naming of variables in the AppleScript language.

Assignment and Retrieval

If a variable is a labelled shoebox (see "Variables" in Chapter 6), then to *assign* a value to a variable is to put something into the shoebox. If the variable already has a value, that value is replaced.

Assignment is performed with one of two commands: set or copy.

---

set

Syntax

set *variableName* to *value*

Description

Assigns *value* to *variableName*.

Example

```
set x to 5
```

There is a synonym using the word returning instead of set, with the parameters in reverse order, like this: 5 returning x. But I have never seen this synonym used.

---

copy

Syntax

copy *value* to *variableName*

Description

Assigns *value* to *variableName*.

Example

```
copy 5 to x
```

An abbreviation for copy is put; an abbreviation for to is into. Thus you could type put 5 into x—although it would still come out as copy 5 to x. These abbreviations were designed to accommodate HyperCard users, who were habituated to this idiom.

There is no simple assignment operator, such as the equals sign (=). You cannot, for example, perform an assignment like this:

```
x = 5
```

That is a comparison, and returns a boolean result revealing whether x is already 5. That code is legal (and therefore does not cause a compile-time error) but is not an assignment (as any mildly experienced programmer would expect); this is a frequent cause of bugs in my scripts. See "The "English-likeness" Monster" in Chapter 4.

Set by Reference

As they both perform assignment, you might think set and copy must be completely interchangeable. In most cases, they are; but with regard to four types of value—lists, records, dates, and script objects—they are not. With these data types, set sets *by reference*, meaning that you can end up with more than one name for the same value.

The reason why these four data types are singled out for special treatment is that they are the only kinds of value that can be mutated in place. Thus, after a set by reference, whatever mutation is performed upon such a value under one of its names applies to it under its other names as well. For example:

```
set L to {1, 2, 3}
set LL to L -- set by reference
set end of L to 4 -- mutate a list in place
LL -- {1, 2, 3, 4}, because it is the same list as L
```

For other datatypes, use whichever command you prefer; I habitually use set.

Multiple Assignment

In an assignment, *variableName* and *value* can optionally be lists—of variable names and values, respectively—allowing multiple assignments in one command. The first item in the *value* list is assigned to the first item in the *variableName* list, the second to the second, and so forth. If the *value* list is longer than the *variableName* list, the extra values are not assigned to anything; if the *value* list is shorter than the *variableName* list, there is a runtime error. This remarkably elegant feature is probably underutilized by beginners. (For a parallel construction involving assignment to a record, see "Record" in Chapter 13.) For example:

```
set {x, y, z} to {1, 2, 3}
z -- 3, and can you guess what x and y are?
```

Retrieval

To *retrieve* the value of a variable (or *fetch* the value, or *use* the value, or whatever you want to call it), simply use the variable's name in code. As with most computer languages, there is no problem retrieving from and assigning to the same variable in a single statement:

```
set x to x + 1
```

There is no circularity, because the value of x is first retrieved, and 1 is added to that value; then the result of this addition is assigned to x, replacing the original value.

The result of a line consisting of just the name of a variable is the value of that variable. So, for example:

```
set x to 5
x
```

The result of that script is 5. This can be useful when you want to see the implicit result of a script for testing or debugging (see "Implicit Result" in Chapter 5).

It is possible to retrieve a variable's value by using the get command:

```
set x to (get x) + 1
```

But no one ever talks this way in real life, and as far as I know this use of get with a variable adds nothing. However, get with an object reference is another matter; see "Get" in Chapter 11.

Declaration and Definition of Variables

There is no requirement in AppleScript that variables be declared explicitly. The rule is basically that if you use a word that AppleScript doesn't understand, the word is assumed to be the name of a variable. The following code, as a complete script, will compile just fine:

```
set x to x + 1
```

Although it is not *necessary* to declare a variable, it is *possible* to declare a variable. I'll explain how you do this, and argue that there are good reasons for doing it, in Chapter 10.

Definition

The code in that last example, as a complete script, will compile, but it won't run; at runtime, it generates an error. The error message reads: "The variable x is not defined." The problem is *not* that the variable x has never been declared! There is no need to declare it. AppleScript understands (or assumes) that x is supposed to be a variable. Nor is the problem that you are trying to assign to it. The problem is that you are trying to fetch its value, and it has no value. That's because x has never been assigned a value. An AppleScript variable is not defined until you first explicitly give it a value. To continue our shoebox analogy, there is no "x" shoebox to fetch the contents of, because you've never put anything into it.

This code both compiles and runs:

```
set x to 5
set x to x + 1
```

During execution of the first line, AppleScript observes that you're putting something into the "x" shoebox, but there is no such shoebox as yet. No problem; AppleScript creates the shoebox, labels it "x", and puts 5 into it. Now the second line runs fine, because there is a shoebox "x" from which to fetch a value.

Once a variable has been defined, it generally stays defined until its scope finishes executing. There is no command explicitly letting you "undefine" a variable or assign the "undefined" value to it. There are a couple of constants, such as null and missing value, that you can assign as a sort of placeholder to signify that a variable hasn't been assigned any other value (see Chapter 17). However, you can in fact genuinely undefine a variable by assigning to it the result of a command that has no result. This is typically an accident: you were expecting a command to return a value, but it doesn't. Code for doing it on purpose appears under "Returned Value" in Chapter 9.

There is no way to ask whether a variable's value is defined; all you can do is fetch its value, and if it's undefined you'll get an error. It would then be up to your code to handle this error (see "Errors" in Chapter 19); otherwise your script will simply stop running at that point.

Initialization

A variable is *initialized* (given its first value) when you explicitly assign it its first value. Even when you explicitly declare a variable, there is no autoinitialization in AppleScript. A variable is undefined until you assign it a value; at that moment it is defined and initialized—the variable now exists, it has a value, and it is possible to fetch that value.

In general, there is no special syntax for initializing variables. There are, however, three exceptions: a script object definition, a handler definition, and the definition of something called a *script property* (it's a kind of global variable; I'll explain further in "Script Properties" in Chapter 8). In all three cases, a variable is defined and initialized by a special syntax not involving set or copy. For example, consider the definition of this script object called s:

```
script s
    display dialog "howdy"
end script
```

When you say that, you're actually defining a *variable* called s and initializing it with a value—namely, the script object itself. A handler definition works just the same way. This may seem an odd way to think of such entities, but I assure you that it is strictly true and is part of what makes AppleScript cool: a script object and a handler are actually variable values just like any other value (such as 5 or "howdy"), and you can do with them, and with the variables that name them, all sorts of stuff that you can do with any other values and variables. It's no coincidence, either, that script object definitions, handler definitions, and script properties have a special syntax of definition and initialization, as they have other things in common as well—they are the three top-level entities of a script object, and their scopes work in parallel ways. We'll return to all these matters in detail later.

Typing

A variable in AppleScript has *no fixed type*. By this I mean simply that it is permissible to assign any value to any variable at any time. The following code is legal:

```
set x to 5
set x to 5.2
set x to "hello"
set x to string
set x to {"fee", "fie", "fo", "fum"}
set x to (path to current user folder)
```

In that code, x becomes successively an integer, a real, a string, a class, a list, and an alias. A defined variable (one that has a value) has a type, called its *class*; this is simply the class (datatype) of its current value, and it changes if a value of a different class is assigned to it.

The various built-in datatypes, and the ways in which AppleScript lets you coerce implicitly and explicitly from one to another, are discussed later in this book (Chapters 13, 14, and 15).

Variable Names

The name of a variable must begin with a letter or underscore and must consist entirely of alphanumeric or underscore characters. So a variable name must begin with a character in the character set [a-zA-Z_] and must consist entirely of characters in the character set [a-zA-Z0-9_].

Case-Insensitivity of Variable Names

Variable names are *case-insensitive at compile time*. That means the following code will compile and run:

```
set myVar to 5
set myvar to myvar + 1
```

AppleScript assumes that myvar in the second line is the same variable as myVar in the first line. Furthermore, as a reflection of this assumption, AppleScript rewrites the variable names after compilation (that is, during decompilation) so that their case matches the first usage of the name:

```
set myVar to 5
set myVar to myVar + 1
```

This phenomenon suggests a trick that can help you spot mistakes: when you first define a variable, use an uppercase letter in its letter; elsewhere, never use an uppercase letter in a variable name. Then, after compilation, any variable name without an uppercase letter must be a mistake. For example, here's some code that I typed following these rules, before compilation:

```
set myVar to 5
set mybar to myvar + 1
```

Here's the same code after compilation:

```
set myVar to 5
set mybar to myVar + 1
```

In that code I have accidentally created and set the value of an unwanted variable mybar in the last line. I meant to say myvar, but I mistyped it. This won't cause Apple-Script to generate any error, and the script will misbehave. The chances that I will spot my mistake are increased by my use of the case trick.

 But this trick is not easy to implement, and it's unreliable because you still might not spot the mistake. The truth is that incorrect variable names are a notorious cause of bugs in scripts, and can be extremely difficult to track down. The real problem is that AppleScript doesn't require you to declare your variables (and unlike Perl with its strict mode, it doesn't let you require it to require you). In my view, this is one of many instances where a feature probably intended to make the language easier actually makes it harder.

Memory of Variable Names

Once a script has been compiled for the first time, its variable names are remembered as they appear at that moment. (Recall that AppleScript has a memory. See "Maintenance of State" in Chapter 3.) Suppose you compile this script:

```
set avariable to 7
```

You then change the script to give the variable name inner capitalization:

```
set aVariable to 7
```

When you compile, AppleScript removes the inner capitalization!

```
set avariable to 7
```

The reason is that when AppleScript first saw the variable name avariable—the first occurrence during the first compilation of the script—it had no capitalization, and that's how the name is remembered from then on.

In Script Editor, this rule washes over to other scripts that you edit during the same session! To see this, start up Script Editor and compile this script:

```
set myvar to 7
```

Now open a new, different window and compile this script:

```
set myVar to 7
```

Your variable names are changed in this second script! It ends up looking like this:

```
set myvar to 7
```

This is because Script Editor uses just one AppleScript scripting component instance per session (that is, until you quit Script Editor). This instance is shared by all the scripts you compile during that session, so the variable names in one script affect the variable names in another. Two different applications don't share the same Apple-Script scripting component instance, though, so your variable names in Script Editor do not affect your variable names in Script Debugger at the same moment. Furthermore, Script Debugger uses a different AppleScript scripting component for each script window, so variable names in different scripts don't affect one another.

Variable Names and Vertical Bars

You can force an illegal variable name to be legal by surrounding it with vertical bars, also known as "pipes" (|). So, for example:

```
set |1| to 2
if |1| is 2 then
    display dialog "The laws of logic are suspended."
end if
```

The laws of logic aren't really suspended; 1 and 2 have not become the same number. A variable named "1" has been assigned the value 2, that's all. This device is good also for variable names in languages other than English:

```
set |monZéro| to 0
```

or for spaces in a variable name:

```
set |my big long variable name with spaces| to 7
```

A variable name surrounded by pipes *is case-sensitive*. This script will compile, but it won't run:

```
set |MyVar| to 5
set |MyVar| to |Myvar| + 1 -- error
```

The reason is that |Myvar| is not the same variable as |MyVar| and has never been given a value, so its value can't be fetched. AppleScript will not touch the case of names in pipes after compilation.

A variable name surrounded by pipes may include a backslash as an "escape" character. The legal escape expressions in this context are \n, \r, \t, \|, and \\.

The real effect of pipes is to tell AppleScript to suspend its compile-time parsing rules and turn what's inside the pipes into a token. The main reason this is genuinely useful is to avoid a conflict between a token name and a term already in use. For example:

```
set |is| to "ought"
```

You couldn't do that without the pipes, because is is a reserved word, a part of the AppleScript language.

Now, you might say: "So what? I'll never need to worry about that; I just won't use any names that conflict with terms that are in use." But it's not so easy. Lots of terms are in use (by AppleScript, by scripting additions, and by the application you're targeting), you can't possibly know what they are, and conflicts are all too easy to stumble into. The use of pipes is a common way to stumble back out. (See "Extensibility and Its Perils" in Chapter 4, and "Terminology Clash" in Chapter 20.)

CHAPTER 8

Script Objects

A *script object* is a script within a script. In fact, a script really *is* a script object, though it also has a special status as the top-level script object. Script objects have certain remarkable features. They have variables of a special kind—I call these top-level entities—that belong to the script object, but can be retrieved and assigned to from elsewhere. They have a run handler, implicit or explicit; the code in this run handler can be executed. They are persistent over repeated executions of a script. They can be saved to disk as files, and a compiled script file can be turned back into a script object. And script objects can even implement a relationship of inheritance with polymorphism. You can think of a script object as a powerful, semi-autonomous package for some code and variables that go together. This chapter presents script objects and their distinctive features.

Script Object Definition

A script object is defined using a block with the keyword `script`:

```
script scriptName
    -- commands within the script object
end script
```

A script object definition may appear anywhere. If defined at the top level of a script object (or script), it is a top-level entity ("Top-Level Entities," later in this chapter). It functions as a scope block. (The rules of scope appear in Chapter 10.) Read Chapter 6 for an overview of how script object definitions fit into a script's overall structure.

A script object definition is just that—a definition. Merely encountering a script object definition in the course of execution does not cause of any of its commands to be executed. Rather, a script object definition is a form of variable initialization. So, for example:

```
script s
    display dialog "howdy"
end script
```

That code does not cause a dialog to display. It defines a script object with an implicit run handler; that run handler contains code that puts up a dialog, but the mere definition does not cause the run handler to run. The script object itself is the value of a variable. Here, that variable is s; when this code is encountered, the variable s is defined and initialized, and its initial value is the script object described by this block of code.

Run Handler

Every script object has exactly one run handler. This may be explicit (all the code marked off by an on run block) or implicit (all the code at the top level of the script object). See "Code and the Run Handler" in Chapter 6.

To execute the code in a script object's run handler, you send the run message to it. You can do this by making the script object the direct object of the run command, or by saying run within a tell block targeting the script object. So, for example:

```
script s
    display dialog "howdy"
end script
run s -- howdy
```

Or:

```
script s
    display dialog "howdy"
end script
tell s
    run -- howdy
end tell
```

A one-line tell block can be reduced to a single line of code with no block:

```
script s
    display dialog "howdy"
end script
tell s to run -- howdy
```

(On the result of a run handler, see "Returned Value" in Chapter 9. On passing parameters to a run handler, see "The Run Handler" in Chapter 9.)

 If a script object has no explicit run handler and has no executable statements in its implicit run handler, telling it to run can have unpredictable consequences (this fact is almost certainly a bug). For example, this would be a bad thing to do:

```
script myScript
end script
run myScript -- error: stack overflow
```

Script Properties

A *script property* (often just called a *property*) is a variable defined and initialized at the top level of a script object through a special statement called a *property declaration*. The syntax is:

```
property propertyName : initialValue
```

For example:

```
script s
    property x : 5
end script
```

The abbreviation for property is prop.

A property is a variable, so its value can be set and fetched in the normal way. For example:

```
script s
    property x : 10
    display dialog x -- 10
    set x to 5
    display dialog x -- 5
end script
```

A property declaration can appear only at the top level of a script object. But the script as a whole is a script object. Therefore a property declaration can appear at the top level of the script, and the script object that owns it is the script as a whole. This is a legal script:

```
property x : 5
display dialog x
```

A script property declaration is like set, not like copy. When a script property is initialized to a value where this makes a difference (a list, a record, a date, or a script object) it is set by reference (see "Set by Reference" in Chapter 7). Here's proof:

```
property L : {1, 2, 3}
script s
    property LL : L
    set end of LL to 4
end script
run s
L -- {1, 2, 3, 4}
```

Script Objects as Values

A script object is a datatype in AppleScript. This means that a variable's value can be a script object. In fact, a script object definition defines exactly such a variable. You can refer to this variable, and get and set its value, just as you would any other variable. Here, we fetch a script object as a value and assign it to another variable:

```
script myScript
    display dialog "Howdy"
end script
set x to myScript
run x -- Howdy
```

You can also assign a new value to a variable whose value is a script object. No law says that this new value must be another script object; you're just replacing the value of the variable, as with any other variable. The original script object is lost if this variable name is your only way of referring to it. So, you could do this if you wanted:

```
script myScript
    display dialog "Howdy"
end script
set myScript to 9
display dialog myScript -- 9
```

You can assign to a variable whose value is a script object the value of another script object, in effect replacing its functionality with new functionality. Of course, that new functionality must be defined somewhere to begin with. The old functionality is lost if this variable name is your only way of referring to it. For example:

```
script sayHowdy
    display dialog "Howdy"
end script
script sayGetLost
    display dialog "Get Lost"
end script
set sayHowdy to sayGetLost
run sayHowdy -- Get Lost
```

When you use set (as opposed to copy) to set a variable to a value that is a script object, you set the variable by reference (see "Set by Reference" in Chapter 7). So the script object is not copied; the variable's name becomes a new name for the script object, in addition to any existing names for the script object. This fact has two important implications:

- Setting a variable to a script object with set is extremely efficient, no matter how big the script object may be.
- If a script object has more than one name, then whatever mutation is performed upon it by way of one name applies to it under its other names as well.

Here's an example:

```
script sayHello
    property greeting : "Hello"
    display dialog greeting
    set greeting to "Get Lost"
end script
```

```
set x to sayHello
run sayHello -- Hello
run x -- Get Lost
```

In that example, running the script object sayHello changed the greeting property of sayHello; when we ran the script object x we found that its greeting property had been changed as well. That's because sayHello and x are merely two names for the same thing. And *that's* because we used set to set x by reference, making its value the very same script object that sayHello was already the name of.

Top-Level Entities

A script object's *top-level entities* are variables defined at the top level of the script object having the special feature that even though they belong to the script object, and even though the rules of scope protect them from being visible to code outside the script object, they can be accessed (retrieved and assigned to) by code outside the script object. A top-level entity is either a script property, a handler, or a script object.

Accessing Top-Level Entities

The most important fact about a script object's top-level entities is that even though they are not directly visible to code outside the script object, they are *accessible on demand* to any code that can see the script object. This means that they can be both retrieved and assigned to (fetched and set) by such code.

A special way of talking is required for doing this. Because a script object's top-level entities are not visible outside the script object, it is necessary, in effect, to ask the script object politely to yield access to a top-level entity (and the script object always politely complies). We say that to access a script object's top-level entities, you must *target* that script object. The syntax for doing this comes in two forms:

- Use the of operator (or the 's operator) to specify the top-level entity in relation to its script object. For example:

```
script myScript
    property x : "Howdy"
    on sayHowdy( )
        display dialog x
    end sayHowdy
    script innerScript
        display dialog x
    end script
end script
set x of myScript to "Hello"
myScript's sayHowdy( ) -- Hello
run innerScript of myScript -- Hello
```

- Alternatively, refer to the top-level entity within a tell block addressed to the script object. This requires the use of the keyword its, except in the case of a handler call. For example:

```
script myScript
    property x : "Howdy"
    on sayHowdy( )
        display dialog x
    end sayHowdy
    script innerScript
        display dialog x
    end script
end script
tell myScript
    set its x to "Hello"
    sayHowdy( ) -- Hello
    run its innerScript -- Hello
end tell
```

In the second form, the keyword its (explained more fully in Chapter 11) is required to specify that we mean myScript's top-level entities and not some other variables. If you omit its from the line where you set x, you actually set a different x (an implicit global, as we'll see in Chapter 10), not the property of myScript. If you omit its from the line where you run innerScript, there is a runtime error, because no defined variable called innerScript is visible here.

(It makes no difference whether the keyword its appears before the call to sayHowdy. This special treatment of handler calls will be discussed in "Handler Calls, Commands, and Script Objects," later in this chapter.)

Persistence of Top-Level Entities

Another remarkable feature of a top-level entity of a script object is that it is *persistent*, meaning that its value survives the execution of the script. If a top-level entity's value is changed during the execution of a script, then if you execute the script again, the top-level entity will have this new value at the outset, as long as you haven't done something to reinitialize it.

So, for example:

```
script myScript
    property x : 5
end script
tell myScript
    set its x to (its x) + 1
end tell
display dialog myScript's x
```

In a script editor application, run that code. A dialog appears saying 6. Now, for dramatic effect, without closing the script window or making any other change, walk away and do something else, such as get a cup of coffee. Now run the code again. The dialog says 7!

A script as a whole is a script object, so we can demonstrate the very same thing much more simply with a property of the script as a whole:

```
property x : 5
set x to x + 1
display dialog x
```

The first time you run this, the dialog says 6. Then when you run it again, the dialog says 7.

This amazing behavior is possible because AppleScript has a memory (see "Maintenance of State" in Chapter 3). Your compiled script is in AppleScript's memory. After the script is executed, AppleScript retains the compiled script, and along with it, the values of all its top-level entities. A script property is a top-level entity. So after the first execution of the script, AppleScript is remembering that the script has a property x and that its value is 6. Thus when you run the script a second time and x is incremented again, it becomes 7.

Now, at this point, you are saying: "But wait! I can see x being initialized to 5 right there in the script. So what about that line? Are you saying that, the second time the script is executed, AppleScript is ignoring that line?" Well, it's really just a matter of what *initialize* means. It means to give a value to something that has no value. The second time the script is executed, x has a value already, remembered from the previous execution. So the initialization has no effect, because x doesn't need initializing.

Now let's go back to the previous code, with the script object myScript. What AppleScript is remembering between executions is the script as a whole. So what persists is the top-level entities of the script as a whole. But myScript is a script object defined at the top level, so it is a top-level entity of the script as a whole. Therefore it persists, and therefore *its* top-level entities persist. That's why that example works.

Generalizing, this means we can nest a script object in a script object in a script object to any depth we like, and as long as each script object is defined at the top level of its containing script object and the top script object is defined at the top level of the script as a whole, the properties of even the deepest script object in the nesting will persist between executions.

Here's an example two levels deep:

```
script outerScript
    script innerScript
        property x : 5
        on increment()
            set x to x + 1
        end increment
    end script
    tell innerScript to increment()
    display dialog innerScript's x
end script
run outerScript -- 6, then 7, and so forth
```

Here's an even more dramatic example, where one script object value is replaced wholesale with another:

```
script myScript
    script myInnerScript
        display dialog "Hello"
    end script
    run myInnerScript
end script
script myNastyScript
    display dialog "Get lost"
end script
run myScript
set myScript's myInnerScript to myNastyScript
```

That code displays Hello the first time, but then it displays Get lost every time after that. The reason is that after the first time, myInnerScript has been replaced by myNastyScript, and this new version of myInnerScript persists.

What reinitializes top-level entities

Nothing lives forever, so just how long does all this persistence persist? Well, for one thing, it all comes to an end if you *edit* the script. That's because altering the script means that the entire script must be recompiled, and at that point the contents of the old compiled script, along with the values of the top-level entities from the previous execution, are thrown away from AppleScript's memory. So, compiling reinitializes top-level entities. (That's why throughout this section I've been telling you to execute the script multiple times without doing anything else. If you so much as type a space in the script window, the script's persistence goes away.)

Another thing that reinitializes top-level entities is generating the script object anew in code. To see what I mean, consider this code:

```
repeat 3 times
    script s
        property x : 1
        display dialog x
        set x to x + 1
    end script
    run s
end repeat
```

There is a loop that repeats three times, and each time we see x being incremented. But what about afterwards? Do you think the value of x will persist after it increments three times? (Think about it before reading on.)

Ha ha, it was a trick question! The value of x will never even increment in the first place. Well, it increments, but then it is reinitialized. That code does not display 1 and then 2 and then 3; it displays 1 and then 1 and then 1. Why? Because each time through the loop, the entire script object definition happens again. So the variable s is defined anew, with a new script object. And each time, this new script object's top-level entities are initialized afresh. The script object s is not defined at the top level of a script object; it is not itself a top-level entity. Thus, no persistence.

Similarly, when a script object is defined within a handler, it has no persistence. The script object is created anew each time the handler runs. This is true even in a script object's explicit run handler. This code illustrates that a script object in an explicit run handler does not have persistent top-level entities:

```
script myScript
    on run
        script myInnerScript
            property x : 10
        end script
        tell myInnerScript
            set its x to (its x) + 1
            display dialog its x
        end tell
    end run
end script
run myScript -- 11
```

That code yields 11 every time it runs. As I said in "Code and the Run Handler" in Chapter 6, only stuff in the implicit run handler is at the top level. An explicit run handler is an ordinary handler, and stuff inside it follows the rules for being inside a handler. So myInnerScript is not defined at the top level of a script object; it is not a top-level entity, and has no persistence.

File-level persistence

So far we've talked about persistence only while a script window remains open for editing in a script editor application. But what about when a script is saved as a compiled script file and its window is closed? Does persistence work when the script file is opened for editing again later? And does persistence work when a saved compiled script file is repeatedly executed by a script runner?

The answer, unfortunately, is: it depends. Persistence doesn't work if you save, close, and open a script file using the current Script Editor. When you run the newly opened script, you find that everything is reinitialized. On the other hand, such persistence does work with older versions of the Script Editor (1.9 or before), or with Script Debugger. Create and run this script several times in Script Debugger:

```
property x : 5
set x to x + 1
display dialog x
```

Now save the script as a compiled script file, and quit, just to prove to yourself that AppleScript's own memory of the value of x is well and truly erased. Now open the compiled script file again (in Script Debugger) and execute it. The incrementing of x picks up right where it left off previously.

It would be really nice if persistence always worked in a compiled script file, but unfortunately this mechanism is not automatic, and in fact has nothing to do with AppleScript itself. AppleScript has no way to enforce file-level persistence, because AppleScript doesn't deal with files. It is up to the environment that's talking to the AppleScript scripting component, after it asks AppleScript to run a compiled script file, to save AppleScript's copy of the compiled script back into the compiled script file after execution. If it doesn't do this, then the compiled script file won't contain the new values, and the values won't persist. Script Editor and Script Debugger behave differently in this regard.

Similarly, script runners and other environments that execute compiled script files can behave differently. Some environments do save the compiled script file back to disk after each execution along with any changed top-level entities. For example, applets do this. So does Apple's Script Menu, and so does BBEdit with its Script menu. But Entourage's Script menu, for example, does not.

Actually, persistence in Apple's Script Menu (and perhaps some other environments) is itself inconsistently implemented. It turns out that the Script Menu implements persistence only if execution of the script returns a value (even though this value is otherwise ignored). Some actions, such as the user canceling out of a dialog, can cause the script to return with no value, and in that case, persistence fails. You can guarantee persistence in this situation by trickery, making sure that the script returns a value no matter what. In the case of display dialog you can catch the error produced by the user canceling and return a value anyway:

```
property x : 5
set x to x + 1
try
    display dialog x
on error
    return 0
end try
```

All this inconsistency can be troublesome. You can't depend on file-level persistence; you must test each intended environment to see whether (and how) it works there. In the next section, I'll describe a mechanism for implementing file-level persistence from within a script, in such a way that it is guaranteed to work.

Compiled Script Files as Script Objects

A script can read a compiled script file and incorporate its contents as a script object. Similarly, a script can save a script object out to disk as a compiled script file. You might use this mechanism as a means of implementing file-level persistence, or to build a separate library of commonly needed code that all scripts can share.

The mechanism depends upon three verbs. They're not part of AppleScript proper, but are implemented in a scripting addition (Chapter 3) that's standard on all machines.

load script

Syntax

```
load script aliasOrFile
```

Description

Returns the top-level script of the compiled script file or applet *aliasOrFile* as a script object.

Example

```
set myScript to load script alias "myDisk:myFile.scpt"
```

run script

Syntax

```
run script aliasOrFile [with parameters list]
```

Description

Tells the top-level script of the compiled script file, applet, or text file *aliasOrFile* to run (compiling first if necessary), optionally handing it the *list* as the parameters for its explicit run handler, and returns the result.

Example

```
run script alias "myDisk:myFile.scpt"
```

store script

Syntax

```
store script scriptObject [in aliasOrFile [replacing yes|no]]
```

Description

Saves *scriptObject* to disk as a compiled script file or applet. Returns no value. If no further parameters are supplied, presents a Save File dialog; if the user cancels, a runtime error is raised. If *aliasOrFile* is supplied, the Save File dialog is suppressed, but if the file exists already, presents a dialog asking how to proceed; if the user cancels, a runtime error is raised. If replacing is supplied, this dialog is suppressed; if yes, the file is just saved, and if no, an error is raised if the file exists. The filename extension determines the format of the resulting file: *.scpt* (or nothing) for a compiled script file, *.scptd* for a script bundle, *.app* for an applet. (The applet will be an applet bundle unless a nonbundle applet already exists.)

Example

```
store script sayHello in file "myDisk:myFile.scpt" replacing yes
```

(On aliases and file specifiers and the differences between them, see Chapter 13. The verb run script, instead of a file, can take a string, and it then functions as a kind of second level of evaluation; see Chapter 19.)

When you save a script object with `store script`, the lines delimiting the script object definition block (if any) are not included. This fact makes sense, since those lines were never part of the actual script object to begin with. So, for example:

```
script sayHello
    display dialog "Hello"
end script
store script sayHello in file "myDisk:myFile.scpt" replacing yes
```

What is saved in *myFile.scpt* is the single line:

```
display dialog "Hello"
```

Data Storage

Recall from earlier in this chapter that top-level script object entities are persistent, but that at the level of a file on disk, this persistence is unreliable, because it depends upon the environment where the script runs. For example, Entourage's Script menu doesn't save a compiled script file back to disk after execution, so top-level entities don't persist between executions. We can get around this uncertainty by storing needed data ourselves in a separate compiled script file. A script object that we save with `store script` is saved along with the current values of its top-level entities. Thus we can guarantee file-level persistence by saving a script object as a compiled script file separately from our main script.

If you load a script as a script object with the `load script` command, and top-level entity values within this script object change, and you wish to write these changes back to disk, it is up to you do so explicitly, with `store script`.

The `run script` command does not save its script, so any changes in the script's top-level entity values do not persist.

Here's an example where we display the user's favorite color. This information will be stored persistently in a file on the desktop called *myPrefs.scpt*. (The `path to` command is discussed in Chapter 21.) First we try to load this file. If we succeed, fine; if we fail, we ask for the user's favorite color and store it in *myPrefs.scpt*. Either way, we now know and can display the user's favorite color. If the user doesn't move *myPrefs.scpt*, the next time the script runs there will be no need to ask for the user's favorite color; we will already know it.

```
set thePath to (path to desktop as string) & "myPrefs.scpt"
script myPrefs
    property favoriteColor : ""
end script
try
    set myPrefs to load script file thePath
on error
    set favoriteColor of myPrefs to text returned of ¬
        (display dialog "Favorite Color:" default answer ¬
            "" buttons {"OK"} default button "OK")
```

```
        store script myPrefs in file thePath replacing yes
    end try
    display dialog "Your favorite color is " & favoriteColor of myPrefs
```

You might object that a file sitting on the user's desktop is a silly place to store our data. You're perfectly right; it's only an example! How might we solve this problem in real life? We need a place to put the data where the user won't see it or object to it. One solution, if it is supported by the environment where the script will run, would be to make this script a script bundle and store the secondary script inside the bundle. A script bundle looks like a file, so the secondary script is out of sight inside it. The first line of the script could then be something like this:

```
    set thePath to (path to me as string) & "Contents:Resources:myPrefs.scpt"
```

Unfortunately, a script runner environment that doesn't implement persistence might not know about script bundles either. Perhaps a better place might be the user's Preferences folder:

```
    set thePath to (path to preferences as string) & "myPrefs.scpt"
```

If you open the file *myPrefs.scpt* in a script editor application, you may be surprised to find that it doesn't actually seem to contain your favorite color:

```
    property favoriteColor : ""
```

Don't worry! The decompiled version of the script, which is what you're seeing, shows the original bytecode, not the persistent data stored internally with the script. But the persistent data is there. (The only way I know of to get a look at the persistent data stored internally with a script is to use Script Debugger. Script Editor doesn't show it, and destroys it if you open and run the script directly.)

Library

A compiled script file may be used to hold commonly needed routines. A running script can access the contents of the script file using load script. The script file's top-level entities, including its run handler, are then available to the running script that loads it. A compiled script file used in this way is called a *library*.

For example, AppleScript has no native command to remove one item from a list (that is, to return a list without its *n*th item). Let's write one. Ooooh, we've already done it; see "LISP-likeness" in Chapter 4. Save that script (the AppleScript version, not the LISP version); for now, let's save it as *library.scpt* on the desktop. Here's how to use the library:

```
    -- load the library . . .
    set f to (path to desktop as string) & "library.scpt"
    set lib to load script alias f
    -- . . . and use it
    set L to {"Mannie", "Moe", "Jack"}
    set L2 to lib's remvix(2, L)
    L2 -- {"Mannie", "Jack"}
```

What are the advantages and disadvantages of using a library? An obvious advantage is that it makes code reusable and maintainable. Here, remvix is a useful handler. We don't want to have to keep copying and pasting it into different scripts. If its code lives in a library, it becomes accessible to any script we write. Furthermore, if we improve remvix in its library file, those improvements are accessible to any script; a script that already calls remvix by way of load script acquires any new improvements the next time it runs. Finally, a library may consist of many interrelated handlers that call each other (and may even share values by way of top-level properties). When you load the library, you load that entire functionality and the handlers work properly without your having to worry about the complexities of dependency.

A disadvantage is that a library reduces portability. We cannot just copy a script that calls remvix to another machine, or send it to a friend, because it depends on another file, *library.scpt*, and refers to it by a pathname that won't work on any other machine.

With Script Debugger, a trick for working around this problem is to load any library files as part of your script property initialization:

```
-- load the library . . .
property f : (path to desktop as string) & "library.scpt"
property lib : load script alias f
-- . . . and use it
set L to {"Mannie", "Moe", "Jack"}
set L2 to lib's remvix(2, L)
L2 -- {"Mannie", "Jack"}
```

This works because, as explained earlier in this chapter, Script Debugger saves top-level entities into the compiled script file. So when you run this script and then save it as a compiled script file with Script Debugger, the property lib is saved in its initialized state, meaning that it contains the script object loaded from disk. The resulting compiled script file thus contains the library that it uses, and will run correctly in a script runner on another machine. In fact, this compiled script file can even be opened and executed using Script Debugger on another machine.

However, if you open this script with Script Editor, the script is ruined, because Script Editor strips out the saved top-level entities when it opens a file. Furthermore, if you edit this script on another machine, the script is ruined. At that point, the values of the script properties will be thrown away, AppleScript will try to reinitialize them, the load script command will fail because the file it refers to doesn't exist, and the script will no longer compile or run. Thus, this trick is probably most appropriate when you can afford to distribute a script as run-only.

(Actually, Script Debugger helps you further in this situation as well. It lets you "flatten" a script so that it incorporates all library files on which it depends, and so has no load script dependencies.)

An interesting attempt to rationalize the library mechanism is the freeware utility Loader. The idea is to try to make it as easy to install and take advantage of libraries, even if they involve mutual dependencies, as in languages like Perl and Python. I haven't tried this myself, but it looks intriguing.

Inheritance

Script objects may be linked into a *chain of inheritance*. One script object inherits from another if the second script is the *parent* of the first. Then, suppose an attempt is made to access a top-level entity of the first script object (using the special syntax described in "Accessing Top-Level Entities," earlier in this chapter). If the script object has no such top-level entity, the attempt is passed along to its parent to see whether *it* has such a top-level entity.

It turns out that every script object has a parent property. This property is set for you if you don't set it (and so there is always an inheritance chain, even though you might not be aware of this). To link two script objects explicitly into a chain of inheritance, *initialize the* parent *property of one to point to the other*.

 The parent property may be set only through initialization (that is, through a script property declaration). You cannot use copy or set to set it.

In this example, we explicitly arrange two script objects, mommy and baby, into an inheritance chain (by initializing baby's parent property). We can then tell baby to execute a handler that it doesn't have, but which mommy does have. Here we go:

```
script mommy
    on talk()
        display dialog "How do you do?"
    end talk
end script
script baby
    property parent : mommy
end script
baby's talk() -- How do you do?
```

In that example, we told the child from outside to execute a handler that it doesn't have but the parent does. The child can also tell itself to execute such a handler:

```
script mommy
    on talk()
        display dialog "How do you do?"
    end talk
end script
script baby
    property parent : mommy
    talk()
end script
run baby -- How do you do?
```

Getting and setting properties works the same way. In this example, we get and set the value of a property of baby that baby doesn't have:

```
script mommy
    property address : "123 Main Street"
end script
script baby
    property parent : mommy
end script
display dialog baby's address -- 123 Main Street
set baby's address to "234 Chestnut Street"
display dialog mommy's address -- 234 Chestnut Street
```

Again, the same thing can be done from code within the child; but now the name of the property must be prefixed with the keyword my. Like its when targeting a script object, my specifies that we're talking about a top-level entity of this script. (In fact, instead of my, you can use its; but that seems less intuitive, somehow.)

```
script mommy
    property address : "123 Main Street"
end script
script baby
    property parent : mommy
    on tellAddress()
        display dialog my address
    end tellAddress
end script
baby's tellAddress() -- 123 Main Street
```

Similarly, we can refer to a script object that the child doesn't have but the parent does:

```
script mommy
    script talk
        display dialog "How do you do?"
    end script
end script
script baby
    property parent : mommy
end script
run baby's talk -- How do you do?
```

Again, if the child wants to do this, it must use my (or its):

```
script mommy
    script talk
        display dialog "How do you do?"
    end script
end script
script baby
    property parent : mommy
    run my talk
end script
run baby -- How do you do?
```

With a handler call, there is no need for my:

```
script mommy
    on talk()
        display dialog "How do you do?"
    end talk
end script
script baby
    property parent : mommy
    talk()
end script
run baby -- How do you do?
```

Polymorphism

When code within a script object refers to a top-level entity, the search for this top-level entity starts in the script object to which the message that caused this code to run was originally sent. This is called *polymorphism*. Again, when accessing a property or script object, you must use the keyword my (or its) to get polymorphism to operate.

An example will clarify:

```
script mommy
    on tellWeight()
        display dialog my weight
    end tellWeight
end script
script baby
    property parent : mommy
    property weight : "9 pounds"
end script
baby's tellWeight() -- 9 pounds
```

We ask baby to tell us its weight, but baby doesn't know how to do this (a baby can't talk), so the message is passed along to the parent, mommy. There is now an attempt to access my weight. But mommy has no weight property. However, the search for weight starts with baby, because our original message was to baby (mommy is involved only because of inheritance). The property is found and the code works.

If we take away my, polymorphism fails to operate and the entire mechanism breaks down. With the previous example, we would get a runtime error message: "The variable weight is not defined." Without my, the name weight is not an attempt to access a top-level entity. Instead, it's just a name. AppleScript looks for a defined variable weight in scope at the point where the name is used, and fails to find it.

The reason for the "poly" in the name "polymorphism" is that the response to the parent's use of a term can mean different things, depending on who the original target was. A parent whose code is running because of inheritance has no idea of this fact, so it has no idea exactly what its own code will do. This is officially cool, and is one of the key principles of object-based programming. For example:

```
script mommy
    property weight : "120 pounds"
    on tellWeight( )
        display dialog my weight
    end tellWeight
end script
script baby
    property parent : mommy
    property weight : "9 pounds"
end script
script baby2
    property parent : mommy
    property weight : "8 pounds"
end script
mommy's tellWeight( ) -- 120 pounds
baby's tellWeight( ) -- 9 pounds
baby2's tellWeight( ) -- 8 pounds
```

In that example, the parental phrase my weight gets three different interpretations, depending solely on what script object was targeted originally.

Again, there is no need to use my (or its) with a handler call; polymorphism operates automatically, as this example shows:

```
script mommy
    on cry()
        display dialog "Boo-hoo, sniff sniff..."
    end cry
    on beSad()
        cry()
    end beSad
end script
script baby
    property parent : mommy
    on cry()
        display dialog "Waaaaaaa!"
    end cry
end script
baby's beSad() -- Waaaaaaa!
```

It's mommy that implements beSad, but the original target was baby, so it's baby's cry that is called.

Continue

A child can call an inherited handler by using the continue command. The syntax is the keyword continue followed by a complete handler call (parameters and all).

You might wonder why this is needed, as after all the child can just send a message directly to the parent. It could do this, for instance, by referring to the parent as parent. But there's a crucial difference. If a message is sent to the parent by referring to it as parent, that's a new message with a new target. On the other hand, the continue command takes place in the context of the current message and the current target; it passes the current flow of control up the inheritance chain. Thus, the one breaks polymorphism, the other does not.

This example demonstrates the difference:

```
script mommy
    property weight : "120 pounds"
    on tellWeight()
        display dialog my weight
    end tellWeight
end script
script baby
    property parent : mommy
    property weight : "9 pounds"
    parent's tellWeight() -- no polymorphism
    continue tellWeight() -- polymorphism
end script
run baby -- 120 pounds, 9 pounds
```

The Implicit Parent Chain

A script object without an explicitly specified parent has as its parent the script as a whole. That fact is surprising and is worth stressing. Mere physical nesting is *not* implicit parenthood:

```
script myScript
    script myInnerScript
        my parent -- the top-level script, not myScript
    end script
    run myInnerScript
end script
run myScript
```

Nor, indeed, can a nested script object be made to have a containing script object as its parent. AppleScript will balk if you try this:

```
script myScript
    script myInnerScript
        property parent: myScript -- compile-time error
    end script
end script
```

(I think the reason for this restriction must be that the demands of parenthood would conflict irresolvably with the rules of scoping.)

The implicit parent chain explains why certain things work that look like they shouldn't work. Here's an example:

```
property x : 10
script outer
    property x : 20
    script inner
    end script
end script
get outer's inner's x -- 10
```

If you go by your intuitions alone, you might think the search for x starts in inner and works its way up the nest. We come immediately to x in outer. So the result of the script should be 20. Your intuitions are wrong. They are right for how scope works (see Chapter 10), but this isn't about scope; it's about accessing top-level entities. Top-level entities are sought up the parent chain, and the top-level script, not outer, is inner's parent. Similarly:

```
on sayHowdy()
    display dialog "Howdy"
end sayHowdy
script s
end script
tell s to sayHowdy() -- Howdy
```

That works not because s can "see" sayHowdy but because sayHowdy is a top-level entity of s's parent. If you don't believe me, I can prove it by breaking the inheritance chain. This isn't easy, because if I set s's parent to a different script object, the script itself will be the parent of *that* script object, and we'll get the same result. So I'll set s's parent to something that isn't a script object:

```
on sayHowdy()
    display dialog "Howdy"
end sayHowdy
script s
    property parent : 3
end script
tell s to sayHowdy() -- Error: Can't get sayHowdy of 3
```

We can take advantage of the inheritance chain to refer to a top-level entity of the script itself, even though the script itself has no name. Consider this code:

```
property x : 5
script myScript
    property x : 10
    display dialog x
end script
run myScript -- 10
```

It looks like we can never access the top-level property x from within the script object myScript, because the name x is overshadowed by myScript's own property x. A script object's top-level entities can be accessed by using the name of the script object, as we know. But the script as a whole has no name. But now we know another way to refer to the script as whole—as mySCript's parent:

```
property x : 5
script myScript
    property x : 10
    display dialog my parent's x
end script
run myScript -- 5
```

Unfortunately, that trick won't work if myScript has a different parent. In that case the solution is to give the script as a whole a name. You can do this by initializing a top-level property to the value me (see "Me" in Chapter 11).

```
property topLevel : me
property x : 5
script scriptOne
    property x : 10
end script
script scriptTwo
    property x : 20
    property parent : scriptOne
    display dialog topLevel's x
end script
run scriptTwo -- 5
```

Surprisingly, there's a parent beyond the script as a whole. The script as a whole has as its parent the AppleScript scripting component. This appears to your code as a script object called AppleScript.

The AppleScript script object has some properties that you can access (listed in Chapter 16). Normally you do this without having to refer to AppleScript explicitly, because these properties are in scope globally; it's as if every script were surrounded by another invisible script with property declarations for these properties. But in a context where a name overshadows the name of one of these properties, it would be necessary to be explicit, in order to jump past the current scope and up to the level of AppleScript:

```
set pi to 3
display dialog pi -- 3
display dialog AppleScript's pi -- 3.141592...
display dialog parent's pi -- 3.141592...
```

The AppleScript scripting component has a parent too—the current application. This is the host application that summoned the AppleScript scripting component to begin with. The current application is the absolute top of the inheritance chain, and can be referred to in code as current application. For example:

```
display dialog (get name of current application) -- Script Editor
```

To sum up:

```
script myScript
    my parent -- «script», the anonymous top level
    my parent's parent -- «script AppleScript»
    my parent's parent's parent -- current application
end script
run myScript
```

Non-Script Parent

A script object's parent doesn't have to be a script object. It can be a value of a different type altogether. In that case, the script object suddenly appears to be that other object, in cases where it cannot respond to a message itself. I have never seen this feature employed usefully in code, but it's definitely cool:

```
script s
    property parent : {"Mannie", "Moe", "Jack"}
    on greeting()
        return "Howdy"
    end greeting
end script
tell s
    greeting() -- "Howdy"
    get item 2 -- "Moe"
end tell
```

In effect, the script object s is now a kind of list wrapper; it can do things that a list can do, such as report on its items, but it can also respond to the greeting() message. However, this trick breaks down against other features of AppleScript; for example, operators treat the script object as a script object, not as a list:

```
script s
    property parent : {"Mannie", "Moe", "Jack"}
end script
get s & "Pep" -- {«script s», "Pep"}, not {"Mannie", "Moe", "Jack", "Pep"}
```

Handler Calls, Commands, and Script Objects

Several times in this chapter I've pointed out that you don't need to use its (or my) with a handler call when accessing a handler that is a top-level entity of a script object. You do have to use its in order to access the handler as a value. It's the *call* that gives you access without its.

So, as you know, you can't say this (without its):

```
script s
    property p : 10
end script
tell s
    get p
end tell
```

At runtime, you get an error saying that p is undefined. That's because without its, AppleScript doesn't know you're talking about s's property p. It thinks you must be talking about some other p, and there isn't one.

This is true for a handler too, if we simply treat the handler as the value of a variable:

```
script s
    on h()
        return 10
    end h
end script
tell s
    get h
end tell
```

Again, we get an error that h is undefined.

But a handler *call* is different. This works without its:

```
script s
    on h()
        return 10
    end h
end script
tell s
    h() -- 10
end tell
```

So a handler call is automatically treated as an attempt to access a top-level entity. It's important to stay conscious of this, because if you go by your intuitions alone you may be confused. Consider this script:

```
script x
    property greeting : "Howdy"
    on myHandler()
        display dialog greeting
    end myHandler
    script y
        display dialog greeting
        myHandler()
    end script
end script
run x's y -- Howdy, then error: «script y» doesn't understand the myHandler message
```

It looks like the property greeting and the handler myHandler are in the same place, so they should have the same status. And that's true, as far as it goes. But y apparently can see greeting, yet it fails in its attempt to call myHandler. That is also true. The reason is that a handler call is not the same thing as just saying the name of some variable. A handler call is routed as a search for a top-level entity. The search starts in y. myHandler isn't there, so we pass to the parent. The parent isn't x; it's the top-level script. myHandler isn't there either. So the search fails. This is not to say that you can never call myHandler at all. You simply have to target x explicitly when you do:

```
script x
    property greeting : "Howdy"
    on myHandler()
        display dialog greeting
    end myHandler
    script y
        x's myHandler() -- explicit target
    end script
end script
run x's y -- Howdy
```

I think the reason for this special status of a handler call is that AppleScript wants to treat a handler call as a command. Its status is like that of the built-in commands, such as run and count. When you give a command to a script object, you don't want to have to talk in some special way; you are sending a message and you want that message to go to the right place all by itself. So a handler call works that way too.

To see that this probably the right sort of explanation, consider how the message-passing mechanism works when you send a built-in command to a script object:

```
script s
end script
tell s to count -- 0
```

The count message is routed just the way a handler call is routed. If a script object implements count, it is this count that is called:

```
script theCount
    on count
        return "1, 2, 3, ha ha ha"
    end count
end script
tell theCount to count -- "1, 2, 3, ha ha ha"
```

Alternatively, if we give s a parent that implements count in a different way, then the count command is routed to that parent:

```
script s
    property parent : {"Mannie", "Moe", "Jack"}
end script
tell s to count -- 3
```

(We'll return to weird handlers like count in Chapter 9, and to objects and the message-sending mechanism in Chapter 11.)

So it appears that the inheritance chain is involved in *every* command. Whether it's a handler call or a built-in command, it has some target and is passed up the inheritance chain from that target until we come to someone who can obey. This probably also explains the curious language of the error message you get when you misdirect a handler call to a scriptable application:

```
tell application "Finder"
    sayHowdy() -- Finder got an error: Can't continue sayHowdy.
end tell
```

It's as if the Finder were a sort of script object, saying, "I don't know what this command means, and I haven't got a parent to pass it along to."

Because handler calls and commands are passed up the inheritance chain, the current application is the implicit target of every command not otherwise targeted. This fact is rarely useful, though. For example, in theory, if a script that drives BBEdit is to run in BBEdit's Script menu, it doesn't need to target BBEdit in a tell block; BBEdit is the current application, so BBEdit is implicitly the target of all commands. But in reality such a script usually will target BBEdit in a tell block, not as a way of directing its commands but as a way of getting its terminology to compile. The script could, however, get its terminology to compile with a terms block (see Chapter 19), and then it would indeed have no need to target BBEdit explicitly.

CHAPTER 9
Handlers

A *handler* is a subroutine within a script. A handler is an important form of flow control, and leads to better-behaved, better-organized, more reusable, and more legible code. With a handler, the same code can be executed from different places in a script. Even if a handler is going to be called only once in the course of a script, it's a useful organizational device because it names a block of code, and this name can describe the block's purpose.

Handler Definition

A handler is defined using a block with the keyword on:

```
on handlerName()
    -- commands within the handler
end handlerName
```

A synonym for on is to.

What follows the name of the handler in the on line of the block might be parentheses, but it might not. The real story is complicated; the details appear later in this chapter ("Syntax of Defining and Calling a Handler").

A handler definition may appear only at the top level of a script object (or a script as a whole). It is a top-level entity of the script object ("Top-Level Entities" in Chapter 8). It functions as a scope block. (The rules of scope appear in Chapter 10.) Read Chapter 6 for an overview of how script object definitions fit into a script's overall structure.

A handler definition is just that—a definition. Merely encountering a handler definition in the course of execution does not cause the handler to be executed. Rather, a handler definition is a form of variable definition. So, for example:

```
on sayHowdy()
    display dialog "howdy"
end sayHowdy
```

That code does not cause a dialog to display. It defines a handler whose code, if executed, would display a dialog. The handler itself is the value of a variable. Here, that variable is sayHowdy; when this code is encountered, the variable sayHowdy is defined and initialized, and its initial value is the handler described by this block of code.

What causes a handler's code to run is code that *calls* the handler. This looks essentially like using the handler's name, with some special syntax that signifies you're actually calling and not merely mentioning the name of the variable that contains the handler. So, for example:

```
on sayHowdy()
    display dialog "howdy"
end sayHowdy
sayHowdy()
```

That code first defines a handler, then calls it. The call is in the last line. Because of that last line, the code does cause a dialog to be displayed.

 It is not an error to refer to a handler by its name alone, with no parentheses or parameters. This can be a useful thing to do, if you wish to refer to the handler as a value (see "Handlers as Values," later in this chapter); but it *doesn't call the handler*. If you refer to a handler by its name alone, intending to call it, your script will misbehave in ways that can be difficult to track down.

Returned Value

When a handler is executed, it may *return* a value. This value is the handler's *result*.

 The term *result* is used here in a technical sense. A handler may do other things besides return a result, and these other things may be quite significant in the world outside of the handler; but although these things may result from calling the handler, in a nontechnical sense, technically they are the handler's *side effects*, not its result. Thus, if you call a handler that erases your hard drive and returns the number 1, you might say, "The result of calling the handler was that my hard drive was erased," but technically you'd be wrong: the result was 1; the erasure of your hard drive was a side effect. (Clearly a side effect can be much more important than a result.)

When a handler is called, the result of executing the handler is essentially substituted as the value of the call that executed the handler.

For example:

```
on getRam()
    set bytes to system attribute "ram "
    return bytes div (2 ^ 20)
end getRam
```

The handler getRam returns the amount of RAM installed on the user's machine, in megabytes. On my machine, it returns the number 1024. This means that a call to getRam( ) can presently be used wherever I would use the number 1024; in effect, it *is* the number 1024. For example:

```
on getRam( )
    set bytes to system attribute "ram "
    return bytes div (2 ^ 20)
end getRam
display dialog "You have " & getRam( ) & "MB of RAM. Wow!"
```

The call to getRam( ) in the last line behaves exactly as the number 1024 would behave in this context: it is a number, it is implicitly coerced to a string and concatenated with the other two strings (as explained under "Concatenation Operator" in Chapter 15), and the full resulting string is displayed to the user.

The value returned by a handler is determined in one of two ways:

An explicit return
> The handler, in the course of execution, encounters a line consisting of the keyword return, possibly followed by a value. At that point execution of the handler ceases, and the returned value is whatever follows the return keyword (which could be nothing, in which case no value is returned).

An implicit result
> The handler finishes executing without ever encountering an explicit return. In that case, the returned value is the result of the last-executed line of the handler.

> For the same reason that I recommend that you not use the result keyword (see "Result" in Chapter 5), I recommend that you not use a handler's ability to return an implicit result. If you're going to capture a handler's result, use an explicit return statement in the handler.

If a handler returns no value, there is no error; but in that case it is a runtime error to attempt to use the call as if it had a value. The status of such a call is similar to that of a variable that has never been assigned a value (see "Declaration and Definition of Variables" in Chapter 7). So, for example, there's nothing wrong with this:

```
on noValue( )
    return
end noValue
set x to noValue( )
```

After that, even if x was previously defined, it is now undefined. That outcome is actually useful if you wanted to undefine x; there's no other way to do it. But remember, a subsequent attempt to fetch x's value will generate a runtime error:

```
on noValue( )
    return
end noValue
```

```
set x to 1
set x to noValue( )
set x to x + 1 -- error: The variable x is not defined
```

The result of a handler is volatile. It is substituted for the call, but the call itself is not storage (it isn't a variable), so the result is then lost. If you wish to use the result of a handler again later, it is up to you to capture it at the time you make the call—for example, by setting a variable to it. Of course, you could just call the handler again; but there are good reasons why this strategy might not be right:

- The handler might yields different results on different occasions; if you wanted the particular result of a particular call, calling it again won't do.

- The handler might do other things besides return a result (side effects); to perform these side effects again might not be good, or might not make sense.

- Storing a result and using it later is far more efficient than calling the handler a second time.

So, for example, this code works, but it is very poor code:

```
on getRam( )
    set bytes to system attribute "ram "
    return bytes div (2 ^ 20)
end getRam
set s to "You have " & getRam( ) & "MB of RAM. Wow! "
set s to s & getRam( ) & "MB is a lot!"
display dialog s
```

The handler is called twice to get the same unchanging result, which is very inefficient. The right way would be more like this:

```
on getRam( )
    set bytes to system attribute "ram "
    return bytes div (2 ^ 20)
end getRam
set myRam to getRam( )
set s to "You have " & myRam & "MB of RAM. Wow! "
set s to s & myRam & "MB is a lot!"
display dialog s
```

The second version calls the handler and immediately stores the result in a variable. Now it suffices to fetch the value from the variable each time it is needed.

The result of a handler may be ignored, though, if the caller doesn't care about it (or knows that no value will be returned). In this case the handler is called entirely for its side effects. Generally the call will appear as the only thing in the line:

```
eraseMyHardDisk( )
```

The same is equally true for the run handler of a script object (or a script as a whole), whether implicit or explicit. A run handler is a handler, and can have a result (possibly a useful result). After you run a script in a script editor application, the result is displayed; if no return statement was encountered, the result displayed is the implicit result of the run handler of the script as a whole. (This fact can be useful in developing and testing a script; see "Implicit Result" in Chapter 5.) A script runner, on the other hand, will usually ignore a script's result, neither capturing it nor displaying it; the script is executed entirely for its side effects.

Handlers as Values

A handler is a datatype in AppleScript. This means that a variable's value can be a handler. In fact, a handler definition defines exactly such a variable. You can refer to this variable, and get and set its value, just as you would any other variable. Here, we fetch a handler as a value and assign it to another variable:

```
on sayHowdy( )
    display dialog "Howdy"
end sayHowdy
set sayHello to sayHowdy
sayHello( ) -- Howdy
```

As the example shows, after the assignment of the handler to another variable, we can call that variable as if it were a handler. That's because the variable *is* a handler.

You can also assign a new value to a variable whose value is a handler. No law says that this new value must be another handler; you're just replacing the value of the variable, as with any other variable. The original handler functionality is lost. For example, you could do this if you wanted:

```
on sayHowdy( )
    display dialog "Howdy"
end sayHowdy
set sayHowdy to 9
display dialog sayHowdy -- 9
```

You can assign to a variable whose value is a handler the value of another handler, in effect replacing its functionality with new functionality. Of course, that functionality has to be defined somewhere to begin with, and the old functionality is lost. For example:

```
on sayHowdy( )
    display dialog "Howdy"
end sayHowdy
on sayGetLost( )
    display dialog "Get Lost"
end sayGetLost
set sayHello to sayGetLost
sayHello( ) -- Get Lost
```

An elegant use of this feature is a list that acts as a dispatch table. The idea is that sometimes we want to call one handler and sometimes another, depending on the circumstances. Rather than code the handler calls within a branching construct, we make a list of handlers and call the desired item of the list:

```
on sayHello()
    display dialog "Hello"
end sayHello
on sayGetLost()
    display dialog "Get Lost"
end sayGetLost
set L to {sayHello, sayGetLost}
-- for this example, we decide randomly which one to call
set h to item (random number from 1 to 2) of L
h()
```

Parameters

One of the key features of a handler is that it can accept parameters. A *parameter* is a value passed to the handler as it is called. The handler can see these values, and can react to them. Thus, the handler can do different things depending on the values actually passed as parameters on each occasion when the handler is called.

For example, here's a definition of a handler that takes two parameters, and a call to that handler:

```
on subtract(x, y)
    return x - y
end subtract
subtract(3, 2) -- 1
```

In the last line, the handler is called with the two parameters it requires. The value 3 is passed as the first parameter; the value 2 is passed as the second parameter. In the handler definition, names that effectively designate variables belonging to the handler have been declared. When the handler is called, and before it actually starts executing, these names are paired with the parameters that were passed, and the corresponding values are assigned. Thus, when add( ) is called on this occasion, it is as if it had a variable x which has been initialized to 3, and a variable y which has been initialized to 2. Thus, the result is 1. But the result would have been different if the parameter values passed in the last line had been 10 and 8. That's the point of parameters.

The names of the parameters within the handler, such as x and y in this example, designate variables *local* to the handler. The meaning and significance of this is explained in Chapter 10, but the key fact is that the names of the parameters in the handler definition have nothing to do with the names of the values passed as parameters. Consider this example:

```
on subtract(x, y)
    return x - y
end subtract
set x to 2
set y to 3
subtract(y, x) -- 1
```

The handler subtracts y from x. If these were the same as the y and x at the top level of the script, you'd expect the result to be negative (we'd be subtracting 3 from 2). But in the handler call, the names are not what matters—the values are. The value 3 is passed as the first parameter and becomes x within the handler. The value 2 is passed as the second parameter and becomes y within the handler.

Pass by Reference

Parameters passed to a handler, and the value returned from a handler, are normally *passed by value* in AppleScript. This means that a *copy* of the value is passed to, and used by, the handler code.

But four datatypes—lists, records, dates, and script objects—when they are passed as parameters to a handler, are *passed by reference*, meaning that no copy is made; the handler and the caller both end up with access to the very same value. These are the only *mutable* datatypes—the only datatypes whose values can be modified in place. Whatever mutation is made to the parameter by the handler applies to it in the context of the caller as well. (Compare "Set by Reference" in Chapter 7.)

Here's an example showing that a list is passed by reference:

```
on extend(LL)
    set end of LL to "Jack"
end extend
set L to {"Mannie", "Moe"}
extend(L)
L -- {"Mannie", "Moe", "Jack"}
```

Even though the caller didn't capture the value of the handler call extend( ), and even though the caller didn't change L, and even though the handler extend never speaks explicitly of L, yet after the call, L has changed in the caller's context. The handler extend was able to modify L.

Here's an example showing that a script object is passed by reference:

```
script myScript
    property x : 10
end script
on myHandler(s)
    set s's x to 20
end myHandler
myHandler(myScript)
display dialog myScript's x -- 20
```

It makes sense that these datatypes *can* be passed by reference, but it is a little disturbing that they are passed by reference *automatically*, without giving you any choice in the matter. Passing by reference gives the handler great power over the parameter, which the handler can misuse. So, to prevent accidents, it is up to you to remember that list, record, date, and script object parameters are passed by reference, and that things you do in a handler to such parameters have an effect outside the handler. If you wish to avoid this, then if you like you can pass them by value, by making a copy and passing the copy:

```
on byValue(x)
    copy x to y
    return y
end byValue
on extend(LL)
    set end of LL to "Jack"
end extend
set L to {"Mannie", "Moe"}
extend(byValue(L))
L -- {"Mannie", "Moe"}
```

What about values that are not lists, records, dates, or script objects? How can they be passed by reference? They can't. Well, sometimes they can, but only in situations where it is pointless to do so. See "Reference as Parameter" in Chapter 12.

Syntax of Defining and Calling a Handler

The way a handler is defined (in the on line) states how many parameters the handler takes (and also supplies names for variables in the handler to which the parameter values will be assigned during a call). A call to the handler must correspond, supplying parameters correctly. It is a runtime error to call a handler with fewer parameters than the definition of the handler requires:

```
on greet(what)
    display dialog what
end greet
greet() -- error: {} doesn't match the parameters {what} for greet
```

The nitty-gritty of *how* a handler's definition states how many parameters there are, and how a corresponding call to that handler must be phrased, is remarkably complicated. There are actually four cases that must be distinguished (though you are most likely to use only the first two in handlers that you define). I'll discuss these four cases in a moment, but first I want to talk about the problem of optional parameters.

Optional Parameters

Officially, there is no way to declare a parameter optional in AppleScript. On the other hand, you really don't need a way to do this, because a parameter can be a list or a record, which can have any number of items. (Gosh, all we need is a shift command and this would be Perl!)

For example, here's a handler that calculates the area of a rectangle given the lengths of the two sides. If you pass the length of only one side, the rectangle is assumed to be a square:

```
on area(L)
    set a to item 1 of L
    if (count L) = 2 then
        set b to item 2 of L
    else
        set b to item 1 of L
    end if
    return a * b
end area
area({3, 4}) -- 12
area({3}) -- 9
```

A record used as a parameter is often an even better way to simulate optional parameters because it allows you to simulate default values for missing parameters as well. A single concatenation lets you merge the defaults into the parameter record without upsetting the values that are already there (see "Record" in Chapter 13; use of this device in this context was suggested to me by Scott Babcock). For example:

```
on greet(R)
    set defaults to {greeting:"Hello", whom:"World"}
    set R to R & defaults
    display dialog R's greeting & ", " & R's whom & "!"
end greet
greet({whom:"Everybody"}) -- Hello, Everybody!
greet({greeting:"Howdy"}) -- Howdy, World!
greet({greeting:"Bonjour", whom:"Monde"}) -- Bonjour, Monde!
greet({}) -- Hello, World!
```

It is not an error to include extra parameters in a handler call. They are simply ignored by the handler. You might think this feature would be useless, but it's not. It allows the caller to be somewhat ignorant of the details of the handler it's calling. This is valuable particularly when the caller and the handler are written by two different people. Suppose, for example, that I'm a script runner and you are supplying the script for me to run. I can specify in the documentation that I'm going to call the person handler in your script, with four parameters: firstName, lastName, age, and place. You can define your person handler, omitting any parameters that you happen not to care about. So, I might call your handler like this:

```
person given firstName:"Matt", lastName:"Neuburg", age:51, place:"Ojai"
```

But you might define your handler like this:

```
on person given firstName:fir, lastName:las
    display dialog fir & space & las
end person
```

That's legal. (The application Phlink actually works like this; see Chapter 26.)

No Parameters

If a handler takes no parameters, the name of the handler in the definition is followed by empty parentheses:

```
on handlerWithNoParameters( )
    -- code
end handlerWithNoParameters
```

The call consists of the name of the handler followed by empty parentheses:

```
handlerWithNoParameters( )
```

Positional Parameters

Positional parameters are unnamed. The pairing between each parameter value passed and the local variable in the handler that receives it is performed by looking at their respective positions: the first parameter is assigned to the first variable, the second parameter is assigned to second variable, and so forth.

If a handler takes positional parameters, the name of the handler in the definition is followed by one or more variable names in parentheses, separated by commas:

```
on handlerWithOneParameter(x)
    -- code
end handlerWithOneParameter
on handlerWithFourParameters(a, b, c, d)
    -- code
end handlerWithFourParameters
```

The call then consists of the name of the handler followed by parentheses containing the parameter value or values, separated by commas:

```
handlerWithOneParameter(7)
handlerWithFourParameters("hey", "ho", "hey", "nonny no")
```

Prepositional Parameters

Prepositional parameters are also called *labeled parameters*. Each parameter is preceded by a preposition drawn from the list in Table 9-1.

Table 9-1. The prepositions

above	beneath	into
against	beside	on
apart from	between	onto
around	by	out of
aside from	for	over
at	from	thru
below	instead of	under

In addition to the prepositions in Table 9-1, there is also a preposition of. This is used in a special way: if you use it, it must come first, and there must be more than one parameter. (This odd rule seems to be due to a mistake in the original design of AppleScript. In AppleScript 1.0, the of parameter was intended as a way of distinguishing the "direct object," the handler's main parameter. Then it was realized that where there was just one parameter and it was the of parameter, an unresolvable ambiguity with the of operator existed. So AppleScript 1.1 resolved the ambiguity by forbidding of to be used that way. But no alternative way of distinguishing the direct object was supplied, so in a sense this feature has been broken ever since.)

If a handler has prepositional parameters, the name of the handler in the definition is followed by a preposition and a variable name, and then possibly another preposition and another variable name, and so on.

In the call, the name of the handler is followed by a preposition and a value, and then possibly another preposition and another value, and so forth. The prepositions used must match those of the definition, but they may appear *in any order*, except for of, which must be first if it appears at all.

Here are some examples of handlers with prepositional parameters and calls to them:

```
on firstLetter from aWord
    return character 1 of aWord
end firstLetter
display dialog (firstLetter from "hello")

on sum of x beside y
    return x + y
end sum
display dialog (sum of 1 beside 2)

on stopping by woods on aSnowyEvening
    return woods & aSnowyEvening
end stopping
display dialog (stopping on "horse" by "farm")
```

In the call, if the value you wish to pass is a boolean (Chapter 13), you may use with or without (to indicate true and false respectively) followed by the preposition. If you don't use this syntax, AppleScript will probably use it for you when it compiles the script: any prepositional parameters for which you pass the literal value true or false will end up as with or without followed by the preposition. Multiple with parameters or without parameters can be joined using and. This looks quite silly when the labels are prepositions, but here goes:

```
on stopping by woods on aSnowyEvening
    if woods and aSnowyEvening then
        return "lovely, dark and deep"
    else
        return "ugly and shallow"
    end if
end stopping
```

```
display dialog (stopping with on and by)
display dialog (stopping with by without on)
```

There's a weird bug (at least I presume it's a bug) that allows you to define a handler with prepositional parameters but call it using positional parameters. The bug operates only in the case where you use of for the first parameter in the definition (which means that you also have to have a second parameter in the definition). When you call the handler with positional parameters, they all arrive as a list in the first parameter; the second parameter is empty. This bug was pointed out to me by Michael Terry, who notes that you can take advantage of it to implement a handler that can take any number of parameters. As your positional parameters are going to end up in a list anyway, there can be any number of them. AppleScript won't complain, no matter how few parameters there are (including none), and they all end up in a list in your handler, so none of the values is lost. For example:

```
on sum of L beside dummy
    set total to 0
    repeat with aNumber in L
        set total to total + aNumber
    end repeat
    return total
end sum
sum(1, 2, 3, 4, 5, 6, 7) -- 28
```

(On some systems, the bug is not present, and there's an error at runtime. On others, AppleScript may crash. But this trick works fine on Tiger. Still, I wouldn't rely on it, because if it is a bug, it might be fixed some day, breaking the example.)

Named Parameters

Named parameters are a way to take advantage of labeled parameters while escaping the circumscribed repertoire of built-in prepositions (Table 9-1). With named parameters, you get to make up your own labels, though of course you mustn't use a word that's already reserved by the language for something else.

You may combine named parameters with prepositional parameters; if you do, the named parameters must come after the prepositional parameters.

The syntax for defining named parameters is colon-based—the name of the parameter is followed by a colon, which is followed by the name of the handler variable:

```
on handlerName ... given paramName1:varName1, paramName2:varName2, ...
```

The first ellipsis in that syntax schema is the definition for the prepositional parameters, if there are any. The second ellipsis is for as many further named parameters as you like.

The call works just the same way: the keyword given must appear, it must appear after all prepositional parameters if there are any, and the same colon-based syntax is used. The named parameters may appear *in any order*:

```
handlerName ... given paramName1:value1, paramName2:value2, ...
```

As with prepositional parameters, boolean values can be passed using with or without and the parameter name, and for these there is no need to say given. Multiple with parameters or without parameters can be joined by using and. Again, AppleScript will use this syntax for you if you pass the literal value true or false.

Here are some examples of handlers with named parameters, and calls to them.

```
on sum given theOne:x, theOther:y
    return x + y
end sum
display dialog (sum given theOther:2, theOne:3)

on scout given loyal:loyal, trustworthy:trustworthy
    if loyal and trustworthy then
        return "eagle"
    else
        return "sparrow"
    end if
end scout
display dialog (scout with loyal and trustworthy)

on area of side1 beside side2 given measure:m
    return ((side1 * side2) as string) & space & m
end area
area of 4 beside 5 given measure:"inches" -- "20 inches"
```

The first example demonstrates that the order of parameters in the call is free. The second example demonstrates the use of with, and also shows that the parameter labels can be the same as the local variable names. The third examples shows prepositional and named parameters used together.

Event Handlers

Handlers that you define freely in code are *user handlers*. But there are also handlers whose definition comes from the dictionary of some scripting addition or application. These are *event handlers* (a command defined in a dictionary is technically called an event, because it is actually an Apple event, as discussed in Chapter 3).

An event handler's parameter syntax is a little different from that of a user handler:

No parameters
　The handler takes no parentheses.

First parameter
　The first parameter (the direct object) simply follows the handler name directly, without parentheses.

Subsequent parameters
　Subsequent parameters are labeled. Labeled parameters are the same as prepositional parameters, but the labels are not limited to the list in Table 9-1; basically, the dictionary can define any labels it likes.

Also, the name of the command, and any of the labels, can consist of multiple words.

An event handler is often used in connection with an automatic location (Chapter 2). Some application is going to send a message to your script, and it has defined what that message will be. To receive the message, your script must contain an event handler with a matching definition. The event handler is an *entry point* to your script.

Take, for example, folder actions (Chapter 26). You can attach a script to a folder as a folder action, so your script is called (by the System Events application) when certain things happen in the Finder. Let's say you want your script to be called when files are put into that folder. Then your script must contain an event handler with this structure:

```
on adding folder items to ff after receiving L
    -- code goes here
end adding folder items to
```

The event here is called adding folder items to. It takes two parameters: the direct object, and a parameter whose label is after receiving. I've called the direct object ff and the second parameter L, but these handler variable names are up to you.

Similarly, in AppleScript Studio, let's say you want your script to be notified when the user clicks a button in the interface. Then your script will contain an event handler with this structure:

```
on clicked theObject
    -- code goes here
end clicked
```

That's an event called clicked taking one parameter, the direct object. The name of the direct object in the handler definition, theObject, is up to you.

The syntax of event handlers is possible because the script is compiled in the presence of a dictionary that defines the event. The adding folder items to event is defined in the StandardAdditions scripting addition, and a scripting addition's dictionary is always visible. The clicked event is defined in the AppleScriptKit dictionary; this dictionary is not always visible, but it is visible when you're editing and compiling AppleScript Studio code.

Interestingly, your code can call an event handler. This is legal (but silly):

```
on adding folder items to ff after receiving L
    display dialog ff & space & L
end adding folder items to
adding folder items to "howdy" after receiving "there"
```

Most applications that want an entry point to your script do *not* use event handlers. The reason is that they have no way to make a dictionary visible at the time you're editing and compiling your script. Apple Computer installs the StandardAdditions scripting addition by default on every machine, so it can use this scripting addition to define events used by the System Events application as entry points for folder actions. And AppleScript Studio works in a special way, where the AppleScriptKit dictionary is automatically visible while you're editing your code. But third-party scriptable applications can't make their dictionary automatically visible, and they can't usually expect you to install a scripting addition just in order to be able to use their event handler terminology. Typically they resort to a user handler instead. (See Chapter 26 for examples.)

By the way, built-in AppleScript commands are visible at all times, so you can write event handlers for them. That is how the explicit run handler works (see the next section); for another example, see "Handler Calls, Commands, and Script Objects" in Chapter 8. (The commands get, copy, and set work differently; you can't write handlers for them—the compiler will stop you if you so much as try it.)

The Run Handler

The run handler of a script object (or script) has been discussed in "Code and the Run Handler" in Chapter 6 and "Run Handler" in Chapter 8. The run handler is an event handler. Thus it has event handler syntax; it takes no parentheses, either in the definition or in the call.

It turns out that an explicit run handler may take parameters. This ability is useful only under special circumstances, and in fact it prevents the script object (or script) from running at all under normal circumstances, because you usually have no way to supply these parameters in the call.

The official syntax for defining a run handler with parameters is to express all parameters as a single list. For example:

```
script s
    on run {what, what2}
        display dialog what & space & what2
    end run
end script
```

You can't simply tell that script object to run, because you can't supply the parameters. If you try, you'll get an error at runtime:

```
run s -- error: «script s» doesn't match the parameters {what, what2} for run
```

One solution is to use the run script command, which permits parameters to be passed to a run handler:

```
run script s with parameters {"howdy", "there"}
```

That approach is rather extreme; run script is expensive, because it requires the creation (and destruction) of an entire separate instance of the AppleScript scripting component. A clever and inexpensive approach (which I owe to Michael Terry) is to take advantage of script object inheritance (Chapter 8) and the `continue` command, which can pass parameters to any event:

```
property args : null
script s
    on run {what, what2}
        display dialog what & space & what2
    end run
end script
script trampoline
    property parent : s
    continue run args
end script
set args to {"howdy", "there"}
run trampoline
```

If you give your script as a whole an explicit run handler that expects parameters, you won't be able to run your script in the Script Editor or in most script runners. For example:

```
on run {what}
    display dialog what
end run
```

That's an unrunnable script, unless you have some way to supply the parameter. One approach is to save the script as a compiled script file and then use `run script` to run the file along with a parameter.

Clearly a run handler with parameters is an oddity, but there are circumstances where it is useful. For example, an Automator action's script has a run handler that takes parameters (see Chapter 27).

Recursion

A handler is visible from within itself. This means that recursion is possible; a handler may call itself.

Explaining the elegances and dangers of recursion is beyond the scope of this book. The best way to learn about recursion is through a language like Scheme or LISP, where recursion is the primary form of looping. In fact, in conjunction with lists, AppleScript's recursion allows some remarkably Scheme-like (or LISP-like) modes of expression (see "LISP-likeness" in Chapter 4).

 The best way to learn Scheme is to read Harold Abelson et al., *Structure and Interpretation of Computer Programs*, 2nd Edition (MIT Press, 1996), the best computer book ever written.

For example, here's a recursive routine for filtering a list. We'll remove from the list everything that isn't a number:

```
on filter(L)
    if L = {} then return L
    if {class of item 1 of L} is in {real, integer, number} then
        return {item 1 of L} & filter(rest of L)
    else
        return filter(rest of L)
    end if
end filter
filter({"hey", 1, "ho", 2, 3}) -- {1, 2, 3}
```

AppleScript is not a truly recursive language, however; recursion is limited by the depth of AppleScript's internal stack. If you recurse too deep (which usually means recursing through too long a list), you'll get a "stack overflow" error message. Unfortunately there's no way to know in advance what the limit is, as it depends on what happens during each recursion and on what environment is running the script. Just to give a typical example, using Script Editor on my machine, this code runs fine if max is 504 but fails with a stack overflow if max is 505; but in Smile it works even if max is as large as 8159:

```
on remvix(L, ix)
    if L is {} then return {}
    if ix is 1 then
        return rest of L
    else
        return item 1 of L & remvix(rest of L, ix - 1)
    end if
end remvix
set L to {}
set max to 505
repeat with x from 1 to max
    set end of L to x
end repeat
remvix(L, max)
```

Be careful when assigning a recursive handler as a value to a variable. At the point where the handler calls itself, its name is hard-coded into its functionality. After assigning the handler functionality to a different variable name, that name may no longer be in scope and the handler will break when called under its new name:

```
script s
    on filter(L)
        if L = {} then return L
        if {class of item 1 of L} is in {real, integer, number} then
            return {item 1 of L} & filter(rest of L)
        else
            return filter(rest of L)
        end if
    end filter
end script
set f to s's filter
f({"hey", 1, "ho", 2, 3}) -- error: «script» doesn't understand the filter message
```

Power Handler Tricks

A handler takes values as parameters and returns a value. A handler is a value. A script object is a value and can contain a handler. If these facts suggest to your mind an intimation of amazing possibilities, read on.

Handler and Script Object as Parameter

You can pass a handler as a parameter to handler. The difficulty is in calling it. This code fails with a runtime error:

```
on sayHowdy( )
    display dialog "Howdy"
end sayHowdy
on doThis(what)
    what( )
end doThis
doThis(sayHowdy) -- error: «script» doesn't understand the what message
```

The trouble is that AppleScript refuses to identify the what( ) in the handler call with the what that arrived as a parameter. This is actually another case of the rule (see "Handler Calls, Commands, and Script Objects" in Chapter 8) that an unqualified handler call is a message directed to the current script object, which in this case is the script as a whole.

One possible workaround is to use a global. This approach works because by copying the handler to a global we're putting it where a message directed to the script as a whole can find it (see "Scope of Globals" in Chapter 10):

```
on sayHowdy()
    display dialog "Howdy"
end sayHowdy
on doThis(what)
    global what2
    set what2 to what
    what2()
end doThis
doThis(sayHowdy) -- Howdy
```

This solution is clever, but now we've broken encapsulation. Global variables pose risks (other code might access this same global, or we might be tromping accidentally on some other code's global), and besides, if we're going to use a global there's little point to passing a parameter in the first place.

Another possible workaround is to pass a script object instead of a handler:

```
script sayHowdy
    display dialog "Howdy"
end script
on doThis(what)
    run what
end doThis
doThis(sayHowdy) -- Howdy
```

This is very efficient because script objects are passed by reference. But we ended up having to use the run command instead of a handler call. That's not going to be very pretty if our handler takes any parameters, because it's hard to pass parameters to a run handler (as shown earlier in this chapter). But wait—a script object can contain a handler! So we can use it as a kind of envelope. We can define a handler in a script object and pass the script object. In fact, this device permits both the script and the handler that receives it as a parameter to be completely general:

```
script myScript
    on doAnything( )
    end doAnything
    doAnything( )
end script
on doThis(what)
    run what
end doThis
on sayHowdy( )
    display dialog "Howdy"
end sayHowdy
set myScript's doAnything to sayHowdy
doThis(myScript) -- Howdy
```

However, there's another way entirely. This happens to be my favorite solution. We don't pass a script object; we pass a handler, just as in our first attempt. But inside the handler, we have a script object waiting to receive it:

```
on sayHowdy( )
    display dialog "Howdy"
end sayHowdy
on doThis(what)
    script whatToDo
        property theHandler : what
        theHandler( )
    end script
    run whatToDo
end doThis
doThis(sayHowdy) -- Howdy
```

The fact that this code works is astonishing (at least, when I stumbled upon it I was astonished). It depends upon an obscure but powerful rule of scope (see "Scope of Locals" in Chapter 10) which says that a script object within a handler can see that handler's local variables. An incoming parameter is such a variable. Thanks to this rule, our property declaration for theHandler can see the incoming what parameter and store its value. So now the property theHandler is a handler! But it is also a top-level entity of the script object, which means that we can call it from within this same script object. Tricky, eh?

For a useful application of this technique, let's return to the example earlier in this chapter where a handler called filter filtered a list to get only those members of the list that were numbers. That handler is not general; we'd like a way to filter a list on *any* criterion we care to provide. So we want to pass it both a list and a handler (a handler that takes a single argument and returns a boolean saying whether it fits the criterion). We can do so by writing `filter( )` as a handler containing a script object:

```
on filter(L, crit)
    script filterer
        property criterion : crit
        on filter(L)
            if L = {} then return L
            if criterion(item 1 of L) then
                return {item 1 of L} & filter(rest of L)
            else
                return filter(rest of L)
            end if
        end filter
    end script
    return filterer's filter(L)
end filter
on isNumber(x)
    return ({class of x} is in {real, integer, number})
end isNumber
filter({"hey", 1, "ho", 2, 3}, isNumber)
```

I consider that example to be the height of the AppleScript programmer's art, so perhaps you'd like to pause a moment to admire it.

Handler and Script Object as Result

A handler may be returned as the result of a handler. Because you can't define a handler directly within a handler, you might have to define it as a handler within a script object within the handler; but this is no bother. So, for example:

```
on makeHandler( )
    script x
        on greet( )
            display dialog "Howdy"
        end greet
    end script
    return x's greet
end makeHandler
set y to makeHandler( )
y( ) -- Howdy
```

Of itself, however, this device is not terribly useful; in real life, you're more likely to return a script object rather a handler:

```
on scriptMaker( )
    script myScript
        property x : "Howdy"
        display dialog x
    end script
    return myScript
end scriptMaker
set s to scriptMaker( )
run s -- Howdy
```

In the last two lines, we acquire the script object returned by the handler scriptMaker, and run it. Of course, if we didn't want to retain the script object, these two lines could be combined into one:

```
run scriptMaker( ) -- Howdy
```

Why might it be useful to return a script object as the result of a handler? Mostly because the handler can customize the script object before returning it. For example, instead of hard-coding the property x that will be displayed, we can pass that value into the handler as a parameter:

```
on scriptMaker(what)
    script myScript
        property x : what
        display dialog x
    end script
    return myScript
end scriptMaker
set s to scriptMaker("Hello")
run s -- Hello
```

The real virtue of this technique emerges when we retain and reuse the resulting script object. To illustrate, here's one more version of the general list-filtering routine we wrote earlier in this chapter. Previously, we passed a handler both a criterion handler and a list, and got back a filtered list. Now we're going to pass just a criterion handler, and get back a script object, which we will retain. Now we've got a script object containing a filter handler that is already customized to filter any list according the criterion we passed in at the outset. In effect, we've built a custom handler! Now we can reuse that handler repeatedly with different lists. We can even create more than one such handler, each customized to be a certain kind of filter. This architecture is elegant and efficient (and LISPy):

```
on makeFilterer(crit)
    script filterer
        property criterion : crit
        on filter (L)
            if L = {} then return L
            if criterion(item 1 of L) then
                return {item 1 of L} & (filter (rest of L))
            else
                return filter (rest of L)
            end if
        end filter
    end script
    return filterer
end makeFilterer
on isNumber(x)
    return ({class of x} is in {real, integer, number})
end isNumber
on isText(x)
    return ({class of x} is in {string, text, Unicode text})
end isText
```

```
set numbersOnly to makeFilterer(isNumber)
set textOnly to makeFilterer(isText)
tell numbersOnly
    filter ({"hey", 1, "ho", 2, "ha", 3}) -- {1, 2, 3}
    filter ({"Mannie", 7, "Moe", 8, "Jack", 9}) -- {7, 8, 9}
end tell
tell textOnly
    filter ({"hey", 1, "ho", 2, "ha", 3}) -- {"hey", "ho", "ha"}
    filter ({"Mannie", 7, "Moe", 8, "Jack", 9}) -- {"Mannie", "Moe", "Jack"}
end tell
```

Another use for a script object as a result of a handler is as a *constructor*. Here we take advantage of the fact that when a handler is called, it initializes any script objects defined within it. So a handler is a way to produce a copy of a script object whose properties are at their initial value.

As an example, consider a script object whose job is to count something. It contains a property c, which maintains the count, and a handler that increments the count. (This approach is using a sledgehammer to kill a fly, but it's a great example, so bear with me.) A handler is used as a constructor to produce an instance of this script object with its property c set to zero. Each time we need to count something new, we call the handler to get a new script object. Then we can repeatedly count that thing by calling the increment handler of the corresponding script object.

```
on newCounter( )
    script aCounter
        property c : 0
        on increment( )
            set c to c + 1
        end increment
    end script
    return aCounter
end newCounter
-- and here's how to use it
set counter1 to newCounter( )
counter1's increment( )
counter1's increment( )
counter1's increment( )
set counter2 to newCounter( )
counter2's increment( )
counter1's increment( )
display dialog counter1's c -- 4
display dialog counter2's c -- 1
```

CHAPTER 10
Scope

By *scope* is meant the ability of one region of code to see variables in another region of code. The rules of scope for AppleScript are remarkably involved—as involved of those of any computer language I know. They are a perennial source of pitfalls for beginning and experienced programmers alike. If you don't understand the rules of scope, or (even worse) if you try to ignore them, you'll find your scripts mysteriously going wrong in confusing ways. This chapter discusses the rules of scope, along with a powerful advanced scope-related feature of AppleScript—closures.

Regions of Scope

Every AppleScript program has regions of scope. Some regions of scope may be inside others, but they do not partially intersect—given two regions, either one is entirely inside the other or they are completely distinct. In other words, the regions of scope are *nested*. The top level of the script is a script object and is a region of scope. Any other regions of scope are inside this, and are created by the presence of *scope blocks*: handler definitions and script object definitions. (See Chapter 6.)

In Example 10-1, I've sketched a sample script with scope blocks nested in various combinations. At every point where code can go, I've put a comment distinguishing that region of scope by number. So, scope 1 is the top level of the script itself (its implicit run handler); scope 2 is the code within handlerOne, a handler defined at the top level of the script; scope 3 is the code within scriptOne, a script object defined within handlerOne; and so on.

Example 10-1. Regions of scope

```
-- scope 1
on handlerOne()
    -- scope 2
    script scriptOne
```

Example 10-1. Regions of scope (continued)

```
            -- scope 3
      end script
      -- scope 2
end handlerOne
-- scope 1
script scriptTwo
      -- scope 5
      on handlerTwo()
            -- scope 6
      end handlerTwo
      -- scope 5
      script scriptThree
            -- scope 7
      end script
      -- scope 5
end script
-- scope 1
```

The region in which a variable is visible is called its *scope*. A variable that is visible at a certain point is said to be *in scope* at that point. To understand scope is to know what kinds of variable can belong to a given region of scope and in what other regions each variable is in scope.

Note that visibility is visibility and access is access. If code can see a variable in any manner, it can access it, which means it can both get and set that variable. In the examples in this chapter I will mostly use getting rather than setting, because that's the simplest way to detect when code *can't* see a variable (the attempt to fetch the value of an undefined variable results in a runtime error—see Chapter 7).

Kinds of Variable

With regard to scope, we must distinguish four kinds of variable:

Top-level entities
> Top-level entities are script properties declared, and script objects and handlers defined, at the top level of a script or script object. (See "Top-Level Entities" in Chapter 8.)

Explicit locals
> An explicit local is a variable announced by a local declaration, which looks like this:
> ```
> local x
> ```

Explicit globals
> An explicit global is a variable announced by a global declaration, which looks like this:
> ```
> global x
> ```

Undeclared variables

A undeclared variable is none of the above. It's just a name that your code suddenly starts using. This is legal, but when you do it, AppleScript assigns the variable a scope, in ways that may surprise you.

The scope of a variable, and what kind of variable it is (these amount to the same thing), are determined at compile time.

Scope of Top-Level Entities

A top-level entity is visible in the scope where it is defined, and at all deeper levels nested in that scope subsequent to where it is defined.

Let's take, for example, a script property. The script property x here, declared at the top level of the script as a whole, is also in scope inside a script object and a handler:

```
property x : 10
script myScript
    display dialog x
end script
on myHandler()
    display dialog x
end myHandler
run myScript -- 10
myHandler() -- 10
```

If a top-level entity is in scope in a script object, a script object nested at a deeper level may declare a top-level entity with the same name. This deeper name will *overshadow* the first entity's name within that deeper scope. Thus in this example there is never the slightest ambiguity as to what is meant by x at any point:

```
property x : 5
script scriptOne
    property x : 10
    script scriptTwo
        property x : 20
        display dialog x
    end script
    display dialog x
    run scriptTwo
end script
script scriptThree
    property x : 30
    display dialog x
end script
script scriptFour
    display dialog x
end script
display dialog x -- 5
run scriptOne -- 10, 20
run scriptThree -- 30
run scriptFour -- 5
```

Regions of scope outside a script object cannot see that script object's top-level entities. But if they can see a name referring to that script object, they can ask to access that script's top-level entities, as explained in "Top-Level Entities" in Chapter 8. In the same way, a region of scope at a deeper level can access an overshadowed name:

```
script scriptOne
    property x : 10
    script inner
        property x : 20
        display dialog scriptOne's x -- 10
    end script
end script
script scriptTwo
    display dialog scriptOne's x -- 10
    display dialog x -- error: The variable x is not defined
end script
run scriptOne's inner
run scriptTwo
```

In that example, scriptOne is a top-level entity of the top-level script (that's where it's defined). For that reason (and because the name scriptOne is not overshadowed), script inner, which is nested two levels down within the top-level script, can see scriptOne. The name x is overshadowed within inner, so inner cannot see scriptOne's property x. But because it can see scriptOne, it can ask scriptOne for access to it. For the same reason, code inside scriptTwo can see scriptOne. It is outside scriptOne, so it can't see scriptOne's property x. But since it can see scriptOne, it can ask scriptOne for access to it.

A curious fact is that a top-level entity is visible at its own level to code even before it is defined. That's because the initialization takes place during compilation, before any code runs. So, for example, a script object:

```
run myScript -- Howdy
script myScript
    display dialog "Howdy"
end script
```

A handler:

```
myHandler() -- Howdy
on myHandler()
    display dialog "Howdy"
end myHandler
```

And even a property:

```
display dialog x -- Howdy
property x : "Howdy"
```

This sort of thing, however, especially with a property, is generally regarded as confusing and poor style. Also, code at a deeper nested level can see a higher-level entity only after that entity has been defined. This doesn't work:

```
run myScript
script myScript
    display dialog myOtherScript's x -- error: The variable myOtherScript is not defined
end script
script myOtherScript
    property x : "Howdy"
end script
```

A handler appears to be an exception, but it isn't really:

```
run myScript
script myScript
    myHandler()
end script
on myHandler()
    display dialog "Howdy"
end myHandler
```

That worked, but not because code inside myScript can see myHandler. It can't see it—myHandler is not in scope here—but it can call it! That's because of the rules of message-passing, which have nothing to do with the rules of scope. (See "Inheritance" in Chapter 8.) The handler call myHandler() in myScript reaches myHandler at the top level because the top level is myScript's parent. To show that code inside myScript can't see myHandler, consider the same script without the parentheses after myHandler, so that the code is not calling myHandler but merely mentioning it:

```
run myScript
script myScript
    myHandler -- error: The variable myHandler is not defined
end script
on myHandler()
    display dialog "Howdy"
end myHandler
```

Note that a script object defined *not* at the top level of a script object (or script) is *not* a top-level entity. Basically, it's an implicit local (see "Scope of Undeclared Variables," later in this chapter), which means that such a definition must precede any reference to itself, and that it can't be seen outside the scope where it is defined. Interestingly, when you define a script object at the top level of a handler, the rule about the definition preceding a reference to itself is enforced by the compiler (with a mysterious error message):

```
on myHandler()
    run myScript
    script myScript -- compile-time error: The myScript property is specified more than once
        display dialog "Howdy"
    end script
end myHandler
myHandler()
```

Scope of Locals

An explicit local is a variable whose name appears in a local declaration. A local declaration can declare several variables at once, delimited by comma:

```
local a
local b, c, d
```

A local variable is visible only within the very same region of scope where it is declared—not outside it, and not at a deeper level. (But there's an exception, which we'll come to in a moment.)

Local variables completely disambiguate a name within their own scope, and local variables in other scopes can have the same name without conflict. Suppose a script object starts like this:

```
script myScript
    local x
```

The local declaration for x means that from now on when code in this script object's scope says x it means this local x and no other. What's more, other scopes may declare their own local x, they may declare a global x, they may bang the floor and have a temper tantrum, but they absolutely will not be able to have any effect upon myScript's x, nor will anything myScript does with its x have any effect upon them.

Here's an example of a local variable in action:

```
local x
set x to 5
script myScript
    display dialog x -- error: The variable x is not defined
end script
run myScript
```

Observe how completely different this is from what would have happened if x had been a top-level property. Here, there is a variable called x and it is defined, but it is declared local and therefore is visible only within its own scope. That scope is the top-level script. The display dialog x command is in a different scope, that of the script object myScript. Therefore AppleScript takes this to be a different x, and this different x has never been assigned a value. (I'll explain later just what x AppleScript takes the x of display dialog x to be.)

A local declaration overshadows the visibility of a top-level entity from a higher level:

```
property x : 5
script myScript
    local x
    display dialog x -- error: The variable x is not defined
end script
run myScript
```

But this overshadowing affects only the scope of the local declaration—not a deeper scope:

```
property x : 5
script myScript
    local x
    on myHandler( )
        set x to 10
    end myHandler
    myHandler( )
    set x to 20
end script
run myScript
display dialog x -- 10 (not 20)
```

The dialog displays 10, not 20. Even though myScript overshadows the top-level property x with a local x declaration, this has no effect on myHandler, which still sees the top-level property x. (This makes sense, because it can't see myScript's local x.) When myHandler sets x to 10, that is the same x as at the top level. When myScript sets x to 20, that's its local x, and the value displayed in the last line is unaffected.

In a handler, the variable names used for parameters in the definition of the handler are local within the handler. Naturally, a handler may also declare further locals:

```
on myHandler(what)
    local x
    set x to 7
end myHandler
myHandler("howdy")
display dialog what -- error: The variable what is not defined
display dialog x -- error: The variable x is not defined
```

Now we come to the great exception: a script object defined in a handler can see the handler's local variables. To a script object in a handler, the handler's locals are like top-level entities: they are visible to the script object and to scopes nested within it. (We took advantage of this rule in "Power Handler Tricks" in Chapter 9.) Thus:

```
on myHandler()
    local x
    set x to 5
    script myScript
        on h()
            display dialog x
        end h
        h()
    end script
    run myScript
end myHandler
myHandler() -- 5
```

I think the reason for this rule is that a handler can contain a nested scope (a script object) but has no top-level entities. A handler can't declare a property, so without this rule, it would have no encapsulated way to expose values to a nested script object. Similarly, without this rule, code in a script object in a handler would be unable to see a script object earlier in the same handler:

```
on h()
    script s
        display dialog "howdy"
    end script
    script ss
        run s
    end script
    run ss
end h
h() -- howdy
```

Scope of Globals

An explicit global is a variable whose name appears in a global declaration. A global declaration can declare several variables at once, delimited by comma:

```
global a
global b, c, d
```

Globals are rather complicated. I'll divide the discussion into two parts: the downward effect of a global declaration, and its upward effect.

Global Declarations: The Downward Effect

The downward effect of a global declaration is very much like a top-level entity declaration. A variable declared global is visible in the scope where it is defined, subsequent to the point where it is defined, and at all deeper levels within that scope, subsequent to the point where it is defined.

For example:

```
global x
set x to 5
on myHandler()
    display dialog x
end myHandler
myHandler() -- 5
```

The variable x is declared global; it is then visible downward into the scope of myHandler, because myHandler is defined subsequently in the same scope as x.

But the following code does not work:

```
set x to 5
on myHandler()
    display dialog x
end myHandler
global x
set x to 10
myHandler() -- error: The variable x is not defined
```

We keep setting x like mad, but to no avail; the global declaration doesn't come until after the handler definition, so code inside the handler can't see x.

Just as with a top-level entity, a global's downward effect is overshadowed by a local declaration of the same variable name at a deeper level, and this overshadowing affects only the scope of the local declaration—not a deeper scope.

Global Declarations: The Upward Effect

The upward effect of a global declaration of a variable is to identify that variable with a variable at the top level of the script with the same name (creating this variable if it does not already exist). This means that separate regions of scope can share a variable simply by declaring it global:

```
on setX( )
    global x
    set x to 5
end setX
on getX( )
    global x
    display dialog x
end getX
setX( )
getX( ) -- 5
```

That example demonstrates that the two handlers are sharing the same variable x. Now let's demonstrate that this x is being instantiated at the top level:

```
on setX()
    global x
    set x to 5
end setX
setX()
display dialog x -- 5
```

The fact that the last line works, rather than generating a runtime error complaining that x is not defined, shows the call to setX has defined x at the top level.

The status of a global created in this way is interesting. First, observe that it is not automatically visible downwards, as it would be if a global declaration (or a property declaration) were present at the top level. This doesn't work:

```
on setX()
    global x
    set x to 5
end setX
on getX()
    display dialog x
end getX
setX()
getX() -- error: The variable x is not defined
```

Even though x is a global defined at the top level, as we proved in the previous example, yet now getX can't see it. There is no global x declaration at a higher level than getX, so there is no downward effect to endow getX with the ability to see x. And getX itself now contains no global x declaration, so in effect it has failed to put in a request of its own to see x.

Global as static

A local is not persistent—it goes out of scope and is destroyed each time its scope finishes executing—but a global is. So a global is one way to implement a static variable (that is, a variable that will persist between executions of the local scope):

```
on incrementOrReport(report)
    global ct
    if report then return ct
    try
        set ct to ct + 1
    on error
        set ct to 1
    end try
end incrementOrReport
incrementOrReport(false)
incrementOrReport(false)
incrementOrReport(false)
incrementOrReport(true) -- 3
```

However, that is really poor programming style; a script object and a property would let you do this in a far more encapsulated way.

Global as script property

A global is, in fact, persistent between script executions, just like a script property. This is a little tricky to prove, because we need a way to initialize the global only just in case it isn't already defined; to do this, I'll have to use some syntax we haven't discussed yet (see "Errors" in Chapter 19):

```
on setX()
    global x
    try
        set x to x + 1
    on error
        set x to 5
    end try
end setX
on getX()
    global x
    display dialog x
end getX
setX()
getX() -- 5, then 6, and so on
```

Indeed, a global isn't merely *like* a script property; it *is* a script property. Again, I have to be a little tricky to prove it to you:

```
on setX()
    global x
    set x to x + 1
end setX
on getX()
    global x
    display dialog x
end getX
setX()
getX() -- 6, then 7, and so on
property x : 5
```

In that example, I deliberately postponed the property declaration until after all the other code, to show that it isn't the property declaration itself that is making x visible in lower scopes (remember, a top-level entity is visible to nested scopes only after its declaration). Thus it must be the global declarations within setX and getX that are identifying x with the script property x at the top level.

Here's another way to show that a global is a script property: I'll use a global to give the anonymous top-level script a name, and then I'll speak of another global as a property of the top-level script. This is a rewrite of a device from "The Implicit Parent Chain" in Chapter 8, using globals instead of properties at the top level:

```
global topLevel, x
set topLevel to me
set x to 5
script s
    property x : 10
    display dialog topLevel's x
end script
run s -- 5
```

Observe that a global declaration lets a scope region refer to an entity defined at the top level of the script, even when its name is overshadowed by a top-level entity at a deeper level:

```
global x
set x to 10
script outer
    property x : 20
    script inner
        global x
        display dialog x
    end script
end script
run outer's inner -- 10
```

Without the global x declaration in inner, inner's x would be outer's property x, and the script would display 20. This script works the same way if the top-level x is declared as a property, not a global; they are the same thing. Thus we have another solution to the problem of how to speak of the top-level entities of a script as a whole even though it is anonymous (see "The Implicit Parent Chain" in Chapter 8).

The double effect of global declarations

In working with explicit globals, remember that every global declaration has both the downward and upward effect at the same time:

```
script myScript
    global x
    on myHandler( )
        set x to 5
    end myHandler
    myHandler( )
end script
on getX( )
    global x
    display dialog x
end
run myScript
getX( ) -- 5
```

In myScript, the global x declaration does two things: it creates the top-level global x (upward effect), and it gives myHandler access to it (downward effect). Thus myHandler is able to set the value of the top-level global that will later be seen and displayed by getX.

Scope of Undeclared Variables

In AppleScript, you do not have to declare variables. When you use a name that, by the preceding rules of scope, is not an existing variable, AppleScript does not complain; rather, it creates the variable for you. How it does this depends upon the location of the code that uses the nonexistent variable name:

Code at the top level
> The variable is created as a global. There is no explicit global declaration, so there is no downward effect, but other scopes can see this variable through a global declaration. I call this an *implicit global*.

Code not at the top level
> The variable is created as a local. I call this an *implicit local*.

Let's illustrate an implicit global first:

```
set x to 5
on getX()
    global x
    display dialog x
end getX
getX() -- 5
```

The first line never said explicitly that x should be a global. But it clearly is one, since when getX comes along and asks to see a global called x, the x created in the first line is what it sees. (Incidentally, you can move the "set x to 5" line to after the getX handler definition and the script will still work; the important thing is that the global x be defined by the time getX *runs*, not necessarily before getX itself is defined.)

Incidentally, a variable created implicitly in a script's top-level explicit run handler is an implicit global as well, just as if you'd declared it at the absolute top level:

```
on run
    set howdy to "Howdy"
    sayHowdy() -- Howdy
end run
on sayHowdy()
    global howdy
    display dialog howdy
end sayHowdy
```

That's a very odd rule, as in no other respect (I believe) is an explicit run handler treated like the absolute top level; usually, it's treated like a handler, in which case the implicit variable would be local. This shows the extremes the language goes to in order to cope with undeclared variables.

Now for an implicit local:

```
set x to 5
on getX()
    set x to 10
    display dialog x
end getX
getX() -- 10
display dialog x -- 5
```

Clearly we are now talking about two different variables called x. We have already established that the top-level x is global; but getX is evidently not seeing it. It is setting to 10, and displaying, some other x; its actions are having no effect on the top-level x, as the last line proves. So getX's x must be local to getX. To prove that it is truly local and not some sort of magic downward global within getX, we need another test:

```
script s
    set x to 10
    on myHandler()
        display dialog x
    end myHandler
    myHandler()
end script
run s -- error: The variable x is not defined
```

But if we reverse the structure—a script object in a handler, instead of a handler in a script object—then it works:

```
on getX()
    set x to 10
    script s
        display dialog x
    end script
    run s
end getX
getX() -- 10
```

That isn't because x is not local; it's because of the special exceptional rule that a script object in a handler can see the handler's locals.

Declare Your Variables

Sounds like "eat your vegetables," doesn't it? Well, it should. Each motto is good advice, no matter how unpalatable it may seem at first. I strongly advise you to declare all your variables—even (especially!) your locals. Unfortunately, AppleScript gives you no help with this; you can't make it warn you when a variable is undeclared. Rather, it silently declares it for you. This behavior, doubtless intended to make programming in AppleScript easier, is in fact the source of more mistakes and confusion among AppleScript programmers than any other feature of the language.

The trouble is that if you are lulled into a false sense of security because there's no need to declare your variables, then you can be surprised when some other scope tramples them. For example, imagine that your script starts like this:

```
set x to 5
```

That's top-level code, so you've just implicitly declared x a global. This means that any other handler or script object anywhere in this script can access your x and change its value, just by saying this:

```
global x
```

This other code may not have intended to trample on your x; perhaps it was trying to establish a global of its own, possibly in order to communicate its value to code at a lower level, or to function as persistent storage between calls. But the damage is done, just because of the upward effects of a global declaration. And to think that you could have prevented this by declaring your top-level x local to start with.

The converse is also true. Pretend that you have a large script and that this code occurs somewhere within it:

```
on myHandler()
    set x to 5
end
```

Is x a local or a global here? You don't know! It depends upon the context. If x has previously been declared global at a higher level, this x is global (by the downward effect of that declaration). If not, this x is local. But it is intolerable that you should have to search elsewhere to learn the scope of x within myHandler!

A particularly tricky problem is presented by script objects loaded from a compiled script file on disk (see Chapter 8). For example:

```
set f to (path to desktop as string) & "lib.scpt"
run (load script alias f)
x -- "howdy"
```

Hokey smokes! How is that possible? Where did this variable x come from? It came from the script in the file *lib.scpt*, which simply says this:

```
set x to "howdy"
```

The x in *lib.scpt* is an implicit global, and when you load and run that script, the global infects your own script's namespace. This is extremely cool or extremely scary, depending on your point of view. It seems cool to be able to make a variable (which can equally be a script object or handler) magically appear, name and all, in your script. My own view, however, is that globals, implicit or explicit, are for this very reason to be avoided in scripts that will be loaded into other scripts. After all, if you didn't know that *lib.scpt* was going to do this, and your script had its own top-level x, then loading and running *lib.scpt* would make your script malfunction mysteriously.

The ideal way to manage scope, in my view, would be to declare everything. If you need a variable to be visible in this scope and deeper scopes, then declare a property. (In a handler, merely declaring a local will do.) Otherwise, declare a local. Use global declarations sparingly, only for special occasions when separate regions of scope need shared access to a value. If you follow these rules, then any undeclared variable must be a free variable (see the next section). Thus you always know what everything is. Unfortunately, as I've said, AppleScript doesn't help, so you can't easily and reliably follow these rules, even if you want to.

A local or global declaration, by the way, does not have to appear right at the top level of a scope block; it can be embedded in a control structure. However, it isn't an executable statement; it is seen and enforced by the compiler, not the runtime engine. In this example, 1 is not 2, so the local x declaration is never "executed," but the example shows that x is local anyway:

```
if 1 is 2 then
    local x
end if
set x to 7
on myHandler()
    global x
    display dialog x
end myHandler
myHandler() -- error: The variable x is not defined
```

That example is silly, but the ability to declare a variable within a control structure is not, because it encourages and helps you to (you guessed it) declare your variables. You could be deep in the middle of typing a complicated control structure when you suddenly introduce a new variable, and you realize that you want to declare it. You don't have to hunt back through your code looking for a place to declare the variable at the top level; you can declare it where you are and get on with your work.

Free Variables

A variable defined outside a handler or script object, but globally visible within it, and not overshadowed by a declaration of the same name, is called a *free variable* with respect to that handler or script object. A free variable in AppleScript is identified with a top-level entity or global through the downward effect of its declaration. For example:

```
global x, y, z
script myScript
    property x : 1
    local y
    yy
    z
end script
```

Within myScript, x is explicitly defined as a property and y is explicitly defined as a local, so neither is a free variable. The variable yy isn't explicitly defined within myScript, but it isn't defined outside it either, so it is an implicit local and not a free variable. But the variable z is globally visible within myScript (from the global declaration at the start of the code), and the name is not redeclared within myScript, so z within myScript is a free variable, and is identified with the global z declared in the first line.

A free variable takes its value within the handler or script object *at the time the code runs*, not at the time the handler or script object is defined. For example:

```
global x
set x to 5
on myHandler()
    display dialog x -- x is a free variable
end myHandler
set x to 10
myHandler() -- 10 (not 5)
```

The dialog displays 10, not 5. It doesn't matter that x had been set to 5 when myHandler was defined; it only matters what its value is when the code inside myHandler actually runs. By that time, x has been set to 10.

Free variables' *values* are determined at runtime; but the identification of the fact that a variable *is* a free variable, and its association with some particular globally visible variable, happens during compilation. This way of resolving the meaning of free variable names is called *lexical scoping*.

So, in the previous example, it is important that x is declared global before myHandler is defined. If you move the global x declaration to after the myHandler definition, the script generates an error at runtime. Even if x is declared global before (temporally) myHandler runs, that's not good enough. We must declare x global before (physically) myHandler speaks of it; otherwise, myHandler's x isn't the global x, and when the code runs, myHandler's x isn't defined. This is another reason why you should declare your variables, and not only declare them but declare them early, even though Apple-Script doesn't require you to do so.

Here's an example with two top-level entities as free variables. One is a property, the other is a script object:

```
property x : 5
script myScript
    display dialog x -- x is a free variable
end script
script myOtherScript
    set x to 20 -- x is a free variable
    run myScript -- myScript is a free variable
end script
set x to 10
run myScript -- 10
run myOtherScript -- 20
```

Redeclaration of Variables

Redeclaration of variables is a nasty edge case, testing the limits of the language. Luckily, the compiler mostly stops you from doing it. But there is a great deal of legal nuttiness, especially among declarations at the top level of a script. Essentially Apple-Script is hoist with its own petard: having ruled that variables can be declared implicitly, and that global variables exist at top level even when they are declared elsewhere, AppleScript is simply trying to cope coherently with the consequences.

Here are some examples of what happens when you redeclare a variable.

It is a compile-time error to redeclare an implicit global as local:

```
set x to 5
local x -- compile-time error: Can't declare x as both a local and global variable
```

It is a compile-time error to redeclare an implicit local as global:

```
on getX( )
    display dialog x
    global x -- compile-time error: Can't declare x as both a local and global variable
end getX
```

By the same token, it is a compile-time error to declare a handler parameter as global within the handler:

```
on myHandler(what)
    global what -- compile-time error: Can't declare x as both a local and global variable
end
```

It is a compile-time error to redeclare as local a variable declared global in the same scope (except at the top level):

```
on getX( )
    global x
    local x -- compile-time error: Can't declare x as both a local and global variable
end getX
```

It is a compile-time error to redeclare as global a variable declared local in the same scope (except at the top level):

```
on getX( )
    local x
    global x -- compile-time error: Can't declare x as both a local and global variable
end getX
```

At the top level, it is *not* an error to declare a variable local and then declare it global in the same scope. But it doesn't have any effect within the top-level scope either. For example:

```
local x
global x
set x to 5
on setX( )
    set x to 10
end setX
on getX( )
    display dialog x
end getX
setX( )
getX( ) -- 10
display dialog x -- 5
```

Once x is declared global, both setX and getX have automatic access to a global variable x. But the code in the top level does not have such access. There, x has already been declared local; nothing can change this. Once a local, always a local. The x that is set to 5, and that is displayed at the end, is this local x, which is different from the global x.

At top level, it is *not* an error to declare a variable global and then declare it local in the same scope. But the global variable is effectively overshadowed by the local in the top-level scope. For example:

```
global x
set x to 5
local x
on getX( )
    display dialog x
end getX
getX( ) -- 5
display dialog x -- error: The variable x is not defined
```

After the first two lines, there is a global variable x and its value is 5, and code at a deeper level can access it; the subsequent local declaration has no effect on this fact, even though it precedes the definition of the deeper-level code. But the top-level code has apparently lost its access to this global variable. It can recover this access, however, through the use of the keyword my:

```
global x
set x to 5
local x
set x to 10
x -- 10
my x -- 5
```

The same thing happens if a global is implicitly redeclared as local by a repeat block (see "Repeat With" in Chapter 19):

```
global x
set x to 10
repeat with x from 1 to 5
end repeat
x -- 5
my x -- 10
```

It is *not* a compile-time error to redeclare a top-level entity as a local or a local as a top-level entity, but access to the top-level entity is lost within that scope:

```
script myScript
    property x : 4
    display dialog x
    local x
    display dialog x
end script
run myScript -- 4, then error: The variable x is not defined
```

The second attempt to display x fails because by that point x has been redeclared as local, and this local has no value. But the downward effect of the property declaration remains, so the property remains accessible at a deeper scope. Thus:

```
script myScript
    property x : 10
    local x
    set x to 20
    on myHandler( )
        display dialog x
    end myHandler
    myHandler( )
    display dialog x
end script
run myScript -- 10, then 20
```

It is a compile-time error to redeclare as global a variable declared as a top-level entity in the same scope:

```
property x: 10
global x -- compile-time error: Can't declare x as both a local and global variable
```

It is *not* a compile-time error to do it the other way around, redeclaring a global as a top-level entity. This is merely taken as a delayed declaration of the top-level entity, and the global declaration has no effect. So:

```
global x
set x to 10
script myScript
    global x
    set x to 5
    property x : 20
    display dialog x
end script
run myScript -- 5
display dialog x -- 10
```

Within myScript, x is a property throughout; the global declaration inside myScript has no effect. The property x starts out with the value 20 before myScript runs, but myScript then sets it to 5, and this is the value that is displayed in the first dialog. The second dialog shows that the global x is unaffected. This code was written and executed on a closed course by a trained driver; please, do not attempt.

Closures

A *closure* is one of those delightfully LISPy things that turns up in AppleScript. The subject is rather advanced, though, so don't feel you have to understand everything in this section at once.

It turns out that a script object may capture certain aspects of its context, maintaining this context even though the script object may run later in a different context. For example:

```
property x : 5
script myScript
    display dialog x
end script
set x to 20
set dummy to myScript
set x to 10
run myScript -- 20
```

That is extremely odd. It violates the rule stated earlier ("Free Variables") about the value of free variables being determined at runtime. By the time myScript runs, its free variable x has been set to 10, yet the dialog displays 20. The proximate cause turns out to be the mysterious line "set dummy to myScript." If that line is removed, the dialog says 10, just as we expect. Yet it is hard to see what difference that one line can make. It's not as if we ever do anything with the variable dummy, after all. We simply assign to it and forget about it. So what's going on?

The rule appears to be that the mere act of assigning a script object variable to another variable—it can equally be a copy as a set—causes the script object to become a closure. A closure is a scope block *plus the values of its free variables at that moment*.

The example is structured in three parts so as to demonstrate the phenomenon fully. First, a property declaration precedes the script definition; this is how x inside the script definition becomes a free variable at compile time. Then, the script object is assigned to another variable; at that moment the closure is formed. The free variable has a different value by this time, so this is the value that gets frozen into the closure. Finally, the free variable's value is changed again and the script object is executed; but the script object was already turned into a closure, so the change in the value of top-level x has no effect on it.

If, at the start of that example, we substitute a global declaration for the property declaration, the example doesn't work: we don't get a closure. Rather, the dialog displays 10, the value of x at the moment the handler is executed—the normal, nonclosure behavior. So *only free variables whose value is supplied by a top-level entity can form a closure*.

Closures and Handlers

So far, we've generated a closure in accidental circumstances. In fact, this feels like a bug; the mere act of assigning a script object to a variable hardly seems to warrant freezing that same script object into a closure, and seems to be more a trap we might fall into, causing our script to misbehave mysteriously, than a feature we would use deliberately. Now, however, let's turn our attention to a situation where we might actually like to generate a closure: when returning a script object from a handler.

Sure enough, it works. A closure is generated at the time we run the handler and generate the script object. Whatever the value of the script object's free variables are at that moment, if that value comes from a top-level entity, that's the value they retain:

```
property x : 5
on h()
    script myScript
        display dialog x
    end script
    return myScript
end h
set x to 10
set s to h()
run s -- 10
set x to 20
run s -- 10
set x to 30
run s -- 10
```

As before, if we replace the property declaration in the first line with a global declaration, there's no closure, and the dialogs say 10, then 20, then 30. Similarly, if we put a global x declaration at the start of h, there's no closure. To get a closure, we need a top-level entity to come shining down from above into our script object's scope.

Because we're inside a handler, there's one more type of variable we need to consider. Remember, a script object inside a handler can see the handler's locals. So a handler's locals can be free variables in the script object. Can *they* generate a closure? Yes, they can:

```
on h()
    local x
    set x to "howdy"
    script myScript
        display dialog x
    end script
    return myScript
end h
set s to h()
run s -- howdy
```

A handler's parameter variables are locals. This means we can feed a parameter into a handler and capture it in a closure produced by the handler:

```
on scriptMaker(what)
    script myScript
        display dialog what
    end script
    return myScript
end scriptMaker
set s to scriptMaker("Hello")
run s -- Hello
```

Wait—do you recognize that example? It comes from "Handler and Script Object as Result" in Chapter 9, except that there's a line missing. Previously, we captured the handler's parameter in the script object by initializing a property to it:

```
        property x : what
```

Now it turns out that, thanks to closures, there was no need for that line. Similarly, we could rewrite the makeFilterer example (from the same section) to use a closure, changing the name criterion to crit everywhere and eliminating this line:

```
        property criterion : crit
```

I hope I'm communicating a sense of how marvelous closures are. A script like this shouldn't even be possible. The parameter what is local to the handler scriptMaker, and goes out of scope—ceases to exist—when scriptMaker finishes executing. Nothing in myScript explicitly copies or stores the value of this what. Yet in the last line, a copy of myScript is executed successfully in a context where there isn't even a name what in scope. That's because, mysteriously, invisibly, it brings along its own context where there *is* a name what in scope. That's a closure.

Closures and Stored Script Objects

Closures also come into play when a compiled script file is to be executed with `load script` or `run script` (see "Persistence of Top-Level Entities" in Chapter 8). There's more to a compiled script file than meets the eye. The `store script` command saves a script object into a compiled script file, but it also saves that script object's *context*, so that if the script object has free variables, it will still work. (You can't see this context unless you use Script Debugger, but it's there.) The `load script` command loads this context, and the `run script` command runs within it.

Consider what happens when we create a compiled script file like this:

```
set f to (path to desktop as string) & "myScript.scpt"
global greeting
set greeting to "Howdy"
property farewell : "Byebye"
script s
    display dialog greeting
    display dialog farewell
end script
store script s in file f replacing yes
```

Both `greeting` and `farewell` are free variables in the script object `s`. Only the two `display dialog` lines are being stored in a compiled script file, but that is not enough information to make sense of these variables. Therefore their context is stored in the file as well.

> Actually, AppleScript makes no attempt to decide at this point what's a free variable and what's not. It just stores the script object's *entire* context in the file. Thus, in this case, f ends up in the compiled script file as well. This makes no difference to how the stored script object will run, because the script object makes no reference to f. It might make a difference to you if you are strongly security-minded, though, as prying eyes with the proper tools can read the value of f. Also it can make the resulting compiled script file unnecessarily large. A trick to prevent `store script` from storing unwanted contextual material is to set the script object's parent to `AppleScript`—but then of course no local context is stored at all (and the rest of the examples in this section will break). Storage of context is an all-or-nothing proposition.

With `run script`, the situation is simple. No script object is generated. The compiled script file runs within its stored context and that's that:

```
set f to (path to desktop as string) & "myScript.scpt"
run script alias f -- Howdy, then Byebye
```

If we use `load script` to load the compiled script file into a script, things are more complicated. Now we have a script object, and that script object has a context within the current script as well as the context with which it was saved. How will those two contexts interact?

```
set f to (path to desktop as string) & "myScript.scpt"
set s to load script alias f
global greeting
set greeting to "Bonjour"
property farewell : "Au revoir"
run s -- Bonjour, then Byebye
```

The first dialog displays the value of greeting from the new, current context. But the second dialog displays the value of farewell from the old, stored context. This result actually makes sense in light of what we already learned about closures. Recall that a free variable whose value is a top-level entity, such as a property, makes a closure; a free variable whose value is a global does not. So the value of farewell, which was stored in the compiled script file as a free variable whose value was a property, is unaffected when the compiled script is loaded into a new context. But in the case of greeting, things are different. This was a global originally, so it does not form a closure. The *fact that this is a free variable*, however, is remembered; and the variable remains free. When the compiled script file is loaded into our script, it looks to our script to supply a value for this free variable. The supplied value can be a top-level entity (usually a property); it can be a declared global, as in our example; it can even be an *implicit* global. This last fact is surprising, so I'll demonstrate:

```
set f to (path to desktop as string) & "myScript.scpt"
set s to load script alias f
set greeting to "Bonjour"
property farewell : "Au revoir"
run s -- Bonjour, then Byebye
```

The point is that there must be *something* named greeting at a higher level to which the script object's free variable greeting can look to obtain a definition, or there will be a runtime error saying that greeting is not defined.

The same thing happens if there is a global declaration in the stored script object. Let's say we store our script object like this:

```
set f to (path to desktop as string) & "myScript.scpt"
script s
    global greeting
    display dialog greeting
end script
store script s in file f replacing yes
```

When we load the stored script into a new context, there's no closure for greeting. But greeting is declared global, so we can supply a value:

```
set f to (path to desktop as string) & "myScript.scpt"
set greeting to "Howdy"
run (load script alias f) -- Howdy
```

CHAPTER 11

Objects

The purpose of AppleScript is to communicate with scriptable applications. Within the language, these applications present themselves as *objects*—things to which you send messages, asking for access to their private world of attributes. This metaphor has been extended in AppleScript in a general way (though not, perhaps, with perfect rigor or consistency) to pervade the whole language, so that *every* value within it is, to a greater or lesser degree, somewhat like a scriptable application. Thus, whether or not AppleScript is an object-oriented language, or even an object-based language, it has a general flavor of involving objects: at every moment in your code, you are talking *to* something, and most of the things to which you talk have attributes. This chapter is about aspects of the language that involve talking to objects and referring to their attributes.

Messages

The fundamental activity in AppleScript is that of sending messages. Every line of code contains at least one imperative verb. There are actually two kinds of imperative verb: a handler call, which matches a handler definition in your script, and a *command*, which matches an *event* defined in a dictionary. The imperative verb is always directed to some specific *target*, which is supposed to obey it. The medium of communication between the imperative verb in your code and the target that you're talking to is a *message*.

An *object* is anything that can be targeted by a message. The most important targets in AppleScript are scriptable applications, but a script object can be a target too, and indeed, in some sense, every value can be a target. So, to that extent, everything in AppleScript is a kind of object. (See also "Object-likeness" in Chapter 4.) For example, count is a command. In a context where the target is the Finder, saying count causes a message to be sent to the Finder. In a context where the target is a script object, saying count causes a message to be sent to that script object. In a context where the target is a string, saying count causes a message to be sent to that string.

AppleScript tries to give the impression that all messages have the same status. Consider, for instance, what happens when an object can't obey a message. If the target is anything other than an application, we are told that the object "doesn't understand the so-and-so message." If the target is an application, we are told: "Can't continue so-and-so." The wording of the error is the same, though, no matter whether the imperative verb that generated the message is a handler call or a command.

```
tell 1
    count -- error: 1 doesn't understand the count message
end tell

script s
end script
tell s
    h() -- error: «script s» doesn't understand the h message
end tell

tell application "Finder"
    tell folder 1
        using terms from application "iPhoto"
            start slideshow
            -- error: Finder got an error: Folder 1 doesn't understand the start slideshow message
        end using terms from
    end tell
end tell

tell application "Finder"
    tell folder 1
        h() -- error: Finder got an error: Folder 1 doesn't understand the h message
    end tell
end tell

tell application "Finder"
    using terms from application "iPhoto"
        start slideshow -- Finder got an error: Can't continue start slideshow
    end using terms from
end tell

tell application "Finder"
    h() -- error: Finder got an error: Can't continue h
end tell
```

The get and set commands (and also sometimes copy) are treated in a special way: they are not messages in the sense just mentioned, but are instead somehow short-circuited so that they always work. The reason is, I suppose, that otherwise it might be possible for code or a target application to break or interfere with them and then nothing would work at all.

The message-target metaphor is also made somewhat problematic by the existence of scripting additions (see Chapter 21). Scripting additions cannot be targeted, but the commands they implement are available everywhere.

Attributes

The second way in which values are object-like in AppleScript is that they can have *attributes*. A attribute is a named value belonging to the object. The most intuitive way to understand attributes is through the notion "has." A list has a length; a string has characters; a folder has a name; an iTunes track has an artist.

There are two important things to understand about attributes. First, attributes are values like any other values, which means they are themselves objects. There is thus a relationship between two objects as owner and attribute. The object that is the attribute may itself have attributes, and so we can end up with a vast chain or tree linking many objects. This structure is called an *object model* and is crucial to your understanding of how to talk to a scriptable application. Every scriptable application has an object model, which functions as your map of that application's world.

Second, attributes are accessible only through their owner. For example, iTunes has a huge object model representing all the tracks in all your playlists, and all the various attributes of those tracks; but there is only one object to which you have direct access—the iTunes application. All the rest of iTunes's object model belongs to iTunes, and to access any object in it, you have to ask iTunes. If this reminds you of how script objects and their top-level entities work, it should (see "Top-Level Entities" in Chapter 8).

Class

Every value is of some fixed and definite type. I usually refer to this as its *datatype*, but the AppleScript term for speaking of a value's type is *class*. You can use the term class to inquire of any value what its datatype is:

```
class of 7 -- integer
class of "howdy" -- string
class of {"Mannie"} -- list
class of class of 1975 -- class
```

As the last line shows, even something's class is a value and therefore has to have a class, namely class.

 Strictly speaking, the datatype of terms like integer and class is not really class but rather type class. It's as if every value has an attribute called class whose value is itself a type class. However, AppleScript will never tell you that the class of anything is type class. You may see a class referred to as *type*, though, in a dictionary or error message:

> 2 as boolean -- *error: Can't make 2 into type boolean*

You can assign a value of any class to any variable, but at a given moment a variable has only one value and that value has only one class (so it is customary to speak of a variable's class, meaning the class of the value it has at that moment).

It is the class of something that determines what messages can be sent to it and what attributes it has. For example, a list has a length because it is a list. I am guaranteed that I can ask any list for its length and get back a meaningful answer. I am also guaranteed that I can send the count message to any list and get back a meaningful response (the same as its length, actually).

The classes of many of the objects you'll be interested in when you're working with AppleScript will be classes defined by some particular scriptable application. This is unfortunate, because such classes are much harder to work with than, say, a list. A list is always a list, but two classes with the same name, defined by two different applications, might well be nothing like one another. The Finder has a folder class and Entourage has a folder class, but a Finder folder and an Entourage folder have virtually nothing in common; they have totally different sets of attributes. Indeed, both the Finder and Entourage themselves belong to the application class, but they have very little in common too. And when it comes to messages, things are even worse; the Finder knows very well what messages it is legal to send to one of its folders, but the Finder's dictionary does little or nothing to tell you what they are. There will be much more groaning about this in Chapter 20.

Target

At every moment in AppleScript code, you are speaking to some object. That object is the *target*, to which all messages will be sent, unless you specify otherwise. Knowing what object is the target, and how to specify a desired target, is very important to your successful use of AppleScript.

The implicit target is the current script or script object. (See "Handler Calls, Commands, and Script Objects" in Chapter 8.) In this code, the implicit target is the script itself:

```
count
```

In this code, the implicit target is the script object myScript:

```
script myScript
    count
end script
```

There are three ways to specify an explicit target: as a direct object of a command, with a tell block, and with the of operator or one of its synonyms. These three ways may be combined to specify the complete target. (If they remind you of ways you can talk to a script object and access its top-level entities, they should; see Chapter 8.)

Direct Object

Most commands take at least one parameter. The unnamed parameter that directly follows the name of the command is the *direct object*. In the absence of any other target information, the target can occupy the place of the direct object.

In this example, we see the count message being sent to various targets, each of which interprets it in a different way:

```
script s
    on count
        return "1, 2, 3, ha ha ha"
    end count
end script
count s -- "1, 2, 3, ha ha ha"
count "hello" -- 5
count {1, 2, 3} -- 3
count application "Finder" -- 32 (the number of desktop items)
```

It is permitted to insert the word of between the command and the direct object (unless the command is get, set, or copy). It is also permitted to insert the word get before the command. This is rather confusing because it makes a command (such as count) look like an attribute, and I do not recommend talking this way.

```
count of "hello" -- 5
get count of "hello" -- 5
script s
    display dialog "howdy"
end script
get run of s -- howdy, but no one ever talks like this
get display dialog of "howdy" -- howdy (now stop that!)
```

This of is related to the special of that can mark the first parameter when using prepositional parameters in a handler call (see Chapter 9). The 's operator is *not* a synonym.

Don't confuse a command's direct object with the target. The target can occupy the direct object slot even if the command itself does not take a direct object. For example, the quit command has no direct object; it is sent to the target, and that is what quits.

```
quit application "Finder"
```

Tell Block

A tell block is a block introduced by the keyword tell. Immediately after that keyword comes the target. Commands within the block are directed to the target, unless they specify a different target. A tell block consisting of a single command can be written as a single line, using the syntax tell *target* to. Things I say about a tell block apply to this variant as well.

Here are some of the earlier direct object examples rewritten to use a tell block. They could all be rewritten in the same manner:

```
tell "hello"
    count -- 5
end tell
tell "hello" to count -- 5
tell application "Finder"
    count -- 32
end tell
tell application "Finder" to count -- 32
```

An important feature of a tell block is that it causes terminology within it to be resolved using the dictionary of the target application. Thus you can say things that would be illegal (without trickery) as a simple direct object.

```
sleep application "Finder" -- compile-time error, because the word "sleep" is not understood
tell application "Finder" to sleep -- snore...
```

The role of a tell block in resolution of terminology, and the trickery you can employ to resolve terminology without one, is discussed in detail in Chapters 19 and 20.

Of

Objects, as we have already seen, can have attributes. The only way, ultimately, to access an object's attributes is through some object that you can see directly. The way to express the relationship between the object that you can see directly and the attribute you want to access is with the of operator.

A synonym for of is in. (I never use this.) Another synonym, for most purposes, is the 's operator: instead of saying *x* of *y*, you can say *y*'s *x*.

(Do not confuse the of operator here with the of that can optionally appear before the direct object of a command.)

The of operator can appear in a target specifier either in a direct object or in the announcement line of a tell block. For example:

```
open file 1 of application "Finder"
tell file 1 of application "Finder" to open
open application "Finder"'s file 1
tell application "Finder"'s file 1 to open
```

The Chain of Ofs and Tells

Material nested within a tell block is joined by an implicit of to the target specified in the announcement line of the tell block. (This device doesn't always work, and I'm being deliberately vague about some of the details; I'll provide them in "Get" and "It," later in this chapter.) So the previous example can be rewritten like this:

```
tell application "Finder"
    open file 1
end tell
```

This is in fact the canonical and most frequently used form. In the earlier forms, the entire target (with of) appears either after tell or after open. Here, the target is effectively divided into two: half of it appears in the announcement line in the tell block (application "Finder") and the other half appears as the direct object of the open command (file 1). Each half is a *partial target*. AppleScript joins them with of to form the *complete target*.

This form has two great advantages, explaining why it is the most frequently used:

Resolution of terminology

A tell block causes the terminology inside it to be resolved in accordance with the target application's dictionary. Thus you can say things in a tell block that you can say in no other way, because the terms you're using are not part of AppleScript itself and would cause a compile-time error outside a tell block.

Multiple commands to the same target

A tell block is a block, so it can contain more than one command. It is very frequently the case that you want to give more than one command to the same target or partial target, so a tell block is the most convenient construct. For example:

```
local n, c
tell application "Finder"
    tell folder 1
        tell file 1
            set n to name
            set c to comment
        end tell
    end tell
end tell
```

The chain of ofs needed to form a complete target is often longer than just two parts. In this case, you can divide the target into partial targets in whatever way is convenient: each part by itself in a nested tell block, or some parts joined together with of. These snippets all do the same thing:

```
tell application "Finder"
    tell folder 1
        tell file 1
            open
        end tell
    end tell
end tell

tell application "Finder"
    tell file 1 of folder 1
        open
    end tell
end tell

tell application "Finder"
    open file 1 of folder 1
end tell

tell application "Finder"
    tell folder 1
        open file 1
    end tell
end tell
```

(You'll notice that I didn't try to crowd any more of the target onto the first line; I didn't say `tell folder 1 of application "Finder"`, for example. This expression is syntactically legal, but it won't compile, because the term `folder` is defined in the Finder's dictionary and must appear within a tell block targeting the Finder.)

Thus there is a sense in which `tell` and `of` are interchangeable. In determining the target, AppleScript actually works its way up the chain of `of`s and `tell`s until it assembles a complete target. (I am deliberately waving my hands over what I mean by "a complete target," but it means something like an application, a script, or a value within your script.)

Whether you use `of` or `tell` on any particular occasion will depend on various circumstances. Sometimes it's just a matter of style and legibility, but sometimes you'll be constrained by other factors. Suppose you want to open file 1 of folder 1, and then file 1 of folder 2. And suppose your code starts this way:

```
tell application "Finder"
    tell folder 1
```

From within this nested tell block, there is absolutely no way to speak of folder 2. You could use the words "folder 2," but you're already inside a tell block targeting folder 1, so this would mean "folder 2 of folder 1," which is not what you want. There isn't any notation that backs you out one level (like `..` in a POSIX pathname). You must actually *be* one level higher. An experienced AppleScript programmer will plan ahead and not nest tell blocks too deeply:

```
tell application "Finder"
    open file 1 of folder 1
    open file 1 of folder 2
end tell
```

Another solution is, as you're working your way down the nest of tell blocks, to capture a reference to something you're going to need later at a level too deep to refer to it. For example:

```
tell application "Microsoft Entourage"
    tell in box folder
        move message 1 to folder "temp"
        -- error: Microsoft Entourage got an error: Can't get message 1 of in box folder
    end tell
end tell
```

Despite the very misleading error message, the actual problem here is that there is no such thing as `folder "temp" of in box folder`—`folder "temp"` is a top-level folder. One way out would of course be not to dive into a tell block:

```
tell application "Microsoft Entourage"
    move message 1 of in box folder to folder "temp"
end tell
```

But in a bigger script or with a long chain of ofs, we might not like that solution. So we'll capture a reference to folder "temp" at a point where we *can* speak of it, and use that reference later:

```
tell application "Microsoft Entourage"
    set ftemp to folder "temp"
    tell in box folder
        move message 1 to ftemp
    end tell
end tell
```

Terms in Scope

The rules for targeting do not override the scoping rules described in the previous chapter. A tell block does not cut off access to the surrounding context—and a good thing too, because if it did, you wouldn't be able to use terms that are in scope while explicitly targeting something. AppleScript does not blindly send messages to the target; it looks at the target's terminology, but it also looks to see whether you might be using a term that's in scope from your script. You can therefore quite freely mingle terms defined in the current context of your script with terms defined by the target.

(The mechanism is actually quite subtle, and if you press up against its limits, conflicts can arise. I'll give some examples in this chapter, and there is further detail in the section "Resolution of Terminology" in Chapter 20.)

For example:

```
set x to "howdy"
tell application "Finder"
    count x
end tell
```

AppleScript knows that x is something meaningful in the context of the script itself, so it doesn't send any message to the Finder asking about x. (That's a good thing, because the Finder doesn't know about anything called x.)

Here's an example with considerable mingling of terms from the two namespaces, yours and the Finder's:

```
set newname to "someFolder"
tell application "Finder"
    set oldname to name of folder 1
    set name of folder 1 to newname
end tell
display dialog oldname
```

Here, oldname and newname are (implicit) globals within the script, and their values are set and retrieved without involving the Finder. To accomplish this, AppleScript must unravel your phrases into separate commands. Consider this line:

```
set oldname to name of folder 1
```

AppleScript actually does two things here. First it sends to the Finder this message (see the later section "Get"):

```
get name of folder 1
```

Then it uses the result to set the value of oldname within your script. There is a clear division of labor: the Finder does not somehow lay hands on any of your script's variables.

But handler calls are different. A handler call will always send a message to the target. This won't work:

```
on whatNumber( )
    return 1
end whatNumber
tell application "Finder"
    get folder whatNumber( ) -- error: Finder got an error: Can't continue whatNumber
end tell
```

The Finder is sent the whatNumber message, but it knows of no whatNumber command. (The section "Me," later in this chapter, will provide the solution to this problem.)

Nested Targets

The innermost target of a command is the target. Once AppleScript, working its way outward from a command, has determined a complete target, it stops, ignoring any further ofs or tells that surround it. Consider, for example, the following:

```
tell application "iTunes"
    tell application "Finder"
        count folders
    end tell
end tell
```

iTunes is not in fact targeted in any way here; no message will be sent to it when the code runs. AppleScript works its way outwards from the count command until it reaches the Finder; now AppleScript has assembled a complete target, and stops. In fact, if you try to write the same thing this way:

```
count folders of application "Finder" of application "iTunes"
```

AppleScript literally throws away the mention of iTunes after decompilation:

```
count folders of application "Finder"
```

The direct object has primacy in this regard. It always has the potential to constitute a complete target and override all surrounding ofs and tells. For example:

```
tell application "Finder"
    count "howdy"
end tell
```

The string "howdy" is a complete target, and no message is sent to the Finder.

Get

The default command is get. In effect, a sentence or clause with no verb is assumed to have get as its verb. So, for example:

```
tell application "Finder"
    name of folder 1
end tell
```

The get command is supplied here and is the actual message sent to the Finder. It's exactly as if you had said get explicitly:

```
tell application "Finder"
    get name of folder 1
end tell
```

One even sees code written like this:

```
tell application "Finder" to name of folder 1
```

AppleScript can also supply get in the middle of a line where needed. As we have already seen, this code:

```
tell application "Finder"
    set oldname to name of folder 1
end tell
```

is actually treated by AppleScript as if it said this:

```
tell application "Finder"
    set oldname to (get name of folder 1)
end tell
```

Do not imagine, however, that it makes no difference whether you ever say get, and that you can blithely omit it. On the contrary, it's probably better to err in the other direction and say get whenever you mean get. There are no prizes for obfuscated AppleScript, and you're most likely to confuse yourself (and impress no one else) if you get into bad habits. More important, omission of get from expressions of any complexity can cause runtime errors. For example, this:

```
tell application "Finder" to display dialog (name of folder 1)
-- error: Finder got an error: Can't make name of folder 1 into type string
```

is not the same as this:

```
tell application "Finder" to display dialog (get name of folder 1) -- Mannie
```

In the first example, name of folder 1 is a reference to an attribute; that's not something that can be displayed by display dialog, so we get an error. In the second, the get command fetches the *value* of that attribute, a string, and all is well. AppleScript programmers like to say that get resolves references.

Sometimes, just the other way around, you don't want references resolved. This works (the first word of the document is deleted):

```
tell application "TextEdit" to delete word 1 of document 1
```

But this doesn't work (there is no error, but nothing happens):

```
tell application "TextEdit" to delete (get word 1 of document 1)
```

In the second case, get resolves the reference, effectively evaluating the expression and yielding a string (the text of the first word). Let's say it's the word "This." Then we're telling TextEdit to delete the string "This"—not as an attribute of some document but in the abstract. That's a meaningless command. (The fact that TextEdit doesn't complain should probably be regarded as a bug.)

As mentioned earlier, get (along with set) is implemented in a special way; it isn't a message to an object in the manner discussed through this chapter. Thus it can't be sent to a direct object by means of a tell block; you must always say what you want to get, immediately after the word get, or the compiler will complain:

```
tell 7 to get -- compile-time error: Expected expression but found end of script
```

It

The keyword it represents the target. (In situations where you would say of it after a word, you may say its before that word instead.)

The keyword it can be useful in helping you understand who the target is. It can also be useful as an explicit target, in situations where AppleScript would otherwise misinterpret your meaning.

This example shows it used while debugging, to make sure we understand who the target is:

```
tell application "Finder"
    tell folders
        it -- every folder of application "Finder"
    end tell
end tell
```

Sometimes when you get yourself deep in a nest of tell blocks (see "The Chain of Ofs and Tells," earlier in this chapter), it can be helpful for referring to the target one level up. For example, this code opens file 1 of folder 1 and also opens folder 1 itself:

```
tell application "Finder"
    tell folder 1
        open file 1
        open it
    end tell
end tell
```

You have already seen ("Accessing Top-Level Entities" in Chapter 8) the need for it when accessing a script object's top-level entities within a tell block addressed to the script object. When targeting an attribute of a scriptable application, there is generally no need for it used in this way. Unlike a script object, an application has a dictionary, so AppleScript knows when you're saying the name of an attribute of that application. For example, the Finder has an attribute home; there is no need for its to tell AppleScript that we mean the Finder's home rather than a variable in scope:

```
set home to "Ojai"
tell application "Finder"
    get home -- folder "mattneub" of folder "Users"...
end tell
```

In fact, here the problem is more likely to be how to refer to the variable home from within this tell block. The next section ("Me") solves the problem.

However, there is one situation where it *is* needed when targeting an application. It may happen that an application's dictionary gives a property (a kind of attribute) and a class the same name. Applications really shouldn't do this, but in fact they do it quite often. Without it, such a term may be treated as the class, causing the script to malfunction. For example:

```
tell application "Finder"
    tell folder 1
        get container -- container, a class
    end tell
end tell
```

This was not the desired result. To get the *value* of the container property of a folder, we must use its or (what amounts to the same thing) the of operator:

```
tell application "Finder"
    tell folder 1
        get its container -- folder "Desktop" of...
    end tell
    get container of folder 1 -- folder "Desktop" of...
end tell
```

This problem is particularly insidious, because there is usually no error, so you're mystified when the script doesn't behave as you expect. The following script is intended to change all instances of "o" to "a" in Word. The script compiles and runs, but the change is not performed:

```
tell application "Microsoft Word"
    tell find object of selection
        set content to "o"
        tell replacement
            set content to "a"
        end tell
        execute find replace replace all
    end tell
end tell
```

The trouble is that replacement is both a property of the find object and the name of a class. The solution is to change the fourth line to this:

```
tell its replacement
```

Sometimes when a script is being troublesome I make both get and it explicit everywhere just to eliminate misunderstandings as a possible source of error. For example, I might rewrite the previous script like this:

```
tell application "Microsoft Word"
    tell (get find object of its selection)
        set its content to "o"
        tell (get its replacement)
            set its content to "a"
        end tell
        execute find replace replace all
    end tell
end tell
```

You'd be amazed by how many problems vanish before a little extra verbosity of this sort.

Me

The keyword me represents the current script—the script or script object that is running the code where the keyword me appears. (In situations where you would say of me after a word, you may say my before that word instead.) Thus:

```
script myScript
    me -- «script myScript»
end script
run myScript
me -- «script», the anonymous top-level script
parent of me -- «script AppleScript»
```

See also "The Implicit Parent Chain" in Chapter 8.

We saw the keyword me used earlier (Chapter 8) as a way to force AppleScript to interpret a term as belonging to the current script object, so that it will use the inheritance chain.

When targeting an application in a tell block, me can be helpful as a specifying that the target should be your script instead. For example, this doesn't work:

```
on reverseString(s)
    set text item delimiters to ""
    return (reverse of characters of s) as string
end reverseString
tell application "Finder"
    set name of folder 1 to reverseString(get name of folder 1)
    -- error: Finder got an error: Can't continue reverseString
end tell
```

When we come to the handler call reverseString( ) in the next-to-last line, the target is the Finder. So AppleScript passes it along to the Finder. The Finder doesn't know what to do with this message. The target for reverseString, and only reverseString, needs to be the current script. This is a job for me (a "can't continue" error usually is):

```
set name of folder 1 to my reverseString(get name of folder 1)
```

But me won't also resolve a *terminology clash* between a term defined by the target and a term within your script. In that case, you'll have to use pipes (vertical bars) around the term, to prevent its resolution by the target dictionary. For instance, how might I refer to the global variable home in a tell block directed at the Finder, which has a home attribute? I can try using my, but I just get a mysterious error message:

```
set home to "Ojai"
tell application "Finder"
    get my home -- error: Can't make home directory into type reference
end tell
```

The problem is not that my failed to retarget the message. It did retarget it! But the term home is still being resolved in accordance with the Finder's dictionary. So when the message arrives at my script, it doesn't speak of my variable home, but of some Finder-based attribute that my script doesn't know how to interpret. Use of pipes solves the problem:

```
set home to "Ojai"
tell application "Finder"
    get |home| -- "Ojai"
end tell
```

There is no need for my, because the pipes cause AppleScript to take home as a name in scope within the script, and so it targets the script rather then the Finder.

Occasionally you may have to use pipes around the name of a handler call, too. In this case you need me as well as the pipes, because a handler call is always directed at the target unless you explicitly say otherwise. For example, here we'd like to call our own reveal, but the message goes to the Finder instead:

```
on reveal(what)
    display dialog (get name of what)
end reveal
tell application "Finder"
    reveal(file 1) -- the Finder highlights the file's icon
end tell
```

Adding my just causes a mysterious error message:

```
on reveal(what)
    display dialog (get name of what)
end reveal
tell application "Finder"
    my reveal (file 1) -- error: Expected expression but found command name
end tell
```

Using pipes without my causes a different error message:

```
on reveal(what)
    display dialog (get name of what)
end reveal
tell application "Finder"
    |reveal|(file 1) -- error: Finder got an error: Can't continue reveal
end tell
```

The solution is to use both:

```
on reveal(what)
    display dialog (get name of what)
end reveal
tell application "Finder"
    my |reveal|(file 1)
end tell
```

The trouble is that the Finder has its own reveal command. The pipes suppress the use of the Finder's terminology; the my routes the message to your script instead of the Finder. If you use me but no pipes, the message is sent to your script using the Finder's terminological encoding, and your script doesn't understand it; if you use pipes but no me, the message is sent to the Finder with no terminological encoding, and the Finder doesn't understand it.

Properties and Elements

The purpose of the chain of ofs and tells is to navigate a structure formed by objects standing in a relationship of owner and attribute to one another. For example, the phrase folder 1 of application "Finder" is needed because folder 1 is an attribute of the Finder, and because I can refer directly to the Finder but not to its attributes. Figuring out how to form a chain of ofs and tells that will let you refer successfully to a desired object constitutes much of the effort of AppleScript programming, as Appendix A vividly illustrates. An application's dictionary is supposed to help you with this, though it often falls short (Chapter 20). AppleScript's own dictionary is not typically visible, so later in the book I'll list the attributes of the built-in datatypes (Chapter 13).

An attribute is either a property or an element. (In fact, I had to coin the term "attribute" because the official AppleScript documentation lacks any comprehensive term for "property or element.") A *property* is an attribute that this class of object has exactly one of. An *element* is an attribute that this class of object may have any number of, and in order to refer to one (or more), you have to say which one(s) you mean.

For example, given a list, length is a property; every list has a length, and that's the end of that. But item is an element; a list might not have any items, and if it does have some, it can have any number of them. To speak of an item or items we have to say which one(s) we mean, as in item 1. Similarly, with regard to a folder in the Finder, name is a property but file is an element.

Some properties are *read-only*: you can get but not set their value. For example:

```
tell application "Finder"
    get startup disk
    set startup disk to disk "gromit"
    -- error: Finder got an error: Can't set startup disk to disk "gromit"
end tell
```

Elements in general are read-only in the sense that you can't say "set folder 1 to" something. However, you can set an element's properties (except those that are read-only, of course), and applications usually implement verbs that permit to you create and manipulate elements.

When you get an attribute's value, that value will be of some particular class. If this is one of AppleScript's built-in datatypes, what you get will usually be a copy. So, for example:

```
tell application "Finder"
    set s to name of disk 1
    set s to "yoho"
end tell
```

That code has no effect upon the name of the disk. A string came back and was stored in the variable s, and you then set the variable s to some other value, throwing away the string the Finder gave you.

But when the class of the returned value is an object type defined by and belonging to the application you're targeting, the value will usually be a reference to that object. Such a reference is a complete target. You can send a message to it, and you can get an attribute of it. You are not in control of what this reference looks like, and the way it looks may surprise you, but you shouldn't worry about that; it's a valid reference and a complete target, and that's all you should care about. For example:

```
tell application "Finder"
    set d to disk of folder 1
end tell
d -- startup disk of application "Finder"
```

What I may have expected to see as a result of asking for this property doesn't matter; I must have faith that the Finder has given me a reference to what I asked for. To justify this faith, I can proceed to target this reference:

```
tell application "Finder"
    set d to disk of folder 1
end tell
get name of d -- "feathers"
```

As d is a complete reference to a Finder object, I can target it; in the last line, the get message is sent to the Finder, and the name of the disk comes back. (The term name is understandable outside of a tell block targeting the Finder because it is defined within AppleScript itself; see Chapter 20.)

We have already, in several examples, taken advantage of this ability to obtain a reference and operate on it. References will be fully discussed in Chapter 12. But for now I must warn you: a reference is not a copy! So what you do to it will truly be done in the real world. For example:

```
tell application "Finder"
    set d to disk of folder 1
end tell
set name of d to "yoho" -- Don't say this unless you mean it!
```

That code really will change the name of your hard disk, even though you're not explicitly targeting the Finder.

Element Specifiers

Referring to a property is easy; you just use the name of the property. For example:

```
get version of application "Finder" -- 10.4.2
```

Referring to an element is harder. An object can have any number of each class of element, so you must say which one(s) you mean. To do this, you use an *element specifier* (or just *specifier* for short—AppleScript also calls this a *key form*). A specifier has two components: the name of a class and some way of picking out the right one(s). AppleScript has eight built-in forms of specifier, and these are the only ones you are allowed to use. The next eight sections describe those eight specifier forms.

(Actually, there are actually nine element specifiers. I don't discuss middle because it is rarely used. Plus, a reference to a property is actually a form of specifier, so I guess that makes ten. The variety of specifier forms makes a specifier quite an interesting and complicated part of an Apple event. The repeated pattern involving the four terms form, want, seld, and from in Example 3-1 denotes a specifier.)

In real life, it will rarely be open to you to use just whichever specifier form you please on a particular occasion. Given a certain application, object, and class of element, only certain specifier forms will work, and experimentation is the best guide as to which ones they are. An application's dictionary is supposed to help you here, but it might not, or might not be accurate (see "Defective Element Specifiers" in Chapter 20).

Name

An element may have a name, which is some kind of string. (I say "some kind of" because it might, for example, be Unicode text, which is not the same class as string.) To specify an element by name, say the class followed by the name:

```
tell application "Finder" to get disk "main"
```

You may insert the keyword named between the class and the name, but I never do.

Typically, there is also a name property, so that you can learn, based on some other element specifier, how to specify a particular element by name:

```
tell application "Finder" to get name of disk 2 -- "gromit"
```

Index

Elements are usually ordered, and numbered in accordance with this ordering. The number is an index. The first element has index 1, the next element has index 2, and so forth. The last element can be referred to by index -1, the next-to-last by index -2, and so forth. (If you want to know just how many elements of this class there are, you have to find out in some other way, such as count.)

To specify an element by index, say the class followed by the index number:

```
tell application "Finder" to get disk 2
```

You may insert the keyword index between the class and the number, but I never do. Instead of a cardinal number, you're allowed to use a wide variety of English-like ordinal numeric literals followed by the class name. So you can say such things as 1st disk, third disk, last disk, front disk, and back disk.

There is sometimes also an index property, so that you can learn, based on some other element specifier, how to specify a particular element by index, but this is not implemented anywhere near as often as one would like, and is sometimes buggy:

```
tell application "Finder" to get index of disk 2 -- 3, for heaven's sake
```

ID

Elements may have a unique and unchanging ID, which is often a number but needn't be. For example, in Entourage a message's name can be changed, and its index within its folder may change, but its ID is constant.

To specify an element by ID, say the class followed by the keyword id followed by the ID value. This value will have been obtained at some earlier point, typically by asking for an element's ID property:

```
tell application "Microsoft Entourage"
    set messageID to ID of message 1 of in box folder -- 2849, if you must know
    -- more code goes here . . .
    get message id messageID
end tell
```

Some

A random element may be specified by saying some followed by the class:

```
tell application "Finder"
    name of some disk -- "gromit"
    name of some disk -- "feathers"
    name of some disk -- "feathers"
end tell
```

Every

It may be possible to get a list of every element of a class. To ask for such a list, say the keyword every followed by the class; alternatively, you may be able to say just the plural of the class:

```
tell application "Finder" to get every disk
tell application "Finder" to get disks
```

If asking for just one element would result in a reference, the result in this case is a list of references.

Range

Elements may be ordered, and you may be able to obtain a list of contiguous elements (a range) by giving the first and last index number you're interested in. It is generally not important in what order you give these index numbers.

To specify elements by range, say the class in a plural form (or every and the class) followed by an index number, the keyword thru (or through), and another index number. You can say beginning or end instead of an index number:

```
get words 1 thru 4 of "now is the winter of our discontent"
get words beginning thru 4 of "now is the winter of our discontent"
```

Alternatively, you may be able to get a list of contiguous elements of a class where the range is marked off by two element specifiers for some *other* class. In this case, you say the class in a plural form (or every and the class) followed by the keyword from, an element specifier for the starting point, the keyword to, and an element specifier for the ending point. Again, you can say beginning or end instead of an element specifier:

```
get words from character 12 to character 17 of "now is the winter"
get words from character 12 to character -1 of "now is the winter"
get words from character 12 to end of "now is the winter"
```

There is a tendency to confuse or conflate these two forms, and to try to say something like this:

```
get words 1 to 3 of "now is the winter of our discontent"  -- compile-time error
```

You can't do that. "To" is not "thru"! Keep these two constructions straight. Practice them before going to bed.

Relative

Elements may be ordered, and it may be possible to refer to an element as the successor or predecessor of another element. To ask for an element in this way, say the name of the class, the keyword before or after, and an element specifier:

```
tell application "TextEdit"
    tell document 1
        get word after word 1
    end tell
end tell
```

A synonym for before is in front of. Synonyms for after are behind and in back of.

That wasn't a very useful example, because we could have asked for word 2. But relative specifiers are useful when you can obtain an object of one class in positional relation to another. For example, in BBEdit all text has insertion point elements lying between the characters. Thus you can say this:

```
tell application "BBEdit"
    tell text of window 1
        get insertion point before word 4
    end tell
end tell
```

Given an insertion point in BBEdit, you can set its contents property to alter the text. This code changes "This is a test" to "This is a great test":

```
tell application "BBEdit"
    tell text of window 1
        set pt to insertion point before word 4
        set contents of pt to "great "
    end tell
end tell
```

Similarly, some applications have a class called location reference (or "insertion location," depending on how the dictionary is displayed). Unlike BBEdit's insertion point, you usually can't get one directly; instead, you form one, primarily as the at or to parameter of the duplicate, make, and move commands. An insertion location is specified using before or after and an element specifier (yielding bizarre locutions like at after); or using beginning of or end of and a reference to an object, or just beginning or end alone; or using just an element specifier.

Applications can be extraordinarily touchy about how they expect an insertion location to look, with results differing from application to application. Here are some examples:

```
tell application "TextEdit"
    tell text of document 1
        make new word at after word 2 with data "not "
        -- changes "this is a test" to "this is not a test"
```

```
        end tell
    end tell

    tell application "TextEdit"
        tell text of document 1
            duplicate word 1 to end
            -- changes "fair is foul and foul is " to "fair is foul and foul is fair"
        end tell
    end tell

    tell application "TextEdit"
        tell text of document 1
            duplicate word 1 to beginning of word 3
            -- changes "wonder of s" to "wonder of wonders"
        end tell
    end tell

    tell application "TextEdit"
        tell text of document 1
            duplicate word 1 to word 7
            -- changes "fair is foul and foul is foul" to "fair is foul and foul is fair"
        end tell
    end tell

    tell application "Script Debugger"
        move window 2 to beginning
        -- bring the second window frontmost
    end tell
```

That last example shows that this locution manipulates more than text.

Boolean Test

It may be possible to get a list of those elements that satisfy a boolean test. What you test may be a property of the target, or it may be the target itself. The test may involve any boolean operator (see "Comparison Operators" and "Containment Operators" in Chapter 15).

A boolean test also involves an index-based specifier: index, range, or every (or some). This is because the answer is a list, and you can ask for the whole list or for particular elements of it.

To specify elements by boolean test, start with an index-based specifier for a class and the keyword where (or whose), followed by a property of that class or the word it, followed by a boolean operator and any value that can function as that operator's second operand. In this context, the word it means the element to be tested.

How you select among the various synonyms and options will probably depend on what feels most English-like to you:

```
tell application "Finder" to get files where name begins with "s"
tell application "Finder" to get every file where name begins with "s"
tell application "Finder" to get files where name of it begins with "s"
tell application "Finder" to get files where its name begins with "s"
tell application "Finder" to get files whose name begins with "s"
```

Those are all equivalent. The index-based specifier is the every specifier, with file as its class; the plural files is a synonym. Then comes where or whose. Now every file will be tested, and name means the name property of the file being tested; the words of it or its are redundant but harmless. The boolean operator is begins with, and its second operand is the string "s".

When a boolean test specifier tests the value of a boolean property, you can say it is (or it is not) and the name of the property. Doing so can make your expression more English-like (if the property name is an adjective); the following two formulations are equivalent, the latter being more English-like:

```
tell application "System Events"
    get process 1 whose frontmost is true
    get process 1 where it is frontmost
end tell
```

The keyword it is needed when an application has defined a property with the same name as a class, just as we saw earlier ("It"). The problem is troublesome, because there's no error; you just don't get the right answer. This comes up empty:

```
tell application "Microsoft Entourage"
    get every POP account whose email address contains "matt" -- {}
end tell
```

Saying its disambiguates. You might also change whose to where for the sake of English-likeness, but you don't have to:

```
tell application "Microsoft Entourage"
    get every POP account whose its email address contains "matt"
    -- {POP account id 1...}
end tell
```

You definitely need it when what you want to test is each object itself, not a property of it:

```
tell application "TextEdit"
    tell text of document 1
        get every word where it contains "t"
        get words whose it contains "t"
    end tell
end tell
```

The two formulations shown are equivalent, but most people prefer the former, as being more English-like. (AppleScript has no equivalent for where it, such as "which" or "that"; it doesn't let you be as English-like as all that.)

That example works because when you ask TextEdit for words, you get a list of strings; each string then functions as the first operand of contains. But this is by no means how every application works. For example, in BBEdit, when you ask for words you get a list of references. To obtain the text of each word you ask for its contents, so you don't end up using it at all:

```
tell application "BBEdit"
    tell text 1 of window 1
        get every word whose contents contains "t"
    end tell
end tell
```

Finally, here's an example involving an index specifier other than every:

```
tell application "BBEdit"
    tell text 1 of window 1
        get word 1 whose contents contains "t"
    end tell
end tell
```

When you use every, if no elements satisfy the text, you get an empty list. But when you specify the index, if that index doesn't exist, you get an error. (This is because you get an error if you ask for a nonexistent item of *any* list.) You can easily catch such an error and handle it (see Chapter 19), but it's something to watch out for.

If the target application is willing, you may even be able to combine multiple boolean tests (see "Boolean Operators" in Chapter 15). The syntax rules require that you supply a first operand for the second test, even if this is the same as the first operand of the first test:

```
tell application "TextEdit"
    tell document 1
        words where it begins with "t" and it ends with "t" -- {"test"}
    end tell
end tell
```

The boolean test, where it works, is a very powerful specifier; with a single Apple event you're getting the target application to do a lot of searching for you. Unfortunately, you never know whether it will work; only experimentation will tell you.

AppleScript itself, most disappointingly, fails to implement boolean test specifiers for its own lists. The two halves of this example are parallel, yet the second fails:

```
tell application "Finder"
    get every disk whose name begins with "g" -- "gromit"
end tell
set pepBoys to {"Mannie", "Moe", "Jack"}
tell pepBoys
    get every item whose text begins with "M" -- error: Can't get...
end tell
```

As a workaround, use the list-filtering handler developed earlier in this book (under "Power Handler Tricks" in Chapter 9).

Operations on Multiple References

When an element specifier would return a list of references, it may be possible to ask for an attribute of this list as a shorthand for asking for that attribute of each element of the list in turn; the request to fetch the attribute is applied *distributively* to each item of the list.

For example, this works, and returns a list of strings, the names of each disk in turn:

```
tell application "Finder" to get name of every disk
```

Similarly:

```
tell application "iTunes"
    tell view of browser window 1
        get name of every track
    end tell
end tell
```

Possibly you can even apply this construct to the result of a boolean test:

```
tell application "iTunes"
    tell view of browser window 1
        get database ID of every track whose name contains "Palestrina"
    end tell
end tell
```

Those examples illustrate a property; the same thing may work for an element:

```
tell application "Finder"
    get file 1 of every folder
end tell
```

When you request multiple elements distributed across a list in this way, whether you get back a list of lists or a single flattened list depends upon the individual application. For example:

```
tell application "Address Book"
    get every email of every person
end tell
```

The result of that code is a list of lists—the outer list has as many items as there are persons, with each item being a list of every email address of the corresponding person. But when you try something similar in the Finder, the result is a single list of files:

```
tell application "Finder"
    get every file of every folder
end tell
```

An application may also be willing to accept a list as the direct object of a command, applying the command distributively to each member of the list. You can't know until you try:

```
tell application "Microsoft Entourage"
    move (every message of in box folder where address of its sender ¬
        contains "lambert") to folder "temp"
end tell
```

Despite the parentheses inserted by AppleScript's compiler, there's only one Apple event here. You're not getting the list and then sending it back to Entourage for processing: you're describing the list and telling Entourage to construct and process it.

Distribution over a list is a tremendously powerful and efficient construct, where a single Apple event causes the target application to do a lot of work for you. But keep in mind that you can't be certain it will be implemented until you try it. For example, let's say you want to know how long each word of a BBEdit document is. A word has a length property, but you can't fetch this property distributively over the items of a list, possible because length is already a property of a list. So, for example, you can say this:

```
tell application "BBEdit"
    contents of every word of window 1 -- {"this", "is", "a", "test"}
end tell
```

But you can't say this:

```
tell application "BBEdit"
    length of every word of window 1 -- 4
end tell
```

Well, you can say it, but it doesn't yield the desired answer. Instead of a list of lengths, we were given the length of the list (that is, the number of words in the window). The workaround, when distribution doesn't work, is to loop through the list yourself:

```
tell application "BBEdit"
    tell document 1
        set L to get contents of every word
        set L2 to {}
        repeat with aWord in L
            set end of L2 to length of aWord
        end repeat
    end tell
end tell
```

In this case, the workaround was not particularly expensive or unpleasant. But when it involves sending an Apple event every time through the loop, it's a poor substitute.

Assignment of Multiple Attributes

Recall from Chapter 7 that it is possible to assign multiple values in a single command by using a list:

```
set {x, y, z} to {1, 2, 3}
```

You can use this syntax to fetch multiple attributes, using either tell or of:

```
tell application "Finder"
    set {x, y} to {name, comment} of folder 1
end tell
{x, y} -- {"Mannie", "howdy"}
```

That code fetches name of folder 1 and comment of folder 1 from the Finder in a single command.

You can use this construct to set multiple properties as well, but only in a tell block (trying to do it with of will cause a runtime error):

```
tell application "Finder"
    tell folder "Mannie"
        set {comment, name} to {"zowie", "Jack"}
    end tell
end tell
```

Be careful of the order in which you list the properties when assigning to them. The values are assigned from left to right. This wouldn't have worked:

```
tell application "Finder"
    tell folder "Mannie"
        set {name, comment} to {"Jack", "zowie"} -- error
    end tell
end tell
```

That code sets the name first, and afterwards there is no longer a folder "Mannie" to set the comment of, so the attempt to set the comment of folder "Mannie" causes a runtime error.

Object String Specifier

For certain objects in the "real world" (that is, the real world inside the computer), AppleScript has a bootstrap problem. It needs a way to refer to these objects, yet they are not attributes of anything. In fact, they are the things that have attributes. So in order to talk about anything at all outside of the script, AppleScript must pull itself up by its bootstraps.

The solution is an object described using the name of the class followed by a string. It looks rather like an element specifier by name; but the object isn't an element of anything, and the string isn't exactly a name. There is no official term for this construct in Apple's documentation, so I call it an *object string specifier*. The main real-world objects for which object string specifiers are used are applications, files and aliases, and dates. Details appear in Chapter 13, but here are some examples.

Throughout this chapter I've constructed application targets using an object string specifier with the application class:

```
tell application "BBEdit"
```

In the case of a file or an alias, the string is a pathname:

```
get POSIX path of file "myDisk:myFile"
```

The string doesn't have to be a literal; a variable will work just as well:

```
set f to "myDisk:myFile"
get POSIX path of file f
```

CHAPTER 12

References

References are an important feature of AppleScript, and many values that you'll encounter using AppleScript will be references. A reference is a special type of data. It isn't the actual data; it's more like a pointer to the data. But it isn't a pointer, either; if you're used to pointers or indirect addressing from some other computer language, a reference is something else again. Remember, AppleScript is all about communicating with scriptable applications. In replying to a communication, the scriptable application might hand you a reference. In this context, a reference is a very powerful thing; it's like an Apple event primed and ready to communicate with an object in that application's world. A reference can be a great convenience, or it can be a danger: if you're not careful, you can send that Apple event and tell that scriptable application to do something you never intended. Unfortunately, Apple-Script goes to some lengths to make it difficult for you to know that you've got a reference in the first place! This chapter explains what references are and how to know when you've got one. It also shows how to make a reference deliberately, and how to do some powerful things with references.

 The phrase "by reference," as in "Set by Reference" in Chapter 7 and "Pass by Reference" in Chapter 9, is *not* what this chapter is about. When you pass a list "by reference" as a parameter to a handler, you do not pass a reference; you pass a list in a certain way. To make things even more complicated, we'll talk about passing a reference as a way to simulate passing by reference! The identity of the terminology is unfortunate but unavoidable.

Reference as Target

It's hard to explain what a *reference* is. In a sense, it is simply a complete target, such as `folder 1 of application "Finder"`. But it isn't the target "out there" in the world; it's the target as expressed in your code. This way of putting it makes a reference sound like *merely* an expression. But it's more than that. It's a value embodying such an expression.

To see what I mean, let's imagine obtaining such a value in a way that's very common—as a result returned by a scriptable application. Any time you fetch an attribute of a scriptable application, if the result is not a built-in datatype such as a string, it is likely to be a reference. For example:

```
tell application "Finder"
    set x to (get folder 1)
end tell
```

Now, what's x? On my machine, it's the following:

```
folder "Mannie" of desktop of application "Finder"
```

It sounds natural enough. But think a little more about this. What can it mean? What *is* x, really? A folder is a thing in the Finder's world. Surely the Finder cannot have literally handed this folder to our script. Rather, the Finder has handed us a *way of talking* about this folder, a *means of access* to this folder. That's a reference.

Reference as Incantation

One very productive way to think of a reference is as an incantation. It's like frozen speech. It encapsulates a bit of phraseology, a particular utterance. If a variable's value is a reference, that value is something you can use to access the object it refers to. What I mean by "use" is "say": a reference is an encapsulation of the words you would have to utter (in your code, of course) in order to access the object. In a way, a reference is like a miniature package of suspended evaluation; it's a little phrase that isn't evaluated until you use it. When you do use it, it works just as if you'd said the phrase at that point in your code.

For example, consider this code:

```
tell application "Finder"
    set x to (get folder 1)
    display dialog (get name of x) -- Mannie
end tell
```

The dialog shows the name of the folder. Why does this work? As we have said, x is this reference:

```
folder "Mannie" of desktop of application "Finder"
```

This means that *using* x is like *using those words*. Therefore, when you say this:

```
get name of x
```

it's just like saying this:

```
get name of folder "Mannie" of desktop of application "Finder"
```

A reference answers the "What would I have to say?" question. What would I have to say in order to speak of the Finder's folder 1? The Finder tells us one answer; I could say this:

```
folder "Mannie" of desktop of application "Finder"
```

You may be disconcerted at first by that fact that this is not what you *did* say. You said folder 1, referring to the folder by index number; the Finder said folder "Mannie", referring to it by name. You didn't say of desktop; the Finder did. You shouldn't worry about this. You just have to have faith, when an application gives you a reference, that this reference will access the thing you asked for access to.

Preresolution of Terminology

When the time comes to use a reference, you don't have to be in the context of a tell block. The reference is not only a complete target; it's a complete target whose vocabulary has *already been resolved* according to the context in which the reference was originally formed.

As a result, this works (see Chapter 11):

```
tell application "Finder"
    set x to (get folder 1)
end tell
name of x -- "Mannie"
```

How can this be? Look at just the last line of that code, in isolation:

```
name of x
```

That line contains no folder; it contains no Finder! Yet it causes a message to be sent to the Finder, asking for the name of a particular folder. The entire target:

```
folder "Mannie" of desktop of application "Finder"
```

is frozen into x. So the effect of the last line of that code is exactly—I mean *exactly*—as if you had said this:

```
tell application "Finder"
    get name of folder "Mannie" of desktop
end tell
```

The whole incantation involving the folder, the desktop, and the Finder is effectively frozen into x, ready to use. The terms folder and desktop have already been resolved, just as they would be in the context of a tell block targeting the Finder—because they were frozen into x in just such a context.

Being Careful with References

A reference is full of hidden power. You can send an Apple event without realizing it, merely by using a reference. It's easy to be lulled into thinking you'll always know when you're sending an Apple event to a target application, because you'll see the chain of ofs and tells culminating in the name of the application. But with a reference, you won't see any of that; the whole chain is hidden inside the reference.

The Event Log in a script editor application can be a big help here, because it tracks Apple events. When you execute this code:

```
tell application "Finder"
    set x to (get folder 1)
end tell
name of x -- "Mannie"
```

the Event Log says this:

```
tell application "Finder"
    get folder 1
    get name of folder "Mannie" of desktop
end tell
```

That makes it very clear what's happening.

A reference is mere words, not a magic pointer. Keep that fact firmly in mind, or you'll be confused when the unexpected happens. Consider the following:

```
tell application "Finder"
    set x to folder 1
    display dialog (get name of x) -- Mannie
    set name of x to "Moe"
    display dialog (get name of x) -- error!
end tell
```

The reason for the error is perfectly clear if you imagine a reference as an incantation. What's x during the first `display dialog` command? It's this:

```
folder "Mannie" of desktop of application "Finder"
```

And that's what it is during the second `display dialog` command, too; the incantation doesn't change. But at that point there is no `folder "Mannie"`—because we just changed the name of that folder to "Moe"! Our reference no longer works, because the incantation no longer speaks of the thing we want to speak of. The speech is frozen, while the world has changed.

Creating a Reference

We've seen that a reference might be handed to you by some application, but you can also create one yourself. To do so, you use the a `reference to` operator. (An abbreviation is `ref`, which is a lot easier to type. Intermediate abbreviation forms like a `ref` and `ref to` are legal as well.) For example:

```
set x to 100
set y to a reference to x
```

When you create a reference, the phrase you use is effectively what gets frozen into the reference as an incantation. Thus, in a situation where you would have been handed a reference anyway, asking explicitly for a reference could get you a different reference:

```
tell application "Finder"
    set x to a reference to folder 1
end tell
x -- folder 1 of application "Finder"
```

What you say is what you get. And what you say doesn't have to exist, either—it doesn't even have to make sense! As long as the compiler can resolve the terminology, it will compile your phrase. The fact that it's unusable doesn't matter; you're *not* using it, you're just freezing it for later. Thus no error arises, no matter how silly your phrase may be. Of course, later on if you *do* try to use it, you'll find out if it's a valid thing to say at that point:

```
tell application "Finder"
    set x to a reference to disk 99 of folder 1 of label "yoho"
end tell
get name of x -- error: Can't get name of disk 99 of folder 1 of label "yoho"
```

What that shows is that asking explicitly for a reference does not send an Apple event; it merely creates the Apple event so you can save it for later.

Identifying References

AppleScript goes to some lengths to hide the existence of references, making it remarkably difficult to find out that a value is a reference. Properly speaking, a reference should be a class, a datatype like string or integer (see "Class" in Chapter 11, and Chapter 13). If you ask a string about its class, it says string. If you ask an integer about its class, it says integer. But if you ask a reference about its class, it will never tell the truth and say reference.

```
set x to a reference to "hey"
set y to a reference to 9
tell application "Finder" to set z to folder 1
class of x -- string
class of y -- integer
class of z -- folder
```

Here are a couple of tricks you can use to learn that a value is a reference. (I don't guarantee any of them, but they do seem mostly to work.)

The reference coercion trick
> The only thing that can be coerced to a reference is a reference. If you try to coerce anything else to a reference, you'll get a runtime error. So try to coerce a value to a reference, and if there's no error, it is a reference. For example:
>
> ```
> tell application "Finder" to set x to folder 1
> x as reference -- no error; it's a reference
> ```

The editor value trick
> If a value, as shown in your script editor application, contains the word of, it is a reference. For example:
>
> ```
> tell application "Finder" to set x to folder 1
> x -- folder "Mannie" of...; it's a reference
> set x to a reference to y
> x -- y of «script»; it's a reference
> ```

When I'm debugging or developing a script, I like the second method best; I look at a variable's value and I can usually see right away whether it's likely to be a reference. If I'm writing code where the code itself needs to test whether something is a reference, I like the first method best. Here's a general handler that returns a boolean value telling whether its parameter is a reference:

```
on isRef(valueToTestAsRef)
    try
        valueToTestAsRef as reference
        return true
    on error
        return false
    end try
end isRef
-- and here's how to call it
tell application "Finder"
    set x to folder 1
end tell
isRef(x) -- true
set x to "haha"
isRef(x) -- false
isRef(a reference to x)) -- true
```

Dereferencing a Reference

Once you have a variable whose value is a reference, AppleScript behaves with confusing inconsistency when you try to use it. In some cases, you can't use the reference unless you explicitly dereference it; in other cases, AppleScript dereferences it for you implicitly when you use it. AppleScript can even behave both ways with one and the same reference.

When AppleScript performs implicit dereferencing, the reference is completely transparent; it acts precisely as if you were saying the incantation that's frozen inside it. This is exactly the same phenomenon noted in the previous section—you can't learn from a reference that it is a reference, because it acts as if it were the thing referred to.

```
tell application "Finder"
    set x to folder 1
end tell
name of x -- Mannie
class of x -- folder
set name of x to "Moe"
```

None of that ought to be possible. A reference's class isn't folder, and a reference doesn't have a name property that you can get and set. In this case, though, it happens that the reference is a reference *to a thing* whose class is folder and that has a name property. AppleScript dereferences the reference implicitly; it treats the reference as if it were the thing referred to.

But in this example, an attempt to use the same reference transparently runs up against a brick wall:

```
tell application "Finder"
    set x to a reference to name of folder 1
end tell
set x to "Moe"
```

If you were hoping that this code would set the name of the Finder's folder 1 to "Moe", you're doomed to disappointment. It didn't: you set the variable x to the string "Moe" (and you lost your reference).

The reason is that the transparency of references can't be permitted to destroy your access to your own variables. Thus, when you perform an assignment, not to a property of a variable that's a reference but to the variable itself, AppleScript stops treating the reference transparently. The assignment is an ordinary assignment to a variable; what's inside the shoebox is thrown away and a new value is put into the shoebox.

Similarly, the boolean equality and inequality operators do not treat references transparently by dereferencing them (see "Comparison Operators" in Chapter 15). Here's a simple example:

```
set x to 3
set y to a reference to x
x = y -- false
y = 3 -- false
```

There's no implicit dereferencing here, and 3 is not the same as a reference to x. With other operators, though, AppleScript does dereference, which makes for some paradoxical-looking results:

```
set x to 3
set y to a reference to x
x = y -- false
x + 0 = y + 0 -- true
x is not less than y and x is not greater than y -- true
```

In situations where AppleScript doesn't implicitly dereference a reference for you, you can dereference it yourself. The way you do this is with the contents of operator. So, this code successfully renames a folder in the Finder:

```
tell application "Finder"
    set x to a reference to name of folder 1
end tell
set contents of x to "Moe"
```

Here's another example:

```
set x to 10
set y to a reference to x
set contents of y to 20
x -- 20
```

Here's the equality example again:

```
set x to 3
set y to a reference to x
x = contents of y -- true
```

The contents of operator works on any value. If the value isn't a reference, the result of applying the contents of operator is simply the value itself. In this example, the use of the contents of operator (twice) is essentially pointless; AppleScript basically just throws it away, and you end up saying the very same thing you'd say if you simply omitted the words contents of from the code:

```
set x to contents of "Mannie"
contents of x -- "Mannie"
```

You can take advantage of this in dealing with the equality example. Let's say you don't know which of x and y is a reference. That's okay—dereference them both, as it does no harm:

```
set x to 3
set y to a reference to x
contents of x = contents of y -- true
```

However, this is not to imply that you can simply use the words "contents of" capriciously. They do mean something, after all! So, this will cause a runtime error:

```
set x to "Mannie"
set contents of x to "Moe" -- error
```

This is like saying set "Mannie" to "Moe", which doesn't work, because "Mannie" is a literal, not the name of a variable.

If a value is a reference to an object belonging to an application, the contents of operator might or might not get you a different reference. So, for example:

```
tell application "Finder"
    set x to folder 1
end tell
x -- folder "Mannie" of desktop of application "Finder"
set x to contents of x
x -- folder "Mannie" of folder "Desktop" of folder "mattneub" of ¬
    folder "Users" of startup disk of application "Finder"
set x to contents of x
x -- folder "Mannie" of folder "Desktop" of folder "mattneub" of ¬
    folder "Users" of startup disk of application "Finder"
```

The exact behavior here is entirely up to the target application, and doesn't have any particular significance. In each case you're just telling the application to do a get whose direct object is the very same "phrase" the application handed back to you previously as a reference. Whether the application returns the same phrase or a different phrase referring to the same object is entirely its own business.

Trouble with Contents

A problem arises when you're targeting an application whose dictionary defines a contents property for one of its object types. Applications shouldn't do this; it's bad behavior, because they're overlapping with a piece of AppleScript's own built-in vocabulary. In the context of a tell block directed at such an application, there is an ambiguity as to whether the word contents will be seen as the contents of operator or the application's contents property.

 I'm told that the problematic nature of the contents property is actually an AppleScript bug. And AppleScript itself is to blame for taking the lead here; it defines a contents property for its selection-object class, luring application developers into doing the same sort of thing.

An example of such an offender is BBEdit. In BBEdit, when you ask for a text element such as a word, it gives you a reference rather than a string. That's good, because it's then possible to access that element in its context and do things to it. But then BBEdit does something bad: it defines the contents property as your way of obtaining the actual string. But it can be quite tricky to get AppleScript to ask BBEdit for the contents of something, because it often sees this as an attempt to dereference a reference instead.

So this works to obtain an actual string:

```
tell application "BBEdit"
    set w to contents of word 4 of window 1
end tell
w -- "test"
```

But this doesn't:

```
tell application "BBEdit"
    set w to contents of (get word 4 of window 1)
end tell
w -- characters 11 thru 14 of text document 1 of application "BBEdit"
```

And therefore neither does this:

```
tell application "BBEdit"
    set x to word 4 of window 1
    set w to contents of x
end tell
w -- characters 11 thru 14 of text document 1 of application "BBEdit"
```

And of course if you start by asking for a reference, things are even worse:

```
tell application "BBEdit"
    set x to a reference to word 4 of window 1
    set x to contents of x
    set w to contents of x
end tell
w -- characters 11 thru 14 of text document 1 of application "BBEdit"
```

It looks as if, having gotten a reference to a word, you can never get from there to the actual text of that word. But there's a trick:

```
tell application "BBEdit"
    set x to a reference to word 4 of window 1
    get contents of text of x -- "test"
end tell
```

The proper behavior would have been for the application to define some other term for obtaining the contents of a thing. A typical approach is to use the term content instead. No confusion arises; AppleScript doesn't know that this is the singular of contents. Microsoft Word, Entourage, Apple Mail, and AppleScript Studio are examples of applications that do this.

Creating References to Variables

You can't make a reference to a local variable. Well, you can, but if you try to use it you'll get a mysterious error. For example:

```
local x
set x to {1, 2, 3}
set y to a reference to x
get item 1 of y -- error: Can't make item 1 of x into type reference
```

But a reference can itself be stored *in* a local variable:

```
local y
set x to {1, 2, 3}
set y to a reference to x
get item 1 of y -- 1
```

You can make a reference to anything that isn't a local, such as a global or a top-level entity:

```
script myScript
    property x : 5
    set y to a reference to x
    set contents of y to y + 1
    display dialog x
end script
run myScript -- 6
```

That works just as well from outside of the script object:

```
script myScript
    property x : 5
    display dialog x
end script
tell myScript
    set y to a reference to its x
    set contents of y to y + 1
    run -- 6
end tell
```

Reference as Parameter

You can pass a value that is a reference as a parameter to a handler, and it remains a reference. So, for example:

```
local x
tell application "Finder"
    set x to folder 1
end tell
on setName(theRef)
    set name of theRef to "Jack"
end setName
setName(x)
```

That code successfully changes the name of a folder in the Finder.

You can pass as a parameter a reference to anything you can usefully make a reference to. Thus, the reference to operator almost provides a solution to the problem of passing by reference (see Chapter 9):

```
on doubleRef(theRef)
    set contents of theRef to 2 * theRef
end doubleRef
script s
    property x : 5
    display dialog x
end script
doubleRef(a reference to s's x)
run s -- 10
```

But this solution is not completely general, and indeed no completely general solution is possible, because you can't usefully make a reference to a local. Also you'll notice that the example worked only because the handler doubleRef knew *in advance* that it was going to be handed a reference—it explicitly dereferenced the reference in order to change the thing referred to. So passing a reference is a way to allow a handler to change a value in place, but this is not the same thing as passing by reference, and it doesn't work if the value to be changed is a local variable.

The use of a reference as a parameter can permit a handler to perform dynamic targeting. As long as a handler doesn't use any vocabulary that depends on a specific target, it can target an application whose identity is not known until runtime. In this example, the same code in the same handler is able to target the Finder and Mailsmith indiscriminately:

```
on getNameOfAnything(theRef)
    return name of theRef
end getNameOfAnything
tell application "Finder" to set x to folder 1
tell application "Microsoft Entourage" to set y to message 1 of in box folder
getNameOfAnything(x) -- "Mannie"
getNameOfAnything(y) -- "Order Confirmation"
```

A handler or script object can also return a reference. Of course, this cannot be a reference to a local variable. It must be a reference to something that the handler or script object can obtain a reference to. For example, it can be a reference to a property:

```
script myScript
    property x : 3
    return a reference to x
end script
set y to run myScript
set contents of y to 10
myScript's x -- 10
```

Or it can be a reference obtained from a scriptable application:

```
on getFolderByNumber(n)
    local x
    tell application "Finder"
        set x to folder n
    end tell
    return x
end getFolderByNumber
getFolderByNumber(1) -- folder "Moe" of desktop of application "Finder"
```

And it can be a reference to a parameter that is a reference or was passed by reference. You can get some rather powerful effects that way:

```
on findInList(what, L)
    repeat with i from 1 to count L
        if item i of L is what then
            return (a reference to item i of L)
        end if
    end repeat
    return
end findInList
local pep
set pep to {"Mannie", "Moe", "Jack"}
set contents of findInList("Moe", pep) to "Larry"
pep -- {"Mannie", "Larry", "Jack"}
```

That's quite similar to return-by-reference in C++. The handler findInList returns a reference to a particular item of L; in this case, it returns the reference item 2 of {"Mannie", "Moe", "Jack"}. Thus what is returned from findInList is a direct pointer to the desired item of the original list, and so we can change that item, in place.

CHAPTER 13

Datatypes

A *datatype* is a classification of a value; every value is of one datatype or another. This is what AppleScript calls a class. For example, `string` is a datatype, `integer` is a datatype, and so forth. AppleScript provides a number of native datatypes; this chapter describes them.

Scriptable applications can extend the language through additional classes. For example, the Finder implements a `folder` class. But such additional classes are confined to the application that defines them; a value returned by a scriptable application must be either a reference to an object belonging to that application or one of AppleScript's native datatypes.

Script objects, handlers, and references are not dealt with in this chapter (see respectively Chapters 8, 9, and 12). The details of *coercion*, the conversion of certain values from one datatype to another, will be explained in Chapters 14 and 15.

Application

The *application* class is used mainly to specify a target. This, in effect, is the primary act of AppleScript programming. You specify a target so that you can send messages to it, and sending messages to an application is the purpose of AppleScript.

You specify an application using an object string specifier—the word `application` followed by a string representing the application's name or (colon-delimited) pathname. An abbreviation for `application` is `app`. For further details on how to target an application using an application specifier, see "Local Applications" in Chapter 23.

Machine

The *machine* class is used to form a machine specifier, which appears in conjunction with an application specifier to target an application running on another computer. See "Remote Applications" in Chapter 23 for further details.

Data

The *data* class represents raw data, a stream of bytes. It's a catch-all for situations when a value cannot be displayed in any other way. For example:

```
tell application "Finder"
    activate
    get (the clipboard)
end tell
-- {«class RECT»:«data RECT0000000000B40075», ¬
    picture:«data PICTFA480000000000B40075001102FF0C...»}, and so on for pages and pages
```

Here we see a record with two items; the value of each item (after the colon) is a data object. What was on the clipboard was a picture, and the Script Editor can't display it (though Script Debugger can), so it shows you the data as a sequence of hex bytes. Evidently what we have is a rectangle (probably the bounds of the picture) and a picture resource in PICT format.

It is also possible to form a data object yourself, by typing just the sort of thing you see here: the word data, a space, and then the resource type and the data, in guillemets (« »). However, this is an advanced technique and shouldn't arise much in real life (though an example of it appears later in this chapter).

Boolean

A *boolean* is a datatype consisting of exactly two possible values: true and false. The main use for a boolean is as a condition in a control statement, such as if or repeat while (see Chapter 19). It often appears also as a way of setting yes-or-no options in a command; for example, the choose file command (discussed in Chapter 21) lets you submit a boolean to indicate whether invisible files and folders should be displayed. Some common commands, such as exists, return a boolean. AppleScript has a number of operators that generate or combine booleans (listed in Chapter 15).

```
class of true -- boolean
class of (1 < 2) -- boolean
```

Integer, Real, and Number

The *integer* and *real* datatypes are the numeric classes. Integers and reals are used for arithmetic calculation (Chapter 15 will discuss AppleScript's operators for this purpose); they are also used, of course, for communicating numeric values between your script and a target application.

```
class of 1 -- integer
class of 1.1 -- real
```

A literal integer is a series of digits, possibly preceded by a minus sign. The maximum integer is 536870911, positive or negative. Any integer value outside this range is implicitly coerced to a real. This is a very strange limit—it's $2^{29}-1$, two bits short of the four-byte standard—and I don't know the reason for it.

A literal real is a series of digits with a decimal point, possibly preceded by a minus sign. You may also use "scientific notation": that's a number followed by small or capital e, possibly followed by a plus sign or a minus sign, followed by an integer. AppleScript might rewrite a scientific notation number for you, but it remains a real:

```
1e2 -- rewritten: 100.0
2.1e26 -- rewritten: 2.1E+26
```

A literal number consisting of too many digits (I have not been able to determine exactly how many is too many) may be rounded, or may be rewritten using scientific notation, at compile time. Alternatively, it may generate an incomprehensible error:

```
0.123456789012345 -- Syntax error. some object [sic]
```

You can't include a comma as a thousands separator in a literal number.

The class number is purely for purposes of coercion. See "Number, String, and Date Coercions" in Chapter 14.

A dictionary may occasionally mention a class small integer, which is two bytes (ranging from -32768 to 32767). You can create one by coercion, but there should be little need to do so (though an example appears later in this chapter). Small integers are typically used transparently; they evidently become integers before you get a look at them:

```
set x to 4 as small integer
class of x -- integer
class of (ASCII number "a") -- integer, even though the dictionary says "small integer"
```

There is also a class double integer, which is eight bytes. This is sometimes used when communicating with the system, and seems to be simply a real within the integer range. Again, there should be little need to create one; a double integer in your code is reported as a real. There are other rarely encountered numeric classes, such as fixed, extended real, and so forth, which are reported as (or transparently coerced to) integer or real.

Date

A *date* is a date-time. A literal date is an object string specifier. In constructing a date, you may use any string value that can be interpreted as a date, a time, or a date-time; AppleScript (or more probably the system) is quite liberal in what it will accept, provided that the string makes sense in terms of the date and time format settings in your International System Preferences. AppleScript supplies missing values such as today's date (if you give only a time) or this year (if you don't give a year) or midnight (if you give only a date). To form a date object for the current date-time, use the current date scripting addition command (see Chapter 21).

AppleScript presents a literal date specifier in long date-time format in accordance with your International preferences. It does this even within your script, on decompilation, if you use a literal string in a date specifier:

```
date "5/25/2005" -- rewritten: date "Wednesday, May 25, 2005 12:00:00 AM"
```

If the expression "5/25/2005" isn't a date according to your International preferences, this code won't compile. For example, if you have U.K. settings, you'd need to type date "25/5/2005". Scripts that form dates dynamically by coercing from a string, like most of the examples in this section, are subject to the same caveat (and are thus not very portable).

AppleScript knows nothing of time zones, and assumes the Gregorian calendar even for dates before its invention. An attempt to form a date specifier earlier than the start of 1000 AD will fail:

```
set s to "December 25, 800"
date s -- date "Monday, December 25, 2800 12:00:00 AM"
```

Confusingly, however, you can obtain such a date by calculation:

```
set s to "December 25, 1000"
set d to date s
set year of d to 800
d -- date "Monday, December 25, 0800 12:00:00 AM"
```

Internally, a date is stored as a number of seconds; precision higher than a second is thrown away during calculation. There are three ways to do calculations with dates:

Date arithmetic

You can derive one date from another by adding or subtracting a number representing seconds. (Chapter 16 lists some global properties that can help you calculate the desired number of seconds.) One date may also be subtracted from another to obtain the number of seconds between them. For example:

```
set s to "8/10/2005 4:45 PM"
(date s) + 56845 -- date "Thursday, August 11, 2005 8:32:25 AM"
```

Date specifier property

By a curious syntax, a new time part or date part may be combined with an existing date by treating a date specifer as a property of another date. The result is a new date object. For example:

```
set s to "2/25"
set d to date s -- date "Friday, February 25, 2005 12:00:00 AM"
set d2 to date "10:30" of d -- date "Friday, February 25, 2005 10:30:00 AM"
set d3 to date "1/24" of d2 -- date "Monday, January 24, 2005 10:30:00 AM"
```

Date properties

Setting a property of a date mutates the date in place. You can change a property in a calendrically impossible way, and AppleScript will compensate:

```
set s to "May 31"
set d to date s
set month of d to June
d -- date "Friday, July 1, 2005 12:00:00 AM"
```

Now that a date has hours, minutes, and seconds properties (new in Tiger), this technique is actually useful for date calculations:

```
set s to "8/10/2005 10:00 PM"
set d to date s
set hours of d to ((hours of d) + 100)
d -- date "Monday, August 15, 2005 2:00:00 AM"
```

When you use set (as opposed to copy) to set a variable to a value that is a date, you set the variable *by reference*. This means that the date is not copied; the variable's name becomes a new name for the date, in addition to any names for the date that may already exist. The same is true when a date is passed as a parameter to a handler. This special treatment is in common between lists, records, dates, and script objects, the four datatypes that can be mutated in place. (See "Set by Reference" in Chapter 7 and "Pass by Reference" in Chapter 9.)

For example:

```
set s to "May 31"
set d to date s
set d2 to d
set month of d2 to June
d -- date "Friday, July 1, 2005 12:00:00 AM"
```

Date Properties

The following are the properties of a date value:

year
> The year number. A positive integer.

month
> The month. A constant (not a string!): January, February, and so on. However, you can set a date's month using an integer (this is new in Tiger).

day
> The day of the month. A positive integer.

hours
> Whole hours since the start of the day (at midnight). A positive integer.

minutes
> Whole minutes since the start of the hour. A positive integer.

seconds
> Seconds since the start of the minute. A positive integer (hours, minutes, and seconds are new in Tiger).

time
> Seconds since the start of the day (at midnight). A positive integer.

weekday
> A constant (not a string!): Monday, Tuesday, and so on. In practice this property is read-only; setting it is not an error, but it has no effect.

```
date string
short date string
time string
```
A string consisting of just the date or time part of the date-time. In practice these properties are read-only; setting them results in a stack overflow (I'd have to call that a bug). They are formatted in accordance with your International preferences.

The time string and date string are suitable for combining with an existing date to form a new date, using the syntax described earlier. For example:

```
set s to "5/25/2005"
set d1 to date s
set t to "4PM"
set d2 to date t
set d3 to date (time string of d2) of d1 -- date "Wednesday, May 25, 2005 4:00:00 PM"
```

String

A *string* is the basic text datatype. It has the MacRoman encoding; see "Unicode Text," later in this chapter, for more about the implications of this. Strings are your primary medium for communicating text information to a scriptable application. AppleScript provides some basic string operators (discussed in Chapter 15).

A literal string is delimited by quotation marks:

```
set s to "howdy"
class of s -- string
```

The empty string is symbolized by "".

In typing a string literal, you may enter certain characters in "escaped" form; they are listed in Table 13-1. These are the only "escaped" characters.

Table 13-1. "Escaped" string literals

What to type	ASCII equivalent	Result
\"	ASCII character 34	Quotation marks
\t	ASCII character 9	Tab
\r	ASCII character 13	Return
\n	ASCII character 10	Newline
\\	ASCII character 92	Backslash

Other untypeable characters may be generated using the ASCII character scripting addition command and incorporated into a string by concatenation (see chapters 15 and 21). There are also a few global properties expressing character values (listed in Chapter 16); these too can be incorporated into a string by concatenation.

After compilation, any tab, return, and newline characters within a literal string are unescaped and turned into whitespace; they remain intact, but you can no longer see directly what characters they are, which is a pity (see "Lines" in Chapter 5). Script Debugger, however, can display such "invisibles."

Don't confuse AppleScript's built-in string type and its native manipulations of this type with how scriptable applications implement their own string behavior. When you ask an application to perform manipulations on text of its own, it might behave differently from AppleScript. For example:

```
tell application "Tex-Edit Plus"
    set text of window 1 to "Now is the winter"
    get word after character 3 of text of window 1 -- "is"
end tell
get word after character 3 of "Now is the winter" -- error: Can't get word after "w"
```

In the tell block, everything belongs to Tex-Edit Plus; you're speaking of Tex-Edit's implementation of the text class, and you're taking advantage of Tex-Edit's idea of a word and a character and what can be done with them. In the last line, you're working with a string and talking to AppleScript itself.

String Properties

The following are the properties of a string. They are read-only.

length
> The number of characters of the string. You can get this same information by sending the count message to the string.

quoted form
> A rendering of the string suitable for handing to the shell as an argument to a command. The string is wrapped in single quotation marks and internal quotation marks are escaped.

You probably shouldn't look at the result of quoted form, because you might not understand it; it's meant for the shell's eyes, not yours, and an extra level of (mis)representation is added by AppleScript as it shows you the string. For example:

```
quoted form of "life's a \"bowl\" of cherries"
-- "'life'\\''s a \"bowl\" of cherries'"
```

That looks pretty dreadful, but it's right, as you'll discover if you hand it to the shell:

```
set s to quoted form of "life's a \"bowl\" of cherries"
do shell script "echo " & s -- "life's a \"bowl\" of cherries"
```

String Elements

The following are the elements of a string. Bear in mind that you can't set them; you cannot mutate a string in place! Elements may be specified by index number, by range, or with every.

character
> A string representing a single character of the string.

word
> A string representing a single word of the string. It has no spaces or other word-boundary punctuation.

paragraph
> A string representing a single paragraph (or line) of the string. It has no line breaks. AppleScript treats a return, a newline, or both together (CRLF) as a line break.

text
> A run of text. Its purpose is to let you obtain a single continuous string using a range element specifier; see "Range" in Chapter 11. So, for example:
>
> ```
> words 1 thru 3 of "Now is the winter" -- {"Now", "is", "the"}
> text from word 1 to word 3 of "Now is the winter" -- "Now is the"
> ```

text item
> A "field" of text, where the field delimiter is AppleScript's text item delimiters property.

The text item property needs some explanation. There is a global property (see Chapter 16) called text item delimiters. You can set this to any string you like. (The documentation claims that the text item delimiters is a list of strings, but in fact only the first item of the list is effective.) When you speak of a text item of a string, the current value of the text item delimiters is used to "split" the string; no text item contains the value of the text item delimiters, and the number of text items of a string is exactly one more than the number of times it contains the value of text item delimiters. For example:

```
set text item delimiters to ":"
text items of "feathers:Users:mattneub" -- {"feathers", "Users", "mattneub"}
set text item delimiters to "tt"
text items of "Matt" -- {"Ma", ""}
set text item delimiters to "s"
set howMany to (count text items of "Mississippi") - 1
howMany -- 4, the number of s's in Mississippi
```

The value of the text item delimiters persists as long as this instance of the AppleScript scripting component does. Because you might run more than one script in the presence of this scripting component, any of which might set the text item delimiters, it is wise to make no assumptions as to the value of the text item delimiters. In other words, don't use it without setting it first. Apple's documentation makes a big deal of this, but it's really no different from any of the other AppleScript global properties, such as pi (see Chapter 16).

Observe that other string elements may equally be used to split a string, often more conveniently: characters splits a string into individual characters, words splits a string at its word boundaries, and paragraphs splits a string at its line breaks.

Unicode Text

Like the Macintosh itself, the AppleScript string class has long been bedeviled by the existence of text encodings representing characters outside its own native encoding, which is MacRoman. With the coming of Mac OS X, this problem is essentially solved at system level: text is now Unicode. Unicode expresses tens of thousands of characters in a single massive encoding, and in its fullest form will express about a million characters, embracing every character of every written language in history. Unfortunately, AppleScript precedes Mac OS X, and the string class is still its primary text class. Over the years, various secondary classes have been fudged into Apple-Script in an attempt to increase a string's representational power and to improve AppleScript's compatibility with text in the world around it. At the moment, the most important of these is the *Unicode text* class, which has the UTF-16 encoding.

Text supplied by the system is often Unicode text rather than a string. For example:

```
tell application "Finder" to set x to (get name of disk 1)
class of x -- Unicode text
```

Similarly, some Mac OS X–native applications, such as TextEdit, return text values as Unicode text.

The trouble is that Unicode text remains very much a second-class citizen within AppleScript. Perhaps someday all AppleScript text will be Unicode text, but that day has not yet come. A literal string (the stuff between quotes in your code) is still a string, not Unicode text. Thus, you can't even enter a Unicode string directly; you can try, but non-MacRoman characters are lost at compile time. AppleScript's supplied string manipulation commands, such as the scripting addition command ASCII character, don't work outside the MacRoman range. The character string element knows nothing of composed characters. Unicode text display (in a result, for example) isn't particularly good either; many non-MacRoman characters are not displayed properly. Unicode text communication between a script and a Unicode-savvy application works, but problems can arise.

Then there's the business of how a Unicode text value will interact with a string value, or with a command that expects a string. The good news is that in Tiger such interaction is much improved over previous versions of AppleScript. Whatever you can do to a string, you can do to Unicode text. If you get an element of a Unicode text value, the result is Unicode text. If you concatenate Unicode text and a string, the result is Unicode text (in earlier versions of AppleScript this was not true, which was a big source of trouble). You can explicitly coerce between a string and Unicode text; AppleScript also implicitly coerces for you as appropriate. And scripting addition commands have now mostly been revised to accept Unicode text parameters.

Forming Unicode Text

As I mentioned earlier, you can't type a non-MacRoman literal directly. This section provides some workarounds, all of them more or less horrible.

Behind the scenes, a Unicode text string is a `'utxt'` resource consisting of a stream of UTF-16 hex bytes. This suggests that you can form such a resource directly as raw data (see "Data," earlier in this chapter) and coerce it to Unicode text. For example:

```
set n to «data utxt03910313030103BB03BA03B703C303C403B903C2»
set n to n as Unicode text
tell application "Finder"
    set name of folder "Mannie" to n
end tell
```

(To enter guillemets on a U.S. keyboard layout, type Option-\ and Option-Shift-\.) The result is shown in Figure 13-1. We've successfully given a folder the name of an Ancient Greek tragedy, creating that name *ex nihilo* in AppleScript.

Figure 13-1. A Finder item named with Unicode text

Another approach is to write the data out to a file and read it back in, which works because AppleScript gives you more ways to treat file data than it gives you to treat text data. Here's an example (on reading and writing files, see Chapter 21). We start with a decimal representation of the same bytes as in the previous example; we write these bytes to a file:

```
set L to {913, 787, 769, 955, 954, 951, 963, 964, 953, 962}
set s to (path to desktop as string) & "tempFile"
set f to a reference to file s
open for access f with write permission
repeat with aChar in L
    write aChar to f as small integer -- two bytes per character
end repeat
close access f
```

If we were to open this file as UTF-16 in a word processor, we would see that we've successfully written out the desired string (Figure 13-2).

We can obtain this string by reading the file back into AppleScript as Unicode text:

```
set s to (path to desktop as string) & "tempFile"
set f to a reference to file s
open for access f
```

Figure 13-2. A Unicode text file generated in AppleScript

```
set s to read f as Unicode text
close access f
```

After that, s is the desired Unicode text. There is also support for exchanging data with a file as UTF-8; but there is no internal support for AppleScript text in UTF-8 encoding, so you have to express this as «class utf8», and if you read text as UTF-8, it is converted to UTF-16.

Still another approach is to talk to the shell. The do shell script scripting addition command returns Unicode text by default, so if you can get a Unix scripting language, such as Perl, to construct the string for you, you can obtain it. So:

```
set p to "print pack(\"U10\", 0x0391, 0x0313, 0x0301, 0x03BB, 0x03BA, " & ¬
    "0x03B7, 0x03C3, 0x03C4, 0x03B9, 0x03C2);"
set s to do shell script "perl -e " & quoted form of p
```

After that, s is that same Unicode text. No doubt there's a better way to do this (there's always a better way to do things in Perl), but you get the idea.

Other Text Classes

Various older text classes, fudged into AppleScript (as I mentioned before) to grapple with the problem of encodings, are still around. These are generally to be avoided nowadays, though they can crop up occasionally.

For example, the international text class was a way of representing text in accordance with a particular language and script (where "script" means a writing system); each language–script combination had its own rules (an encoding) for how particular sequences of bytes were mapped to characters (glyphs). The mess created by this multiplicity of encodings is the reason why Unicode is a Good Thing.

The styled text class is another case in point. A *style* is an attribute of text, such as its font and size, whether it's underlined, that sort of thing. AppleScript defines a styled text class, but you can't manipulate it in any interesting way; in fact, you can barely even detect that it exists, because if you happen to encounter one and ask for its class, you're told it's a string. Nor is it used very much for representing style information; most applications that provide scriptable text styling use a more sophisticated class that lets you access and manipulate styles. Nevertheless, you might encounter styled text from time to time, such as when retrieving text data from the clipboard. You can detect that this has happened by coercing the text to a record:

```
tell application "Finder"
    activate
    set x to (the clipboard)
end tell
x as record
-- {«class ktxt»:"test", ¬
«class ksty»:«data styl000100000000000D000A00100000000C000000000000»}
```

As you can see, the string is actually made up of text information and style information. But the text information is all that AppleScript is normally willing to show you.

The style resource can be used (perhaps one should say "misused") as a way of carrying encoding information, by associating a font with an encoding. When you coerce an alias to a string, for example, AppleScript actually returns styled text, on the off chance (I suppose) that if the pathname contains any characters outside the Mac-Roman encoding, the extra encoding information in the style resource can help represent them. But AppleScript conceals from you the fact that it's doing this:

```
class of ((path to desktop) as string) -- string
```

Despite AppleScript's answer here, the result is really styled text. As before, we can detect this fact by coercing to a record:

```
(path to desktop) as string
result as record -- {«class ktxt»:"feathers:Users:mattneub:Desktop:", «class ksty»:
«data styl000100000000010000E00030000000C000000000000»}
```

Similarly, any Unicode text coerced to a string is secretly coerced to styled text:

```
"howdy" as Unicode text as string as record -- {«class ktxt»:"howdy", «class ksty»:
«data styl000100000000010000E00030000000C000000000000»}
```

To make things even more complicated, international text and styled text sometimes give the impression of being interchangeable. For example:

```
get name of application "Tex-Edit Plus"
```

According to Tex-Edit Plus's dictionary, the result should be international text, but in fact it is styled text. All this is fairly mystifying, and the undeniable impression is that AppleScript text handling is messy and it's trying to conceal the mess (mostly by sweeping it under the carpet).

File and Alias

A *file* object is a reference to a file or folder on disk. To construct one, use an object string specifier—the word file followed by a string representing a colon-delimited pathname:

```
file "feathers:Users:mattneub:"
```

By "colon-delimited" I mean an old-style Macintosh-type path. This is not the same as the new-style Unix-type path (new to Mac users, anyway), also known as a POSIX path. AppleScript has a long history on Macintosh, so it is not surprising that its native representation of file paths is not the Unix representation. Macintosh paths start with a disk name, and the delimiter between the disk name, folder names, and filename is a colon. A pathname ending in a colon is a folder or a disk. (A partial pathname, one whose first element is not a disk, is taken to start inside the "current directory," but the interpretation of this notion is unreliable, and partial pathnames should be avoided.)

Oddly, you can't assign a file object specifier to a variable, or return it as a value. If you try, you get a runtime error message:

```
set x to file "feathers:Users:mattneub:"
-- error: Can't make file "feathers:Users:mattneub:" into type reference
```

Instead, you must generate a reference to the file object, like this:

```
set x to a reference to file "feathers:Users:mattneub:"
x -- file "feathers:Users:mattneub:" of «script»
```

A file specifier is not resolved until the script actually runs. This means that the item on disk need not exist at compile time. At runtime, however, when the file specifier is handed to some command, either the item must exist, or, if the command proposes to create it, everything in the path must exist except for the last element, the name of the item you're about to create. Otherwise the command will generate a runtime error on the grounds that it can't find or create the item. We've already met one command that accepts a file specifier to create a file—store script (see "Compiled Script Files as Script Objects" in Chapter 8).

Alias

An *alias* object is very much like a file object. You can form an alias specifier in just the same way as you form a file specifier, and an alias object can often be used in the same places where a file object would be used. But there are some important differences:

- If an alias specifier uses a literal pathname string, then the item on disk that it represents must exist at compile time.

- If an alias specifier uses a string variable, then the item on disk that it represents must exist when the specifier is encountered at runtime.

- An alias can be assigned directly to a variable as its value.

- An alias is an alias. That means it has the wonderful ability of a Macintosh alias to continue pointing to an item on disk even if the item is moved or renamed.

Alias objects are commonly used by scriptable applications as a way of returning a pointer to an item on disk. For example:

```
tell application "BBEdit"
    get file of window 1 -- alias "feathers:Users:mattneub:someFile"
end tell
```

In that code, the term file is merely the name of a window property, and has nothing to do with the file class from the previous section. (Well, almost nothing. Its raw four-letter code is the same as that of the file class. See Chapter 20.)

There is a longstanding confusion in AppleScript about how to specify the file to which a new document is to be saved. The dictionaries of many applications, such as GraphicConverter and TextEdit, say that the save command takes an alias. But this is impossible, because an alias must exist in order to speak of it, and clearly it doesn't, as what you're trying to do is create it. Because the dictionary is lying, you must experiment in order to find out what the application really wants. For example:

```
tell application "GraphicConverter"
    set s to "feathers:Users:mattneub:Desktop:joconde"
    save window 1 in alias s as PICT
    -- error: File feathers:Users:mattneub:Desktop:joconde wasn't found
end tell
```

That code fails because the file doesn't exist. If you write the same code using a file specifier, there is a different mysterious error:

```
tell application "GraphicConverter"
    set s to "feathers:Users:mattneub:Desktop:joconde"
    save window 1 in file s as PICT
    -- error: GraphicConverter got an error: Can't get window 1. Access not allowed
end tell
```

After a great deal of banging around, you finally try this, and it works:

```
tell application "GraphicConverter"
    set s to "feathers:Users:mattneub:Desktop:joconde"
    save window 1 in s as PICT
end tell
```

It turns out that what GraphicConverter wanted was a pathname. Indeed, some newer applications' dictionaries explicitly ask for Unicode text, implying that they expect a pathname. Even then you're not home free, because there are two forms of pathname string. Only experimentation will reveal whether an application wants a Macintosh (colon-delimited) path or a POSIX-type path here.

Other File Classes

You can specify a file using a POSIX-type path, where the delimiters are slashes and an initial slash means the top level of the startup disk. To do so, use an object string specifier for a POSIX file instead of a file. If the path is a literal string, or if you ask to see a POSIX file as a result, AppleScript presents it as a file specifier with the delimiters changed to colons. So, for example, if I write this:

```
POSIX file "/Users/mattneub/"
```

AppleScript changes it to this at compile time:

```
file "features:Users:mattneub:"
```

The really weird part is that, despite appearances, this is not the same thing as a file object specifier! There are two ways to know this. First, it describes itself as a different class: it says it's a «class furl», which I take to be a file URL. Second, unlike a file specifier, a file URL can be assigned directly to a variable.

To see how insane this situation is, start with this (uncompiled):

```
set x to POSIX file "/Users/mattneub"
set y to file "feathers:Users:mattneub"
```

When you run that, you get this:

```
set x to file "feathers:Users:mattneub"
set y to file "feathers:Users:mattneub"
-- error: Can't make file "feathers:Users:mattneub" into type reference
```

The two lines look identical, but the first line is a file URL. AppleScript complains only about the second line, which is a file object specifier. But now if you deliberately compile the script and run it again, look what happens:

```
set x to file "feathers:Users:mattneub"
-- error: Can't make file "feathers:Users:mattneub" into type reference
set y to file "feathers:Users:mattneub"
```

The file URL in the first line has been turned into a file object specifier, and now AppleScript complains about the first line! You can avoid a lot of this madness by using a variable instead of a literal in your specifier:

```
set s1 to "/Users/mattneub"
set x to POSIX file s1
set s2 to "feathers:Users:mattneub"
set y to a reference to file s2
```

The string used to form a file URL specifier must not contain a colon. If it does, various bad things can happen, depending on the version of AppleScript and the environment: an incorrect pathname might be generated (a bug in AppleScript), or the script could fail to compile or to run (silently, in the Tiger version of Script Editor—a bug in Script Editor).

The string used to form a file URL specifier need not denote an existing path:

```
set s to "/alice/in/wonderland"
POSIX file s -- file "feathers:alice:in:wonderland"
```

You may regard this as a bug, but in any case, don't use such a string in the first place. Similarly, don't form a file URL specifier with a string that does not start with a slash; partial pathnames are unreliable.

The file URL class pops up in various contexts, lurking behind the file class. For example, the choose file name scripting addition is documented as returning a file object, and appears to do so, but in reality it's a file URL.

A few old applications still expect or generate a deprecated, outmoded class called file specification (class 'fss '). For example:

```
tell application "BBEdit"
    set r to check syntax file "feathers:Users:mattneub:Desktop:testing.html"
    class of result_file of item 1 of r -- file specification
end tell
```

You can even form a file specification object using an object string specifier, but don't. They can behave oddly; that's why they are deprecated. The file class replaces the file specification class transparently. So stick to a file object and let the transparency work for you.

File Properties

The following is a property of a file, an alias, or a file URL:

POSIX path
This is the Unix-type pathname of the file. No element of the pathname need exist, but you should not deliberately misuse this feature: apply it only to valid files. When you do, it is very helpful; for example, it supplies the */Volumes* directory before the name of a nonstartup disk.

```
POSIX path of file "alice:in:wonderland" -- "/alice/in/wonderland", a misuse
POSIX path of file "gromit" -- "/Volumes/gromit/"
```

That is the only file property, but there are some scripting addition commands (see Chapter 21) that supplement the file classes in valuable ways. For example, you can obtain a host of useful information about a file, such as its creation date, whether it's invisible, whether it's a folder, how big it is, what application opens it, and lots of other cool stuff, with the info for command:

```
info for file "feathers:Users:mattneub:someFile"
```

The result comes back as a record, which is easy to read and well documented in the StandardAdditions dictionary, so I won't go into details here. You can also obtain a list of the names of a folder's contents with the list folder command. There are also commands for reading and writing a file, and there's even some interface for letting the user choose a file.

File Classes in Applications

Don't confuse the AppleScript file object with the file class as defined by a particular scriptable application. For example, the Finder defines a file class, but it's a completely different file class. One way you can tell this is that, on the one hand, it has no POSIX path property, and on the other hand, it has lots of elements and properties not defined in AppleScript itself. For example:

```
tell application "Finder"
    get owner of file "feathers:Users:mattneub:myFile" -- mattneub
end tell
```

You couldn't do that without the Finder, because the owner property is defined by the Finder. It's true that the second line appears to contain a file object specifier, but it doesn't. Rather, this is a name element specifier, just like saying folder "Mannie". It just so happens that the Finder lets you use a pathname as the "name" for many of its classes.

Another way to see that the Finder's file class is not AppleScript's file class is to try handing an AppleScript file object to the Finder. You can't do it:

```
set f to a reference to file "feathers:Users:mattneub:myFile"
tell application "Finder"
    get owner of f
    -- error: Can't make «class sown» of file "feathers:Users:mattneub:myFile" into type reference
end tell
```

What that error tells you is that you're not even targeting the Finder. The variable f is a file object reference belonging to your script, not an object in the Finder at all.

Similarly, the Finder's alias file class is not an alias object.

List

A *list* is a collection corresponding roughly to what many other languages would call an array—it's an ordered set of values. These values are its *items*. Each item can be of any datatype (including a list). Lists are returned by scriptable applications from element specifiers such as every and boolean tests. They are useful for passing as parameters to commands and handlers because they can contain any number of items. AppleScript provides some operators for testing the contents of a list and for concatenating lists to form a new list (see Chapter 15).

A literal list is delimited by curly braces. Its contents can be literal values, variable names, or any other expressions that AppleScript can evaluate meaningfully; they are separated by commas. The literal empty list is just a pair of curly braces:

```
set empty to {}
set pep to {"Mannie", "Moe"}
set pep3 to "Jack"
empty & pep & {pep3} -- {"Mannie", "Moe", "Jack"}
```

You can assign a list of values to a literal list of variable names or other references as a shorthand for performing multiple assignments. The assignments are performed pairwise in order: item 1 to item 1, item 2 to item 2, and so on. If the list of values is too long, the extra values are ignored; if it's too short, there's a runtime error. (See "Assignment and Retrieval" in Chapter 7 and "Assignment of Multiple Attributes" in Chapter 11.) For example:

```
tell application "Finder"
    set L to {name of folder 1, name of folder 2}
    set {oldname1, oldname2} to L
    set {name of folder 1, name of folder 2} to {"f1", "f2"}
end tell
```

When you use set (as opposed to copy) to set a variable to a value that is a list, you set the variable *by reference*. This means that the list is not copied; the variable's name becomes a new name for the list, in addition to any names for the list that may already exist. The same is true when a list is passed as a parameter to a handler. This special treatment is in common between lists, records, dates, and script objects, the four datatypes that can be mutated in place. (See "Set by Reference" in Chapter 7 and "Pass by Reference" in Chapter 9.) For example:

```
set L1 to {"Mannie", "Moe"}
set L2 to L1
set end of L1 to "Jack"
item 3 of L2 -- "Jack"
```

In a literal list, a variable representing a list, record, date, or script object is itself set by reference. For example:

```
set L1 to {"Mannie", "Moe"}
set L2 to {L1, "Pep"}
set end of L1 to "Jack"
item 3 of item 1 of L2 -- "Jack"
```

A list can be mutated in place in two ways: you can replace individual items, and you can add a new item to the beginning or end of a list. The reason is that a list is stored internally as a data structure called a *vector*. In this data structure, the items of the list are accessible with equal efficiency; if a list has 100 items, it doesn't matter whether you refer to item 1 or item 100—AppleScript can access the item instantly. By the same token, setting an existing item of a list to a new value is efficient, because all that happens is that the new value is copied to the location in memory where the old value used to be.

```
set L to {"Mannie", "Moe"}
set item 1 of L to "Larry"
L -- {"Larry", "Moe"}
```

Also, setting the beginning or end of a list (as a way of appending to the list) is efficient; nothing moves in memory except the new value, and the list is told it is one item longer than it was. So:

```
set L to {"Moe"}
set end of L to "Jack"
set beginning of L to "Mannie"
L -- {"Mannie", "Moe", "Jack"}
```

The speed and efficiency (and mutability) of a list is often a reason for using a list, instead of a string, for an extended series of operations, and then coercing to a string afterwards; an example appears in "Concatenation Operator" in Chapter 15. See Chapter 22 for some hints on speed of list access.

The vector implementation of a list has its downside, though: it means that there is no efficient way to insert an item into the middle of an existing list, or to delete an item of a list. Thus there are no built-in commands for these operations, nor can they be performed by mutation in place. You'll probably want to arm yourself with a small arsenal of list utility handlers. For an item-deletion handler, see "LISP-like-ness" in Chapter 4. See "Power Handler Tricks" in Chapter 9 for a filter handler, and "Reference as Parameter" in Chapter 12 for a find-in-list handler. Here's an item-insertion handler:

```
on listInsert(L, what, ix)
    if ix = 1 then
        return {what} & L
    else
        return {item 1 of L} & listInsert(rest of L, what, ix - 1)
    end if
end listInsert
listInsert({"Mannie", "Jack"}, "Moe", 2) -- {"Mannie", "Moe", "Jack"}
```

List Recursion

A surprising feature of AppleScript lists is that they can recurse. This feature is actually a natural consequence of the foregoing. We know that when you use set to assign a list as a value, you set by reference; you create a pointer to the existing list. We know that a list item can be a list. So if a list item is created using set, it's a pointer to a list. Well then, it can be a pointer to the *same* list. For example:

```
set L to {"Mannie", "Moe", "Jack"}
set end of L to L
count L -- 4
count item 4 of L -- 4
count item 4 of item 4 of item 4 of item 4 of item 4 of L -- 4
items 1 thru 3 of item 4 of item 4 of item 4 of L -- {"Mannie", "Moe", "Jack"}
```

Where did all these items of items of items come from? We've formed a recursive list. L now consists of four items. The first three items are unchanged. The fourth item of L is a pointer to L itself. So if we look at the fourth item of L, we dereference this pointer and presto, we're looking at L. The fourth item of that is a pointer to L itself—and so forth. In other words, this is not an infinite list in the sense that it genuinely goes infinitely deep or far in memory; if it were, flames would come out of your computer. It's just a data structure of four items that goes round and round in a tight little circle.

Multiple lists can mutually recurse:

```
set L1 to {"Mannie", "Moe", "Jack"}
set L2 to {"Curly", "Larry"}
set end of L1 to L2
set end of L2 to L1
item 1 of item 4 of L1 -- "Curly"
item 1 of item 3 of L2 -- "Mannie"
```

I don't know of any practical use for this curious feature, and I wouldn't count on its being supported in future versions.

Secondary List Classes

AppleScript contains a couple of built-in classes that are really just lists by another name, along with some coercion rules. For example, bounding rectangle is a list of four integers, rgb color is a list of three integers, and point is a list of two integers. There may be others like this that I haven't stumbled upon.

List Properties

The following are the properties of a list. They are all read-only.

length
> The number of items in the list. You can get the same information by sending the list the count message.

rest
> Everything in the list except its first item.

reverse
> The list in reverse order.

List Elements

The following are the elements of a list:

item
> An item of the list, specified by index number, by range, or with every.

classname
> An item whose class is *classname*, specified by index number, by range, or with every. This is the closest thing a list has to a boolean test element specifier. For example, you can't say:
>
> ```
> item 2 of {23, "skiddoo", "catch", 22} whose class is integer -- error
> ```
>
> but you can say:
>
> ```
> integer 2 of {23, "skiddoo", "catch", 22} -- 22
> ```
>
> This does not work if the class you're asking about is class (a known bug).

Record

A *record* is an unordered collection of name–value pairs. Each value may be of any type. Records are passed to a few important commands, such as make, and are returned by scriptable applications and scripting additions as a way of providing a "table" of information (see Chapter 21). They are useful for passing as parameters to handlers because they can contain any number of items. AppleScript provides some operators for testing the contents of a record and for concatenating records to form a new record (see Chapter 15).

A literal record looks like a literal list except that each item has a name. The name is separated from the corresponding value with a colon:

```
set R to {who:"Matt", town:"Ojai"}
```

There is no empty record as distinct from the empty list; the empty list is treated as the empty record for purposes of containment and concatenation. A record has no item elements, its items cannot be referred to by index number, and you can't talk about the beginning or end of a record.

You can assign a record of values to a literal record of variable names or other references as a shorthand for performing multiple assignment. The assignments are performed pairwise by name, independently. If the record of values includes names that aren't in the record of variables, the extra values are ignored; if it's missing any names that are in the record of variables, there's a runtime error. See "List," earlier in this chapter. For example:

```
local who, town
set {who:who, town:town} to {town:"Ojai", who:"Matt"}
{who, town} -- {"Matt", "Ojai"}
```

When you use set (as opposed to copy) to set a variable to a value that is a record, you set the variable *by reference*. This means that the record is not copied; the variable's name becomes a new name for the record, in addition to any names for the record that may already exist. The same is true when a record is passed as a parameter to a handler. This special treatment is in common between lists, records, dates, and script objects, the four datatypes that can be mutated in place. (See "Set by Reference" in Chapter 7 and "Pass by Reference" in Chapter 9.) For example:

```
set R2 to {who:"Matt", town:"Ojai"}
set R1 to R2
set who of R2 to "Jaime"
R1 -- {who:"Jaime", town:"Ojai"}
```

In a literal record, a variable representing a list, record, date, or script object is itself set by reference. For example:

```
set L to {"Mannie", "Moe"}
set R to {pep:L}
set end of R's pep to "Jack"
item 3 of L -- "Jack"
```

The only mutation you can perform in place on an existing record is to replace the value of an individual item by assignment. Other changes in the record require generation of a new record. So, for example, if you wish to add to a record an item with a name that doesn't already exist in that record, you must make a new record using concatenation:

```
set R to {who:"Matt", town:"Ojai"}
set who of R to "Jaime"
R -- {who:"Jaime", town:"Ojai"}
set R to R & {friend:"Steve"}
R -- {who:"Jaime", town:"Ojai", friend:"Steve"}
```

There is no penalty for concatenating an item with a name that already exists in a record, but it has no effect. For example:

```
set R to {who:"Matt", town:"Ojai"} & {who:"Jaime"}
R -- {who:"Matt", town:"Ojai"}
```

Clearly, order is all-important here, and you can use this fact to your advantage. Suppose you want to assign a friend value within a record. If the record already has such an item, you can do it by assignment. If it doesn't, you can do it by concatenation. But what if you don't know whether it has such an item or not? You can do it regardless by concatenating in the opposite order:

```
set R to {who:"Jaime", town:"Ojai"}
set R to {friend:"Steve"} & R
R -- {friend:"Steve", who:"Jaime", town:"Ojai"}

set R to {who:"Jaime", town:"Ojai", friend:"Matt"}
set R to {friend:"Steve"} & R
R -- {friend:"Steve", who:"Jaime", town:"Ojai"}
```

A record can recurse, for the same reason that a list can:

```
set R to {who:"Matt", town:"Ojai", cycle:null}
set cycle of R to R
who of cycle of cycle of cycle of cycle of R -- "Matt"
```

You can make records mutually recurse; you can even make a list and record that mutually recurse. Does anyone have an aspirin?

Record Properties

The following are the properties of a record:

length
> The number of items in the record. This property is read-only. You can get the same information by sending the record the count message.

The names of the items
> Every name of every item is a property of the record.

Please pretend now that I'm jumping up and down, waving a big red flag and screaming: *the names of a record's items are properties*. The names are not strings; the names are not any kind of variable or value. They are effectively tokens created by AppleScript at compile time, like the names of variables. Actually, these tokens are created in two different ways. If the name is an existing property or class name, the token is its four-letter code, and the item is stored as a property. Otherwise, it is a string and is called a *user property*; internally, user property–value pairs are stored as a list (called a 'usrf') of alternating names and values.

Thus, a record consisting of two predefined properties and two user properties actually contains three items internally: the two predefined properties, followed by a list of four items (the name and value of each user property). For example:

```
set R to {name:"Matt", character:"impeccable", town:"Ojai", age:51}
```

It happens that name is a property and character is a class implemented in Apple-Script itself, so these are tokenized as their four-letter codes, 'pnam' and 'cha ' respectively. But town and age are user properties, so the third item of storage in the record is a 'usrf' list containing the strings "town" and "age" and their values:

```
{
    'pnam':"Matt",
    'cha ':"impeccable",
    'usrf':[
        "town",
        "Ojai",
        "age",
        51
    ]
}
```

You can avoid having AppleScript treat existing property names as properties by putting those names in pipes (vertical bars). If you do this, you must put that name in pipes to refer to that item of the record later on, as otherwise AppleScript thinks you're talking about a property, which isn't defined for this record.

```
set R to {|name|:"Matt", |character|:"impeccable", town:"Ojai", age:51}
get |name| of R -- "Matt"
get name of R -- error: Can't get name of...
```

When you talk to a record, it is the target, and its item names are used to interpret the vocabulary you use. The first thing AppleScript does is look to see whether any of this vocabulary is the name of an item of the record. That's why you can't assign to a nonexistent item in a record—the name you're using for that item is meaningless. No terminological confusion normally arises, because the context is clear. So:

```
set town to "Ojai"
set R to {name:"Matt", town:null}
set town of R to town -- no problem
```

Of course, you can confuse AppleScript if you set your mind to it. This code just sets the existing value of the variable town to itself; the record is untouched:

```
set town to "Ojai"
set R to {name:"Matt", town:null}
tell R
    set town to town
end tell
R -- {name:"Matt", town:null}
```

But you know how to fix that—right? (Hint: see Chapter 11.)

```
set town to "Ojai"
set R to {name:"Matt", town:null}
tell R
    set its town to town
end tell
R -- {name:"Matt", town:"Ojai"}
```

There is no built-in way to obtain a list of the names of the items of a record. A record has no such introspective abilities. You (a human being) can see the names of the items of a record in AppleScript's display of the record's value. But your code can't see this information; the names of the items are not values of any kind, and cannot easily be turned into values. I have seen many elaborate attempts to work around this problem, but I'm not going to show you any of them. This is a big short-coming of AppleScript itself, and it needs to be fixed on the level of AppleScript itself. Until it is, you can get assistance from Late Night Software's free List & Record Tools scripting addition. For example:

```
set R to {name:"Matt", town:"Ojai"}
get property IDs of R -- {"pnam"}
get user property names of R -- {"town"}
```

It is possible to fetch or assign to the value of an item of a record using a variable to represent the name, through a second level of evaluation (through the run script command, as explained in Chapter 19). Here's a way to fetch an item's value:

```
global r
set r to {name:"Matt", age:51}
on getWhat(what)
    set s to "on run {r}
get " & what & " of r
end"
    run script s with parameters {r}
end getWhat
getWhat("name")
```

It's a pity that such trickery is needed, and I don't really recommend this approach. Again, the List & Record Tools scripting addition provides a better alternative. See also "List Coercions" in the next chapter.

CHAPTER 14

Coercions

A *coercion* is a conversion of a value of one datatype to a value of another datatype. In AppleScript, not just any old value can be turned into a value of just any old datatype. To put it more strictly: for some pairs of datatype, call them Datatype A and Datatype B, it is the case that at least some values of Datatype A can be coerced to a value of Datatype B. For example, the string "30" can be coerced to a number; when that happens, you get the number 30. There are other strings that can be coerced to other numbers, and there are strings that can't be coerced to any number at all. This implies that there is some sort of equivalence or formula that determines the new value given the old value. This chapter presents these equivalences for every pair of datatypes, describing what coercions are possible and the rules by which they are performed.

The discussion is confined almost entirely to AppleScript's native datatypes (listed in Chapter 13). Coercions between these datatypes are defined by the language. Coercions between nonnative datatypes, or between a native datatype and a nonnative datatype, must be implemented by the application that defines the nonnative type. Applications do this, if they do it at all, on an individual basis, so no documentation is possible here. Additional coercions of native (and other) types can be implemented by scripting additions (Chapter 21), but these are not discussed here either.

Implicit Coercion

Implicit coercion is performed automatically when you supply a value where a value of another datatype is expected. This happens only in connection with AppleScript's operators. These operators have definite rules about what datatypes they expect, and what implicit coercions they will perform if other datatypes are provided. Details appear in Chapter 15.

Otherwise, AppleScript has no implicit coercion.

No implicit coercion takes place when assigning a value to a variable, because variables have no declared datatype; the variable simply adopts the new value.

No implicit coercion takes place when a parameter is passed to a user handler, because such handlers are not protected by any mechanism such as prototypes or datatype declarations in their definition from receiving parameters with undesirable datatypes. If your handler has reason to be choosy about what sorts of values it's willing to accept, then it needs to test those values and respond accordingly. For example, it might coerce explicitly, or it might throw an error, like this:

```
on sendMeAString(s)
    if {class of s} is not in {string, Unicode text} then
        error "Can't make some data into the expected type."
    end if
    -- remaining code goes here, secure in the knowledge that s is a string . . .
end sendMeAString
```

Coercion might take place when passing a parameter to a command, but then the coercion is probably not being performed by AppleScript, and whether it is implicit becomes a moot point. For example:

```
tell application "Finder"
    set sidebar width of window 1 to "123"
end tell
```

You shouldn't have done that, but it works anyway. The sidebar width property is distinctly said, in the Finder's dictionary, to be an integer. You provided a string, but the Finder, instead of complaining, coerced it to an integer. This has nothing whatsoever to do with AppleScript itself! AppleScript did not look in the Finder's dictionary, see that the Finder expects an integer, and implicitly coerce the string. It sent the string to the Finder, and let you take your chances. You gambled, and luckily, this time, you won.

You should not, however, count on such behavior. For one thing, you have absolutely no way of knowing when it will work; a scriptable application's dictionary doesn't tell you (see "Coercions" in Chapter 20). The Finder's dictionary here says "integer," not "I'd like an integer, but if you're fool enough to send me a string, I suppose I'll coerce it for you." For another thing, it doesn't always work. For example, suppose you say this:

```
tell application "Finder"
    set name of folder 1 to 6
    -- error: Finder got an error: Can't make some data into the expected type
end tell
```

Again, as you can see, AppleScript does not help out; it just sends the Finder what you said to send it. It is then up to the Finder to decide whether it's happy with what was sent. In this case, the Finder is not happy, and lets you know with an error.

Explicit Coercion

Explicit coercion is performed with the as operator. There are actually two cases, depending on whether the value to be coerced is a native AppleScript datatype and belongs to your script. These two cases amount to two different operators, even though AppleScript (in its usual misguided attempt to make things "easy") makes them look the same.

---

as coercion

Syntax

value as *class*

Description

If *value* is a native datatype, you're asking AppleScript to coerce it to *class*. If this is a coercion AppleScript is willing to perform, the result is a new value of the requested datatype. If not, there's a runtime error.

---

get . . . as coercion by target

Syntax

[get] *reference* as *class*

Description

If *reference* is an object or attribute of some application, you're asking that application to fetch it and coerce it to *class*. If the application is willing, the result is a value of the requested datatype. If not, there's a runtime error.

Coercion by AppleScript

Coercion by AppleScript is the subject of this chapter, which tells you what coercions AppleScript is willing to perform. For example:

```
9 as string -- "9"
9 as boolean -- error: Can't make 9 into type boolean
```

Even though a variable's value can be a class, you can't use a variable as the second operand in a coercion. This won't even compile:

```
set className to string
9 as className -- compile-time error: Expected class name but found identifier
```

AppleScript must see a class name right there in the script at compile time, or it won't parse the line. (I regard this as a bug.)

Do not confuse a coercion with an object string specifier! (See "Object String Specifier" in Chapter 11.) This is a coercion:

```
"feathers:" as alias
```

This is an object string specifier:

```
alias "feathers:"
```

The distinction can be crucial. There are circumstances where the coercion will compile but the object specifier will not. You can't compile an alias specifier that uses a literal string unless the file exists, but you can compile a coercion from any string to an alias. And there are circumstances where the object string specifier will compile but the coercion will not. You can form a file specifier using a pathname string, but you can't coerce a string to a file object. (See "File Coercions," later in this chapter.)

Coercion by a Scriptable Application

Here's an example of an application being asked to perform a coercion:

```
tell application "Finder"
    folder 1 as string
end tell
```

That does not involve a coercion performed by AppleScript. AppleScript can't coerce a folder to a string. It doesn't even know what a folder is. It is a coercion request targeted entirely at the Finder. It happens that the Finder is happy to comply—it returns the pathname of the folder.

How do you know when a coercion will be performed by AppleScript and when it will be performed by a scriptable application? It depends on what is to be coerced. This code is in a tell block, but no message is sent to the Finder; AppleScript performs the coercion:

```
tell application "Finder"
    get "9" as integer
end tell
```

The value "9" is a complete target. One might equally have said:

```
tell application "Finder"
    tell "9"
        get it as integer
    end tell
end tell
```

The presence of the Finder in a tell block surrounding this code is ignored. At the other extreme:

```
tell application "Finder"
    set x to folder 1
end tell
name of x as integer
```

In that code, x is a reference to an object in the Finder, so obtaining name of x involves sending a message to the Finder. That message is modified by as; the Finder is asked to perform the coercion. All of this makes sense in terms of who the target is, as explained in Chapters 11 and 12.

However, when a coercion request is sent to an application and it refuses, if the datatype to be coerced is something AppleScript knows about, then AppleScript will also take a turn. This affects the error message that you'll see if the coercion fails:

```
tell application "Finder"
    get folder 1 as integer -- error: Finder got an error: Unknown object type
end tell
```

The error in that example is attributed to the Finder. AppleScript doesn't know what a folder is so it doesn't get involved. But compare this:

```
tell application "Finder"
    get name of folder 1 as integer -- error: Can't make "Mannie" into type integer
end tell
```

The error comes from AppleScript itself. The Finder was sent the coercion request as part of the get command, but it didn't obey that part; it returned a string (actually, Unicode text). AppleScript sees this, and attempts to perform the coercion itself—and fails.

An application can refuse to perform even the most elementary coercion:

```
tell application "Finder"
    folder 1 as list -- error: Finder got an error: Unknown object type
end tell
```

That is an easy trap to fall into, because you are likely to become accustomed to turning a value into a one-item list easily with as list, so you're not expecting it to fail. This object, however, belongs to the Finder, so any attempt to coerce it to anything is going to be passed on to the Finder. Because the Finder won't perform this coercion, and because AppleScript itself doesn't know what a folder is, there is absolutely no way the coercion can be performed. Luckily there are other ways to achieve the same effect:

```
tell application "Finder"
    {folder 1}
end tell
```

As I've said, you generally have no way of knowing in advance what coercions an application is willing to perform for you, or what the rules of those coercions may be. The application's dictionary doesn't tell you. You just have to find out by experimentation. The rest of this chapter is about AppleScript's native datatypes; what coercions can be performed on a nonnative type belonging to some application is anybody's guess.

Boolean Coercions

A boolean may be coerced to a string; depending on whether the boolean is true or false, this string will be either "true" or "false".

A string may be coerced to a boolean. The string "true" (not case-sensitive) will be true; any other string will be false.

A boolean may be coerced to an integer; depending on whether the boolean is true or false, this integer will be either 1 or 0.

The integers 1 and 0 may be coerced to a boolean, yielding true and false respectively; other integers can't be coerced to a boolean.

Number, String, and Date Coercions

An integer may be coerced to a real.

A real (within in the integer range) may be coerced to an integer; it is rounded to the nearest integer. This was a new feature starting in Panther; in earlier versions of AppleScript, a real could be coerced to an integer only if it *was* an integer (that is, it had no fractional part). The old behavior is still present in repeat with (see Chapter 19) and, as you'll see in a moment, in coercion from a string (I regard this as a bug).

 Observe that AppleScript's real-to-integer coercion rule is not like that of other computer languages you may know, such as in C, where the fractional part is thrown away. To throw away the fractional part of x, say x div 1 (see Chapter 15). The round scripting addition command can also help here (see "Numbers and Dates" in Chapter 21), as it can be used to dictate the desired rounding behavior.

A number may be coerced to a string.

A string may be coerced to a number, provided that the string looks like a literal number; whitespace will be ignored, but nothing else will be. So for example "1a" can't be coerced to a number. But the empty string, or a string consisting solely of whitespace, will be coerced to 0.

Distinguish between the classes integer and real, on the one hand, and number on the other. A string may be coerced to a real, provided that the string looks like a number. A string may be coerced to an integer, though, only if the string looks like an integer value:

```
"1.1" as real -- 1.1
"1" as real -- 1.0
"1.0" as integer -- 1
"1.1" as integer -- error: Can't make "1.1" into type integer
```

But a string that looks like an integer or a real can be coerced to a number, and it will be coerced to whichever datatype is appropriate—integer or real. This is nice because it saves *you* from having to worry about which is appropriate.

```
class of ("1" as number) -- integer
class of ("1.1" as number) -- real
```

Thus we have a workaround for the problem of coercing a string representing a real to an integer:

```
"1.1" as number as integer -- 1
```

 However, number cannot be used in every situation where a numeric coercion is possible. For example, true as integer is legal, but true as number is not. I regard this as a bug.

A version can be coerced to a real; this coercion is useful for ascertaining that the version of something is at least as high (or low) as some requirement. However, with Tiger, the algorithm has changed. Previously, version 1.9.3 (for example) would coerce to 1.93. Now, a version such as 1.10 is possible; this would coerce to 1.1, which is less than 1.93. Therefore, starting in Tiger, two digits are used for each section of the version, and version 1.10.3 now coerces to 1.1003. But most applications supply their version as a string property anyway, which can't be coerced to a real:

```
tell application "Finder"
    set v to (get version)
end tell
v as real -- error: Can't make "10.4.2" into type real
```

A class or constant may be coerced to a string. For example:

```
string as string -- "string"
italic as string -- "italic"
```

However, if you allow a class to be coerced to a string by some command, you may get a different result. Here, the display dialog command turns the class into its four-letter code:

```
display dialog string -- TEXT
```

A date may be coerced to a string; this is the same string that appears in the literal date specifier after compilation or in a result.

A string may be used to form a date specifier, but it cannot be coerced to a date.

A month may be coerced to a string (because it is a class). A month may also be coerced to an integer; this was a new feature in Panther. An integer cannot be coerced to a month, but it can be used to set a date's month property (new in Tiger). A weekday can be coerced to an integer (new in Tiger): Sunday is 1.

A string, Unicode text, and styled text may be coerced to one another. When coercing to a string, you can say as text instead of as string. This way of talking is confusing, though, because the class of the result is still string, and text is actually the name of a completely different class (string is 'TEXT', text is 'ctxt').

In the past, you could not rely on all commands, especially in scripting additions, to coerce a parameter between Unicode text and string. Thus something like this would mysteriously fail:

```
tell application "Finder"
    say (get name of disk 1)
    -- error: Finder got an error: "feathers" doesn't understand the say message
end
```

The problem, although you'd never know it from the error message, is that say couldn't take Unicode text as a parameter. In Tiger, this problem is generally fixed.

File Coercions

The various coercions and other forms of conversion that are and are not possible between a file specifier, a POSIX file (file URL), an alias, and a string or Unicode text (which might represent a Macintosh pathname or a POSIX pathname), are enough to make your head swim. The trouble is that there are many things you can't do; at the same time, there's always a workaround if you're willing to jump through hoops.

A Macintosh pathname string can be used to form a file specifier or alias. (A file specifier cannot be assigned to a variable or displayed as a result, but a reference to it can be.) A POSIX pathname string can be used to form a POSIX file specifier. (See Chapter 13.) As I pointed out earlier in the chapter, these are *not* coercions.

An alias can be coerced to a string representing its Macintosh pathname, and its POSIX path property is a string representing its POSIX pathname. An alias cannot be coerced to a file object, but a string can be used as an intermediary to form a file specifier:

```
set a to alias "gromit:Users:matt2:reason:Resources:"
POSIX path of a -- "/Volumes/gromit/Users/matt2/reason/Resources/"
a as string -- "gromit:Users:matt2:reason:Resources:"
a reference to file (a as string)
-- file "gromit:Users:matt2:reason:Resources:" of «script»
```

A Macintosh pathname can be coerced to an alias. (The item denoted by the pathname must exist at runtime; see Chapter 13.)

```
set s to "gromit:Users:matt2:reason:Resources:"
s as alias -- alias "gromit:Users:matt2:reason:Resources:"
```

A file object cannot be coerced to a string. But a file object can be coerced to an alias (though in the Panther version of Script Editor there's a bug that makes it appear that it can't be), which in turn can be coerced to a string. A file object's POSIX path property is a string representing its POSIX pathname.

```
set f to a reference to file "gromit:Users:matt2:reason:Resources:"
f as alias -- alias "gromit:Users:matt2:reason:Resources:"
POSIX path of f -- "/Volumes/gromit/Users/matt2/reason/Resources/"
```

A POSIX file can be coerced to a string representing its Macintosh pathname. A string representing a POSIX path can be coerced to a POSIX file:

```
set s to "/Volumes/gromit/Users/matt2/reason/Resources/"
POSIX file s as string -- "gromit:Users:matt2:reason:Resources:"
s as POSIX file -- file "gromit:Users:matt2:reason:Resources:"
```

Because an item must exist in order to form an alias to it, coercion to an alias is a good way to test whether the item denoted by a pathname exists:

```
on pathExists of s given posixStyle:b
    try
        if b then
            POSIX file s as alias
        else
            s as alias
        end if
        return true
    on error
        return false
    end try
end pathExists
pathExists of "gromit:Users:matt2" without posixStyle -- true
pathExists of "/Volumes/gromit/Users/matt2" with posixStyle -- true
```

Throughout the preceding, wherever I say "string," you should understand "or Unicode text," as, strictly speaking, a string might not express all the characters that the filesystem text encoding can express—whereas Unicode text should be able to do so.

 I have found, though, that with some items on disk whose names contain Unicode-only characters, coercion between an alias and Unicode text, in either direction, can fail with a runtime error. This is probably a bug. The workaround is to construct an alias with an alias specifier, and use an alias's POSIX path property to obtain its pathname. To get a Macintosh pathname from an alias reliably, get its POSIX path property, form a POSIX file specifer, and coerce that to Unicode text.

List Coercions

Anything may be coerced to a list. How it is treated depends on what you start with:

A list
> The result is identically the same list.

A record
> The result is a list of the values from the record:
> ```
> set R to {name:"Matt", age:51}
> R as list -- {"Matt", 51}
> ```

Anything else
> The result is a list of one item, that item being the thing you started with.

Coercion to a list is very useful for making sure you have a list; if the thing you start with isn't a list, it becomes one, and if it is a list, it is unchanged. Recall, however, that this coercion might not work if the thing you start with belongs to an application, because that application might not implement it (see "Coercion by a Scriptable Application," earlier in this chapter).

Officially you can't coerce a list to a record, but there's a trick for doing it using a second level of evaluation. (Consider the warnings at "Second-Level Evaluation" in Chapter 19 before resorting to this trick; it involves a lot of overhead.) The value of every odd item of the list (which should be a string) becomes the name of a record item, whose value in turn is the corresponding even item of the list:

```
on listToRecord(L)
    script myScript
        return {«class usrf»:L}
    end script
    return run script myScript
end listToRecord
set R to listToRecord({"name", "haha", "age", 51})
R -- {|name|:"haha", age:51}
```

To understand the trickery involved here, see "Record" in Chapter 13. Observe that because we are forming a user record, the term name ends up in pipes; it is not the predefined name property, and its value cannot be accessed without pipes around the term name.

A list of one item may be coerced to the datatype of that item, and the result will be that item. Of course, the result can then be coerced to any datatype that it can be coerced to, so you can also coerce a list of one item to that datatype in a single step. For example:

```
{true} as string -- "true"
```

That's possible because the list of one boolean is first coerced to a boolean, and a boolean can be coerced to a string.

A list of multiple items may be coerced to a string, provided that every individual item may be coerced to a string. This coercion is performed using the current value of the text item delimiters. (See "String" in Chapter 13.) The rule is that every item of the list is coerced to a string, and the resulting strings are joined into a single string with the text item delimiters value between each pair. The text item delimiters value can be the empty string; this is in fact its default value. If an item of the list is a list, it is coerced to a string by the same rule; so this coercion in effect flattens a list, to any depth, into a single string.

So, assuming the text item delimiters is the empty string:

```
{"Manny", {"Moe", "Jack"}} as string -- "MannyMoeJack"
```

Or, assuming the text item delimiters is a comma followed by a space:

```
{"Manny", {"Moe", "Jack"}} as string -- "Manny, Moe, Jack"
```

A common technique is to transform a string to a list (using text items or some other element), process the list in some way, and then transform it back to a string by coercion. This technique can help you perform string manipulations, making up somewhat for the fact that AppleScript's native string functionality is so thin. (Also, a list, unlike a string, can be mutated in place, so operating on a list can be faster and more efficient.) As a simple example, here's how to get the containing folder from a Macintosh pathname:

```
on containingFolder(s)
    set text item delimiters to ":"
    return (items 1 thru -2 of text items of s) as string
end containingFolder
containingFolder("feathers:Users:mattneub:Documents:someDoc")
-- "feathers:Users:mattneub:Documents"
```

 A list can be *implicitly* coerced to a string. (See Chapter 15 for the situations in which this can occur.) Beware of allowing this to happen without taking into account the current state of the text item delimiters.

A common complaint is that with display dialog you can't display a list as a list (that is, as it would be displayed as a result by the Script Editor). A workaround is to coerce the list to something impossible, such as a record, and capture the resulting error message. This trick is based upon the observation that the error message has somehow performed precisely the coercion you had in mind:

```
on coerceForDisplay(L)
    try
        L as record
    on error s
        set c to characters of s
        set u to count c
        repeat with i from 1 to u
            if item i of c is "{" then exit repeat
        end repeat
        repeat with j from u to 1 by -1
            if item j of c is "}" then exit repeat
        end repeat
        set text item delimiters to ""
        return (items i thru j of c) as string
    end try
end coerceForDisplay
display dialog coerceForDisplay({"pep", 3, {"Mannie", "Moe", "Jack"}})
-- {"pep", 3, {"Mannie", "Moe", "Jack"}}
```

Unit Conversions

AppleScript provides a number of classes whose sole purpose is to allow you to perform measurement unit conversions. They are implemented as classes so that you can use the as operator to perform the conversion; that is, the conversion is really a coercion.

Because of this implementation, the way you have to speak in order to perform a conversion ends up looking fairly silly. You can't say 3 feet; you have to coerce 3 (a number) to the feet class, by saying 3 as feet. Now you coerce to the desired class; suppose this is yards. But now you have a value of the yards class. You can't do anything with it, so you have to coerce it to a number (or a string). So, for example:

```
on feetToYards(ft)
    return ft as feet as yards as number
end feetToYards
feetToYards(3) -- 1.0
```

The implemented units are themselves a mixed lot. Many important units, such as acres and hectares, aren't implemented at all. Accuracy of some of the conversions has also been called into question, but this is said to be fixed in Tiger. Table 14-1 provides a list.

Table 14-1. Conversion unit classes

meters	inches	feet	yards
miles	kilometers	centimeters	square meters
square feet	square yards	square miles	square kilometers
liters	gallons	quarts	cubic meters
cubic centimeters	cubic feet	cubic inches	cubic yards
kilograms	grams	ounces	pounds
degrees Celsius	degrees Fahrenheit	degrees Kelvin	

A better list of conversion units is built into Mac OS X by way of the Unix tool units. Here's a way to use it:

```
on convert(val, unit1, unit2)
    set text item delimiters to " "
    set conv to do shell script ({"units", unit1, unit2} as string)
    return val * (word 1 of paragraph 1 of conv as real)
end convert
convert(4, "feet", "meters") -- 1.2192
```

CHAPTER 15

Operators

An *operator* is a token that transforms a value or a pair of values to produce a new value. These transformations are *operations*, and the values operated upon are the *operands*. An operator with two operands is *binary*; an operator with one operand is *unary*. This chapter lists the AppleScript operators and explains what they do, with special attention to implicit coercions performed by the operators. It also talks about parentheses, because they help determine the effects of the operators. Finally, there's a section on the differences between what happens when AppleScript performs an operation and when a scriptable application performs it.

(For the coercion operator, as, see Chapter 14; for the object containment operator, of, see Chapter 11.)

Implicit Coercion

In Chapter 14, I explained coercion and described the coercions that are possible between built-in datatypes in the AppleScript language. Binary operators can (and will) perform coercion without your specifically asking for it. This is called *implicit coercion*, and is one of the most confusing aspects of AppleScript—and a frequent source of mistakes in scripts. If you are not prepared for what implicit coercions an operator will perform, you will be surprised when the result of an operation is not what you expected. That's why this chapter spends so much time on the implicit coercions performed by the various operators.

What coercions AppleScript will perform implicitly is not the same as what coercions you can get it to perform explicitly (with the as operator). AppleScript's error messages in this regard can add to the confusion. For example:

    1 and 1 -- *compile-time error: Can't make 1 into type boolean*

That error message, on its face, is lying. AppleScript *can* make 1 into a boolean. What AppleScript really means by the error message here is: "In order for me to perform this operation, I would need to coerce the first 1 (before the and) to a boolean, implicitly; and I refuse to do that." Even weirder is what happens when you proceed to coerce the first 1 to a boolean explicitly:

```
1 as boolean and 1 -- true
```

It works—which means that even though AppleScript refused to coerce the first 1 to a boolean implicitly, it now happily coerces the second 1 to a boolean implicitly!

But do not imagine that there is some simple rule governing this behavior (such as that AppleScript never coerces the first operand implicitly). In this next example, AppleScript happily coerces both operands implicitly (to a number):

```
"3" + "4" -- 7
```

You see now why the rules for implicit coercion need to be made explicit.

Arithmetic Operators

The arithmetic operators combine numbers to get new numbers in accordance with the usual rules of arithmetic. As in most computer languages, multiplication and division take precedence over addition and subtraction (in the absence of parentheses). So, for example:

```
3 + 4 * 2 -- 11
3 * 4 + 2 -- 14
```

An operand that is a list consisting of one number will be coerced to a number. An operand that is a string representing a number, or a list consisting of one such string, will be coerced to a number.

The class of the result of the addition, subtraction, multiplication, and remainder operators is as follows: the result is an integer if the first operand is an integer and if the second operand either is an integer or is a real that can be coerced to an integer without loss of information. Otherwise, the result is a real.

 If you have some programming experience and you know a language such as C or LISP (where if *either* arithmetic operand is a real, the result is a real), you're going to find AppleScript's behavior surprising. Think of it like this. For the result to be a real, it is not enough that one operand be a real; the *first* operand must be a real, or else the second operand must have a significant fractional part, not merely a decimal point. Saying x * 1.0, for example, is *not* a way of making sure you've got a real. When in doubt, coerce explicitly.

Do not blame AppleScript for the phenomena inherent in doing floating-point arithmetic in any language on any computer. It is the nature of computer numerics that most values can only be approximated. Modern processors are extraordinarily clever about compensating, but rounding operations can easily expose the truth:

```
2.32 * 100.0 div 1 -- 231
```

Similarly, there may be situations where instead of comparing two values for absolute equality, you will do better to test whether the difference between them lies within some acceptable small epsilon.

+   addition

Syntax
```
number1 + number2
date + integer
```

Description
Adds the operands. The addition operator is not overloaded to perform string concatenation; see "Concatenation Operator" (&) later in this chapter. On date arithmetic, see Chapter 13.

−   subtraction; unary negation

Syntax
```
number1 - number2
date - integer
date - date
-number
```

Description
Subtracts the second operand from the first, or negates the single operand. Unary negation has very high precedence. On date arithmetic, see Chapter 13.

---

*   multiplication

Syntax
```
number * number
```

Description
Multiplies the operands.

/   real division

Syntax
```
number1 / number2
```

Description
Divides the first operand by the second. Both numbers are treated as reals, and the result is a real.

div

Syntax

number1 div *number2*

Description

Obtains the integer part of a division. Both numbers are treated as reals; the first is divided by the second, and the result is coerced to an integer by throwing away its fractional part. Notice that this is *not* the same as AppleScript's normal real-to-integer coercion behavior. Thus, the way to get the integer part of a real in AppleScript is x div 1, not x as integer.

Example

```
4 div 5 -- 0
(4 / 5) as integer -- 1
```

mod

Syntax

number1 mod *number1*

Description

Obtains the remainder from a division. The first operand is divided by the absolute value of the second, and the remainder is returned.

^

Syntax

number1 ^ *number2*

Description

Raises the first number to the power of the second. The result is a real.

Boolean Operators

The boolean operators implement the basics of logic, working on boolean operands to produce a boolean result. The second operand, but not the first, will be coerced from a string or an integer, or a list of one string or one integer, to a boolean. Either operand will be coerced from a list of one boolean to a boolean.

and

Syntax

boolean1 and *boolean2*

Description

Returns true if both operands are true. If the first operand is false, the second operand won't even be evaluated ("short-circuiting").

or   logical or

Syntax

boolean1 or *boolean2*

Description

Returns false if both operands are false. If the first operand is true, the second operand won't even be evaluated ("short-circuiting").

---

not   logical not

Syntax

not *boolean*

Description

Changes true to false and false to true.

Comparison Operators

The comparison operators test whether one operand is the same as the other, or whether, if they can be ordered, they are ordered in a given direction. The result is a boolean.

The nature of comparisons involving strings can be influenced by a considering clause; see Chapter 19.

Lists are internally ordered, but records are not:

```
{1, 2} = {2, 1} -- false
{name:"Matt", age:"51"} = {age:"51", name:"Matt"} -- true
```

The equality (=) and inequality (≠) operators do *not* coerce their operands; operands may be of any datatype, and operands of different datatypes are unequal. So:

```
{"2"} = 2 -- false
```

In that example, the first operand is a list, the second operand is a number, and no coercion takes place. So the operands are not equal, and the comparison is false.

With the other comparison operators, operands must ultimately be a string, a number, or a date. The first operator is coerced to a string, a number, or a date, and then the second operator is coerced to match the datatype of the first:

```
{"2"} ≥ 2 -- true
```

In that example, the first operand is a list of one string, so it is coerced to a string. Now the second operand is coerced to a string; the two strings are equal and the comparison is true.

Thus, although you cannot use the equality operator to learn whether two values would be equal if implicitly coerced to the same datatype, you can work around the problem like this:

```
{"2"} ≤ 2 and {"2"} ≥ 2 -- true
```

As noted in "Assignment and Retrieval" in Chapter 7, the equality operator is not overloaded as an assignment operator. This code will compile and run, but it won't assign 4 to x (it will report whether they are equal):

```
x = 4
```

= (is)   equality

Syntax

operand1 = *operand2*

Description

Yields true if the operands are equal. No coercion is performed; different datatypes are not equal. Synonym is equal to has abbreviations equal, equals, and equal to.

≠ (is not)   inequality

Syntax

operand1 ≠ *operand2*

Description

Yields true if the the operands are unequal. No coercion is performed; different datatypes are not equal. The not-equals sign is typed using Option-=. is not has abbreviation isn't. Synonym is not equal to has abbreviations is not equal, isn't equal, does not equal, and doesn't equal. There are no synonyms <> or !=.

<   less than

Syntax

operand1 < *operand2*

Description

Yields true if the first operand is less than the first. Synonyms are is less than (abbreviation less than) and comes before.

>   greater than

Syntax

operand1 > *operand2*

Description

Yields true if the first operand is greater than the first. Synonyms are is greater than (abbreviation greater than) and comes after.

Syntax

operand1 ≤ *operand2*

Description

Yields true if the first operand is less than or equal to the first. Abbreviation is <=, or the ≤ symbol may be typed using Option-comma. Synonym is less than or equal to has abbreviations omitting is, to, or both. There are also synonyms does not come after and is not greater than.

Syntax

operand1 ≥ *operand2*

Description

Yields true if the first operand is greater than or equal to the second. Abbreviation is >=, or the ≥ symbol may be typed using Option-period. Synonym is greater than or equal to has abbreviations omitting is, to, or both. There are also synonyms does not come before and is not less than.

Containment Operators

The containment operators test whether the value of one thing is to be found "inside" the value of another. For example, the string "test" contains the string "e". Containment may apply to two strings, two lists, or two records. The result is a boolean.

Containment implies comparison, and the nature of comparisons involving strings can be influenced by a considering clause; see Chapter 19.

It is worth stressing that in the case of list containment, both operands must be lists. In other words, the second operand is not an *element*; it's a *sublist*. This is a little counterintuitive at first. To complicate matters, AppleScript fools you by apparently letting you say just what you (wrongly) think you should be allowed to say:

    {1, 2} contains 2 -- **true**

You can say that, but not because it is correct on its face; it's because 2 is coerced to {2} implicitly to get the right syntax, which would be this:

    {1, 2} contains {2} -- **true**

Because the second operand is a sublist, you can ask about more than one element at once:

```
{1, 2, 3} contains {2, 3} -- true
```

Lists are ordered, so the items of the sublist you ask about must appear consecutively and in the same order in the target list. These are false:

```
{1, 2, 3} contains {1, 3} -- false
{1, 2, 3} contains {3, 2} -- false
```

Because lists can contain lists, you may have to use an explicit extra level to say what you mean:

```
{{1}, {2}} contains {2} -- false
{{1}, {2}} contains {{2}} -- true
```

The first is false because 2 is not an element of the first list, and {2} is not going to be coerced to {{2}} for you—it's a list already, so there's nothing to coerce.

With regard to record containment, both the label and the value must match for containment to be true:

```
{name:"Matt", age:"51"} contains {name:"Matt"} -- true
{name:"Matt", age:"51"} contains {title:"Matt"} -- false
{name:"Matt", age:"51"} contains {name:"Socrates"} -- false
```

Records are not internally ordered:

```
{name:"Matt", age:"51"} contains {age:"51", name:"Matt"} -- true
```

For purposes of containment, the empty list is treated as the empty record:

```
{name:"Matt", age:"51"} contains {} -- true
{} contains {name:"Matt", age:"51"} -- false
```

Because the containment operators are overloaded to apply to both strings and lists, the first operand is never implicitly coerced to a string, because AppleScript can't know that this is what you mean; it is coerced to a list unless it is a string (or record). The second operand is then coerced to match the datatype of the first. For example:

```
"51" contains 5 -- true; string containment, "51" contains "5"
51 contains 5 -- false; list containment, {51} doesn't contain {5}
```

It's important not to confuse the implicit coercion rules here with those for certain other operators. For example, your experience with arithmetic operators might lead you to expect a certain kind of implicit coercion:

```
{"7"} * 7 -- 49
```

The list of a single string is coerced to a single string and from there to a number. But that isn't going to happen with contains:

```
{"7"} contains 7 -- false
```

The first operand isn't coerced at all; the second operand is coerced to {7}, and that's the end. The second operand isn't a sublist of the first, so the comparison is false.

Do not rely on implicit coercion of nonnative classes to a list; it usually doesn't work. For example:

```
tell application "Microsoft Entourage"
    every contact contains contact 1
    -- error: Can't make «class cAbE» id 1 of application "Microsoft Entourage" into type vector
end tell
```

You should have said {contact 1}, or contact 1 as list (Entourage implements coercion to a list, unlike the Finder example in "Explicit Coercion" in Chapter 14). For the mysterious "vector" type mentioned in the error message, see "List" in Chapter 13.

---

contains, does not contain, is in, is not in
containment

Syntax

string1 contains *string2*
string2 is in *string1*
list1 contains *list2*
list2 is in *list1*
record1 contains *record2*
record2 is in *record1*

Description

Tests whether the first operand contains the second. The is in synonyms reverse the operand order of the contains synonyms—that is, with is in, the second operand comes physically before the first operand (as deliberately shown in the syntax listings), but it is still the second operand. This is relevant in the rules for implicit coercions.

---

begins with
initial containment

Syntax

string1 begins with *string2*
list1 begins with *list2*

Description

Same as contains with the additional requirement that the second operand come first in the first operand. Records are not ordered, so they aren't eligible operands. Synonym is starts with.

---

ends with
final containment

Syntax

string1 ends with *string2*
list1 ends with *list2*

Description

Same as contains with the additional requirement that the second operand come last in the first operand. Records are not ordered, so they aren't eligible operands.

Concatenation Operator

Concatenation is the joining of two things in sequence. It may be performed on a pair of strings (resulting in a string), a pair of lists (resulting in a list), or a pair of records (resulting in a record). Implicit coercions are performed in exactly the same way as for the containment operators (see the previous section). So, for example:

```
"three" & 20 -- "three20"
3 & "twenty" -- {3, "twenty"}
```

That example shows the difference the order of operands can make; the reason is perfectly obvious if you know the implicit coercion rules, and baffling otherwise.

In earlier versions of AppleScript, concatenation of Unicode text and a string was troublesome, because the class of the result depended the class of the first operand. Now (starting in Tiger), if either operand is Unicode text, the result is Unicode text. This behavior makes string concatenation effectively transparent.

To turn string concatenation into list concatenation, it suffices to coerce the first operand to a list; this can be done simply by expressing it in list delimiters:

```
{"Mannie"} & "Moe" & "Jack" -- {"Mannie", "Moe", "Jack"}
```

Without the list delimiters, we'd end up with "MannieMoeJack".

Recall (from Chapter 14) that coercion of a list to a string is another way to concatenate. Thus concatenation of a string and a list concatenates the string with all the elements of the list, each coerced to a string and joined by the text item delimiters:

```
set text item delimiters to ""
"butter" & {"field", 8} -- "butterfield8"
```

Recall what was said in the previous section about both operands having to be of the same type, and what this implies for lists. Concatenation is a way to append one or more items to a list:

```
{1, 2, 3} & {4, 5, 6} -- {1, 2, 3, 4, 5, 6}
```

The result is not {1, 2, 3, {4, 5, 6}}; if that's what you wanted, you can use an extra level of list delimiters:

```
{1, 2, 3} & {{4, 5, 6}}
```

Concatenation of a list to the empty list yields exactly the same list, not a copy. This is probably intended as an optimization, but you are more likely to experience it as a bug. For example:

```
set L1 to {}
set L2 to {"mannie"}
set L1 to L1 & L2
set item 1 of L1 to "moe"
L2 -- {"moe"}
```

Evidently L1 has been set (by reference) to L2; L1 and L2 are now two names for the same thing. This would not have happened if the first operand in the concatenation had originally been anything other than an empty list. One wants to say, "So just don't do that," but the problem is that if (as in this example) the first concatenation operand is a variable, you might not know that it is an empty list, and it seems onerous to suggest that you should test it every time. A workaround is to use copy instead of set in the third line:

```
copy L1 & L2 to L1
```

The operation set end of is more efficient than the concatenation operator because no extra copies have to be made internally. Strings are not mutable in place, but lists are. Thus it is common practice to perform an extended series of string operations by operating on a list instead. For example, instead of this:

```
set s to "anti"
set s to s & "dis"
set s to s & "establishment"
set s to s & "arianism"
```

it is more efficient to say this:

```
set text item delimiters to ""
set L to {}
set end of L to "anti"
set end of L to "dis"
set end of L to "establishment"
set end of L to "arianism"
set s to L as string
```

Concatenating records yields a record consisting of all the items of the first record along with just those items of the second record whose name isn't the name of any item in the first record (see Chapter 13):

```
set r to {who:"Jaime", town:"Ojai"} & {who:"Matt", friend:"Steve"}
r -- {who:"Jaime", town:"Ojai", friend:"Steve"}
```

Concatenating a record with an empty list (in either order) yields the same record. For a use of this, see "Parameters" in Chapter 9. If the empty list is the first operand, the result is the very same record, just as we saw a moment ago for lists:

```
set R1 to {}
set R2 to {name:"Matt"}
set R1 to R1 & R2
set name of R1 to "Neuburg"
R2 -- {name:"Neuburg"}
```

Scripting additions can provide further interesting variations on the notion of concatenation. For example, the Satimage scripting addition's special concat command concatenates lists from items with the same name in different records:

```
special concat {who:{"Matt"}} with {who:{"Neuburg"}} -- {who:{"Matt", "Neuburg"}}
```

Syntax

```
string1 & string2
list1 & list2
record1 & record2
```

Description

Concatenates the operands. The result is a string, list, or record respectively.

Parentheses

Parentheses may be used to determine the order of operations at runtime:

```
3 + 4 * 2 -- 11
(3 + 4) * 2 -- 14
```

Parentheses can also help determine the order of interpretation of vocabulary at compile time. Thus they can make the difference between successful compilation and failed compilation. For example, this compiles fine, because all the expressions are legal:

```
set r to random number
round r rounding up
```

Now try to save a line by combining them, and you get this ungrammatical and mysterious error:

```
round random number rounding up
-- compile-time error: A application constant [sic] or consideration can't go after this identifier
```

The problem is that `random number` is a command that can optionally take various labeled parameters, and `rounding up` isn't one of them. Instead of rethinking its interpretation ("So, maybe `random number` isn't taking any parameters here!"), AppleScript just gives up. You have to help it out, by using parentheses:

```
round (random number) rounding up
```

Sometimes AppleScript will insert parentheses for you, on compilation. For example, I didn't put any parentheses when I typed this code:

```
tell application "System Events"
    copy name of every process where it is frontmost to theProc
end tell
```

But AppleScript did, when it compiled:

```
tell application "System Events"
    copy (name of every process where it is frontmost) to theProc
end tell
```

The reason seems to be to delimit a phrase implying a get command. But if you actually use get explicitly here without parentheses, AppleScript refuses to compile at all:

```
tell application "System Events"
    copy get name of every process where it is frontmost to theProc
    -- compile-time error: Expected "into", "to", etc. but found "get"
end tell
```

The problem seems to be that AppleScript doesn't like the phrase copy get, which is two commands in a row. If you add the parentheses, AppleScript compiles:

```
tell application "System Events"
    copy (get name of every process where it is frontmost) to theProc
end tell
```

Parentheses can also make a difference at runtime. AppleScript will compile this, but it causes an error at runtime:

```
tell application "System Events"
    set L to name of every process
    frontmost of process item 1 of L
    -- error: No result was returned from some part of this expression
end tell
```

This runs fine:

```
tell application "System Events"
    set L to name of every process
    frontmost of process (item 1 of L)
end tell
```

The moral is: if things don't seem to be working out, try playing with parentheses.

Who Performs an Operation

Some operations within an interapplication communications context can be performed by the target application rather than by AppleScript. There are two cases to consider. The operation may appear as a bare expression (for example, the condition in an if clause); I will call this a *direct operation*. Or, the operation may be part of a boolean test element specifier.

Direct Operations

According to Apple's documentation, if the first operand of a direct operation is a reference to an object of the target application, the target application should perform the operation. So, for example:

```
tell application "Finder"
    if name of folder 1 contains "e" then
```

The object name of folder 1 is a Finder object, so in this case, according to Apple, the Finder should perform the operation. However, experimentation shows that the

Finder does *not* perform the operation; AppleScript does try to get it to do so, but the target application replies with an error indicating that it doesn't wish to perform that sort of operation. AppleScript thereupon adopts a new strategy: it asks the target application for the values in question, and performs the operation itself.

So, here's how that example really works. AppleScript starts by sending the Finder a single Apple event that means: "Please tell me whether the name of your folder 1 contains "e"." The Finder replies with an error message. So then AppleScript tries the other strategy: it goes back to the Finder and sends it another Apple event that means: "Okay, never mind that, just tell me the name of your folder 1." The Finder complies, and now AppleScript looks, itself, to see whether the result contains "e".

This approach seems wasteful, but it is wasteful only the first time. The second time the same sort of code is encountered, the AppleScript scripting component remembers that the Finder doesn't do this sort of operation, and skips the first step; it just asks the Finder for the value of the operand and does the operation itself.

In fact, I have not found *any* application that appears willing to perform direct operations when AppleScript asks it to! The entire matter is therefore moot. One can see, all the same, that the mechanism is a good idea. For example, there is no way to ask an application whether two references are references to the very same thing:

```
tell application "Finder"
    set f1 to folder 1
    set f2 to folder "Mannie"
    f1 = f2 -- false
end tell
```

These are in fact one and the same folder, and it would be really great if the Finder could tell us so. In order for this to happen, though, the Finder would have to perform the comparison, and it simply isn't going to. Similarly, in this code:

```
tell application "Finder"
    if name of folder 1 is name of folder 2 then
```

It would be efficient to be able to ask the Finder, with a single Apple event, to perform this comparison and report on the result. As it is, AppleScript ends up sending the Finder two Apple events (one asking for the name of folder 1, the second asking for the name of folder 2) and performing the comparison itself.

Boolean Test Element Specifiers

In a boolean test element specifier (see Chapter 11), the target application *always* performs the comparison itself. For example:

```
tell application "Finder"
    name of every folder whose name contains "E"
end tell
```

That is a single Apple event; the Apple event includes instructions to use contains "E" as the criterion for returning folder names, so the Finder must implement contains in order to obey.

Differences between an application's implementation of an operator and Apple-Script's implementation can arise under these circumstances. This seems rather scary, but if the application is well-behaved, these differences should be minor. The primary case in point is the use of considering clauses. For example:

```
tell application "Finder"
    considering case
        name of every folder whose name contains "E"
    end considering
end tell
-- {"emptyFolder", "Test Me"}
```

The Finder gives the wrong answer; if you consider case, neither of these folder names contains "E". The Finder is simply ignoring the considering clause. In fact, I don't know of *any* application that considers considering clauses in a string comparison. (See "String Considerations" in Chapter 19.)

The workaround in a situation like this is a two-step approach: fetch all the values and then have AppleScript perform the test itself. AppleScript does not implement boolean test element specifiers for lists, so the test must be performed as a loop:

```
tell application "Finder"
    set L to name of every folder
end tell
set L2 to {}
considering case
    repeat with aName in L
        if aName contains "E" then
            set end of L2 to contents of aName
        end if
    end repeat
end considering
```

After that, L2 contains the right answer. Fortunately, such an approach is not particularly expensive in this case; luckily, the Finder implements get name of every (see "Operations on Multiple References" in Chapter 11), and the test we perform in the loop doesn't involve sending any Apple events.

CHAPTER 16

Global Properties

AppleScript's *global properties* are essentially predefined variables; they are named values that exist automatically, without your code having to define them. Your code can access them because they are in scope in every script, thanks to the inheritance mechanism (see "Inheritance" in Chapter 8). Your script as a whole is a script object whose parent, by default, is another script object called AppleScript, which represents the AppleScript scripting component instance. These predefined variables are properties of the AppleScript script object. Thus the inheritance mechanism makes them global; no matter where you are when you access one of them, it is sought as a top-level entity up the parent chain until the AppleScript script object is reached. Even if the name of a global property is overshadowed in some scope of your script, it can still be accessed through the name AppleScript. For example:

```
property pi : 3
AppleScript's pi -- 3.14159265359
```

The global properties are like any other script properties, and as such:

- They are settable.
- Their values are shared by all scripts running under this instance of the Apple-Script scripting component.
- They persist along with this instance of the AppleScript scripting component.

The status of the global script properties is thus somewhat counterintuitive. You might have thought values such as pi and tab would remain constant. That's not the case. You can change the value of one of them, and then this script and any other scripts that run under the same AppleScript scripting component instance will share this new value. This mechanism introduces a certain fragility, because if a script assumes that these properties always have their default values, it can break. The only thing standing between you, the programmer, and this fragility is a sort of tacit agreement about which global script properties it is customary to change. It is common practice to change the value of the text item delimiters; it is not common practice to change things like pi or tab. This is rather a silly state of affairs but there's nothing that can be done about it now.

If you really, really want to, you can completely cut off your own access to the global properties: you can overshadow all their names, overshadow the name AppleScript, and alter the parent chain. So Don't Do That.

Strings

return

"\r"

Description
Macintosh line-break character. There does not seem to be any conflict with the keyword return (see "Returned Value" in Chapter 9). The only place where a conflict could occur is when return is the first word of a line. The rule in that situation seems to be that if return is followed by an operator, it can't be the keyword, so it must be this property.

Example
```
"This is a line." & return & "This is another line."
```

tab

"\t"

Description
Tab character.

Example
```
"an item" & tab & "another item"
```

quote

"\""

Description
Quote character. (This is new in Tiger.)

Example
```
quote & "This is cool," & quote & " said Tom frigidly."
```

space

" "

Description
Space character.

Example
```
"word" & space & "otherWord"
```

text item delimiters

"" (the empty string)

Description
The text item delimiters global property has two uses: it is used to split a string into its text item elements (see "String" in Chapter 13), and it is used to join list items when a list

is coerced to a string (see "List Coercions" in Chapter 14). In theory it is a list of strings, but in fact it can be set to a string, and if it is a list, only the first item of the list matters.

Example

```
set text item delimiters to ":"
text item 1 of (path to system folder as string)
```

Numbers

The minutes property and its ilk are intended to help you convert to seconds. This is because date arithmetic uses seconds (see "Date" in Chapter 13 and "Arithmetic Operators" in Chapter 15).

---

pi   3.14159265359

Description

The ratio of a circle's circumference to its diameter.

Example

```
set area to pi * (radius ^ 2)
```

---

minutes   60

Description

The number of seconds in a minute.

Example

```
(current date) + 30 * minutes -- half an hour from now
```

---

hours   3600

Description

The number of seconds in an hour.

Example

```
(current date) + 2 * hours -- two hours from now
```

---

days   86400

Description

The number of seconds in a day.

Example

```
(current date) + 2 * days -- two days from now
```

weeks

Description

The number of seconds in a week.

Example

```
(current date) + 2 * weeks -- two weeks from now
```

Miscellaneous

version

Description

The version of AppleScript. The name of this property is also the name of a class, and the appearance that its value is a string is an illusion; this value is actually a version, which is coerced to a string for display.

Example

```
display dialog AppleScript's version -- "1.10.3"
AppleScript's version as real -- 1.1003
```

CHAPTER 17

Constants

A *constant* in AppleScript is a term that functions as a value. It isn't a variable, which is a name that *has* a value. A constant *is* a value. The fixed value of a constant will appear to you as the name of the constant. For example, the value of yes is yes; it cannot be reduced to any other form (though a constant can be coerced to a string). You can use it as a value, but that's about all you can do with it. You cannot set the value of a constant; if you try, you'll get a compile-time error, "Access not allowed." You cannot create a variable whose name is that of a constant; if you try, you'll get a compile-time error, "Expected variable name or property but found application constant or consideration." The datatype (class) of a constant is usually constant; but as we shall see, some of them are a class instead.

Behind the scenes, many constants are implemented as *enumerations*, meaning a set of fixed values (called *enumerators*), any of which may occupy a certain syntactic slot. For example, the replacing clause of the store script command (see "Compiled Script Files as Script Objects" in Chapter 8) may consist of any of the constants yes, no, or ask. Nothing stops you, however, from supplying some other value, in which case it is up to the target to decide how it wants to respond. If you say replacing 42 in a store script command, the script will compile and run. If you try to set a date's weekday to yes, the script will compile but not run.

Applications are free to extend AppleScript's vocabulary by implementing constants of their own. For example, GraphicConverter can save an image file in many formats, and it needs a way to let you specify a format; it does this with some four dozen constants, such as PICT, TIFF, GIF, BMP, and JPEG. An application's dictionary will show you the constants that can be used in any connection with a given command. See "Enumerations" in Chapter 20.

true, false

Description

Boolean values. See "Boolean" in Chapter 13 and "Boolean Operators" in Chapter 15.

Example

```
open for access f write permission true
```

yes, no, ask

Description

Options when saving a file. For a description of some typical behavior in response to these options, see "Compiled Script Files as Script Objects" in Chapter 8.

Example

```
store script s in f replacing yes
```

missing value

Description

This is actually a class, but it has no values; all you'll ever see is the class itself, so it works as if it were a constant. It seems to be a way for an application to return a value while signaling a nonvalue; it isn't an error, and it isn't a failure to return any value at all.

Example

```
tell application "Finder" to get description of folder 1 -- missing value
```

null

Description

Like missing value, this is implemented as a class with no values. I've never found a use for it in communicating with a scriptable application, nor have I ever seen an application return it as a result. But I do sometimes use it in my own scripts, as a way of giving a variable or record item a value that signifies "No value has been assigned yet" without its being undefined. Examples have appeared in "The Run Handler" in Chapter 9 and "Record" in Chapter 13.

Example

```
set aPerson to {name:null, age:null, town:null}
```

plain, bold, italic, outline, shadow, underline, superscript, subscript, strikethrough, small caps, all caps, all lowercase, condensed, expanded, hidden

Description

Text styles, for applications that wish to speak of such things. The example here shows Tex-Edit Plus returning a text style record. (See "Records" in Chapter 20.) This is a record consisting of two lists, the on styles (those that are applied to a piece of text) and the off styles (those that are not applied to a piece of text). The items of each list are text styles. The piece of text we're asking about here is underlined.

Example

```
tell application "Tex-Edit Plus"
    set tsr to style of word 4 of document 1
    on styles of tsr -- {underline}
end tell
```

case, diacriticals, white space, hyphens, expansion, punctuation, numeric strings

Description

String considerations; see "Considering/Ignoring" in Chapter 19.

Example

```
considering case
    "heyho" contains "H" -- false
end considering
```

application responses

Description

See "Considering/Ignoring" in Chapter 19.

Example

```
ignoring application responses
    tell application "GraphicConverter" to quit
end ignoring
```

current application

Description

The top-level object. See "The Implicit Parent Chain" in Chapter 8.

Example

```
name of current application -- Script Editor
```

Sunday, Monday, Tuesday, Wednesday, Thursday, Friday, Saturday

Description

Days of the week; see "Date Properties" in Chapter 13. These terms are actually implemented as class names (I don't know why).

Example

```
weekday of (current date) -- Wednesday
```

January, February, March, April, May, June, July, August, September, October, November, December

Description

Names of months; see "Date Properties" in Chapter 13. These terms are actually implemented as class names (I don't know why).

Example

```
month of (current date) -- May
```

CHAPTER 18

Commands

A *command* is basically a verb. Technically, a command is called an *event* (because it really is an Apple event, as discussed in Chapter 3). This chapter catalogues the built-in commands of the AppleScript language—those not described elsewhere in this book. AppleScript defines very few commands of its own, leaving it to other applications to extend the language by defining further verbs as necessary.

(For the syntax of a command, see "Event Handlers" in Chapter 9; on how to use a command, see Chapter 11. For set, copy, and get, see "Assignment and Retrieval" in Chapter 7. For run, see "Run Handler" in Chapter 8. For error, see "Errors" in Chapter 19.)

Application Commands

A few commands may be sent to applications to start them up, bring them to the front, and make them quit. An application does not have to be scriptable to obey them (see Table 20-1 and the discussion there).

launch

Syntax

```
launch application
```

Description

Makes sure an application is running, without bringing it frontmost or making it perform any actions. This command is not commonly needed, because AppleScript, as it runs a script that targets an application locally, will automatically attempt to start up that application if it isn't running already (a good thing, since an application that isn't running can't receive any Apple events). Some applications, however, perform special actions when started up automatically in this way, such as opening a document or coming to the front. The launch command can be a way of running the application while avoiding these special actions, and there is no penalty for issuing it if the application is already running, as nothing will happen.

activate

Syntax

activate *application*

Description

Brings an application frontmost.

reopen

Syntax

reopen *application*

Description

Tells an application to behave as if it had been opened from the Finder. Some applications behave specially when told to do this. For example, in the case of the Finder, reopen makes a window open if no Finder windows are open at that moment; launch and activate don't.

quit

Syntax

quit *application*

Description

Tells an application to quit.

Standard Commands

The standard commands are basic events that should be implemented by any scriptable application. The only standard command implemented by AppleScript itself is count (with strings, lists, and records; see Chapter 13).

count

Syntax

count *object* [each *class*]
count every *class* of *object*
count *class-plural* of *object*

Description

Reports the number of *class* elements of *object*.

The count command is implemented in an unusual way. The *class* represents the element that is to be counted; it is optional, and most users prefer the second or third formulation if it is to be specified. (So, one tends to say "count items of L" rather than "count L each item.") If it is *not* specified, then it is up to the target to supply a default element and count it. Users tend to be unconscious of this fact. For example, when you say "count s," where s is a string, you're probably not aware that AppleScript is reinterpreting this as "count s each character." That's because character is the default element for a string; you could also specify a different element ("count words of s"). This syntax is sometimes the cause of misunderstandings, especially when talking to some scriptable application. See "Repeat With . . . In" in Chapter 19.

Logging Commands

These commands have to do with the script editor application's logging window or pane. They control the generation of the AppleScript messages that this window or pane is "watching" while it is open.

log

Syntax

```
log value
```

Description

If the event log pane or window is open, writes *value* to the log pane or window. This is useful for debugging. See Appendix A for an example.

stop log, start log

Syntax

```
stop log
start log
```

Description

If the event log pane or window is open, disables and enables automatic logging of Apple events sent between applications; has no effect on the log command.

Only the old version of Script Editor (version 1.9), and Script Debugger, implement stop log and start log properly. If you try to use them in Smile or in the current Script Editor, you get a runtime error.

CHAPTER 19

Control

Control structures are the basis of a computer program's overall logic and "intelligence." They dictate the flow of a script. They are not commands; they are the signposts that describe how commands should be treated. They tell AppleScript how to decide what command should be executed next, or what to do if a command fails at runtime. They also modify how certain commands and operators are interpreted.

 When typing any block in this chapter, in the termination line just type the word end. AppleScript fills in the missing term after compilation. (So, for example, don't type end if; just type end.) This shortcut saves time and is helpful for confirming that you have correctly structured your blocks.

Branching

The "intelligent" behavior of a computer program depends upon its ability to make choices at runtime. These choices generally take the form of evaluating some expression and executing or not executing a particular block of code depending on how the evaluation turns out at that moment.

One major form of choice is *branching*. We have a line or block of code that can be executed optionally. The computer evaluates a boolean expression, called a *condition*. If the condition is true, the line or block of code is executed; if it isn't, the line or block of code is skipped, and execution jumps to the line that follows it.

In AppleScript, branching control is performed with if. An if block comes in several forms. The basic form is a single block of code that is executed only if a condition is true. If the condition is false, the block is skipped, and execution resumes after the end if line.

```
if condition then
    -- what to do if condition is true
end if
```

It is also permitted to supply a second block with else, to be executed if the condition is false. One or the other of the two blocks will be executed.

```
if condition then
        -- what to do if condition is true
else
        -- what to do if condition is false
end if
```

Another syntax lets you specify multiple conditions. AppleScript will execute the first block whose condition is true, skipping the others. It is permitted to supply, with else, a final block that will be executed if none of the conditions is true.

```
if condition1 then
        -- what to do if condition1 is true
else if condition2 then
        -- what to do if condition2 is true
-- ... same for condition3, condition4, etc.
[else]
        -- what to do if none of them is true
end if
```

So, for example:

```
set x to random number from 1 to 10
set guess to text returned of ¬
    (display dialog "Pick a number from 1 to 10" default answer "")
try
    set guess to guess as number
on error
    return
end try
if guess < 1 or guess > 10 then
    display dialog "I said from 1 to 10!"
else if guess < x then
    display dialog "Too small. I was thinking of " & x
else if guess > x then
    display dialog "Too big. I was thinking of " & x
else
    display dialog "Just right."
end if
```

There's also a single-line form:

```
if condition then whatToDo
```

In the single-line form, whatToDo is any valid expression or single-line command (it can even be another single-line if).

 When typing a multiline if block, don't bother to type the word then. AppleScript will add it at compile time.

Looping

The other major form of choice is *looping*, which involves branching back to the start of a block repeatedly. In AppleScript, looping is performed with repeat. There are several varieties of repeat, but repeat blocks all take same basic form:

```
repeat whatKindOfRepeat
    -- what to do
end repeat
```

 Loops involve repetition—perhaps a lot of repetition. Therefore, although I'm no great believer in worrying too much about optimization, if you're going to optimize your code anywhere, loops are the place to do it. A small increase in speed can add up tremendously over multiple repetitions. See Chapter 22.

The big question with a repeat block is how you're going to get out of it. Obviously you don't want to repeat the repeat block forever, because that would be an infinite loop and would cause the computer to hang. Most kinds of repeat block include some instruction (as symbolized by *whatKindOfRepeat* in the syntax template), such as a condition to be evaluated, as a way of deciding whether to loop again.

There are also some special commands for hustling things along by leaping completely out of the repeat block from inside it. These are the *premature terminations* of a repeat block. They can be used with any form of repeat block. Here they are:

exit repeat
> This statement exits the innermost repeat block in which it occurs. Execution resumes after the end repeat line.

try block
> If the repeat block is inside a try block, throwing an error exits the repeat block by virtue of the fact that it exits the try block. See "Errors," later in this chapter.

return
> A return statement exits the repeat block by virtue of the fact that it terminates execution of the handler or script.

Repeat Forever

A repeat block with no *whatKindOfRepeat* condition repeats forever. Obviously you don't *really* want it to repeat forever, so it's up to you to supply a way out by using one of the three premature terminations.

```
repeat
    display dialog "Prepare to loop forever."
    exit repeat
end repeat
display dialog "Just kidding."
```

Repeat N Times

A repeat block where *whatKindOfRepeat* is an integer followed by the keyword times repeats that number of times (unless the block terminates prematurely). The integer can be a variable.

```
repeat 3 times
    display dialog "This is really boring."
end repeat
display dialog "Zzzzzz...."
```

An interesting misuse of this construct is as a workaround for AppleScript's lack of a next repeat or continue keyword. (This idea was suggested to me by Paul Berkowitz, who attributes it to Ray Robertson.) The problem is that you can short-circuit a repeat block by exiting it completely, but you cannot, as you can in many languages, short-circuit it by proceeding immediately to the next iteration of the loop. The workaround is to embed a one-time repeat block within your repeat block; an exit repeat within this one-time repeat block works as a next repeat with respect to the outer repeat block. This device has some shortcomings (it prevents exit repeat from doing its proper job), and it doesn't accomplish anything you couldn't manage with an if block, but in a large script it can make your code easier to read and maintain.

In this (silly) example, we add only the positive items of a list:

```
set L to {2, -5, 33, 4, -7, 8}
set total to 0
repeat (count L) times
    repeat 1 times
        set x to item 1 of L
        set L to rest of L
        if x < 0 then exit repeat
        set total to total + x
    end repeat
end repeat
total -- 47
```

For another useful misuse of this construct, see "Blocks" in Chapter 5.

Repeat While

A repeat block where *whatKindOfRepeat* is the keyword while followed by a boolean condition tests the condition before each repetition. If the condition is true, the block is executed. If the condition is false, the block is not executed and that's the end of the loop; execution resumes after the end repeat line. The idea is that in the course of looping something will eventually happen that will make the condition false.

```
set response to "Who's there?"
repeat while response = "Who's there?"
    set response to button returned of ¬
        (display dialog "Knock knock!" buttons {"Enough!", "Who's there?"})
end repeat
```

Repeat Until

A repeat block where *whatKindOfRepeat* is the keyword until followed by a boolean condition tests the condition before each repetition. If the condition is false, the block is executed. If the condition is true, the block is not executed and that's the end of the loop; execution resumes after the end repeat line. This construct is technically unnecessary, as the very same thing could have been achieved by reversing the truth value of the condition of a repeat while block—that is to say, repeat until is exactly the same as repeat while not.

```
set response to ""
repeat until response = "Enough!"
    set response to button returned of ¬
        (display dialog "Knock knock!" buttons {"Enough!", "Who's there?"})
end repeat
```

 Those accustomed to the do...until construct in C and similar languages should observe that it is possible for an AppleScript repeat until block not to be executed even once.

Repeat With

The syntax of a repeat with announcement line is as follows:

```
repeat with variableName from startInteger to endInteger [by stepInteger]
```

Here's how a repeat with works:

1. When the repeat with announcement line is encountered for the first time, *startInteger* and *endInteger* (and *stepInteger*, if supplied) are evaluated once and for all. Each must be an integer (or a real or string representing an integer); if not, there's a runtime error.

2. If *startInteger* is larger than *endInteger* (or smaller if *stepInteger* is negative), that's the end of the loop and execution resumes after the end repeat line.

3. The value *startInteger* is assigned to the variable *variableName*, which is created as a local if not in scope already. (Note that *variableName*, if declared implicitly at the top level, will *not* be a global; this contradicts "Scope of Undeclared Variables" in Chapter 10.)

4. The block is executed. (If code within the block terminates the repetition prematurely, that's the end.)

5. The value 1 (or *stepInteger* if supplied) is added to the value that *variableName* was assigned before the previous repetition. If the resulting value is larger than *endInteger* (or smaller if *stepInteger* is negative), that's the end of the loop and execution resumes after the end repeat line. Otherwise, *variableName* is assigned this new value, and it's back to step 4 for another execution of the block.

If you read the description carefully, you will realize that:

- There's no extra overhead involved if any of the integers in the repeat with line are derived from handler calls or commands, as the evaluation is performed only once. This behavior is in contrast to repeat while and repeat until.
- After a repeat with is all over, the variable *variableName* has the value it had when the last repetition terminated.
- Setting the variable *variableName* within a repeat with block affects the code that executes subsequently within the block, but it has no effect on the test performed at the top of the next repetition or on what value *variableName* will take on as the next repetition begins.

Here's a simple example of repeat with in action:

```
repeat with x from 3 to 1 by -1
    display dialog x
end repeat
display dialog "Blast off!"
```

Repeat With . . . In

The syntax of a repeat with...in announcement line is as follows:

```
repeat with variableName in list
```

This construct is a convenient way of cycling through each item of a list. Here's how to visualize the way it works:

1. The variable *variableName* is created as a local if it is not already in scope.
2. The size of the list is obtained. Call this number theCount.
3. A reference to the list is obtained. Call this theListRef.
4. A counter is initialized to zero. Call it x.
5. Before each repetition, x is incremented. If x exceeds theCount, that's the end of the loop, and execution resumes after the end repeat line. Otherwise, *variableName* is assigned this value:

```
a reference to item x of theListRef
```

6. The block is executed.

(In this sequence of steps, none of the variable names are real: there is nothing called theCount, theListRef, or x. But AppleScript is truly maintaining these values internally; I gave them names simply for clarity.)

The big surprise here is step 5, which sets the value of *variableName*. At the start of each repetition, nothing is copied from the list into *variableName*. It's a reference (see Chapter 12). So, for example, in this loop:

```
repeat with x in {1, 2, 3}
    -- code
end repeat
```

the variable x does *not* take on the values 1, 2, 3. It takes on these successive values:

```
a reference to item 1 of {1, 2, 3}
a reference to item 2 of {1, 2, 3}
a reference to item 3 of {1, 2, 3}
```

References are often transparently dereferenced, so the fact that *variableName* is a reference might not make a difference to your code. For example:

```
repeat with x in {1, 2, 3}
    display dialog x -- 1, 2, 3
end repeat
```

In that example, the reference is implicitly dereferenced, and the value of each item is retrieved from the list. But consider what happens when the reference is *not* implicitly dereferenced. For instance, you might apply to *variableName* the equality or inequality operator:

```
repeat with x in {1, 2, 3}
    if x = 2 then
        display dialog "2"
    end if
end repeat
```

The dialog never appears! That's because x is never 2. The second time through the loop, x is a reference to item 2 of {1, 2, 3}; that's not the same thing as the integer 2, and AppleScript doesn't implicitly dereference the reference. Clearly your script will misbehave if you're unprepared. The solution is to dereference explicitly:

```
repeat with x in {1, 2, 3}
    if contents of x = 2 then
        display dialog "2"
    end if
end repeat
```

Here's another example; we'll retrieve each value and store it somewhere else:

```
set L1 to {1, 2, 3}
set L2 to {}
repeat with x in L1
    set end of L2 to x
end repeat
```

What do you think L2 is after that? If you said {1, 2, 3}, you're wrong; it's this:

```
L2 -- {item 1 of {1, 2, 3}, item 2 of {1, 2, 3}, item 3 of {1, 2, 3}}
```

L1 is a list of values; L2 is a list of references. If you want L2 to end up identical to L1, you must dereference each reference:

```
set L1 to {1, 2, 3}
set L2 to {}
repeat with x in L1
    set end of L2 to contents of x
end repeat
L2 -- {1, 2, 3}
```

A powerful consequence of the fact that *variableName* is a reference to an item of a list is that you can use it to assign back into the original list:

```
set L to {1, 2, 3}
repeat with x in L
     set contents of x to item x of {"Mannie", "Moe", "Jack"}
end repeat
L -- {"Mannie", "Moe", "Jack"}
```

We can take advantage of this technique to rewrite the return-by-reference example from the end of Chapter 12 in a different way:

```
on findInList(what, L)
     repeat with anItem in L
          if contents of anItem is what then
               return anItem
          end if
     end repeat
     return
end findInList
local pep
set pep to {"Mannie", "Moe", "Jack"}
set contents of findInList("Moe", pep) to "Larry"
pep -- {"Mannie", "Larry", "Jack"}
```

On the whole, you should probably not make more radical alterations to the list during the course of a repetition, but it is not unsafe to do so. If you assign a completely new value to the list variable, there is no change in the behavior of the loop, because a reference to the old list was already captured at the outset (that is the significance of the listRef variable in my explanation of how this construct works). So:

```
set L to {1, 2, 3}
repeat with x in L
     set L to {"Mannie", "Moe", "Jack"}
     display dialog x -- 1, then 2, then 3
end repeat
```

Why does that work? It's because on each repetition, x takes on these values, just as before:

```
a reference to item 1 of {1, 2, 3}
a reference to item 2 of {1, 2, 3}
a reference to item 3 of {1, 2, 3}
```

You changed what L points to, but listRef already holds a reference to the original list. On the other hand, if you mutate the list in place, listRef is still a reference to that same list, so it acquires the mutations:

```
set L to {1, 2, 3}
repeat with x in L
     display dialog x -- 1 (every time)
     set beginning of L to contents of x
end repeat
L -- {1, 1, 1, 1, 2, 3}
```

The dialog says "1" every time because, for example, by the time we come to the third loop and get a reference to item 3 of L, item 3 of L is 1. Observe that this code did not cause an infinite loop. That is the significance of step 2 in my explanation of how this construct works: theCount was evaluated once, before the first repetition, and you won't repeat more times than that.

A very odd thing happens when you combine repeat with...in directly with a class name as a way of gathering a list of elements, like this:

```
repeat with x in every class
```

To see what I mean, consider this code:

```
set total to 0
tell application "Finder"
    count folders -- 6
    repeat with x in every folder
        set total to total + 1
    end repeat
end tell
total -- 50
```

I've got only six folders on my desktop, so where did the number 50 come from? To put it another way, what did we just cycle through? The answer is that we didn't cycle through each folder; we cycled through each item *inside* each folder. (So 50 is the total number of files and folders inside the six folders on my desktop.) Here's why. When you talk like this, AppleScript does *not* ask the target application for a list of all the things you specify. Instead, it merely asks the target application for a *count* of those things. And it asks for this count in a very strange form:

```
count every class each item
```

Most applications simply shrug off this extra "each item"; most of their classes don't have an element called item, so they ignore this part of the command. For example, when you say this:

```
tell application "Microsoft Entourage"
    repeat with x in every contact
```

AppleScript asks Entourage to "count every contact each item." Entourage contacts don't have an item element, so Entourage treats this as if it were "count every contact" and simply reports the number of contacts. But in the Finder, a folder *does* have items, so the Finder obligingly totals up the number of items within each folder and reports that total.

This is not, however, simply an odd behavior on the part of the Finder; my point is what AppleScript does. We've just seen that when you say this:

```
repeat with x in every class
```

AppleScript does not gather a list. It merely obtains a number. So how on earth does it perform the loop? In other words, what is x every time through the loop? When you say this:

```
tell application "Microsoft Entourage"
    repeat with x in every contact
```

then on successive passes through the loop the value of x is this:

```
a reference to item 1 of every contact
a reference to item 2 of every contact
a reference to item 3 of every contact
```

And so on. AppleScript uses the class you asked for to form a reference to a particular item of the list that *would* be generated if we actually asked for it. But it doesn't ask for that list unless you try to fetch that item. This looks at first blush like an optimization, but if you think about, it's really quite the opposite. Consider what happens when you run this script:

```
tell application "Microsoft Entourage"
    repeat with x in every contact
        get name of x
    end repeat
end tell
```

That is already a wasteful script, as you could have obtained the names of all contacts with a single Apple event by asking for "name of every contact." But it's even more wasteful than you might suppose. Each time through the loop, you are not asking for "name of contact 1," "name of contact 2," and so forth. You are asking for "name of item 1 of every contact," "name of item 2 of every contact," and so forth. In other words, you are asking Entourage to form a list of all contacts, *every time through the loop!* That's unnecessary, because the list doesn't change.

This situation gets even worse if the list you're asking for is to be generated in a more complicated way. Here is some code where we try to get BBEdit to change all words that start with "t" to the word "howdy":

```
tell application "BBEdit"
    repeat with w in (every word of document 1 where its text begins with "t")
        set text of w to "howdy"
    end repeat
end tell
```

There are two problems with this code. First, it's incredibly wasteful, because every time through the loop, w is something like this:

```
a reference to item x of every word of window 1 of application "BBEdit" ¬
    where its text begins with "t"
```

Thus, if we do anything with w, we are asking BBEdit to perform this complicated boolean test (every word of window 1 where its text begins with "t") every time through the loop!

The second problem is that the code doesn't work. If there are two words starting with "t" in the document, it fails with a runtime error. The reason is that the second time through the loop, we are asking for this:

```
a reference to item 2 of every word of window 1 of application "BBEdit" ¬
    where its text begins with "t"
```

But there is no such item, because there were originally two such words and we just changed one of them to "howdy," so now there is only one such word.

The solution to this entire issue is: Don't Do That. Simply don't talk like this:

```
repeat with x in every class
```

AppleScript's response to this way of talking may have been intended as an optimization, but it's just a mess. The simple solution is to gather the list explicitly, in the same line or an earlier line. So, say this:

```
repeat with x in (get every class)
```

Or this:

```
set L to (get every class)
repeat with x in L
```

All the problems with repeat with...in vanish in a puff of smoke if you do this. You ask for the list just once, at the start of the loop. That's the only time the application has to form the list, so execution is far less wasteful. You actually obtain the list you ask for, so you're looping through what you think you're looping through. So, for instance, this works properly:

```
tell application "Finder"
    repeat with x in (get every folder) -- loops 6 times, as expected
```

And here's a quick, efficient, and correctly working version of our BBEdit script:

```
tell application "BBEdit"
    set L to (get every word of document 1 where its text begins with "t")
    repeat with w in (reverse of L)
        set text of w to "howdy"
    end repeat
end tell
```

Tell

A tell block, like an if block, comes in two forms: a genuine block and a single-line version. The block form is like this:

```
tell target
    -- code targeting this target
end tell
```

The single-line version is like this:

```
tell target to command
```

A tell block performs two distinct functions:

- It determines (at runtime) the *target* of the commands within the block.
- It dictates (at compile time) the source that will be used for the resolution of the *terminology* that appears within the block.

The fact that a tell block does both these things makes a certain sense. After all, if you're going to be sending messages to the Finder, you're probably going to want to use the Finder's terminology. Nevertheless, the two functions are distinct, and it is possible to do either one without the other:

- To target an application without resolving any terminology, address it entirely by means of of, without using tell:

  ```
  get frontmost of application "Finder" -- false
  ```

  That works because the term frontmost is defined by AppleScript itself, so there is no terminology to resolve; the Finder is targeted and a reply comes back.

- To resolve an application's terminology without targeting it, use a terms block (see the next section, "Using Terms From"):

  ```
  using terms from application "Finder"
      set f to a reference to folder 1
  end using terms from
  ```

  That works because the terms block uses the Finder's dictionary to resolve the term folder; the Finder is not targeted (we're just forming a reference).

If the *target* in a tell block is an application, that application can be expressed as a variable rather than a literal application specifier. This variable may have as its value an application specifier, or it might be a reference to an object belonging to an application. Or, the target could be an application specifier, but the name of the application is a string variable instead of a literal string. In these situations, you'll probably have to use a terms block in order to get the code inside the tell block to compile.

On the need for a target application to be present at compile time, decompile time, and runtime, see "Missing External Referents" in Chapter 3. On determination of the target, see Chapter 11. On resolution of terminology, see Chapter 20.

Using Terms From

A terms block has the following structure:

```
using terms from application
    -- code containing terms to be resolved
end using terms from
```

A terms block dictates which application's dictionary AppleScript should get the enclosed terminology from, without actually targeting that application. Terminology is resolved at compile time; therefore the *application* must be a literal application specifier (otherwise there's a compile-time error, "Can't make some data into the expected type"). A terms block is important *only* at compile time (and decompile time); it is effectively ignored at runtime.

A question immediately arises of what happens when a tell block and a terms block are nested inside one another. The short answer is that the innermost block takes precedence. Here's an example of how to screw things up:

```
tell application "Finder"
    using terms from application "Microsoft Entourage"
        get name of folder 1 -- error: Finder got an error: Can't get name of folder 1
    end using terms from
end tell
```

The problem there is that you're forcing AppleScript to resolve folder by means of Entourage's dictionary. Entourage defines folder, but using a different four-letter code from the Finder. You're still targeting the Finder, though, so when you do, you're talking to it in Entourage's language, which the Finder doesn't understand.

But if an innermost tell block would not permit AppleScript to resolve terminology, a terms block surrounding it may do so. This will compile just fine:

```
using terms from application "Finder"
    tell application someVariable
        get name of folder 1
    end tell
end using terms from
```

And it's completely equivalent to nesting the blocks the other way around:

```
tell application someVariable
    using terms from application "Finder"
        get name of folder 1
    end using terms from
end tell
```

Those examples illustrate how a terms block is typically used—it lets you target an application in a tell block without saying explicitly what application it is. Here, the application's name is expressed as a variable, someVariable; AppleScript has no idea what this will be at runtime, so it follows the instructions of the terms block and thus is able at compile time to obtain a dictionary that resolves the enclosed terminology. Successful compilation, of course, does not guarantee that the code will run. Perhaps someVariable will specify an application that understands the Finder's notion of what a folder is; perhaps not. Basically you're telling AppleScript to suspend judgment and just believe that the Finder's notion of a folder will work here.

Why would you want to do something like that? One reason would be to allow compilation of a script targeting a remote application (see "Remote Applications" in Chapter 23). You have seen that AppleScript must be able to resolve all terminology at compile time, and that normally it attempts to do this by using the dictionary of the targeted application. When an application is on another computer, this might not be possible at the time the script is compiled: the remote machine might be unavailable, the remote application might not be running, or the script might specify the target machine dynamically. A terms block lets you get past these hurdles by specifying a local source for the terminology you're using.

In this example, I'll talk to my iBook in the next room. I've turned on Remote Apple Events in the iBook's Sharing preferences. The script specifies a machine dynamically. It compiles on my iMac because I use a terms block to get the Finder's terminology from the local Finder, the Finder on my iMac. It runs because I specify a valid machine name in the dialog (and because I know the username and password for that machine):

```
set whatMachine to text returned of ¬
    (display dialog "Machine to connect to:" default answer "eppc://")
-- I enter eppc://duck.local and hit OK; the password dialog appears and I fill it out correctly
tell application "Finder" of machine whatMachine
    using terms from application "Finder"
        get name of disk 1 -- "OmniumGatherum"
    end using terms from
end tell
```

This next example shows how applications can be targeted dynamically through references. There is no tell block anywhere in the script! The handler getThing acts as a general dispatcher; it dereferences whatever reference it is handed, and reports back the result. It has no notion of what application this involves, or even that it involves an application. AppleScript must be able to resolve all terminology at compile time, so we form our references with terms blocks.

```
using terms from application "Microsoft Entourage"
    set n1 to a reference to name of folder 1 of application "Microsoft Entourage"
end using terms from
using terms from application "Finder"
    set n2 to a reference to name of folder 1 of application "Finder"
end using terms from
on getThing(R)
    return (get contents of R)
end getThing
getThing(n1) -- "Inbox"
getThing(n2) -- "Mannie"
```

A terms block can also be used to solve the puzzle of how an applet can be made to behave like a compiled script file when a targeted application might be missing. (See "Missing External Referents" in Chapter 3.) Normally, an applet attempts to locate all targeted applications at launch time. A compiled script file, on the other hand, postpones this attempt until the script is running and code targeting an application is actually encountered; if such code is never encountered, the question never arises. The problem is to get an applet to behave that way—to launch and start running even if, somewhere in its code, it targets an application that might not be present. The trick here is to refer to the target application in its tell block by means of a variable, wrapping the whole thing in a terms block so that compilation will succeed:

```
using terms from application "someAppThatMightBeMissing"
    set s to "someAppThatMightBeMissing"
    tell application s
        doYourThing
    end tell
end using terms from
```

If this code is actually encountered during the course of execution, then the application had better be present or there will be a runtime error. But the point is that at least the applet will launch! Other code might decide whether to execute this code, based on the presence of the application or some other criteria, or this code could be enclosed in a try block that will catch the error and proceed in some other way (see "Errors," later in this chapter).

With

A with block is used to specify certain external attributes of Apple events sent to target applications from inside the block. Two types of with block are defined: a timeout block and a transaction block.

Timeout

Recall from "Apple Events" in Chapter 3 that during interapplication communications, the sender of an Apple event may attach to that Apple event a specification of how long it is willing to wait for a reply. This is the Apple event's *timeout* period. If the target does not reply within the specified timeout period, for whatever reason (the requested operation might be too lengthy, the target application might be otherwise engaged, and so forth), the system stops waiting for a reply and reports to the sender that the Apple event timed out. This report arrives as an error; your script can handle this error and proceed (see "Errors," later in this chapter).

This entire mechanism is valuable, because (among other things) it rescues the sender from hanging indefinitely while waiting for the target to reply; if the target takes too long, the sender is able to proceed nonetheless. Of course, the sender must then do without any reply from the target, but a script can take account of this possibility. For example, reporting the problem to the user and proceeding, or even terminating in good order, is surely preferable to hanging or appearing to hang while waiting for a reply that is taking a long time to arrive and that may, indeed, never come.

All Apple events sent to target applications have a default timeout value of *one minute*. This is a good compromise between waiting sufficiently long for lengthy operations to complete and waiting so long (or not having any timeout at all) that a script can hang or appear to hang. If this value is acceptable to you, you don't need a timeout block to change it.

To change the timeout value temporarily using a timeout block, use this syntax:

```
with timeout of integer second[s]
    -- code affected by timeout value
end timeout
```

This affects only code within the block; afterwards, Apple events revert to the default timeout value. To wait indefinitely, use an extremely large *integer*. The maximum permissible value is 8947848. In Tiger there is no penalty for using a larger number, but it will be treated as 8947848; on earlier systems, a larger number will cause a runtime error ("The result of a numeric operation was too large").

To illustrate, we'll command the Finder to perform an operation so long that without a timeout specification, it probably wouldn't have time to reply—we'll ask it to cycle down the entire hierarchy looking for a certain kind of file:

```
with timeout of 100000 seconds
    tell application "Finder"
        get every application file of entire contents ¬
            of disk 1 where its creator type is "aplt"
    end tell
end timeout
```

If we don't provide a timeout block, this code will time out before the Finder is finished, and we'll get an error: "Finder got an error: AppleEvent timed out." (Even if the Apple event times out, the Finder will still be cycling down the entire hierarchy, and it will keep doing so until it finishes. So don't run that example unless you're not planning on using the Finder for a while!)

Transaction

A problem that can arise with interapplication communications is that a target application is promiscuous. While you're being a sender and talking to a target application, some other sender can come along and talk to it as well. If this happens in the middle of a series of Apple events from you, it can alter the state of the target application, messing up what you're trying to accomplish.

The Apple event solution to this is the *transaction*. A transaction is a kind of permission slip allowing you to unify multiple commands. You start by asking for this permission slip, and the target application returns a transaction ID of some sort. You then continue sending the target application Apple events, showing it the transaction ID every time. When you're done, you tell the target that you're done (showing it the transaction ID, of course), and that transaction comes to an end. Not every scriptable application implements transactions (would that they did); a commonly used application that does is FileMaker Pro.

The target application itself is responsible for deciding how to implement the notion of a transaction. All you care about is that state should be conserved throughout the multiple commands of a single transaction. FileMaker's approach is to implement a transaction as monopolization; once you've asked for the permission slip and obtained the transaction ID, FileMaker will simply refuse to respond to any Apple event that does not show the transaction ID until you tell it the transaction is over, at which point it returns to its normal state of promiscuity.

The way to obtain, show, and release the transaction ID is by wrapping your transactional communications in a transaction block, which looks like this:

```
with transaction
      -- transactional code
end transaction
```

All the actual business of dealing with the transaction ID is handled transparently for you. The with transaction line causes an Apple event to be sent to the current target asking for the transaction ID. Then all the application-targeted Apple events inside the block are accompanied by this transaction ID. Finally, the end transaction line sends the current target an Apple event (accompanied by the transaction ID) telling it to leave transaction mode.

In this example, we monopolize FileMaker Pro long enough to create a Find request and perform it:

```
tell application "FileMaker Pro"
    with transaction
        tell database 1
            show every record
            set f to create new request
            set cell "lastname" of f to "neuburg"
            find
        end tell
    end transaction
end tell
```

There is one important thing to notice about that code: the transaction block is inside the tell block. It is essential to structure your code this way; the application with which you want to carry on a transaction must be the target when the with transaction line is encountered, so that AppleScript knows where to send that first Apple event asking for the transaction ID. Unfortunately, this means we run smack into a bizarre terminology problem. It turns out that FileMaker Pro's dictionary also implements the opening and closing transactional Apple events as the commands begin transaction and end transaction. This means that when you say end transaction inside a tell block addressed to FileMaker Pro, it is seen as FileMaker's end transaction command, not as the closing of the transaction block. The script then won't compile. The workaround, which is terribly annoying, is to delete the word transaction from the end transaction line whenever you are about to compile.

You might worry about what happens if something goes wrong in the middle of the transaction block. What if we say something that generates an error? We'll never reach the end of the transaction block, and that means we'll leave FileMaker Pro in a transaction state, refusing to respond to Apple events. You're perfectly right to worry about this; you certainly don't want to leave FileMaker Pro in transaction mode. If FileMaker Pro were to get into such a state, you couldn't even quit it, because the Quit menu item is implemented with an Apple event—and FileMaker Pro won't listen to that Apple event, because it doesn't supply the transaction ID! It turns out, though, that AppleScript solves this problem transparently. If an error is encountered during a transaction block, AppleScript sends the target the Apple event that ends the transaction. I suspect that the transaction block is wrapped in a sort of invisible try block. In any case, it's really all very nicely implemented.

Considering/Ignoring

There are two kinds of considering/ignoring block. One is the "ignoring application responses" block, which affects the nature of Apple events targeting an application. The other affects the details of string comparisons.

Ignoring Application Responses

Recall from "Apple Events" in Chapter 3 that during interapplication communications the sender of an Apple event may specify that it has no intention of waiting around for a reply. It doesn't care what the result is; it doesn't care if there's an error. It just wants to send the Apple event and be done with it, proceeding immediately to its own next step. In AppleScript, here's how to send such an Apple event:

```
ignoring application responses
    -- code
end ignoring
```

Within the block, only Apple events sent to other applications are affected. Apple events sent to scripting additions, for example, are sent in the normal way and receive whatever replies they normally receive.

For an example, see "Reduction" in Chapter 1. The code that opens a URL from the clipboard is wrapped in an "ignoring application responses" block, because I want the browser or mail client or whatever to open in the background and without my waiting for it; thus I can get on immediately with what I was doing.

Inside an "ignoring application responses" block, it is possible to override the block by embedding a "considering application responses" block. You might use this construct, for example, to ignore responses from one application but not another.

String Considerations

String considerations are optional switches that govern the nature of a string comparison (see "Comparison Operators" and "Containment Operators" in Chapter 15). For example, string comparison may be case-sensitive or case-insensitive. You can use a considering/ignoring block to govern this behavior.

Until recently there was no mechanism for making string considerations visible to a targeted application. This meant that string considerations could operate only within AppleScript; a string comparison performed as part of a boolean test element specifier, for example, could not be affected by string considerations (see "Boolean Test" in Chapter 11 and "Who Performs an Operation" in Chapter 15). This limitation has changed, but applications must be rewritten if they are to notice and take account of string considerations (and I do not know of any application that has been rewritten in this way). See also "String and Clipboard" in Chapter 21 on the offset scripting addition command.

Here are the string considerations:

case
> If ignored, uppercase and lowercase variants of the same letter are taken to be equivalent. Ignored by default.

diacriticals
> If ignored, variants of the same letter with different accent marks (or no accent mark) are taken to be equivalent. Considered by default.

expansion
> If ignored, ligatures are taken to be equivalent to their component characters. Considered by default.

hyphens
> If ignored, hyphens are taken not to exist. Considered by default.

punctuation
> If ignored, word-boundary punctuation and quotation marks and apostrophes are taken not to exist. Considered by default.

white space
> If ignored, spaces, tabs, and line-break characters are taken not to exist. Considered by default.

numeric strings
> (New in Tiger.) If considered, the string is treated as a version number, consisting of sections delimited by a period; order is determined by successive numeric comparison of these sections.

Here's the syntax for writing a string consideration:

```
considering | ignoring considerations [but ignoring | considering considerations]
    -- code
end considering | ignoring
```

Each set of *considerations* is any number of string considerations separated by comma; AppleScript will rewrite the last comma as and. Entire string consideration blocks may also be nested. So, for example:

```
ignoring hyphens, expansion and punctuation
    considering white space but ignoring case and diacriticals
        "a-" = "Å!" -- true
    end considering
end ignoring
```

String considerations are Unicode-savvy:

```
set bigEpsilon to «data utxt0395» as Unicode text
set littleEpsilon to «data utxt03B5» as Unicode text
ignoring case
    bigEpsilon = littleEpsilon -- true
end ignoring
```

Here's an example illustrating the new numeric strings consideration:

```
"1.10" > "1.9.3" -- false
considering numeric strings
    "1.10" > "1.9.3" -- true
end considering
```

In the comparison inside the considering block, 1 is equal to 1 so we proceed to the next section; 10 is greater than 9 so that's the result of the comparison.

Errors

An *error* is a message at runtime saying, in effect, that something bad has happened and execution cannot continue. The sender of such a message is said to *throw* an error. The message percolates up through the chain of handler calls (the *call chain*), looking for an error-handling block surrounding the line currently being executed; such a block is said to *catch* the error. If no such block catches the error, it percolates all the way up to AppleScript, and the script terminates prematurely (possibly with an error dialog).

This entire mechanism is extremely nice, because it provides a target application, or AppleScript itself, with a way to signal that it's impossible to proceed, interrupting the flow of code while leaving it up to the caller whether and how to recover. Your script can implement no error handling, in which case any runtime error will bring the script to a grinding halt. Or your script can implement error handling in certain areas where it expects an error might occur. It can recover from some errors and re-throw others, allowing them to terminate the script. It can even throw an error deliberately as a way of controlling the flow of code.

An error can be a positive thing, and can be built into the structure of a command's implementation. For example, display dialog throws an error if the user clicks the Cancel button in the dialog. This need not kill your script. It will if you let it, and this can be a good thing (because Cancel often means "stop"). But alternatively, your script can catch the error as a way of learning that the user has cancelled, and can then proceed in some other appropriate manner.

I'll talk first about how to throw an error, then about how to catch one.

Throwing an Error

To throw an error, use the error command. It has five optional parameters:

```
error [messageString]
      [number shortInteger]
      [partial result list]
      [from anything]
      [to class]
```

Here are the default values of the parameters:

messageString
    Nothing

number
    -2700

partial result
    The empty list

from
    The currently executing script or script object

to
    The class item

You can use any of the parameters when throwing an error, but in real life you are likely to use only the first two. The others are present because this is also the structure of an error message from an application, which can supply this further information to help explain what the problem was.

If you throw an uncaught error, it will percolate all the way up to AppleScript and will be presented to the user as a dialog. The *messageString* is your chance to dictate what appears in that dialog. You will probably want to say something meaningful about what went wrong. For example:

```
error "Things fall apart, the centre cannot hold."
```

Figure 19-1 shows how that error is presented to the user in the Script Editor.

If an error is thrown in an applet, the applet puts up a similar dialog, which also offers a chance to edit the script. If this is a Stay Open applet ("Applet Options" in Chapter 27), the error does not cause it to quit.

If you don't supply any parameters at all to your error command, the error dialog reads: "An error has occurred." If you don't supply a *messageString* but you do supply an error number—let's say it's 32—the dialog reads: "An error of type 32 has occurred."

Figure 19-1. An error dialog

An error number is not highly communicative to the user, unless the user happens to have a table of error numbers and their meanings, but it is certainly useful within code, particularly when you're implementing internal error handling. If different kinds of things can go wrong, you can use this number to signal which one did go wrong. An example appears in the next section.

Error number -128 is special. If an error with this number percolates up to Apple-Script, the script stops but no error dialog is displayed. This is the error number generated when the user presses Cancel in a dialog presented by an interface scripting addition command such as `display dialog`. Thus, the user can cancel without automatically being presented with an error message immediately after. ("User canceled." "I *know* that!")

Some milieus never present an error message, regardless of the error. For example, if a script being run by Apple's Script Menu generates a runtime error, the script will simply fail silently. I regard this as a bug.

Catching an Error

The only way to catch an error is for that error to be thrown within a try block. The thrown error percolates up through the call chain, and if it eventually finds itself within a try block, it may be caught. The point of the call chain here is that the error need not occur *directly* within a try block; it may occur within in a handler that was called within a try block, or the call to *that* handler may be within a try block, and so forth.

There are two forms of try block. In the first, there is no actual error-handling code:

```
try
    -- code in which errors will be caught
end try
```

This form of try block handles the error by ignoring it. If an error occurs within the try block, the block terminates; execution resumes after the end try, and that's the end of the matter. Thus, you have no way to learn directly that an error was caught (though you can learn indirectly, because some code may have been skipped). But at least the error didn't bring your script to a halt. Here's an example:

```
set x to "Cancel"
try
    set x to button returned of (display dialog "Press a button.")
end try
display dialog "You pressed " & x
```

Without the try block, this code would never reach the last line after the user presses the Cancel button.

In this next example, we use a try block as a form of flow control, to terminate a loop prematurely (see "Looping," earlier in this chapter). We want to get the name of every disk. (Ignore the fact that we could just ask the Finder for this information directly.) Instead of asking how many disks there are and looping that number of times, we loop inside a try block. The loop is ostensibly endless, but in actual fact, when we exceed the number of disks, the Finder throws an error and the loop ends.

```
set L to {}
set x to 1
tell application "Finder"
    try
        repeat
            set end of L to name of disk x
            set x to x + 1
        end repeat
    end try
end tell
L -- {"feathers", "gromit", "Network"}
```

In the second, fuller form of try block, you supply a second block, an error block, presumably containing some error-handling functionality:

```
try
    -- code in which errors will be caught
on error [parameters]
    -- error-handling code
end try
```

If an error is occurs within the try block (the part before the error block), the try block terminates; execution resumes at the start of the error block. If no error occurs in the try block, the error block is skipped.

If an error occurs within the error block, it is not caught by this try block, because we are past that already; but it might be caught by some other try block that we are nested inside, either directly or further up the calling chain. Indeed, it is perfectly legitimate, and possibly useful, to throw an error within an error block.

The *parameters* of an error block are exactly the same as those for an error command, so your error block can capture and respond to any information that may have been included when the error was thrown. You don't have to include any parameters and you can include any subset of the parameters; thus you aren't forced to capture information you don't care about. Parameter variable names are local to the error block.

A not-uncommon technique is to include all the parameters and rethrow the very same error, or a slightly modified version of it, from within the error block. This could be a way, for instance, to shut things down in good order before letting the error percolate all the way to AppleScript and display a message. It can also be a way to tell yourself more about where the error occurred:

```
on num(what)
    try
        return what as number
    on error s number i partial result p from f to t
        set s to "Handler num got an error: " & s
        error s number i partial result p from f to t
    end try
end num
num("howdy") -- error: Handler num got an error: Can't make "howdy" into type number
```

Error handling and error throwing can be the basis of useful flow control. You can do some powerful things with errors that can't easily be accomplished in any other way. You can also structure your scripts better through the use of errors.

In this example, flow control is implemented entirely through handler calls and errors. We ask the user for a number; if the user tries to cancel, or supplies something that can't be coerced to a number, AppleScript throws an error, and we start over recursively. The error thrown at the end of the askUser handler is a trick for returning the user's number directly without unwinding the entire recursion:

```
on askUser()
    try
        set x to text returned of ¬
            (display dialog "Give me a number:" default answer "")
        set x to (x as number)
    on error
        askUser()
    end try
    error x
end askUser
try
    askUser()
on error what
    display dialog "Your number is " & what
end try
```

This next example is somewhat similar: it asks the user to enter the name of a color, and persists until the user complies. (In this example, unlike the previous one, if the user cancels, the script politely stops.) The example demonstrates how errors and error handling can help you organize the structure of a script:

```
on getFavoriteColor()
    try
        set r to display dialog "What is your favorite color?" default answer ""
    on error
        error number 1001
    end try
    set s to text returned of r
    if s = "" then error number 1000
    return s
end getFavoriteColor
set c to ""
repeat until c is not ""
    try
        set c to getFavoriteColor()
    on error number n
        if n = 1000 then
            display dialog "You didn't enter a color!" buttons "OK"
        else if n = 1001 then
            display dialog "Why did you cancel? Tell me!" buttons "OK"
        end if
    end try
end repeat
display dialog "Aha, you like " & c & ", eh?"
```

In that example, the handler getFavoriteColor has just one job—to try to get the user's favorite color and report what happened. Either it returns the user's favorite color, or it throws error 1000 to signal that the user left the field blank in the dialog, or it throws error 1001 to signal that the user cancelled. It's up to the caller to decide how to proceed based on on this report. This particular caller has a different dialog ready to show the user in case of either error, and is perfectly prepared to loop all day until the user enters something in the dialog. But all of that is the caller's own decision; the handler itself just performs the single task for which it was written. Distribution of responsibilities makes for more reusable code, and the example shows how throwing errors contributes to this.

A common technique in an error handler is to handle only those errors that are in some sense yours—those that you expect and are prepared to deal with. Unexpected errors are simply allowed to percolate on up the call chain, possibly all the way to AppleScript, causing the script to terminate; this makes sense because they're unexpected and you're not prepared to deal with them. There are two ways to accomplish this.

One way is to catch all errors and then rethrow any errors you aren't prepared to handle. If you're going to do that, you should probably use all the parameters, both in the on error line as you catch the error and in the error command as you rethrow it; otherwise you might strip the error of some of its information, which might reduce its value to the user (or to any code at some higher level that catches it).

In this example, we ask the user for the number of a disk to get the name of. If the number is not the number of an existing disk, the Finder throws error number -1728, so if we get an error and that's its number, we deliver a meaningful response. If we get any other error—for example, the user enters text in the dialog that can't be coerced to a number—we rethrow it and let AppleScript inform the user that this is not an integer.

```
set n to text returned of ¬
    (display dialog "What disk would you like the name of?" default answer "")
try
    tell application "Finder" to set x to name of disk (n as integer)
    display dialog x
on error e number n partial result p from f to t
    if n = -1728 then
        display dialog "I don't think that disk exists. " & e
    else
        error e number n partial result p from f to t
    end if
end try
```

The other approach is to use a *filtered error handler*. In this approach, some of the parameters in the on error line are not variable names but literals. AppleScript will call the error block only if all such literals are matched by the corresponding error parameter value. Otherwise, the error percolates up the call chain, of its own accord.

Thus, we can rewrite the entire error block from the previous example in a much briefer form, as follows:

```
on error e number -1728
    display dialog "I don't think that disk exists. " & e
end try
```

There's no way to list alternative literals; you can't write an error block that catches errors with either of just two particular error numbers, for instance. A workaround is to nest try blocks. To illustrate, here's the same example again, but this time we'll catch both error -1728 (no such disk) and error -1700 (not an integer).

```
set n to text returned of ¬
    (display dialog "What disk would you like the name of?" default answer "")
try
    try
        tell application "Finder" to set x to name of disk (n as integer)
        display dialog x
    on error e number -1728
        display dialog "I don't think that disk exists. " & e
    end try
on error e number -1700
    display dialog "I don't think that was an integer."
end try
```

If you don't like the look of literally nested try blocks ("lexical nesting"), you can nest them by means of the calling chain ("dynamic nesting"):

```
on askUser()
    set n to text returned of ¬
        (display dialog "What disk would you like the name of?" default answer "")
    try
        tell application "Finder" to set x to name of disk (n as integer)
        display dialog x
    on error e number -1728
        display dialog "I don't think that disk exists. " & e
    end try
end askUser
try
    askUser()
on error e number -1700
    display dialog "I don't think that was an integer."
end try
```

An expired timeout (see "Timeout," earlier in this chapter) is an error like any other; this example shows a way to handle it:

```
try
    tell application "Finder"
        activate
        with timeout of 1 second
            display dialog "Press a button." giving up after 2
        end timeout
    end tell
on error number -1712
    activate
    display dialog "Ha ha, not fast enough!"
end try
```

Second-Level Evaluation

By "second-level evaluation" I mean constructing and executing code at runtime. AppleScript has no built-in way of performing second-level evaluation. However, you can achieve much the same effect through the use of the run script scripting addition command, which allows you to compile and run a string. (See "Compiled Script Files as Script Objects" in Chapter 8.)

The use of run script is rather resource-expensive, because it requires that a completely new instance of the AppleScript scripting component be generated and torn down. It's also rather slow, because it takes time to compile the string. Finally, it's rather clunky, because a string run in this way has no communication with its surroundings; indeed, because a new instance of the AppleScript scripting component is generated, it has no surroundings at all. In other words, it isn't like a script object that can "see" globals at the point where it is defined and run.

Nevertheless, there are things you can accomplish with run script that can be accomplished in no other way. For example, all terminology must be resolved at compile time, so the only way to construct completely dynamically, at runtime, a command involving terminology is by means of run script.

In this example, we permit the user to enter part of an expression to be evaluated by saying it to the Finder:

```
set d to "window 1"
set p to "What Finder object would you like the name of?"
set r to display dialog p default answer d
set s to text returned of r
set s to "tell app \"Finder\" to get name of " & s
try
    set res to run script s
    display dialog res
on error
    display dialog "Sorry, that didn't work."
end try
```

For another example of run script used for second-level evaluation, see "Record Properties" in Chapter 13.

AppleScript In Action

Part III is about AppleScript in practice. The previous section described the Apple-Script language; that is your sword. Now, wielding this sword, you will go forth to do battle; this section is about the battle—the practical side of actually using Apple-Script to get something done.

The chapters are:

CHAPTER 20

Dictionaries

In Part II you learned the AppleScript language. It's essential to know this language if you're going to write AppleScript code; yet, ironically, the AppleScript language on its own won't get you very far. That's because AppleScript, all by itself, doesn't do very much; its real power and purpose lies in communicating with scriptable applications, which provide powers that AppleScript lacks. In order that you, the Apple-Script programmer, may harness its powers, a scriptable application extends the vocabulary of the AppleScript language. For example, AppleScript can't make a new folder on your hard drive, but the Finder can; therefore the Finder extends Apple-Script's vocabulary, supplementing it with terms such as make and folder so that you can use AppleScript to command it (the Finder) to make a folder. This extended vocabulary is called a scriptable application's *terminology*. A *dictionary* is the means by which a scriptable application or scripting addition lets the world know how it extends AppleScript's vocabulary.

A dictionary has two audiences—AppleScript and the AppleScript programmer. Let's consider how each of these audiences uses a dictionary:

AppleScript

AppleScript uses an application's dictionary at compile time to look up the terms that the programmer uses. In this way, AppleScript confirms that the terms really exist; as they don't exist within AppleScript itself, AppleScript cannot know without a dictionary that the programmer isn't just talking nonsense. At the same time, AppleScript uses the dictionary to *resolve* the terms into their corresponding Apple event form; otherwise, it wouldn't know what actual Apple event messages to send to the scriptable application at runtime. And it uses the dictionary when decompiling, to translate those Apple event terms back into English-like words for display to the programmer.

The AppleScript programmer

The AppleScript programmer studies a human-readable display of a dictionary to learn what English-like terms, beyond those built into the AppleScript language itself, may be used when targeting a particular application, or in the presence of a particular scripting addition. Studying a dictionary to figure out how to use AppleScript to get an application to do your bidding is a major part of the typical AppleScript programming experience. Such study must often be combined with experimentation when the dictionary is insufficiently informative.

The dictionary mechanism pervades the life of the AppleScript programmer in several ways:

- The dictionary is used by AppleScript for resolution of terminology. Therefore you have to make certain that your script points AppleScript properly to any required dictionaries, and that it can find these dictionaries at key moments (compilation, decompilation, and runtime).

- The dictionaries of scriptable applications and scripting additions invade the available namespace. This invasion creates clashes between terminology used in one dictionary and another, or between one dictionary and the terms that you, the programmer, would like to use. The result is a high probability that something you'd like to say will be misinterpreted or forbidden.

- The dictionary is usually your only documentation on how to communicate with a given application. But a dictionary, in and of itself, by the very nature of its format, is almost certainly going to fulfill this function inadequately. To make matters worse, dictionaries are often badly written or downright misleading. You therefore face the paradox of being dependent upon the dictionary for information that may be insufficient, hard to understand, or wrong.

This chapter discusses all these aspects of dictionaries. See also Chapter 3 for the format in which a dictionary is stored and for the implications when a needed dictionary is missing. See "Target" in Chapter 11, and "Tell" and "Using Terms From" in Chapter 19, for details on how the target is determined, how messages are sent, and how AppleScript decides what application's dictionary it will use to resolve terminology. In Chapter 21 I'll talk more about what scripting additions and their dictionaries add to the mix, and in Chapter 27 we'll actually construct a small dictionary to make an application scriptable. Also, see Appendix A for an example of a real programmer struggling valiantly with a real dictionary.

Resolution of Terminology

Example 20-1 exhibits some common patterns of terminology usage. With it, we'll model AppleScript's interaction with dictionaries during the process of compilation.

Example 20-1. Simple terminology resolution

```
tell application "Finder"
    set c to display dialog ((count folders) as string)
end tell
```

Compilation of code like Example 20-1 proceeds in two distinct stages:

1. The tell block causes AppleScript to locate a particular application and load its dictionary.
2. The terms inside the tell block are resolved.

Let's consider these stages one at a time.

Loading the Dictionary

As AppleScript's compiler encounters a tell block (or a terms block) targeting a literal application, it attempts to locate this application and load its dictionary. If the compiler can't find the application, it will ask the user where it is; if the user cancels out of this process, refusing to choose an application, AppleScript will not compile the script (see "Missing External Referents" in Chapter 3).

AppleScript will proceed happily at this point, provided that it can find the application, or the user chooses an application for it—*any* application. The compiler has not yet reached the stage of trying to resolve any actual terminology, so it doesn't matter whether there is any terminology to resolve, or even whether the application has a dictionary. All that matters so far is that the application referred to in code should be identified with some actual application.

Loading a dictionary takes time, and may even require launching the application in question, which takes even more time. Once the current instance of the AppleScript scripting component has already loaded a particular application's dictionary, however, it doesn't need to do so again, because it now has a copy of the dictionary cached in memory. These are some of the reasons why a script typically takes longer to compile the first time.

Translating the Terms

Presume that the compiler has reached the interior of the innermost tell block or terms block that caused a dictionary to be loaded. The compiler now proceeds to resolve the actual terms of the block.

The innermost application dictionary

Only one application dictionary is involved in the resolution of terminology in a given context. This is the dictionary corresponding to the innermost surrounding terms block or tell block where an application is explicitly specified. Let's call this the *innermost application dictionary*.

The interaction between nested terms blocks and tell blocks in determining the target and the innermost application dictionary was described in Chapter 11 and Chapter 19. Recall that iTunes is not targeted in this code:

```
tell application "iTunes"
    tell application "Finder"
        count folders
    end tell
end tell
```

So iTunes's dictionary will be loaded at compile time (and this will necessitate launching iTunes if it isn't running already) but it will not be consulted because it isn't targeted. iTunes knows nothing of folders, but this doesn't matter. On the other hand, it does matter in a case like this:

```
tell application "Finder"
    using terms from application "iTunes"
        count folders -- error: The variable folders is not defined
    end using terms from
end tell
```

The terms block deliberately perverts AppleScript's use of dictionaries. AppleScript, instructed explicitly to look in iTunes's dictionary, never learns that folder is defined in the Finder's dictionary, nor does it find folder in iTunes's dictionary. Thus it thinks folders is the name of a variable; that variable is undefined at runtime, causing an error.

Hunting for each term

Every term used in a given context must be found in a dictionary in order to be resolved. But the innermost application dictionary is not the only place where AppleScript may have to look, because some of the terms may be defined elsewhere. The hunt for terminology thus involves several steps. Here's how it goes:

1. The commands get and set (and sometimes copy) are specially short-circuited and are not sought in any dictionary.
2. The term is sought in the innermost application dictionary. (But see "No Terminology Clash," later in this chapter.)
3. The term is sought in AppleScript's own dictionary (described later in this chapter, under "The 'aeut' Resource").
4. The term is sought in the dictionaries of any scripting additions that are present.
5. The term is sought in the script itself.

Let's trace the resolution of the terms in Example 20-1, according to these rules:

- The term set (and its parameter to) are short-circuited (rule 1).
- The term folder is defined in the Finder's dictionary (rule 2).

- The term `count` appears both in the Finder's dictionary and in AppleScript's own dictionary. The former is used in the present case (rule 2).
- The term `string` appears in AppleScript's own dictionary (rule 3).
- The term `display dialog` is defined in a scripting addition's dictionary (rule 4).
- The term `c` isn't found anywhere, so it's sought in the script, and is resolved as the name of an implicitly defined local variable (rule 5).

As part of the terminology resolution process, AppleScript translates terms into their corresponding four-letter codes and constructs any Apple events that are called for (Chapter 3). So in Example 20-1, the Finder defines folder as `'cfol'` and count as `'core\cnte'`, and AppleScript constructs this Apple event:

```
core\cnte {
    kocl:'cfol',
    ----:'null'()
}
```

The Apple event is written into the compiled code, ready to be sent to the Finder at runtime.

Terminology Clash

Things don't always go smoothly when AppleScript resolves terminology. Terms are sought in the dictionaries of the innermost application, of AppleScript itself, and of all scripting additions, as well as in the script. Given such a large namespace comprising contributions from multiple independent entities, it is possible for conflicts to arise. Such a conflict is called a *terminology clash*. Either the programmer generates the clash by an unwise choice of variable names, or different dictionaries generate it by defining the same term in different ways.

When the programmer causes a terminology clash, various things can happen. Sometimes the code won't compile; sometimes it won't run; sometimes it runs but gets an unexpected result; sometimes the clash is resolved sensibly and there's no problem.

Compile-time Error

When the compiler stops you from using a term, the term is probably defined elsewhere as a different "part of speech" from how you're trying to use it.

For example, this won't compile:

```
local count
-- compile-time error: Expected variable name or property but found command name
```

The term count is defined by AppleScript itself as a command. Thus you're effectively trying to use a verb where a noun is expected.

This won't compile:

```
set sel to {length:2, offset:4}
-- compile-time error: Expected variable name, class name or property but found command name
```

This is similar to the previous example: `offset` is defined as a command in a scripting addition. Observe that `length` doesn't cause a clash here, even though it's defined in AppleScript's own dictionary; that's because it's defined as a property, and you're using it as a property (see "Record Properties" in Chapter 13).

This won't compile:

```
local desktop
-- compile-time error:
-- Expected variable name or property but found application constant or consideration
```

Again, the problem is a scripting addition; `desktop` is a constant, part of an enumeration used in the path to command. (See "Enumerations," later in this chapter.)

When you don't declare a variable, the error message is different, though the cause is the same:

```
set desktop to 7 -- compile-time error: Can't set desktop to 7. Access not allowed
```

A constant isn't something that can be assigned to.

In those examples, the clash was with a term defined by AppleScript or a scripting addition. Within a tell block, the same sort of thing can happen with respect to a term defined by the target application:

```
tell application "Finder"
    set container to 7 -- compile-time error: Can't set «class ctnr» to 7. Access not allowed
end tell
```

Within the context of a tell block targeting the Finder, `container` is resolved as the Finder's term container, which is a class name. A class can't be assigned to.

Here's an example where the error message is particularly unhelpful:

```
tell application "Finder"
    script eject -- compile-time error: Expected "tell", etc. but found "script"
    end script
end tell
```

The cause is that `eject` is a command defined by the Finder.

One more example. One day I was confused when the `filter` example at the end of "Handler and Script Object as Parameter" in Chapter 9 refused to compile. The troublesome line was apparently this one:

```
return filterer's filter(L)
-- compile-time error: Expected expression but found command name
```

It turned out that a recently installed scripting addition (the Satimage osax) contained a `filter` command.

Runtime Error

As we've just seen, you can't use the name of a command as a declared variable. If you don't declare it, though, you can get away with using the name of a command as a variable at compile time—only to be caught out at runtime, with a very strange and ungrammatical form of error:

```
set count to 0 -- error: Can't set count of 0 to
```

It's okay to use a defined property name as the name of a variable, but not if you don't declare it:

```
set year to 2005 -- error: Can't make year into type reference
```

If you do declare it, it's fine:

```
local year
set year to 2005 -- fine
```

No Error, Surprising Behavior

A terminology clash where the compiler doesn't complain and there is no runtime error is potentially the worst case for the programmer, because the code runs but it doesn't behave as expected. Here's an example:

```
local container, x
set container to "howdy"
tell application "Finder"
    set x to container
end tell
x -- container, not "howdy"
```

The programmer was trying to set the variable x to the value of the variable container. But in the context of a tell block targeting the Finder, container is the name of a class, so the variable x ends up with that class as its value.

Here's a similar example from "Me" in Chapter 11:

```
set home to "Ojai"
tell application "Finder"
    get home
    -- folder "mattneub" of folder "Users" of startup disk of application "Finder"
end tell
```

If you create a handler name that clashes with the name of a scripting addition command, you can make it impossible to call the scripting addition command. For example, the beep scripting addition command is supposed to take one optional parameter, the number of times to beep. If you define a handler called beep, the beep scripting addition command becomes inaccessible:

```
on beep (what)
    display dialog what
end beep
beep 3 -- 3, not beep beep beep
```

AppleScript accepts the syntax beep 3 because that's correct syntax for the event as defined in the scripting addition; but at runtime it routes the call to your handler.

Detecting Terminology Clash

Terminology clash that prevents compilation is good; the script won't compile, but at least you were saved from the problem before execution of the script was underway. Terminology clash that doesn't prevent compilation is a tougher nut to crack: either there's going to be a runtime error or, even worse, the script will execute without error but will do the wrong thing. How can this situation be avoided?

An important clue that a terminology clash is brewing is the pretty-printing of the compiled and decompiled script in your script editor application. (The pretty-printing occurs after compilation but before execution, so this is a good reason to compile and run in two separate steps.) AppleScript's preferences can be set so that, when your script is pretty-printed, terms defined in your script have a different color or style from other terms. (To set these preferences, use the Preferences dialog of a script editor application.) If you think a term is being defined in your script, but it doesn't have correct color and style, trouble may lie ahead. For example:

```
set count to 0
set myVar to 10
```

On my machine, count and myVar are colored differently. This is a bad sign, and should make me stop and think before executing this script. *Why* don't they have the same status? Aren't they both variable names defined by my script? Thinking about this, I might realize that count is the name of a command defined by AppleScript, and is a bad choice of name for a variable.

Look back over earlier examples. In the example with home, the local variable home and the home in the tell block targeting the Finder appear in different colors in my script editor application; this should tell me they refer to two different things, which is not my intention, so the script is going to misbehave. Exactly the same thing happens in the example with container. In the example with beep, the term beep is the wrong color everywhere; this should warn me that I may be trying to use a term that's already defined elsewhere, which may have unexpected results.

No Terminology Clash

Sometimes the pretty-printed terminology colors seem to threaten a terminology clash, but there isn't one. For instance:

```
local year
set year to 2005 -- fine
```

The term year is the wrong color, but the script runs fine. We may conclude that *an explicitly declared variable* whose name is that of a defined *property* is not problematic. The reason, apparently, is that a variable name and a property name are very much alike, and can be used in similar ways. If a name is invented by the programmer, it is one color; if it is already defined as a property name, it's another color (and behind the scenes its four-letter code is used). But syntactically they are largely interchangeable, as long as AppleScript doesn't get confused about what role the name is playing in its current context. That, presumably, is why the declaration is necessary: it says to AppleScript, "I know this is an existing property name, but I'm using it as the name of a variable here." (Recall how the name of a record item can be an existing property name or a "user property" name—see "Record Properties" in Chapter 13.) As a result, and rather surprisingly, this code works perfectly:

```
local bounds
tell application "Finder"
    set bounds to (get bounds of item 1)
end tell
bounds -- {-33, -33, 31, 31}
```

Within the tell block, the term bounds is being used in two different ways, yet AppleScript knows which is which. The reason, ironically, is that bounds is already defined by AppleScript as the name of a property. Thus all four occurrences of bounds are the same color when pretty-printed: they are *all* property names. Just as important, they have the same four-letter code: they are all the *same* property name. The variable declaration at the start puts bounds in scope as a variable name; inside the tell block, it can also be resolved as the name of a Finder property. In the third line, AppleScript identifies the second bounds (the one after get) with the Finder's bounds, but it identifies the first bounds (the one after set) with the variable bounds defined in the first line. The difference is that the first bounds (the one after set) has no of (or its, which would amount to the same thing); thus it is not explicitly said to be a property of the Finder, and is identified with the variable bounds instead.

To understand better the circumstances under which this sort of thing works, contrast some situations in which it doesn't work. It doesn't work if there is no explicit declaration of the variable bounds:

```
tell application "Finder"
    set bounds to (get bounds of item 1)
    -- error: Finder got an error: Can't set bounds to {-33, -33, 31, 31}
end tell
```

In that example, the first bounds *is* identified with the Finder's bounds property, because there's nothing else for it to be identified with.

And here, the variable name home, though declared explicitly, cannot be identified with the home in the tell block, because the former is a name created by the user; it is not an existing property name whose four-letter code matches that of the Finder's home:

```
local home
tell application "Finder"
    set home to (get bounds of item 1)
    -- error: Finder got an error: Can't set home to {-33, -33, 31, 31}
end tell
```

Resolving Terminology Clash

If you are aware of a terminology clash caused by your choice of name, your best option is to avoid the conflict altogether: don't use problematic names in the first place! If you insist upon using a problematic name, however, you can usually resolve the conflict (as explained earlier in the section "Me" in Chapter 11) by using pipes (vertical bars) to suppress AppleScript's interpretation of something as a dictionary term. Many of the examples that wouldn't compile or run correctly earlier in this section work perfectly if you add pipes:

```
local |count|
set |count| to 0
set |year| to 2005
set sel to {length:2, |offset|:4}
local |desktop|
tell application "Finder"
    set |container| to 7
end tell
tell application "Finder"
    script |eject|
    end script
end tell
on |beep|(what)
    display dialog what
end |beep|
beep 1 -- beeps
|beep|("howdy") -- howdy
```

If a scripting addition was not present when a script was compiled and is present when the script is decompiled, pipes can appear spontaneously around terms that would cause a conflict with the scripting addition. In effect, AppleScript has inserted the pipes to resolve the terminology clash! That's a useful mechanism, but it can surprise the user. So, for example, if the `filter` example at the end of "Handler and Script Object as Parameter" in Chapter 9 is compiled and saved, and then you install the Satimage osax and open the compiled script, all instances of `filter` will have been changed to `|filter|`.

Bear in mind that there may be more at stake than terminology clash. There is also the problem of who the target is. Recall this earlier example:

```
set home to "Ojai"
tell application "Finder"
    get home
    -- folder "mattneub" of folder "Users" of startup disk of application "Finder"
end tell
```

The programmer wanted to refer from inside the tell block to the home in the first line. The problem is that there is a terminology clash *and* the second home is being directed to the Finder instead of the script. It isn't enough retarget the second home:

```
set home to "Ojai"
tell application "Finder"
    get my home -- error: Can't make home directory into type reference
end tell
```

That's because there's still a terminology clash. The correct solution is to resolve the terminology clash:

```
set home to "Ojai"
tell application "Finder"
    get |home| -- "Ojai"
end tell
```

This example from Chapter 11, on the other hand, is *not* a terminology clash:

```
on reverseString(s)
    set text item delimiters to ""
    return (reverse of characters of s) as string
end reverseString
tell application "Finder"
    set name of folder 1 to reverseString(get name of folder 1)
    -- error: Finder got an error: Can't continue reverseString
end tell
```

The color of the term reverseString in the tell block shows that, to the compiler, this is the same reverseString defined as a handler earlier. But that doesn't matter; the handler call is still going to be sent as a message to the Finder, not to the script. Adding my solves the problem. (See "Handler Calls, Commands, and Script Objects" in Chapter 8, as well as "Terms in Scope" and "Me" in Chapter 11. If your choice of names is sufficiently perverse, you may have to use both my and pipes, as in the reveal example in Chapter 11.)

Clash Between Dictionaries

If a clash is caused by the programmer, the programmer can choose different terms and avoid the clash. But what happens when the same term is defined in two different dictionaries, which are not in the programmer's power?

Clashes between the dictionaries of scriptable applications are not problematic, as you can target only one scriptable application at a time. For instance, both Entourage and the Finder define the term folder, but unless you deliberately pervert the terminology-resolution mechanism with a terms block, no conflict will ever arise.

A term defined in both AppleScript's and an application's dictionary is not necessarily problematic either. In fact, it's expected, provided they are the very same term—the same English-like term and the same underlying four-letter code should be used (and, I should probably add, both dictionaries should use the term as the same part of speech). For example, AppleScript defines the term name ('pnam') as a property of a script object; the Finder defines it as a property of an item. As they both use the same English-like term and the same four-letter code, and they both use it as a property, this is not a conflict. Similarly, both AppleScript and the Finder implement the count command.

Nevertheless, a dictionary can be badly written. The authors of a dictionary are supposed to do their homework, making sure they don't use any terminology that might conflict with AppleScript itself. Sometimes, they don't do their homework (see "Clashes with AppleScript," later in this chapter). Even more insidious is what happens when a scripting addition's dictionary gets into the act. After all, even if an application's dictionary generates a terminology clash, at least the problem arises only if you're targeting that application. But when a scripting addition makes the same kind of mistake, it conflicts *everywhere*, and there's nothing you can do about it (short of not using that scripting addition). You can't target a scripting addition explicitly, and you can't hide the scripting addition's terminology from your script. And an application developer, creating an application's dictionary, even by doing all the homework in the world, can't guess what third-party scripting additions you might install and what conflicts these might cause. Thus the real trouble lies in the nature of the scripting addition mechanism itself, which invites such clashes; this is one of the reasons why Apple discourages developers from writing scripting additions (Chapter 21).

Not surprisingly, there have historically been many instances of clashes caused by scripting additions. Thoughtful scripting addition developers give their terms deliberately improbable names to reduce the likelihood of clashes. Sometimes a user notices a clash and notifies the scripting addition's developer, who responds by creating a new version of the scripting addition with an altered dictionary. Nonetheless, there are probably still some scripting additions where terminology clash is simply part of the price of using them.

Here's a mysterious terminology clash that isn't solved by pipes:

```
local folder
set folder to 5
tell application "Finder"
    set |folder| to 10
end tell
folder -- 5, not 10
```

The trouble is that folder is also defined in a scripting addition, as the name of a property. (It's a property of the file information record returned by the info for command. The scripting addition defines folder as 'asdr', but the Finder defines it as 'cfol'.) To use folder as a variable name successfully, if we are going to put pipes around it anywhere, we must put pipes around it *everywhere*, so that it isn't identified with this scripting addition property:

```
local |folder|
set |folder| to 5
tell application "Finder"
    set |folder| to 10
end tell
|folder| -- 10
```

An infamous example for many years was this:

```
tell application "BBEdit"
    tell text window 1
        offset of "i" in (get contents of word 1)
        -- compile-time error: access not allowed
    end tell
end tell
```

The trouble was caused by a conflict between BBEdit's offset property and the offset scripting addition command. Consequently there was no straightforward way to use this scripting addition command while targeting BBEdit. Fortunately, recent changes in BBEdit's dictionary have effectively resolved the problem.

Nonsensical Apple Events

As we saw in a previous section ("Compile-time Error"), AppleScript will sometimes blow the whistle at compile time to indicate that you are using a term as the wrong "part of speech." This is extremely helpful. For example, you can't use a verb as a noun:

```
tell application "Finder"
    get name of eject -- compile-time error: Expected expression but found command name
end tell
```

And you can't assign to a class:

```
tell application "Finder"
    set container to "howdy"
    -- compile-time error: Can't set «class ctnr» to "howdy". Access not allowed
end tell
```

You have to supply valid parameter names:

```
tell application "Finder"
    duplicate x by y -- compile-time error: Expected end of line but found "by"
end tell
```

The duplicate command doesn't have a by parameter, and the compiler knows this.

You can't make an element specifier out of something that isn't a class name:

```
tell application "Finder"
    get name 1 -- compile-time error: Expected end of line but found number
end tell
```

The compiler also displays some intelligence about singular and plural forms of a class name. The plural form of a class name is taken to be a synonym for the every element specifier; otherwise, if you use a plural where a singular is expected or vice versa, the compiler will usually change it for you, silently:

```
tell application "Finder"
    folder -- folder (the class name)
    folders -- {...}, a list of references to every folder
    folders 1 -- compiles as folder 1
    folder 1 thru 2 -- compiles as folders 1 thru 2
end tell
```

This might lead you to believe that the AppleScript compiler will use an application's dictionary to confirm that what you're saying is valid. Don't believe that. It is all too easy to form a nonsensical expression and get it past the compiler—which will then form a nonsensical Apple event, which will be sent to the application at runtime. In general, you should not expect compilation to serve as a "sanity check."

For example, the dictionary describes certain definite relationships between particular terms—this property is a property of this class, this element is an element of this class, this name is a class, this name is a property—but AppleScript largely ignores such information. As far as the compiler is concerned, property and element names are *not encapsulated* with respect to their class, and property names and class names are *not distinguished*. The result is a namespace mess; indeed, this is one reason why terminology clashes can so easily occur.

The examples that follow illustrate the staggering willingness of the compiler to form a nonsensical Apple event. When you send such an Apple event, there is no hope that any good can come of it. It's up to the target application to notice the problem and return an error message.

For instance:

```
tell application "Finder" to get column 1 of desktop
```

That's total nonsense; column is an element of the list view options class, not of the desktop. But the compiler doesn't care; it can see the dictionary, but it doesn't draw even such elementary, straightforward conclusions from it. So that code compiles. Of course there's an error at runtime.

Here we use a class name where a property name is expected:

```
tell application "Finder" to eject the item of file 1
```

The Finder's dictionary makes it clear that item isn't a property of file, and that it isn't a property name but a class name. But the compiler ignores such matters.

Here we use a property name where a class name is expected:

```
tell application "Finder"
    tell folder 1
        make new extension hidden
    end tell
end tell
```

The make command expects a class after new. But extension hidden isn't a class; it's a property. The code compiles anyway.

In this example, we seem to be using a noun as a verb; yet the compiler accepts it:

```
tell application "Finder" to folder the item
```

It probably looks to you as if AppleScript has treated folder as a verb; but in fact AppleScript is supplying get, as it typically does if the verb is missing. AppleScript is parsing your words like this:

```
tell application "Finder" to get folder index item
```

It thinks you're asking for a folder by index (e.g., folder 1), except that you've put the class name item as your index instead of an integer value. The fact that a class name is not a valid index value doesn't seem to faze the compiler one bit.

Raw Four-Letter Codes

When AppleScript compiles a script, it uses the dictionary to translate your English-like terminology into Apple events. When AppleScript decompiles a compiled script, it uses the dictionary to translate Apple events to English-like terminology.

It is possible to do AppleScript's job for it and type a raw Apple event directly into a script. There is then no translation to be performed, and no dictionary is needed. Apple events, as we observed in Chapter 3, are constructed of four-letter codes. The notation is a keyword stating what "part of speech" this four-letter code is (such as constant, property, class or event), followed by a space, followed by the four letters (or, in the case of an event, eight letters). The entire thing is wrapped in guillemets, also called chevrons («»). On the U.S. keyboard layout, these are typed using Option-\ and Shift-Option-\ (backslash).

Using raw Apple events, we can target an application using its own terminology but without a tell block and without AppleScript's making any use of the application's dictionary. For example:

```
get name of «class cdis» 1 of application "Finder" -- "feathers"
```

The term name is defined by AppleScript, but the term disk is not. Yet we can use the term disk outside a tell block by entering it in its raw form.

There are not many situations where this sort of thing is necessary, but it can be a useful strategy to know about. There are times when it can be a way of resolving a terminology conflict. Recall that earlier I mentioned a longstanding conflict between BBEdit and the offset scripting addition command. A similar problem exists when trying to use the path to scripting addition command while targeting System Events (I owe this example to John Gruber):

```
path to application support from user domain
-- alias "feathers:Users:mattneub:Library:Application Support:"
tell application "System Events"
    path to application support from user domain
    -- alias "feathers:Library:Application Support:"
end tell
```

The very same scripting addition command gives a different answer depending on whether the context targets System Events or not. The System Events answer is wrong, and is caused by the fact that System Events defines a user domain property, which conflicts with the user domain enumerator in StandardAdditions. (It's the same four-letter code with the same English-like terminology, but used as a different "part of speech.") You can work around the problem by using raw four-letter codes:

```
tell application "System Events"
    path to application support from «constant fldmfldu»
    -- alias "feathers:Users:mattneub:Library:Application Support:"
end tell
```

You may find use of four-letter codes not very satisfactory as a solution to terminology conflict, because the original problem recurs the next time the script is compiled. Take the previous example. When we run the script, the four-letter code decompiles to user domain. That's fine as long as the script doesn't need recompilation; but if the script is edited, then the next time we compile, this term is misunderstood by the compiler in the same way as before, and the raw Apple event has to be substituted again. One easy fix is to capture the enumerator as a variable:

```
set userdomain to user domain
tell application "System Events"
    path to application support from userdomain
    -- alias "feathers:Users:mattneub:Library:Application Support:"
end tell
```

An even more robust approach is to use run script to get a second level of evaluation. It's true that run script is expensive, but we can mitigate this somewhat by calling it in a script property initializer, so that the result is obtained just once (until we recompile, of course). The four-letter code appears as a literal string, which has the further advantage of clarifying the purpose of our trickery:

```
property userdomain : run script ("«constant fldmfldu»")
tell application "System Events"
    path to application support from userdomain
    -- alias "feathers:Users:mattneub:Library:Application Support:"
end tell
```

If decompilation of a script runs into trouble, you may see bits and pieces of original Apple events as raw four-letter codes. We saw earlier ("Missing External Referents" in Chapter 3) what happens if an application or scripting addition is present when a script file is compiled but is missing when you open the compiled script file in a script editor application. AppleScript needs the dictionary in order to decompile the script. If a scripting addition is missing, or if AppleScript can't find an application and you nominate some other application, the script opens anyway, but any Apple events that can't be translated into English appear as raw four-letter codes:

```
tell application "Finder"
    get «class euSu» of «class euMS» 1 of «class euMB» "Trash"
end tell
```

Something similar can happen in the display of a dictionary, if the dictionary is defective. For instance, BBEdit's print settings class has a property cover page whose class is described as lwec (or, in older presentations of the dictionary, «class lwec»). Evidently this refers to some class or enumeration whose definition is missing from the dictionary, so it has to be displayed using its four-letter code. Because the definition is missing, it is impossible to learn what BBEdit expects here.

In a compiled script executed by a script runner, or in an applet, no decompilation takes place. Therefore, if you ask AppleScript to do something involving translation through a dictionary, you may end up seeing four-letter codes. Here's an example. This works in a script editor application:

```
tell application "iTunes"
    display dialog (kind of source 1 as string) -- library
end tell
```

The kind property of a source in iTunes is an enumeration, so what comes back from iTunes here is a constant. A constant can't be shown by display dialog, but it can be coerced to a string (Chapter 17) and then shown. iTunes does not implement this coercion, so AppleScript performs it (see "Coercion by a Scriptable Application" in Chapter 14). In a script editor application, it can do this satisfactorily, thanks to decompilation: AppleScript has access to iTunes's dictionary, so it knows that the English-like term for this constant is library and can coerce it to the string "library". But when executing in a script runner or an applet, there is no decompilation, and AppleScript is left holding the bag. All it knows is the four-letter code for this constant, because that's what came back from iTunes. It has no way to translate it into English, so it coerces the four-letter code to a string:

```
tell application "iTunes"
    display dialog (kind of source 1 as string) -- «constant ****kLib»
end tell
```

The workaround in this situation is to construct a table of constants and their string equivalents and perform the translation yourself:

```
set R to {«class kACD»:"audio CD", «class kLib»:"library", ¬
    «class kTrk»:"track listing"}
tell application "iTunes"
    set k to (get kind of source 1)
    display dialog (get property k in R) -- library
end tell
```

(The next-to-last line uses Late Night Software's List & Record Tools scripting addition to make the lookup process more elegant. It allows a record property to be expressed as the value of a variable.)

All this assumes, of course, that you have a way to learn what the four-letter codes are. One very easy way is to use Script Debugger, whose dictionary display and Apple Event Log allow you to view the four-letter codes directly. Alternatively, if the dictionary is a text file, you can read it in any text editor; if it is (or if you can turn it into) an 'aete' resource in a resource fork, you can read it with the freeware Eighty-Rez.

Multiple-Word Terms

Many terms, especially commands in scripting additions, consist of multiple words. An example frequently used in this book is display dialog. You might think that such a term would present extra challenges for resolution, but in actual fact just the opposite appears to be the case; multiple-word terms are a good thing:

You can't make one
> Terms that you create in a script can't contain spaces unless surrounded by pipes—and pipes mean that no dictionary will be consulted. Therefore the probability of your creating a term in a script that clashes with a dictionary-based multiple-word term is zero.

Clash is improbable
> The more words a term consists of, the more likely it is that this term is unique among all dictionaries. This is especially important with scripting additions, whose terms are globally visible; for this reason, well-behaved scripting additions tend to use multiple-word commands.

There is no clash with single-word terms
> This is the really surprising part. Consider, for example, the scripting addition command set the clipboard to. Even though set...to is a command, and the is usually ignored, and clipboard could be a variable name (and is in fact a property defined by AppleScript), no confusion arises:
> ```
> local clipboard, tester
> set clipboard to "Mannie" -- sets the variable clipboard
> set the tester to "Moe" -- sets the variable tester (ignoring "the")
> set the clipboard to "Jack" -- sets the system scrap
> ```

Though I don't know the details, a natural explanation of AppleScript's success in resolving multiple-word terms would be that it tries the longest possible combinations of words first.

A multiple-word property name can be a little troublesome. The most commonly encountered example is text item delimiters (Chapter 16). Here's what happens when you use this term in a tell block targeting a scriptable application:

```
tell application "Finder"
    get text item delimiters -- error: Finder got an error: Can't get text item delimiters
end tell
```

In that code, AppleScript successfully resolves text item delimiters as the 'txdl' property, but then it makes a mistake: it sends an Apple event to the Finder, asking for this property. The Finder has no 'txdl' property, so it returns an error. The usual workaround is to add my or AppleScript's:

```
tell application "Finder"
    get my text item delimiters -- fine
end tell
```

But no Apple event is sent to the Finder in the case of a one-word global property:

```
tell application "Finder"
    get space
end tell
```

I believe this is the same behavior discussed in "No Terminology Clash," earlier in this chapter: space is a name already in scope, and we don't say this is the Finder's space, so it is assumed to be our space (meaning AppleScript's space). Evidently this rule breaks down with multiple-word properties. Fortunately, multiple-word properties that you might be tempted to use unqualified (without saying of something) are very rare—indeed, text item delimiters is probably the only one.

What's in a Dictionary

Dictionaries are not presented to you as a verbal explanation with instructions for their use. They are structured in tabular form and typically displayed through a special dictionary viewer window within a script editor application. It takes time and practice to learn to use this dictionary viewer and to get the most out of its display. You need to be adept at reading and understanding a dictionary display if you are to communicate successfully with scriptable applications and scripting additions.

The good news is that, starting in Tiger, the Script Editor's dictionary display has been improved (for the first time since the dawn of AppleScript). Back in the bad old days, the dictionary was shown in a simple, primitive way (Figure 20-1). Its table of contents was a simple scrolling list down the left side, organized by "suites" that were not alphabetically arranged. Because you didn't know what "suite" a particular item was in, you had to scroll through the list looking for it in each suite. Clicking an entry in the list displayed its information in the main pane; that information was static and terse.

In Tiger, the list on the left is an outline whose headings can be opened and closed; alternatively, you can use a columnar browser at the top of the window (Figure 20-2). A search field at the top lets you jump directly to a desired entry. The information for an entry is more copious: you learn not only what elements a class contains but also what classes it is an element of. And class names are hyperlinks, which you can click to jump to their entries and read their information.

In Script Debugger, the dictionary display is even better. (See Figure 20-3; the screenshot has been doctored to shorten the window by omitting some of the elements.)

The columnar browser at the top of Script Debugger's dictionary window has categories grouping commands and classes, letting you escape the tyranny of "suites." In the information displayed for an entry, the plural is given; properties and elements are shown in a clean, tabular layout; all datatypes (not just classes) are hyperlinked; and an extra section at the bottom of the display lists all classes of which this is an

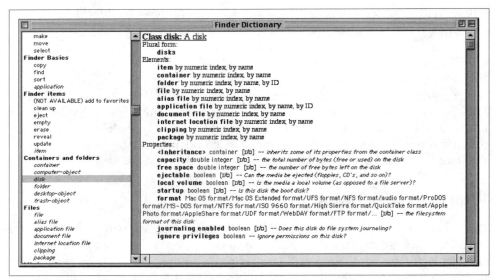

Figure 20-1. The dictionary display in Script Editor 1.8.3

element or property and all verbs of which this is a parameter type. There is also an option, not shown here, to display the raw four-letter codes in addition to their English-like translations. (I'll talk about further features of the Script Debugger dictionary display later on.)

Not only the dictionary *display* has been improved; starting with Tiger, applications can take advantage of a new dictionary *format*. In the past, an application expressed its dictionary as an 'aete' resource; starting in Tiger, an application can express its dictionary as an sdef file (an XML text file), which AppleScript can read directly (see "Dictionary" in Chapter 3). The new sdef format will give dictionaries more flexibility and allow their display to be more expressive and helpful than in the past; for instance, an sdef dictionary can include extensive comments and examples. However, AppleScript on pre-Tiger systems can't read an sdef, so it may be some time before applications actually start relying on the new dictionary format. (In fact, I don't know any major application that uses it.) Thus, in the discussion that follows, I'll treat 'aete' format as the default case.

Value Types

There are many places where a dictionary specifies a value's type. Every property is of some type, and the dictionary tells you what it is. (Examples appear in Figure 20-2; a disk object's capacity is a double integer, its ejectable is a boolean, and so forth.) Each of a command's parameters is of some type, and the command's returned value, if any, is of some type (Figure 20-4).

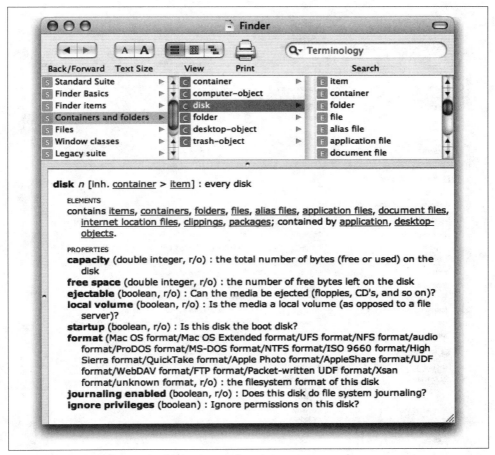

Figure 20-2. The dictionary display in Script Editor 2.1

In the dictionary itself, such value types are expressed as four-letter codes. Such a four-letter code may designate a built-in AppleScript datatype (see Chapter 13) or a class defined by the application (see "Enumerations" and "Classes," later in this section). This allows, say, iTunes's dictionary to specify that a value should be a string or a track. However, this is not enough to express all that a dictionary might want to tell you, so the dictionary specification permits certain further value types and options:

anything
    A complete wildcard type ('****'). Might appear as "any."

reference
    A less wild wildcard type ('obj '), indicating that the value is some object belonging to the application. Might appear as "specifier."

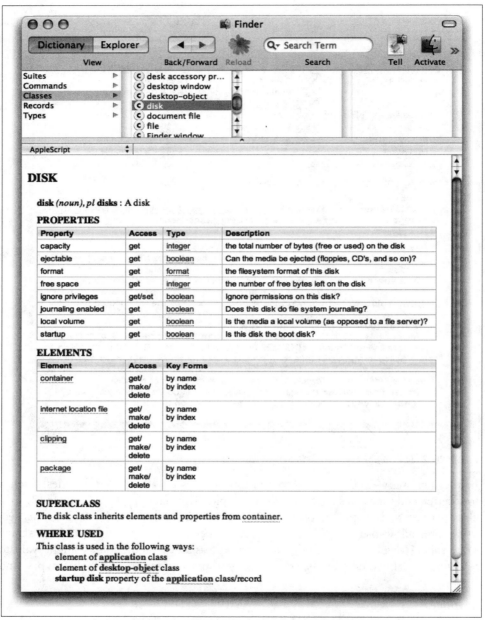

Figure 20-3. The dictionary display in Script Debugger 4 (abbreviated)

location reference

A relative element specification ('insl'). See "Relative" in Chapter 11. Might appear as "insertion location."

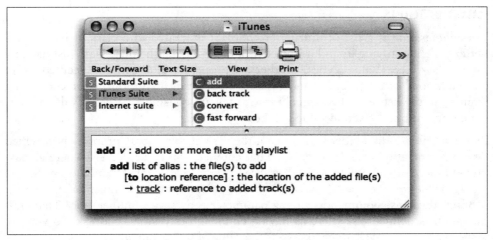

Figure 20-4. A command as displayed in Script Editor

type class

> A class; a datatype ('type'). Might appear as "type." See "Class" in Chapter 11.

property

> A property ('prop'). Might appear as "property specifier."

list of

> A type may be qualified in the dictionary to indicate a list of that type (like "list of alias" in Figure 20-4).

or

> Where a limited set of alternative types is legal, these may be specified explicitly, separated by "or." Historically, this option is rarely used. The sdef format makes it easier to implement, so we may see more of this sort of thing in the future.

Value type information is for the human reader only. The AppleScript compiler, for example, does not check to see whether the value you actually supply as a command parameter or to set a property is of the type specified by the dictionary; and the runtime engine doesn't care what type of value a scriptable application returns.

This being so, it is difficult to see why the dictionary specification requires that types be encoded as four-letter codes; four-letter codes are a machine-readable format, but no machine is going to read this information. The communicative worth of value types in the dictionary is thus limited unnecessarily.

Take, for example, iTunes's convert command. Its direct object is described in the dictionary as list of reference. This is both too restrictive and too general. It's too restrictive because the direct object need not be a list. It's too general because "reference" could mean anything, whereas in fact what iTunes wants is quite specific: a track or an alias. The dictionary specification provides no convenient way to say "a track or an alias, either singly or a list" by means of four-letter codes; so iTunes's developers have effectively left the truth to be discovered by experimentation.

Enumerations

An *enumeration* is a list of four-letter codes. It is treated as a class, it has a four-letter code identifying it, and it is used as a value type in the dictionary just like any other class (see "Value Types," earlier); a property value can be specified as an enumeration, as can a command parameter or result. The four-letter codes that constitute the list are called *enumerators*; they are constants. When a value type is an enumeration, the actual value will be an enumerator.

For example, in the Finder's dictionary, the disk class's format property is specified as an enumeration called an 'edfm'. That enumeration is defined elsewhere as having enumerators including Mac OS Extended format, audio format, and so on. So the actual value will be Mac OS Extended format or some other member of the list. In BBEdit, the close command's saving parameter is a 'savo' enumeration. That enumeration is defined elsewhere as having enumerators yes, no, and ask. So you are expected to supply yes, or no, or ask as the value of this parameter.

In the Script Editor's display of a dictionary, enumerations are not listed along with classes. Rather, an enumeration is shown as a value type by listing its enumerators (separated by slashes). In Figure 20-2, the format property is not said to be a certain kind of enumeration; instead, a list of that enumeration's enumerators is displayed. Similarly, in the Script Editor's display of BBEdit's dictionary, the close command's saving parameter is not said to be a certain kind of enumeration; its value is given as yes/no/ask, a list of that enumeration's enumerators. This way of displaying an enumeration rapidly becomes all but illegible as the number of enumerators increases (as Figure 20-2 demonstrates). Also, enumerations and enumerators may have comments describing their meaning and usage; this information is completely stripped from the display.

Script Debugger's display is much more like what's actually in the dictionary. Enumerations are listed separately in tabular form, showing their enumerators and any comments. A property or parameter whose value is an enumeration gives the enumeration as a hyperlink; you click the hyperlink to see the listing of its enumerators.

In your code, when you supply a value that is stated in the dictionary to be an enumeration, the AppleScript compiler does not check to see whether that value is in fact an enumerator of the specified enumeration.

Classes

A *class* is a datatype (see Chapter 13). Applications are free to define new datatypes in addition to those provided by AppleScript. These will generally correspond to the various types of thing the application operates on. For example, the Finder is all about files and folders on disks, so it has a file class, a folder class, and a disk class.

Internally, the dictionary expresses a class as a four-letter code. Where a class is already defined by AppleScript, the dictionary uses (or should use) the same four-letter code that AppleScript uses. In the dictionary display, you will see the English-like name of the class. (See "Value Types," earlier in this chapter.)

Plurals

For most classes, the dictionary will provide both a singular and a plural form for the English-like term. So, for example, the Finder defines both `file` and `files`, both `folder` and `folders`, both `disk` and `disks`. In the Script Editor's display of the dictionary, a class's plural appears when that class is listed as an element of another class (Figure 20-2). In Script Debugger, the plural is given explicitly along with the class's name (Figure 20-3).

The AppleScript compiler uses this information to treat singular and plural alternatives with some intelligence (see "Nonsensical Apple Events," earlier in this chapter). For example, a bare plural is often interchangeable with every plus the singular: you can tell the Finder equivalently to get `disks` or to get every `disk`. This is not because AppleScript has any natural-language intelligence; it's because the dictionary explicitly says that `disks` is the plural of `disk`.

Sometimes, a dictionary won't provide a plural form for a class name. Perhaps there is only one object of that class (it occurs only as a property, not an element). For example, the Finder provides only the singular for `desktop-object`, the class of the desktop. In a case like this, you can't use the plural or every with the singular.

It is also possible for a class to be declared as its own plural (`text` does this, for example). In such a case, you can use every but not a separate plural term.

Class inheritance

At an early stage in the history of AppleScript, it was observed that dictionaries were becoming large and repetitive. Several classes might share some of the very same attributes, and it seemed silly, both in the dictionary resource and in its display, to repeat the information about these attributes in the entry for each of those classes. Also, in those early days there were limits on how large a dictionary could be, so there were practical reasons for wanting to prevent unnecessary repetition.

Thus a mechanism was instituted for separating out attributes common to multiple classes. This is done by having the dictionary specify that one class *inherits* from another class. For example, in the Finder, there is a class `item`; both the `file` class and the `container` class inherit from `item`. This simply means that whatever properties the `item` class has, both the `file` class and the `container` class have also—though of course the `file` class and the `container` class might have other properties that the `item` class does not. The `item` class has a `name` property; therefore, so does the `file` class, and so does the `container` class. Similarly, the `folder` class inherits from the container class. Therefore it also inherits from item, and so a folder has a name property too. Furthermore, the container class has an entire contents property; therefore, so does the folder class. We also say that item is the *superclass* of file and container, and that file and container are two of its *subclasses*.

Thus we have a hierarchy of inheritance. An application's dictionary can include more than one such hierarchy. For example, the Finder also has a class desktop window, which inherits from Finder window, which inherits from window.

It must be stressed that this inheritance is not a true object-oriented relationship among classes! It has nothing to do with object-orientation, and it doesn't reflect any reality about how these datatypes are implemented in the application. There is no sense, in AppleScript, in which a folder "is" a container because the folder class inherits from the container class. Inheritance here is merely a notational device for expressing commonality of attributes in the dictionary.

Because of class inheritance, it is possible for a class to be *abstract*—that is, a class may exist *only* as a way of encapsulating a set of attributes so that other classes can inherit them; it is not the class of any actual object to which the programmer will ever refer. For example, BBEdit's dictionary defines an item class whose sole function is as an ultimate superclass, just so that every other class will have an ID property and a container property inherited from it; there's no property or element anywhere in the dictionary whose class is item.

The Finder, too, has an item class that acts primarily as a superclass. No Finder object is of the item class, so it is reasonable to describe this class as abstract. Nevertheless, it's a bit different from BBEdit's item class: in the Finder, some classes have an item element. So you can use the term item when scripting the Finder, in ways that you never would when scripting BBEdit. For example:

```
tell application "Finder"
    class of item 1 of desktop -- document file (not item)
end tell
```

We come now to the question of how inheritance is portrayed in a dictionary display. In the Script Editor, inheritance is simply stated as a fact. For example, in Figure 20-2, the disk class listing says: "inh. container > item." This means that disk inherits from container, which inherits from item. The implication is that when you look at the disk class listing in Script Editor, you're not being shown all the properties of disk. To see the rest of disk's properties, you need to look at container and item as well. Thus inheritance may actually make it harder for you to see a class's properties; you have to keep shuttling from class to class, up the entire inheritance chain, finding what properties each superclass has, and trying to remember them all.

Script Debugger is more helpful. The listing for a class in Script Debugger can *include* its inherited attributes. Thus you are shown all of a class's properties in one place.

Another nice feature of Script Debugger is that it graphs each of an application's inheritance hierarchies (Figure 20-5). (Script Editor can display classes organized by inheritance in its browser, but it shows only the single hierarchy starting with the item class, if there is one.)

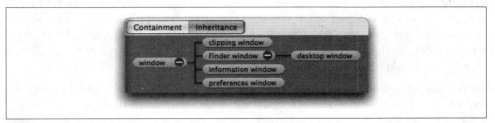

Figure 20-5. Script Debugger's display of the Finder's class inheritance hierarchies

Elements (as well as properties) are inherited by subclasses, but most application developers do not bother to take advantage of this in constructing the dictionary. For example, in the Finder the elements of the folder class are exactly the same as the elements of the container class; yet the dictionary explicitly repeats them in both classes—it does not, as it does for properties, include them only in the container class, even though this would be perfectly sufficient, as the folder class would inherit them.

Properties and Elements

A class can have two kinds of attribute: properties and elements (compare "Properties and Elements" in Chapter 11). A class's properties and elements are part of that class's listing in the dictionary.

A property in the dictionary involves two four-letter codes—one for the property's name and one for its value type (see "Value Types," earlier in this chapter). If a property name is the same as the name of a property defined by AppleScript, they should have the same four-letter code. For example, in the Finder the item class's name property has the four-letter code 'pnam' and a value type 'utxt' (Unicode text); the code 'pnam' matches the code for the name property defined by Apple-Script itself. A property can be specified as read-only; this is displayed in Script Editor as "[r/o]", and in Script Debugger as "get" (as opposed to "get/set").

An element in the dictionary is the four-letter code of a class (see "Classes," earlier). Thus an element name in the dictionary display is a class name. The dictionary can also provide the forms of element specifier that may be used to access this element; in the Tiger Script Editor this information is stripped from the dictionary display, but Script Debugger includes it (contrast Figure 20-2 with Figure 20-3). An element can also be specified as read-only; this is much rarer than a read-only property. Script Debugger marks such an element as "get" (as opposed to "get/make/delete," the default).

The complete schema of a scriptable application's properties and elements constitutes its *object model* (see "Attributes" in Chapter 11). The object model is what makes it possible to refer to any actual object within the application. In theory, all actual objects should be connected as a kind of tree, which should be navigable in its entirety starting at a single point—namely, the application itself, the only thing to which you have a reference when you start targeting that application—and it should be possible to deduce this tree correctly from the dictionary. The tree should start at the application class. For this reason, the application class is usually the first thing you'll turn to when you begin your study of an application's dictionary.

In real life, things are not so simple, for various reasons. Objects can be mutually linked as elements of one another; class inheritance can muck up the tree; there can be more than one tree, with orphaned classes; there can be shortcuts, sometimes undocumented, that jump through levels of the tree implicitly; and the dictionary can simply lie ("Defects in the Object Model," later in this chapter). Nevertheless, the object model is one of your basic keys to successful scripting of an application, and much of the struggle of using a dictionary involves trying to deduce the object model so that you refer to a desired object (see, always see, Appendix A).

The Script Editor helps you with a "containment" view of a dictionary's classes (Figure 20-2; to see the containment hierarchy, you would press the second segment of the View button in the toolbar). Script Debugger goes further, drawing a graph of the tree rooted at any class that has elements. Even more important, Script Debugger has an Explorer view that probes a running application's object model in real time, showing all elements and properties for every actual object in the hierarchy at that moment, telling you their values and showing you how to refer to them (see Figure 2-4).

The AppleScript compiler does not enforce the distinction between a property and an element, and does not enforce encapsulation—for example, it doesn't look in the dictionary to see whether the property you are ascribing to an object really is a property of that object. See "Nonsensical Apple Events," earlier in this chapter.

Records

When the result of a command sent to a scriptable application is an object of a class defined by that application, it is usually a reference to an object in that application's world (Chapter 12). For example, when you ask BBEdit to get document 1, what comes back is a reference to document 1—you aren't handed the entire literal document. If you want to know more about document 1, you can explore its properties, and when you do, an Apple event is sent to BBEdit. That's because this object lives in BBEdit's world; all you've got is a reference:

```
tell application "BBEdit"
    set d to document 1 -- result is a reference
    get name of d -- sends Apple event to BBEdit
end tell
```

But sometimes what happens is quite different. You receive from the application what appears to be an object. It has properties. It seems to be an object of a class defined by the target application. But examining its properties doesn't cause any Apple event to be sent. What you have isn't a reference: it's the entire object itself:

```
tell application "BBEdit"
    set d to find tag "style" start_offset 0
    class of d -- tag result
    start_offset of tag of d -- 225; no Apple event is sent
    end_offset of tag of d -- 259; no Apple event is sent
end tell
```

What you've got is actually a record (Chapter 13) disguised as a class. You can think of it as a *pseudo-class*. In the dictionary, it's listed as a class. You have no certain way of knowing, from the dictionary display, that this command yields a record rather than a reference to an object. And if you ask it what class it is, this thing says tag result, not record. But that's just trickery. It *is* a record—a record with an item named class! Thus when you ask it for its class, you're given the value of that item, which is tag result.

The example illustrates why this device is useful. BBEdit wants to hand you a package of information consisting of a whole bunch of values at once. These values have names so that you can examine the ones you're interested in. A record is a perfect vehicle for conveying this, because that's precisely what a record is—a package of name–value pairs. At the same time, this record needs to be described in the dictionary, because if it weren't, it would be useless to you. A record has no introspection! You can't ask a record: "So, what properties have you got?" You have to know in advance. The description of the record in the dictionary tells you what properties the record has and what they signify. To provide you with this description, the dictionary simply treats the record as a class; the record properties are treated as class properties (and the "class" has no elements).

Because the names of the properties of this record are defined in the target application's dictionary, you may not be able to extract them outside a tell block targeting that application. For example, this doesn't work:

```
tell application "BBEdit"
    set d to find tag "style" start_offset 0
end tell
start_offset of tag of d -- error: Can't get tag of...
```

There's no formal marker in an 'aete'-format dictionary to distinguish a record from a class. Script Editor's dictionary display thus does nothing to let you know that a class might really be a record. Script Debugger, on the other hand, does some detective work. If a class has no elements and is not an element of any class, Script Debugger calls it a record. This results in some false positives (the Finder's Finder preferences property, for example, is not a record, though Script Debugger calls it one), but it's still a helpful heuristic. In an sdef-based dictionary, the distinction can be made formally, so we can expect dictionary displays to be positively useful in this regard as applications begin to adopt the sdef format.

Events

Events are the verbs of the AppleScript language. An event is an Apple event (Chapter 3). An Apple event is specified using two four-letter codes. So, for example, the Finder's reveal command is the event 'misc\mvis'.

(In reality the two four-letter codes together are simply a 64-bit integer. The exact convention used to present them to a human reader is unimportant. I like to separate them with a backslash. Others use a forward slash, or put each half in single quotes, or whatever.)

An Apple event can take parameters. The default parameter is the "direct object"; its four-letter code is '----', which has no English equivalent. Others parameters have names; the name is a four-letter code, like a property. (See "Event Handlers" in Chapter 9 and "Target" in Chapter 11.)

The dictionary entry for an event lists the following information:

The event itself
> The event's four-letter codes and its English name are provided.

The direct object
> The direct object is marked as existing or not existing. If it exists, its value type is given, and it is marked as either optional or required.

Other parameters
> Each parameter's four-letter code and English name are provided. The value type is specified. The parameter is marked as either optional or required.

Returned value
> The event's returned value (result) is marked as existing or not existing. If it exists, its value type is given, and it is marked as either optional or required.

The dictionary display expresses essentially the same information: it tells you a command's name, the names and value types of the parameters (and whether they are optional), and the value type of the result, if any. Figure 20-6 shows the Script Editor's display of iTunes's add command. The direct object is said to be a list of alias; the to parameter is said to be a location reference, and optional (that's the meaning of the square brackets); and the result is said to be a track. Script Debugger's display (Figure 20-6) includes a template for actually using the command and a tabular display of its parameter information; if you press the Tell button in the toolbar, the command template is pasted into your script.

In an sdef-based dictionary, a distinction can be made formally between commands (Apple events that your script sends) and events (Apple events sent by an application to your script, as discussed in "Event Handlers" in Chapter 9). In the future, therefore, we can expect dictionary displays to reflect this distinction.

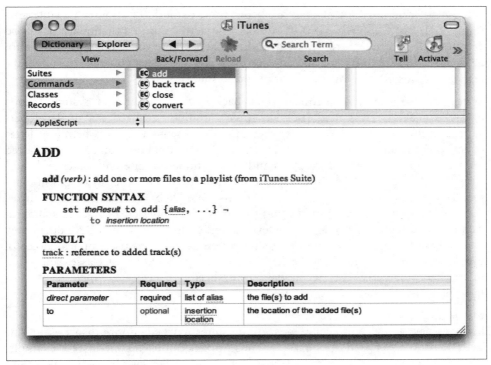

Figure 20-6. Script Debugger's display of a command

The AppleScript compiler enforces the rule that the only parameters following a command should be the direct object and the labeled parameters defined by that particular command. It knows nothing about required and optional parameters, and it does not enforce the value types expected for each parameter.

Suites

At the top level of a dictionary, events and classes are grouped into *suites*. You can see this in Figure 20-2, where the first column of the browser at the top of the Script Editor dictionary display consists of suites: the Standard suite, the Finder Basics suite, the Finder Items suite, and so forth.

A suite is in large part just a device for organizing the top level of a dictionary. Whether this is a *good* organizational device is a matter of opinion. Some people profess to like them; I think they're the work of the devil. In part my opinion goes back to the days (Figure 20-1) when the only way to find anything in a dictionary window was through a scrolling list that clumped things into suites. You didn't know what suite anything was in, and the suites weren't listed in alphabetical order, so you could never find anything. Things are better now. I still don't know what suite anything is in, but I don't need to know, because Script Editor's dictionary has good searching. Best of all is Script Debugger's approach, where you can ignore suites altogether: the first column of the browser (Figure 20-6) lets you view commands, classes, records, and so forth without regard to suites.

Suites are also a kind of historical fossil. Back in the early days of System 7, even before AppleScript was made public, Apple Computer realized that if developers started freely adding Apple events to their applications and assigning them four-letter codes, there would be massive conflict and duplication of effort. Imagine a hundred different versions of the delete command, with a hundred different names and four-letter codes and sets of parameters; multiply that by the number of common commands and classes that scriptable applications were likely to need, and you can see the nightmare vision that was starting to unfold. So Apple created some standardized sets of commonly needed Apple events and classes, not telling developers how to implement them, but requesting them, where possible, to use Apple's choice of four-letter codes and English-like terminology, Apple's choice of classes and commands and parameters. The result was a centralized database—the *Apple event registry*. The suites resulted from this codification.

Interestingly, much of the Apple event registry contents still exist, as part of AppleScript—even though, ironically, most of the suites have fallen into disuse (see "The 'aeut' Resource," later in this chapter). Thus AppleScript itself contains, for example, a suite of Macintosh Connectivity Classes, with names like bus slot, which you can't see and which no application (as far as I know) has ever bothered to implement. On the other hand, certain suites present in AppleScript are quite commonly implemented, in whole or in part. The Standard Suite, sometimes referred to as the Core Suite, is the source of commands like exists, make, and select. The Text Suite, containing terms like word and text style info, is sometimes used as a starting point for applications that manipulate text. On the other hand, the Miscellaneous Suite, a frequent repository for commands like copy, cut, and undo, is a product of the Apple event registry but is not built into AppleScript itself.

You may recall that in Chapter 1 I said ("Is This Application Scriptable?") that the mere presence of a dictionary wasn't enough to prove that an application was scriptable. Apple's own Dictionary application, which I used as an example, essentially reflects in its dictionary the Standard Suite and the Text Suite from AppleScript itself. But this is really just a bug, a kind of automatic reflex of the framework used to build the application (basically, any Cocoa application that claims to be scriptable inherits this meaningless dictionary even if it isn't really scriptable).

A word needs to be said about the Required Suite. In the current implementation of AppleScript this is empty, but in the early days of System 7 these were the four Apple events to which every application, scriptable or not, had to respond in order to be System 7–native in the first place. That's because these were the fundamental messages sent by the Finder to do such basic things as launch and quit the application. The old Required Suite Apple events have been moved to the Standard Suite, and to this day, every application responds to them. They are shown in Table 20-1.

Table 20-1. The original Required Apple events

Command	Four-letter code	Effect
run	`'aevt\oapp'`	Launch the application
open	`'aevt\odoc'`	Open a document or documents
print	`'aevt\pdoc'`	Print a document or documents
quit	`'aevt\quit'`	Quit

The 'aeut' Resource

When terminology is resolved, AppleScript itself is represented by a dictionary (see "Resolution of Terminology," earlier in this chapter). This fact comes as a surprise to many AppleScript users, because they don't think of AppleScript as having a dictionary. And no wonder, as they don't normally get to see this dictionary. Nevertheless, it is there. It's called the 'aeut' resource, and it lives in the AppleScript scripting component file, *AppleScript.component* (inside the package, it's at *Contents/Resources/AppleScript.rsrc*). It is loaded when the AppleScript scripting component comes into being, it looks basically like any other dictionary, and it defines the terminology for all of AppleScript's built-in commands and classes (except for get and set, which are treated specially).

If you'd like to get a look at the 'aeut' resource, you can; both Smile and Script Debugger permit you to see it, by choosing File → Open Dictionary → AppleScript.

The 'aeut' resource contains the terms for virtually the entire AppleScript language, including comparison operators, prepositions, global script properties, and so forth. There are even some terms not discussed in this book (because in practice they don't arise, or may never even have been implemented, like the upper case class or the print depth global property). You can learn a lot from perusing the 'aeut' resource; at the very least, it can help to explain why certain variable names generate terminology conflicts (when the name is already defined in the 'aeut' resource).

Here's a quick guided tour of what you'll see if you decide to gaze directly upon the 'aeut' resource (don't worry, it won't turn you to stone). The AppleScript Suite contains the global terms that make the AppleScript language work. The Type Names Suite contains many minor types without elements or properties, including secondary arithmetic classes such as small integer (see Chapter 13) as well as the location reference type so crucial to the make command (see "Relative" in Chapter 11); however, you might not see this in the display, because the Type Names Suite is normally suppressed from a dictionary display. (Applications take advantage of this to define terms needed for compilation but not suitable for human view.) The Standard

Suite (also called the Core Suite) and the Text Suite are visible to the compiler but are usually overridden and extended by individual applications; not all the terms within them have any intrinsic implementation in AppleScript. So, for example, the count command works on lists and strings, but the exists command does nothing unless a scriptable application implements it. Other suites and their contents are not visible to the compiler; they seem to be present for historical and information purposes (see "Suites," earlier in this chapter).

Inadequacies of the Dictionary

One function of the dictionary is to show the human user how to speak AppleScript to a scriptable application in order to drive that application. But the very nature of a dictionary renders it insufficiently expressive to fulfill this function. A dictionary is merely a list of words. Words don't make a language. The problem, as Austin famously put it, is how to *do things with words*. That's what you want to know, but it's just what the dictionary is incapable of telling you. Dictionaries can be more discursive and explanatory thanks to the new sdef format, and it is to be hoped that developers will take advantage of this to improve them; but few dictionaries use this format, and even when they do, the fundamental problem will remain: a vocabulary list is not documentation.

Here's an eclectic collection of some of the various ways in which the dictionary can fail the user. Forewarned is forearmed; I hope this discussion will make you a sharper reader of dictionaries and a wiser AppleScript programmer.

> This discussion is not meant to imply that all dictionaries are bad. On the contrary, some developers have worked hard to write careful, informative dictionaries. But it is hard work. You have to know AppleScript, you have to anticipate your users' needs and expectations, and you have to know the dictionary format and how to make the best of it. Most important, your application's scriptability has to have been well implemented to start with; for some useful guidelines from Apple, see *http://developer.apple.com/technotes/tn2002/tn2106.html*.

Defects in the Object Model

An application's object model is a hierarchy, essentially equivalent to the chain of ofs allowing you specify any of the application's objects (see "Properties and Elements," earlier in this chapter). Clearly this hierarchy requires a starting point; there must be some ultimate, top-level object in terms of which all others may be specified. In an Apple event, that top-level object is null(). But in AppleScript there is no way to express this null() explicitly; it is simply supplied for you as the end of the chain, whenever you specify an object. (You can see this in Example 3-1.) Therefore you must rely on convention. And the convention is that the application class should correspond to the top-level null() object. This makes sense, as in a tell block the application is ultimately the only thing you can get a reference to in order to start referring to its objects. That's why your starting place when you study a dictionary is usually its application class. You assume that this is the top of the object model hierarchy, and you look to see what properties and elements it has, in the expectation that these will lead you wherever you want to go.

The object model, however, may not be a simple hierarchy. A number of things can undermine this straightforward picture.

Secret shortcuts

Here are the elements of iTunes's application class: browser window, encoder, EQ preset, EQ window, playlist window, source, visual, window. You'll notice that none of these is your library, and none of them is a playlist. Yet these are the things you're most likely to want to refer to. So how are you expected to talk about them? You can spend ages mucking about in the dictionary looking for some way to reach playlist level from here—but it turns out that you could have asked for a playlist directly all along. Indeed, it turns out your library *is* a playlist:

```
tell application "iTunes"
    get playlist "library" -- library playlist id 40 of source id 35
end tell
```

Notice the discrepancy between what you said to iTunes and the reference iTunes handed you. In theory a playlist is an element of a source, and a source is an element of the application, and that's the path you should have to travel to reach a playlist. But in actual fact there's a shortcut that lets you jump right from the application to a playlist. That's excellent, but the dictionary never told you so.

This book has been full of examples of the Finder doing the same sort of thing:

```
tell application "Finder"
    get folder 1 -- folder "Mannie" of desktop
end tell
```

As you can see, folder 1 is not the first folder at the top of your startup disk, as you might expect: it's the first folder on your desktop. Again, the dictionary never told you about this.

Your main source in iTunes (called the Library source), and the desktop in the Finder, are *implicit subcontainers* supplied when you speak of certain elements without qualification. The application gives you a shortcut for reaching certain places in its object model with traversing the whole path explicitly. But this fact isn't documented in the dictionary.

Such shortcuts needn't start at the top level. Consider the following:

```
tell application "Microsoft Entourage"
    get email address 1 of contact 1 -- "matt@tidbits.com"
    get label of email address 1 of contact 1 -- home
end tell
```

The first line makes it appear that "email address 1 of contact 1" is a string, but that makes the second line anomalous, as a string has no label property. The truth is that the email address class has a contents property; when you ask for an email address object (as opposed to a property of such an object), Entourage takes a secret short-cut and returns the value of its contents property instead.

Some applications are particularly badly behaved in this regard. A good example is Eudora. There is a mailbox class in Eudora, but how can you speak of any particular mailbox? The only place a mailbox element appears in the dictionary is under the mail folder class. But in fact not every mailbox in Eudora is in a mail folder, so how can you ever speak of such a mailbox at all? It looks impossible. Yet it turns out (after some experimentation) that you can speak of a mailbox directly:

```
tell application "Eudora" to count messages of mailbox "In"
```

That's nice, but if it's legal, why doesn't the dictionary say so? Why isn't mailbox an element of the application class? In Eudora's dictionary, mailbox is an *orphan class*.

A dictionary may also simply omit pieces of the puzzle, such as not bothering to list all of a class's elements. If you read Appendix A you'll see me spending much of my time discovering that in FrameMaker an anchored frame can be an element of a paragraph or of a document. This discovery comes as a relief, and makes the ultimate solution possible, but the dictionary says no such thing; only experimentation reveals the facts.

Something quite similar happens in the Finder's dictionary. The dictionary quite clearly states that a Finder window has no elements (and it doesn't inherit from anything that has elements). Yet the following is both legal and useful:

```
tell application "Finder" to get item 1 of Finder window 1
```

Thus an application can have a perfectly reasonable object model in its head, as it were, but fail to reveal it to you in its dictionary. In the dictionary, the object model is defective. And the dictionary is all you've got.

Defective Element Specifiers

There are many ways to refer to an element (see "Element Specifiers" in Chapter 11), but you can't be sure from the dictionary which ones are implemented for any particular element. The dictionary format has a place for this information, but developers often fail to provide it correctly, leaving you to discover the truth by experimentation. Even if the correct information is present in the dictionary, the Tiger version of Script Editor omits it altogether from its dictionary display.

For example, according to the Finder's dictionary, a container's file elements can be specified by name and by index. But those are not, in fact, the only specifier forms that work. The range specifier form works too:

```
tell application "Finder" to get files 1 thru 2 of folder 1
```

The Finder also lists in its dictionary specifier forms that do *not* work. For example, the dictionary says you can specify a folder by ID. But you can't get a folder's ID, so that's not true.

An application can implement element specifier forms in bizarre ways. For example, in Eudora, you can't say this:

```
tell application "Eudora" to get mailbox 1 -- error: Can't get mailbox 1
```

But you can say this:

```
tell application "Eudora" to get name of mailbox 1 -- "In"
```

Or this:

```
tell application "Eudora" to count messages of mailbox 1
```

So you can't get a mailbox by index, but you can get its name and messages by index? What's the underlying logic here? Weirdest of all, you can't say this:

```
tell application "Eudora" to count mailboxes -- error: Can't get every mailbox
```

So how are you supposed to learn how many mailboxes there are? You can't. So how can you cycle through all mailboxes? As far as I know, the only way is to keep cycling by index number, incrementing the index, until you get an error.

Boolean test specifiers are, of course, the most chancy, but when they work they are wonderfully elegant and powerful. A simple listing in the dictionary could never tell you everything you want to know about boolean test specifiers, because it can't possibly let you know all the various tests that work and don't work; so experimentation is your only option. The same goes for properties of multiple references, such as "get name of every..." (Chapter 11); the dictionary has no way to tell you whether expressions like these will work, so you just have to try them and see.

Properties with Eponymous Classes

A common developer mistake is to give a property the same name and four-letter code as a class. This causes errors in the user's script that can be difficult to track down. Also, it's just confusing.

For example, in Entourage, a message has recipients, and a recipient has an address property which is itself of the address class. To learn, as a string, who the addressee is, you have to ask for an address's address property. This requires a nutty way of talking ("address of address"?); and to make things worse, it doesn't seem to work:

```
tell application "Microsoft Entourage"
    tell folder 1
        tell message 1
            tell recipient 1
                get address of address -- error: Can't get address of address
            end tell
        end tell
    end tell
end tell
```

The problem is that a property and a class have the same name; this causes the script to resolve the terms incorrectly. To solve the problem, you must help AppleScript to understand that you mean the property, not the class:

```
tell application "Microsoft Entourage"
    tell folder 1
        tell message 1
            tell recipient 1
                get address of its address -- "matt@tidbits.com"
            end tell
        end tell
    end tell
end tell
```

Even worse is what happens when a property and a class have the same four-letter code but different English-like names. For example, in Panther, here's what happens when you ask the Finder for the class of its desktop property:

```
tell application "Finder" to get class of desktop -- desktop
```

But there is no desktop class! The correct answer is desktop-object; the problem is that the four-letter codes for desktop-object and desktop are the same. (The term desktop comes first in the dictionary and hides the term desktop-object during decompilation.) The mistake is fixed in Tiger's version of the Finder dictionary.

Clashes with AppleScript

An application's dictionary should not clash with the AppleScript language itself. When it does, the language is perverted, and scripts that should compile don't, or compile oddly.

We've already seen some examples of trouble caused by poor choice of terminology in an application's dictionary. The use of the term end transaction by FileMaker Pro as the English-like equivalent of the 'misc\endt' Apple event conflicts with AppleScript's own use of end transaction as the closing phrase of a transaction block. BBEdit's use of the term contents as a property of a text-object conflicts with AppleScript's own contents of operator.

Another example is Entourage's recipient class, which has a recipient type property whose four-letter code is 'rtyp'. This conflicts with a fundamental feature of the AppleScript language—it's the same as the as in get...as (see Chapter 14). Thus if you enter this code:

```
tell application "Microsoft Entourage"
    get path to desktop as string
end tell
```

it compiles and decompiles to yield this (after which, of course, it won't compile at all):

```
tell application "Microsoft Entourage"
    get path to desktop recipient type string
end tell
```

Wrong Value Types

Dictionaries are notorious for stating incorrectly the value type of a property, a command parameter, or a command return type. Only experimentation will reveal the truth.

For example, Entourage's application class lists the value type of most of its properties as "reference" (meaning `'obj '`; see "Value Types," earlier in this chapter). This is true as far as it goes, but it's unnecessarily vague. The class of the in box folder property, for example, is folder; it will never be anything else. So why not say so in the dictionary?

We saw earlier that iTunes misstates the class of the direct object of the convert command. Recall also that GraphicConverter's dictionary says it expects an alias as the in parameter of the save command. That puts the user in a quandary, because you might want save to create a new file, but you can't use an alias where the file doesn't already exist. Experimentation reveals that a string will do:

```
tell application "GraphicConverter"
    set s to "feathers:Users:mattneub:Desktop:joconde"
    save window 1 in s as PICT
end tell
```

Interestingly, the AppleScript `'aeut'` resource contains an alias or string class, presumably intended exactly for this situation—that is, it exists just so that a dictionary has a way to tell the user that an alias or a string is acceptable as a parameter. GraphicConverter's dictionary fails to take advantage of this. However, the real problem here is a shortcoming in the underlying dictionary format, which makes it hard to express alternative value types. (The new sdef format goes some way towards solving this.)

Then there's the matter of the result returned from a command. Sometimes a result's value type will be documented incorrectly. For example, the StandardAdditions dictionary says that do shell script returns a string, but it returns Unicode text (and the distinction can be crucial). It says that choose URL returns a URL; it returns a string. StuffIt Expander's dictionary contains just one entry—the verb expand—so wouldn't you think that the developers could be bothered to write it truthfully? Well, they couldn't. The dictionary says that this verb returns an integer representing the number of files that were successfully expanded. It doesn't. Because of this falsehood in the dictionary, a simple script that should take minutes to write can take hours (I speak from experience).

Sometimes a command will be documented as not returning any result when in fact it does, or vice versa. The Finder's reveal command is an example; the dictionary does not say it returns any value, but it actually returns a reference to the item revealed. This sort of thing is crucial to know, especially as it can affect the value of the implicit result of a line of your code, or even of a handler or the script as a whole.

A related problem is that the dictionary doesn't distinguish between a reference and a record as returned value types (see "Records," earlier in this chapter). This can make a big difference to your script. As a careful programmer you will probably want to know whether what you have is a reference, and whether fetching a property of it will send an Apple event. Yet experimentation is the only way to find out.

It also doesn't help matters that the very same command can return different types of value under different circumstances. A common source of error is a construct of this form:

```
tell application "Finder"
    repeat with d in (get every disk)
        -- do something here
    end repeat
end tell
```

The problem is that every disk returns a list unless there is only one disk, in which case it returns a reference to a single disk object. Thus, this script can break in a subtle way: if you have more than one disk, you're cycling through disks; if you have just one disk, you're cycling through top-level folders. And you may have no way to find this out! You can test your script until you're blue in the face, believe that it works fine, and distribute it to others, only to learn later that it mysteriously breaks on someone else's computer.

Wrong Parameter Details

Aside from their value types, command parameters are all too often described incorrectly in the dictionary. First, is a parameter optional? The dictionary has a place for this information, but developers sometimes get it wrong. Second, if a parameter is optional, what is the default? (That is, what will happen if the parameter is omitted?) There is no formal provision for answering this question, but there's a place for a comment on each parameter, and you'd think the developers would answer it here. But sometimes they don't.

For example, the Finder's dictionary says that when you're using the make command, the at parameter is compulsory, not optional. That just isn't true; this works:

```
tell application "Finder" to make Finder window
```

With iTunes's add command, the to parameter is optional. If you omit it, what will this file be added to? You can probably guess—but you shouldn't have to. The dictionary should tell you what this command will do, so you don't have to waste time experimenting to find out.

Make

Some common commands are particularly troublesome, and none more so than the verb make, used to create objects in AppleScript. No action is so fundamental as creating something—a window, a document, a mail message, a piece of text—and yet nothing in AppleScript is more difficult to do. The make command typically has the same basic set of parameters in every application, yet it is implemented in a bewildering variety of ways (sometimes it seems that every application implements it differently) and usually little or no assistance is provided by the dictionary.

 The make command appears in the dictionary with its first parameter preceded by new. But in actual fact you can omit the word new; what follows the word make, where the direct object would go, is taken to be the new parameter. The dictionary fails to express this fact, which is hard-coded into the inner workings of AppleScript itself.

The first question is *what* to make. It's going to be a class belonging to the target application, and it will almost surely be a class that functions as an element in the application's object model. Nevertheless, for a given act of creation, it is not always clear what class you should try to make. You might think, for example, that to make a new email message in Mailsmith—I mean a new outgoing message, one that you intend to populate with an address, a body, and so forth, so as to send it later— you'd ask to make a new message; but it turns out that this creates a new *incoming* message (which makes no sense whatsoever—why in the world would you ever want to do such a thing?). The way to make a new outgoing message is to ask for a new message window. Nothing in the dictionary would lead you to this solution. Similarly, the way you create a new window in AppleWorks isn't to ask for a new window, which just gets you an incomprehensible error message, but to ask for a new document. The way you create a new window in the Finder isn't to ask for a new window but to ask for a new Finder window.

Often (but not always) you must also say *where* to create the new object. The dictionary lists this parameter:

at **location reference** `--` *the location at which to insert the element*

Every application seems to have a different idea of what constitutes an appropriate location. (See also the section "Relative" in Chapter 11.) In Eudora, for example, if you're trying to make an outgoing message, it turns out that the place to create it is at the end of the "Out" mailbox:

```
tell application "Eudora"
    make new message at end of mailbox "Out"
end tell
```

This seems particularly nutty. In Eudora's interface, it's easy to make a new outgoing message: you just choose Message → New Message. You don't have to say *where* to make this new message! You just say you want one, and Eudora makes it in some sensible place. This is exactly what I'm trying to do in AppleScript; surely I should be able to say simply "make new message" and Eudora should create the outgoing message in precisely the same manner. But that's not the case. You must say the magic words or you won't get any new message. And don't expect the dictionary to tell you what the magic words are, either.

With Cocoa applications, the at parameter must typically refer to a collection (sometimes imaginary) of the same things you're trying to make one of. For instance, in the outliner NoteTaker, to make a new outline entry, you have to say something like this:

```
tell application "NoteTaker"
    tell current notebook
        tell current page
            make new entry at beginning of entries
        end tell
    end tell
end tell
```

If you target the wrong object, or if you don't say at beginning of entries, you get an error, or nothing happens, or NoteTaker crashes.

Not only the at parameter, but also the *meaning* of at, varies from application to application. This code inserts a new word *after* word 2:

```
tell application "BBEdit"
    tell window 1
        make new word at word 2 with data "howdy"
    end tell
end tell
```

This code inserts a new word *replacing* word 2:

```
tell application "TextEdit"
    tell text of document 1
        make new word at word 2 with data "howdy"
    end tell
end tell
```

This code inserts a new folder *inside* folder 1:

```
tell application "Finder"
    make new folder at folder 1
end tell
```

Then there's the with parameter. This is the most troublesome at all. Actually your choices are usually with data and with properties; some applications let you say only a particular one of these, but some let you say either (or both).

In the case of with data, you are probably setting some fundamental aspect of the new object's initial state; but you don't know, until you try it, exactly what aspect this will be. In the examples with BBEdit and TextEdit, it turns out that with a word, its data is its text.

In the case of with properties, what you're providing is a record; the properties and values you supply will be used to set the inital values of the corresponding properties in the newly created object. You don't usually need to supply an initial value for all of the new object's properties, but sometimes you have to supply an initial value for at least some of them. You might expect that you would be permitted to make a new, essentially blank object; the make command returns a reference to the new object, so you could then proceed to populate its properties afterwards. But some applications don't let you do this; they require you to provide certain initial values—and the problem is that you don't know which ones.

For example, the way to add an address to a Mailsmith message window is as follows:

```
tell application "Mailsmith"
    tell message window 1
        make new to_recipient with properties {address:"matt@tidbits.com"}
    end tell
end tell
```

If you leave out the with properties parameter, you'll get a runtime error.

Selection

Another extraordinarily difficult concept to express in AppleScript is the selection, which is usually implemented through a selection property. The selection can be tricky to get and tricky to set.

Some applications give you no access to the selection at all. For example, in TextEdit there is no provision for learning what is selected. Similarly, Apple Mail lets you learn what messages are selected but not what text is selected in a message. This is a clear deficiency and should be regarded as a bug, as it is perfectly reasonable that you would want a script to operate on the selected text.

Of what should the selection be a property? Different applications have different philosophies about this. Be sure to look through the dictionary to see where the selection is implemented. The safest assumption is that there is an application-wide selection, and so it is the application class's selection property that is most likely to be appropriate. If an application has multiple windows, and you have selected something in several of them, only the selection in the frontmost window is the application-wide selection. But an application may also let you specify the selection in terms of some other physical container, such as a window. Thus, for example, BBEdit lets you work with the selection of a non-frontmost window; but the Finder does not.

When you ask for the selection, what kind of result is returned? The answer will vary from application to application, but what you hope for is a reference (or list of references). Learning what kind of object this is a reference to, and what you can do with this information, might require experimentation. If it is a list, you might have to cycle through its items to work further with them. For example, in Address Book, this doesn't work:

```
tell application "Address Book"
    name of selection
    -- error: Address Book got an error: Can't make name of selection into type reference
end tell
```

The selection is a list, and Address Book is not willing to distribute a property over the items in that list (see "Operations on Multiple References" in Chapter 11). You have to cycle through the list yourself:

```
tell application "Address Book"
    set L to {}
    repeat with aThing in (get selection)
        set end of L to (get name of aThing)
    end repeat
    L
end tell
```

Sometimes, the selection property is not what you really want. If you're simply trying to get a reference to what's frontmost in the application, look for properties with "current" in their name, such as iTunes's current playlist. Similarly, in Entourage, the selection might be a list of references (to messages selected in a window that lists messages, for example), or it might be the selected text (as Unicode text, not a reference); but Entourage implements a current messages property that always returns a list of messages, which is far more likely to be useful.

Then there is the matter of how to set the selection. An application that implements selection will usually implement a select command to go with it. Most applications don't let you say "set selection," and those that do mean something else. For example, in BBEdit, "set selection" is a way of replacing the selected text. Microsoft Word, where the selection is often crucial for performing operations on text, provides many ways to manipulate the selection.

Idioms for Common Tasks

Think of AppleScript as an interface to an application, just like the interface you see on the screen. One is a programming interface, the other is a graphical interface. It is not always easy to see how the latter maps to the former. You are accustomed to doing things in an application's graphical interface, in what you think of as a simple, straightforward way. When you're using AppleScript, you often want to "translate" a common interface operation into the AppleScript language. The trouble is that the command repertory, the object model, and the dictionary are often structured quite differently from the graphical interface. Thus the object model is often not at all like the mental picture of the application you've built up from using it in the ordinary way. The verbs you think you need aren't there, or the verbs that are there don't do what you expect. This is probably somewhat inevitable, given the nature of Apple-Script (the AppleScript interface to an application is *necessarily* different from the graphical interface) and the nature of the dictionary (it is a list of words, not to a how-to manual). But it's also very frustrating. Your mind thinks in terms of *tasks*; you're presented with some *vocabulary*. You're told some words, but not how to do things with them.

No matter how inevitable this disconnect may be, there is little doubt that some applications carry it much further than necessary. Eudora is a classic example. As we've already seen ("Make," earlier in this chapter), you can't create a new outgoing message with AppleScript in Eudora as simply as you would do it in the graphical interface; you have to say the magic words that tell Eudora where to create the new message, even though there is only one place where it could ever be meaningfully created. Similarly, deleting a message in Eudora is extraordinarily difficult. Once again, the simplicity of the graphical interface misleads you. You're used to simply selecting a message and deleting it (with the Delete key). This sounds like the delete event, so you try it:

```
tell application "Eudora"
    delete message 1 of mailbox "Out"
    -- error: Message 1 of mailbox 'Out' doesn't understand the delete message
end tell
```

So how on earth are you supposed to delete it? The solution, it turns out, is to move the message into the trash:

```
tell application "Eudora"
    move message 1 of mailbox "Out" to end of mailbox "Trash"
end tell
```

Who would ever have thought of saying something like that? And the dictionary doesn't tell you to say it, so how are you supposed to find out?

Another good example is how you insert text into a BBEdit window. There is no insert verb, and make turns out to be unreliable. The best way, apparently, is to position the selection where you want to insert the text and then say "set selection to" the new text.

Events and Classes

A dictionary lists events (verbs) and classes (nouns), but it doesn't tell you *what* verbs apply to *what* nouns. The verb make creates a new object, but *what* objects am I allowed to create? The verb delete deletes things, but *what* objects am I allowed to delete? The dictionary doesn't say.

The problem is particularly acute when the dictionary entry for a verb doesn't provide any meaningful information. For example, here's how delete is listed in most dictionaries:

```
delete reference -- the element to delete
```

That could mean anything, so it means nothing. The only way to find out what it does mean is by trying it. Another good example is close; there are usually very few objects in an application that can be closed (windows, typically) so why doesn't the dictionary tell you?

Script Debugger is particularly helpful here, because for every class it lists all the places in the dictionary where it's used. But of course this is only as good as the dictionary itself; Script Debugger doesn't have xray eyes that can peer into the workings of an application, and if a dictionary is not specific about what class or classes can serve as the object of a verb, no amount of cross-referencing can tell you.

Part of the problem here is that the dictionary is not designed to communicate the desired information in any complete and coherent manner. The new sdef format may, in some cases, improve the situation. A Cocoa application's sdef can actually include implementation information in the dictionary; a class can list the commands it responds to, and a dictionary display will then be able to pass this along to the human reader.

Until the new sdef format is widely adopted, we're left with trial and error. If Apple-Script or an application doesn't want to apply a particular verb to a particular object, it will usually return an error message that "such-and-such an object doesn't understand the so-and-so message." In other words: sorry, guess again.

Coercions

Dictionaries don't list the coercions that can be performed by an application in response to get...as. (See "Explicit Coercion" in Chapter 14.) Only trial and error can give you this information.

A rare exception is the Finder, which defines a class alias list and almost tells you (but not quite) that the purpose of this class is to let you coerce to it:

```
tell application "Finder"
    get every disk as alias list
    -- {alias "feathers:", alias "gromit:", alias "Network:"}
end tell
```

Sometimes, for particular verbs, a comment can help to fill the gap. But sometimes the comment is lying. The path to scripting addition command has an as parameter; the comment tells you that your choices are string and alias. But you can also say Unicode text, and it might be important to do so; the dictionary fails to mention this.

The problem is particularly acute for scripting additions. A scripting addition can implement a coercion, which then works as if it were part of the AppleScript language. (A good example is Jon's Commands, which lets you coerce a script object to a string.) But because coercions are not listed in the dictionary, you have no way to find out about this (except from some other documentation). Even worse, if you then run a script in the absence of that scripting addition, this coercion will break and you might not know why, because you didn't realize that it was working in the first place only because of that scripting addition.

Bad Grammar

When developers decide on the English-like terminology for a dictionary, do they think about the experience of the users who will actually employ this terminology in typical AppleScript expressions? I sometimes wonder, when I find myself saying something like this to the Finder:

```
if application file n has scripting terminology then
```

That's illegal, and generates a compile-time error. Instead, you have to say this ungrammatical-sounding phrase:

```
if application file n is has scripting terminology then -- "is has"???
```

The trouble is that `has scripting terminology` is the name of a property. Why would anyone make a property name a verb? If the name of this property were an adjective, such as `scriptable`, it could be used without sounding unnatural. (See "The "English-likeness" Monster" in Chapter 4.)

Multiple Listings

Sometimes an entry in a dictionary will appear as several different entries, distributed over different suites. For example, in the Finder's dictionary, the application class appears twice, once in the Finder Basics suites, and again in the Legacy suite. This sort of thing probably arises out of decent motives—to categorize different parts of a thing (here, different properies of the same class) by their functionality—but it is utterly maddening for the user. The prospect of having to flip back and forth between two listings of something is unbearable, assuming that one is even aware to start with that there *are* two listings for it, which is unlikely. If suites are the work of the devil, splitting something over two different suites is punishable in the eighth circle.

Once again, Script Debugger comes to the rescue; if it finds an entry repeated between multiple suites, it collapses them into a single entry in the dictionary display.

Busted Scriptability

Sometimes the reason why you can't figure out how to do something is that it can't be done. For instance, there is no way to close a "dirty" TextEdit document without saving it. (The `close` command is documented as having a `saving` parameter to which you can supply a value `no`, but it doesn't actually work.) And, as we've already seen, you can't get or set the selection in TextEdit. The best approach here is, if at all possible, just to walk away! Don't expect every application to be equally scriptable. TextEdit's scriptability is fundamentally busted, so find some other application that can do what you want to do. (For example, if you need a text processor or word processor, BBEdit, Tex-Edit Plus, and Microsoft Word are wonderfully scriptable.)

Bad Comments

A dictionary is, as I've argued, by the very nature of its underlying format, inadequately informative to users. But everything in a dictionary has a feature that can help compensate for this inadequacy—a *comment*. A comment is simply a string, so it is a developer's opportunity to say anything at all to the user, in what amounts to a free form, untramelled by the formal restrictions of dictionary structure. A comment is not a perfect medium of communication (it's just a string, it is of limited length, and it can appear only in a restricted set of places in the dictionary), but it is certainly the developer's best chance to make up for the shortcomings of a dictionary entry.

It's surprising, then, that developers fail so often to take advantage of comments. For example, earlier I mentioned that the close command is likely to operate on a restricted set of objects. The comment might be a good place to explain what these are. But here's the Finder's comment on the close command: "Close an object." And here's its comment on the close command's direct object: "The object to close." Thanks for nothing, Finder!

Here's an example of a good comment—the to parameter from the Finder's make command: "When creating an alias file, the original item to create an alias to or when creating a file viewer window, the target of the window." That tells me exactly what this parameter is for; it's used on a limited set of occasions, and the comment says just what they are.

A dictionary with some really splendid comments is Mailsmith's. In a few words it explains how to think about an entry, and even provides examples. Here's how Mailsmith's dictionary describes the text_object class: "Abstract class describing a text object and its basic properties." That is really superb. The dictionary itself has no way to let you know a class is abstract, so the Mailsmith folks come right out and tell you in a comment. And here's what it says about the text_object class's offset property: "Offset of a text object from the beginning of the document (first char has offset 1)." This description actually explains how the characters are numbered! Would that all comments were like these.

Possibly the greatest promise of the new sdef format is that it provides the opportunity for unlimited comments. A comment can be of any length, and it can be formatted (using XHTML). This means that we may hope some day soon to see dictionary presentations that read more like proper documentation.

CHAPTER 21

Scripting Additions

A *scripting addition* (or *osax*) is a compiled code fragment, typically written in a language such as C, that extends the AppleScript language (see "Scripting Addition" in Chapter 3). A scripting addition has a dictionary, but it can't be targeted, and doesn't need to be; the commands that it implements are present as if built into AppleScript itself (see Chapter 20).

A scripting addition can define events (commands), records (pseudo-classes), and coercions. Generally speaking, a scripting addition can fulfill two purposes:

Add to AppleScript's powers
> AppleScript is a "little language" (see Chapter 4), and in some ways it's just too little. A scripting addition can supplement AppleScript's powers by implementing additional commands.

Define events
> A scripting addition's dictionary can provide terminology for an event that some application might send to your script. Using this terminology, you can write an event handler to respond to the event. (See "Event Handlers" in Chapter 9.)

The default Tiger installation includes one scripting addition that adds to AppleScript's powers—the StandardAdditions osax. Many of the commands that it implements are so fundamental that this book treats them as part of the core language—for example, `display dialog`, which is used in examples throughout the book, and the very important `load script` and `store script` commands (see Chapter 8). (The other installed scripting addition, Digital Hub Scripting, implements no functionality; it defines events, which are discussed in Chapter 26.)

Writing a scripting addition is beyond the scope of this book. If you're interested, Appendix C lists some resources that may prove helpful.

For some tips about speed when accessing a scripting addition command, see "Scripting Additions" in Chapter 22.

Pros and Cons of Scripting Additions

A scripting addition implements functionality along with terminology for accessing it. So does a scriptable application. So why use a scripting addition rather than a scriptable application? There are clearly some things that scripting additions do better than scriptable applications. An application must be running in order to be targeted; if it isn't running, it must be found, which may require user intervention, and it must be launched, which takes time. But a scripting addition, once installed, is always present. If a scripting addition puts up some interface, that interface appears to be part of whatever application is being targeted at that moment. An application's dictionary has to be loaded (using a tell block or a terms block) in order for its terminology to be accessible; a script addition's terminology is simply part of the language. For this reason, a scriptable application can't be used to define the terminology for an event handler. And communicating with an application is slower than calling a scripting addition command (though less so than formerly).

On the other hand, in some ways scripting additions are clearly a Bad Thing. There are some considerations of memory management, though these are too technical to describe here. A scripting addition is inconvenient, as in order to be available to a script, it must be not merely present on the user's machine (like a scriptable application) but installed in a particular location. Scripting additions can define coercions, but these cannot be documented in the dictionary. Finally, scripting additions invade the global AppleScript namespace, in ways that can be confusing and frustrating. A scripting addition may conflict with terminology the programmer would like to use; if a scripting addition was present when a script was compiled and absent when the script is run, the script may break, and the cause may be difficult to track down. (See Chapter 20 for examples and further discussion.)

For these reasons and others, Apple actively discourages, by word and deed, the proliferation of scripting additions. The words include official statements such as the following: "There are severe limitations to what you can do in the context of a scripting addition, and the system costs of managing large numbers of scripting additions are high." (The main limitation Apple refers to here is that a scripting addition cannot define any classes. The Apple document I'm quoting also says that scripting additions can't maintain state between calls, but this is no longer true.)

The deeds consist of Apple's own steady retreat from the use of scripting additions, replacing them with scriptable applications (which may be faceless background applications). On Mac OS 9, of the nine files present by default in the *Scripting Additions* folder, five are applications; under Mac OS X, of the seven files present in */System/ Library/ScriptingAdditions*, five are applications. (There's no particular reason why such an application should live in the *ScriptingAdditions* folder; it must still be launched and targeted like any other application. So the placement of these applications in this folder is a way of ensuring their presence while suggesting that they fulfill a utility function similar to a scripting addition.)

Nonetheless, scripting additions have a venerable history and don't show signs of going away anytime soon. In the early days of AppleScript, developers enthusiastically provided freeware or shareware scripting additions, which users have collected with something approaching the fervor with which HyperCard users once collected XCMDs. (A popular and definitive repository of scripting additions is *http://www.osaxen.com*.) Scripting additions are a convenient way to provide AppleScript with system-level abilities and powers of rapid calculation that it otherwise lacks. They are a fact of life with AppleScript.

Classic Scripting Additions

There is a difference between a scripting addition intended to be used with Mac OS 9 or before and a scripting addition intended to be used with Mac OS X. A Mac OS X–type osax will not work on Mac OS 9. A Mac OS 9–type osax will work on Mac OS X only if it has been Carbonized, meaning that internally its Toolbox calls have been linked against CarbonLib. In general, any particular osax file will probably be intended for one system or the other, not both. You may not be able to tell just by looking; if the Show Package Contents menu item appears in the Finder's contextual menu for an osax, it is certainly for Mac OS X, but otherwise you may need to consult the osax's documentation.

Mac OS X on the one hand, and Classic running under Mac OS X on the other, implement AppleScript separately, but the two are compatible and Apple events travel back and forth between them. This raises the question of how the presence of Classic osaxen affects scripts running under Mac OS X. The answer seems to be that any osax terminology *in code that targets a Classic application* is handled by a Classic osax if possible. You can see this with a term like `display dialog`, because the dialogs put up by the Mac OS X and Classic versions of this command differ in appearance. So, for example:

```
set f to "gromit:Applications (Mac OS 9):SimpleText"
tell application f to display dialog "hello" -- clearly the Classic display dialog
```

On my computer, it is impossible to use English-like terminology to call a Classic scripting addition command from Mac OS X unless the same terminology is defined by an installed Mac OS X scripting addition. (The Apple documentation claims there's a way to do it with a terms block, but I have not gotten that to work.) So, for example, this works when run in the Classic Script Editor:

```
min monitor depth -- 8
```

But this won't even compile in the Mac OS X Script Editor:

```
set f to "gromit:Applications (Mac OS 9):SimpleText"
tell application f to get min monitor depth
-- compile-time error: Expected end of line, etc. but found identifier
```

The simplest solution is to employ the raw four-letter code to call the scripting addition command:

```
set f to "gromit:Applications (Mac OS 9):SimpleText"
tell application f to «event aevtgmnd» -- 8
```

But remember, you have to be targeting a Classic application. On its own, the same Apple event will fail:

```
«event aevtgmnd» -- error: «script» doesn't understand the «event aevtgmnd» message
```

Loading Scripting Additions

A scripting addition is not targeted; it is loaded. In particular, in order to be seen and used by a script, a scripting addition must be loaded by the AppleScript scripting component instance that is going to compile or run that script (see Chapter 3). For that to happen, the scripting addition file must be physically installed in any of a specific set of locations at the time that the AppleScript component instance is summoned into existence. On Mac OS X, those locations are, in the first instance, the three */Library/ScriptAdditions* directories—in */System*, at the top level, and in the user directory. (On previous systems, there was one location, the *Scripting Additions* folder; this was originally in the *Extensions* folder but was moved into the System Folder starting in Mac OS 8.)

This architecture has historically caused headaches for script developers. If you wanted to write a script relying on a third-party scripting addition and distribute that script to others, you had to worry about how to guarantee that your end user had the right scripting addition in the right location by the time the script ran. Typically this involved social engineering. First you had to ascertain what scripting additions your script was calling. (Script Debugger is especially helpful here; it lists the scripting additions on which your script depends, even looking up any unresolved event codes on *http://macscripter.net* for you.) Then you had to distribute the required scripting additions with your script, or otherwise include instructions for acquiring them, along with loud and clear instructions on installing the scripting additions, in the hope of staving off complaints when your end user heedlessly tried to use the script without installing the scripting additions and got an error.

Starting in Panther, an elegant solution to this longstanding difficulty was implemented at last: if you are willing to distribute your script as an application—either as an applet bundle or as an AppleScript Studio application—then if that bundle contains a directory *Contents/Resources/Scripting Additions*, any osaxen in that directory will be loaded when the application starts up. The needed osaxen must, however, be installed in one of the standard locations on *your* machine ("you" being the developer) as otherwise the script cannot be compiled in the first place. And of course the effectiveness of this solution is limited to systems that implement the mechanism involved, which means Panther and later. (On what an applet bundle is, see "Applet and Droplet" in Chapter 3. For examples, see Chapter 27.)

In your Library directory, the *ScriptingAdditions* directory has no space in its name. In a bundle-style applet or AppleScript Studio application, the *Scripting Additions* directory does have a space. Somebody goofed but it's too late to fix things now. This inconsistency makes things tricky; you must get the names right or things won't work.

There is one other trick for making a scripting addition available on an end user's machine, and that is for your script to install it into a *ScriptingAdditions* folder. You might think this couldn't possibly work, because by now the script is running, the AppleScript scripting component instance has already been created, and any scripting additions that are going to be loaded have already been loaded. You're right, but there's a magic spell for telling the AppleScript component to reload osaxen:

```
try
        tell me to «event ascrgdut»
end try
```

The Apple event must be issued in raw form, as it has no English-like equivalent (it's not in any dictionary). It's enclosed in a try block because it will probably generate an error; but the error is spurious and may be safely ignored.

Thus, your script can install a scripting addition on the fly and call a command within it. Here's an example using the Jon's Commands osax. We will call the ticks, a command within Jon's Commands; we use run script so that the osax doesn't have to be installed in order to compile and test the script (alternatively, we could use the command's four-letter code, «event JonstikC»). To install Jon's Commands, we have to find a copy of it; here, we ask the user to locate it:

```
try
    run script "get the ticks"
on error -- evidently it isn't installed
        set jons to choose file with prompt "Please find Jon's Commands:"
        set sa to path to scripting additions from user domain
        tell application "Finder" to duplicate jons to sa
        try
                tell me to «event ascrgdut»
        end try
end try
display dialog (run script "get the ticks") -- 1974834
```

Standard Scripting Addition Commands

The scripting addition commands present in a standard installation of Tiger (Mac OS X 10.4) are all implemented by the StandardAdditions scripting addition. You can consult the StandardAdditions dictionary to learn what commands it contains and to get the full details on their syntax, and it would be a waste of trees for me to repeat the information you'll find there. However, I'll list all the commands and provide some basic explanations and comments (and examples) that go beyond what the dictionary tells you. For most of these commands, where I or the dictionary might say "string," you should understand "or Unicode text," since StandardAdditions has been generally revised to be Unicode-savvy.

(For load script, store script, and run script, see "Compiled Script Files as Script Objects" in Chapter 8. For the POSIX file class, see "File and Alias" in Chapter 13 and "File Coercions" in Chapter 14. For do shell script, see Chapter 25. For digital hub scripting, folder actions, and CGI events, see Chapter 27.)

Dialogs

These scripting addition commands put up dialogs, thus providing a modicum of user interaction. The dialog will appear in whatever application is being targeted at the moment, or in the host application if no application is being targeted. They should not be used in an environment where no user interaction is allowed (for example, in a Unix osascript command). Recall (from "Errors" in Chapter 19) that the -128 ("User canceled") error thrown when the user clicks the Cancel button in one of these dialogs, if it percolates all the way up to AppleScript, does not normally result in an error dialog (though it will cause the script to terminate prematurely).

---

display dialog   general informational, text entry, and button-choice dialog

Description

A remarkably flexible little command. You can put up an information dialog. It can have an icon and a title. It can include a user text entry field; optionally, the user's text can appear as bullets (for password entry and so forth). You can dictate the names of up to three buttons, specify which is the OK button (which responds to Return) and which is the Cancel button (which responds to Esc or Command-Period, generates error -128), and learn which one the user pressed. The dialog can be set to time out if the user does not respond, and you can learn that this is what happened. By default, the buttons are "Cancel" and "OK"; a button called "Cancel" is the Cancel button by default. Returns a record.

Examples

```
set r to display dialog "Quick! Pick a Pep Boy!" buttons {"Mannie", "Moe", "Jack"} ¬
    with icon caution giving up after 3
set favoritePepBoy to button returned of r
if favoritePepBoy is "" and gave up of r then set notFastEnough to true
set whoIsIt to text returned of (display dialog "What is your name?" ¬
    default answer "" buttons {"OK"} default button "OK")
```

---

display alert   informational dialog

Description

Syntactically, a simpler version of display dialog; there is no user text entry. Has a more Cocoa-like appearance than display, dialog; there can be title text and smaller message text, and the icon has the proper look for the host application. The default is a single button ("OK"), and there is always a default button (the rightmost, by default). A button named "Cancel" is *not* automatically the Cancel button. The third (leftmost) button is gapped away from the others. Returns a record. (New in Tiger.)

Example

```
tell application "Finder"
    display alert "Pep Alert" message "Mannie, Moe, and Jack welcome you."
end tell
```

choose from list

listbox selection dialog

Description

Puts up a scrolling list of strings or numbers for the user to choose from. Returns a list of chosen strings or numbers, or false (not an error!) if the user cancels. There are two buttons, and you can set their titles; you can add a prompt and a window title. You can specify whether to permit multiple selections and/or an empty selection.

Example

```
set p to choose from list {"Mannie", "Moe", "Jack"} with prompt "Pick a Pep Boy:"
```

choose file

file selection dialog

Description

Puts up a standard Open File dialog, with title "Choose File" and default button "Choose." You can add a prompt; you can set the initial folder displayed. You can specify whether invisible files should be shown, whether packages should be treated as folders, and what types of file to display (can be a list of either four-letter file type codes or UTIs—see *http://developer.apple.com/macosx/uniformtypeidentifiers.html*—but not both). Returns an alias.

Example

```
set f to choose file of type {"public.text"} without invisibles
```

choose folder

folder selection dialog

Description

Puts up a standard Choose Folder dialog, with title "Choose a Folder." The user can also create a new folder. Your options are similar to choose file. Returns an alias.

Example

```
set f to choose folder with prompt "Pick a folder:"
```

choose file name

file save dialog

Description

Puts up a standard Save File dialog (default button "Save"), with title "Choose File Name" and default prompt "Specify new file name and location." The user can also create a new folder. If the user specifies an existing file, goes through the usual "Replace?" rigmarole. You can set the initial folder, the initial filename, and the prompt. Returns a file URL (which appears as a file specifier). Does not actually save anything.

Example

```
set f to choose file name with prompt "Where shall I save this stuff?"
```

choose application

Description

Puts up a standard Choose Application dialog, listing all applications, with title "Choose Application" and default prompt "Select an application." The user can switch to browsing in a standard Open File dialog. You can specify the window title and prompt. Returns an application specifier, or optionally an alias, or a list if multiple selections are allowed.

Example

```
set theApp to choose application as alias
tell application "Finder"
    set isScriptable to has scripting terminology of theApp
end tell
if isScriptable then display dialog "It's scriptable!"
```

choose URL

Description

Puts up a standard Choose URL dialog (with a Connect button); this is rather like the Finder's Connect to Server dialog, useful for finding servers on the local network, with an option to let the user choose various categories of server. The user can also just type a URL unless you prevent it; this can be basically any string at all. Does not actually connect! Returns a string.

Example

```
choose URL showing File servers -- "afp://duck.local."
```

choose remote application

Description

Puts up a dialog with title "Choose Remote Application" and two panes, one for selecting a local machine or entering an IP number, the other with default prompt "Select an application." The target machine must have Remote Apple Events turned on in the Sharing system preferences. I have not been able to get the local-machine choice to work (where the Bonjour names of local machines are listed automatically) but using the IP number works, and a Bonjour name can be entered manually. You can supply the title and prompt. Returns an eppc URL string suitable for targeting the application remotely; see Chapter 23. (New in Tiger.)

Examples

```
choose remote application
-- application "Finder" of machine "eppc://192.168.0.4/?uid=501&pid=178"
using terms from application "Finder"
    set ap to choose remote application -- I choose Finder on remote machine
    -- username/password dialog appears, I fill it out
    tell ap
        get name of window 1 -- Desktop
    end tell
end using terms from
```

choose color

Description

Puts up a standard Color Picker dialog, where the user may choose a color. You can specify the initially selected color. Returns a color. A color is expressed as an `rgb color`, which is a list of three integers representing the red, green, and blue components.

Example

```
choose color default color {9000, 10000, 50000} -- {50000, 9000, 10000}
```

Noises

These commands produce sounds and modify sound settings.

beep

Description

Plays the system beep sound. Optionally takes an integer saying how many times to beep.

Example

```
beep
```

get volume settings

Description

Reports the loudness of sound output, input, and alert volume, as a record.

Example

```
alert volume of (get volume settings) -- 75
```

set volume

Description

Sets the loudness of sound output, input, and alert volume.

Example

```
set volume output volume 100 alert volume 100
beep
```

say

Description

Reads text aloud, either in real time or saving the synthesized speech as a sound file. Can also be used in conjunction with speech recognition to determine what text appears below the microphone window.

Example

```
tell application "SpeechRecognitionServer"
    set s to listen for {"yes", "no"} with prompt "Would you like me to beep?" ¬
        giving up after 10
end tell
if s is "yes" then
    say "Okay, I will beep now." displaying "Okay."
    beep
else
    say "Okay, then I won't." displaying "Okay."
end if
```

File and Machine Information

The following commands provide information about a file or the system.

system info

system information

Description

Returns a record of basic system information, such as the computer name, CPU speed and type, Ethernet address, and so forth (new in Tiger). If the desired information is not part of this record, use the more general (but harder to use) system attribute command.

Example

```
set v to system version of (system info)
display dialog "You are running system " & v & "!"
```

system attribute

gestalt and environment variables

Description

Returns the value of gestalt selectors (see *http://developer.apple.com/documentation/Carbon/Reference/Gestalt_Manager/index.html*).

Example

```
set n to system attribute "sysv"
set s to "print sprintf \"%lx\", " & n
set v to do shell script "perl -e " & quoted form of s
set L to characters of v
set v to "." & item -1 of L
set v to "." & item -2 of L & v
set v to ((items 1 thru -3 of L) as string) & v
display dialog "You are running system " & v & "!"
```

Also returns the value of user environment variables (see Chapter 25 for an example). To find out what they are, issue the system attribute command with no parameters.

Example

```
system attribute "SHELL" -- "/bin/bash"
```

path to

Description

Locates various standard folders, such as the system folder. If the designated folder is legal but doesn't exist, the path to command silently creates it unless you specify without folder creation, in which case an error is returned if the folder doesn't exist. If a standard folder isn't listed as an enumerator, you can use its four-letter code (see *http://developer.apple. com/documentation/Carbon/Reference/Folder_Manager/index.html*). Returns an alias, or a string, if desired (or Unicode text—the dictionary fails to document this fact).

Example

```
path to desktop -- alias "feathers:Users:mattneub:Desktop:"
path to "cmnu" -- alias "feathers:Library:Contextual Menu Items:"
```

path to

Description

Locates an application by name, including the current application (the host application). Launches the application if it uses Cocoa scripting (I regard this as a bug). The special phrase path to me is supposed to give the alias of the current compiled script file, but in the past this has been unreliable; it is somewhat better in Tiger, though it can still go wrong depending on the script runner environment and the script file format (script bundles are problematic), and it doesn't work in Script Editor (works fine in Script Debugger).

Example

```
path to application "Finder"
-- alias "feathers:System:Library:CoreServices:Finder.app:"
```

path to resource

Description

Locates a file in the Resources folder of a bundle. Intended primarily for script bundles and applet bundles (and AppleScript Studio applications), so they can see inside themselves; doesn't work in Script Editor, but works fine in Script Debugger. You can optionally designate any bundle to look in (such as an application), and a subfolder within the bundle.

Examples

```
display dialog ((path to resource "description.rtfd") as string)
-- feathers:Users:mattneub:Library:Scripts:myScriptBundle.scptd:Contents:
    Resources:description.rtfd
set f to path to resource "app.icns" in bundle ¬
    alias "feathers:Applications:Mail.app:"
display dialog "Time to check your mail!" with icon f
```

list disks

Description

Gets the names of all mounted volumes. Returns a list of strings (meaning Unicode text).

Example

```
list disks -- {"feathers", "gromit", "Network"}
```

list folder

Description

Gets the names of all items within a folder. Includes invisible files and folders if you don't prevent it. Returns a list of strings (meaning Unicode text).

Example

```
list folder (path to home folder)
-- {".bash_history", ".CFUserTextEncoding", ".DS_Store", ".ssh", ...}
```

info for

Description

Gets information about an item on disk. Returns a file information record packed with useful stuff. If you ask for the info for a folder, the script may take some time to run, in order to sum the sizes of all the files within it; you can prevent this by saying without size.

Example

```
set uf to (path to home folder as string)
set L to list folder uf
set s to {}
repeat with f in L -- collect sizes of all items
    set end of s to size of (info for file (uf & f))
end repeat
set maxItem to 0
set maxVal to 0
repeat with i from 1 to (count s) -- find biggest size
    if item i of s > maxVal then
        set maxItem to i
        set maxVal to item i of s
    end if
end repeat
display dialog "The biggest thing in your home folder is: " & item maxItem of L
```

File Data

These commands perform sequential read and write of file data. ("Sequential" means that each read or write will start, by default, just after the last character read or written in the same session.)

open for access

Description

Opens a file for read access—optionally, for write access—creating the file as a text file if it doesn't exist (it does this even if you're opening for read access only; I regard this as a bug). Returns a file reference number that can be used with the other commands.

Example

```
set f to (path to desktop as string) & "newfile.txt"
set ff to open for access file f
close access ff
```

read

Description

Reads data from a file, optionally treating it as a specified datatype (for an example, see "Forming Unicode Text" in Chapter 13); the default is string (not Unicode text). There are options for where to start (character position values start at 1), how many characters to read, and where to stop. The using delimiter parameter is poorly documented: this is a list of one-character strings, any of which will be used to break the data into a single-level list of strings (which will lack all the delimiter characters). The until and before parameters fail when reading as string if they are out of the basic ASCII range (over 128), but they work using Unicode text.

Example

```
set f to (path to desktop as string) & "someUTF16file.txt"
set ff to open for access file f
set d1 to read ff as Unicode text
d1 -- "Mannie¬Moe¬Jack"
-- testing delimiter parameter
set notsign to "¬" as Unicode text
set L to read ff from 1 as Unicode text using delimiter notsign
L -- {"Mannie", "Moe", "Jack"}
-- testing before parameter
set d2 to read ff from 1 as Unicode text before notsign
close access ff
d2 -- "Mannie"
```

write

Description

Writes data to a file, optionally treating it as a specified datatype; thus you can store any kind of data in a text file and retrieve it later (it will be read correctly if you specify the same class when writing and when reading). There are options for where to start and how much data to write; writing at the end of a file appends, but writing in the middle of the file overwrites existing data (it doesn't insert).

Example

```
set f to a reference to file ((path to desktop as string) & "justTesting")
open for access f with write permission
write {"Mannie", "Moe", "Jack"} as list to f
close access f
open for access f
set L to read f as list
close access f
L -- {"Mannie", "Moe", "Jack"}
```

Description

Returns the index of the last character of a file (which is also the size of the file). Because character position values start at 1, and because the eof is the position of the last character, if you want to append to a file you must start writing at a position one greater than the eof (and that is the largest position at which you are permitted to start writing).

Example

```
write "Howdy" to f
set ourEof to get eof of f
write "Doody" to f starting at ourEof + 1
```

set eof   set file end position

Description

Sets a file's size, truncating its data or filling the new excess with zeros. To replace an existing file's data, set its eof to 0 before writing to it.

close access   close file

Description

Closes a file. Always close a file you have opened for access!

The file data commands let you describe the file you want to operate on as either a file reference number returned by open for access, or a file specifier or alias. In the read example earlier, I capture a file reference number and use it throughout; in the write example, I start with a file specifier and use that instead. The open for access command will also take a pathname string, but other commands will not. So, this works:

```
set f to open for access ((path to desktop as string) & "testing")
close access f
```

And so does this:

```
set f to ((path to desktop as string) & "testing")
open for access f
close access alias f
```

But this doesn't:

```
set f to ((path to desktop as string) & "testing")
open for access f
close access f
-- error: Can't make "feathers:Users:mattneub:Desktop:testing" into type file
```

You should ensure sufficient error handling so as not to leave a file open (unlike all the examples thus far!). If you do accidentally leave a file open, you might have to quit the current application, such as the Script Editor, in order to close it. Script Debugger helps you here; it notifies you if you've left a file open, and permits you to close it without quitting.

In this example, we use AppleScript to construct a miniature "database." We have some strings; taking advantage of the write command's starting at parameter, we write each string into a 32-character "field." Notice the cautious error handling:

```
set pep to {"Mannie", "Moe", "Jack"}
set f to (path to current user folder as string) & "testFile"
try
    set fNum to open for access file f with write permission
on error
    close access file f
    return
end try
try
    set eof fNum to 0 -- erase if exists
    set eof fNum to (count pep) * 32
    repeat with i from 1 to (count pep)
        write item i of pep to fNum starting at (i - 1) * 32
    end repeat
    close access fNum
on error
    close access fNum
end try
```

Now we'll fetch the data from the "database." We take advantage of the fact that all data that isn't part of a string is null.

```
set f to choose file of type "TEXT"
try
    set fNum to open for access f
on error
    close access f
    return
end try
set L to {}
try
    set ct to (get eof fNum) / 32
    repeat with i from 1 to ct
        set end of L to read fNum from (i - 1) * 32 ¬
            before ASCII character 0 -- read up to but not including null
    end repeat
    close access fNum
on error
    close access fNum
end try
L -- {"Mannie", "Moe", "Jack"}
```

String and Clipboard

These commands give string-related information or work with the Clipboard.

ASCII character

number to character

Description

Converts an ASCII numeric value to a one-character (MacRoman) string.

Example

```
ASCII character 82 -- "R"
```

ASCII number

character to number

Description

Converts the first character of a (MacRoman) string to an ASCII numeric value.

Example

```
ASCII number "Ribbit" -- 82
```

offset

substring position

Description

Reports the position of a substring within a target string. Character position values start at 1. Returns 0 if the substring isn't found. Formerly considered case and ignored diacriticals, which is backwards from AppleScript's own defaults; staring in Panther, this is fixed, and string considerations are obeyed (see "String Considerations" in Chapter 19).

Example

```
offset of "bb" in "Ribbit" -- 3
```

summarize

summary of content

Description

Summarizes the content of a string or textfile, like the Summarize Service.

set the clipboard to

set clipboard

Description

Puts data onto the clipboard.

clipboard info

describe clipboard

Description

Describes the contents of the clipboard as a list of class–size pairs.

Example

```
-- user has copied a file's icon in the Finder
clipboard info
-- {{string, 20}, {«class ut16», 44}, {«class hfs », 80}, {«class utf8», 20},
{Unicode text, 42}, {picture, 2616}, {«class icns», 43336}, {«class furl», 62}}
```

Description

Gets the clipboard text, or you can specify some other class. A common trick is to specify as record; in the resulting record, the names of the items are their classes, and the values are their values.

```
-- user has copied a file's icon in the Finder
set r to the clipboard as record
-- {string:"Hawaii Itinerary.pdf", «class ut16»:"Hawaii Itinerary.pdf", «class hfs »:
«data hfs 0000...0000», «class utf8»:"Hawaii Itinerary.pdf", Unicode text:"Hawaii
Itinerary.pdf", picture:«data PICT0A38...000FF», «class icns»:«data icns6963...0000»,
«class furl»:file "feathers:Users:mattneub:Desktop:Hawaii Itinerary.pdf"}
type identifier of (info for «class furl» of r) -- "com.adobe.pdf"
the clipboard as «class furl» -- works too
```

Numbers and Dates

These commands add some extra arithmetic and date-time powers to AppleScript.

round

Description

Rounds a real to an integer, in various ways (one of which is called rounding as taught in school, showing that AppleScript has a sense of humor).

Example

```
round 1.3 -- 1
```

random number

Description

Generates a random number. By default, this is a real between 0 and 1, but you can specify a different upper bound or both bounds. If every number you specify is an integer, the result is an integer, which could be either of the bounds; otherwise it is a real. You can seed the generator to get it started; this is useful for generating a fixed pseudo-random sequence.

Example

```
random number
set L to {}
repeat 10 times
    if (random number 1) as boolean then
        set end of L to "heads"
    else
        set end of L to "tails"
    end if
end repeat
L -- {"heads", "tails", "heads", "heads", "heads",
    "tails", "heads", "heads", "heads", "heads"}
```

current date

now

Description

Generates a date object corresponding to the current date and time.

Example

```
time string of (current date) -- "10:41:13 AM"
```

time to GMT

time zone

Description

Reports the time zone that has been set via the Date & Time preference pane, as an offset from Greenwich Mean Time, in seconds.

Example

```
(time to GMT) / hours -- -7.0
```

Miscellaneous

These are scripting addition commands I couldn't categorize.

delay

wait

Description

Pauses for a specified number of seconds. Starting with Panther, this number can be a real.

Example

```
delay 1
beep
```

mount volume

AppleShare

Description

Mounts an AppleShare volume (a machine where Personal File Sharing is turned on). The machine is specified as an afp URL string, such as is returned from the choose URL command. To avoid the dialog for choosing a particular volume, add the volume name as a second path element. To avoid the dialog asking for username and password, supply them as parameters or as part of the URL. A Windows server can be mounted using an smb URL. Returns a file URL (but no result if the volume is already mounted). If the syntax of the mount volume command is insufficiently flexible, consider using do shell script to call mount_afp.

Examples

```
-- this first one lets user choose, presents the "Select volumes to mount" dialog
set s to choose URL showing File servers
mount volume s as user name "mattneub" with password "teehee"
-- these next ones present no dialogs
mount volume "afp://matt%20neuburg:teehee@duck.local/OmniumGatherum"
mount volume "afp://duck.local/OmniumGatherum" ¬
```

```
        as user name "matt neuburg" with password "teehee"
-- this one presents username/password dialog and volume dialog
mount volume "afp://duck.local"
```

scripting components

list OSA components

Description

Returns a list of strings giving the names of the installed OSA scripting components. One of these will be "AppleScript".

open location

open a URL

Description

Given a URL string, opens the URL with the appropriate helper application. For an example, see "Reduction" in Chapter 1.

CHAPTER 22

Speed

There are people who worry about squeezing every last possible ounce of speed out of AppleScript. They like nothing better than to sit down with a script and find clever ways of rearranging or reexpressing it so as to make it run faster. They have developed ingenious tricks and devices to optimize AppleScript code for speed. They even hold little contests to see whose script can complete a given task fastest! Personally, I'm not a great believer in optimizing code, but it's certainly true, as a practical matter, that most AppleScript programmers, sooner or later, do become concerned about speed. You've developed a script, and it's working, but when it runs it's taking longer than you think it should. You want to know whether there's anything you can do to make your script faster.

A few general considerations will put speed into perspective:

Things are better than they used to be
> AppleScript is a lot faster than it once was, not just because we're all using vastly quicker computers these days, but because the runtime engine has been made more efficient. AppleScript used to be downright sluggish, and this was very noticeable back in the old days when computers had floppy disk slots and less than 4MB of RAM (and we all had to clean the streets with our tongues on the way to school). That's no longer the case.

Interapplication communication is a bottleneck
> AppleScript is all about communicating with other applications. It (AppleScript) isn't supposed to be fast, because it isn't supposed to be doing much of anything. It's supposed to be sending Apple events to scriptable applications, and as soon as it does that, speed is completely out of its hands; having handed an Apple event to the system to dispatch, AppleScript can do nothing but wait— and that's what most of a script's execution time probably consists of, waiting for some target application to receive an Apple event, do what it says to do, and return a reply.

Only repetition really matters

Considerations of speed are probably not worth raising at all unless your script performs some sort of repetition, meaning either a handler calling itself recursively or a repeat block—and even then, not until the number of repetitions becomes significant. It is here, in a repetition, that a small difference in speed one way or the other can accumulate, as the same code is performed again and again, so as to have a big impact on how long your script takes to run.

Tools of the Trade

In order to improve speed, you have to measure it. At the crudest level, you can do this with the current date command, which captures the date-time at the moment it is issued, but this is good only to the nearest second. A better choice is the command the ticks from the Jon's Commands osax; this is particularly good for timing things, since a tick is about one-sixtieth of a second. Examples will appear later in this chapter.

Script Debugger can also help you quantify speed. It doesn't yet provide true code profiling (reporting the time spent on different sections of your code), but it does report how long the script took to run and how much of that time was spent within AppleScript and how much was spent sending Apple events and how many Apple events were sent. It also provides code coverage, indicating what lines of your code were actually executed, so you don't waste effort optimizing areas of your script that aren't doing anything.

Apple Events

Apple events are expensive, and some Apple events are *very* expensive. You can't do anything about the time spent waiting for each Apple event to execute, but perhaps you can minimize the number of Apple events sent. At the same time, you may be able to improve the efficiency of the particular Apple events you do send.

The boolean expression at the top of a repeat while block must be evaluated before every repetition of the block, and then once more in order to decide not to repeat the block any further. This means that it should not contain any commands whose result will not change during the repetition, as it would be needless and wasteful overhead to issue those commands each time through the loop.

Here's a silly but telling example. Suppose we have two folders in the Finder, and we want to create enough new folders inside the first folder so that it contains the same number of items as the second folder. The following code expresses neatly and elegantly what we want done:

```
set x to 1
tell application "Finder"
    set f1 to folder "f1"
    set f2 to folder "f2"
    repeat while ((count items of f1) < (count items of f2))
        make new folder at f1 with properties {name:("f" & x)}
        set x to x + 1
    end repeat
end tell
```

But in the world of AppleScript, neat and elegant isn't always good. That code sends the count message to the Finder twice for each time through the loop, when in fact we need only send it twice at the outset as we prepare for the loop:

```
set x to 1
tell application "Finder"
    set f1 to folder "f1"
    set f2 to folder "f2"
    set c1 to count items of f1
    set c2 to count items of f2
    repeat while c1 < c2
        make new folder at f1 with properties {name:("f" & x)}
        set x to x + 1
        set c1 to c1 + 1
    end repeat
end tell
```

Observe that the same issue would not arise if I had coded this using repeat with x from...to, because that construct evaluates everything once at the outset and then never again.

Special considerations arise when using repeat with...in (see Chapter 19). The Apple events you send may be needlessly numerous *and* needlessly complex. Suppose we want to ask BBEdit to make uppercase every word starting with "t":

```
tell application "BBEdit"
    repeat with w in every word of document 1
        if contents of text of w begins with "t" then
            change case w making raise case
        end if
    end repeat
end tell
```

That looks very neat, but looks are deceptive. Each time through the loop, w is set to this:

```
a reference to item 1 of every word of document 1 of application "BBEdit"
a reference to item 2 of every word of document 1 of application "BBEdit"
a reference to item 3 of every word of document 1 of application "BBEdit"
```

And so on. Our code is sending BBEdit an Apple event for every word in the document, and this Apple event asks BBdit to evaluate the concept every word afresh each time, even though the meaning of that concept is not changing significantly as we loop. If there are a thousand words and just two beginning with "t", that's a massive waste.

We can eliminate the repeated evaluation of every word by gathering the words of the document once, before the loop:

```
tell application "BBEdit"
    set L to (get every word of document 1)
    repeat with w in L
        if contents of text of w begins with "t" then
            change case w making raise case
        end if
    end repeat
end tell
```

But we are still sending one Apple event for every word in the document. With a single much more efficient Apple event at the outset, we can ask BBEdit to give us a list of just those words we will need to change:

```
tell application "BBEdit"
    set L to ¬
        (get every word of document 1 where contents of text of it begins with "t")
    repeat with w in L
        change case w making raise case
    end repeat
end tell
```

That way, even if our document consists of a thousand words, if there are just two words beginning with "t", our code will send just three Apple events: one to gather the list of references to the two words, and then two more to change their case.

Be alert for implicit Apple events you may be sending without intending to do so. Reread Chapter 12 to see how capturing a reference implies the possibility that using that reference might send an Apple event. In a loop, that sort of thing can add up.

Finally, consider that you might not have to loop at all. The target application may be smart enough do what you want with a single command. There's no need for the loop in this code to gather the names of Finder folders:

```
tell application "Finder"
    set L to (get every folder)
    set L2 to {}
    repeat with f in L
        set end of L2 to name of f
    end repeat
end tell
```

Instead, you can say this (see "Operations on Multiple References" in Chapter 11):

```
tell application "Finder"
    set L to (get name of every folder)
end tell
```

List Access

When you access an attribute of a list, it is much faster to target a reference to the list, or the list as a script property, than to target the list directly. It's not entirely clear why this is; it seems like a bug. But it's a venerable and acknowledged bug, because even Apple's earliest documentation on AppleScript contains an example illustrating this point.

In this code (based on Apple's example) we total the numbers in a long list:

```
set L to {}
set total to 0
set bignum to 5000
repeat with i from 1 to bignum
    set end of L to i
end repeat
repeat with i from 1 to bignum
    set total to total + (item i of L)
end repeat
total -- 12502500, and it takes about 22 seconds to run on my machine
```

The big slowdown here is the second repeat block, accessing items of the list. If we access these items by way of a reference to the list, things speed up dramatically:

```
set L to {}
set refL to a reference to L
set total to 0
set bignum to 5000
repeat with i from 1 to bignum
    set end of L to i
end repeat
repeat with i from 1 to bignum
    set total to total + (item i of refL)
end repeat
total -- 12502500, and it took less than a second
```

Instead of a reference, you can get the same extraordinary speed bump by referring to the list as a script property:

```
set L to {}
set total to 0
set bignum to 5000
repeat with i from 1 to bignum
    set end of L to i
end repeat
repeat with i from 1 to bignum
    set total to total + (item i of my L)
end repeat
total -- 12502500, and it took less than a second
```

The magic word in that code is my. Take it away, and the code takes 22 seconds to run; with it, the code runs in less than a second. (Discovery of this remarkable device is generally credited to Serge Belleudy-d'Espinose.)

Now suppose all of that code is part of a handler, where L is a local variable. You can't take a reference to L, so you'd have to use the trick of making L a script property. To do so, you might have to create a script object expressly for this purpose; that may seem silly, but it's worth it:

```
on myHandler()
    set L to {}
    script myScript
        property refL : L
    end script
    set total to 0
    set bignum to 5000
    repeat with i from 1 to bignum
        set end of L to i
    end repeat
    repeat with i from 1 to bignum
        set total to total + (item i of myScript's refL)
    end repeat
    return total
end myHandler
myHandler() -- 12502500, and it took less than a second
```

I've been unable to arrive at a rule explaining what causes list access to be slow and when it isn't. In the examples in this section, the first repeat block (containing set end of) is fast; it's the second repeat block that's slow. But this does not mean that set end of is *always* fast. Sometimes it's slow too, and I don't know why. However, all you need to know is that, in such cases, the tricks with reference-based or property-based access will speed it up. So these should be among the first weapons in your arsenal when you're looking for ways to optimize your code.

Scripting Additions

One of the main reasons for using scripting additions is speed. For repeated trigonometric calculations, for example, it is certainly going to be a lot faster to use a scripting addition, such as the Satimage osax, than to roll your own calculation (as disingenuously suggested at Apple's web site). Similarly, a scripting addition that implements transformations to a list, such as returning a list with a particular element deleted, is going to be faster than coding the same operation in AppleScript (see "LISP-likeness" in Chapter 4). Just how quickly a scripting addition is called, however, depends on how you call it.

The osax architecture is such that a scripting addition appears to be present "inside" whatever application is being targeted when the scripting addition command is called. This behavior is noticeable, and useful, when a scripting addition puts up some user interface. For example, if the display dialog command is called from within a tell block targeting the Finder, the dialog appears within the Finder; it's as if you'd given the Finder a new dialog.

Behind the scenes, though, this architecture involves a serious inefficiency. The application itself is sent the Apple event denoting a scripting addition command. Obviously the application can't deal with this Apple event, so at that point the message is sent on up to the realm of scripting additions as a kind of fallback. This means that when you use a scripting addition command while targeting an application, that command must be routed through an extra step. This takes time, and in a context of repetition, the time adds up significantly.

If, on the other hand, you use a scripting addition command outside of any tell block, or within a "tell me" block, the message is sent directly to the scripting addition, which is faster by about an order of magnitude—a very significant difference. Here's a script that demonstrates.

```
set t to the ticks
repeat 5000 times
    tell application "Finder" to get offset of "i" in "ticks"
end repeat
set t1 to (the ticks) - t
set t to the ticks
repeat 5000 times
    tell me to get offset of "i" in "ticks"
end repeat
set t2 to (the ticks) - t
return {t1, t2} -- {944, 71}
```

Context

The context or environment from which a script is executed can make a huge difference to its speed. This is in large measure because Apple events are expensive. In particular, what makes them expensive is the context switch involved in communicating between one application and another. Thus it is typically fastest, where possible, to run a script from within the application it targets. If an application has a Script menu, therefore, it is worth putting the script there and executing it from there to see if this makes it faster.

(But also, there are some contexts that are inherently slower than others, for no discernable reason; it has something to do with how these contexts are programmed and that's that.)

Here's a test script:

```
set x to (get current date)
repeat 500 times
    tell application "iTunes"
        get name of it
    end tell
end repeat
set y to (get current date)
set z to (y - x)
```

```
tell application "Finder"
    activate
    display dialog z
end tell
```

Table 22-1 shows some rough timings on my machine for running that script from within various contexts.

Table 22-1. *Timings for the same script executed in different contexts*

Context	Timing
iTunes's Script Menu	0.15 second
Red Sweater FastScripts	0.5 second
Script Debugger	1.5 seconds
Apple's Script Menu	8 seconds
Script Editor	9 seconds
DragThing	Timed out after 500 seconds

Many external factors affect speed, so no absolute lessons can be drawn from a simple, unscientific test such as this; but clearly it can be worthwhile to consider the context in which a script will run when evaluating its speed.

CHAPTER 23
Scriptable Applications

AppleScript's chief purpose is to let you communicate with scriptable applications. How you target a scriptable application using AppleScript depends on whether the application is *local* (run on the same computer and by the same user as your script) or *remote* (run on a different machine, or on the same machine but by a different logged-in user). You might also like to know what scriptable applications are included with a default installation of Tiger. (On creation of scriptable applications using applets, AppleScript Studio, and Cocoa, see Chapter 27.)

This book won't teach you how to script any particular application (see "The Scope of This Book" in the Preface). If the application comes with documentation or examples showing how to script it, start with that. For certain applications, there may be third-party books or web pages devoted to the topic of scripting it. The application will in any case have a dictionary (see Chapter 20).

Targeting Scriptable Applications

To *target* a scriptable application is to aim Apple events at it, like arrows. The principal linguistic device for targeting an application in AppleScript is the tell block containing an application specifier. Such a tell block actually has two purposes: it determines the target, if no other target is specified within the block, and (at compile time) it also causes a dictionary to be loaded, which may be used in the resolution of terminology. If the target of the tell block is expressed as a variable rather than a literal application specifier, no resolution of terminology is performed and the application is not sought for targeting until runtime when the code is actually encountered. Instead of a tell block, the of operator (or its equivalents) can be used to form a target; this does not cause any resolution of terminology either. Terminology can be resolved independently of any tell block by means of a terms block.

A reference to an object belonging to an application can also be used to target that application. The terminology within the reference has already been resolved (otherwise the reference could not have been formed in the first place); any further terminology accompanying the reference when you actually use it will have to be resolved independently.

(See "Missing External Referents" in Chapter 3; "Target" in Chapter 11; Chapter 12; "Application" in Chapter 13; "Tell" and "Using Terms From" in Chapter 19; and "Resolution of Terminology" in Chapter 20.)

Local Applications

A *local* application is an application on the same computer and under the same user as the script. The specifier for a local application may consist of a full pathname string (colon-delimited) or simply the name of the application; the name should usually be sufficient.

Specifying an application's name can be trickier than you might suppose. Back in the pre–Mac OS X days, typing the name of an application could be a maddening and tedious exercise. BBEdit's name wasn't `"BBEdit"`; it was `"BBEdit 6.5"`. Excel's name was `"Microsoft Excel"`. Frontier's name was `"UserLand Frontier™"`, and you'd better not omit that `"™"` (and good luck remembering how to type it). Fortunately, if you got the name wrong, AppleScript would put up a File Open dialog giving you a chance to locate the application, and the correct name would then be substituted in your script. I remember I often used to supply a false name deliberately, such as `tell application "xxx"`, just to get this dialog, because locating the application through the dialog was faster than trying to type (let alone remember) its "real" name.

With the coming of Mac OS X, things got even worse. The File Open dialog was replaced by a Choose Application dialog asking "Where is . . . ?" and listing all your applications; this dialog is slow to open and impossibly sluggish to navigate. For the programmer, the horror of this dialog becomes an incentive to enter the application's name correctly to begin with. At the same time, applications often contrive to disguise their real names. For example, Excel's name is `"Excel"` in both the Application menu and the Dock, but its real name is `"Microsoft Excel"`. Before Tiger, that's what you had to type in order to specify it. In Tiger, though, you can specify an application by its short name, such as `"Excel"`; on compilation, provided the application is running, it will be found and the long name will be substituted.

Script editor applications now generally provide shortcuts for entering application names. In Script Editor, if an application is listed in the Library palette, you can select it and click the New Script button (in the palette's toolbar) to create a new script containing a tell block targeting that application. Script Debugger helps even more: there's a Recent Applications palette similar to Script Editor's Library window; every dictionary window contains a Paste Tell button; you can drag an application's icon into a script window or onto Script Debugger's icon to get a tell block targeting it; and there's a Paste Tell menu item, which lists all currently running scriptable applications and all applications whose dictionary you've recently viewed. Thus there is usually no need to type an application's name manually in order to target it.

Specifying a full pathname should not usually be necessary, but can sometimes be useful; for example, it could be a way to distinguish two versions of the same application on your machine. Unfortunately, this trick doesn't work if one version is already running. For example, I have FileMaker Pro version 7 and FileMaker Pro version 5.5. This script is meant to launch version 5.5, but it misbehaves if version 7 is already running (I regard this as a bug in AppleScript):

```
tell application "gromit:Users:matt2:Info Process:FileMaker 5.5:FileMaker Pro.app"
    launch
    get version -- "7.0v3"
end tell
```

Remote Applications

A *remote* application is an application running on a different computer from the script, or on the same computer but under a different user already logged in (through Fast User Switching). Communication is performed over IP (not AppleTalk, as in the past); this has the advantage that it works over the Internet. Thanks to Bonjour (formerly called Rendezvous), a machine on the local network can be specified by name. On the target computer, Remote Apple Events must first be turned on; this can be done in the Sharing preference pane.

> Worried about the insecurity of Remote Apple Events being left on all the time? (It requires only a password, and anyone can use choose remote application to see what processes are running *without* a password.) If you can get into a remote machine via ssh (which can be set to use the far more secure public–private key authentication method), you may be able to turn on Remote Apple Events from the command line. This formula, for example, works if the target machine is running Tiger (substitute **unload** to turn Remote Apple Events off again):
>
> `% sudo launchctl load -w /System/Library/LaunchDaemons/eppc.plist`

To target a remote application, you have to specify the machine on which it is running. To do so, you use an eppc URL. You can learn a lot more about the format of this URL—indeed, you can easily create such a URL, suitable for targeting a remote application—through the choose remote application command (Chapter 21). For example, if I use choose remote application to select the Finder on my iBook in the next room, I get this result:

```
application "Finder" of machine "eppc://duck.local/?uid=501&pid=179"
```

The application specifier is followed by a machine specifier that uses an eppc URL with my iBook's Bonjour name as the first path element. Actual connection to this machine will require a username and password; you can supply these as part of the eppc URL using the format username:password@ just before the machine name. The question mark and the material that follows it is optional, but can be useful. The uid is the user number, and you're going to need this parameter if you want to target a particular user's applications when multiple users are logged in. The pid is the process number of this application, so it's redundant given that we are already targeting the process by name, and in any case this number can change if an application quits or the computer is restarted, so you will probably have no use for it (though you can certainly use it instead of the name if you like). You can also incorporate the machine specifier into the application specifier by putting the application name as a second path element after the machine name (if you do this with a literal specifier, decompilation will rewrite the specifier in canonical form).

So, here are some ways of targeting the Finder on my iBook:

```
tell application "Finder" of machine "eppc://duck.local"
    -- puts up the username/password dialog
    get name of every window
end tell

tell application "Finder" of machine "eppc://mattneub:teehee@duck.local"
    -- avoids the username/password dialog
    get name of every window
end tell

set s to "eppc://mattneub:teehee@duck.local/Finder"
-- incorporates machine specifier into application specifier
tell application s
    get name of window 1
end tell

set s to "eppc://mattneub:teehee@192.168.0.4/Finder"
-- uses IP number instead of Bonjour name
tell application s
    get name of window 1
end tell

set s to "eppc://mattneub:teehee@duck.local/?uid=501&pid=179"
-- uses pid instead of application name
tell application s
    get name of window 1
end tell
```

If you use a variable rather than a literal to specify the target, a terms block referring to a local application may be needed to resolve terminology at compile time (see "Using Terms From" in Chapter 19). It wasn't needed in the previous examples, because name and window are defined in AppleScript itself (see "The 'aeut' Resource" in Chapter 20). If possible, it's probably a good idea to use a terms block in any case, because it is much faster to get the dictionary from a local copy of an application than to get it across a network, and besides, you probably don't want to bother forming the connection to the remote machine every time you compile the script. So, for example:

```
set s to "eppc://mattneub:teehee@duck.local/Finder?uid=501"
using terms from application "Finder"
    tell application s
        get name of every disk
        -- {"OmniumGatherum", "Network", "SecretSharer", "Puma"}
    end tell
end using terms from
```

Some scripting addition commands you call while targeting a remote application are run on the remote machine. For example:

```
tell application "Finder" of machine "eppc://duck.local"
    say "Watson, come here, I want you."
end tell
```

Starting in Tiger, however, scripting addition commands that put up a user interface are disabled from operating remotely; this makes sense because there might be no one at the remote machine to dismiss a dialog:

```
tell application "Finder" of machine "eppc://duck.local"
    display dialog "Watson, come here, I want you."
    -- error: Finder got an error: No user interaction allowed
end tell
```

The scripting addition commands `store script` and `run script` are disabled, probably as a security measure (but `load script` works).

Passing object references back and forth between machines can work, because the reference is usually endowed with a machine specifier as well as an application specifier. But aliases can't usually be handed between one machine and another, because they are resolved on the wrong machine; instead, try to obtain a pathname string.

You cannot target a remote machine merely; you must target some application on that machine. This raises the question of how to launch a remote application in order to target it. You cannot simply target the application by name as a way of launching it, because a literal application specifier will be resolved on the local machine. A remote application must thus already be running *before* you target it. Accordingly, you must always start with some application you know is running; likely possibilities are Finder and Dock. Then you can worry about whether the application you want to target is running. Here's how to find out:

```
set s to "eppc://mattneub:teehee@duck.local/Finder?uid=501"
using terms from application "Finder"
    tell application s
        get name of every process
        -- {"loginwindow", "Dock", "SystemUIServer", "Finder", "LaunchBar",
            "UniversalAccess", "System Events"}
    end tell
end using terms from
```

In theory you shouldn't be able to talk like that, because the Finder no longer handles the process class—System Events does (see "System Events," later in this chapter). However, the process class is grandfathered into the Finder, and as a bonus, it is implemented by routing the Apple event to System Events, so not only do you get the answer, you also cause System Events to launch, which is good because you might want to target it.

This still doesn't answer the more general question of how to launch an application remotely. If you know its full pathname, then you can just tell the Finder to open it:

```
tell application "Finder" of machine "eppc://duck.local"
    open item "OmniumGatherum:Applications:Utilities:Terminal.app"
end tell
```

Otherwise, the official solution is to ask the Finder to open the application file using its ID, which can be a four-letter creator code or the application's bundle identifier. Thus, this works even if BBEdit is not running:

```
set m to "eppc://mattneub:teehee@duck.local"
tell application "Finder" of machine m
    using terms from application "Finder"
        open application file id "com.barebones.BBEdit"
    end using terms from
end tell
tell application "BBEdit" of machine m
    using terms from application "BBEdit"
        set contents of document 1 to "Hello, world!"
    end using terms from
end tell
```

(It is also possible to launch an application remotely using do shell script and osascript, but I'm told that this is regarded as a security hole and may be closed.)

If multiple users are logged into the remote computer simultaneously, you can target a specific user with the uid parameter of the machine specifier. Indeed, you really should do so, because otherwise you can't be certain which user you're talking to (Apple-Script seems to decide this in a somewhat random manner; I regard this as a bug). Again, the choose remote application dialog can be helpful here, as it distinguishes applications running under different users and tells you the user's uid number. Another approach is trial and error: just throw uid numbers at the machine and try to communicate with a running application, and see if you get an error or not:

```
set L to {}
repeat with i from 501 to 520
    set m to "eppc://mattneub:teehee@duck.local/?uid=" & (i as string)
    using terms from application "Finder"
        try
            tell application "Finder" of machine m
                get (desktop as string)
                set end of L to i
            end tell
        end try
    end using terms from
end repeat
L -- {501, 502}
```

Once we know the uid numbers of the logged-in users, we can target the applications run by a specific user. Observe that the username and password is still the username and password for the machine as a whole, not the user:

```
on test(m)
    tell application "Finder" of machine m
        set n to (get name of window 1)
    end tell
    display dialog n
end test
test("eppc://mattneub:teehee@duck.local/?uid=501") -- mattneub
test("eppc://mattneub:teehee@duck.local/?uid=502") -- guest
```

The identical syntax allows you to target a different user logged into the *local* machine. In other words, if a machine has multiple users logged in, you can run a script under one user and target an application under another user. You can describe the present machine as localhost. Don't forget to turn on Remote Apple Events on your own machine!

```
tell application "Finder" to get name of window 1 -- mattneub
set m to "eppc://mattneub:teehee@localhost/?uid=502"
tell application "Finder" of machine m
    get name of window 1 -- mrclean
end tell
```

XML-RPC and SOAP

XML-RPC and SOAP are *web services*. This means they are ways for one computer (the client) to query or command another computer (the server) over the Internet. The server defines certain commands to which it is prepared to respond. The client somehow knows what these are, and issues one of the commands with appropriate parameters; it also knows what sort of reply to expect, so it can parse the reply that it receives and extract desired pieces of data from it. If this sounds a lot like what Apple events and AppleScript are all about, it should! AppleScript is a good fit with XML-RPC and SOAP, and it makes sense that the AppleScript language should be capable of functioning as a client.

XML-RPC and SOAP do not themselves use Apple events for communication. They use the HTTP protocol. This is clever, because HTTP is the protocol you use in your browser when you type in a URL or click a link to ask for a web page. It's a common, well-understood, and widely implemented protocol. An XML-RPC or SOAP message can be sent anywhere that a web page request can be sent—because it *is* a web page request. And any CGI-enabled web server can function as an XML-RPC or SOAP server; it treats the message from the client just as it would an ordinary web page request—because it *is* a web page request. A message from the client to server is actually XML, structured according to certain conventions; this XML is wrapped up in an HTTP post argument (a post argument is the same sort of thing that gets sent when you press the Submit button in a web page form in your browser). The server looks at the requested URL and passes the message along to the appropriate CGI application, which pulls the XML out of the post argument, parses it, does whatever it's supposed to do, and hands back the reply. The reply is structured as a web page consisting of XML, so the web server just sends it back in the same way that it would send an ordinary web page back to your browser.

The web server here need not in fact be elsewhere on the Internet. It could be on your local network, even on the same machine. It isn't difficult to set up your own web server to function as an XML-RPC or SOAP server; there are standard modules for doing this with Perl or PHP, for example. This means you can use AppleScript to communicate with a Perl or PHP script. I know someone who does this as a way of storing certain email messages in a MySQL database. PHP has a good interface to MySQL, so it makes a good intermediary. His email client is scriptable; when he receives an email message that he wants to store, he runs a script that captures the information from the email message and sends a SOAP message containing it to the web server running on the same machine; the web server processes the SOAP message through PHP, which stores the email message in the MySQL database. (For a similar architecture, with AppleScript speaking to Perl instead of PHP, see *http://developer.apple.com/internet/applescript/applescripttoperl.html*.)

AppleScript targets XML-RPC and SOAP services through support built into the Apple Event Manager. Your AppleScript command is translated into an Apple event, which in turn is translated into XML. The XML is shoved into the post argument of an HTTP request, and the request is sent across the Internet. (Your script waits synchronously for a reply.) When the reply comes back, the XML is extracted from the reply and interpreted as AppleScript data (usually a record)—and that's the result of your command. You specify the server in a tell block, but instead of saying the name of an application, you provide a URL string. Within the tell block, you use one of two commands: either the call xmlrpc command or the call soap command. (These terms are resolved only when the target is an http URL; otherwise, they are illegal.)

The target can be expressed in this form:

```
tell application "http://www.xxx.com/someApplication"
```

or you can say this, which decompiles to the previous syntax:

```
tell application "someApplication" of machine "http://www.xxx.com"
```

The syntax for call xmlrpc is as follows:

```
call xmlrpc {method name: methodName, parameters: parameterList}
```

The syntax for call soap is as follows:

```
call soap {method name: methodName, ¬
    method namespace uri: uri, ¬
    parameters: parameterRecord, ¬
    SOAPAction: action}
```

You can omit an item of the parameter record (such as method namespace uri or parameters) if it isn't applicable.

Now let's test these commands. There's a copy of UserLand Frontier on the Internet that is intended for users to test with XML-RPC and SOAP requests. By default, we access this server's XML-RPC functionality through a URL whose path is /rpc2. The server includes some simple test verbs, one of which is examples.getStateName. We can call this verb using AppleScript, as follows:

```
tell application "http://superhonker.userland.com/rpc2"
    call xmlrpc ¬
        {method name:"examples.getStateName", ¬
        parameters:30} -- "New Jersey"
end tell
```

Frontier is also a SOAP server. We can call the SOAP equivalent of the same verb using AppleScript, as follows:

```
tell application "http://superhonker.userland.com"
    call soap ¬
        {method name:"getStateName", ¬
        SOAPAction:"/examples", ¬
        parameters:{statenum:30}} -- "New Jersey"
end tell
```

If you happen to have a copy of Frontier or Radio UserLand, you can test all this on your own machine, without using the Internet. These programs run the very same server on port 8080. So with Frontier or Radio UserLand running, you can substitute "http://localhost:8080/rpc2" and "http://localhost:8080" as the application URLs for the tell block.

If you tell AppleScript to look for a dictionary in an application that is a web URL, AppleScript won't actually look there, but will assume that this application is a SOAP or XML-RPC server. We can use this as a trick to treat the target as a variable when doing a SOAP call over the Internet. This example, based on a script distributed by Apple, shows how to write a general SOAP-calling handler. The handler generalSOAP contains no hard-coded information at all, except the application URL named in the terms block—but this URL is a fake, merely to satisfy the compiler that the call soap command is legal. In the last line of this script, we test our general SOAP-calling handler by handing it some parameters; in this case, we are fetching the current Apple stock price over the Internet:

```
on generalSOAP(u, m, s, a, p)
    using terms from application "http://www.apple.com/placebo"
        tell application u
            return call soap ¬
                {method name:m, ¬
                method namespace uri:s, ¬
                parameters:p, ¬
                SOAPAction:a}
        end tell
    end using terms from
end generalSOAP
generalSOAP("http://services.xmethods.net:80/soap", ¬
    "getQuote", "urn:xmethods-delayed-quotes", ¬
    "", {Symbol:"AAPL"}) -- 74.93
```

For another example of call soap, see "Combining Specialties" in Chapter 1. In general, call xmlrpc and call soap are not difficult to use, but you'll have to study the documentation for the service you're trying to call, and it may take a little trial and error to get the parameters just right.

 Some SOAP servers are not compatible with the XML syntax used by the Apple Event Manager. There are two common SOAP formats, "rpc/encoded" and "document/literal," and call soap does not support the second format. I regard this as a bug.

Some Scriptable Applications

As part of the default Tiger installation, Apple ships a number of applications with varying degrees of useful scriptability. Some of these are in places where you might think to look, but a number of them are not, so here's a quick survey of the scriptable applications you'll find on your computer. (Third-party applications, which are often the most important scriptable applications in a workflow, are not discussed here.)

iApps and Utilities

Of the applications in your /Applications directory, quite a number are usefully scriptable. iTunes is probably the most popular target; it is, perhaps, the only one of the iApps whose powers emerge to their fullest extent only in the presence of AppleScript. Address Book and iCal are essentially databases, and provide scriptable access to their data. Mail is scriptable, though there are many bugs and functionality holes.

Safari, aside from control over its preferences and interface, responds to just one important command, do JavaScript, but this command should not be underestimated, as it opens the door to some powerful capabilities. System Profiler is another one-trick pony: you can retrieve an XML version of its report, from which you can retrieve any desired information. Script Editor is scriptable enough to allow insertion of templated control structures through its contextual menu. If you see the Internet via modem or PPPoE, Internet Connect is a good way to query and manipulate your connection; you can connect and disconnect, and learn whether you are connected. iChat is scriptable enough to let you get buddy list information and send a message. TextEdit's scriptability is substandard. Other applications that are scriptable in a rudimentary way are Automator, DVD Player, Font Book, iPhoto, iSync, and Quick-Time Player.

Finder

The Finder, located in /System/Library/CoreServices, is the favorite target application for examples in this book—and with good reason. For all its faults, Finder scripting is a solid way to interact with the hierarchy of files and folders on your hard disk. It's very good at such things as renaming files, copying files, deleting files, creating folders and aliases, and describing the folder hierarchy. The Finder is also one scriptable application that is almost certain to be running (so that, for example, you have somewhere to start when targeting a remote machine).

System Events

In Mac OS 9 and before, the Finder was the locus of scriptability for a lot of system functionality that had nothing to do with files and folders, such as what applications were running. This was somewhat irrational, as the Finder wasn't involved in such matters; it was being used as a kind of stand-in for the system itself. In Mac OS X, scripting of system functionality of this kind has been moved to a faceless background application called System Events (located in the *CoreServices* folder, along with the Finder). Here are some of the things you can do with System Events:

- Sleep, restart, and shut down the computer.
- Manipulate login items and access users:

```
tell application "System Events"
    get full name of current user
    make new login item at end of login items with properties ¬
        {path:"/Applications/Safari.app"}
end tell
```

- Navigate the hard disk hierarchy. The object model is similar to the Finder, but not identical; you have to start with a disk or with a domain:

```
tell application "System Events"
    name of folder 1 of desktop folder of user domain -- "Mannie"
end tell
```

- Manipulate running processes, determining such things as what processes are running, which ones are visible, and which one is frontmost.
- Perform elementary parsing of XML and property list files.
- Explore QuickTime file attributes.

Here we examine some features of an audio file:

```
tell application "Finder" to set f to (get file 1 as string)
tell application "System Events"
    try
        set f to audio file f
    on error
        error "Not an audio file."
    end try
    set k to kind of f
    tell (get contents of f)
        set t to (its duration) / (its time scale)
        set min to t div 60
        set sec to round (t mod 60) rounding as taught in school
    end tell
    return k & ", " & min & ":" & sec -- MP3 Audio File, 2:43
end tell
```

Here's an illustration of System Events's support for parsing XML. This is very crude: we have to know the schema of the XML beforehand, and all we can do is cycle through elements and attributes looking for a desired value. (We cannot, for example, extract data through an XPath query.) In this example, I cycle down into the System Profiler report to find out what kind of computer I've got:

```
tell application "System Profiler"
    set s to (XML text of document 1)
end tell
on findElementWithValue(e, v)
    tell application "System Events"
        repeat with i from 1 to (count XML elements of e)
            if value of XML element i of e is v then
                return i
            end if
        end repeat
    end tell
    error "not found"
end findElementWithValue
tell application "System Events"
    set x to make new XML data with data s
    set e to XML element 1 of XML element 1 of x
    set e to first XML element of e where ¬
        value of XML element 2 of it is "SPHardwareDataType"
    set i to my findElementWithValue(e, "_items")
    set e to XML element 1 of XML element (i + 1) of e
    set i to my findElementWithValue(e, "machine_name")
    return value of XML element (i + 1) of e -- iMacG5
end tell
```

In this particular case the XML in question is actually a property list, and we can do a much more elegant job of retrieving the desired data by treating it as such:

```
tell application "System Profiler"
    set s to (XML text of document 1)
end tell
tell application "System Events"
    set p to make new property list item with data s
    set p to property list item 1 of p
    set p to property list item "_items" of p
    set p to property list item 1 of p
    return value of property list item "machine_name" of p -- iMacG5
end tell
```

System Events is also responsible for GUI scripting (see Chapter 24) and for folder actions (see Chapter 27). Plus, it is System Events that actually runs menu items chosen in Apple's global Script Menu (see Chapter 2), which operates by passing the chosen script to System Events as the parameter of the do script command. System Events is thus a very important application, and its dictionary deserves study. Another example of scripting System Events appeared in Chapter 1.

SpeechRecognitionServer

This application, hidden away in the Carbon framework, is the scriptable front end for the system's built-in speech recognition functionality. For an example, see "Noises" in Chapter 21.

URL Access Scripting

This is a background-only application in the *ScriptingAdditions* folder. When it was invented (back in Mac OS 8.5, I believe), it was a good thing, because it provided a way to download and upload via HTTP and FTP across the Internet without the overhead a full-featured client. However, I find it undependable, and as we're now in the Unix-based world of Mac OS X, I recommend do shell script and curl instead (see Chapter 25).

Keychain Scripting

This is another background-only application in the *ScriptingAdditions* folder, and acts as a scriptable front end to the user's keychain, where passwords are stored. This is analogous to the functionality accessed through the Keychain Access utility. In order to access a password, however, Keychain Access itself must be launched by a different process from your script, which calls for a certain amount of extra song-and-dance (see *http://docs.info.apple.com/article.html?artnum=301858*):

```
set f to (path to application "Keychain Scripting")
tell application "Keychain Scripting" to quit
tell application "Finder" to open f
delay 5 -- that ought to do it!
tell application "Keychain Scripting"
    tell (get current keychain)
        set k to (get first generic key whose name is "mattneub")
        get {account, description, service, password} of k
        -- {"mattneub", "application password", "iTools", "teehee"}
    end tell
end tell
```

When I run that example, the Confirm Access to Keychain dialog appears twice (once for the Keychain Scripting application and once for the host application in which the script is running), because this is a password whose access control is set to require confirmation. Thus, this script could not run successfully without human intervention, which is a good thing. As a further security measure, you cannot access the access control rules for a key through Keychain Scripting.

Image Events

This is another background-only application living in the *CoreServices* folder along with the Finder and System Events. It is a front end to sips (type **sips --help** in the Terminal for more information), which performs some basic manipulations on image files, such as scaling, rotating, and manipulating color profiles, as well as supplying information about monitors. For example:

```
tell application "Image Events"
    set f to (path to desktop as string) & "bigImage.tiff"
    set f2 to POSIX path of (path to desktop) & "/smallerImage.tiff"
    set im to open file f
    scale im by factor 0.5
    save im in f2
end tell
```

Database Events

Database Events, yet another background-only application located in *CoreServices*, is for manipulating "databases." Here we create and populate a tiny database:

```
property fieldnames : {"firstname", "lastname", "book"}
property theData : {{"Matt", "Neuburg", "AppleScript"}, ¬
    {"Charles", "Dickens", "Pickwick"}, ¬
    {"William", "Shakespeare", "Hamlet"}}
tell application "Database Events"
    set d to (make new database with properties {name:"people"})
    tell d
        repeat with i from 1 to (count theData)
            set r to (make new record with properties {name:""})
            repeat with j from 1 to (count fieldnames)
                tell r to make new field with properties ¬
                    {name:item j of fieldnames, value:item j of item i of theData}
            end repeat
        end repeat
        save
    end tell
    delete every database -- actually, just closes the database
end tell
```

Observe that we do not try to tell Database Events where to save the database; this is because every database, rather annoyingly, is automatically saved in and retrieved from your *~/Documents/Databases* folder. Now we'll query the database:

```
tell application "Database Events"
    tell database "~/Documents/Databases/people.dbev"
        get value of field "book" of ¬
            (every record where value of field "firstname" is "Matt")
        -- "AppleScript"
    end tell
end tell
```

The syntax illustrated here is extraordinarily clumsy and touchy, even for Apple, and the object model's approach to databases is unhelpful and nonstandard; you cannot execute an SQL command, nor does Database Events understand that a true database consists of tables (so you could not use it to make a relational database, and even the claim that it makes "databases" seems dubious). Furthermore, files created by Database Events cannot be opened by SQLite (the excellent lightweight open-source database engine included with Mac OS X starting in Tiger; see *http://www.sqlite.org*), which makes it hard to credit Apple's boast that Tiger includes a "Data Events suite" that "lets you create and parse SQLite databases." In sum, Database Events is nowhere near as powerful, coherent, and complete as the `sqlite3` command-line tool. So it's best to disregard Database Events as a bad job, and use the command line instead. Here we create and populate the database:

```
set d to space & "~/Desktop/people.db" & space
set s to "sqlite3" & d & quote
set s to s & "create table people(firstname, lastname, book); "
set s to s & "insert into people values('matt','neuburg','AppleScript'); "
set s to s & "insert into people values('charles','dickens','Pickwick'); "
set s to s & "insert into people values('william', 'shakespeare', 'Hamlet');"
set s to s & quote
do shell script s
```

And here we query it:

```
set d to space & "~/Desktop/people.db" & space
set s to "sqlite3 -list" & d & quote
set s to s & "select book from people where firstname = 'matt';"
set s to s & quote
do shell script s -- "AppleScript"
```

CHAPTER 24

Unscriptable Applications

Some applications are not scriptable; they have no repertory of Apple events to which they are prepared to respond. The developers simply omitted this feature, like the tinsmith who forgot to give the Woodsman a heart. Other applications are scriptable, but not in the way you'd like; the thing you'd like to make the application do isn't among its scriptable behaviors. How can you script the unscriptable? In theory, of course, you can't, and this book shouldn't be discussing this situation at all. AppleScript is about talking to applications with Apple events, and these applications are refusing to listen. It turns out, however, that in many cases you can use AppleScript in a different way, to direct simulated user actions at an unscriptable application. If you can do something with the mouse and keyboard, you may be able to automate those same mouse and keyboard movements using AppleScript, by means of a technology called *GUI scripting*.

When you use GUI scripting, you are essentially driving a a *macro program* that functions as an intermediary between AppleScript and the target application. Such a program has the power to "see" an application's interface and to act as a kind of ghost user, pressing buttons, typing keys, and choosing menu items. Anything a user can do in an application can presumably be performed through some definable sequence of mouse and keyboard gestures; therefore it might be possible to emulate that sequence of gestures with a macro program. The result might not be as fast, elegant, or flexible as true scripting by means of Apple events, but might get the job done. The macro program used here will be System Events (see Chapter 23).

Historical Perspective

Back in the pre–Mac OS X days, there were a number of very strong macro programs, such as QuicKeys, PreFab Player, and OneClick (see Appendix C for URLs). These depended upon a feature of the system architecture whereby third-party code fragments called *system extensions* (or *INITs*) could be loaded into the system at startup in such a way as to modify the system's response to Toolbox calls. The code fragment would effectively interpose itself into the Toolbox call dispatch architecture, so that when the system was about to execute a certain piece of its functionality, this code fragment would be called instead; usually it would also call the system's original functionality, so as not to break the computer altogether, but along the way it would introduce functionality of its own. (On INITs, see Joe Zobkiw, *A Fragment of Your Imagination* [Addison-Wesley, 1995], Chapter 4.)

The trouble with this approach was that INITs were a threat to stability and reliability. They caused no end of headaches for users, who often found that different INITs conflicted with one another, and for application developers, who would learn that their application misbehaved in the presence of some INIT. The ability of users to customize their own systems meant that every user's system could be essentially different from every other's.

On Mac OS X, INITs are abolished. In fact, that's part of the point of Mac OS X: at bottom, every system should be a clean system, and all machines should reliably work the same way. But without INITs, there's no way for a third-party macro program to hook into the system's functionality at a level low enough for it to do the things that a macro program needs to do. This, in the early days of Mac OS X, made scripting the unscriptable next to impossible; and there was serious doubt as to whether there could ever be a macro program on Mac OS X.

Then, however, a solution emerged from Apple itself. As part of an effort to make Mac OS X accessible to people who may not be able to use a mouse and keyboard or see a computer screen, Apple created the Accessibility API, a set of Toolbox commands that can do just what a macro program would do—"see" an application's interface and manipulate it like a ghost user wielding an invisible mouse and keyboard. Going even further, they made the Accessibility API itself scriptable via Apple-Script, by way of System Events. When you do GUI scripting, you use AppleScript to send Apple events to System Events, which translates your commands into terms that the Accessibility API can understand.

Although GUI scripting definitely has its uses, some of them very serious (such as automating a suite for testing the interface of an application under development), and although it is valuable for working around holes in scriptability (as the examples in this chapter will illustrate), it is not a panacea. It doesn't work everywhere; a particular interface item, a window, or an entire application might not use the standard interface elements. In that case, the Accessibility API can do nothing for you. And in any case, for your purposes as an AppleScript programmer, real scriptability is always better. If you're reduced to using GUI scripting to accomplish some goal, and if the target application is still being actively developed, then consider writing to the developer and requesting that the desired aspect of the target application be made properly scriptable.

Getting Started with Accessibility

The prerequisite for GUI scripting to work is that the Accessibility API must be turned on. This may be done through the "Enable access for assistive devices" checkbox in the Universal Access system preferences. Unless this checkbox is checked, the scripts in this chapter will fail.

Now examine System Events's dictionary; in particular, look at the Processes Suite. Here you'll find events such as click and keystroke and classes such as radio button and menu item. The classes in question are all UI element subclasses. So your task is to use these events to operate on these classes, as a way of simulating clicks and keystrokes in the target application. The target application itself is expressed as an application process element of System Events. Thus, AppleScript code that does GUI scripting will have a structure similar to the following:

```
tell application "TextEdit" to activate
tell application "System Events"
    tell application process "TextEdit"
        tell menu 1 of menu bar item "Format" of menu bar 1
            click menu item 4
        end tell
    end tell
end tell
```

If you try that script, you'll see that it toggles the format of the frontmost TextEdit document between plain text and rich text (RTF). And you can see why: it literally chooses the fourth menu item of the Format menu. Observe that the target here is not TextEdit! It's System Events. The phrase tell application process "TextEdit" is not the same as tell application "TextEdit"—it isn't an application specifier, it's merely an element specifier sent to System Events as part of the chain of ofs and tells specifying the complete target (see "The Chain of Ofs and Tells" in Chapter 11).

The problem now, for any given task you'd like to perform by means of GUI scripting, is to express each desired interface element in terms of the UI element object model. This is not at all easy; ultimately, you must probably resign yourself to a certain amount of experimentation. There are, however, some utilities that can help you. These take advantage the fact that the Accessibility API can not only drive interface elements; it can also see them.

AppleScript
AppleScript itself can be used to drive System Events to use the Accessibility API to explore the interface of an application. Example utility scripts appear in Apple's global Script Menu (see "Script Runner" in Chapter 2), or you can find them on your hard disk at */Library/Scripts/UI Element Scripts*. Some of these are scripts you can run; others are intended just to show you the sort of thing you can say.

UIElementInspector

This is an application from Apple that probes an interface. Confusingly, there is more than one version of this application floating around at Apple's site; download the most recent one, included with the source code at *http://developer.apple. com/samplecode/UIElementInspector/UIElementInspector.html*. It's clumsy to use, however, as you can focus on only one interface item at a time, and the interface item is described in Accessibility API terms, not in terms of System Events and AppleScript.

PreFab UI Browser

This inexpensive commercial utility is indispensable if you're going to be doing any serious GUI scripting. You can use a column browser or the mouse to reach the interface item you're interested in, and UI Browser tells you about the attributes of that item and the entire UI element hierarchy leading to it, and even generates AppleScript code for talking to it. Figure 24-1 shows how I used UI Browser to learn how to refer to the menu item of TextEdit for the preceding example code.

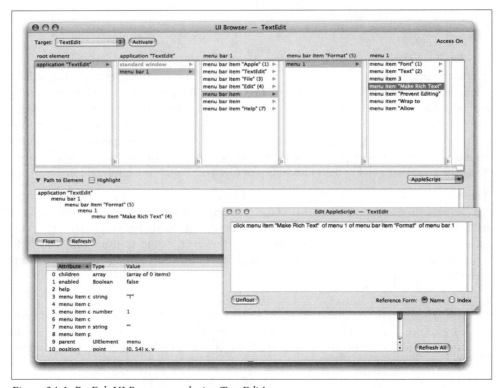

Figure 24-1. PreFab UI Browser exploring TextEdit's menu

GUI Scripting Examples

GUI scripting is something of an art, and needs either a big treatment providing the fruits of plentiful experience or a small treatment that shows a few useful examples and leaves you to explore further on your own. I've opted here for the latter; I'll just give a few practical examples of GUI scripting, without further elaboration.

First I'll show how to toggle File Sharing on and off through the System Preferences application. System Preferences itself is not particularly scriptable; all you can really do is go to the desired preference pane. GUI scripting does the rest:

```
tell application "System Preferences"
    activate
    set current pane to pane "com.apple.preferences.sharing"
end tell
tell application "System Events"
    tell application process "System Preferences"
        tell tab group 1 of window "Sharing"
            click radio button "Services"
            select row 1 of table 1 of scroll area 1
            click button 1
        end tell
    end tell
end tell
```

Now let's work around the fact that TextEdit doesn't let you learn what text is selected. We can use GUI scripting to learn both what text is selected and where the selection is:

```
tell application "TextEdit" to activate
-- front window contains "this is a test of GUI scripting"; "test" is selected
tell application "System Events"
    tell application process "TextEdit"
        tell window 1
            tell text area 1 of scroll area 1
                get value of attribute "AXSelectedText" -- "test"
                get value of attribute "AXSelectedTextRange" -- {11,14}
            end tell
        end tell
    end tell
end tell
```

In this example, we work around the fact that you can't script TextEdit to close a window without saving it. The idea here is to close the window and allow the dialog to appear asking whether we want to save this document; when that happens, we press the Don't Save button using GUI scripting:

```
tell application "TextEdit"
    activate
    close window 1
end tell
tell application "System Events"
    tell application process "TextEdit"
```

```
        tell window 1
            repeat while not (exists sheet 1)
                delay 0.5
            end repeat
            click button "Don't Save" of sheet 1
        end tell
    end tell
end tell
```

Finally, we work around (sort of) the Dictionary application's not being scriptable:

```
set s to text returned of (display dialog "Word to define:" default answer "")
-- prestidigitation
tell application "Dictionary" to activate
open location "DICT:///" & (s as string)
tell application "System Events"
    tell application process "Dictionary"
        tell UI element 1 of scroll area 1 of scroll area 1 of group 1 of window 1
            set s to value of it
        end tell
    end tell
end tell
s -- Dictionary
prestidigitation |?prest??dij??t? sh ?n| noun formal magic tricks performed as
entertainment. DERIVATIVES prestidigitator |-?dij??t?t?r| noun ORIGIN mid 19th cent.:
from French, from preste 'nimble' + Latin digitus 'finger' + -ation .
```

CHAPTER 25

Unix

Once upon a time, Apple's Mac OS operating system and the Unix operating system were two completely separate worlds, each with its own idea of what constituted "scripting." On Mac OS, there was AppleScript and the OSA. On Unix, there was the command line, shell scripting, and the various shell scripting languages such as Perl. Now, with Mac OS X, those two worlds are united; both kinds of "scripting" are present, and there is communication between them, in both directions. Thus, you can combine the power of Unix scripting with the power of AppleScript.

The way you call a Unix tool from AppleScript is with the do shell script scripting addition command. The way you call from Unix into AppleScript is with the osascript tool. This chapter discusses both, along with some examples; you'll see how Perl, curl, and AppleScript can work together to perform a web query, and you'll see Ruby, AppleScript, and Microsoft Excel joining forces to perform textual analysis and graph the results.

Do Shell Script

Your first step in getting acquainted with the do shell script scripting addition command should be to read Apple's excellent technical note documenting it (*http:// developer.apple.com/technotes/tn2002/tn2065.html*).

The direct object of do shell script is a string representing the text you would type at the command-line prompt in the Terminal. Actually, that's not quite true, so do not imagine that you can blithely test a prospective do shell script command simply by typing it in the Terminal, as there might be some differences. Your Terminal shell is probably bash or tcsh, whereas the shell for do shell script is sh (you probably won't experience this as a difference in Tiger, though, where sh *is* bash). Also, the default paths used by do shell script might not be the same as your own shell's paths, so to specify a command, you might have to provide a full pathname, such as /usr/bin/perl instead of just perl. (That's not a real example, though, as perl will probably work just fine.)

The result of do shell script is whatever is returned from the command via standard output (stdout). Unix newline characters are converted to Mac return characters by default, but you can prevent this if you wish. If the command terminates with a non-zero result (an error), an error by the same number is thrown in your script, and you can use this number (along with the man pages for the command) to learn what went wrong.

For example, the following code requests a (decimal) number from the user and converts it to hex by means of the Unix printf command:

```
set theNum to text returned of (display dialog "Enter a number:" default answer "")
set s to "printf %X " & theNum
display dialog (do shell script s)
```

The do shell script command both accepts and returns Unicode text. But the actual medium of communication between AppleScript and the shell is UTF-8—that is, the direct object of do shell script is converted to UTF-8 before passing to the shell, and the reply from the shell is assumed to be UTF-8 and is converted to Unicode text (UTF-16) before arriving in your script. This is a sensible approach. Most Unix tools are probably unprepared to deal with Unicode input, and for characters in the ASCII range, the UTF-8 representation is the ASCII representation, so in effect the direct object is coerced automatically from Unicode text to a string, as long as it consists of just ASCII characters—which it usually will, so you usually won't have to worry about it. On the other hand, some Unix tools produce UTF-8 output, and it's nice to know that you can capture this seamlessly as the result; indeed, this can be a useful technique, as you saw in "Unicode Text" in Chapter 13.

The optional parameter with administrator privileges lets you run a command as root. Such a command will require administrator authentication; you can provide it as part of the command (with the user name and password parameters) or permit the authentication dialog to appear. The implementation of this option has been tweaked several times over the course of its history; this is unfortunate, as it means that the precise version of AppleScript your script runs on can make a crucial difference to the script's behavior. For example, before Tiger, multiple commands (separated by semicolons) in a do shell script command with the with administrator privileges parameter broke; in early versions of Tiger, scripts that called sudo or perl from do shell script along with the with administrator privileges parameter broke. Be careful, and test thoroughly.

The shell set up by do shell script is not interactive, so beware of tools that expect an interactive shell. Many such tools provide a noninteractive alternative, though, so you can still use them. For instance, if you wanted to call top, you could call it in a noninteractive form such as top -l1 and parse the result. The following (rather silly) example converts a number to a hex string by way of bc by writing out a small bc program file and calling bc to process it:

```
set theNum to text returned of (display dialog "Enter a number:" default answer "")
set t to path to temporary items
set posixT to POSIX path of t
set f to open for access file ((t as string) & "bctemp") with write permission
write "obase = 16\n" to f
write (theNum as string) & "\n" to f
write "quit\n" to f
close access f
set s to "/usr/bin/bc " & quoted form of (posixT & "bctemp")
display dialog (do shell script s)
```

(The text returned of display dialog is Unicode text in Tiger; I don't want to write Unicode text to the file, because bc won't be able to read it, so I coerce to a string.)

The Unix shell parsing and quotation rules can be something of a headache. A simple solution is to protect a string from the parsing rules completely by wrapping it in single quotes; AppleScript makes this easy with the quoted form property of a string (see "String Properties" in Chapter 13). But this does not absolve you from Apple-Script's own rules for forming literal strings (see Table 13-1). So, for instance, in the system attribute example in "File and Machine Information" in Chapter 21, quotes are escaped in the literal string s, to get AppleScript to do the right thing; then the entire string is munged with quoted form to get the shell to do the right thing.

Using a file as an intermediary can simplify things. When talking to Perl, for example, there is no problem forming a short Perl script and handing it to Perl directly by means of the -e switch; but for a longer Perl script it might make sense to write it into a file and then tell Perl to run the file. The Perl script can be created on the fly, but often there is no need; it might make more sense to prepare it beforehand.

Here's an example. I write for the weekly online Macintosh journal *TidBITS*, whose archives are searchable online: their web site has a page (*http://db.tidbits.com*) where you can enter words to search for, returning a page of links to past articles containing those words. We'll simulate this page, acting as a web client ourselves, with the help of curl (a brilliant Internet client Unix tool—read the man pages for more information). We have researched the HTML format of the results page, and we've prepared a Perl script to parse it and extract the URLs and titles of the found articles. The Perl script expects as argument the pathname of the file containing the HTML:

```
$s = "";
while (<>) {
    $s .= $_;
}
$s =~ m{search results (.*)$}si;
$1 =~ m{<table(.*?)</table>}si;
@rows = ($1 =~ m{<tr(.*?)</tr>}sig);
for ($i=0;$i<$#rows;$i++) {
    ($links[$i], $titles[$i]) =
        ($rows[$i+1] =~ m{<a href="(.*?)">(.*?)</a>}i);
}
print join "\n", @links, @titles;
```

Now for the AppleScript code. First we put up a dialog where the user can enter the terms to search for. We URL-encode these terms in a primitive way (substituting a plus sign for any spaces) and assemble the post data for the form submission. We use curl to submit this post data to the TidBITS server. The TidBITS server receives essentially the same HTML it would receive if a user entered the same search terms in the first field of the TidBITS search page and pressed the Submit button. The results come back as a page of HTML, which curl writes out to a file. We now hand this file over to our Perl script for parsing. The results come back from the Perl script, and now we have a list which is really two lists: first the URLs of the found pages, then the titles of those same pages. We put up a list showing the titles; if the user chooses one, we ask the browser to display the corresponding URL.

```
set t to text returned of ¬
    (display dialog "Search TidBITS for:" default answer "")
set text item delimiters to "+"
set t to (words of t) as string
set d to "'-response=TBSearch.lasso&-token.srch=TBAdv"
set d to d & "&Article+HTML=" & t
set d to d & "&Article+Author=&Article+Title=&-operator"
set d to d & "=eq&RawIssueNum=&-operator=equals&ArticleDate"
set d to d & "=&-sortField=ArticleDate&-sortOrder=descending"
set d to d & "&-maxRecords=20&-nothing=MSExplorerHack&-nothing"
set d to d & "=Start+Search' "
set u to "http://db.tidbits.com/TBSrchAdv.lasso"
set f to POSIX path of file ((path to temporary items as string) & "tempTidBITS")
do shell script "curl -d " & d & " -o " & f & " " & u
set perlScript to ... -- where is the Perl script?
set r to do shell script "perl " & perlScript & " " & f
set L to paragraphs of r
set half to (count L) / 2
set L1 to items 1 thru half of L
set L2 to items (half + 1) thru -1 of L
set choice to (choose from list L2) as string
repeat with i from 1 to half
    if item i of L2 is choice then
        open location (item i of L1)
        exit repeat
    end if
end repeat
```

The only unsettled question is the line in the middle of the AppleScript code where the variable perlScript must be set to the POSIX pathname of the Perl script file. If we happen to know the name and location of this file, then of course the problem is solved and we can just hardcode this information into the AppleScript code; for example:

```
set perlScript to POSIX path of file ((path to desktop as string) & "perlScript.pl")
```

But this seems a rather fragile approach, as we are relying on an important file to be in a certain location; the file could accidentally be moved or renamed. This situation is just the sort where the script bundle format comes in handy (see "Compiled Script

Files" in Chapter 3). We'll put the Perl script file inside the AppleScript compiled script file's bundle; the user will never see it, the two files won't be accidentally separated, and the AppleScript code will know where the Perl file is.

Create the AppleScript compiled script file using a script editor application, and save it as a script bundle (let's call it *searchTidBITS*). Create the Perl script in some other way (using a text editor such as BBEdit), save it as *parseHTML.pl*, and then move it into *Contents/Resources* inside *searchTidBITS*—you can do this manually using the Show Package Contents command in the Finder, or you can use Apple's Script Editor, which represents *Contents/Resources* in the Bundle Contents drawer of the script window (you can drag *parseHTML.pl* directly from the Finder into that drawer). The missing line of our code will then read:

```
set perlScript to quoted form of POSIX path of (path to resource "parseHTML.pl")
```

Note, when testing, that this script won't work when run from Apple's Script Editor, because path to resource in that context looks inside the Script Editor bundle, not the script bundle. Instead, use Script Debugger for testing, or else put the script bundle into your *~/Library/Scripts* folder and run it from the Script Menu. (In Chapter 27 we'll take this approach one step further with AppleScript Studio: we'll build the Perl script into the application bundle and we'll wrap a nicer interface around our AppleScript code.)

Osascript

Three command-line tools are provided for accessing AppleScript from Unix—osalang, osacompile, and osascript—of which osascript is the most important. So let's talk about the other two first.

osalang lists the scripting components present on your machine (see "The Open Scripting Architecture" in Chapter 3):

```
% osalang -l
ascr appl cgxervdh  AppleScript
scpt appl cgxervdh  Generic Scripting System
```

If you have other OSA components installed, they will also appear. (For example, if you use Script Debugger, you'll see AppleScript Debugger X and JavaScript.) The two four-letter codes identifying each component are used by OSA programmers, but typically won't arise in the context of your AppleScript experience. Then comes a series of flags describing the capabilities of this scripting component (see the osalang man page for their meanings). Finally, we have the name of the component. The "Generic Scripting System" is the general front end to the OSA (what Chapter 3 calls the generic system component or GSC); "AppleScript" is the AppleScript scripting component in particular. You can use either of these two terms as a language specifier in calling the other two command-line tools, but their effect will be identical, because the GSC will treat AppleScript as the default component. In general, unless you are using other OSA scripting components, you'll have no need for osalang.

osacompile takes as argument a text file, or some text provided on the command line, and generates a compiled script file or applet. For example:

```
% cat > textfile.txt
tell app "Finder"
display dialog "Hello, world!"
end
^D
% osacompile -o compiledfile.scpt textfile.txt
```

The result is a compiled script file *compiledfile.scpt* that can be opened in Script Editor, executed by a script runner, and so forth. You can avoid the intermediate text file by including the script text as part of the osacompile command; the ensuing discussion of osascript shows how. The extension on the filename supplied in the -o parameter determines the type of file that's created; the *.scptd* extension makes a script bundle, the *.app* extension makes an applet bundle, and otherwise you get a compiled script file. Further switches let you determine which fork the compiled script bytecode is saved into (the default is the resource fork; see "Compiled Script File Formats" in Chapter 3) and the characteristics of a created applet (see "Applet Options" in Chapter 27). Consult the osacompile man pages for more information.

The osascript command executes a compiled script file, a text file, or text provided from the command line. This command is the real key to bridging the gap between Unix and AppleScript from the Unix side.

Here's how to execute a text file or a compiled script file (these are the same files we made earlier in connection with osacompile):

```
% osascript textfile.txt
% osascript compiledfile.scpt
```

You can enter the script text manually after the osascript command:

```
% osascript
tell app "Finder"
display dialog "Hello, world!"
end
^D
```

To include the script text on the command line, use the -e switch. The shell's usual quotational hoops will have to be jumped through; the bash shell helps by permitting a literal string to be entered in ANSI-C form:

```
% osascript -e $'tell app "Finder"\rdisplay dialog "Hello, world!"\rend'
```

Another approach to entering a multiple-line script is to repeat the -e switch multiple times. For example:

```
% osascript -e 'tell app "Finder"' -e 'display dialog "Hello, world!"' -e 'end'
```

The result of osascript is formatted differently depending on whether you supply the -ss flag. If you include it, delimiters are used, as in the Script Editor, to show the nature of the result. If you omit it, a list of strings is flattened into a series of comma-delimited tokens:

```
% osascript -ss -e 'tell app "Finder" to get name of every disk'
{"feathers", "gromit", "Network"}
% osascript -e 'tell app "Finder" to get name of every disk'
feathers, gromit, Network
```

The same list flattening extends to a deeper level:

```
% osascript -e '{"Mannie", {"Moe"}}'
Mannie, Moe
```

Such a flattened, unquoted list does have its uses, especially in conjunction with other Unix tools. In this example (suggested to me by Chris Nebel), I find all persons who appear more than once in my Address Book:

```
% osascript -e 'tell app "Address Book" to get name of every person'
    | tr , "\n" | sort -bf -k2 | uniq -d
Mark Anbinder
Mary Byrd
Jeff Carlson
[and so on]
```

The line-break character represented by the keyword return is a Macintosh line-break character (\r), which can confuse the display in a Unix context. This is purely a cosmetic issue. For example (in the Terminal):

```
% osascript -e 'set pep to "Manny" & return & "Moe"'
Moeny
% osascript -e 'set pep to "Manny" & (ASCII character 10) & "Moe"'
Manny
Moe
```

What happened in the first reply is that "Moe" overprinted "Manny". If you expect that Macintosh line breaks will appear in the output, you can pipe it through tr:

```
% osascript -e 'set pep to "Manny" & return & "Moe"' | tr "\r" "\n"
Manny
Moe
```

Do not use any scripting addition commands that put up a user interface, such as display dialog, directly from within osascript. The problem is that osascript is not an application context, so it has no provision for user interactivity. That's why we targeted the Finder in the earlier examples involving display dialog. In Tiger, an attempt to use an interactive scripting addition command will be blocked coherently with a nice error message ("No user interaction allowed"); in earlier systems, however, the dialog would appear, but you couldn't click the buttons to dismiss it, and the only escape was to kill the osascript process.

Arguments after the script on the command line with `osascript` are treated as a list of strings to be passed to the script's run handler (see "The Run Handler" in Chapter 9); this feature is new in Tiger. For example:

```
% cat > textfile.txt
on run what
set total to 0
repeat with anItem in what
set total to total + anItem
end
return total
end
^D
% osascript textfile.txt 1 2 3
6
```

You are most likely to use `osascript` not directly from the command line, but from within a shell script written in a language such as Perl. In this situation it's rather easy to tie oneself in knots escaping characters when constructing a string intended for `osascript`, because two environments, the shell script language and the shell, are going to munge this string before it reaches AppleScript. This line of Perl shows what I mean:

```
$s = `osascript -e "tell app \\"Finder\\" to get name of every disk"`;
```

The Perl backtick operator hands its contents over to the shell for execution, but first there's a round of variable interpolation within Perl; during that round, the escaped backslashes are mutated into single backslashes, and these single backslashes correctly escape the double quotes around `"Finder"` in the string that the shell receives as the argument to `osascript`.

One solution is to single-quote the string, which avoids the round of interpolation. This example is a Perl script that single-quotes everything in sight, and also illustrates how easily Perl lets you create a literal string representing multiline AppleScript code:

```
$howdy = 'tell app "Finder"
display dialog "howdy"
end';
`osascript -e '$howdy'`;
```

An even better approach is to use a "here document," which is supported by most scripting languages. This eliminates worries about escaping characters while letting you construct the AppleScript code dynamically through variable interpolation. To illustrate, here's a rather silly Perl program intended to be run in the Terminal; it asks the user for the number of a disk and then fetches the name of that disk:

```
#!/usr/bin/perl
$s = <<"END_S";
    tell application "Finder"
        count disks
    end tell
```

```
END_S
chomp ($numDisks = `osascript -ss -e '$s'`);
print "You have $numDisks disks.\n",
    "Which one would you like to know the name of?\n",
    "Type a number between 1 and $numDisks: ";
while (<>) {
    chomp;
    last if $_ < 1 || $_ > $numDisks;
    $ss = <<"END_SS";
        tell application "Finder"
            get name of disk $_
        end tell
END_SS
    print `osascript -ss -e '$ss'`,
        "Type a number between 1 and $numDisks: ";
}
```

Observe that the result of osascript has an extra return character appended to it, which has to be chomped if that isn't what we wanted. Here's the game in action, played in the Terminal:

```
% ./disker.pl
You have 3 disks.
Which one would you like to know the name of?
Type a number between 1 and 3: 1
"feathers"
Type a number between 1 and 3: 2
"gromit"
Type a number between 1 and 3: 4
```

Here's a serious real-life example of osascript in action. It started out as a Ruby script written to construct a histogram of a text file, showing the 30 most frequently used words in the file. When the question arose of how to store the results, it seemed a good idea to put them into a Microsoft Excel spreadsheet; the obvious way to transfer the data from Ruby to Excel was AppleScript. At that point, it also seemed a good idea to have Excel chart the the results (as shown in Figure 25-1).

Here's the script:

```
#!/usr/bin/ruby
class Histogram
    def initialize
        @tally = Hash.new(0)
    end
    def analyze(s)
        s.split.each do |word|
            myword = word.downcase.gsub(/[^a-z0-9]/, "")
            @tally[myword] = @tally[myword] + 1 if !myword.empty?
        end
        @tally.sort { |x,y| y[1]<=>x[1] }
    end
end
analysis = Histogram.new.analyze(File.new(ARGV[0]).read)
counter = 1
```

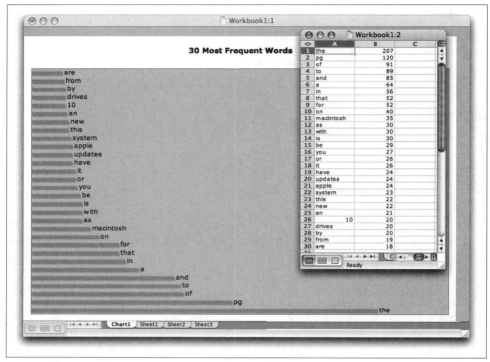

Figure 25-1. Excel data and chart generated by a Ruby script

```ruby
oneline = ""
analysis[0..29].each do |entry|
    oneline = oneline + "set the value of cell 1 of " +
        "row #{counter.to_s} to \"#{entry[0]}\"\n"
    oneline = oneline + "set the value of cell 2 of " +
        "row #{counter.to_s} to #{entry[1].to_s}\n"
    counter = counter + 1
end
script = <<DONE
    tell application "Microsoft Excel"
        activate
        tell worksheet 1
            #{oneline}
        end tell
        select range "A1:B30"
        set chartSheet to make new chart sheet at beginning of active workbook
        set c to active chart
        tell c
            set chart type to bar clustered
            set has title to true
            set caption of its chart title to "30 Most Frequent Words"
            set has legend to false
            apply data labels type data labels show label without legend key
        end tell
```

```
            repeat with axt in {category axis, series axis, value axis}
                repeat with ax in {primary axis, secondary axis}
                    try
                        tell (get axis c axis type axt which axis ax)
                            set has major gridlines to false
                            set has minor gridlines to false
                            set has title to false
                        end tell
                        set has axis c axis type axt axis group ax without axis exists
                    end try
                end repeat
            end repeat
        end tell
    DONE
    `osascript -ss -e '#{script}'`
```

The script is called from the Terminal command line like this:

```
% histogram.rb somefile.txt
```

CHAPTER 26

Triggering Scripts Automatically

What causes a script to run? It might be that you deliberately run it—you press the Run button in a script editor application, for example, or you choose the script from the menu of a script runner environment. However, there is a whole class of situations where your script just sits there patiently and eventually some other process comes along and runs it, with no direct intervention or action on your part. I call this sort of milieu an *automatic location* (see Chapter 2). In an automatic location, AppleScript takes a passive instead of an active part. Instead of you personally setting a chain of events in motion, AppleScript operates in response to other events or activities taking place on your computer: someone inserts an audio CD, someone moves a file into a certain folder, a certain web page request appears at your server, a certain time of day arrives, the computer wakes from sleep, a certain hard drive is mounted, the telephone rings.

There are a number of distinct automatic locations built into Tiger, and there are many varieties of circumstance in which third-party applications may trigger your scripts. A complete compendium of the ways in which scripts can be triggered automatically would be impossible, so the chief purpose of this chapter is to awaken you to the range of possibilities. You may be surprised by the sorts of role AppleScript can play on your computer.

Preparing a script to operate in an automatic location is different from simply writing a script and running it. The reason is that you're not in charge. Some other process is—the process that will actually call your script—and you must know and obey the strictures imposed by that process. In general, you'll need to know two things:

How to position your script

> Some arrangement will have to be made so that the calling process knows where and when to find your script. The script may have to be in a particular folder. It may have to have a particular name. You may have to make some sort of preparatory arrangement, explicitly informing the process beforehand that when a certain thing happens, a certain script should be called.

What the caller will say to your script

Your script might simply be executed (its run handler will be called, just as if you executed the script from a script editor application); but this is very often not the case. Rather, a particular event or handler call may be sent to your script, and it is up to you to know what it is, and to prepare your script to receive it.

Finding out all of this is up to you, and will usually involve reading some sort of documentation. You are making a highly specific prearrangement with the triggering process, in accordance with a kind of contract; you must know the terms of that contract and abide by them, or things won't work.

Digital Hub Scripting

On your computer, when you insert a music CD, likely as not, the application iTunes runs. But it doesn't have to be that way. This is one example of a general phenomenon called *digital hub scripting*: when a DVD, or a CD that doesn't consist of ordinary files, is inserted into your computer, the system can react by notifying a designated application. A little-known fact is that you can interpose your own code in this process; instead of iTunes, when an event like this occurs, a script of your choice is triggered, and can react in any desired manner.

In the CDs & DVDs pane of System Preferences are the settings that determine how the system responds to a disk-insertion event. Here you can determine what application should be notified when the disk is inserted; alternatively, there's an option to run a script. The system will send one of five events to your script, and so your script will need to contain a handler for the appropriate event (see "Event Handlers" in Chapter 9). To learn what these events are, examine the dictionary of the *Digital Hub Scripting* scripting addition, where their terminology is defined.

Let's say we want to take charge of what happens when an audio CD is inserted. This means that in our script there must be a `music CD appeared` handler. Suppose we call our script *musicListener.scpt*. In the CDs & DVDs preferences, we choose from the "When you insert a music CD" popup menu; the Run Script menu item lets us set *musicListener.scpt* to be called when a music CD is inserted. Here, we offer the user a choice of playing just one track of the audio CD:

```
on music CD appeared d
    set diskName to d as alias as string
    set text item delimiters to ":"
    set diskName to text item 1 of diskName
    tell application "Finder"
        set L to name of every file of disk diskName
    end tell
    tell application "iTunes"
        activate
        set temp to {diskName, choose from list L}
        play file (temp as string)
    end tell
end music CD appeared
```

Folder Actions

A *folder action* involves a script being called automatically when certain events take place in a designated folder in the Finder. A script to be used as a folder action does not live in the folder with which it is associated; rather, it should live in your user library, at *~/Library/Scripts/Folder Action Scripts*. Alternatively, such a script may live in the top-level */Library/Scripts/Folder Action Scripts*, where you'll find some useful examples of folder action scripts, but the location in your user library is the default.

Because the script and the folder are in different places, an extra step is required in order to form the explicit association between a particular script and a particular folder. In essence, this association is the folder action. To form such an association is to *attach* the script to the folder; to break the association is to *remove* the script from the folder. The script is not actually moved; attachment and removal are conceptual, not physical. Attachment and removal are implemented through the System Events application (see "System Events" in Chapter 23). System Events associates a folder with a script through a folder action object. These folder action objects are maintained as top-level elements of the System Events application class. System Events is then responsible for watching those folders to see whether an appropriate event takes place in the Finder, and, when it does, for sending the corresponding messages to any attached scripts. System Events doesn't do this, though, unless you also enable the folder actions mechanism as a whole—you do this through its `folder actions enabled` property, which functions as a kind of master switch.

> It is necessary for the System Events application to be running in order for folder actions to work. Therefore, when you enable the folder actions mechanism, System Events is added to your Login Items. This is not a very robust approach, and it is easy to be puzzled when your folder actions stop working (because System Events is not running).

The relationship maintained by a folder action object is one-to-many: a folder action object has one folder path property, but it can have many script elements, meaning that more than one script is attached to that folder. Thus, the same folder can trigger multiple scripts. You might take advantage of this architecture, for example, to have different scripts respond when different kinds of event occur. Furthermore, a folder action object can be disabled (without turning off the folder actions mechanism), and a script attached to a folder action object can be disabled (without removing it from the folder action object, and without disabling the folder action object).

> Nothing prevents you from setting more than one folder action object to point to the same folder, but this is useless, as all but the first folder action object will be ignored when an event occurs. I regard this as a gross flaw in the folder actions architecture.

Because System Events is a scriptable application, you can give it all appropriate instructions explicitly by means of AppleScript. In general, however, there is no need to do so. Apple provides a graphical interface through the Configure Folder Actions application, located in */Applications/AppleScript*. (You can start up Configure Folder Actions directly, or launch it from a button in the AppleScript Utility application.) With the checkbox at the top of the window, you toggle on or off the folder actions mechanism as a whole. Beneath this are two lists. The list on the left is called "Folders with Actions," but it is *not* a list of folders; it is a list of folder action objects. So, using the list on the left, you maintain the list of folder actions: you can create a new folder action, destroy an existing one, and even rename a folder action (this does not rename the assocated folder, of course). The list on the right shows the scripts associated with the folder action object selected on the left; here you can attach or remove a script from a folder action object. You can also toggle the enablement of a folder action object or an attached script, and you can open a script for editing.

Another interface is provided by way of a folder's contextual menu within a Finder window. This is a much simpler interface than the Configure Folder Actions application, because it is clear from the outset what folder is in question—it's the one whose contextual menu you're using—and because only commands appropriate to the state of the folder actually appear in the menu. Thus, if the folder actions mechanism is turned off, the only thing you can do here is turn it on. If the folder actions mechanism is turned on, you can attach, remove, or edit an associated script. The only thing you can't do is toggle the enablement of an existing folder action object or attached script.

If, on the other hand, you want to configure folder actions directly by using AppleScript to drive System Events, it is not difficult to do. There are some scripts located in */Library/Scripts/Folder Actions* (accessible through the Script Menu—see "Script Runner" in Chapter 2) that can serve as useful examples of common tasks:

Enable Folder Actions
> Turns on the folder actions mechanism.

Disable Folder Actions
> Turns off the folder actions mechanism.

Attach Script to Folder
> Prompts the user for a script and folder and attaches the script to that folder.

Remove Folder Actions
> Prompts the user for a folder and a script and removes that script from that folder so that it is no longer a folder action for it.

The Attach Script to Folder script has a major bug: can you spot it? When the user selects a folder to attach a script to, then if a folder action object with the same name as that folder already exists, the script will be attached to that folder action object. But this folder action object's folder might not be the folder the user just selected! Still, even a bug can be instructive; fixing it is left as an exercise for the reader. (Hint: don't look at the folder object's name; look at its path.)

So much for how to associate a script with a folder. What about the code that goes into a folder action script? The StandardAdditions scripting addition defines (in the Folder Actions suite) five events that may be sent to a folder action script:

adding folder items to
Called when an item newly appears in the folder.

removing folder items from
Called when an item in the folder disappears.

opening folder
Called when the folder's window is opened in the Finder.

closing folder window for
Called when the folder's window is closed in the Finder.

moving folder window for
Called when the folder's window is moved or resized in the Finder.

Your folder action script will contain a handler for each event to which you'd like it to respond. (One and the same script can respond to more than one event.) In this example, our folder automatically decodes any *.hqx* files that are put into it (it is assumed that you've installed StuffIt Expander, which doesn't come with Tiger):

```
on adding folder items to ff after receiving L
    tell application "Finder"
        repeat with f in L
            set n to name of f
            if n ends with ".hqx" then
                tell application "StuffIt Expander" to expand f
            end if
        end repeat
    end tell
    tell application "System Events"
        if process "StuffIt Expander" exists then
            tell application "StuffIt Expander" to quit
        end if
    end tell
end adding folder items to
```

The script runs when any file is put into that folder, so the first step is to ignore everything except *.hqx* files. We call StuffIt Expander to decode each appropriate file. This leaves StuffIt Expander running, so at the end we look to see whether StuffIt Expander is running, and if it is, we quit it. A folder with this script attached functions as a kind of magic decoder drop box for *.hqx* files.

A common error is failing to take account of the fact that the folder action script may do something to an item in the folder such as to trigger the same (or a different) folder action script. This circularity is not a problem as long as it is not vicious. This is one reason why, in the previous script, we test the name of each file; as we expand a file whose name ends in *.hqx*, we create a new file that triggers the script again, but we ignore it because its name doesn't end in *.hqx*.

CGI Application

A *CGI* application (for *common gateway interface*, if you must know) is a process that supplements a web server. When a request arrives for a page, instead of simply fetching a file on disk, the web server can turn to a CGI application and ask it for the page; the CGI application is expected to compose the entire HTML of the page, including headers, and hand it back to the web server, which sends it on as the reply to the client that made the request.

Before Mac OS X, the communication between a web server and a CGI application was conventionally performed on Mac OS through Apple events. In particular, an Apple event usually known (for historical reasons) as the WebSTAR event is sent by the web server to the CGI application, describing the page request. The CGI application hands back the page as the reply to this Apple event (see *http://www.4d.com/ products/wsdev/internetspecs.html*). This means that an AppleScript applet could be used as a CGI application; such, indeed, was the traditional approach. Terminology for the WebSTAR event is defined in the *StandardAdditions* scripting addition; it is the handle CGI request event. So in the past, you would write an applet implementing an event handler for handle CGI request, and point your web server at that applet as the CGI application for certain web page requests.

With the coming of Mac OS X, however, all this has changed. Of course if you're still using WebSTAR or some other web server that implements CGIs in the traditional Mac OS manner, you can continue using it directly with an applet. However, you are more likely to be using the web server that comes with Mac OS X, namely Apache, which doesn't work this way. Apache is a Unix web server, and Unix doesn't have Apple events. In Unix, environment variables, along with stdin and stdout, are used as the communication medium between the server and the CGI process.

If you really want to, you can still use an AppleScript applet as a CGI application with Apache, but in order to do so, you need some intermediary application that swings both ways, as it were. On the one hand, this intermediary application must behave as an Apache-style CGI process, so that Apache has someone to talk to. On the other hand, this intermediary application must translate a CGI request from Apache into an Apple event and forward this Apple event to the appropriate applet; when the result comes back from the applet, it must then translate that result into the form Apache expects, and pass it back to Apache.

So, where will you get this intermediary application? Mac OS X Server, I believe, comes with one; but ordinary Mac OS X does not. Instead, you can use James Sentman's *acgi dispatcher* utility. Here is a description of how to write and implement a basic CGI applet in AppleScript using *acgi dispatcher*. (What's documented here is version 2.5, the latest version at the time this was written; these instructions will not work for earlier versions.)

For purposes of the example, we'll write an "echo" CGI, whose job is to return a web page simply describing the original request. This is always a valuable thing to have on hand when you're doing CGI, because it can be used for testing and debugging, and in any case it exemplifies the two basic tasks of a CGI applet, namely to receive the Apple event and to respond by constructing and returning a web page.

The code is straightforward. The main requirements are that we implement the handle CGI request event as defined in StandardAdditions, and that we return a valid page of HTML preceded by some minimal HTTP headers. (*acgi dispatcher* provides an extra parameter, a list of URL-decoded form elements, saving your applet the tedious job of parsing the form information; you can capture this by adding an extra parameter, given «class TraL», to the parameters, but this example doesn't.)

```
property crlf : "\r\n"
property http_header : "MIME-Version: 1.0" & crlf & ¬
    "Content-type: text/html" & crlf & crlf
property s : ""

on makeLine(whatName, whatValue)
    return "<p><b>" & whatName & ":</b> " & whatValue & "</p>" & return
end makeLine
on addLine(whatName, whatValue)
    set s to s & makeLine(whatName, whatValue)
end addLine

on handle CGI request path_args ¬
    from virtual host virtual_host ¬
        searching for http_search_args ¬
        with posted data post_args ¬
        using access method method ¬
        from address client_address ¬
        from user username ¬
        using password pword ¬
        with user info from_user ¬
        from server server_name ¬
        via port server_port ¬
        executing by script_name ¬
        of content type content_type ¬
        referred by referer ¬
        from browser user_agent ¬
        of action type action_path ¬
        from client IP address client_ip ¬
        with full request full_request ¬
        with connection ID connection_id ¬
        using action action
```

```
            set s to http_header
            set s to s & ¬
                "<html><head><title>Echo Page</title></head>" & return
            set s to s & "<body><h1>Echo Page</h1>" & return
            addLine("virtual_host", POSIX path of virtual_host)
            addLine("path_args", path_args)
            addLine("http_search_args", http_search_args)
            addLine("post_args", post_args)
            addLine("method", method)
            addLine("client_address", client_address)
            addLine("username", username)
            addLine("password", pword)
            addLine("from_user", from_user)
            addLine("server_name", server_name)
            addLine("server_port", server_port)
            addLine("script_name", script_name)
            addLine("content_type", content_type)
            addLine("referer", referer)
            addLine("user_agent", user_agent)
            addLine("action_path", action_path)
            addLine("client_ip", client_ip)
            addLine("full_request", "</p><pre>" & full_request & "</pre><p>")
            addLine("connection_ID", connection_id)
            addLine("action", action)
            set s to s & "<hr><i>" & (current date) & "</i>"
            set s to s & "</body></html>"
            return s
    end handle CGI request
```

We start by defining the header that will precede our HTML. Then comes a pair of utility handlers that will make the code for generating each line of our HTML a bit less tedious. Our plan for generating the HTML is to append line after line of this format:

```
<p><b>param_name:</b>param_value</p>
```

and these utilities make the job a bit more elegant. Finally we have the actual handler for the Apple event that will come from *acgi dispatcher*. As long as this returns a correct HTTP header followed by some reasonably legal HTML, it should work.

Save the script as a Stay Open applet. (Chapter 27 will explain the implications of this designation.) Let's name it *echo.acgi*. (After saving the applet, you may have to use the Finder's Get Info dialog to remove the *.app* suffix appended by your script editor application. It is crucial that the file extension should be *.acgi*, not *.app*.)

Now let's set up Apache to use *acgi dispatcher* as a CGI process. This is easy because *acgi dispatcher* automates the configuration for you. Start up *acgi dispatcher* and provide your admin password when requested, and the configuration will be performed. Go into the Sharing pane of System Preferences and confirm that Personal Web Sharing is turned on (turn it on if not). Confirm that Apache is serving by opening a browser and asking for the default web page. For example, from the same machine you would ask for *http://localhost*; from another machine on the same network you would use the machine's Bonjour name (so, for example, my test machine is called *tangerineScream.local*, so I would ask for *http://tangerineScream.local*).

Now move *echo.acgi* into */Library/WebServer/CGI-Executables*, and double-click it to start it up. Take a deep breath and, in your browser, ask for it by appending */cgi-bin/echo.acgi* to the working URL of your Apache server. For example, I would ask for *http://localhost/cgi-bin/echo.acgi* in a browser on the same machine, or *http://tangerineScream.local/cgi-bin/echo.acgi* in a browser on a different machine. Presto! You should get a web page in response, containing such information such as your IP number and what browser you're using, and showing the current date and time at the bottom. That's the script in *echo.acgi* doing its thing! You've successfully written an AppleScript CGI script.

A question that arises with CGI applets (or any applet, really) is what happens if a request arrives when the applet is already in the middle of handling a pending request. Your web server and your CGI dispatcher may be multithreaded, but AppleScript is not, so Apple events that arrive during execution must be queued and then handled in some definite order. Starting with Panther (AppleScript 1.9.2), that order is FIFO—first in, first out. This means that CGI requests are processed in the order in which they arrive; if a request arrives while another request is already being processed, the new request must wait its turn and will be taken as soon as all currently pending requests are handled.

(This is a big improvement over past systems, where the order was LIFO—last in, first out. Under LIFO ordering, if an Apple event arrives, all pending execution is put on hold until the execution triggered by this latest Apple event has finished. This used to mean that if many requests arrived close to one another, it was quite possible for the earliest ones to be edged out of the queue by newcomers; if this went on for long enough, then from the client's point of view, the web page request would time out, which was thoroughly unfair.)

Timers, Hooks, Attachability, Observability

A number of applications will trigger your script in response to the arrival of a certain day or time. Your choice of such an application will depend upon your particular needs (and possibly what you're willing to spend). Possibilities to examine include Script Timer, iDo Script Scheduler, and various cron front ends. There is also QuicKeys X, though this is rather pricey for what it does. Another option might even be iCal (which is already present on your computer); the alarm for an event or to-do item can involve running a script.

A *hook* is a point in an application's operation where it is willing to turn to you—or more exactly, to a script you've supplied—to ask what to do. Many sorts of application use a hook to let you customize their behavior at key moments. Such, for the most part, are the applications listed in "Automatic Location" in Chapter 2. Thus, one example is iCal: as I mentioned a moment ago, when an alarm fires, iCal can run a script in response. Similarly, Apple's Mail program and Microsoft Entourage let you create rules that are performed in response to the arrival of mail messages meeting certain criteria; one of the things a rule can do is to run a script.

Some applications have hooks as their life blood, so to speak. An example is Salling Clicker, which is all about responding to a handheld device (such as a Bluetooth phone) by running a script. Another example is Ovolab Phlink, which answers the phone and turns at every stage of the phone call to your scripts to see what to do— when the phone rings, when it answers, when the caller presses keys on a touchtone phone, when the call ends, and so forth.

Phlink calls into your script by taking advantage of named parameters. For example, when a phone call arrives on your computer, if you have a script called *ring* in the proper location, it will be called. In order for this to work, your script must contain a handler with this definition:

```
on incoming_call given call:theCall, ¬
    callername:theName, ¬
    callerid:theId, ¬
    ringcount:theCount
    -- code
end incoming_call
```

This is a user handler; you can define it without any scripting addition because it contains no special terminology. With named parameters, the names are up to you— except that you've purposely used the names that Phlink will use when it calls your script. Phlink does define these handlers in its dictionary, but only for informational purposes; it can't enforce them on your script, because your script isn't targeting Phlink at the point where the handler is defined. A nice thing about this choice of syntax is that you can omit, in your definition, parameters you're not interested in receiving; there is, you remember, no penalty when a handler is called with extra parameters (they are simply ignored; see "Syntax of Defining and Calling a Handler" in Chapter 9).

An application may be considered *attachable* if it treats ordinary user actions as hooks (see "Modes of Scriptability" in Chapter 3). For example, BBEdit will run scripts located in its *Menu Scripts* folder, in response to your choosing from any of BBEdit's built-in menus. Thus, any of BBEdit's menus can do what it normally does, but optionally it can include, or can be overridden by, functionality that you provide as a script. Such a script must contain a handler with the following structure:

```
on menuselect(menuName, itemName)
    -- code
end menuselect
```

The fact that an application can call into a user handler that takes positional parameters in your script is surprising, and involves a cool mechanism under the hood; this same mechanism is also how scriptability is implemented in an applet (see Chapter 27).

An event is *observable* if another application can see it. So for example QuicKeys, mentioned earlier, can run a script in response to a certain application starting or quitting, or becoming or ceasing to be frontmost, or when a certain drive is mounted or unmounted. That events at a high system level should be observable is not surprising, because it is reasonable that they should be so; an application certainly has a need and a right to know when it becomes frontmost, so why shouldn't it be able to tell when some other application becomes frontmost? On the other hand, the notion that one application can observe what's happening *internally* within some other application is surprising, both technically and, as it were, morally: an application that "sees" what characters I'm typing into FrameMaker at this moment could justly be accused of spying. Nevertheless, in recent versions of Mac OS X the range of observable application-internal events has been greatly increased, to include not simply when an application is activated or hidden, but also when a menu item is chosen, when a window is created, moved, resized, or miniaturized, as well as what happens at an even more detailed level of the application's interface. This means that your script can react to such internal events occurring in a particular application.

The mechanism here is the Accessibility API, just as for GUI scripting (see Chapter 24), except that it's being used in reverse. When an item in an appropriately written application's user interface is affected, the application gives off a little squawk called a *notification*. A second application can register to receive such notifications, and so it is effectively observing what goes on in the first. Not every application can be observed in this way; but every Cocoa application can, at the least. To experience the full power of this observation mechanism, try PreFab's UI Actions.

An example used in the tutorial included with UI Actions is a modification of Script Editor (I can't think how else to express it—attachability really does, in effect, modify an application's behavior) so that every time a new (untitled) script window is created, a comment is inserted giving the current date:

```
tell application "UI Actions"
    tell UI action "Script Editor-AXWindowCreated"
        set d to date string of (get timestamp)
        set w to affected UI element
    end tell
end tell
tell application "System Events"
    set n to title of w
    if n begins with "Untitled" then
        tell application "Script Editor"
            set text of document n to "-- " & d
        end tell
    end if
end tell
```

As with folder actions (see earlier in this chapter), UI Actions lets you associate an observed event in an application with a script that should be executed when that event occurs. So, using UI Actions, the user will "attach" this script to Script Editor's "AXWindowCreated" notification, so that when a new window is created in Script Editor, the script will be called. When the script *is* called, it targets UI Actions to get a reference to the window that generated the notification; then it targets System Events to learn (through GUI scripting) the name of this window; finally, if this appears to be a new script window (because its name starts with "Untitled"), it enters the current date into the window.

UI Actions can be an elegant solution to the problem of making sure that your script is triggered at an appropriate moment. The UI Actions application itself is scriptable, so you could write a script that creates a script and attaches it to a particular action, or that enables or disables a particular attached script. In fact, such a script could itself be triggered through being attached to some action. The mind boggles.

CHAPTER 27

Writing Applications

You might wish to create a standalone application, perhaps as a way of distributing your script to other users in a form that's easy to use. AppleScript provides the simplest way in the world to write an application: just save your script as an applet. An applet is a true standalone application; it can even accept drag-and-drop of files and folders onto its icon, and (most surprising) it's scriptable. However, an applet has essentially no interface (except for display dialog and other user-interactive scripting addition commands). You can wrap your script in a full-fledged interface, with windows, buttons, text fields, menus, and similar bells and whistles, using Apple-Script Studio, a free development environment that lets you create a Cocoa application even if the only programming language you know is AppleScript. Another use of AppleScript Studio is to wrap your script in the smaller interface of an Automator action; users can then customize it through its interface and link it to other actions to create their own workflows. This chapter also deals with some more advanced issues related to writing applications: how to get started adding scriptability to a Cocoa application, and how an AppleScript Studio application can communicate internally from Cocoa to AppleScript. (See also "Application" in Chapter 2.)

Applets

An *applet* is a compiled script wrapped up in a simple standalone application shell (see "Applet and Droplet" in Chapter 3). To make a script into an applet, save it from a script editor application as an application instead of as a compiled script. You select this option in the Save As dialog. When you launch the resulting application (by double-clicking it in the Finder, for example), the script runs.

It is also possible to save a script as an application bundle. From the outside, this looks and works like an applet. Because it's a bundle, though, you can do things with it that you can't do with an old-style applet, such as storing extra resources inside it; for an example, see "Persistence," later in this chapter. Also, an application bundle can call scripting additions contained within itself; see "Loading

Scripting Additions" in Chapter 21. Keep in mind that this format is not compatible with systems earlier than Panther.

For applet formats, and for special applet behaviors when an application is missing as an applet starts up, see "Applet and Droplet" and "Application Missing When an Applet Launches" in Chapter 3, and "Using Terms From" in Chapter 19. Persistence works in applets; see "Persistence of Top-Level Entities" in Chapter 8. For the behavior of an applet when a runtime error occurs, see "Errors" in Chapter 19. When an applet runs, no decompilation takes place; for one way this can affect the behavior of your script, see "Raw Four-Letter Codes" in Chapter 20.

Applet Options

When you elect to save a script as an applet, you are given some options that affect how the applet will behave:

Stay Open

> The normal behavior of an applet when started up is to run its script and then automatically quit. A stay-open applet does *not* automatically quit; it just sits there running, like any application. An applet has some built-in menus, and in a stay-open applet the user has time to access them; they include a Quit menu item, which the user can choose to quit the applet. If stay-open applet has already run its script, what's the point of its staying open? For the answer, see "Applet Event Handlers," later in this section.

Startup Screen

> (Also called Show Startup or Show Startup Screen; in older versions of Script Editor this option was reversed and was called Never Show Startup Screen.) The startup screen, if it is to be shown, is a kind of introductory splash screen displaying the script's description when the applet is started up. In a script editor application, there is a text view into which a script's description may be entered. The description is styled text, and the styling is maintained in the startup screen dialog. The splash screen also offers the choice to run the applet's script or to quit without running it.
>
> In a stay-open applet, where the user has time to access the applet's menus, the user can toggle the startup screen option by choosing File → Use Startup Screen. Even in an ordinary applet, the user can compel the startup screen to appear by holding down the Control key as the applet starts up.

Editing an Applet

A script saved as an applet is normally still legible and editable. The only way to prevent this is to save the applet as Run Only. Keep in mind that this means even *you* can't edit the applet's script; if you have no other copy of the script, you lose all ability to edit the applet's script, forever.

Let's presume the applet is not run-only. How can its script be edited? Not by double-clicking the applet from the Finder, because that runs the applet. However, a script editor application can still open it (through its Open dialog, for example). In fact, you can even keep an applet script open for editing in a script editor application, save it without closing it, and then double-click it in the Finder to run it, as a way of testing while developing. But, for obvious reasons, you can't save an applet's script into the applet while the applet is actually running—well, you actually can, but the changed functionality won't be available until you quit the applet and start it up again.

Another way to edit an applet is to choose its Edit → Edit Script menu item. In a stay-open applet, that menu item can be chosen whenever the applet is idle. In non-stay-open applet, the menus are visible while the startup screen is displayed; thus, the user can start up the applet while holding down the Control key, to force the display of the startup screen, and then choose Edit → Edit Script.

Applet Event Handlers

An applet script may contain certain event handlers (see "Event Handlers" in Chapter 9) which, if present, will be called automatically at specific moments in the lifetime of the applet:

run

> The run handler, whether implicit or explicit (see "The Run Handler" in Chapter 9), is called when the applet is started up, either by the user opening it from the Finder or by a script targeting it. (To start up an applet without calling its run handler, tell it to launch.)

reopen

> A reopen event handler, if present, is called when the already running applet is summoned to the front by such means as being double-clicked in the Finder or having its icon clicked in the Dock. Merely switching among applications with ⌘-Tab, or telling the applet to activate, does *not* send a reopen event.

idle

> An idle event handler, if present, is called as soon as the run handler finishes executing, and then again periodically while a stay-open applet is running. The value returned by the idle handler is a real number, representing how many seconds later the idle handler should be called again. A return value of 0, or any other value that can't be coerced to a positive real, is treated as 30.

quit

> A quit event handler, if present, is called when the applet is about to quit. If it is a stay-open applet, this might be because the user has chosen its Quit menu item; if not, it might be because the applet has been started up and its run handler has finished executing. If the quit handler wishes to permit the applet to quit, it must give the continue quit command.

An applet having a quit handler that does not give the `continue quit` command will appear to the user to be impossible to quit (except by force-quitting).

So, for example, here's an annoying little stay-open applet:

```
on run
    display dialog "Howdy!"
end run
on reopen
    display dialog "Get to Work!"
end reopen
on quit
    display dialog "Farewell!"
    continue quit
end quit
on idle
    beep
    activate
    display dialog "Get to Work!"
    return 1 * minutes
end idle
```

An applet is scriptable with respect to its event handlers; that is, you can tell an applet to run, reopen, idle, or quit, and it will execute the respective handler if it has one. If you tell an applet to quit and it has no quit handler, it simply quits. If you tell an applet to idle and it has no idle handler, or to reopen and it has no reopen handler, nothing happens (but the calling script may receive an error).

If an applet is not running, do not tell it to run or you'll confuse yourself. The run handler will be called *twice*—once because you targeted the applet, and again because you told it to run—and the idle handler will be called as well. To prevent this, tell the nonrunning applet to activate (the run handler will be called once, and the idle handler will be called).

Alternatively, you can tell the nonrunning applet to launch. In that case, neither the run handler nor the idle handler will be called, and no other event handler is called either; if you immediately tell the applet to quit, not even its quit handler is called. An applet launched in this way "comes to life" only if you send it some further Apple event (for example, tell it to launch and *then* tell it to run).

An idle handler should not be treated as ensuring a precise measure of time; the time interval returned is merely a request not to be called until after that interval has elapsed. (I am not entirely clear on what the time interval is measured *from*; experiments returning 0 seemed to suggest that it was measured from when the idle handler was last called, not from when it last returned, but this didn't seem to be true for other values.) If your goal is to run a script at certain times or intervals, you might be happier using a timer utility to handle this for you (see "Timers, Hooks, Attachability, Observability" in Chapter 26).

A question arises of how to interrupt a time-consuming applet. (This problem, and its solution, were suggested to me by Paul Berkowitz.) Suppose the run handler takes a long time and the user wishes to stop it and quit. The user can press Command-. (period), which raises an error (-128, "User canceled") that stops the run handler dead in its tracks, but the user might not know this. The Quit menu item doesn't work; if the user chooses it, the applet doesn't quit—if it has a quit handler, the quit handler is called, but when the quit handler says continue quit, the applet goes right back to executing the run handler where it left off! (I regard this as a bug.) There is also the question of how you can make sure that any required clean-up actions are performed as the applet quits. The best strategy is probably something like this:

```
global shouldQuit
global didCleanup
on run
    set shouldQuit to false
    set didCleanup to false
    try
        -- lengthy operation goes here
        repeat with x from 1 to 10
            if shouldQuit then error
            say (x as string)
            delay 5
        end repeat
    on error
        tell me to quit
    end try
end run
on quit
    if not didCleanup then
        -- cleanup operation goes here
        say "cleaning up"
        set didCleanup to true
    end if
    set shouldQuit to true
    continue quit
end quit
```

When the user chooses Quit from the menu bar, our quit handler is called, but when we say continue quit we will merely resume the run handler, so we also set a global indicating that the user is trying to quit. The resumed run handler notices this and deliberately errors out, and we catch the error and call our own quit handler, and quit in good order. We would perform our cleanup operations twice in this case, but that is prevented by another global. It's all very ingenious, but it's messy, and ultimately not very satisfactory. If the user chooses Quit from the applet's Dock menu, our applet's quit menu handler isn't called (another bug), and if the user force-quits our applet then of course no cleanup is performed.

Droplets

A *droplet* is an applet onto whose icon the user can drop Finder items (files and folders). Internally, it is simply an applet with an open event handler:

open

An open event handler, if present, will be called when items are dropped in the Finder onto the droplet's icon. It should take one parameter, through which your code will receive a list of aliases to the items dropped.

If a droplet is started up by double-clicking it from the Finder, then its run handler is executed and its open handler is not. But if it is started up by dropping items on it in the Finder, then it's the other way around: its open handler is executed and its run handler is not. Once a droplet is running (assuming it is a stay-open droplet), the open handler can be executed by dropping items onto the droplet's icon in the Finder. The open handler is also scriptable, using the open command, whose parameter should be a list of aliases.

In this simple example, the droplet reports how many folders were dropped on its icon:

```
on open what
    set total to 0
    repeat with f in what
        if folder of (info for f size no) then set total to total + 1
    end repeat
    display dialog (total as string) & " folder(s)"
end open
```

Persistence

Persistence of top-level entities (see Chapter 8) works in an applet. The script is resaved when the applet quits, maintaining the state of its top-level environment.

So, for example, the following modification to the previous example would cause an applet to report the count of folders that had *ever* been dropped on it, not just the count of folders dropped on it at this moment:

```
property total : 0
on open what
    repeat with f in what
        if folder of (info for f size no) then set total to total + 1
    end repeat
    display dialog (total as string) & " folder(s)"
end open
```

On the other hand, this persistence naturally ends as soon as the applet's script is edited. If you're still developing an applet, or are likely to edit it further for any reason, you might like a way to store data persistently with no chance of losing it. The application bundle format supplies a solution. An application bundle looks, and behaves in the Finder, just like an applet, but is in reality a folder. We can perform persistent data storage in a separate file inside the bundle; the user won't see this separate file, and its data will persist even when we edit the applet's main script.

To illustrate, let's return to the example in "Data Storage" in Chapter 8. This code is just the same as in that example, except that we now assume we are an application bundle, and the opening lines have been changed to store the data inside the bundle:

```
set thePath to (path to resource "applet.icns") as string
set text item delimiters to ":"
set thePath to ((text items 1 thru -2 of thePath) as string) & ":myPrefs.scpt"
script myPrefs
    property favoriteColor : ""
end script
try
    set myPrefs to load script file thePath
on error
    set favoriteColor of myPrefs to text returned of ¬
        (display dialog "Favorite Color:" default answer ¬
            "" buttons {"OK"} default button "OK")
    store script myPrefs in file thePath replacing yes
end try
display dialog "Your favorite color is " & favoriteColor of myPrefs
```

The first three lines of the script are a rather elaborate song-and-dance to obtain the pathname of the bundle's *Resources* directory. We could hardcode the path from the top of the bundle, like this:

```
set thePath to (path to me as string) & "Contents:Resources:myPrefs.scpt"
```

Instead, we use the path to resource command. But this command has an odd functionality hole: we can obtain the pathname of a resource file inside the *Resources* directory, but not the pathname of the directory itself. So we start with a resource file we know is present and work our way up the folder hierarchy and back down again.

Applet Scriptability

We have seen already that an applet is scriptable with respect to its event handlers: you can tell an applet to run, open, reopen, idle, or quit, and the corresponding event handler will be called. An applet is scriptable also with respect to user handlers. You call them like ordinary handlers. For example, suppose we have a stay-open applet *howdy* whose script goes like this:

```
on sayHowdy(toWhom)
    activate
    display dialog "Howdy, " & toWhom
end sayHowdy
```

Then we can say in another script:

```
tell application "howdy"
    sayHowdy("Matt")
end tell
```

The value is returned as one would expect; here, the calling script receives the value {button returned:"OK"} if user presses the OK button.

The reason this is possible is that AppleScript's mechanism for calling a user handler in a script object is extended to work even when you're talking to an applet. The call is translated into a special event, the Call•subroutine command ('ascr\psbr'). This is a sort of meta-command; its parameters are the name of the handler you're calling and the parameters you're passing. At the other end, the target applet unpacks the handler call and performs it within its script. Thus it's just as if you said sayHowdy("Matt") from inside the applet's script. If the script defines such a handler, the result comes back as the reply. If it doesn't, you get a "Can't continue" error message. (This error message is familiar from when you *accidentally* use this same mechanism to send a user handler call to an ordinary scriptable application, which, as we have seen in Chapter 11 and elsewhere, is all too easy to do.)

An applet is also scriptable with respect to its other top-level entities. If an applet has a top-level property x, you can get and set its x. And if an applet defines a top-level script object s, you can refer to s, and you can get and set *its* properties.

In short, an applet behaves like a script object, whose top-level entities you can access in the normal way (see "Top-Level Entities" in Chapter 8). You might think of it as a stored script object that you can target without loading it, and that is automatically persistent without your storing it.

Of course, this means that when you're scripting an applet, no special dictionary is involved. An applet doesn't have a dictionary, and it doesn't need one, any more than a script object needs a dictionary. Therefore an applet has no way to publish information about what top-level entities it contains. The user who wishes to script the applet must know in some other way how to do so (by reading the applet's script, or through some other documentation).

AppleScript Studio

AppleScript Studio is a free development environment from Apple allowing you to write Cocoa applications using the AppleScript language. It would require an entire book to discuss AppleScript Studio adequately, so in this section I'll just explain what AppleScript Studio is and how it works, and talk about how you might go about learning it more fully; I'll also provide a simple hands-on example of Apple-Script Studio in action.

Cocoa and AppleScript Studio

AppleScript Studio is Cocoa. The precise sense in which I mean this will be clearer in a moment, but it's a simple truth on the face of it, and it means that to understand what AppleScript Studio is, you need to know what Cocoa is.

Cocoa is a massive application framework included as part of Mac OS X. This framework knows how to do all the things that an application might typically wish to do. For example, it can put up windows, in which it can display many different kinds of interface elements for interacting with the user, such as buttons and text fields and sliders and tables and so forth. It also provides very strong text and graphics capabilities. Cocoa is a remarkably well-constructed application framework, striking an excellent balance between power and flexibility; with Cocoa, it's easy to write a simple standard application quite quickly, while at the same time the framework usually provides enough leeway so that the programmer can fully customize the application's behavior if desired. The presence of Cocoa as part of Mac OS X makes it much easier for programmers to write sophisticated, powerful, Mac OS X–native applications, while at the same time such applications often require relatively little code, because so much of the code that does the work resides in the framework.

AppleScript Studio is Apple's way of letting you, the AppleScript programmer, take advantage of the Cocoa application framework without having to learn a different programming language. The "native" Cocoa programming language is Objective-C, and to use Cocoa fully, you would want to learn that language. But as an AppleScript programmer, you might already have written a working script. You don't want to rewrite its functionality in some other language; you want to enhance your script with a more sophisticated user interface than AppleScript alone can provide. AppleScript Studio can let you do this. Think of it as a way to leverage an existing script into a Cocoa application, a way to wrap a Cocoa interface around AppleScript functionality with relative ease.

AppleScript Studio is not, however, a way to take *full* advantage of the power of Cocoa. By this I mean that you should not expect AppleScript Studio to let you do *everything* that Objective-C/Cocoa would let you do. If that's what you want, learn Objective-C! AppleScript Studio gives you access to a limited portion of Cocoa's power; that portion is usually enough to let you write a satisfactory application pretty quickly and easily, provided that your needs are fairly simple and your ambitions don't get out of hand. You should not feel disappointed about the fact that AppleScript Studio exposes to the AppleScript programmer only a simplified fraction of Cocoa's abilities. Simple is good. After all, Cocoa is very big, and can require years to learn fully. AppleScript Studio, on the other hand, is relatively tractable.

Let me explain in a bit more technical depth how AppleScript Studio exposes Cocoa to the AppleScript programmer. You'll need a sense of this in order to use AppleScript Studio effectively in any case. Cocoa is an application framework, so it operates through messages that travel back and forth between *its* code (the code inside the framework) and *your* code (the code that you actually write, whether you're writing in Objective-C, AppleScript, or whatever). Cocoa is like a gigantic lock, and your code must be structured as a key that fits that lock; you have to write code that will slot into Cocoa's expectations of how an application should work. Thus, even though you can't see inside Cocoa, you do need to know what messages to send to Cocoa and what messages Cocoa will send you, so that its code and your code can work together properly. These messages come under some basic headings:

Built-in methods

The interface elements, such as windows and menus and buttons and text fields, as well as the application as a whole, are prepared to respond to certain messages that you can send. For example, you might like to tell a button to change its title, or ask a text field what the user has typed in it, or tell a window to close, or ask the application whether it is frontmost. You can do these things because the entity to whom you're speaking defines an appropriate message. A button "knows" how to change its title and defines a way for you to tell it to do so; a text field "knows" how to report what the user has typed in it; and so forth. These predefined messages that you can send are the *built-in methods*.

Action messages

Certain interface elements have a single special behavior when the user performs a certain special operation on them. In the case of a button, that operation is pushing the button. In the case of a text field, it's typing Return within the text field. This is the interface element's *action*, and when the action occurs, your code can receive an *action message* so that it can respond.

Lifetime notifications

Cocoa will, if you wish, notify your code of things that routinely take place over the lifetime of an application. For example, you might like your code to be called when your application first starts up, when it comes to the front, or when it is about to quit; or you might like to be informed when the user selects a line in a table or types a character in a text field. These are the *lifetime notifications*, and again, they exist so that your code has a chance to respond to what's happening.

Delegation queries

Cocoa will sometimes offer your code the opportunity to intervene in its behavior. For example, suppose that the user clicks the mouse to select a line in a table. Normally that line would just be selected, but perhaps your code might have some reason for making it unselectable at that moment. Cocoa can delegate the responsibility for this sort of decision to your code, querying your code as to whether it should proceed normally; if you elect to receive such *delegation queries*, your code must give a definite answer as to how Cocoa should proceed.

Thus there are two kinds of messages in Cocoa—those you send to Cocoa (the built-in methods) and those that Cocoa will send to you (the action messages, lifetime notifications, and delegation queries). Furthermore, your code is essentially idle until something triggers some part of it. An application does nothing unless it is somehow told to do it. And the only way your code can be told to do anything is through a message that Cocoa sends it. In other words, *all* your code will run only in response to action messages, lifetime notifications, and delegations queries; so your code must be structured, not independently, but as responses to messages from Cocoa.

The architecture I've just described does not perfectly match how AppleScript code works. So to make it match, the Apple folks have interposed a kind of interpreter between Cocoa and your AppleScript code. The interpreter's job is to take care of all the differences between Cocoa and AppleScript, so that you don't have to worry about them. Cocoa sends out a delegation query or a notification message; the interpreter receives this and turns it into AppleScript and routes an appropriate event handler call to your script. Your AppleScript code obtains references to interface elements and targets them with commands, and gets and sets their properties; the interpreter turns this into Objective-C and calls the corresponding built-in method of the relevant Cocoa object. This interpreted linkage between AppleScript and Cocoa is often referred to as a *bridge*, and we say that the Apple folks have bridged AppleScript to (certain parts of) Cocoa.

The first thing to do in learning AppleScript Studio is to consider learning more about Cocoa. After all, AppleScript Studio *is* Cocoa, and even if you'd rather not learn any Objective-C, it can be really helpful to have some familiarity with the location of the Cocoa documentation on your hard drive, and perhaps to read a couple of good introductory Cocoa books. (My favorite is Aaron Hillegass, *Cocoa Programming for Mac OS X* [Addison-Wesley, 2004], 2nd ed.) Furthermore, it's possible that you might end up wanting to learn some Objective-C after all. You can easily find your programming desires thwarted when you encounter an area where AppleScript is *not* bridged to Cocoa. There are four solutions when this happens:

Give up
> If you restrain your desires, your desires can't be thwarted. If something you want to do isn't bridged, stop wanting to do it and confine yourself to what is bridged. This is not an ignoble way out; all programming involves a trade-off of time and effort, and it may be that simplifying your needs is the wisest course.

Use call method
> You can call directly from AppleScript into an Objective-C method with the call method command (I'll illustrate its use later on).

Make a hybrid
> It's perfectly possible for some of your code to be written in AppleScript, in a script, and for other parts of your code to be written in Objective-C, in a custom class. In effect, such an application is a hybrid of Objective-C/Cocoa and AppleScript Studio.

Give up, the other way
> Sometimes AppleScript in Cocoa is a square peg in a round hole. Consider learning Objective-C and writing your application in Objective-C/Cocoa. You can

still use AppleScript from within Objective-C (see "Application" in Chapter 2). It may seem paradoxical, but *not* using AppleScript Studio can sometimes be the wisest development strategy.

The Pieces of AppleScript Studio

AppleScript Studio is like Los Angeles: it isn't actually anywhere. It isn't a thing or a place; it's many tools and resources, used in a certain way. Let's talk about those tools and resources.

The developer tools
> The developer tools, collectively known as the Xcode Tools, are on the Tiger DVD, but they are an optional installation. If you don't install them, you won't have any of the AppleScript Studio tools and resources on your hard disk. So install them! An even better approach, as the version on your copy of the Tiger DVD may be outdated, is to obtain the latest version from Apple. First you must join the Apple Developer Connection; the "online" membership level is free (*http://developer.apple.com/membership/online.html*). Then you'll be able to log in and download the Xcode Tools.

Interface Builder
> Interface Builder, an application located (after you've installed the developer tools) in */Developer/Applications*, is where you'll design your application's interface. It's worth perusing the Interface Builder Help early in the game.

Xcode
> The Xcode application (not to be confused with the Xcode Tools as a whole) is also in */Developer/Applications*. This is where you create and work with a *project* (the collection of files that will be combined to create your application); it's where you write your code, it's where you access the files that constitute the project, and it's where you'll ask to have your code turned into a real application (called *building* the project). What makes your project an AppleScript Studio application is that you specify "AppleScript Application" when you create the project.

> The fact that you design your interface in one application but edit your code and build the application in another is a tricky aspect of the Cocoa development experience, and takes some getting used to. As a beginner, you should work on only one project at a time; while doing so, keep both Interface Builder and Xcode running but hide whichever you're not using at that moment.

Tutorial
> There is a hands-on tutorial at */Developer/ADC Reference Library/documentation/ AppleScript/Conceptual/StudioBuildingApps/*. I have reservations about its appropriateness (it employs some techniques I regard as inadvisable), but it's probably worth going through it, if only as a way of becoming familiar with Xcode and Interface Builder.

Reference

The most important AppleScript Studio documentation is the reference document at */Developer/ADC Reference Library/documentation/AppleScript/Reference/ StudioReference/*. You should skim through this at the outset and then expect to refer to it constantly while working.

The dictionary

The terminology for the repertory of things you can say in an AppleScript Studio application is defined in a dictionary. (You don't have to target any application in your AppleScript Studio code in order to gain access to this terminology; it is made automatically available.) This dictionary appears in your project as *AppleScriptKit.sdef*; double-click it to view it in a dictionary display. This is essentially the same information as in the reference, but not as well presented, so you're less likely to use it.

Examples

There are many AppleScript Studio examples located in */Developer/Examples/ AppleScript Studio*. They explore and demonstrate most of the important aspects of using AppleScript Studio to drive the user interface; it's very worthwhile to study them.

Cocoa documentation

There are good links to help you find your way into Cocoa, Objective-C, and Cocoa documentation in an introductory document at */Developer/ADC Reference Library/referencelibrary/GettingStarted/GS_Cocoa/*. Furthermore, each page about an AppleScript class in the AppleScript Studio reference document is cross-linked to the page about the corresponding Cocoa class; the discussion of the Cocoa class is well worth consulting, as it often explains things better, and frequently has links to even more useful pages on general topics about how things work in Cocoa.

AppleScript Studio Example

As a tutorial example, let's return to the code presented earlier for searching the TidBITS online archive (in Chapter 25). Recall what it does. We allow the user to enter search terms. We use curl to submit those terms to the TidBITS search engine. The reply is a page of HTML listing the pages found. We use Perl to parse the HTML, and present the results to the user as a list. If the user double-clicks a listed article, we present the corresponding page in the web browser. The purpose of the tutorial is to illustrate AppleScript Studio development by wrapping this script in a nice interface. We'll have two windows, a Search window where the user enters search terms and a Results window where the results will be listed.

Begin by creating the project. Start up Xcode. Choose File → New Project and select "AppleScript Application"; in the dialog that appears, name the project *SearchTidBITS* and finish creating it.

We must embed the Perl script into the bundle of the built application. This must be done by the build process, so the Perl script must be incorporated into the project. Select the Resources folder on the left side of the project window and choose Project → Add Files. In the Open File dialog, find and select the Perl script, which is called *parseHTML.pl*. In the next dialog, check the box at the top which asks whether you want to copy the file into the project, and click the Add button.

Now we'll design the interface. In the project window, double-click *MainMenu.nib*. Interface Builder will open. I'm going to skip some details ("drag this interface element from this palette onto this window, resize it, make these settings in the Attributes pane of the Inspector," and so forth) and simply show you the interface design we're going to construct. It consists of two windows and some changes to the menu bar:

- The Search window contains an NSForm displaying three fields the user can search on (text, title, and author) and a Search button, along with a spinning progress indicator to provide feedback while we're talking to the Internet (Figure 27-1).

Figure 27-1. Search window

- The Results window contains a single-column table for displaying the titles of the found articles, along with some explanatory text telling the user what to do (Figure 27-2).
- In the menu bar, I remove the File menu and replace it with a Search menu consisting of a single New menu item; also, I add a Close menu item to the Window menu. Finally, I run through the menu items of the application menu and the Help menu and replace the placeholder "NewApplication" with "SearchTid-BITS," the name of our application (Figure 27-3).

Now comes the really interesting part. As you'll recall, the Cocoa framework defines certain action messages, lifetime notifications, and delegation queries that can be sent to your code. In Interface Builder, we must specify which of these messages we want to receive, with respect to each element of our interface as well as

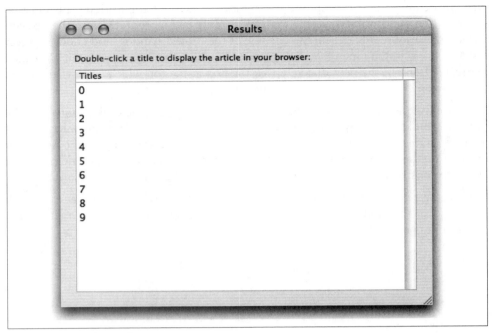

Figure 27-2. Results window

Figure 27-3. The menu bar

the application as a whole. (Remember, we *must* elect to receive some of these messages or our code will never run.) At the same time, we should also give at least some of our interface elements AppleScript names, so that our AppleScript code can refer to them. All of this is done in the AppleScript pane of the Inspector window.

Figure 27-4 shows the process. I've selected the Search window (not shown) and now I focus my attention on the Inspector and its AppleScript pane. In the Name field I've entered an AppleScript name, "search"; this will allow our code to refer to this window by name, as window "search". In the list of event handlers, I've checked the "will open" checkbox; this means that our code will receive a will open event at the appropriate moment in the lifetime of this window (namely, when it is about to open). Somewhat confusingly, it is not sufficient to check this checkbox; it is also necessary to check the Script checkbox specifying the file *SearchTidBITS.applescript*, so that AppleScript Studio knows what script to send the will open event to (even though our project has in fact only one script).

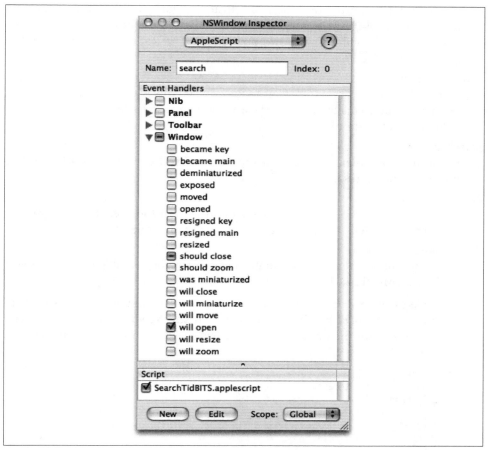

Figure 27-4. AppleScript Inspector for the Search window

Here are the interface items of our project and the treatment I apply to each:

File's Owner
This icon in the main Interface Builder window represents the application as a whole. I want to know when the application has launched so that I can perform some initializations, so I check Application: launched (a lifetime notification).

Search → New menu item
I want to know when the user chooses this menu item, so I check Menu: choose menu item (the menu item's action message).

Window → Close menu item
I want the frontmost window to close when the user chooses this menu item. I could check Menu: choose menu item for this menu item as well, but the knowledge of how to close a window is already built into Cocoa, so there is no need to

involve AppleScript or any code at all. Instead, I form a Cocoa connection. To do so, I Control-drag from this menu item to the First Responder icon in the main Interface Builder window, and connect it to the First Responder's performClose: method.

Search window

I name this window search. I want to know when this window is about to open, because I want to make some interface adjustments; so I select Window: will open (a lifetime notification).

Search window: the Search button

I want to know when the user clicks this button, so I select Action: clicked (the button's action message).

Results window

I name this window results. I want to know when the user tries to close this window, so I check Window: should close (a delegation query).

Results window: the table view

I want to know when the user double-clicks a row of the table view, so I select Action: double clicked.

This completes our use of Interface Builder, so we save our work and switch to Xcode. Find the *SearchTidBITS.applescript* file in the Xcode project window and open it. Templates for the event handlers that we specified in Interface Builder have already been created:

```
on will open theObject
    (*Add your script here.*)
end will open

on launched theObject
    (*Add your script here.*)
end launched

on choose menu item theObject
    (*Add your script here.*)
end choose menu item

on clicked theObject
    (*Add your script here.*)
end clicked

on double clicked theObject
    (*Add your script here.*)
end double clicked

on should close theObject
    (*Add your script here.*)
end should close
```

Now we'll write our script's code, filling in these event handlers and adding any further user handlers of our own. Let's tour the final code a little at a time. In Example 27-1 we declare some top-level globals. We also write code for the launched handler that will be called right after the application has started up; this is the best place for general initializations, which is just what we use it for here, locating the Perl file within our application's bundle and retaining its POSIX pathname as a global.

Example 27-1. Globals and launched handler

```
global perlScriptPath, L1, L2, textSought, titleSought, authorSought

on launched theObject
    local f
    set f to (path to resource "parseHTML.pl")
    set perlScriptPath to quoted form of (POSIX path of f)
end launched
```

Example 27-2 shows the will open handler. Observe that these event handlers have a parameter, theObject; this contains a reference to the interface element with which this action message, notification, or delegation query is associated. In this case, we know that only the Search window is set to deliver a will open notification, so there is no need to bother checking theObject's identity; we just blithely assume that it's the Search window.

Example 27-2. The will open handler

```
on will open theObject
    tell theObject
        call method "setDisplayedWhenStopped:" of progress indicator 1 with parameter 0
    end tell
end will open
```

The code illustrates the use of call method to form a manual bridge from AppleScript to Objective-C. We want to make sure that the progress indicator is invisible when not spinning. This setting is available through a built-in Cocoa method, but no AppleScript property is bridged to it, so we cross the bridge ourselves; in effect, we form the equivalent of the following line of Objective-C code:

```
[theProgressIndicator setDisplayedWhenStopped: NO];
```

Example 27-3 shows the choose menu item event handler, which is the action message from the Search → New menu item. We hide the Results window and show the Search window, emptying the form cells and selecting the first cell, ready for the user to enter text. Once again, AppleScript is not bridged to a built-in Cocoa method that we want to call, so we use the call method command to call it directly.

Example 27-3. The choose menu item handler

```
on choose menu item theObject
    hide window "results"
    tell window "search"
        tell matrix 1
            set content of cell 1 to ""
            set content of cell 2 to ""
            set content of cell 3 to ""
            call method "selectTextAtIndex:" of it with parameter 0
        end tell
        show
    end tell
end choose menu item
```

Example 27-4 shows the `clicked` handler. This is the Search button's action message, and is the heart of our application. To make the code clearer, I've broken the functionality out into some ancillary user handlers. We start by initializing our globals based on what's in the Search window form; then, after a sanity check, we call the next user handler, `doTheSearch`.

Example 27-4. The clicked handler and an associated utility

```
on clicked theObject
    tell matrix 1 of window "search"
        set textSought to my urlEncode(content of cell 1)
        set titleSought to my urlEncode(content of cell 2)
        set authorSought to my urlEncode(content of cell 3)
    end tell
    if length of textSought < 5 and length of titleSought < 5 and ¬
        length of authorSought < 5 then
        beep
        return
    end if
    doTheSearch()
end clicked

on urlEncode(what)
    set text item delimiters to "+"
    return (words of what) as string
end urlEncode
```

Example 27-5 is a utility hander, `feedbackBusy`, purely for manipulating the interface to provide some user feedback. We're going to be talking to the Internet by way of `curl`, and while we're doing this, nothing will be happening. The user might think that the application is idle or broken. Therefore we spin the progress indicator and disable the Search button to give the user a sense that the application is busy and that he should keep his hands off while it does whatever it's doing. The handler is called with a boolean parameter telling whether to begin or end this feedback. Once again there's a use of call method to make up for a deficiency in the bridging: here, we force the window to update its display so that the disabled or enabled Search button will look disabled or enabled.

Example 27-5. The feedbackBusy handler

```
on feedbackBusy(yn)
    tell window "search"
        if yn then
            set enabled of button 1 to false
            start progress indicator 1
        else
            set enabled of button 1 to true
            stop progress indicator 1
        end if
        call method "display" of it
    end tell
end feedbackBusy
```

Example 27-6 shows the doTheSearch handler. This should seem familiar, being nearly unchanged from the code in Chapter 25. The main differences are:

- The post argument now incorporates values from the three different form fields the user is allowed to fill out.

- We ask for 2,000 articles instead of 20. The reason is that we're hoping to capture the titles of all the found articles. The search was originally constructed so that its results could be displayed in a web page, where you're supposed to find the first 20 results, then ask for another page showing the next 20, and so forth. I originally thought of trying to emulate this in our application. But then it struck me that we've got this nice scrolling table view to play with, and displaying a large number of titles is no problem, so we may as well gather lots of them in one search and be done with it.

- Interface feedback is provided to the user through calls to feedbackBusy before and after the call to curl.

- The call to curl now has a few more parameters—for example, we provide some timeout values, because the TidBITS search server can be rather slow.

- The intermediary file is now located in the temporary items directory, where the user won't see it (it will be deleted automatically when the user logs out).

- Error handling has been added. It's primitive—if there's a problem, we beep—but this is enough to prevent any mysterious error messages from appearing before the user's eyes. The problem will usually be either that no results were obtained from the search or that the search was never run because we couldn't connect to the server; in real life it might be nice to distinguish these cases and to provide nice error messages, but this is left as an exercise to the reader (meaning that I was too lazy to do it myself).

Example 27-6. The doTheSearch handler

```
on doTheSearch()
    local d, f, r
    set d to "'-response=TBSearch.lasso&-token.srch=TBAdv"
    set d to d & "&Article+HTML=" & textSought
    set d to d & "&Article+Author=" & authorSought
    set d to d & "&Article+Title=" & titleSought
    set d to d & "&-operator"
    set d to d & "=eq&RawIssueNum=&-operator=equals&ArticleDate"
    set d to d & "=&-sortField=ArticleDate&-sortOrder=descending"
    set d to d & "&-maxRecords=2000&-nothing=MSExplorerHack&-nothing"
    set d to d & "=Start+Search' "
    set u to "http://db.tidbits.com/TBSrchAdv.lasso"
    set f to (POSIX path of (path to temporary items)) & "tempTidBITS"
    feedbackBusy(true)
    try
        do shell script ¬
            "curl -s --connect-timeout 25 -m 120 -d " & d & " -o " & f & " " & u
        set r to do shell script ("perl " & perlScriptPath & " " & f)
        feedbackBusy(false)
        set L to paragraphs of r
        set half to (count L) / 2
        set L1 to items 1 thru half of L
        set L2 to items (half + 1) thru -1 of L
        displayResults()
    on error
        feedbackBusy(false)
        beep
    end try
end doTheSearch
```

If the doTheSearch handler doesn't error out, it calls displayResults to populate the Results window and present it to the user. Example 27-7 shows the displayResults handler, along with two event handlers connected with the Results window. The double clicked event handler responds when the user double-clicks a line of the table of article titles: the corresponding URL is sent to the web browser for display. The should close handler works around a bug in Tiger's version of AppleScript Studio (at least I think it's a bug): a window that might be shown again later must not be closed, as if it *is* shown again later it will malfunction. Therefore when the user attempts to close the Results window we prevent it (by returning false) and hide the window instead; it looks to the user as if the window has closed, but it hasn't.

Example 27-7. The displayResults handler

```
on displayResults()
    tell table view 1 of scroll view 1 of window "results"
        set contents to L2
    end tell
    show window "results"
end displayResults
```

Example 27-7. The displayResults handler (continued)

```
on double clicked theObject
    try
        open location (item (clicked row of theObject) of L1)
    end try
end double clicked

on should close theObject
    hide theObject
    return false
end should close
```

This completes the development of our application. To test it, choose Build → Build and Run in Xcode. (Figure 27-5 shows the running application in action; we've performed a search for articles by our favorite author mentioning our favorite subject, and the first article found is being displayed in a web browser in the background.) To prepare your application for public release, choose Project → Set Active Build Configuration → Release; then choose Build → Clean All Targets and then Build → Build. The result is a more compact application that will run on other users' machines, with the script saved as run-only to hide it from prying eyes.

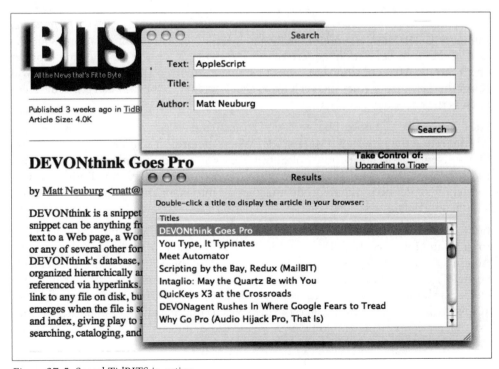

Figure 27-5. SearchTidBITS in action

Automator Actions

An Automator action (see "Automator" in Chapter 2) is an excellent way to wrap some AppleScript code with a lightweight interface. An Automator action is not a standalone application; rather, it is hosted by Automator (or by some other environment that can run Automator workflows). An action typically has no windows or menus; rather, a single pane (technically, an NSView) appears as the action's interface within Automator, and optionally can appear when the workflow runs, as a way of supplying the script with parameters. This isn't much interface, but in many cases it will be just enough. The script also receives as a parameter the output values from the previous action in the workflow. An Automator action thus gives the end user more power and flexibility than a pure script: the end user can position the action within a larger workflow, and can set options in its interface, effectively repurposing the script and customizing its behavior without seeing or editing its code (and without having to know any AppleScript). To write an Automator action is not difficult, and takes only a few minutes; and it can be done using AppleScript Studio.

Here's a hands-on tutorial illustrating the process of writing an Automator action. (See */Developer/ADC Reference Library/documentation/AppleApplications/Conceptual/ AutomatorConcepts* for Apple's full documentation.) For our example, we'll write an action that accepts file aliases and encodes those files as MP3s using lame (*http://lame. sourceforge.net*). It is assumed that lame is installed in its default location, which is */usr/local/bin*. In our action's interface, we'll provide an option for selecting a preset and a bitrate. MP3 encoding is a time-consuming activity, so our implementation will script the Terminal (rather than calling do shell script) so the user can see some feedback as the encoding proceeds.

Start up Xcode. Choose File → New Project and select AppleScript Automator Action; name the project *LAME Encode*. When the project window appears, choose File → New File to create an AppleScript Text File called *ui.applescript* to be added to the project. The reason is that we wish to write some code that will interact with the action's interface, and this code must not go into *main.applescript*, the only script supplied by default.

Now let's create our action's interface. In the project window, double-click *main.nib* to start up Interface Builder. The View window displays the pane in which the Action's interface is to appear. Start by removing the placeholder text ("UI elements go here"). Apple's interface guidelines for Automator actions specify that interface elements should be Small size rather than Regular, and that the NSView should have 10-pixel margins. They also suggest using space economically, and in particular they ask that a popup menu should be preferred to radio buttons.

Figure 27-6 shows our action's interface. The top row contains the interface elements the user can set. The popup menu contains the names of the most important presets: its items are "insane," "extreme," "standard," "medium," a menu item separator, then "studio," "cd," "hifi," "tape," and "mw-us." The second row contains a text field that we'll use to show the user the results of the current settings in the top row. We won't implement VBR bitrates, so the bitrate text field will be disabled unless the "cbr" checkbox is checked. The height of the NSView has been reduced as much as possible; vertical space is at a premium when the user is constructing a workflow in Automator, so we don't want to waste any.

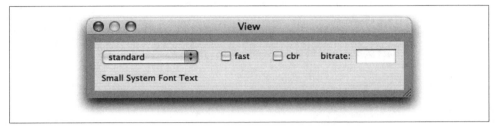

Figure 27-6. The action's interface

Just as in the AppleScript Studio tutorial, earlier in this chapter, we now give our interface elements AppleScript names and arrange for notification when the user changes one of them. The names are namePopup, fastSwitch, cbrSwitch, cbrText, and example. The notifications must all be sent to *ui.applescript*; they are the popup menu's action, the clicked of the two checkboxes, and the bitrate text field's action and changed, along with the NSView's update parameters and awake from nib.

We can use Cocoa bindings to tie our interface items to parameter values that our *main.applescript* code will receive. That's why the NSObjectController called "Parameters" is present in the main window. The use of bindings isn't compulsory, but in this case we can save ourselves a bit of coding by binding the "cbr" checkbox's value to a key "cbrSwitch" and the bitrate text field's value to a key "cbrText." We can now immediately bind the bitrate text field's enabled to the "cbr" checkbox; thus, the text field will be enabled or disabled automatically as the user checks or unchecks the check box. Also, later on we'll be able to supply a default value for the bitrate text field without writing any code. (Figure 27-7 shows the bindings for the bitrate text field as displayed in the inspector after creating them.)

This completes the design of the interface, so save and quit Interface Builder. Back in Xcode, now comes the touchiest part of the process—editing the *Info.plist* file. Starting with Xcode 2.1 this task is has been made somewhat easier, because it can be

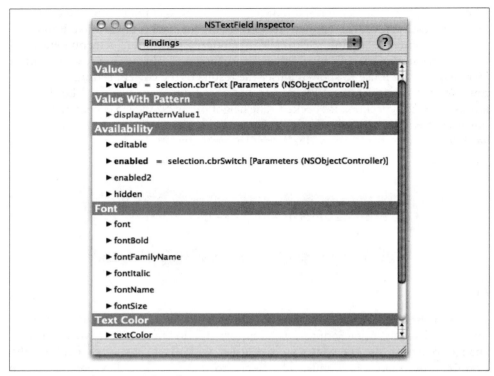

Figure 27-7. Binding an interface element

done mostly in the target's info window. Choose Project → Edit Active Project to bring up the info window, and switch to the Properties pane; in the lower half is the Collection popup menu, and the idea is to choose each of its items in turn and edit, as necessary, the members of that collection. Here are the settings I've elected to use:

Collection	Setting	Value
General	Action name	LAME Encode
General	Application	iTunes
General	Category	iTunes
General	Icon name	iTunes
Parameters	cbrSwitch	Type boolean; value 0
Parameters	cbrText	Type string; value 128
Parameters	exampleText	Type string; value "dummy"
Description	Summary	Encodes files to MP3.

Also, in the General collection, check "Can show when run" at the bottom of the window.

Observe the use of the Parameters settings to supply part of our interface with initial values by way of the bound keys; so, for example, the bitrate field will initially contain "128" because we say so here. It is crucial that the name and spelling for the keys, such as cbrText, should match exactly between Interface Builder (where the interface item is bound to that key) and here (where the key's initial value is given).

You should be wondering what the exampleText parameter is for, as we have no interface element bound to this key. This parameter is part of a trick that will be used later to communicate between our *ui.applescript* and *main.applescript* files, so read on and all will be made clear.

So much for the info window, but unfortunately we still need to edit *Info.plist* a bit further by hand. Select *Info.plist* in the project window and choose File → Open With Finder to bring up the file for editing in Property List Editor. (Under no circumstances should you attempt to edit this file by hand as a text file, as you will invariably make a mistake and render the file invalid as a property list.) Open each triangle and select and delete each line that we've left as a default comment (such as AMDInput and most of the other entries under AMDescription). When you're done with all that, save the file and quit Property List Editor. But, alas, we are *still* not done. We must also edit the localised versions of these settings, in the file called *InfoPlist.strings*. Open this file as a text file and delete everything except the CFBundleName and the AMName, and save it.

We are now ready, at long last, to write our code. Start with *ui.applescript*. Remember, the purpose of this script is to interact with our action's interface. The code is almost identical to what we'd put in a standalone application built with AppleScript Studio. I'll present the code a bit at a time.

Example 27-8 shows start of the code. The very first thing is to capture a reference to the NSView that contains the interface elements so that the rest of our code can refer to them. (Unlike our earlier standalone application example, we have no globally available named window, such as window "search", on which to base a reference to an interface element.) We have set the NSView to send us an awake from nib notification; this notification is guaranteed to arrive very early when our action's interface loads, and since theObject in this case in the NSView itself, we simply copy it to a property. To this and all the other action messages and notifications, we respond by calling our updateInterface handler; thus our interface will be "live," updating itself whenever the user does anything.

Example 27-8. Keeping the interface updated

```
property theView : missing value

on awake from nib theObject
    set theView to theObject
    updateInterface()
end awake from nib
```

Example 27-8. Keeping the interface updated (continued)

```
on action theObject
    updateInterface()
end action

on clicked theObject
    updateInterface()
end clicked

on changed theObject
    updateInterface()
end changed
```

Example 27-9 shows the updateInterface handler. The idea is to construct the lame command based on what the user has selected and typed in the interface, displaying this command in the example text field in the action's interface. To keep things simple, I have omitted to perform certain validations; in particular, the user can enter anything in the bitrate text field. (If the value is an unreasonable number, we use it anyway, and if it's not a number, we treat it as 128.)

Example 27-9. Constructing the lame command

```
on updateInterface()
    tell theView
        set s to title of popup button 1
        set s1 to "lame --preset "
        if (state of button "fastSwitch") is 1 then
            if state of button "cbrSwitch" is 0 then
                if s is in {"medium", "standard", "extreme"} then
                    set s1 to s1 & "fast "
                end if
            end if
        end if
        if (state of button "cbrSwitch") is 1 then
            try
                set s to "cbr " & (content of text field "cbrText" as integer)
            on error
                set s to "cbr 128"
            end try
        end if
        set content of text field "example" to s1 & s
    end tell
end updateInterface
```

Now comes the clever part (Example 27-10). We want *main.applescript* to receive, among its parameters, the updated value of the example text field, as this is the lame command to be sent along to the Terminal. These parameters are supplied as a record whose items are based on the parameters listed in *Info.plist*. That's why we created the exampleText parameter in *Info.plist*—to make it appear in the parameters record. In addition, we have implemented the update parameters event handler, whose purpose is exactly to give us a chance to modify the values in the parameters record. This event handler will be called just before the workflow runs; the record containing the parameters arrives under the name theParameters. So we update the interface one last time, and then we modify the exampleText item of theParameters and hand back the modified record.

Example 27-10. Passing a parameter to main.applescript

```
on update parameters theObject parameters theParameters
    updateInterface()
    set |exampleText| of theParameters to (content of text field "example" of theView)
    return theParameters
end update parameters
```

Now we are ready for *main.applescript* (Example 27-11). This script contains just one event handler, the run handler, which has been created for us. It takes two parameters: input, which is the output from the previous step in the workflow, and parameters, which contains the bound values from the interface along with the modifications made in our update parameters handler. We assume that input is a list of aliases; we convert these aliases to POSIX pathnames. We extract the exampleText item from the parameters record; this is the lame command the user wants us to perform. Now we form a shell command that will loop through each POSIX pathname in turn and hand it to our lame command. (The shell is assumed to be bash.) We send this shell command to the Terminal for execution. The Terminal will execute this command asynchronously (we have specified that are ignoring application responses), so our handler will end immediately; we must return something to serve as our action's output, even though the action produces no meaningful output, so on the principle of doing least harm we return the same list we received as input.

Example 27-11. The action's main script

```
on run {input, parameters}
    set myInput to (input as list)
    set L to {}
    repeat with anAlias in input
        set end of L to quoted form of POSIX path of anAlias
    end repeat
    set text item delimiters to space
    set theFiles to L as string
    set s to "arr=(" & theFiles & "); "
    set s to s & "for i in \"${arr[@]}\"; "
    set s to s & "do echo /usr/local/bin/" & |exampleText| of parameters & space
    set s to s & "\"$i\" \"${i%\\.*}.mp3\"; done"
    ignoring application responses
        tell application "Terminal" to do script s
    end ignoring
    return input
end run
```

The really cool part is that, because we have allowed it in *Info.plist*, the user can now choose "Show Action When Run" to display our action's interface in a workflow at runtime (Figure 27-8).

Figure 27-8. Choosing to show the action's interface at runtime

This gives the user maximum flexibility. Let's say, for example, that the user creates a workflow consisting of just our LAME Encode action, with "Show Action When Run" checked, and saves it as a Finder plug-in. This means that in the Finder this workflow will appear as a contextual menu item. The user can select some sound files in the Finder and, using the contextual menu, run this workflow. Our action's interface will appear as a dialog in the Finder! (See Figure 27-9.) The user can then specify the desired settings and continue with the workflow; the files will be converted to MP3 format, with feedback in the Terminal. This illustrates my point about an Automator action having just enough interface.

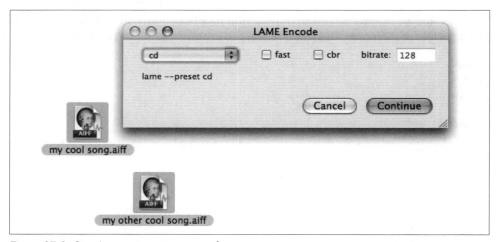

Figure 27-9. Our Automator action at work

Cocoa Scripting

Adding scriptability to an application that you write has been, in the past, not a task for the faint of heart. An 'aete'-format dictionary is difficult to create and maintain. On the programming side, the system needs to be able to call into your application when an Apple event arrives, so as your application starts up it must register the appropriate functions with the Apple Event Manager, and when an Apple event arrives, your code must parse it (no mean feat, especially if it involves a reference to an object in your application) and respond appropriately.

For this reason, programmers have often relied on sample code and application frameworks for assistance in making an application scriptable. There was some concern among programmers, therefore, when Mac OS X first emerged, over how it would be possible to take advantage of the Cocoa application framework and make an application scriptable at the same time. Since those early days, support for scriptability has gradually been folded into Cocoa; this is called *Cocoa scripting*. Cocoa scripting is still not perfect, but at least it has passed its infancy, and in Tiger it is easier than ever, thanks in part to the introduction of the sdef-based dictionary.

Thus, if you're a Cocoa programmer, Cocoa scripting in Tiger is a good way to start adding scriptability to your application. Getting started is the hardest part, though, for several reasons:

Multiple workplaces
> You have to coordinate the sdef dictionary with your code. If you make a mistake in either of them, or if you cause one of them not to match the other, some aspect of scriptability can fail mysteriously.

Scattered documentation
> The documentation is copious, but it's scattered in many different places, and elementary tasks and common problems are often not explained clearly. Also, Cocoa scripting uses "key-value coding," which means that often there is no way to look up a troublesome method in the documentation (because it *isn't* documented, except as a kind of template).

Tiresome testing
> Testing is tedious and difficult. Basically, you have to test by scripting your application; you must think of everything an end user might say with AppleScript to your application, and see whether your application responds coherently.

To help you get started with Cocoa scripting, here's a tutorial that adds the rudiments of scriptability to an existing Cocoa application, a little bit at a time. In order to make the example useful, this scriptability will include elements, properties, an enumeration, and a command. I'll assume you're using Tiger for development, and our example application will be scriptable on Tiger only; once you've achieved Tiger scriptability, it is possible to extend your scriptability to work on earlier systems (I'll talk about how to do that in the next section, "AppleScript Studio Scriptability").

Our Cocoa application, which is called Pairs, is very simple. We have a Person class, and we can create multiple instances of it. A Person has a name. Two Person instances can be paired, and this works like a monogamous marriage: once a Person is united to another, it can't be united to any other Person. The application presumably has some sort of interface, but I'm not going to concern myself with that. We assume that the application's basic functionality is working, and that it initializes itself on startup into some useful state—for example, it creates two initial Persons, named "Jack" and "Jill"—and now we want to go back and make it scriptable.

Here's the structure of the application before we start adding scriptability. The main controller class, instantiated in the nib, is MyObject. Here is its interface:

```
@interface MyObject : NSObject
{
    NSMutableArray* persons;
    NSMutableArray* pairs;
    // outlets go here
}
// method declarations go here
@end
```

The persons mutable array is made up of Person objects; each Person instance, as it is created, is added to this array. Here is the interface for Person:

```
@class Pair;
@interface Person : NSObject {
    NSString* name;
    Pair* pair;
}
- (NSString *)name;
- (void)setName:(NSString *)aName;
- (Pair *)pair;
- (void)setPair:(Pair *)aPair;
// other method declarations go here
@end
```

As you can see, we have accessors for our name instance variable. We also have a pair instance variable in the Person class, plus there is a pairs array in MyObject. It happens that the rest of our implementation is as follows. A Pair has two Person pointers, called person1 and person2. To pair two Persons, we make a new Pair object, add it to the pairs array, and point its two Person pointers at the two Persons; we also point the pair pointer of each of these paired Persons at this Pair object. Thus, a Pair and its Persons are double-linked; a Person knows it is paired because its `pair` instance variable isn't nil, and it can find the Person to which it is paired by looking at its Pair's Persons and finding the one different from itself.

The question of whether this way of implementing pairings is a particularly good one is beside the point. What's important is that we do *not* intend to expose this to the end user. You don't have to show the user everything that goes on behind the scenes! The end user will be thinking in terms of persons, not pairs, and we want our scripting interface to match the user's conceptual thought processes, not to reveal our backstage implementation.

So how should our scripting interface look to the AppleScript programmer? Clearly there needs to be a `person` class, and a `person` should have a `name` property. There can be multiple persons, so there should be a `persons` element. This is not a document-based application, so the only coherent location for the `persons` element is at the top level of the object model—that is, it will be an element of the `application` class.

Now we'll create our sdef-format dictionary and add it to the project. The best way to make the dictionary is with the wonderful Sdef Editor application (see Appendix C for this and other Cocoa scripting resources). Let's call the dictionary *pairs.sdef*. Then to make our application scriptable through this dictionary, we must add the following lines to our project's *Info.plist* file:

```
<key>NSAppleScriptEnabled</key>
<string>YES</string>
<key>OSAScriptingDefinition</key>
<string>pairs.sdef</string>
```

The first step in creating an sdef is to give it whatever common commands we intend to implement. For example, we want the user to be able to ask how many persons there are, using the `count` command. This won't be possible all by itself; we have to include the `count` command in the dictionary. Common commands can be found in the Standard Suite (see "Suites" in Chapter 20), which you can access in Sdef Editor by choosing File → Open Standard Suite → NSCoreSuite. The idea here is to put NSCoreSuite into the dictionary and then immediately remove from it everything we don't need; in this case, the remaining commands will be just `count`, `delete`, `exists`, and `make`—the bare minimum needed for working with a collection of persons. (There is no need to include `get` and `set`, because they are short-circuited, and we don't need an entry for `quit` because every application can do that.)

Now we make a new suite, which I'll call the Pairs Suite. I like to move the application class into this, and I'll simplify the application class, leaving just the `name`, `frontmost`, and `version` properties, which are implemented automatically. Now we can add the `person` class with its `name` property, and give the application class a `person` element.

I assume you can figure out how to work with Sdef Editor, so let's focus on the text version of the result. I'll present it in two parts. First we have the automatically generated Standard Suite:

```xml
<?xml version="1.0" encoding="UTF-8"?>
<!DOCTYPE dictionary SYSTEM "file://localhost/System/Library/DTDs/sdef.dtd">
<dictionary title="Pairs Dictionary">
    <suite name="Standard Suite" code="????"
    description="Common classes and commands for most applications.">
        <cocoa name="NSCoreSuite"/>
        <command name="count" code="corecnte" description="Return the number of
         elements of a particular class within an object.">
            <cocoa class="NSCountCommand"/>
            <direct-parameter description="the object whose elements are to be
             counted" type="specifier"/>
            <parameter name="each" code="kocl" description="The class of objects to
             be counted." type="type" optional="yes">
                <cocoa key="ObjectClass"/>
            </parameter>
            <result description="the number of elements" type="integer"/>
        </command>
        <command name="delete" code="coredelo" description="Delete an object.">
            <cocoa class="NSDeleteCommand"/>
            <direct-parameter description="the object to delete" type="specifier"/>
        </command>
        <command name="exists" code="coredoex"
        description="Verify if an object exists.">
            <cocoa class="NSExistsCommand"/>
            <direct-parameter description="the object in question"
             type="specifier"/>
            <result description="true if it exists, false if not" type="boolean"/>
        </command>
        <command name="make" code="corecrel" description="Make a new object.">
            <cocoa name="Create" class="NSCreateCommand"/>
            <parameter name="new" code="kocl"
            description="The class of the new object." type="type">
                <cocoa key="ObjectClass"/>
            </parameter>
            <parameter name="at" code="insh" description="The location at which to
             insert the object." type="location specifier" optional="yes">
                <cocoa key="Location"/>
            </parameter>
            <parameter name="with data" code="data" description="The initial data
             for the object." type="any" optional="yes">
                <cocoa key="ObjectData"/>
            </parameter>
            <parameter name="with properties" code="prdt" description="The initial
             values for properties of the object." type="record" optional="yes">
                <cocoa key="KeyDictionary"/>
            </parameter>
            <result description="to the new object" type="specifier"/>
        </command>
    </suite>
```

Next comes the Pairs Suite. The application's name, frontmost, and version properties were generated automatically; the application's person element, and the person class itself, were added by you. The material you've actually had to create is shown here in bold type:

```
<suite name="Pairs Suite" code="pAIR" description="The Pairs suite">
    <class name="application" code="capp" description="An application&apos;s top
    level scripting object.">
        <cocoa class="NSApplication"/>
        <element description="The persons." type="person">
            <cocoa key="persons"/>
        </element>
        <property name="name" code="pnam"
        description="The name of the application." type="text" access="r"/>
        <property name="frontmost" code="pisf" description="Is this the
         frontmost (active) application?" type="boolean" access="r">
            <cocoa key="isActive"/>
        </property>
        <property name="version" code="vers"
        description="The version of the application." type="text" access="r"/>
    </class>
    <class name="person" code="pRSN" description="A person." plural="persons">
        <cocoa class="Person"/>
        <property name="name" code="pnam"
        description="The person&apos;s name." type="text">
            <cocoa key="name"/>
        </property>
    </class>
</suite>
</dictionary>
```

Even though only a dozen lines were added by you, there's lots of room to go wrong here. (I speak from experience.) The following points are worth emphasizing:

You must make up some four-letter codes.

The codes 'pAIR' and 'pRSN' are arbitrary. It is crucial, however, that they not overlap with existing four-letter codes. One way to feel confident of this is to use some capital letters, as we've done here; Apple reserves to itself all four-letter codes consisting entirely of lowercase letters.

You must use existing four-letter codes.

The name property of the person class has code 'pnam'. This is a standard property, already defined in AppleScript, and it is essential to get the code right.

You must match Cocoa keys with your code.

The Cocoa key for the person element of the application class is "persons"; that's because persons is the name of the instance variable in MyObject through which the collection of Person objects is accessed. The Cocoa key for the person class is "Person"; that's because Person is the name of the Cocoa class implementing this AppleScript class. The Cocoa key for the person class's name property is "name"; that's because name is the name of the instance variable in Person representing the name property. A mistake here—even a discrepancy in capitalization between the Objective-C code, on the one hand, and the Cocoa key in the sdef, on the other—will cause scriptability to fail.

The reason Cocoa keys in the sdef are so crucial is that Cocoa scripting uses key-value coding to find its way through your code. *Key-value coding* (or *KVC*) is an informal protocol that takes advantage of Objective-C's dynamism and introspection. It uses a string as a key to hunt for names among your instance variables and methods. The object model is navigated by way of a path leading down from the application class. At every step of a path, your classes must be KVC-compliant (meaning that the right instance variables or methods are present) or things won't work.

In our application, so far, there is just one simple little path. The scriptability framework will start with the application class. It has a person element whose Cocoa key is "persons." So the framework looks in MyObject to see if it is KVC-compliant with respect to to the key "persons." Is it? Yes, because it has an instance variable named persons. That instance variable is an NSMutableArray; that's a built-in class which is itself KVC-compliant. The contents of this NSMutableArray are Person objects; that fits with the Cocoa key for this class, which says that everything in persons should be a Person. And Person is KVC-compliant with respect to "name," because it has a name accessor method and a setName: accessor method.

We build our application and run it, and point Script Editor at it, to test our scriptability—and it doesn't work! For example, we say:

```
tell application "Pairs"
    get person 1
end tell
```

and we get an error message in the console:

```
[<NSApplication 0x314220> valueForUndefinedKey:]: this class is not key value coding-
compliant for the key persons
```

The reason is simple: the very first step in the path is incorrectly set up. As our sdef says, the application class's Cocoa key is "NSApplication." But we want the path to start in MyObject, not in NSApplication. We must not change the Cocoa key for the application class; rather, we need a way to tell the scriptability framework to jump from NSApplication to MyObject as it descends the path. One very simple way to do this is to make MyObject the *delegate* of NSApplication; you can specify this by a connection in the nib. We must also write some code in MyObject announcing that it, as the application delegate, implements certain keys:

```
- (BOOL)application:(NSApplication *)sender delegateHandlesKey:(NSString *)key {
    if ([key isEqualToString: @"persons"]) return YES;
    return NO;
}
```

We add that code to MyObject, which is now also NSApplication's delegate. We build and run the application, and we test it in Script Editor; lo and behold, it works!

```
tell application "Pairs"
    count persons -- 2
    name of person 1 -- "Jack"
    name of person 2 -- "Jill"
    name of every person -- {"Jack", "Jill"}
    name of every person whose name ends with "k" -- {"Jack"}
    exists person "Jack" -- true
    exists person "Matt" -- false
    delete person "Jack"
    count persons -- 1
    get name of person 1 -- "Jill"
    set name of person 1 to "Mannie"
    name of every person -- {"Mannie"}
end tell
```

This shows the advantage of starting with an application framework. We've added to an existing application no more than a couple of lines of code and a dozen lines of dictionary, and presto, we're scripting our application. We can get and set a property; we can count elements, delete an element, and test by property for the existence of an element; we can even use a boolean test specifier.

Having achieved this initial intoxicating success, we should consider some improvements and refactoring before proceeding any further:

Better accessors

So far, our code lends itself more or less by accident to KVC. For example, access to the person element is possible only because there happens to be an instance variable called persons in MyObject. We should implement our accessors in a more deliberate fashion, in accordance with the expectations of key-value coding and the scriptability framework.

Separate accessors

It will be wise to separate the scriptability accessors from the programming accessors. For example, when the user changes the name property of a person, the scriptability framework is using the setName: accessor, which is exactly the same method our own Objective-C code would use to change the name instance variable of a Person. But our code might need to respond differently depending on who is calling; our code should be able to do things that a user should not be able to do through AppleScript (think of a read-only property). We should nominate a different Cocoa key in the dictionary and create a different set of scriptability framework accessors.

Separate code

As long as we're going to have separate accessors, we might want to separate the code that responds to scripting from the code that implements our application's internal functionality. A common architecture is to implement scriptability as an Objective-C category on the existing classes.

Add checks and error handling

At present, our application is very open to the user's commands; for example, a script can delete a person, give two persons the same name, or create a person with no name. We will want to close some of these doors and return a runtime error message to the script when the user tries to do something we disapprove of.

Implement objectSpecifier

Every AppleScript class that our application declares should have in its corresponding Objective-C class an implementation of the `objectSpecifier` method. This is what allows an object reference such as `person "Matt" of application "Pairs"` to be returned to a script when the user says something like `get person 1` or `make new person`. Without an `objectSpecifier` implementation, the script will receive a meaningless reference.

Here's code that illustrates these points. First, I've changed two of the Cocoa keys in the dictionary: the `person` element of the `application` class now has Cocoa key "personsArray," and the `name` property of the `person` class now has Cocoa key "personName." These changes will allow our code to respond separately to the messages sent by the scriptability framework. I've moved all the scriptability code into its own file, where it is implemented through categories on the existing classes. I'll present it a piece at a time. First we have a general utility routine implemented as a category on NSObject, because every scriptable class will need it:

```
@implementation NSObject (MNscriptability)

- (void) returnError:(int)n string:(NSString*)s {
    NSScriptCommand* c = [NSScriptCommand currentCommand];
    [c setScriptErrorNumber:n];
    if (s) [c setScriptErrorString:s];
}
@end
```

Observe how to return an error to AppleScript: you fetch the pending command and assign it an error number and, optionally, an error message to accompany it. (See Figure 3-1 in Chapter 3; the system holds out the incoming Apple event to your application like an envelope, from which you read the message and into which you insert any response, whether it's a result or an error.)

Next, we have the category on Person:

```
@implementation Person (MNscriptability)

- (NSScriptObjectSpecifier *)objectSpecifier {
    NSScriptClassDescription* appDesc
        = (NSScriptClassDescription*)[NSApp classDescription];
    return [[[NSNameSpecifier alloc]
        initWithContainerClassDescription:appDesc
        containerSpecifier:nil
        key:@"personsArray"
        name:[self name]] autorelease];
}
```

```
- (NSString *)personName {return name;}

- (void)setPersonName:(NSString *)aName {
    if ([[NSScriptCommand currentCommand] isKindOfClass: [NSCreateCommand class]])
        [self setName:aName];
    else
        [master scripterWantsToChangeName:aName of:self];
}
@end
```

The implementation of objectSpecifier allows proper object references to be returned to AppleScript. We must specify the object's container, which in this case is the application class, and we must provide a key ("personsArray") matching the Cocoa key in the dictionary for how this element is accessed from that container.

Next we have the scriptability accessors for the name property, now keyed through "personName." A tricky architectural difficulty arises immediately, illustrating why it's so hard to get started with Cocoa scripting.

In good object-oriented programming, objects are assigned appropriate tasks. Some objects are just data ("model"); other objects control that data ("controller"). In my application, a Person in MyObject's persons array is just data; it is MyObject that should be responsible for creating and validating a Person. But key-value coding slams into your existing application like a sudden side wind, ignoring your architecture and surprising your code. When the user tries to change the name of an existing person, it is Person's setPersonName: that is called, even though it is MyObject that should decide whether the new name is valid. Accordingly, I've given Person a master instance variable pointing at its creator, which in this case is MyObject; when the user asks to change a person's name, the request is shuttled off to MyObject, which will decide the suitability of the requested change and comply if appropriate.

But it gets worse. We have an additional problem when the user says make new person, because at that moment the scriptability framework creates a Person object by calling alloc and init directly on our Person class; any designated initializer is ignored, and MyObject doesn't have a chance to perform initializations or pass judgment. There is no easy way to prevent this (such as saying to the framework, "When you want to create a Person, call such-and-such a method"). Furthermore, if the user's command also says with properties {name:"whatever"}, setPersonName: is called to set the new name. This puts our code in a quandary; there is no master, so there is no one to judge the suitability of the new name.

Fortunately, if the user is creating this person (a condition for which we can test, as the code demonstrates), the scriptability framework will send the resulting Person object to MyObject anyway, for insertion into the persons collection. So we set the name as requested, because MyObject will eventually get a chance to pass judgment on this proposed new person—and initialize it properly.

Now let's talk about the category on MyObject. Here's the first part of it:

```objc
@implementation MyObject (MNscriptability)

- (BOOL)application:(NSApplication *)sender delegateHandlesKey:(NSString *)key {
    if ([key isEqualToString: @"personsArray"]) return YES;
    return NO;
}
- (unsigned int)countOfPersonsArray {
    return [persons count];
}
- (Person *)objectInPersonsArrayAtIndex:(unsigned int)i {
    return [persons objectAtIndex: i];
}
```

First, we have our same old application:delegateHandlesKey: method. Next, we've implemented our own access to the persons array through the Cocoa key "personsArray"; we will report its size and return an object in it, so that the scriptability framework never gets its hands on the array directly.

Here's more of the MyObject category:

```objc
- (BOOL) canGivePerson:(Person*)p name:(NSString*)name {
    if (!name || [name isEqualToString:@""]) {
        [self returnError:errOSACantAssign
            string:@"Can't give person empty name."];
        return NO;
    }
    if ([self existsPersonWithName: name]) {
        [self returnError:errOSACantAssign
            string:@"Can't give person same name as existing person."];
        return NO;
    }
    return YES;
}
- (void) scripterWantsToChangeName:(NSString*)n of:(Person*)p {
    if ([n isEqualToString: [p name]]) return; // nothing to do
    if (![self canGivePerson:p name:n]) return;
    [p setName: n];
}
- (void)insertObject:(Person *)p inPersonsArrayAtIndex:(unsigned int)index {
    if (![self canGivePerson:p name:[p name]]) return;
    [p setMaster: self];
    [persons insertObject:p atIndex:index];
}
- (void)insertInPersonsArray:(Person *)p {
    if (![self canGivePerson:p name:[p name]]) return;
    [p setMaster: self];
    [persons addObject:p];
}
```

First we have a general name-checking routine. If the user wants to assign a person a name, either as part of creating that person or altering the name of an existing person, we report an error to AppleScript if the name is the empty string or matches that of an existing person. Then we have the method that will be called by Person if the user tries to change the name of an existing person: either we return an error or we comply by setting the name. Finally, we have two methods that may be called when the user says make new person; I don't actually know which is called when, but it appears they are both needed for KVC-compliance so I've implemented both.

This is indicative of another difficulty that besets the new scriptability programmer. There is no straightforward documentation stating directly what methods will be sought and called, and when, and in what order, and what the scriptability framework will do if it fails to find a method it's looking for (will it default to a different method, or will it throw an error declaring your class not KVC-compliant, or will it return a mysterious error to the script, or what?). So you can never be quite sure what you need to implement and what method the framework may decide to call at any moment. Here you can see me working around this difficulty by implementing the same functionality twice. And I do the same thing in the last part of the MyObject category:

```
-(void)removeObjectFromPersonsArrayAtIndex:(unsigned int)index {
    [self returnError:OSAMessageNotUnderstood string:nil];
}
-(void)removeFromPersonsArrayAtIndex:(unsigned int)index {
    [self returnError:OSAMessageNotUnderstood string:nil];
}
@end
```

That code is to prevent the user from deleting a person. I've implemented two methods that do the same thing because the framework seems to complain on different occasions if I fail to implement either one, and I don't know why; lacking clear documentation, it seems easiest to fall back on a double implementation and move on.

With all of that in place, the previous test script still works perfectly. In addition, our application can now successfully return an object reference; and it now responds coherently to the user's attempts to do things we don't permit:

```
tell application "Pairs"
    get name of every person -- {"Jack", "Jill"}
    delete person "Jack"
    -- error: Pairs got an error: person "Jack" doesn't understand the delete message
    make new person
    -- error: Pairs got an error: Can't give person empty name
    make new person at end with properties {name:"Moe"}
    -- person "Moe" of application "Pairs"
    set name of person "Jill" to "Mannie"
    set name of person 1 to "Mannie"
    -- error: Pairs got an error: Can't give person same name as existing person
    make new person with properties {name:"Mannie"}
    -- error: Pairs got an error: Can't give person same name as existing person
end tell
```

Now let's add some more features. Let's give a person an additional property: gender, which is either male or female. This is simply to illustrate how you implement an enumeration. The Person class will need an instance variable, gender, whose value is an int, and we should probably add accessors gender and setGender. To define the enumeration and its enumerators for AppleScript, you want something in the dictionary like this:

```
<enumeration name="genders" code="gEND" description="A gender." inline="2">
    <enumerator name="male" code="gMAL" description="Male gender."/>
    <enumerator name="female" code="gFEM" description="Female gender."/>
</enumeration>
```

Back in our Objective-C code, we define the same enumeration, like this:

```
enum {
    MALE='gMAL',
    FEMALE='gFEM'
} genders;
```

The match between the four-letter codes in the dictionary and our Objective-C code is crucial. Now, in the dictionary, we add the property to the person class:

```
<property name="gender" code="gNdR" description="The person&apos;s gender.">
    <cocoa key="personGender"/>
</property>
```

(Observe that I do not make the common mistake of giving the property the same four-letter code as the class.) The Cocoa key "personGender" means that in our Person class the accessors personGender and setPersonGender: will be called. Implementation of these in the category on Person is straightforward; in my implementation I've allowed (and indeed required) the user to supply a gender when creating a person, but I've made it illegal for the user to change the gender of an existing person.

Now let's implement a verb. Let's call this pair, and we'll have it apply to two person objects. One will be the direct object; the other will appear after a parameter, to:

```
pair person 1 to person 2
```

Verbs (commands) are implemented in two different ways in Cocoa scripting. If a verb basically applies to a single object, it can appear in the Objective-C code as a method in the class that corresponds to the class of that object. This is called *object-first dispatch*. (The other way of implementing a command, *verb-first dispatch*, is demonstrated later in this chapter.) Having defined the command in the dictionary, you then specify in the dictionary every class that can serve as the direct object to this command. So the dictionary will contain this definition of the command:

```
<command name="pair" code="pAiRpAiR">
    <direct-parameter description="One person." type="person"/>
    <parameter name="to" code="othR" description="The other person." type="person">
        <cocoa key="otherPerson"/>
    </parameter>
</command>
```

And in our person class, the dictionary now contains the following:

```
<responds-to name="pair">
    <cocoa method="scripterSaysPair:"/>
</responds-to>
```

What this means is that when the user invokes the pair command, a message scripterSaysPair: will be sent to the Person object who represents the direct object of the command. The parameter to this method is an NSScriptCommand object whose evaluatedArguments method yields an NSDictionary containing the command's additional parameters, accessible through their Cocoa keys; in this case, there is just one additional parameter, and its key will be "otherPerson." So now we can implement scripterSaysPair: in our category on the Person class:

```
- (void)scripterSaysPair:(NSScriptCommand*)command {
    Person* p1 = [command evaluatedReceivers];
    Person* p2 = [[command evaluatedArguments] valueForKey:@"otherPerson"];
    if (self != p1 || self == p2) {
        [self returnError:errOSACantAssign string:@"Invalid pairing."];
        return;
    }
    [master scripterWantsToPair:p1 with:p2];
}
```

After an error check, the command is passed on to MyObject for processing. The routine in MyObject (not shown here) does some more error-checking (making sure neither of the person objects is already paired) and then does whatever it usually does to pair two Persons. I use this architecture in order to distribute responsibilities appropriately; a Person can look to see whether the pair command makes basic sense, but it is MyObject, as master of the persons collection, who decides whether two Persons can be paired and, if so, pairs them.

It would be nice to complete the picture by adding a read-only boolean paired property to the person class, stating whether the person has been paired, along with a read-only partner property that returns a reference to the other person in the pair. These correspond to no instance variable of the Person class, which just goes to show that a sensible scripting interface needn't be like the underlying implementation.

```
- (id) personPartner {
    Pair* myPair = [self pair];
    if (!myPair) return [NSNull null];
    return ([myPair person1] == self ? [myPair person2] : [myPair person1]);
}
- (void) setPersonPartner:(id)newPartner {
    [self returnError:errOSACantAssign string:@"Partner property is read-only."];
}
- (BOOL) personPaired {
    return ([self pair] != nil);
}
- (void) setPersonPaired:(BOOL)newPaired {
    [self returnError:errOSACantAssign string:@"Paired property is read-only."];
}
```

The personPartner method returns an NSNull instance if the person hasn't been paired; that's how you cause missing value to be returned to AppleScript. Finally, observe that you must implement setter accessors even though the dictionary marks these properties as read-only.

 When the user requests an object that doesn't exist (a person whose index number is too large, for example), an ugly and obnoxious "NSReceiverScriptError" runtime error message is returned by the scriptability framework. Various workarounds have been proposed, and I have elsewhere tentatively proposed one of my own, but the truth is that this is a serious flaw in the underlying framework and needs to be corrected at that level.

AppleScript Studio Scriptability

It is natural to wonder whether an AppleScript Studio application is scriptable. The news here is something of a mixed bag.

AppleScript programmers who are accustomed to writing applets, which are inherently scriptable, will be disappointed to learn that AppleScript Studio applications are not scriptable in quite the same easy way. The mere presence of a top-level entity in an applet's script makes the applet scriptable with respect to that entity, but no such thing is true of an AppleScript Studio application. So, for example, you cannot simply tell our SearchTidBITS application to displayResults() (see Example 27-7). The problem is that an AppleScript Studio application is not merely an application shell wrapped around a script; it's a true Cocoa application. So your message isn't magically routed to the correct script, because in the way stands the entire mechanism of a Cocoa application.

On the other hand, an AppleScript Studio application is scriptable with respect to the entire *AppleScriptKit.sdef* dictionary, which is actually visible to users though a script editor application as if it were your application's own dictionary. This means that whatever built-in commands you can give from within the code of an AppleScript Studio application, a user can give from outside it. For example:

```
tell application "SearchTidBITS"
    activate
    tell window "search"
        tell matrix 1
            set content of cell 1 to "AppleScript"
            set content of cell 3 to "Matt Neuburg"
        end tell
        tell button 1 to perform action
    end tell
end tell
```

That's exactly the same as if the user had typed values into two of the text fields and then pressed the Search button! Initially this may sound exciting, but most Apple-Script Studio programmers ultimately regret that things work this way, for the following reasons:

It's messy.

The user who looks at your AppleScript Studio application's dictionary sees the entire confusing *AppleScriptKit.sdef* dictionary, which says nothing as to your application's purpose or what the user can appropriately do when scripting it.

It's overly free.

The user can do things to your application that a user really shouldn't be able to do. To give a simple example, if an interface element is tied to a script, that script is available through that interface element; the user can get its script, and even worse, can set its script. For example:

```
tell application "SearchTidBITS"
    script s
    end script
    set the script of button 1 of window "search" to s
end tell
```

That code disables the Search button; its functionality has been replaced, and the only way to restore it is to quit the application and start it up again.

It's incomplete.

The user can manipulate the interface, but can't call any event handlers. You'll notice that in the earlier example it was possible to press the Search button programmatically because there is a perform action command, but it is impossible to tell the application to clicked:

```
tell application "SearchTidBITS"
    clicked button 1 of window "search"
    -- error: SearchTidBITS got an error: NSReceiversCantHandleCommandScriptError
end tell
```

You might wonder, as you can get the script of an interface element, whether it might be possible to route a message to that script. This is a clever idea, and at first it looks promising:

```
tell application "SearchTidBITS"
    set s to (get script of button 1 of window "search")
    tell s
        urlEncode("hi there") -- "hi+there"
    end tell
end tell
```

It turns out, however, that when you get the script of an interface element, it's a copy. The real script object, the one that the interface element is actually using at that moment, was copied and loaded when the application started up; what you've got is a different script object, completely unbound from its proper context in the running application—for example, its top-level entity values are not the same as the current top-level entity values of the real script. (This is a serious problem for Apple-Script Studio programmers as well, because it complicates communication between scripts and makes the reliable storage of true globals rather an elaborate exercise.)

Thus an AppleScript Studio application is automatically scriptable, but only in a messy, disordered way. On the other hand, because an AppleScript Studio application is a Cocoa application, you might wonder whether you can add customized scriptability to your AppleScript Studio application through Cocoa scripting. You can, although there are two major shortcomings to this approach:

Big dictionary

You can add your own suite and your own terms to the dictionary, but you can't at the same time suppress the default AppleScript Studio dictionary. The user might not even notice your custom scriptability amid the vast wash of confusing and useless information.

Communication between languages

It's obvious how AppleScript can talk to Objective-C classes and instances (using call method), but it is far from clear how Objective-C can talk to AppleScript. This is essentially the same problem raised a moment ago; your Objective-C code can't get direct access to the AppleScript script objects that are currently loaded and functioning as the scripts attached to the interface.

With those caveats, it is possible to add Cocoa scripting to an AppleScript Studio application. The procedure is straightforward, except for one thing: you can't use the sdef dictionary format to implement your scriptability. To put it technically, if you add the OSAScriptingDefinition key to your *Info.plist*, AppleScript Studio itself will break and your application will be stripped of its functionality. Therefore you must implement scriptability the old way, with a resource file. This is not such a terrible thing, as it's what you would have to do in order to implement scriptability for a pre-Tiger application anyway. And besides, you can *develop* your scriptability using an sdef file; you simply can't *implement* it with an sdef file in the built application. Thus, as the application is built, you must transform your sdef file into a different format, one that is compatible with earlier systems; and it happens that there's a Unix tool, sdp, that makes this easy to do.

To illustrate, we'll add some basic custom scriptability to the SearchTidBITS application developed earlier in this chapter with AppleScript Studio. The first step is to whip out the Sdef Editor application and create the sdef file. Here it is (for brevity, descriptions are omitted):

```
<?xml version="1.0" encoding="UTF-8"?>
<!DOCTYPE dictionary SYSTEM "file://localhost/System/Library/DTDs/sdef.dtd">
<dictionary title="Dictionary">
    <suite name="SearchTidBITS Suite" code="sTBs">
```

```
<class name="application" code="capp" plural="applications"
inherits="ASKApplicationSuite.NSApplication">
    <cocoa class="NSApplication"/>
    <property name="search text" code="sTBt" description="" type="text">
        <cocoa key="searchText"/>
    </property>
    <property name="search title" code="sTBi" description="" type="text">
        <cocoa key="searchTitle"/>
    </property>
    <property name="search author" code="sTBa" description="" type="text">
        <cocoa key="searchAuthor"/>
    </property>
</class>
<command name="do search" code="sTIDdSRC" description="">
    <cocoa class="MyScriptCommand"/>
</command>
</suite>
</dictionary>
```

The most important thing here is to hook the application class in this file to the existing AppleScript Studio application class. The lines in boldface are absolutely crucial. Get one of these values wrong and the integration between Cocoa scripting and AppleScript Studio will fail. The four-letter code must be 'capp'; the inheritance must specify "ASKApplicationSuite.NSApplication" as the superclass; and the Cocoa class must be "NSApplication."

Save the sdef file as *searchTidBITS.sdef*. Open the *SearchTidBITS* project in Xcode and import the sdef file into the project; elect to copy it into the project folder but do *not* add it to the target. We want this file to live in the project folder for development purposes, but we do not want it to be copied into the built application.

What we do want copied into the built application is a resource file containing the dictionary, along with *scriptSuite* and *scriptTerminology* files to implement Cocoa scriptability (see "Dictionary Formats" in Chapter 3). To arrange for this to happen automatically, choose Project → New Build Phase → New Shell Script Build Phase. The info window for the run script phase will appear; in the script field, enter this Unix code:

```
/usr/bin/sdp -fast -o "$BUILT_PRODUCTS_DIR/$FULL_PRODUCT_NAME/Contents/Resources"
"$SOURCE_ROOT/searchTidBITS.sdef"
```

When you build and run the application, you'll find that it runs normally; if you examine its dictionary in a script editor application, you'll find that the Search-TidBITS Suite is present and that there are three new application properties (search text, search title, and search author) and a new command (do search).

Now let's add implementation code. We'll need a place to put it, so we'll create a new Cocoa class. (I assume you know how to do this, so my instructions will be very abbreviated.) Open *MainMenu.nib* and, in Interface Builder, create a new NSObject subclass called MyObject, instantiate it, and make the instance the application delegate by making the Cocoa connection between the File's Owner and MyObject. Now save MyObject into the project. Save, and quit Interface Builder. Back in Xcode, here's the implementation code for MyObject:

```
@implementation MyObject

- (BOOL) application: (id) sender delegateHandlesKey:(NSString*) key {
    NSLog(@"handles key? %@", key);
    if ([key isEqualToString: @"searchText"])
        return YES;
    if ([key isEqualToString: @"searchTitle"])
        return YES;
    if ([key isEqualToString: @"searchAuthor"])
        return YES;
    return NO;
}
- (NSAppleEventDescriptor*) doAS: (NSString*) s {
    NSAppleScript* as = [[NSAppleScript alloc] initWithSource:s];
    NSAppleEventDescriptor* d = [as executeAndReturnError:nil];
    [as release];
    return d;
}
- (NSString*) searchText {
    NSString* s = @"tell current application "
        @"to get content of cell 1 of matrix 1 of window \"search\"";
    return [[self doAS:s] stringValue];
}
- (void) setSearchText: (NSString*) t {
    NSString* s = [NSString stringWithFormat: @"tell current application "
        @"to set content of cell 1 of matrix 1 of window \"search\" "
        @"to \"%@\"", t];
    [self doAS:s];
}
// ... and so on ...
@end
```

The accessors for "searchTitle" and "searchAuthor" are omitted for brevity; you should be able to write them easily. (They are exactly the same as the accessors for "searchText" except for the names, and except for the cell numbers, which are 2 and 3 respectively.)

This implementation works around the problem of communicating from Objective-C code to AppleScript code by not even trying to do so. Instead, we communicate with the interface. We know that our AppleScript Studio application is scriptable through the native AppleScript Studio commands, so we use them directly, just as we do in our AppleScript code, to drive the interface. We can do this readily; the current application is SearchTidBITS itself, so we are sending a message to ourselves. But this is still a skanky solution: instead of sending a message from one region of code to another, we are using the interface as a kind of drop box. We can't tell our Apple-Script code to set its internal textSought, titleSought, and authorSought globals, so we content ourselves with leaving the corresponding values in the interface, where the AppleScript code will find them later.

So now let's tell the AppleScript code to find them, by implementing the do search command. This command doesn't take a direct object, so we'll implement it using verb-first dispatch. (See the earlier section "Cocoa Scripting" for the other way of implementing a command, object-first dispatch.) It works like this: in the sdef, you declare a Cocoa class representing your command; in your project, you create an NSScriptCommand subclass with the same name. We've declared in the sdef that our class is called MyScriptCommand, so now we create that class. In Xcode, choose File → New File, making the new file an Objective-C class and calling it MyScript-Command. In the header file, make MyScriptCommand a subclass of NSScriptCom-mand. In the implementation file, enter this code:

```
@implementation MyScriptCommand

- (NSAppleEventDescriptor*) doAS: (NSString*) s {
    NSAppleScript* as = [[NSAppleScript alloc] initWithSource:s];
    NSAppleEventDescriptor* d = [as executeAndReturnError:nil];
    [as release];
    return d;
}
- (id) performDefaultImplementation {
    NSString* s = @"tell current application "
        @" to perform action of button 1 of window \"search\"";
    [self doAS:s];
    return nil;
}
@end
```

In our override of the performDefaultImplementation method, we get to implement our own functionality for this command. Once more we have not tried to solve the problem of communicating from Objective-C to AppleScript; instead, we have again used the interface as a medium of indirect communication. We can't call the clicked handler directly, so instead we effectively press the Search button, using an Apple-Script Studio command that permits us to do so, and this triggers the clicked handler already tied to that button.

Even though we can't send messages from Objective-C to AppleScript, perhaps we can improve the way we send messages to the interface. At present we are forming a script as text on the fly and then compiling and executing it. This way is very slow, uses a lot of unnecessary overhead, and may be justly charged with a certain fragility. To give just one example, if the user says set search text to with a value that contains a quote character, our setSearchText: method will break, because of the blithe way it constructs a literal string. That's clearly a bug.

I will conclude, therefore, by demonstrating a more elegant architecture that uses a compiled script as an intermediary (a "trampoline"). We will call into this compiled script with an Apple event, and the compiled script will send an Apple event to our interface. Apple events are fast, and running a compiled script is fast; it's compiling text on the fly that's slow. And this approach will be immune to the bug with strings containing a quote, because we will never "unpack" an AppleScript string—we will pass it along directly to the compiled script, and we know that this will work because the string must have been a valid AppleScript string to start with (or we could never have received it in the first place).

Start with a script encapsulating the AppleScript code we're already using to get and set the contents of a form cell in the Search window:

```
on setCell(n, s)
    tell current application
        using terms from application "Automator"
            set content of cell n of matrix 1 of window "search" to s
        end using terms from
    end tell
end setCell
on getCell(n)
    tell current application
        using terms from application "Automator"
            get content of cell n of matrix 1 of window "search"
        end using terms from
    end tell
end getCell
```

The terms blocks, targeting Automator, are a trick: in order for the central lines to compile, we must resolve them with respect to AppleScript Studio's terminology; Automator's dictionary contains this terminology.

Now compile the script (at which point Automator's task is done, because it is never actually targeted), and save it as *trampoline.scpt*. Add it to the SearchTidBITS project so that it will be copied into the built application bundle.

Because we might be using this script any time the user targets the SearchTidBITS application, we'll save time by loading it once and for all into an NSAppleScript* instance variable (called trampoline) as our application starts up:

```
- (void) awakeFromNib {
    NSString* path = [[NSBundle mainBundle] pathForResource:@"trampoline"
                          ofType:@"scpt"];
    NSURL* url = [NSURL fileURLWithPath:path];
    trampoline = [[NSAppleScript alloc] initWithContentsOfURL:url error:nil];
}
```

When the user wants to get or set any of the properties search text or search title or search author, we will call the corresponding handler of *trampoline.scpt*, along with appropriate parameter values. We know how to execute a script as a whole in Cocoa using NSAppleScript, but how do we call a particular handler, and how do we pass it parameters? The solution is the very same mechanism by which scriptability of user handlers in an applet is implemented (see "Applet Scriptability," earlier in this chapter)—the 'ascr\psbr' Apple event. We must form this Apple event more or less manually, but it isn't hard to do. Here's how. Observe that for the sake of brevity and clarity I've issued a #define equating "Desc" to the lengthy term "NSAppleEventDescriptor" which would otherwise clutter up the code.

```
#define Desc NSAppleEventDescriptor
- (Desc*) callSub:(NSString*)handler params:(Desc*)firstParam, ... {
    Desc* list = [Desc listDescriptor];
    int i=0; va_list ppp; va_start(ppp, firstParam);
    Desc* aParam = firstParam;
    while(aParam) {
        [list insertDescriptor:aParam atIndex:++i];
        aParam = va_arg(ppp, Desc*);
    }
    Desc* h = [Desc descriptorWithString:[handler lowercaseString]];
    Desc* ae = [Desc appleEventWithEventClass:'ascr' eventID:'psbr'
                          targetDescriptor:[Desc nullDescriptor]
                                  returnID:kAutoGenerateReturnID
                             transactionID:kAnyTransactionID];
    [ae setParamDescriptor:h forKeyword:'snam'];
    [ae setParamDescriptor:list forKeyword:keyDirectObject];
    return ae;
}
- (void) setCell: (int) n toString: (NSString*) s {
    Desc* dn = [Desc descriptorWithInt32:n];
    Desc* ds = [Desc descriptorWithString:s];
    [trampoline executeAppleEvent:
        [self callSub:@"setCell" params:dn, ds, nil] error:nil];
}
- (id) getCell: (int) n{
    Desc* dn = [Desc descriptorWithInt32:n];
    return [[trampoline executeAppleEvent:
        [self callSub:@"getCell" params:dn, nil] error:nil] stringValue];
}
- (NSString*) searchText {
    return [self getCell: 1];
}
- (void) setSearchText: (NSString*) t {
    [self setCell: 1 toString: t];
}
// ...and so on...
```

The callSub: routine is a general utility for helping to form the 'ascr\psbr' Apple event. It takes as its parameters the name of the AppleScript handler you want to call, followed by a nil-terminated series of AppleScript parameter values. Each AppleScript parameter value must have previously been embedded into an NSAppleEventDescriptor of the proper type, but this is not usually difficult to do; the setCell: and getCell: methods exemplify the technique, and show how to call callSub:.

Appendixes

Part IV contains this book's appendixes.

The appendixes are:

The AppleScript Experience

This appendix illustrates informally the process of developing AppleScript code. The idea is to convey to the beginner some sense of what it's like to work with Apple-Script, and to present some typical stages in the development of an AppleScript-based solution. My approach is to demonstrate by example, letting you look over my shoulder as I tackle a genuine problem in my real life. The procedures and thought processes exemplified here are quite typical of my own approach to writing Apple-Script code, and probably that of many other experienced users as well; as such, the neophyte may benefit by witnessing them. Besides, if you've never programmed with AppleScript before, you're probably curious about what you're getting yourself into.

Think of this appendix, then, as a nonprogrammer's introduction to the art of Apple-Script development. It's the art that's important here. The particular problem I'll solve in this chapter will probably have no relevance whatsoever to your own life. But the way I approach the problem, the things I do and experience as I work on it, contain useful lessons. At the end we'll extract some general principles on how to approach a task with AppleScript.

The Problem

I have just completed, working in Adobe FrameMaker, the manuscript for a book about AppleScript. This manuscript is now to be submitted to my publisher. My publisher can take submissions in FrameMaker, which is what the production department uses in-house, and there is a checklist enumerating certain details of the form the manuscript should take. Looking over this checklist, I find an entry from the illustration department informing me that I'm supposed to follow certain rules about the naming of the files that contain the illustrations, and that I'm to submit a list of illustrations providing the number, name, and caption of each figure. Table A-1 presents the example the illustration department provides.

Table A-1. How the O'Reilly illustration department wants figure files named

Fig. No.	Filename	Caption (or description)
1-1	*wfi_0101.eps*	Overview of the Windows NT operating system environment.
1-2	*wfi_0102.eps*	Name space presented by the Object Manager.
1-3	*wfi_0103.eps*	Filter drivers in the driver hierarchy.
2-1	*wfi_0201.eps*	Local File System.
2-2	*wfi_0202.eps*	Hierarchical name space for directories and files.

As the example shows, the illustration department would like each illustration file named according to its place in the book. Each name starts with some letters identifying the book, followed by an underscore. Then there are two digits signifying the number of the chapter in which the figure appears. Then there are two more digits signifying the relative position of the figure within the chapter. Finally, there's the suffix indicating what kind of file it is. The illustration department would also like me to attach a list that looks like the table, associating figure numbers, filenames, and captions.

Naturally, as I've been writing the book, I haven't done any of that. It wouldn't have made sense, because I didn't know, as I wrote the book, exactly how many chapters there would be and what order they would be in, and exactly what illustrations there would be and what order *they* would be in. I've been cutting and pasting and rearranging right up until the last moment. My illustration files simply have whatever names I gave them at the time of creation; these names are generally pretty meaningless, and in the Finder they appear in alphabetical order, which is not at all the order in which they appear in the book. For example, here are the names of the illustration files for Chapter 2, as they appear in the Finder:

> *automator.eps*
> *automator2.eps*
> *cocoa.eps*
> *fileMaker1.eps*
> *fileMaker2.eps*
> *radio.eps*
> *scriptDebugger.eps*
> *scriptDebuggerDict.eps*
> *scriptEditor.eps*
> *scriptEditorDict.eps*

Now, however, the proverbial last moment has arrived. So it's time for me to grapple with the illustration department's requirements. The problem, therefore, is to rename these files in accordance with the chapter in which they appear and their order of appearance within it. Clearly I'm going to have to work in two places at once. In FrameMaker, I need to look at each illustration in order, and see what file on disk it corresponds to. In the Finder, I need to change the name of that file. Then, back in FrameMaker, I need to change the reference for each illustration, so that it points to the correct file under its new name.

This promises to be a massively painful, tedious, and error-prone task—not something I'm looking forward to. Then I get an idea. Adobe FrameMaker is scriptable; in fact, it's extraordinarily scriptable. And so is the Finder. Perhaps this task can be automated using AppleScript.

A Day in the Life

Although I know that FrameMaker is scriptable, I have no idea how to script it. I haven't the slightest notion how to talk to FrameMaker, using AppleScript, about the illustrations in my manuscript. So the first thing I need to do is to try to find this out.

Caught in the Web of Words

My starting place, as with any new AppleScript programming task, is the dictionary of the application I'm going to be talking to, where I examine the terminology I can use in speaking to this application with AppleScript. To see FrameMaker's dictionary, I start up Apple's Script Editor, open the Library window, add FrameMaker to the library, and double-click its icon in the Library window. The dictionary opens, as shown in Figure A-1.

This is a massive document and, to the untrained eye (or even to the trained eye), largely incomprehensible. What are we looking for here? Basically, I'd like to know whether FrameMaker gives me a way to talk about illustrations. To find out, I open each of the headings on the left, and under each heading I study its classes. What I'm trying to find out is what things FrameMaker knows about, so that I can guess which of those things is likely to be most useful for the problem I'm facing. In particular, I'd like to find a class that stands a chance of being what FrameMaker thinks my illustrations are.

The fact is, however, that I don't see anything that looks promising. The trouble is that I don't really understand what an illustration *is*, in FrameMaker's terms. I know that when working with FrameMaker through its graphical user interface, to add an illustration to a FrameMaker document, using the template my publisher has set up, I begin by inserting a table, and then, to make the reference to an illustration file, I choose the Import File menu item. Sure enough, there is a table class in the FrameMaker dictionary, but it is not at all clear to me what kind of entity I generate by choosing Import File.

At this point an idea strikes me. Perhaps I should start with an existing illustration and see if I can find a way to ask FrameMaker, "Hey, what's this?" In fact, very near the start of FrameMaker's dictionary—and you can see this in Figure A-1—there's a

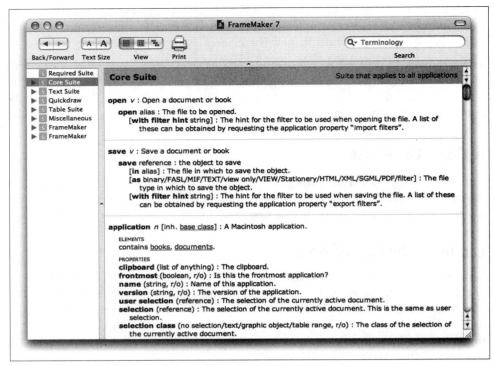

Figure A-1. FrameMaker dictionary

listing called selection. This suggests that perhaps if I select an illustration manually in FrameMaker and then use AppleScript to ask FrameMaker for its selection, I will learn what sort of thing an illustration is.

The word selection is listed as a property of the application class. This means I should be able to talk directly about the selection when I'm targeting FrameMaker. So, in FrameMaker, I manually select an illustration; then, in Script Editor, I make a new script window and enter this code:

```
tell application "FrameMaker 7.0"
    get selection
end tell
```

I run that code, and the result comes back in the lower part of the script window, in the Result pane (I've reformatted the result here to emphasize its structure):

```
inset 1
    of anchored frame 22
        of document "gromit:Users:matt2:extra:astdg:ch02"
            of application "FrameMaker 7.0"
```

Wow! All of a sudden I'm getting someplace. I now have a chain of ofs showing the classes needed to refer to an illustration. So it turns out there's a class called inset, and that an inset belongs to another class called anchored frame. I certainly would never have thought of any of that on my own; even with the help of the dictionary I wouldn't have realized that these were the classes I needed. Now that I know, of course, I see that these classes are indeed listed in the FrameMaker dictionary.

Looking at the dictionary listing for the newly discovered inset class, I see that it has a property inset file, which is described as follows:

```
inset file (alias) : The file where the graphic originated
```

This could be just what I'm after—the link between an illustration in FrameMaker and the illustration file on disk. To find out, I'll ask for the inset file property of the same illustration I just selected a moment ago. So I make a new script window and enter some new code and run it. To form this script, I simply take the reply I just received from AppleScript a moment ago and turn it inside-out, with nested tell blocks instead of the word of:

```
tell application "FrameMaker 7.0"
    tell document "gromit:Users:matt2:extra:astdg:ch02"
        tell anchored frame 22
            get inset file of inset 1
        end tell
    end tell
end tell
```

And here's the answer that comes back:

```
"gromit:Users:matt2:extra:astdg:figs:scriptEditor.eps"
```

Perfect! This is sensational. I've started with a way of referring to an illustration inside FrameMaker, and I've ended up with the pathname of the corresponding illustration file on disk—the very file I'm going to want to rename. Clearly I'm on the right track. I set this script aside and move on to the next part of the problem.

One for All and All for One

I now have some idea of how I'm going to refer to an illustration in FrameMaker and how I'm going to mediate between that reference and the pathname of the file on disk that the illustration comes from. So, having solved this piece of the puzzle for one illustration, I move on to the problem of generalizing. I'm going to want to do this for *every* illustration in the document. How, using AppleScript, am I going to talk about *every* illustration?

In the previous code, I specified a particular illustration by talking about "anchored frame 22." That's an element specifier, referring to a particular member of the anchored frame class by number. So perhaps the way I'm going to solve the problem is by cycling numerically through the anchored frame elements of my document— that is, by talking about "anchored frame 1," then "anchored frame 2," and so on. I'm a little surprised, to be sure, by how the numbers are working here. I don't have 22 illustrations in this document, so why am I talking about "anchored frame 22"? However, I press on regardless; we'll cross that bridge when we come to it.

Let's see if I can list the inset files for *all* the illustrations in the document. To do so, I'll start by gathering up a list of all the anchored frame elements; if FrameMaker will let me, I should be able to do it using the word every. Let's try it:

```
tell application "FrameMaker 7.0"
    tell document "gromit:Users:matt2:extra:astdg:ch02"
        get every anchored frame
    end tell
end tell
```

Here's the response:

```
{anchored frame 1 of document "gromit:Users:matt2:extra:astdg:ch02"
    of application "FrameMaker 7.0",
 anchored frame 2 of document "gromit:Users:matt2:extra:astdg:ch02"
    of application "FrameMaker 7.0",
 anchored frame 3 of document "gromit:Users:matt2:extra:astdg:ch02"
    of application "FrameMaker 7.0",
 ...
}
```

And so on. I've left out most of it, but you get the idea. This seems to be working nicely so far. What I've gotten back is a list, and each item of this list is a reference to one of the anchored frames in the document. So I should be able to run through this list and ask each anchored frame for the inset file property of its "inset 1" element, just as I did with anchored frame 22 earlier. I'll start by making a variable allFrames to store the list in, and then I'll see if I can run through it:

```
tell application "FrameMaker 7.0"
    tell document "gromit:Users:matt2:extra:astdg:ch02"
        set allFrames to get every anchored frame
        repeat with oneFrame in allFrames
        end repeat
    end tell
end tell
```

That code runs, which is good. First I've made a variable allFrames to hold the list; then I've made another variable oneFrame to represent each item of that list as I run through it. But the code doesn't do anything, because I haven't said yet what I want to do with oneFrame; there is no code inside the repeat block.

What I'll do now is create yet another variable, allPaths, to hold my file paths. I'll start this variable as an empty list; every time I get a file path, I'll append it to the list. So here's my code:

```
tell application "FrameMaker 7.0"
    tell document "gromit:Users:matt2:extra:astdg:ch02"
        set allPaths to {}
        set allFrames to get every anchored frame
        repeat with oneFrame in allFrames
            set end of allPaths to inset file of inset 1 of oneFrame
        end repeat
    end tell
end tell
```

I run this code, and—it doesn't work! I get an error message:

```
FrameMaker 7.0 got an error: Can't get inset file of inset 1 of anchored frame 1
    of document "gromit:Users:matt2:extra:astdg:ch02".
```

I don't really know what this error message means. That sort of thing happens a lot when you're working with AppleScript; stuff goes wrong, but you don't get a very helpful error message explaining why. However, I do see that we didn't get far in the list; right at the start, with anchored frame 1, we had a problem. Now, we know that this is going to work for anchored frame 22, so maybe the problem is related to the mystery of the numbering of the anchored frames. Maybe I've got two kinds of anchored frame: those that represent illustrations and those that don't, which apparently is the same thing as saying those that have an inset file and those that don't.

Because I believe this code should work when I get up to anchored frame 22, I'd like to ignore the problem with anchored frame 1 and any other anchored frames that may not be relevant here. There's an easy way to do this: I'll wrap the code in a try block. I expect I'll still get an error, but now the code won't stop; it will shrug off the error and keep going. In this way I hope to cycle far enough through the list of anchored frames that I get to the ones where I don't get an error. Here's the code now:

```
tell application "FrameMaker 7.0"
    tell document "gromit:Users:matt2:extra:astdg:ch02"
        set allPaths to {}
        set allFrames to get every anchored frame
        repeat with oneFrame in allFrames
            try
                set end of allPaths to inset file of inset 1 of oneFrame
            end try
        end repeat
    end tell
end tell
```

I run that code, and there's no error. However, I'm not seeing any result! Oh, wait, I understand what I did wrong. I constructed the list, as the variable allPaths, but I forgot to ask for that list as the final result of the script. The result that you see in the Result pane of the Script Editor after you run a script is the value of the last command that was executed. So the way to display as your result the value of a variable you're interested in is to say the name of that variable as the last executable line of your code. Let's try again, like this:

```
tell application "FrameMaker 7.0"
    tell document "gromit:Users:matt2:extra:astdg:ch02"
        set allPaths to {}
        set allFrames to get every anchored frame
        repeat with oneFrame in allFrames
            try
                set end of allPaths to inset file of inset 1 of oneFrame
            end try
        end repeat
    end tell
end tell
allPaths
```

And here's the result:

```
{"gromit:Users:matt2:extra:astdg:figs:fileMaker1.eps",
 "gromit:Users:matt2:extra:astdg:figs:fileMaker2.eps",
 "gromit:Users:matt2:extra:astdg:figs:cocoa.eps",
 "gromit:Users:matt2:extra:astdg:figs:scriptEditor.eps",
 "gromit:Users:matt2:extra:astdg:figs:scriptEditorDict.eps",
 "gromit:Users:matt2:extra:astdg:figs:scriptDebugger.eps",
 "gromit:Users:matt2:extra:astdg:figs:scriptDebuggerDict.eps",
 "gromit:Users:matt2:extra:astdg:figs:radio.eps",
 "gromit:Users:matt2:extra:astdg:figs:automator.eps",
 "gromit:Users:matt2:extra:astdg:figs:automator2.eps",
 "", "", "", "", "", "", ""}
```

Well, that's pretty good. I have no idea what those last seven items are, the ones that just show up as empty strings (symbolized by empty pairs of quotation marks). But in my final code I guess I could just ignore the empty strings, so that's not really a problem. And we've got ten pathnames, which is exactly right because the chapter has ten illustrations.

But there's a problem. A really big problem. *The pathnames are in the wrong order.*

Remember, our entire purpose is to rename these files in accordance with the order in which they appear in the document. But this is *not* the order in which they appear in the document. I don't know what order it is, but I do know that the first illustration in the document is *scriptEditor.eps*. This is a disaster. Our efforts so far have probably not been a total waste, but there's no denying that we're completely stuck. The "every anchored frame" strategy is a failure.

Seek and Ye Shall Find

At this point I'm exhausted and frustrated, so I do something else for a while and brainstorm subconsciously about the problem to see if I can come up with a new angle. Instead of gathering up all anchored frame references as FrameMaker understands them, we want to run forward through the document itself, looking for anchored frames in order, just as a user would. Hmm…as a user would….

This gives me an idea. How would I, as a user, run through the illustrations in a FrameMaker document? I'd use the Find dialog. Perhaps FrameMaker lets me do the same thing with AppleScript. Yes, by golly; looking in the dictionary, I discover there's a find command. Here's the dictionary entry:

```
find v : Find text, objects, or properties in a Frame document.
    find text/text having paragraph tag/text having character tag/marker/
        marker having type/marker containing text/variable/variable having name/
        anchored frame/table/table having tag/footnote/xref/xref having format/
        unresolved xref/autohyphen : The type of object or property to be found.
    [with value string] : The value of the text, tag, type, format, or name
        being found.
```

```
[with properties list of list] : The properties of the text to be found.
    Most text properties will work here. Finding both value and properties
    is unlikely to work, and some combinations of properties don't work
    well together.
in reference : The document in which to find.
[using use case/whole word/use wildcards/backwards/no wrap/find next] :
    The options to be applied to the find.
→ reference : to the object that was found.
```

The words "anchored frame" in the first paragraph leap right off the screen at me. I can find an anchored frame! I create a new script window in Script Editor, and try it.

```
tell application "FrameMaker 7.0"
    find anchored frame
end tell
```

No, when I run that it generates an error. What's gone wrong? Oh, I see: I've left out the in parameter. I have to tell FrameMaker what document to look in.

```
tell application "FrameMaker 7.0"
    find anchored frame in document "gromit:Users:matt2:extra:astdg:ch02"
end tell
```

It works! The first illustration is selected, and the result is a reference to it, just as the dictionary promises:

```
anchored frame 22 of document "gromit:Users:matt2:extra:astdg:ch02"
    of application "FrameMaker 7.0"
```

So now it begins to look like I can use find repeatedly to get a succession of references to the anchored frames in the document in the order in which they actually appear. To test this idea, I'll just make an artificial loop without worrying for now about how many times I would have to loop in real life:

```
tell application "FrameMaker 7.0"
    set allPaths to {}
    repeat 5 times
        set oneFrame to find anchored frame ¬
            in document "gromit:Users:matt2:extra:astdg:ch02"
        set end of allPaths to inset file of inset 1 of oneFrame
    end repeat
end tell
allPaths
```

Here's the result:

```
{"gromit:Users:matt2:extra:astdg:figs:scriptEditor.eps",
 "gromit:Users:matt2:extra:astdg:figs:scriptEditor.eps",
 "gromit:Users:matt2:extra:astdg:figs:scriptEditor.eps",
 "gromit:Users:matt2:extra:astdg:figs:scriptEditor.eps",
 "gromit:Users:matt2:extra:astdg:figs:scriptEditor.eps"}
```

Oops. We're not moving forward through the document; we're just finding the same illustration repeatedly. In FrameMaker itself, hitting the Find button over and over keeps finding the *next* match, which is what we want; in AppleScript, though, it appears that giving the find command over and over keeps finding the *same* match. But wait; the find command has a using parameter where I can specify find next. Let's try that:

```
tell application "FrameMaker 7.0"
    set allPaths to {}
    repeat 5 times
        set oneFrame to find anchored frame ¬
            in document "gromit:Users:matt2:extra:astdg:ch02" using find next
        set end of allPaths to inset file of inset 1 of oneFrame
    end repeat
end tell
allPaths
```

Darn it; this generates the same result. I guess "find next" simply means to find forwards as opposed to backwards. The trouble is I'm *not* finding forwards. It appears that once I've selected something, finding again just finds that same thing again. All right, then, maybe if I can just somehow move the selection point forward a little after finding an illustration, I'll be able to find the next illustration instead of the current one. So now I have to figure out how to move the selection point forward. I start by selecting some text, and then comes a long round of experimentation, of which I'll spare you the details, at the end of which I come up with this:

```
tell application "FrameMaker 7.0"
    select insertion point after selection
end tell
```

This works just fine when the selection is some text. Unfortunately, as I soon discover, when the selection is an illustration, I get an error message. This is so frustrating! Just when I thought I had the problem solved, I'm completely blocked again, simply because I don't know how to move the selection off an illustration.

Turning the Tables

At this point I remember that every illustration is embedded in a table. According to FrameMaker's dictionary, the find command has an option to find a table. Perhaps this will work better if I start by dealing with tables instead of anchored frames. So I try this:

```
tell application "FrameMaker 7.0"
    find table in document "gromit:Users:matt2:extra:astdg:ch02"
    select insertion point after selection
end tell
```

Gee, there's no error. Could it be that this is actually working? To find out, I'll try to cycle through several tables, collecting references to them to see if I'm finding different ones:

```
tell application "FrameMaker 7.0"
    set allTables to {}
    repeat 5 times
```

```
        set oneTable to find table ¬
            in document "gromit:Users:matt2:extra:astdg:ch02"
        set end of allTables to oneTable
        select insertion point after selection
    end repeat
end tell
allTables
```

Here's the result:

```
{table 33 of document "gromit:Users:matt2:extra:astdg:ch02"
    of application "FrameMaker 7.0",
table 34 of document "gromit:Users:matt2:extra:astdg:ch02"
    of application "FrameMaker 7.0",
table 32 of document "gromit:Users:matt2:extra:astdg:ch02"
    of application "FrameMaker 7.0",
table 35 of document "gromit:Users:matt2:extra:astdg:ch02"
    of application "FrameMaker 7.0",
table 26 of document "gromit:Users:matt2:extra:astdg:ch02"
    of application "FrameMaker 7.0"}
```

That's great. The numbers are once again mystifying; I have no idea why FrameMaker thinks there are at least 35 tables in this document, and of course it is numbering them in a different order than they appear in the document, just as it did with anchored frames. But the important thing is that those are five *different* tables. That means I really can cycle through the tables of the document this way.

Now I need to prove to myself that having found a table, I can get to the anchored frame—the illustration—inside it. This could be tricky, but surely there's a way. Examining the table class listing in the dictionary, I see that a table has cell elements. Well, for a table representing an illustration, that should be simple enough; there's only one cell. Let's see:

```
tell application "FrameMaker 7.0"
    tell document "gromit:Users:matt2:extra:astdg:ch02"
        tell table 33
            get cell 1
        end tell
    end tell
end tell
```

Yes, that runs without error. Now, what's inside a cell? Looking in the cell class listing in the dictionary, I see that it has various possible elements, including paragraph, word, and text. Let's try paragraph:

```
tell application "FrameMaker 7.0"
    tell document "gromit:Users:matt2:extra:astdg:ch02"
        tell table 33
            tell cell 1
                get paragraph 1
            end tell
        end tell
    end tell
end tell
```

Yes, that too runs without error. But can I get from this paragraph to the anchored frame, the actual illustration? There's only one way to find out—try it:

```
tell application "FrameMaker 7.0"
    tell document "gromit:Users:matt2:extra:astdg:ch02"
        tell table 33
            tell cell 1
                tell paragraph 1
                    get anchored frame 1
                end tell
            end tell
        end tell
    end tell
end tell
```

Here's the result:

```
anchored frame 22 of document "gromit:Users:matt2:extra:astdg:ch02"
    of application "FrameMaker 7.0"
```

Son of a gun, it worked. Starting with a reference to a table, I've found a way to refer to the anchored frame inside it. But in that case—dare I say it?—the problem is essentially solved. I know that in principle I can cycle through all the tables in a document, in the order in which they appear. I know that in principle I can get from a reference to a table to a reference to an anchored frame. I know that, given an anchored frame, I can obtain the pathname for the file on disk that is the source of the illustration. So I should be able to put it all together and get the pathnames for the illustration files, in the order in which the illustrations appear in the document.

Let's try it. I'll start things off at the top of the document by selecting the first paragraph. Then I'll cycle through the tables. As I come to each table, I'll get the anchored frame, and from there I'll get the pathname to its source file and append it to a list. I'll continue my policy of cycling some arbitrary number of times, because I don't want to worry yet about the real question of how many times to do it; I just want to prove to myself that I *can* do it.

The first thing is to learn how to select the first paragraph. This turns out to be somewhat tricky. I try this, but it doesn't work:

```
tell application "FrameMaker 7.0"
    tell document "gromit:Users:matt2:extra:astdg:ch02"
        select paragraph 1
    end tell
end tell
```

By once again using my trick of selecting the first paragraph manually and then asking FrameMaker for its selection, so as to learn how it thinks of a paragraph, I finally come up with this:

```
tell application "FrameMaker 7.0"
    tell document "gromit:Users:matt2:extra:astdg:ch02"
        select paragraph 1 of text flow 1
    end tell
end tell
```

Now I'm ready to put it all together:

```
tell application "FrameMaker 7.0"
    tell document "gromit:Users:matt2:extra:astdg:ch02"
        set allPaths to {}
        select paragraph 1 of text flow 1
        repeat 5 times
            set oneTable to find table in it
            set end of allPaths to inset file of inset 1 ¬
                of anchored frame 1 of paragraph 1 of cell 1 of oneTable
            select insertion point after selection
        end repeat
    end tell
end tell
allPaths
```

A change you'll notice here is the use of the word it. Because the current target is the document, the word it refers to this document. This is needed because the find command requires a reference to a document, but all the other commands are already being addressed to that document.

Here's the result:

```
{"gromit:Users:matt2:extra:astdg:figs:scriptEditor.eps",
"gromit:Users:matt2:extra:astdg:figs:scriptEditorDict.eps",
"gromit:Users:matt2:extra:astdg:figs:scriptDebugger.eps",
"gromit:Users:matt2:extra:astdg:figs:scriptDebuggerDict.eps",
"gromit:Users:matt2:extra:astdg:figs:fileMaker1.eps"}
```

That's the right answer: those are the pathnames to the first five illustrations in the document, *in the order in which they appear*. For the first time since starting to work on the problem, I now believe I'm going to be able to solve it.

Refiner's Fire

Now let's make a few refinements. First, it occurs to me that I'm doing something rather stupid here; I'm finding every table. That's going be troublesome, because some tables are illustrations but some are just ordinary tables. I want to find illustration tables only. I know that in my FrameMaker template these are tables whose tag (or style name) is "Figure." The find command, according to FrameMaker's dictionary, lets me find a table having tag. So that's the way I should find my tables. After a short struggle to understand the syntax of this command, I come up with the following new version of my script:

```
tell application "FrameMaker 7.0"
    tell document "gromit:Users:matt2:extra:astdg:ch02"
        set allPaths to {}
        select paragraph 1 of text flow 1
        repeat 5 times
            set oneTable to find table having tag with value "Figure" in it
            set end of allPaths to inset file of inset 1 ¬
                of anchored frame 1 of paragraph 1 of cell 1 of oneTable
```

```
            select insertion point after selection
        end repeat
    end tell
end tell
allPaths
```

The result is just the same, so I haven't wrecked the successes I've already had (known in the programming business as a "regression"), and I believe I've eliminated some possible false positives from the find.

Next, let's worry about how to know how many times to loop. By changing "5 times" to "20 times," which is more times than the number of illustrations in the document, and then running the script again, I discover that when I get to the end of the document the search wraps around and starts from the top once more. I try to fix this by adding the option using no wrap to the find, but it doesn't help. Therefore I'd like to know *beforehand* exactly how many times to loop.

Now, I know from the dictionary that a table has a table tag property. AppleScript's boolean test specifier allows me to specify particular objects of a class in terms of the value of one of that class's properties; not every scriptable application implements this construct when you'd like it to, but the only way to find out whether FrameMaker does in this case is to try it, so I do. After some stumbling about, I realize that a document has a text flow element that I have to refer to before I can refer to a table, and I come up with this:

```
tell application "FrameMaker 7.0"
    tell document "gromit:Users:matt2:extra:astdg:ch02"
        tell text flow 1
            get tables whose table tag is "Figure"
        end tell
    end tell
end tell
```

That works. But I don't really want this entire list; I just want to know how many items it contains. The size of a list can be obtained with the count command:

```
tell application "FrameMaker 7.0"
    tell document "gromit:Users:matt2:extra:astdg:ch02"
        tell text flow 1
            count (get tables whose table tag is "Figure")
        end tell
    end tell
end tell
```

The result is 10. That's correct. So I should be able to use this approach before starting my loop in order to know just how many times to loop. Here's my new version of the script:

```
tell application "FrameMaker 7.0"
    tell document "gromit:Users:matt2:extra:astdg:ch02"
        tell text flow 1
            set howMany to count (get tables whose table tag is "Figure")
        end tell
```

```
            set allPaths to {}
            select paragraph 1 of text flow 1
            repeat howMany times
                set oneTable to find table having tag with value "Figure" in it
                set end of allPaths to inset file of inset 1 ¬
                    of anchored frame 1 of paragraph 1 of cell 1 of oneTable
                select insertion point after selection
            end repeat
        end tell
    end tell
    allPaths
```

And here's the result; it's absolutely perfect, the correct names of the correct illustrations in the correct order:

```
{"gromit:Users:matt2:extra:astdg:figs:scriptEditor.eps",
 "gromit:Users:matt2:extra:astdg:figs:scriptEditorDict.eps",
 "gromit:Users:matt2:extra:astdg:figs:scriptDebugger.eps",
 "gromit:Users:matt2:extra:astdg:figs:scriptDebuggerDict.eps",
 "gromit:Users:matt2:extra:astdg:figs:fileMaker1.eps",
 "gromit:Users:matt2:extra:astdg:figs:fileMaker2.eps",
 "gromit:Users:matt2:extra:astdg:figs:radio.eps",
 "gromit:Users:matt2:extra:astdg:figs:cocoa.eps",
 "gromit:Users:matt2:extra:astdg:figs:automator.eps",
 "gromit:Users:matt2:extra:astdg:figs:automator2.eps"}
```

Naming of Parts

Let's now turn our attention to the business of deriving the new name of each illustration. This will involve the chapter number. How can we learn this number?

It happens that in the FrameMaker template I'm using, every chapter document has exactly one paragraph whose tag (paragraph style) is "ChapterLabel," and that the text of this paragraph is the chapter number. So if FrameMaker gives me a way to refer to this paragraph, I should be home free. The dictionary tells me that the paragraph class has a paragraph tag property. Using the same sort of boolean test specifier construct I used a moment ago to find only those tables with a particular table tag, I try to find just those paragraphs that have this particular paragraph tag, expecting there to be just one:

```
tell application "FrameMaker 7.0"
    tell document "gromit:Users:matt2:extra:astdg:ch02"
        tell text flow 1
            get paragraphs whose paragraph tag is "ChapterLabel"
        end tell
    end tell
end tell
```

This doesn't give me an error, but the result is not quite what I expected:

```
{""}
```

I guess the problem is that the paragraph itself is empty; the chapter number is generated automatically through FrameMaker's autonumbering feature, and doesn't really count as its text. The dictionary lists a couple of paragraph properties that look promising here:

autoNum string (string) : The automatic numbering format string
paragraph number (string) : The formatted string representation of the
    paragraph number

The second one looks like what I'm after, so I try it:

```
tell application "FrameMaker 7.0"
    tell document "gromit:Users:matt2:extra:astdg:ch02"
        tell text flow 1
            get paragraph number of paragraphs ¬
                whose paragraph tag is "ChapterLabel"
        end tell
    end tell
end tell
```

The result is this:

```
{"Chapter 2"}
```

That's the right answer! It's a list because I asked for all such paragraphs, but it's a list of just one item because there is only one such paragraph, and the string "Chapter 2" provides the chapter number for this chapter. Now, of course, I need to extract just the "2" from this string, but that's easy, because AppleScript understands the concept of a word:

```
tell application "FrameMaker 7.0"
    tell document "gromit:Users:matt2:extra:astdg:ch02"
        tell text flow 1
            set chapNum to (get paragraph number of paragraphs ¬
                whose paragraph tag is "ChapterLabel")
        end tell
    end tell
end tell
set chapNum to word -1 of item 1 of chapNum
chapNum
```

The element item 1 extracts the single string "Chapter 2" from the list, and the element word -1 extracts the last word of that. The result is "2", which is perfect.

I want this number formatted to have two digits. Now, this is a piece of functionality I'm going to need more than once, so I write a little handler (a subroutine). This handler's job is to accept a string and pad it with zero at the front until it is two characters long. Having written the handler, I add some code to call the handler and test it, twice, because I want to make sure it works for a string that is either one or two characters long.

```
on pad(s)
    repeat while length of s < 2
        set s to ("0" & s)
    end repeat
```

```
        return s
    end pad
    log pad("2")
    log pad("22")
```

The pad handler makes use of concatenation (via the ampersand operator) to assemble the desired string. The last two lines do two things:

- The pad command calls the pad handler that appears earlier in the code.
- The log command puts the result of the pad command into the Event Log History window. The Event Log History window must be opened manually before running the script.

Logging like this is a good approach when you want to test more than one thing in a single running of a script. The result looks good:

```
(*02*)
(*22*)
```

Those parentheses and asterisks are comment delimiters; I don't quite understand why the log window uses them, but it doesn't matter.

Another problem is that the new name of each illustration is going to be based partly on its old name. I need to break up the illustration file's pathname into its components, and I need to break up the last component, the actual name of the file, into the name itself and the file-type suffix, because the only part of the pathname I want to change is the name itself.

The typical AppleScript way to break up a string into fields based on some delimiter is to set the special variable text item delimiters to that delimiter and then ask for the string's text items. So I'll do that twice, once with colon as the delimiter and again with period as the delimiter. Once again, I'll make this a handler, just because it makes the script so much neater. I'll have the handler return both results, the list of pathname components together with the list of filename components, combined as a single list. That way, when I call this handler, I will have all the pieces and can reassemble them the way I want:

```
on bust(s)
    set text item delimiters to ":"
    set pathParts to text items of s
    set text item delimiters to "."
    set nameParts to text items of last item of pathParts
    return {pathParts, nameParts}
end bust
bust("disk:folder:folder:file.suffix")
```

The result shows that the right thing is happening:

```
{{"disk", "folder", "folder", "file.suffix"}, {"file", "suffix"}}
```

Now I'm ready to practice renaming an illustration file. I'll write a handler that takes two numbers and the current pathname of the illustration file and generates the new pathname for that file:

```
on pad(s)
    repeat while length of s < 2
        set s to ("0" & s)
    end repeat
    return s
end pad
on bust(s)
    set text item delimiters to ":"
    set pathParts to text items of s
    set text item delimiters to "."
    set nameParts to text items of last item of pathParts
    return {pathParts, nameParts}
end bust
on rename(n1, n2, oldPath)
    set bothLists to bust(oldPath)
    set extension to last item of item 2 of bothLists
    set pathPart to items 1 thru -2 of item 1 of bothLists
    set newFileName to "as_" & pad(n1) & pad(n2)
    set newFileName to newFileName & "." & extension
    set text item delimiters to ":"
    return (pathPart as string) & ":" & newFileName
end rename
rename("2", "3", "disk:folder:folder:oldName.eps")
```

The expression as string when applied to a list, as in the very last line of the rename handler, assembles the items of the list, together with the text item delimiters between each pair of items, into a single string. And here's the result:

```
"disk:folder:folder:as_0203.eps"
```

Got it right the first time! It's hard to believe, but I am now ready for a practice run using an actual FrameMaker document.

Practice Makes Perfect

If I've learned one thing about programming over the years, it's to practice before doing anything drastic. I'm going to run through the document and *pretend* to change the illustration names. Instead of really changing them, I'll log a note telling myself what I *would* have changed the name to if this had been the real thing. So, putting it all together, here's my practice script:

```
on pad(s)
    repeat while length of s < 2
        set s to ("0" & s)
    end repeat
    return s
end pad
on bust(s)
```

```
        set text item delimiters to ":"
        set pathParts to text items of s
        set text item delimiters to "."
        set nameParts to text items of last item of pathParts
        return {pathParts, nameParts}
    end bust
    on rename(n1, n2, oldPath)
        set bothLists to bust(oldPath)
        set extension to last item of item 2 of bothLists
        set pathPart to items 1 thru -2 of item 1 of bothLists
        set newFileName to "as_" & pad(n1) & pad(n2)
        set newFileName to newFileName & "." & extension
        set text item delimiters to ":"
        return (pathPart as string) & ":" & newFileName
    end rename
    tell application "FrameMaker 7.0"
        tell document "gromit:Users:matt2:extra:astdg:ch02"
            tell text flow 1
                set howMany to count (get tables whose table tag is "Figure")
                set chapNum to (get paragraph number of paragraphs ¬
                    whose paragraph tag is "ChapterLabel")
            end tell
            set chapNum to word -1 of item 1 of chapNum
            set allPaths to {}
            select paragraph 1 of text flow 1
            set counter to 1
            repeat howMany times
                set oneTable to find table having tag with value "Figure" in it
                set thisFile to inset file of inset 1 ¬
                    of anchored frame 1 of paragraph 1 of cell 1 of oneTable
                set newName to ¬
                    my rename(chapNum, (counter as string), thisFile)
                log "I found " & thisFile
                log "I'm thinking of changing it to " & newName
                select insertion point after selection
                set counter to counter + 1
            end repeat
        end tell
    end tell
```

Observe that I have put in the variable counter, which starts at 1 and is incremented in every loop; this is how I know how many times I've done the find, and therefore tells me the number of the current illustration. I must admit that it took me a couple of tries to get this script to run. When I first tried to run it, I got an error at the point where I call the rename handler. This was because I had forgotten to put the magic word my before it; this tells AppleScript that even though I'm talking to FrameMaker I want to call a handler in my own script. And then, after I made that change and ran the script again, I got another error: it appeared that the rename handler was called but was now choking. The reason was that the variable counter was a number, and the rename handler was passing this on to the pad handler, which was expecting a string. The phrase counter as string converts the number to a string for purposes of passing it to the rename handler.

Here are the first couple of relevant entries of the resulting log:

```
(*I found gromit:Users:matt2:extra:astdg:figs:scriptEditor.eps*)
(*I'm thinking of changing it to gromit:Users:matt2:extra:astdg:figs:as_0201.eps*)
(*I found gromit:Users:matt2:extra:astdg:figs:scriptEditorDict.eps*)
(*I'm thinking of changing it to gromit:Users:matt2:extra:astdg:figs:as_0202.eps*)
...
```

And so forth. That looks as good as I could wish. I'm rapidly becoming very confident that my script, when unleashed for real upon my FrameMaker document, will correctly calculate the new names for the illustration files.

Finder's Keepers

I must not change only the file reference of each illustration within FrameMaker; I must change also the name of the actual illustration file. This involves speaking to the Finder. As a test, I create a file and run a little code to make sure I know how to tell the Finder how to change the name of a file.

```
tell application "Finder"
    set name of file "feathers:Users:mattneub:Desktop:testing.txt" to "itWorked"
end tell
```

This works, and now I'm ready to run my original script for real. Before doing so, I make sure I have backup copies of everything involved, in case something goes wrong. Even with backups, it's a scary business making such possibly disastrous changes, both in a FrameMaker document and on disk, so I start by running the script against a document that has just one illustration—in fact, I run it against this very document, Appendix A.

To make the script work for real, I change it in two places. First, at the start I add another little handler to extract the final component from a pathname, so that I can obtain the new name that the Finder is to give to the illustration file:

```
on justName(s)
    set text item delimiters to ":"
    return last text item of s
end justName
```

Second, I replace the two "log" lines from the previous version with this:

```
set newShortName to my justName(newName)
tell application "Finder" ¬
    to set name of file thisFile to newShortName
set inset file of inset 1 ¬
    of anchored frame 1 of paragraph 1 of cell 1 of oneTable ¬
    to newName
```

The first two lines are simply a rewrite of the Finder file-renaming code just tested a moment ago, with the values coming from variables in the script instead of being hard-coded as literal strings. The second line actually changes the name of the illustration file on disk. (Observe that I can talk to the Finder even inside code where I'm already talking to FrameMaker.) The last line is the only one that makes an actual change in the FrameMaker document—the crucial change, the one I came here to make, altering the illustration's file reference to match the new pathname of the illustration file. I run the script against Appendix A, and it works; the illustration file's name is changed, and the illustration's file reference in the FrameMaker document is changed to match.

I've Got a Little List

Recall that one of my purposes is to generate the figure list requested by the illustration department, as shown in Table A-1. I already know the chapter number, the illustration number, and the illustration file's name. The only missing piece of information is the illustration's caption. The FrameMaker dictionary shows that a table has a `title` property that looks like what I want. A quick test against a specific table shows that it is:

```
tell application "FrameMaker 7.0"
    set theTitle to (get title of table 36 of document ¬
        "gromit:Users:matt2:extra:astdg:appa")
end tell
```

This works, but because of the way the template is constructed, it includes an unwanted return character at the start of the result. To eliminate this, I use an AppleScript expression that extracts all but the first character of a string:

```
tell application "FrameMaker 7.0"
    set theTitle to text from character 2 to -1 of ¬
        (get title of table 36 of document ¬
        "gromit:Users:matt2:extra:astdg:appa")
end tell
```

That works; the result is this:

```
"FrameMaker dictionary"
```

That is indeed the caption of the first illustration of this chapter. AppleScript can write to a file, so all I need now is a handler that appends to a file, nicely formatted, a line containing the information for the illustration currently being processed. Here, then, is the final version of the script, including this handler and a call to it:

```
on pad(s)
    repeat while length of s < 2
        set s to ("0" & s)
    end repeat
    return s
end pad
on bust(s)
    set text item delimiters to ":"
    set pathParts to text items of s
    set text item delimiters to "."
    set nameParts to text items of last item of pathParts
    return {pathParts, nameParts}
end bust
```

```
on rename(n1, n2, oldPath)
    set bothLists to bust(oldPath)
    set extension to last item of item 2 of bothLists
    set pathPart to items 1 thru -2 of item 1 of bothLists
    set newFileName to "as_" & pad(n1) & pad(n2)
    set newFileName to newFileName & "." & extension
    set text item delimiters to ":"
    return (pathPart as string) & ":" & newFileName
end rename
on justName(s)
    set text item delimiters to ":"
    return last text item of s
end justName
on writeInfo(n1, n2, theName, theTitle)
    set s to return & n1 & "-" & n2 & tab & theName & tab & theTitle & return
    set f to open for access ¬
        file "feathers:Users:mattneub:figs" with write permission
    write s to f starting at (get eof of f)
    close access f
end writeInfo
tell application "FrameMaker 7.0"
    tell document "gromit:Users:matt2:extra:astdg:appa"
        tell text flow 1
            set howMany to count (get tables whose table tag is "Figure")
            set chapNum to (get paragraph number of paragraphs ¬
                whose paragraph tag is "ChapterLabel")
        end tell
        set chapNum to word -1 of item 1 of chapNum
        set allPaths to {}
        select paragraph 1 of text flow 1
        set counter to 1
        repeat howMany times
            set oneTable to find table having tag with value "Figure" in it
            set thisFile to inset file of inset 1 ¬
                of anchored frame 1 of paragraph 1 of cell 1 of oneTable
            set newName to my rename(chapNum, (counter as string), thisFile)
            set newShortName to my justName(newName)
            tell application "Finder" to set name of file thisFile to newShortName
            set inset file of inset 1 ¬
                of anchored frame 1 of paragraph 1 of cell 1 of oneTable ¬
                to newName
            set theTitle to text from character 2 to -1 of (get title of oneTable)
            my writeInfo(chapNum, (counter as string), newShortName, theTitle)
            select insertion point after selection
            set counter to counter + 1
        end repeat
    end tell
end tell
```

There is just one thing I don't like about that script, namely this line:

```
tell document "gromit:Users:matt2:extra:astdg:appa"
```

That line hard-codes the pathname of the document file. This works, but it means that I have to change the script manually for each file I process. That's not so terrible, as only a few chapters of this book have any illustrations at all, but it would be nice not to have to do it at all, if only because it seems a possible source of error. Nevertheless, I think we can save this matter for some future round of refinements, and for now at least, consider the problem solved.

Conclusions, Lessons, and Advice

You'll no doubt have noticed that most of my time and effort working on this problem was spent wrestling with the particular scriptable application I was trying to automate. In general, that's how it is with AppleScript. AppleScript itself is a very small language; it is extended in different ways by different scriptable applications. Trying to work out what a particular scriptable application will let you say and how it will respond when you say it constitutes much of the battle of working with AppleScript.

Another feature of the struggle is that AppleScript's error messages aren't very helpful, and it lacks a debugging environment (unless you use Script Debugger as your script editor application), so it's important to proceed with caution and patience. When you try to execute a script, all you really know is that it worked or it didn't; if it didn't, finding out why isn't easy. You can see that I developed my final script slowly and in stages, testing each piece as I went along. I knew that the pieces worked before I put them into place; that way I could be pretty confident that I knew what the script as a whole would do.

Here, to conclude, are a few apophthegms to live by, derived from the foregoing. I hope you'll find this advice helpful in your own AppleScript adventures:

Use the dictionary.
> The biggest problem you face as you approach driving a scriptable application is that you don't know the application's "object model"—what sorts of thing it thinks of itself as knowing about, what it calls these things, and how the things relate to one another. In this regard, nouns (classes) are much more important than verbs (commands). Most scriptable applications, especially if they are scriptable in a deep and powerful way, have lots of nouns and relatively few verbs. Notice how I did almost everything in the script with the basic built-in verbs get, set, and count; even select is fairly standard. The only unusual verb I ended up using was find. I spent almost all of the time worrying about the nouns. The biggest problem in AppleScript is referring to the thing you want to talk about, in the manner that your scriptable application expects and accepts.

Don't expect too much from the dictionary.
> Try to think of other ways to learn how to construct the desired reference. FrameMaker's dictionary let us down quite severely on several occasions; I was much more successful in asking for the selection and letting FrameMaker

describe a thing in its own terms than in trying to construct a reference from scratch based on the dictionary. In fact, although I didn't say anything about it at the time because the matter is rather technical, FrameMaker's dictionary is massively faulty; although I learned by experiment that an anchored frame can be an element of a paragraph or of a document, the dictionary doesn't say this at all. Had it done so, I would have had a much easier time.

Think outside the box.

When FrameMaker wouldn't just hand me references to every anchored frame in the order in which they occur in the document, I was frustrated, but I didn't give up; I tried to think of another way. The `find` command looks broken to me, but I didn't worry about this; I figured out how to move the selection point forward to work around the problem. If you waste your time and energy bewailing things that you feel are broken or quirky or inadequate in AppleScript or in some particular scriptable application, you won't get any work done. Face reality and tighten your belt another notch.

Start small.

Look at how much of the time was taken up testing very short snippets of code over and over just to learn how to construct a reference or to see what some operation would do. Part of the problem here is that you don't know until you try it what an application will permit you to do; the dictionary can't really tell you. Another part of the problem is that AppleScript has no built-in facilities for debugging. Therefore you need to develop the program one line at a time, building it up from individual lines that you already know work (because you've tested them). Don't try to write an entire program in AppleScript and then figure out why it didn't work; you'll never manage it. By the time you put the whole program together, you should be like a lawyer cross-examining a witness in court: ideally, you should never ask a question to which you don't already know the answer.

Test every step.

When you don't know the answer to some question your code is asking in the course of your script, find out. Use the result of running a script. Use logging. You want to know at every step, as you develop a script, whether what's happening is what you want and expect.

Don't be ashamed to experiment.

Don't be afraid to guess! A lot of AppleScript code development is guesswork. As Aristotle said, it is a mark of wisdom to ask from a subject only so much precision as that subject admits of.

Solve the single case before expanding to "every."

Solve the single case before expanding to a loop. Solve an artificial loop before worrying about the boundary cases (that is, before figuring out how to know exactly how many times to loop).

Don't try to understand AppleScript's mysterious error messages.

The important thing isn't what went wrong but where it went wrong. Knowing where the problem is will usually suffice, because you know where you need to make a change, even if you're just guessing when you make it. If you think the error isn't important, use error-handling (a try block) to ignore it, so that it won't stop your code from executing.

Write a practice script before writing the final version of the script.

AppleScript has the power to do very far-reaching things, such as deleting files and wrecking your document. You want to be very sure things are working before you throw the switch that says, "This is not a drill."

Know the language.

It's true that in the course of development I did a lot of guessing about FrameMaker's object model, but I didn't guess about the language itself. I couldn't have written this program at all if I hadn't known already what my and it mean, and how to use tell and of, and how to form a boolean test specifier, and what the difference is between a property and an element. AppleScript may look like English, and that might make you think you already know AppleScript because you already know English. If you think that, you're wrong. AppleScript is a rule-based programming language like any other. It is rigorous, choosy, and precise. This book can't teach you to write that one special script you'd like to write, but it can and does teach you the language.

APPENDIX B
Apple Events Without AppleScript

Considering AppleScript purely as a vehicle for constructing and sending Apple events to scriptable applications (and for receiving and parsing the replies), and in light of the shortcomings and inconveniences of the AppleScript language, one may reasonably wonder why it might not be possible to construct and send Apple events using some other (possibly more attractive) language. Such an approach would have the advantage of letting you work in a language or a development environment you favor, plus at runtime you'd bypass the overhead of the AppleScript compiler and runtime engine. As a matter of fact, there are several such alternative languages to choose from. It is not at all trivial to mold another language to operate on Apple events in a way that parallels AppleScript's own approach, especially because Apple-Script does some odd (or buggy) things under the hood, and also because of the inherent problem of extensible terminology; nevertheless, it can be and has been done. This is not, strictly speaking, an AppleScript matter; indeed, it is quite clearly an anti-AppleScript matter! So in theory, discussion of it should have no place in this book. Nevertheless, my own favorite ways of sending Apple events have often included some non-AppleScript language or other, and the subject is certainly an interesting one, so I've included some information on the topic here, as an appendix.

Here, then, are some ways to send Apple events without using AppleScript. Your choice might depend upon what languages you like or are already using, and upon the nature of a particular language's implementation of Apple events. Throughout this appendix, the "model events" (the Apple events we will attempt to construct and send for purposes of example) will be those corresponding to the following script:

```
tell application "BBEdit"
    make new document
    tell document 1
        set its text to "Hello, world!"
    end tell
end tell
```

At programming level, these events provide a nice balance between simplicity and complexity: we're forming a two-level object specifier, which is a fairly interesting thing, without getting too deep into the nitty-gritty. At the user level, the result is pleasantly satisfying, as (if our code is correct) we can see the new window appear in BBEdit with the words "Hello, world!" proudly emblazoned on it.

Pure Raw Apple Events

If you're a Carbon programmer, you can construct a raw Apple event yourself, directly, in code. A number of other languages, such as Objective-C/Cocoa and REALbasic, give you the wherewithal to do the same thing in a possibly more convenient form. Still, no matter how you slice it, building a raw Apple event is a lot of work, and because every Apple event is different, this approach is not particularly general or flexible. You can compensate by developing libraries of wrapper functions, and Apple provides such libraries (such as the *MoreAppleEvents* sample code available at the developer web site), but it's still a fairly unpleasant procedure.

Here's some code for generating and sending our model events in Objective-C/Cocoa. Actually it's blended with C/Carbon, because Objective-C, curiously, although it provides some fairly convenient ways to construct the pieces of an Apple event, provides no way to *send* the event once it's been constructed. Also it's a lot more convenient to construct an object specifier in Carbon than in pure Cocoa. For simplicity, issue of memory management and error checking are ignored:

```
[[NSWorkspace sharedWorkspace] launchApplication:@"BBEdit"];
NSAppleEventDescriptor* bbedit =
    [NSAppleEventDescriptor descriptorWithDescriptorType:typeApplicationBundleID
            data:[@"com.barebones.bbedit" dataUsingEncoding:NSUTF8StringEncoding]];
NSAppleEventDescriptor* ae =
    [NSAppleEventDescriptor appleEventWithEventClass:'core'
                            eventID:'crel'
                            targetDescriptor:bbedit
                            returnID:kAutoGenerateReturnID
                            transactionID:kAnyTransactionID];
[ae setParamDescriptor:[NSAppleEventDescriptor descriptorWithTypeCode:'docu']
                            forKeyword:'kocl'];
AESendMessage([ae aeDesc], NULL,
                            kAENoReply | kAENeverInteract,
                            kAEDefaultTimeout);
ae =
    [NSAppleEventDescriptor appleEventWithEventClass:'core'
                            eventID:'setd'
                            targetDescriptor:bbedit
                            returnID:kAutoGenerateReturnID
                            transactionID:kAnyTransactionID];
[ae setParamDescriptor:
    [NSAppleEventDescriptor descriptorWithString:@"Hello, world!"]
                            forKeyword:'data'];
AEDesc docu1;
CreateObjSpecifier('docu',
                            [[NSAppleEventDescriptor nullDescriptor] aeDesc],
```

```
                        formAbsolutePosition,
                        [[NSAppleEventDescriptor descriptorWithInt32:1] aeDesc],
                        YES, &docu1);
AEDesc allText;
CreateObjSpecifier('ctxt', &docu1, formAbsolutePosition,
                        [[NSAppleEventDescriptor descriptorWithDescriptorType:
                            'abso' bytes:"all " length:4] aeDesc],
                        YES, &allText);
NSAppleEventDescriptor* allTextDesc =
    [[NSAppleEventDescriptor alloc] initWithAEDescNoCopy:&allText];
[ae setParamDescriptor:allTextDesc forKeyword:keyDirectObject];
AESendMessage([ae aeDesc], NULL,
                        kAENoReply | kAENeverInteract,
                        kAEDefaultTimeout);
```

First we make sure that BBEdit is running. Then we start forming our Apple events. An Apple event is composed of Apple event descriptors, and is itself an Apple event descriptor. Since we're going to be targeting BBEdit, we first form a target descriptor specifying BBEdit. Then we build a "make new" Apple event targeting BBEdit, set its parameter with the four-letter code for "document," and send it. Next we form a "set" Apple event. Filling in the "data" parameter (what we're going to set something to) is easy enough, but filling in the direct parameter is more involved, because this is an object specifier. We form the object specifier in two stages, working from the outside in: first we make an object specifier for "document 1," then we make a second object specifier for "[every] text of" and link it to the first object specifier. We shove the specifier into our Apple event and send it.

For more information about sending raw Apple events with Cocoa and Carbon, see the Apple documentation listed in Appendix C, along with Apple's sample code.

REALbasic's native support for forming raw Apple events remains largely incomplete, but it is sufficient for constructing and sending for the model events. The code is certainly much more compact than doing the same thing in Cocoa and Carbon:

```
dim ae as AppleEvent
dim theDoc, theText as AppleEventObjectSpecifier
dim s as new shell
s.execute("open -a 'BBEdit'")
ae = NewAppleEvent("core","crel", "R*ch")
ae.macTypeParam("kocl") = "docu"
call ae.send
theDoc = getIndexedObjectDescriptor("docu", nil, 1)
theText = getOrdinalObjectDescriptor("ctxt",theDoc,"all ")
ae = NewAppleEvent("core","setd","R*ch")
ae.objectSpecifierParam("----") = theText
ae.stringParam("data") = "Hello, world!"
call ae.send
```

For more information, see the REALbasic online help, along with Chapter 31 of my book *REALbasic: The Definitive Guide*, 2nd ed., O'Reilly Media, 2001 (now out of print).

JavaScript

The free JavaScript OSA component file from Late Night Software (see "Other Scripting Languages" in Chapter 3) implements an OSA language that appears in your script editor application; this language is JavaScript with some additions that allow it to construct and send (and receive) Apple events.

Actually, JavaScript OSA can construct Apple events in two ways. If you like, you can construct raw Apple events by a process quite similar to the earlier REALbasic example. However, JavaScript OSA can also read the dictionary of the target application in real time and incorporate its terminology into the JavaScript language. The target application is, in effect, represented by an object with properties and methods corresponding to AppleScript attributes and commands. Here is code to generate and send our model events:

```
with (MacOS.appBySignature("R*ch")) {
    make(_types.document);
    document[1].valueOf().text = "Hello, world!";
}
```

This mode of expression is extraordinarily compact and direct. A with clause and dot notation replace the chain of ofs and tells; true assignment with an equal-sign replaces set. Elements appear as arrays. Certain distinctions that are muddied by AppleScript are clarified; the term document is different as an element and as a class, for instance.

JavaScript OSA can't express every kind of Apple event (in particular, boolean test specifiers are not supported), but this is compensated for by the powerful combination of the cool and elegant object-oriented JavaScript language with the automatic implementation of AppleScript terminology. Most important, JavaScript OSA is an OSA language, meaning that it's usable just about anywhere you would use an AppleScript compiled script file. For instance, many of the scripts I use with script runners such as Entourage's and BBEdit's Script menus are written in JavaScript.

To learn more about JavaScript OSA, download it and look through the "Introducing JavaScript OSA" manual (written by yours truly).

UserTalk

UserTalk is the native scripting language of UserLand Frontier and its inexpensive "little brother," Radio UserLand. Frontier is now also once again available in a free version, which is open source.

UserTalk does not read an application's dictionary in real time, the way JavaScript OSA does. In UserTalk, all terminology (not only as relates to Apple events, but the entire language) is implemented through a hierarchical namespace table called "the database." Every name in the database corresponds to a value; a value can be a string, an integer, a raw four-character code, a script written in the UserTalk language, a subtable, or any of a dozen other types of value. The namespace is navigated through dot notation, starting at the top level, which is called root. Certain nodes in the database are short-circuited, though, so that an unqualified term is sought at these points directly. English-like AppleScript terminology is implemented through the database, like everything else; to drive an application, you need a table to translate from English-like terms to four-letter codes, scripts, and so forth. This is called the *glue table* for that application. Construction of a glue table must be performed separately before you can start targeting a given application. The process of constructing a glue table is largely automatic (Frontier includes a script that can read an application's dictionary and generate the corresponding table), but too involved to describe here. Let's just assume, therefore, that we have previously constructed a BBEdit glue table. Then the code to generate our model events is as follows:

```
if !(bbedit.isRunning())
    launch.application(bbedit.appinfo.path)
with objectmodel, bbedit
    make(document)
    set(document[1].text,"Hello, world!")
```

The term bbedit refers to our glue table (located in the system.verbs.apps table, one of the short-circuited areas of the database). The term objectmodel refers to a table in system.macintosh (another short-circuited area) where certain common terms are defined. The with clause means: "Look for these terms starting in objectmodel, and if you don't find one, look for it in bbedit instead." As a result, make and set are found in bbedit, whereas document and text are found in objectmodel. As you can see, the code looks very much like the JavaScript OSA expression of the same events, pleasantly compact and legible. As with JavaScript OSA, dot notation and array notation are used to assemble an object reference.

An interesting thing about Frontier is that, because a lot of its innards are implemented in UserTalk and are simply part of the database, we can look under the hood a little further. For instance, here's the script located at bbedit.make:

```
on make (new, at = nil, withProperties = nil)
    return (appleEvent (BBEdit.id, 'core', 'crel', 'kocl', string4 (new), \
        'insh', at, 'prdt', withProperties))}
```

Thus we see that it would have been possible to form and send the raw Apple event ourselves, as that's exactly what UserTalk is doing here. The built-in UserTalk verb appleEvent() constructs and sends an Apple event; its parameters tell it what event to construct. BBEdit.id is the four-letter code for BBEdit, stored in the id entry of the bbedit table. You know what core and crel are (the two four-letter codes of the Apple event we are to send), and kocl is the name of the parameter. The next item, called new, is the value for the kocl parameter, the class we are to make a new one of, which was passed in as the first parameter in the call to make(); in this case it is the value of `objectmodel.document` (namely docu). The remaining parameters are optional; they are not supplied in this call, so they are not used in the construction of the Apple event.

For more information about Frontier, see my book *Frontier: The Definitive Guide*, from O'Reilly & Associates; it's out of print, but you can read it online at *http:// pages.sbcglobal.net/mattneub/frontierDef/ch00.html*. The information in the book is somewhat outdated, but not all that much; Frontier has grown by accretion, not by internal alteration, and the implementation of Apple events is certainly unchanged. In fact, this is something of a problem. Frontier runs on Mac OS X, but has not been revised from its Classic origins to take account of many changed aspects of the file system, and there have even been a few changes in the system-level implementation of Apple events. Thus Frontier has become a bit rusty and unreliable as a way of expressing Apple events, which is a pity, especially because this is what it was originally created to do; indeed, Frontier and UserTalk were constructing and sending Apple events before AppleScript existed, and UserTalk's expression of Apple events remains one of Frontier's most elegant and powerful features. The other great disappointment is that UserTalk on Mac OS X is not an OSA language (as it was under previous systems), so it can be used only from within Frontier.

Perl

Perl has a surprisingly long history on the Macintosh; years before it was present as part of Unix in Mac OS X, it had been ported to the Classic Mac OS by Matthias Neeracher (see *http://www.ptf.com/macperl*). Modules to form and send Apple events were naturally part of this port (see *http://www.ptf.com/macperl/depts/articles/ IPCwMP.html*). Support for these modules has continued, under the guidance of Chris Nandor, and they are available to Mac OS X users.

Once again, you have a choice: you can form the raw Apple events yourself, using Mac::AppleEvents, or you can use AppleScript terminology through Mac::Glue. The operation of Mac::Glue is similar to Frontier with its glue tables (and is probably deliberately modelled after it); a glue table for a given application must be formed and stored on disk before you can target that application using AppleScript English-like terminology. In order to get started, you will need Mac::Carbon (which includes Mac::AppleEvents) as well as Mac::Glue; on Tiger these are installed by default, but it can't hurt to check for more recent versions.

To make glue, run the gluemac Unix tool. For example:

```
% sudo /usr/bin/gluemac /Volumes/gromit/Users/matt2/extra/BBEdit\ 8/BBEdit.app
Making glue for '/Volumes/gromit/Users/matt2/extra/BBEdit 8/BBEdit.app'
What is the glue name? [BBEdit]:
Created and installed App glue for 'BBEdit.app, v8.2.3' (BBEdit)
```

The resulting glue table contains a document in the standard Perl documentation format (*POD*, for "plain old documentation") expressing the dictionary in Perl syntax. You can read it with `perldoc`; another tool, `gluedoc`, provides a shortcut to the desired document:

```
% gluedoc BBEdit
```

Using the POD document and the instructions for Mac::Glue, you can usually figure out the Perl analogue to an AppleScript expression. Here's code to generate our model events:

```
use Mac::Glue;
my $bb = Mac::Glue->new('BBEdit');
$bb->launch();
$bb->make(new => 'document');
my $doc = $bb->obj(document => 1);
my $text = $bb->obj(property => 'text', $doc);
$bb->set($text, to => 'Hello, world!');
```

Personally, I find Perl's notion of object-orientation clunky, and Mac::Glue's expression of AppleScript terminology rather inconsistent. Moreover, a Perl script that uses Mac::Glue takes even longer to get running than the corresponding AppleScript code would take to compile. This makes me wonder why it wouldn't be preferable to use `osascript` and have done with it (Chapter 25). Still, it's Perl, and for people who like this sort of thing, this is the sort of thing they like.

Python

Hamish Sanderson's Appscript brings AppleScript terminology to Python. It comes with a standard installer package; double-click and run the installer and you're good to go. Scripts must be run using `pythonw`, not plain `python`. Here's the code for generating our model events:

```
from appscript import *
bb = app('BBEdit')
bb.make(new=k.document)
bb.documents[1].text.set('Hello, world!')
```

No glue is necessary; like JavaScript OSA, Appscript reads the dictionary and constitutes an appropriate application object behind the scenes. It does this very quickly, and it's even faster if you run the supplied background application *Appscript-TerminologyServer*. The Python code is structured in a compact, intuitive, highly legible manner, incorporating all the best features of UserTalk and JavaScript; this is partly due to Python itself and partly due to Appscript's clean and thoughtful implementation. Appscript is also easy to learn. An included tool, `htmldoc.py`, generates an HTML-formatted display of an application's dictionary with the Python version of its terminology. (Alternatively, you can use the *HTMLDictionary* standalone application, included with the installer, which does the same thing.) And a particularly nice extra is an interactive help command for exploring either the terminology or the live attributes of an application's objects. So, for example, within the interactive pythonw interpreter:

```
>>> bb.documents[1].help('-s')
============================================================================
Appscript Help (-s)

Reference: app(u'/Volumes/gromit/Users/matt2/extra/BBEdit 8/BBEdit.app').documents[1]


----------------------------------------------------------------------------
Current state of referenced object(s)

--- Get reference ---

app(u'/Volumes/gromit/Users/matt2/extra/BBEdit 8/BBEdit.app').text_documents.first

---- Properties ----

properties:
{k.contents: u'Hello, world!',
 k.ID_: 7038242,
 k.file: k.MissingValue,
 k.modifiable: True,
 k.state_modified: False,
 k.name: u'untitled text 3',
 k.modification_date: datetime.datetime(2005, 9, 22, 12, 51, 51),
 k.source_language: '',
 k.FTP_info: k.MissingValue,
 k.line_breaks: k.Unix,
 k.container: None,
 k.text: u'Hello, world!',
 ...
```

And so on. This is like a command-line version of Script Debugger, and greatly eases the trial and error required to develop a script. Appscript clearly attempts to equal and even surpass AppleScript as an environment for creating and sending Apple events. In my view, it succeeds admirably; it is extremely complete and consistent, and takes care of all the heavy lifting for you.

Tools and Resources

This appendix provides sources for software, tools, documentation, and further information on various topics discussed in this book.

Free software from Apple mentioned in this book is already on your hard drive. For AppleScript Studio (Xcode, Interface Builder) you must install the developer tools. Applications mentioned by name only, but not discussed or used in examples, are not listed here.

Scripting Software and Tools

- Script Debugger, a commercial environment for developing and debugging scripts and exploring scriptable applications, crucial to my use of AppleScript (this book couldn't have been written without it):

    http://www.latenightsw.com

- JavaScript OSA, an Apple-event savvy OSA language version of JavaScript:

    http://www.latenightsw.com/freeware/JavaScriptOSA/

- Mac::Carbon and Mac::Glue, modules for using Apple events in Perl:

    http://projects.pudge.net

- Appscript, an Apple events implementation for Python:

    http://freespace.virgin.net/hamish.sanderson/appscript.html

- UserLand Frontier, and its inexpensive little brother Radio UserLand, a brilliant, powerful scripting environment with its own scripting language and built-in persistent storage, great interapplication communications, and Internet server/client capability. There is now also a free open source version:

    http://www.userland.com
    http://sourceforge.net/projects/frontierkernel

- OSABridge, a set of components making Perl, Ruby, Python, PHP, sh, and Tcl available as OSA languages:

    http://homepage.mac.com/philip_aker/

- Loader, a system for rationalizing AppleScript libraries:

    http://applemods.sourceforge.net
- PreFab UI Browser, an indispensable tool for GUI scripting:

    http://www.prefab.com/uibrowser/
- REALbasic, an application development environment:

    http://www.realbasic.com
- HyperCard, a once free, then overpriced, now out-of-date, Classic-only, unsupported, but historically insanely great Mac scripting and interface construction environment. Sales ceased in March 2004. For more information:

    http://pan.uqam.ca/pan/pmwiki.php/Pan/HomePage
- Gary McGath's EightyRez, a free `'aete'` resource editor; this book could not have been written without it:

    http://www.mcgath.com/EightyRez.html
- Smile, a free script editing environment:

    http://www.satimage.fr/software/en/softx.html
- FastScripts, a replacement for Apple's Script Menu:

    http://www.red-sweater.com/RedSweater/FSFeatures.html
- Big Cat, a contextual menu script runner:

    http://ranchero.com/bigcat
- Bellhop, a utility for turning a script into an application service:

    http://www.xendai.com/bellhop/
- *acgi dispatcher*, a utility for using AppleScript applets for CGI with Apache:

    http://www.sentman.com/acgi/
- QuicKeys, a macro program:

    http://www.startly.com/products/qkx.html
- PreFab Player, a Classic macro program:

    http://www.prefab.com/player.html
- iKey, Keyboard Maestro, and DragThing, launcher programs that let you run a script by typing a keyboard shortcut:

    http://www.scriptsoftware.com/ikey
    http://www.keyboardmaestro.com
    http://www.dragthing.com
- Script Timer and iDo Script Scheduler, commercial products for running scripts at specified times:

    http:// www.appsandmore.com
    http://www.sophisticated.com/products/ido/ido_ss.html

- PreFab UI Actions, a scriptable utility for observing applications through the Accessibility API:

  http://www.prefab.com/uiactions/

- Late Night Software's free List & Record Tools scripting addition:

  http://www.latenightsw.com/freeware/RecordTools/

- Jon's Commands scripting addition:

  http://www.seanet.com/~jonpugh/

Scriptable Software

- BBEdit, a scriptable text editor:

  http://www.barebones.com/products/bbedit/

- MultiAd Creator, an extraordinarily scriptable and attachable page layout and drawing program:

  http://www.creatorsoftware.com/products/

- Mailsmith, a scriptable email client:

  http://www.barebones.com/products/mailsmith/

- Eudora, a scriptable email client:

  http://www.eudora.com/email/

- Microsoft Entourage, Word, and Excel—a scriptable email client and an incredibly scriptable word processor and spreadsheet program:

  http://www.microsoft.com/macoffice/

- FileMaker Pro, a scriptable database program:

  http://www.filemaker.com

- GraphicConverter, a scriptable image processing program:

  http://www.lemkesoft.com/en/graphcon.htm

- Tex-Edit Plus, a scriptable styled text editor:

  http://www.tex-edit.com

- NoteTaker, a scriptable outliner:

  http://www.aquaminds.com

- StuffIt Expander, a scriptable file expander/decoder:

  http://www.stuffit.com/mac/

- SpamSieve, a scriptable program that filters spam, communicating with email client programs through AppleScript:

  http://c-command.com

- Salling Clicker, a scriptable remote-control program:

  http://www.salling.com/Clicker/

- Ovolab Phlink, a scriptable phone-answering program:

    http://www.ovolab.com/phlink/

- TextCommands, a scriptable faceless background application supplying valuable text-parsing abilities such as regular expressions:

    http://freespace.virgin.net/hamish.sanderson/

- Adobe FrameMaker, a superb scriptable layout program used to write this book; on Mac OS, it is Classic-only and development has officially ceased:

    http://www.adobe.com/products/framemaker/main.html

AppleScript Documentation

- The main AppleScript page, including a number of example scripts and other resources:

    http://www.apple.com/applescript/

- AppleScript on Mac OS X from the developer's point of view:

    http://developer.apple.com/documentation/AppleScript/Conceptual/ AppleScriptX/

- The AppleScript Language Guide—still the primary official documentation, and an important source of information, even though it often obfuscates more than it explains and is valid only to Version 1.3.7:

    http://developer.apple.com/documentation/AppleScript/Conceptual/ AppleScriptLangGuide/

- Incremental release notes and change notes postdating the Language Guide:

    - AppleScript 1.4 change notes:

        http://developer.apple.com/technotes/tn/tn1176.html#applescript

    - AppleScript 1.4.3 change notes:

        http://docs.info.apple.com/article.html?artnum=75073

    - AppleScript 1.5.5 change notes:

        http://developer.apple.com/technotes/tn/tn2010.html#applescript

    - AppleScript 1.6 change notes:

        http://docs.info.apple.com/article.html?artnum=60835

    - AppleScript 1.7-1.9.2 release notes (at this point Apple seems at last to have recognized the importance of gathering and linking to the release notes from a single location):

        http://www.apple.com/applescript/release_notes/

- A superb detailed historical record of AppleScript changes, maintained by Bill Cheeseman:

    http://www.applescriptsourcebook.com/applescript.html

- The 'aete' resource format:

    http://developer.apple.com/documentation/mac/IAC/IAC-308.html

- The *scriptSuite* and *scriptTerminology* format:

    *http://developer.apple.com/documentation/Cocoa/Conceptual/Scriptability/
    Tasks/SuiteDefs.html*

- GUI scripting:

    http://www.apple.com/applescript/uiscripting/

- AppleScript Studio:

    *http://developer.apple.com/documentation/AppleScript/Conceptual/
    StudioBuildingApps/index.html*

- Scripting on Mac OS X:

    *http://developer.apple.com/techpubs/macosx/Cocoa/TasksAndConcepts/
    ProgrammingTopics/Scriptability/Concepts/ScriptingOnOSX.html*

- XML-RPC and SOAP:

    *http://developer.apple.com/documentation/AppleScript/Conceptual/
    soapXMLRPC/*

- *Inside Macintosh, Interapplication Communication*:

    http://developer.apple.com/documentation/mac/IAC/IAC-2.html

- Apple events:

    *http://developer.apple.com/documentation/Carbon/Reference/Apple_Event_
    Manager/*
    *http://developer.apple.com/documentation/AppleScript/Conceptual/
    AppleEvents/*

- The Open Scripting Architecture:

    *http://developer.apple.com/documentation/Carbon/Reference/Open_Scripti_
    Architecture/index.html*

- Remarkable early white paper on the OSA and AppleScript, by their creators:

    http://www.cs.utexas.edu/users/wcook/papers/AppleScript/AppleScript95.pdf

- Glossary of AppleScript/Apple event terms:

    *http://developer.apple.com/documentation/Cocoa/Conceptual/Scriptability/
    Concepts/ScriptabilityTerms.html*

Writing a Scripting Addition

- Apple's tech note on how to write a scripting addition:

    http://developer.apple.com/technotes/tn/tn1164.html

- A seminal article from *MacTech Magazine*:

    http://www.mactech.com/articles/mactech/Vol.10/10.01/ExtendApplescript/

- Useful notes from an experienced scripting addition coder:

  http://www.latenightsw.com/technotes/ScriptingAddition/
- Sample code for creating a scripting addition:

  http://www.satimage.fr/software/en/downloads_sample_projects.html

Writing a Scriptable Application

- Making a Cocoa application scriptable:

  http://developer.apple.com/documentation/Cocoa/Conceptual/Scriptability/
- Sdef-based scriptability:

  http://developer.apple.com/documentation/Cocoa/Conceptual/ScriptableCocoaApplications
- Apple's scripting interface guidelines:

  http://developer.apple.com/technotes/tn2002/tn2106.html
- Apple's sample scriptability code:

  http://developer.apple.com/samplecode/Sketch-112/Sketch-112.html
- Sdef Editor, a brilliant and absolutely crucial free utility by Jean-Daniel Dupas:

  http://chezjd.free.fr/Creation/logiciel.php?sign=SdEd
- Andrew Stone's tutorial:

  http://www.stone.com/The_Cocoa_Files/Adding_Applescript.html
- Dustin Voss's tutorial:

  http://cocoadev.com/?HowToSupportAppleScript
- Don Briggs's examples and tools:

  http://homepage.mac.com/donbriggs/

Portals, Instruction, and Repositories

It's better to list a few web sites that between them contain virtually all important links than to try to list all those links, so here they are.

- ScriptWeb, a web portal to all things scripting-related:

  http://www.scriptweb.org
- MacScripter, a live collection of news items, examples, and links; now also incorporates AppleScriptCentral:

  http://macscripter.net
- MacScripter's scripting additions repository:

  http://osaxen.com

- Bill Cheeseman's encyclopedic site of history, examples, instruction, links, and more:

    http://www.applescriptsourcebook.com/home.html
- Main portal for XML-RPC and SOAP servers:

    http://www.xmethods.net

Mailing Lists

Mailing lists remain an important source of assistance, and are often haunted by Apple employees and by users of wisdom and experience.

- Apple's AppleScript list:

    http://lists.apple.com/mailman/listinfo/applescript-users
- Dartmouth's venerable MacScrpt list (in whose name the "i" is not only silent, it's downright absent):

    http://www.lsoft.com/scripts/wl.exe?SL1=MACSCRPT&H=LISTSERV. DARTMOUTH.EDU
- Apple's list for developers writing scriptable applications:

    http://lists.apple.com/mailman/listinfo/applescript-implementors
- Apple's AppleScript Studio list:

    http://lists.apple.com/mailman/listinfo/applescript-studio

Books

- Danny Goodman's groundbreaking *AppleScript Handbook*:

    http://www.dannyg.com/pubs/index.html
- Ethan Wilde, *AppleScript for the Internet: Visual QuickStart Guide* (Peachpit Press, 1998):

    http://www.amazon.com/exec/obidos/ASIN/0201353598/
- Ethan Wilde, *AppleScript for Applications: Visual QuickStart Guide* (Peachpit Press, 2001):

    http://www.amazon.com/exec/obidos/ASIN/0201716135
- Shirley Hopkins, *AppleScripting InDesign* (Dtp Connection, 2000):

    http://www.amazon.com/exec/obidos/ASIN/0970726511/
- Shirley Hopkins, *AppleScripting QuarkXPress* (Dtp Connection, 2000):

    http://www.amazon.com/exec/obidos/ASIN/0970726503/
- Ethan Wilde, *Adobe Illustrator Scripting with Visual Basic and AppleScript* (Adobe, 2002):

    http://www.amazon.com/exec/obidos/ASIN/0321112512/

Unix Scripting

- Dave Taylor, *Learning Unix for Mac OS X Tiger* (O'Reilly Media, 2005):
  http://www.oreilly.com/catalog/ltigerunix/
- Larry Wall et al., *Programming Perl*, Third Edition (O'Reilly Media, 2000):
  http://www.oreilly.com/catalog/pperl3/
- Mark Lutz, *Programming Python*, Second Edition (O'Reilly Media, 2001):
  http://www.oreilly.com/catalog/python2/
- "Programming Ruby," an excellent online book:
  http://www.rubycentral.com/book/

Index

Symbols

& (ampersand), concatenation operator, 267
* (asterisk), multiplication operator, 258
\ (backslash)
    in literal strings, 225
    variable names, 107
^ (caret), exponentiation operator, 259
: (colon)
    handler definition and call, 145
    in handler definition and call, 145
    in Macintosh pathnames, 232
    POSIX path, don't use in, 234
    record, name-value separator, 240
, (comma)
    in global declaration, 163
    in local declaration, 161
    separating list items, 236
    separating parameters, 143, 145
    separating record items, 240
    thousands separator illegal, 222
¬ (continuation character), 55, 85
    entering, 85
    how used in this book, 85
    moved or removed by decompilation, 85
    must be last thing in line, 85
{ } (curly braces)
    delimiting lists, 236
    delimiting records, 240
= (equals sign), equality operator, 260, 261
    assignment, not, 102, 261
≠ (not equals sign), inequality operator, 261
!= (not equal to), doesn't exist, 261
> (greater than), 261

≥ (greater than or equal to), 262
>= (abbreviation for ≥), 262
« » (guillemets)
    constructing data class object, 221
    entering, 229, 325
    raw four-letter code, entering, 325
- (minus sign), subtraction and unary
        negation operator, 258
-- (comment delimiter), 88
    inside comment delimiters, 89
---- (direct object), 40, 340
    optional or required, 340
< (less than), 261
<> (not equal to), doesn't exist, 261
≤ (less than or equal to), 262
<= (abbreviation for ≤), 262
( ) (parentheses)
    handler definition and call, 143
    interpretation of commands, 267
    order of operations, 267
(* and *) (comment delimiters), 89
    commenting out, 89
    nesting, 89
+ (plus sign), addition operator, 258
    concatenation, not overloaded for, 258
' (single quote)
    delimiting four-letter code, 40
    string comparisons and, 299
" (quotation marks)
    in comment delimiters, 89
    delimiting literal strings, 225
    in literal strings, 225
    quote global property, 272
    string comparisons and, 299

We'd like to hear your suggestions for improving our indexes. Send email to *index@oreilly.com*.

attribute *(continued)*
    coercion, by scriptable application, 246, 247
    dictionary, how listed in, 337
    fetching or assigning several at once, 206
    inheritance, in dictionary, 335
    value may be a reference, 196
    (see also property; element)
audio file, getting info about, 396
August (constant), 277
Austin, J. L., 344
autocompletion (Script Editor), 16
autoinitialization, 104
automatic location, 25, 418–429
Automator, 32
    action, 32
        Run AppleScript, 32
        virtues of, 452
        writing, 452–458
    documentation, online, 452
    workflow, 32
        in Finder contextual menu, 32

B

Babcock, Scott, 142
backslash (\) character
    literal strings, 225
    variable names, 107
bash, 407
    escaping strings on command line, 412
BASIC, 52
BBEdit, 357, 518
    attachable, 71, 427
    automatic location, 25
    contents property hard to use, 216
    factored, 71
    inserting text, 200, 355
    insertion point elements, 200
    Menu Scripts folder, 25, 427
    offset property, terminology bug, 322
    print settings class defective, 326
    pseudo-classes (records) used by, 339
    recordable, 70
    Script menu, 23
        implements persistence, 118
    Shutdown Items folder, 25
    Startup Items folder, 25
beep command, 367
before keyword, 200
beginning keyword, 199

begins with operator, 264
behind (synonym for after), 200
Belleudy-d'Espinose, Serge, 382
Bellhop, 24, 517
below (preposition), 143
beneath (preposition), 143
Berkowitz, Paul, xxi, xxii, 284, 434
beside (preposition), 143
between (preposition), 143
Big Cat, 24, 517
binary operator, 256
binding name with value, 100
bindings, Cocoa, 453
blank line after continuation character, 85
block, 91, 93
    abbreviating termination line, 92, 281
    arbitrary, 92
    how referred to in this book, 91
    indentation, 91
    level, 95
    nesting, 95
    scope, 93, 156
bold (constant), 276
Bonjour name
    choose remote application bug, 366
    targeting remote computer by, 388
books about AppleScript, 522
boolean, 221
    coercion, 248
        integer, 259
        string, 259
    condition, 281
    operators, 259
    parameter, replaced by "with" or "without", 144, 146
boolean test (element specifier), 201
    dictionary, not listed in, 347
    failure may generate error, 203
    lists, not implemented for, 203
        workaround (sort of), 239
    multiple tests, 203
    performed by target application, 269
    string considerations ignored, 299
bootstrap code (applet), 59
bounding rectangle class, 239
braces, curly
    delimiting lists, 236
    delimiting records, 240
branching, 281
bridge (AppleScript Studio), 440
Briggs, Don, 521

delay command, 376
delegation (Cocoa), 439
delete item of list, 81
dereferencing (a reference), 213
   needed in repeat with . . . in, 287
Description tab (Script Editor), 16
developer tools, 441
diacriticals (constant), 277
dialog, error, 300, 301
   not displayed when user cancels, 302,
      364
dialogs, StandardAdditions, 364
dictionary, 61, 311–358
   AppleScript (see aeut)
   AppleScriptKit (AppleScript Studio), 147,
      442
   applet, 437
   application class as starting point, 338,
      345
   application launched by consulting, 62,
      313
   class with same name as property, 192,
      347
   coercions not listed, 245, 248, 356
   commands not listed by class, 183, 355
      Script Debugger helps, 356
   comments usually inadequate, 358
   compilation and decompilation, how used
      during, 62, 311
   compilation, needed for, 64, 313
   contents of, 329–343
   creating, 461
   datatypes in, 330
      alternative, 333, 349
      inaccurately listed, 233, 333, 349
   decompilation, needed for, 65
   display, 329
      Script Debugger, 329
      Script Editor, 16, 329
   element specifiers listed in, 337
   event handler defined by, 147
   formats, 62
      aete, 62
      scriptSuite and scriptTerminology, 62
      sdef, 63
   four-letter code avoids need for, 325
   four-letter codes mysteriously appear
      in, 326
   graphical interface, might not match, 354
   hidden terminology, 343
   implicit subcontainers not listed, 345

inadequacy, 63, 333, 344–358, 506
inheritance, 335
   how displayed, 336
innermost application, 313
internal implementation, need not
      match, 461
learning to read, 329
loading, 313
   scripting addition, 360
omissions, 346
optional parameter default not listed, 350
remote application, 389
resolution of terminology, 312–323
scripting addition, 359
sdef, can be in Tiger, 63, 330
specifying which to use, 292
static or dynamic, 62
study of, major part of AppleScript
      programming, 311, 505
terminology clash caused by, 321, 322
(see also terminology; aete; sdef)
Dictionary (application), 7
   looks scriptable but isn't, 7, 342
      workaround with GUI scripting, 406
Digital Hub Scripting, 61, 419
direct object, 183
   Apple event, 40, 340
      optional or required, 340
   command, 183
   get command must be followed by, 191
   multiple (as a list), 205
   specifying target, 183
direct operation, 268
disk
   get every (Finder), 350
   list names of (StandardAdditions), 369
   nonexistent, 232
dispatch
   object-first, 470
   verb-first, 477
dispatch table, 138
dispatch-based targeting, 294
display alert command, 364
display dialog command, 364
   constant displayed incorrectly, 327
   error if user cancels, 300
   list, displaying, 254
   Unicode text returned by, 409
distribution of command or attribute over
      list, 204
distribution of script, 32, 55, 122, 362

URL
   applescript, 30
   eppc, 388
   opening, 8, 377
   XML-RPC or SOAP server, 393
URL Access Scripting, 398
user
   actions
      run script in response to, 428
      simulating, 401
   environment variables, 368
   getting info about, 396
   interaction (see interface)
   targeting (see remote application)
user domain, terminology conflict, 325
user handler, 146
   applet, scriptable in, 436
   instead of event handler, 427
user property, 241
UserLand Frontier (see Frontier)
UserTalk, 22, 44
   Apple events, sending with, 511
   bundle construct, 92
   (see also Frontier)
using terms from (see terms block)
usrf (list of user properties), 241
UTF-16 encoding, 228, 408
UTF-8 encoding, 230, 408
UTI (Uniform Type Identifier), 365

V

value
   assigning to variable, 101, 182
      no implicit coercion, 245
   attribute, reference vs. copy, 196
   class, 182
      testing, 245
   coercion, 244
   constant, 275
   datatype, 182, 220
      converting, 244
      testing, 245
   default, of parameter, 142
   file object specifier, 232
   free variable, 171
   global properties, shared between
      scripts, 271
   handler as, 138
   handler call, 135
      none, 136
   initial, 104

missing, 276
numeric, approximation, 257
object-like qualities, 180
pass by, 140
   guaranteeing, 141
passing to handler, 139
placeholders for unassigned, 104
record item name is not, 243
reference, 208
returned, 135
script object as, 111
top-level entity, 113
type (in dictionary), 330
   alternative, 333, 349
   wrongly listed, 349
undefined, 103
variable, 100
   retrieving from, 103
variable, 100
   application object specifier, 292
   assignment, 101
      multiple, 236, 240
      no implicit coercion, 245
   class, 182
      can be assigned value of any, 182
   coercion, can't be used for class in, 246
   constant is not, 275
   declaration legal in control structure, 170
   declaration not required, 103, 169
      called harmful, 106, 169
   defined, learning whether, 104
   definition, 103
   file object specifier, 232
   file URL can be assigned to, 234
   free (see free variable)
   global (see global)
   handler as, 138
   initialization, 104
   kinds, 157
      determined at compile time, 158
   local (see local)
   name, 105
      case of, 105, 107
      legalizing with vertical bars, 107
      misspelled, 106
      persistent and shared between
         scripts, 106
      same as class name, 316, 317
      same as command name, 315
      same as constant name, 316
      same as property name, 317, 318
   object string specifier, 207, 292

About the Author

Matt Neuburg started programming computers in 1968, when he was 14 years old, as a member of a literally underground high school club, which met once a week to do timesharing on a bank of PDP-10s by way of primitive teletype machines. He also occasionally used Princeton University's IBM-360/67, but gave it up in frustration when one day he dropped his punch cards. He majored in Greek at Swarthmore College and received his Ph.D. from Cornell University in 1981, writing his doctoral dissertation (about Aeschylus) on a mainframe. He proceeded to teach Classical languages, literature, and culture at many well-known institutions of higher learning, most of which now disavow knowledge of his existence, and to publish numerous scholarly articles unlikely to interest anyone. Meanwhile, he obtained an Apple IIc and became hopelessly hooked on computers again, migrating to a Macintosh in 1990. He wrote some educational and utility freeware, became an early regular contributor to the online journal *TidBITS*, and in 1995 left academe to edit *MacTech Magazine*. In August 1996, he became a freelancer, which means he has been looking for work ever since. He is also the author of two other books for O'Reilly, *Frontier: The Definitive Guide* and *REALbasic: The Definitive Guide*.

Colophon

The animal on the cover of *AppleScript: The Definitive Guide* is a Boston terrier. The youngest breed in the American Kennel Club (AKC), the Boston is a cross between various types of bulldogs and bull terriers. Originally bred in England, the breed stabilized in the United States, where it was initially favored as a fighter in the underworld rat pits of the seedier areas of late eighteenth- and early nineteenth-century Boston. By the late nineteenth century, however, people started to admire the beauty of the breed's compact, elegant build—the "American Gentleman," as the Boston terrier is now known, had been discovered.

In 1889, the AKC rejected the Stud Book applications put forth by the "American bull terrier" owners only to accept the breed in 1893 under its new name, Boston terrier. Today, its gentle yet playful and protective nature, combined with its willingness to be trained, make it a popular family pet—especially, of course, in Boston, the metropolitan area in which O'Reilly maintains a large editorial and production staff. Although the Boston terrier's fighting days are in its past, the sportsmen and sportswomen at Boston University evoke the breed's heritage each time they take the field or ice.

The cover font is Adobe ITC Garamond. The text font is Linotype Birka; the heading font is Adobe Myriad Condensed; and the code font is LucasFont's TheSans Mono Condensed.

Better than e-books

Buy *AppleScript: The Definitive Guide,*
2nd Edition, and access the digital edition
FREE on Safari for 45 days.

Go to www.oreilly.com/go/safarienabled
and type in coupon code 01234567890234567890

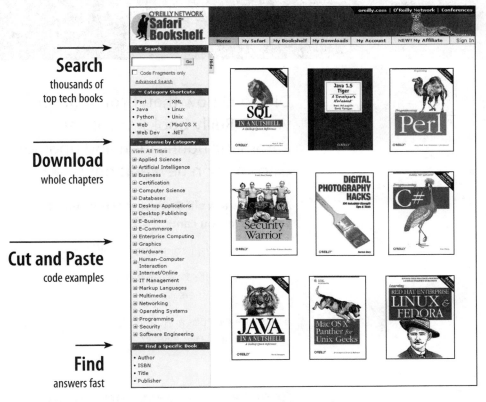

Search
thousands of
top tech books

Download
whole chapters

Cut and Paste
code examples

Find
answers fast

Search Safari! The premier electronic reference
library for programmers and IT professionals.